■ Four million people subscribe to commercial online services

■ Twenty million people use the Internet

■ Twelve million people regularly call a BBS

More and more Americans discover the medium every day. *It's 1954 and your family has just bought a television set! Along with millions of others up and down Maple Street you want to know one thing: **what's on?*** Now that same question echoes out in Cyberspace. As the Net becomes an entertainment as well as an information medium, a program guide becomes an essential tool and a must-have part of the experience. That guide is Net Guide—the first easy-to-use, comprehensive directory to the best "shows" in Cyberspace.

"*Net Guide* is the *TV Guide* to Cyberspace!"
—Louis Rossetto, editor, *Wired*

You've read the book. Now keep up-to-date online.

Every month hundreds of new newsgroups, mailing lists, forums, and BBSs come online. How can you possibly keep up? It's easy. The Net Guide Online Directory is updated round the clock. Call Net Guide Online for the latest offerings on the Net.

Net Guide Online is a service for data.comm.phobes

To watch your favorite show on TV you don't have to know about circuits and tubes. To have fun in Cyberspace you shouldn't have to know about "transmission-control protocols." Net Guide Online Support makes it simple to navigate the Net—you'll get real help from real people.

Busy? No carrier? Host unavailable?

If you've been out in Cyberspace, you know the frustration of not connecting. Net Guide Online can handle the traffic! Call now for your local access number and make an easy connection.

Join us!

The Net is a new medium and a new world. Be a part of it. As a charter member of Net Guide Online you'll get 15 hours of time FREE, plus one of the lowest subscription costs anywhere in Cyberspace!

✓ **Interactive Magazines**

✓ **Regular** *Net Guide* **Updates**
- **Commercial services**
- **Internet**
- **BBSs**

✓ **Special Directories**
- **Adult**
- **Travel**
- **Business**
- **Shareware**
- **Kids**

✓ **BBS Reviews**

✓ **Net News**
- **Usenet Digest**
- **Talk of the Net**

✓ **Easy Navigation Tools**

✓ **Usenet FAQ Archive**

✓ **Chat**

✓ **Games**

✓ **News**

✓ **Shopping**

netguide ™

Your Map to the Services, Information and Entertainment on the Electronic Highway

A Michael Wolff Book

Peter Rutten, Albert F. Bayers III,
and Kelly Maloni

For free updates call 1-800-NET-1133

RANDOM HOUSE
ELECTRONIC PUBLISHING

New York

Net Guide™ has been wholly created and produced by Michael Wolff & Company, Inc., 1633 Broadway, 27th Floor, New York, NY 10019. Net Guide is a trademark of Michael Wolff & Company, Inc. All design and production has been done by means of desktop-publishing technology. The text is set in the typefaces Garamond, customized Futura, Zapf Dingbats, Franklin Gothic, Pike, and Wolff Icons.

Random House Electronic Publishing is a division of Random House, Inc., 201 E. 50th St., New York, NY 10022. Published simultaneously in the U.S. by Random House, NY, and in Canada by Random House of Canada, Ltd.

0 9 8 7 6

ISBN 0-679-75106-8

All of the photographs and illustrations in this book have been obtained from online sources, and have been included to demonstrate the variety of work that is available on the Net. The caption with each photograph or illustration identifies its online source.

The icons have been designed by Nancy Wolff. Copyright © 1994 by Michael Wolff & Company, Inc. The book jacket has been designed by Peter Rutten. Copyright © 1994 by Michael Wolff & Company, Inc.

The author and publisher have used their best efforts in preparing this book. However, the author and publisher make no warranties of any kind, express or implied, with regard to the documentation contained in this book, and specifically disclaim, without limitation, any implied warranties of merchantability and fitness for a particular purpose with respect to listings in the book, or the techniques described in the book. In no event shall the author or publisher be responsible or liable for any loss of profit or any other commercial damages, including but not limited to special, incidental, consequential, or any other damages in connection with or arising out of furnishing, performance, or use of this book.

Trademarks

A number of entered words in which we have reason to believe trademark, service mark, or other proprietary rights may exist have been designated as such by use of initial capitalization. However, no attempt has been made to designate as trademarks or service marks all personal computer words or terms in which proprietary rights might exist. The inclusion, exclusion, or definition of a word or term is not intended to affect, or to express any judgment on, the validity or legal status of any proprietary right which may be claimed in that word or term.

Manufactured in the United States of America

New York   Toronto   London   Sydney   Auckland

Acknowledgments

A project of this scope and detail depends on the enthusiasm, support, counsel, generosity, and kindness of friends, colleagues, spouses, and strangers.

Particular thanks are owed to Amy Arnold at America Online, Debra Young at CompuServe, Rusty Williams and Eric Romanik at Delphi, Barb Byro at GEnie, Jenny Ambrosak at Prodigy, and Christine Taylor at BIX. Indeed, we have received enormous help in the preparation of this book from all areas of the online community.

Undoubtedly, the greatest resource in creating this book was Cyberspace itself. Hundreds of sysops and system administrators have provided us with guidance and information, and thousands of email correspondents have answered our calls for help and suggestions. Truly, this book is a reflection of the vast bounty of the Net, from the far-flung indexes that we've relied on, to the FAQs that we've consulted, learned from, and quoted here, to the posts we've used as "cybernotes" to show the tone and concerns of the Net, to the photographs and illustrations, which we've used as examples of the incredible collection of images that float freely in the great digital scrapbook of Cyberspace.

This project would surely not have happened without the particular talents of our agent, Peter Ginsberg at Curtis Brown; our lawyer, Alison Anthoine at Shea & Gould; and our editor, Tracy Smith at Random House.

Stan Norton, at North Sea Consulting, is the network visionary whose idea inspired *Net Guide*. John Perry Barlow, who has written the foreword, counseled us throughout the process of creating the book.

Ted Williams helped us design the *Net Guide* logo. Nancy Wolff created the icons ⊞ ☻ ⊕ ▥. Matt Weingarden, our copy editor, saved us from a thousand embarrassments. David Wolff helped us develop the database. Onno de Jong ably advised us on a variety of technical issues. Elizabeth Brown worked with us through the final months of the project. And, as always, at the top of the list of people we've counted on, there is Aggy Aed.

Most of all, I'd like to thank my colleagues Peter Rutten, Chip Bayers, and Kelly Maloni, who did it all.

Address all notice of mistakes, misjudgments, omissions, and bad calls to me: MWOLFF@GO-NETGUIDE.COM.

Michael Wolff
New York
November 15, 1993

Table of contents

Part 3: Telecommunications & Electronics

Part 4: Nations, Cultures & Religions

Part 5: Business & Finance

Part 6: Games, Sports & the Outdoors

Part 7: Mind & Body

Part 8: Home, Hobbies & Shopping

Part 9: Lifestyles, Leisure & Travel

Part 10: Public Affairs, Politics & the Media

Part 11: Nature, Science & Technology

Foreword

A State of Minds

It's a state of minds. Or, possibly, in some more realized future condition, The State of Mind. It's the current phase of what I call The Great Work, the hard-wiring of collective consciousness, the end toward which, according to paleontologist-theologian Teilhard de Chardin, the great journey of evolution has been headed all these eons.

It's almost certainly the most important thing to happen to information since Gutenberg let words out of the Abbey. I increasingly suspect it may alter what it is to be human more than any technological development since the capture of fire.

Or maybe it's just noise—the dieseling of a few million cerebrums whose owners could use more sleep, a better diet, and more mature methods for handling disagreements. It's so unedited that I sometimes think it's what the typings of an infinite number of monkeys would look like. Words without voices, ideas without authors, points of view without eyes.

I'm talking about the Net. In the course of my experiences with it or "in" it, I've called it a number of names—Cyberspace, the Datasphere, the Electronic Frontier, the Matrix—each in the service of a different metaphor. The metaphors always fail. It's hard to find the right metaphor for something that is itself so metaphorical.

And then there are all the confusing technical layers, hard and soft, which interrelate like three-dimensional Venn diagrams. Are we talking about phone lines here? Fiber optic-cable? Addressing protocols? Software interfaces? Device drivers? Or the various regions and villages—CompuServe, FidoNet, America Online, the WELL, Delphi—each of which might seem to its inhabitants a complete world unto itself. There is certainly confusion among many residents of these subsets as to their relationship with the rest of the Net.

And who the hell is in charge here? Nobody. Who's paying for this party? It's not that clear.

The National Science Foundation pays for a lot of the connective tissue of the Net, but most of the costs are as distributed as the structure itself. Really, the Net is largely a volunteer project. It is built on little labors of love by millions of grad students, computer scientists, wire-heads, and bit-twiddlers.

This thing is so difficult to wrap one's mind around that it's likely many of the multitudes from whose keystrokes it rises may not have any sense of the immensity of what they are helping create.

Here's what I mean when I say the Net: I mean the great cloud of words, images, and sounds that floats above all the ones and zeroes on all the hard disks of all the connected computers in the world. I mean the enormous conversation taking place among all the people who use those computers.

In practice, this cloud floats primarily above the Internet. The name Internet refers to all of those continuously connected computers that use a method of transmitting packets of data to one another called TCP/IP. That, and a universal addressing scheme that gets those packets from one computer to another without any centralized switching facilities, is what seems to define the Internet these days.

There was a time when both its boundaries and its ownership were a lot clearer. The Internet was originally a project of the Defense Advanced Research Projects Agency (DARPA). Given its pyramidic progenitor, there is a delicious irony to its real genius, which is its ability to form an enormously expandable, utterly ungovernable anarchy.

When it was first patched together in 1968, DARPANET, as it was then called, connected machines in the computer-science departments of seven universities at speeds that were geologically deliberate by today's standards.

But it provided its users with the ability to access systems many miles away, to retrieve and leave information for their colleagues at a rate of exchange many times more rapid than the prevailing methods of scientific publication.

The most remarkable thing about the Internet is that unlike all previous anarchies, this one actually works. Weirder still, it has gone on working, even as it has scaled, over 25 years, from a network of seven host machines to something like 2 million host machines (by present estimate), from which dangle an unknowable but huge number of client computers, upon which tens of millions of users have unique email addresses.

It has gone on working and growing at rates that were occasionally geometric, even as the speed of information transfer between its larger nodes has ascended from a few hundred bits per second to 44 billion bits per second.

It is growing like kudzu. Some months, the number of its host machines increases by as much as 20 percent. If the Internet continued to expand at present rates, every human being on the planet would have an Internet address before the turn of the millennium. (Though I suspect we will see the growth curve go asymptotic before then.)

Its decentralized architecture served the military's desire for a communications network that couldn't be shut down by nuking it in the head. Thus its "head" was distributed evenly throughout. It is rather like the Buddhist notion of Indra's Net—an infinite grid of pearls, each of which reflects perfectly the image of every other pearl in it.

There are other large digital networks besides the Internet, using different communications protocols, addressing schemes, and reproductive strategies.

For example, there's FidoNet, a loincloth-and-machete version of the Internet that connects something like 25,000 computer bulletin boards worldwide, most of them set up on low-end IBM clones. FidoNet is the creation of a gay anarchist punker named Tom Jennings who wrote the free software it's based on back when the Internet was still exclusively a Pentagon product.

FidoNet sites queue up electronic mail and news postings all day and then relay them over ordinary phone lines at night, when long-distance rates are cheaper. It's crude, it's slow, but it's cheap, it works, and there's no one in charge.

Like those of IBM's venerable Bitnet (a university network now largely merged with the Internet) or such commercial services as CompuServe, America Online, and MCI Mail, FidoNet's methods for transporting bits around within itself differ from the Internet's, but it is connected to the Internet with translating gateways through which users can pass electronic mail as though all these networks were one seamless web. Which, increasingly, they are.

The Net seems to me to be, in some loose sense of the word, alive. In its ability to extract resources from the surrounding informational, infrastructural, economic, and mental "ecology," it exhibits many of the characteristics of an organism, albeit a parasitic one. In its spreading dendritic forks and redundant channels, this organism looks a lot like a global nervous system, an almost continuous extension of the wet, gray gauze within the humans who sit at its silicon receptor sites.

What does this nervous system think? Too much for any one of its constituents to comprehend. Unlike the human brain, the Net is not quite capable yet of erecting the cognitive hierarchies through which relevant ideas can rise to the focal plane of individual attention.

The flat, distributed nature of its architecture, while ideally suited to durability under assault, rapid proliferation, and self-organization, is not so well tuned to the stacked categorical methods we customarily use for storing and accessing information.

It's a little like an enormous and rapidly expanding library for which there is no card catalog. Millions of words and thousands of images are added to its hard disks every day, but to many users, they are like a vast desert, shimmering with a white mirage of undifferentiated bits, a Plain of Babel.

Further confusion arises from the different ways in which information might be stored or conveyed within the Net. The largest and most obvious repository of information is Usenet, more than 5,000 "conversations" covering everything from sex with animals to the gaffes of Dan Quayle. Employing any of several different pieces of news-reading software, Internet users can browse through these topics or newsgroups, read new entries that might have been posted from anywhere in the world, and add their own.

Some of these newsgroups are moderated to improve the "signal-to-noise ratio," the disparity between digital hand waving, grandstanding, verbal abuse, and actually informative content.

Then there are thousands of mailing lists to which one may subscribe, some of them edited, most of them simply distributing the mail that any subscriber might generate to every other subscriber on the list.

Another important part of Internet memory is the anonymous FTP archives. These are places on Internet-connected machines where files may be left and retrieved by anyone, regardless of whether he or she has an account on the machine where the archive is based. These archives can also be accessed with searching tools like Gopher, Archie, World Wide Web, and WAIS.

There are also somewhere around a 100,000 computer bulletin boards, ranging from one-modem XT clones maintained by pale young men in basements to large commercial operations that rival CompuServe in subscriber numbers. Many of these are connected to FidoNet and carry, in addition to their own local discussion topics, the postings from FidoNet's equivalent to Usenet newsgroups.

Finally, of course, there are the large commercial operations like CompuServe, America Online, Prodigy, the WELL, Delphi, and GEnie. Of these, only the WELL and Delphi offer their subscribers real-time access to the Internet, which is required to participate in Usenet newsgroups, grab files from FTP archives, or use any of the Net-wide search tools. However, with the exception of Prodigy, the commercial services are open to electronic mail from elsewhere on the Internet, which means, for example, that CompuServe subscribers may participate in mailing-list-based discussions even though they don't have direct access to the Internet. And, of course, subscribers to the large services also have access to the discussion groups and databases within their own virtual malls.

It's kind of a mess, really, just as you might expect an anarchy to be. But it's been estimated that there are already more words "published" on the Net in a week than are bound into books in the United States in a year.

And these words are fresh. They generally reflect the very latest information in fields where the shelf life of thought is brief indeed. In any case, there would be no point in publishing them on paper. By the time they were printed and distributed, they would be well out of date.

Net Guide represents an important step in bringing light and order into the thickets of Cyberspace. This book and its successors will be the Baedekers of the Electronic Frontier, the Yellow Pages of digital discourse.

The "place" this book describes is the most fluid environment human beings have ever tried to inhabit. We're making it up as we go along. It will change us even as we are changing it.

John Perry Barlow
Cognitive Dissident

FAQs

"Frequently Asked Questions" about the Net and Net Guide

1. What is the Net?

The Net is the electronic medium spawned by the millions of computers linked (that is, *net*worked) together throughout the world. The Net is often called the electronic highway or the information highway by the news media as well as by proponents like Vice President Al Gore. It is also called Cyberspace, a termed coined by science-fiction writer William Gibson, meaning something like a fourth dimension created out of information. The largest online network is the Internet, a global, noncommercial system with more than 20 million computers communicating through it. Then there are the major commercial services such as CompuServe, America Online, and Prodigy, and the thousands of local and regional bulletin-board services (BBSs). And there is also a growing variety of special-interest networks, like PeaceNet, KinkNet, Smartnet, FidoNet, and ZiffNet. Gradually, all of these systems and networks are being linked together through the Internet.

2. What can I do on the Net?

You can start relationships, fire off insults, publish your own writings. You can get help on your screenplay. You can get updates on the TV soaps you've missed. You can play games. You can send and receive electronic mail. You can search through libraries around the world. You can trade advice, ask and answer questions, and exchange opinions. You can contribute to one of the greatest written enterprises (or outpourings) in the history of the press. You can lose yourself in a new medium and a new world.

3. Who has access to it?

You do! Twenty million people are out there already.

4. What do I need?

✓A PC (any flavor).

✓A modem, preferably a "14,400," the fastest on the market, which transfers data at speeds up to 14,400 bits per second (bps) and is available for under $300. (By early 1994, there should be modems on the market that will carry data at 28,800 bits per second.)

✓Communications software to control your modem. This software will probably come free with your modem or PC; otherwise you can buy it off the shelf for under $100.

5. How do I start?

Hook up your modem. Join a commercial service (Prodigy, CompuServe, America Online, GEnie, and Delphi are the big ones) by purchasing its software package in your local computer store, using the offers in this book, or just calling a service's 800 number. Try a few local bulletin-board services that pique your interest simply by dialing them up on your modem (see page 315 for listings of BBSs by area

---

Modems

The following modems were used for the research and writing of Net Guide. Using a variety of communications-software packages, these modems transferred thousands of files, made countless BBS connections and commercial service log-ins, and sent untold numbers of faxes. Each of these modems transfers data and faxes at the current maximum industry standard speed of 14,400 bits per second, and comes with communications and fax software.

✓Hayes Smartmodem
   Optima 144
   Current street price:
   $359

✓Practical Peripherals
   PM14400FXSA V.32bis
   Current street price:
   $369

✓Zoom Telephonics
   FaxModem VFX V.32bis
   Current street price:
   $159

code). Find an Internet connection (see page 327).

6. What commercial service should I pick?

Having access to just one commercial service is like having only a single television channel. More and more users join several services. A quick run down on each of the services goes something like this:

✓CompuServe has the greatest range of offerings, and many users regard it as the "must have" service. While a lot of its offerings are consumer-oriented, CompuServe also caters to business and professional users, and its fees tend to be higher than those of the other services.

✓America Online (AOL) is the fastest-growing service; it's like a hot magazine (in fact, you can get many magazines online, including *Time, The New Republic,* and *Wired*). AOL is famous for its chat and its easy-to-use interface (what you see on the screen).

✓Prodigy is far and away the best service for kids; its big drawback is that it doesn't allow you to send email to the other services.

Commercial Services

America Online
- 1-800-827-6364 (voice)
- Monthly fee: $9.95
- Free monthly hours: 5
- Hourly fees: $3.50

CompuServe
- 1-800-848-8199 (voice)
- Monthly fee: $8.95
- Free monthly hours: unlimited for basic services
- Extended services, marked with a + on CompuServe, and including many online games, special-interest forums, and most financial services, are billed on the basis of your modem speed:
  - 300 bps, 1,200 bps, or 2,400 bps—$4.80 per hour
  - 9,600 or 14,400 bps—$9.60 per hour

Delphi
- 1-800-695-4005 (voice)
- Monthly fees: $10 for the basic "$10/4 hrs. plan"; $20 for the premium "$20/20 hrs. plan"—plus $19 enrollment fee
- Free monthly hours: 4 with the 10/4 Plan,

→

✓GEnie offers international coverage and games.

✓Delphi provides Internet access.

✓And then there are the boutique services: for example, BIX and ZiffNet for techie topics; Sierra Online for games; and PeaceNet, EcoNet, and ConflictNet for access to political, social, and environmental news.

7. What exactly is a BBS?

BBS stands for bulletin-board service. A BBS is smaller than a commercial service (but not always; see page 102 for Big Boards); it's often devoted to a specialty topic; it's usually local (but not always—more and more boards have national access); and it's something that might well be tailored just for you and a few like-minded souls. You can chat, download software and pictures, play games, and get info on a vast (and often eccentric) range of topics. By some counts, there are up to 100,000 privately run BBSs in America. When you log in (or try to log in) to a BBS be prepared for busy signals, other connection hiccups, interfaces of varying quality, and, frequently, a range of peculiar log-in questions. Many BBSs have begun offering access to their boards through so-called packet networks, which, for a flat monthly fee, provide a local access number for long-distance dial-up, thus beating regular long-distance charges. Among the popular packet networks are: PC Pursuit, SprintNet, CompuServe

20 with the 20/20 plan
• Hourly fees: $4, 10/4 plan; $1.80, 20/20 plan

GEnie
• 1-800-638-9636 (voice)
• Monthly fee: $8.95
• Free monthly hours: 4
• Hourly fees (by modem speed):
• 2,400 bps—$3 off-prime, $12.50 prime (8 a.m.–6 p.m.)
• 9,600 bps—$9 off-prime, $18 prime

Prodigy
• 1-800-PRODIGY
• Monthly fees: $14.95 ("Standard plan"), $29.95 ("Alternative plan")
• Free monthly hours:
• Standard plan: unlimited in "core" services, 2 hours in "plus" services
• Alternative plan: 25 hours in the "plus" services
• "Plus" includes: access to all bulletin boards, financial information, and on-line travel reservations
• Hourly fees: $3.60 over 2 hours in the Standard Plan

Packet Network, and Tymnet. Check your BBS for more information.

8. FidoNet, RelayNet, Smartnet, KinkNet, and ILink—What are they?

These are BBS networks. FidoNet is the largest BBS network, offering hundreds of what are called echoes or, sometimes, conferences—messages on specific topics contributed by BBS users all over the world. A FidoNet BBS may carry all the FidoNet echoes or a selected few (see page 315 for a list of FidoNet boards). A BBS will often prominently display the names of the networks it belongs to on its opening screen.

9. What the hell is the Internet, anyway?

The Internet is the big enchilada. It's not just a network, it's a network of networks—a collection of thousands of interlinked computer networks that communicate with each other using a common computer language, or "protocol." That protocol allows people on these networks to exchange email, log in to other computers, and bring files back to their own machines. The Internet started in the late 1960s, connecting a few hundred computers. In the past five years it has seen explosive growth, with thousands of new computers joining the network every day. The Internet isn't a company, and you can't call it up; in fact, it isn't really run by anybody at all. Indeed, many of the people who maintain the system are volunteers. And while it may cost you something (usually $15 to $30 a month) to get access to it, once you're on the Internet there are no more charges—not when you spend the night connected to Tokyo and not for the volumes of files you download to your own machine. (See John Perry Barlow's description in the foreword on page XV.)

10. Allright, I've subscribed to a commercial service. Now what?

Say I've subscribed to America Online?

On America Online, after your modem dials the number and logs you in, AOL greets you with a window on your computer screen that says, "Welcome to America Online." You'll see a menu of AOL services, each with a corresponding icon you can select with your mouse, or your tab and space keys if you don't have a mouse. Selecting the newspaper icon, for example, will take you to the day's top news stories. By selecting the "Departments" button, you can view a menu of America Online's broad subject areas, such as "Entertainment" and "Travel & Shopping."

But the quickest way to navigate around AOL is by using its *keyword* system, available under "Go To" on the menu bar. If you know where you want to go, select the *keyword* command from this menu, then type the *keyword*. How will you know the right *keyword*? You'll find it in Net Guide. For example, you can reach the Parents Information Network (see page 199) by typing the *keyword* PIN.

What about CompuServe?

The initial menus you'll see on CompuServe after you've logged in include "What's New This Week," with announcements about new services and upcoming events; "Top," which offers access to the basic services (like the AP newswire and weather); and the broad CompuServe subject areas, including "Computers/Technology" and "Hobbies/Lifestyles/Entertainment." You can search the CompuServe menus, or navigate directly to a subject by using the *go* command from the menu and typing the appropriate *go* word, which is identified in Net Guide. The Graphics Gallery Forum (see page 71), for example, is reachable by using the *go* command (clicking on it or using the key combination) and typing GALLERY (if you don't have CompuServe's Information Manager type, GO GALLERY).

And Delphi?

When you log in to Delphi you'll first see the "Main Menu," which includes its broadest category groupings, like "Groups and Clubs" and "Business and Finance." By choosing any of these categories, you can browse for a specific forum. Or navigate directly to your destination by using Delphi's version of the *go* command. For example, you can reach Delphi's Theological Network (see page 130) by typing GO GR THEO.

And GEnie?

GEnie opens with a menu called "GEnie Announcements," similar to CompuServe's "What's New This Week" or AOL's "Welcome to America Online." This is followed by GEnie's "TOP" menu, which offers broad subject groups similar to the other commercial services'—"News, Sports & Features," for example. Use the menus to navigate or type the appropriate *keyword*. Typing TIS, for instance, will take you to GEnie's Travel RoundTable (page 237).

And Prodigy?

Prodigy's initial screen is labeled "Prodigy Highlights" and contains a news update and menu of the broad Prodigy categories. The direct-navigation command, available at the bottom of the screen, is *jump*. Prodigy's "Education BB" (page 300), for example, is reached by using the *jump* command and typing EDUCATION BB.

You're online. Welcome to Cyberspace!

11. Now what do I do? Can I get email? What is email, anyway?

You can get email if (1) you belong to one of the commercial services (2) you have Internet access, or (3) you belong to a bulletin-board service that offers email. Email lets you receive personal messages in a private online mailbox (the person sending you email doesn't have to belong to your service). If you're on America Online, for example, you can receive email from people with accounts on all the other services, including CompuServe, GEnie, Prodigy, and Delphi, as well as people using the Internet or commercial email providers like MCI Mail. You can also use email to receive Internet "mailing lists" and files from Internet computers, even if you don't have full Internet access.

12. Can I send email?

If you can receive email, you can send email to other users on the commercial services, the Internet, and bulletin-board services. All you need is the address to which you want to send your email. For instance, you can send email to the president with the address PRESIDENT@WHITEHOUSE.GOV (see page 262). (See page 20 for complete sending instructions.)

13. Can I go onto the Internet?

Actually, you may already be on the Internet in a limited way. If you have an account on one of the major commercial networks, you have email access to other people with an Internet address and to Internet mailing lists. If you're on a local BBS that offers Usenet newsgroups, you are receiving messages delivered via the Internet.

14. What is *full* Internet access and how do I get it?

With full access you'll get email and Usenet newsgroups, plus the ability to transfer files (including software), chat live with others around the world (for no additional cost), and log in to other Internet computers. In other words, you'll be able to wander freely throughout Cyberspace.

Many schools and universities offer full Internet access to students and faculty members; some are even extending service to their alumni. Not-for-profit organizations often make Internet access available to members and employees. Some communities offer limited access through Free-Nets (page 111). And some corporations connected to the Net provide their employees with accounts. In addition, full access is available to individuals through public Internet providers (page 327) which have begun to sprout up around the country, for fees that range upward from $15 a month.

15. Do I really need it?

Full Internet access lets you tap into an ever-expanding world of information. The commercial services and bulletin boards more or less control the "content" you'll be able to receive. With full access to the Internet *you* are in control.

Usenet

Usenet is a collection of millions of messages, grouped by specific subject categories called "newsgroups" (e.g., REC.ARTS.STARTREK.MISC—see page 34). Anyone can join a newsgroup and read and contribute to the discussions. Messages in a newsgroup are received and made available by many bulletin boards, Internet access "sites," and some commercial services. There are two kinds of newsgroups, the official ones and the alternative ones.

The designation "official" means that a majority of administrators at Internet sites voted to create the newsgroup. Official newsgroups, organized into a hierarchy of broad categories and subcategories, contain the word or prefix COMP (for computer-related), NEWS (for topics related to Usenet itself), REC (for recreation, hobbies, and the arts), SCI (for science and research), SOC (for society and culture), TALK (for issues and debate), or

→

(Compare it to getting your books by subscribing to a book club and doing your own shopping in a bookstore, or between taking a package tour and traveling solo.) What's more, you'll be part of an active, expanding community of people exploring what cyberguru John Perry Barlow calls the information frontier.

16. How do I find my way around Cyberspace?

A variety of software tools can ferry you around Cyberspace and provide you with information as you go. On the commercial services and many BBSs there is a simple system of menus and command words. On the Internet, navigation and information tools are only slightly more complicated. The two main tools are *FTP* and *telnet.*

FTP, short for file transfer protocol, is the method used on the Internet to copy a file from one computer on to another. Using *FTP*, you can search through directories on computers around the world, locate a file, and transfer a copy of it to your own machine via your Internet access provider.

Telnet is the method used to log in to another computer on the Internet. *Telnet* is often used to log in to computers with library catalogs and other searchable databases. But it is also used to log in to computers that have become giant game centers. It's as if your keyboard were directly plugged into that computer, even if you're in

MISC (for other areas) in their title (which is also their Internet address).

Alternative groups, which can be started by anyone, all begin with the prefix ALT. These are some of the most popular features on the Net. There are more than 2,500 ALT groups, from ALT.FEMINISM (page 263) to ALT.HOWARD.STERN (page 52).

If the BBS or Internet site where you have an account says it receives Usenet news, it may receive all categories, or just a few—it's up to your system operator to decide.

There are also newsgroup categories that cover narrower topics, including BIONET (biology news), BIZ (business), and K12 (education). Messages in these newsgroups are collected and distributed the same way as in other newsgroups but are usually received only at sites interested in the topics.

New York and the other computer is in Australia. You can't transfer files, but you can use programs on the "remote" system.

But knowing *how* to go somewhere is just part of the trip. It's just as important to know *where* you want to go. There's the rub.

Every commercial service has a user manual, sometimes several, but each manual covers only the material on its own service. There are several guides to the Internet, some for sale in bookstores, some available online for free. But these guides (see page 314) are mainly about *how*, not *where*, to go. There are also software programs available on the Internet, one of them called "Archie," another called "Gopher," that help you find files or databases—but each has tremendous limitations in its scope and ease of use.

Perhaps the easiest way to find your way around Cyberspace (all the commercial services, the Internet, and thousands of BBSs) is with the book you're holding in your hand. Net Guide presents almost 4,000 places you can go on the Net. It organizes these places by subject. You can go directly to what you want rather than waste time scanning long lists looking for what might possibly interest you.

Internet Addresses

Internet addresses include a computer name, followed by a location, followed by a domain (or type of site) name, linked by dots. There's an archive file with *Star Trek* information, for example, on FTP.UU.NET. Here, FTP is the name of the machine; UU means it's located at a company called UUNET Technologies; the domain name NET means the machine is part of a group used for network resources. An individual's Internet address might be NETGUIDE@MINDVOX.PHANTOM.COM. In this case, NETGUIDE is the user's name, or "handle;" MINDVOX is the name of the computer; PHANTOM is the company that provides the user with Internet access; COM means that the "site" is a commercial enterprise. Besides NET and COM, the other domain names are EDU for educational institutions, GOV for government sites, MIL for military facilities, and ORG for nonprofit and other private organizations.

17. How does Net Guide work?

Let's say you're interested in *Star Trek*. It's a popular subject on the Net, as you can see if you turn to page 60 in the Arts & Entertainment section. First you'll find a brief introduction to the *Star Trek* choices with some suggestions and recommendations from Net Guide. For instance, Net Guide singles out REC.ARTS.STARTREK.MISC (a Usenet newsgroup available from the Internet and on selected BBSs) as one of the most comprehensive catalogs of *Star Trek* lore and trivia. Then there's a wide range of choices on the page, including the Star Trek Club on America Online; tlhIngan Hol, an Internet mailing list devoted to the Klingon language; The Flagship Enterprise, a BBS for Trekkies; discussion about *Star Trek*–inspired games on the Usenet newsgroup REC.GAMES.NETREK and the Internet mailing list Stargame; and 25 other entries. Each entry offers all the information you'll need to get from the Net Guide page to the proper location in Cyberspace.

A Net Guide entry consists of three major parts: The name of the entry (in boldface), a description of the entry, and the address information (preceded by a ✓).

"ML" after the name of the entry indicates a mailing list; "NG," a newsgroup; "BBS," a bulletin-board service. Other entries, such as commercial services, as well as *FTP*, *telnet*, and other Internet sites, can be clearly identified by their addresses.

In between the description and the address you'll often find one or more of the following icons: 🎲 💬 ♠ ▦. The icon 🎲 means that you can play games here; 💬 indicates that there's a place to chat in real time with other

> ### Hyphenation in a Net Guide entry
> Addresses in Cyberspace are often long and they aren't always in plain English. Internet, FidoNet and Smartnet addresses, in particular, consist of one uninterrupted string of characters, hyphens, and underline marks. (The occasional port number in an Internet "telnet" address is not part of the uninterrupted string.) If an Internet, FidoNet or Smartnet address breaks to the next line in a Net Guide entry, *there will be no hyphen to indicate the break* (to avoid confusion with hyphens that *are* part of the address). The absence of a hyphen *does not mean that the address consists of two words*—just type the address as one uninterrupted string.

users; ⊕ lets you know that you can shop online at this site; and ▦ tells you that the service provides news.

After the ✓ you'll see the name of a network, followed by an arrow. The arrow means "go to…" It is followed by all the steps you have to take, such as typing a command or starting a program, to get to the site. (Additional ✓'s indicate the other networks through which the site is accessible; triple dots indicate another address on the same network.)

The following chart highlights in red the elements in a Net Guide entry:

The Site Name	Activity Icon	Command or Program
Weather Underground Sites U.S. and Canadian weather forecasts, ski conditions, earthquake reports, severe-weather reports, hurricane advisories, and weather conditions in some international cities. ▦ ✓**INTERNET** …→*telnet* DOWNWIND.SPRL.UMICH.EDU 3000 …→*telnet* MEASUN.NRRC.NCSU.EDU 3000 …→*telnet* WIND.ATMOS.UAH. EDU 3000 …→*telnet* UCSU.COL ORADO.EDU 3000	**Weather Underground Sites** U.S. and Canadian weather forecasts, ski conditions, earthquake reports, severe-weather reports, hurricane advisories, and weather conditions in some international cities. ▦ ✓**INTERNET** …→*telnet* DOWNWIND.SPRL.UMICH.EDU 3000 …→*telnet* MEASUN.NRRC.NCSU.EDU 3000 …→*telnet* WIND.ATMOS.UAH. EDU 3000 …→*telnet* UCSU.COL ORADO.EDU 3000	**Weather Underground Sites** U.S. and Canadian weather forecasts, ski conditions, earthquake reports, severe-weather reports, hurricane advisories, and weather conditions in some international cities. ▦ ✓**INTERNET** …→*telnet* DOWNWIND.SPRL.UMICH.EDU 3000 …→*telnet* MEASUN.NRRC.NCSU.EDU 3000 …→*telnet* WIND.ATMOS.UAH. EDU 3000 …→*telnet* UCSU.COL ORADO.EDU 3000
The Site Description	The Network	The Address(es)
Weather Underground Sites U.S. and Canadian weather forecasts, ski conditions, earthquake reports, severe-weather reports, hurricane advisories, and weather conditions in some international cities. ▦ ✓**INTERNET** …→*telnet* DOWNWIND.SPRL.UMICH.EDU 3000 …→*telnet* MEASUN.NRRC.NCSU.EDU 3000 …→*telnet* WIND.ATMOS.UAH. EDU 3000 …→*telnet* UCSU.COL ORADO.EDU 3000	**Weather Underground Sites** U.S. and Canadian weather forecasts, ski conditions, earthquake reports, severe-weather reports, hurricane advisories, and weather conditions in some international cities. ▦ ✓**INTERNET** …→*telnet* DOWNWIND.SPRL.UMICH.EDU 3000 …→*telnet* MEASUN.NRRC.NCSU.EDU 3000 …→*telnet* WIND.ATMOS.UAH. EDU 3000 …→*telnet* UCSU.COL ORADO.EDU 3000	**Weather Underground Sites** U.S. and Canadian weather forecasts, ski conditions, earthquake reports, severe-weather reports, hurricane advisories, and weather conditions in some international cities. ▦ ✓**INTERNET** …→*telnet* DOWNWIND.SPRL.UMICH.EDU 3000 …→*telnet* MEASUN.NRRC.NCSU.EDU 3000 …→*telnet* WIND.ATMOS.UAH. EDU 3000 …→*telnet* UCSU.COL ORADO.EDU 3000

18. Okay, I need to *telnet*. Explain step by step what I have to do.

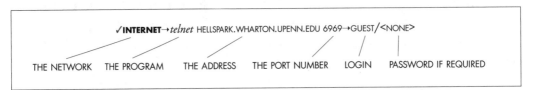

✓**INTERNET**→*telnet* HELLSPARK.WHARTON.UPENN.EDU 6969→GUEST/<NONE>

THE NETWORK   THE PROGRAM   THE ADDRESS   THE PORT NUMBER   LOGIN   PASSWORD IF REQUIRED

1. Log in to your Internet site and locate the *telnet* program. This is the software program that will transport you to another computer on the Internet. Since *telnet* is a widely used feature, you will most likely find it in the main menu of your Internet access provider. On Delphi, for example, *telnet* is available in the main Internet menu. Just type TELNET.

2. Once you've started the program, you should see a *telnet* prompt (for instance, TELNET> or TELNET:). Type OPEN <TELNET ADDRESS>, replacing the bracketed text with the address of the machine you want to reach. (Note: Some systems do not require you to type OPEN. Also, don't type the brackets.) Let's say you want to go to the New York Public Library. The New York Public Library and its catalogs are at the address NYPLGATE.NYPL.ORG, so that after the *telnet* prompt you would type OPEN NYPLGATE.NYPL.ORG. Some addresses include a port number with the *telnet* address; type a space to separate the port number from the address. To reach the Weather Underground, for example, type OPEN DOWNWIND.SPRL.UMICH.EDU 3000 after the *telnet* prompt. (Remember: 3000 is a port number. Port numbers are placed after the uninterrupted string. It's the only time when an Internet address contains a space.)

3. The *telnet* program will connect you to the remote computer—in our example, the New York Public Library. Once you're connected, you'll see a prompt that reads LOGIN:. Type the remote computer's login name as listed in the Net Guide entry. The New York Public Library login is NYPL. If no login is needed, the Net Guide entry will say <NONE>—just press the <RETURN> or <ENTER> key. Now the remote system will ask you for a password, probably with the prompt

PASSWORD:. Type the password as indicated in Net Guide. If no password is requested, the Net Guide entry will say <NONE>, meaning you should press <RETURN>. Oh, and you may be asked about the type of terminal you're using. If you're unsure, vt-100 is a safe bet.

4. You're logged in. Now just follow the instructions on the screen, which will differ with every *telnet* site.

19. I want to *FTP.* Explain step by step what I have to do.

When you're *FTP*ing, you're copying a file from another Internet-connected computer to your own.

1. Log in to your Internet site. Then, start the *FTP* program on your local computer—in most cases, by typing FTP or choosing it from a menu, probably the main menu.

2. When you see the *FTP* prompt, type OPEN <FTP.ADDRESS> to connect to the other computer. The Star Trek Archive, for example, is at the address FTP.UU.NET, so you would type: OPEN FTP.UU.NET. (By the way, OPEN is not always required.)

3. Most *FTP* sites offer what is called "anonymous login," which means that you won't need a personal account and password to access the machine. When you connect to an "anonymous" *FTP* machine, you will be asked for your

name with the prompt NAME:. Type ANONYMOUS after the prompt. Next, the remote system will ask you for your password with the prompt PASSWORD:. Type your email address.

4. Once you're logged in to an *FTP* site, you can change directories by typing CD <DIRECTORY NAME>. For example, the Star Trek Archive at FTP.UU.NET is in USENET/REC.ARTS.STARTREK. After login, type CD USENET to change to the Usenet directory, then CD REC.ARTS.STARTREK to change again (to move back up to the original directory, you must type CDUP or CHDIRUP).

5. To transfer files from the *FTP* site to your home directory use the GET command. For example, in the Star Trek Archive there's a picture of Mr. Spock. Retrieve it by typing GET spock.gif and <RETURN>. The distinction between upper- and lowercase in directory and file names is important. Type a lower case letter when you should have typed upper case and you'll leave empty-handed.

20. I want to read the messages in a newsgroup. Explain step by step what I have to do.

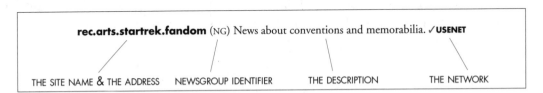

rec.arts.startrek.fandom (NG) News about conventions and memorabilia. ✓USENET

THE SITE NAME & THE ADDRESS   NEWSGROUP IDENTIFIER   THE DESCRIPTION   THE NETWORK

1. Usenet newsgroups are the "forums" that travel the Internet—accessible to anyone without subscribing. Reading Usenet newsgroups is easy—all you need is an Internet site that offers them. On Delphi, for example, you simply choose Usenet from the menu of Internet services.

2. The messages in a newsgroup, called "posts," are listed and numbered chronologically—in other words, in the order in which they were posted. You can scan a list of message headers, which includes a subject line for each message as well as the name of the person who wrote it, before deciding to read a particular message.

3. If someone posts a message that prompts responses, the original and all follow-up messages are called a "thread." The subject line of subsequent posts in the thread refers to the subject of the original. For example, if you were to post a message with the subject "How Do I Sell My Script?" in ALT.STARTREK.CREATIVE, all responses would have the subject line "RE: How Do I Sell My Script?" In practice, however, topics in a thread tend to wander off in many directions.

4. Different services offer different kinds of software for reading the newsgroups, called "readers." Some readers let you follow message threads, others organize messages chronologically. You can also use a reader to customize the newsgroup menu to include only the newsgroup you're interested in. Follow the instructions for the reader offered by your service. (Typing ? will usually direct you to the instructions.)

Note: In some of the Net Guide listings, an asterisk (*) has been used to represent collections of related newsgroups—for example on page 93, COMP.SYS.SGI* indicates a set of newsgroups that includes COMP.SYS.SGI.APPLICATIONS, COMP.SYS.SGI.HARDWARE, and COMP.SYS.SGI.TECH.

21. I want to email. Explain step by step what I have to do.

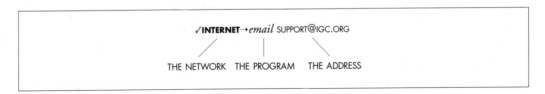

If you have an Internet account, email is simple. Most likely, the main menu at the Internet provider you use has "send" or "mail" options, and "to" or "for" when you're in "mail." Just address your email to a person's user name. For instance, mail to John Doe (user name: JDOE) at the World, an Internet service provider, would be addressed to JDOE@WORLD.STD.COM (note: Don't put a dot at the end of an email address).

What about sending email *from* CompuServe?

Enter the CompuServe mail area by choosing the *go* command from the menu and typing MAIL (if you don't have CompuServe's Information Manager software, type GO MAIL). If you want to send a message to someone on another commercial service, your email will be routed through the Internet, so you must address it with the prefix INTERNET:. Mail to John Doe at American Online, for instance, would be addressed INTERNET:JDOE@AOL.COM; to John Doe at The World, it would be addressed INTERNET:JDOE@WORLD.STD.COM.

And *to* CompuServe?

Use the addressee's CompuServe I.D. number. If John Doe's I.D. is 12345,678 you'll address mail to 12345.678@COMPUSERVE.COM (make sure to replace the comma in the CompuServe I.D. with a period).

How do I send email *from* America Online?

Use AOL's Internet mail gateway (*keyword:* INTERNET). Then address and send mail as you normally would on any other Internet site, using the JDOE@SER VICE.ORG address style.

And *to* America Online?

Just address email to JDOE@AOL.COM.

And *from* GEnie?

Use the *keyword:* MAIL and address email to JDOE@SERVICE.ORG@INET#.

And *to* GEnie?

Address email to JDOE@GENIE.GEIS.COM.

From Delphi?

Use the command GO MAIL and address mail to INTERNET"JDOE@SERVICE.ORG" (make sure to include the quotation marks).

To Delphi?

Address mail to JDOE@DELPHI.COM.

From Prodigy?

To send mail from Prodigy, first download Prodigy's Mail Manager by using the command JUMP MAIL MANAGER. Address mail to JDOE@SERVICE.ORG. Mail Manager is available for DOS and Windows only.

To Prodigy?

Address mail to the addressee's user I.D. For John Doe (user I.D.: ABCD12A), for example, you would address it: ABCD12A@PRODIGY.COM.

Finger
Anyone with an Internet address has an automatically maintained personal "log" that contains such basic information as when you last logged in, your full name, sometimes even your postal (aka "snail mail") address. Logs can be viewed by anybody with Internet access, generally by typing FINGER along with the Internet address of the person you want information about. Many systems allow you to customize your personal log so that someone "fingering" you will see whatever news you choose to include about yourself. There are even information services linked to finger files—FINGER YANOFF@CSD4. CSD.UWM.EDU, for example, for the latest list of interesting Internet services.

22. What's a mailing list, and how do I get put on or taken off one?

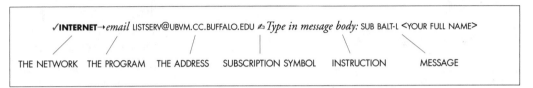

√**INTERNET**→*email* LISTSERV@UBVM.CC.BUFFALO.EDU ✍*Type in message body:* SUB BALT-L <YOUR FULL NAME>

THE NETWORK   THE PROGRAM   THE ADDRESS   SUBSCRIPTION SYMBOL   INSTRUCTION   MESSAGE

Mailing lists are electronic discussions distributed via the Internet email system. There are numerous mailing lists, each dedicated to a very specific topic. You become a member of an "ML" by "subscribing" to it. This means that from then on you will receive via email everything that is posted on the list by the administrator and by the other subscribers. Mailing lists are maintained and distributed by a human moderator, or by an automated system.

To subscribe to a mailing list, send an email to the mailing list's subscription address containing the following information:

1. Where it says SUBJECT in your email message, enter the text from the Net Guide listing that appears after ✍*Type in subject line:*. If ✍*Type in subject line:* does not appear, leave the subject line blank. For example, Strek-L does not require a subject, so you would press <RETURN> when you see the prompt SUBJECT:.

2. If the subscription service is automated, you'll be asked to type a short line of text in the message body. The Net Guide listing for Strek-L, for example, says ✍*Type in message body:* SUB STREK-L <YOUR FULL NAME>. Enter only this text, replacing the bracketed text with your name. Other subscription requests require that you include your email address, noted in Net Guide as <YOUR EMAIL ADDRESS>. Don't include any other text (or the brackets).

3. If the Net Guide listing says ✍*Subscribe by request*, do just that—write a short note asking to be added to the mailing list. As a courtesy, include your email address (to help things along, include the word SUBSCRIBE in the subject line).

4. To unsubscribe you use the same address that you used to subscribe—not the list address, but the subscription address mentioned in Net Guide. If the list is automated (i.e., if you had to type something in the message body), sending SIGNOFF <LIST NAME> or UNSUBSCRIBE <LIST NAME> will generally do the job—don't include your full name. If the list is maintained by a human (i.e., if you had to subscribe by request, or type something in the subject line), then send a message, such as PLEASE UNSUBSCRIBE ME FROM THIS LIST. Here, it's a good idea to type UNSUBSCRIBE in the subject line.

23. What's *WAIS*, and how do I use it?

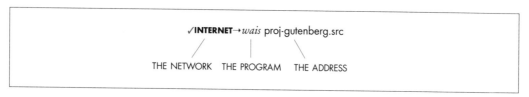

A Wide Area Information Server (*WAIS*) is a program that allows you to find and retrieve files on a large number of Internet computers through keyword searches. Some 500 databases residing on Internet computers are searchable this way.

If your Internet access provider does not offer *WAIS* (and most of them don't), you can use a "public *WAIS* server" by *telnet*ting to it (see the explanation on how to *telnet* to an Internet computer on page 15; a list of public *WAIS* servers can be found on page 314). The machine will start running the *WAIS* program by listing all the available databases.

If you know which database you want all you have to do is type /, and the *WAIS* will ask you to enter the name of the database after the prompt SOURCE NAME. Type the database name, hit <RETURN>, and the *WAIS* will find and highlight your database. Select it by hitting the spacebar. You can select more than one database to search simultaneously.

Now you can start a keyword search in that database—not to be confused with America Online's *keywords*. In a *WAIS* keywords are words that the files you hope to find will probably contain (in the Project Gutenberg database, the keyword ALICE will find a full-text version of *Alice in Wonderland*). Type W, and when you see the prompt KEYWORDS type one or more keywords separated with a space, then hit <RETURN>.

First the public *WAIS* server establishes a connection with the Internet computer that your database is on. Next it does a search of all the files as it looks for your keywords. Finally, it reports back to you with a list of "hits"—files that contain your keywords.

These files have a number ranging from 0 to 1,000 in front of their names. The higher the number, the more on target the file probably is. Use the up and down keys to browse through the list. You can now retrieve any file by highlighting it and hitting the <RETURN> key. The file's text will be scrolled onto your screen, with pages separated by a colon. At a colon, hit the spacebar.

24. I want to chat. Explain step by step what I have to do.

The live chat service on the Internet is called Internet Relay Chat, or IRC (page 219). The chat is real-time, which means that if you type something, the people you're chatting with—in Sweden, Switzerland, or the Sudan—see your words appear immediately on their screens. People from around the world gather in "channels" that are usually focused on a specific theme or subject. When a channel is "hot," there may be as many as fifty chatters. Sometimes, though, it's just you and a friendly stranger. If you would like to join the channel #hottub, for instance, where conversation is supposed to mimic that found in a hot tub, do the following:

1. If your Internet site offers IRC (sometimes called an IRC client), follow the site's access instructions. This may be as simple as typing IRC at the main-menu prompt.

2. Once you're there, you can go to a particular channel. For example, to go to the channel #hottub all you have to do is type /CHANNEL #HOTTUB and <RETURN>. (Whatever you type on IRC appears on the other users' screens as dialogue, so if you don't want to converse but want to give an IRC command, you have to first type a back slash.)

3. If you want to see a list of available channels, with the number of people participating, and a short description of what the channels are about, type /LIST and press <RETURN>.

4. If you would like to create your own channel, follow the same steps you would to join an existing channel, but substitute the new channel name you want. If there isn't already a channel named #NETGUIDE on IRC, for example, you would type /CHANNEL #NETGUIDE to create it.

5. To quit IRC, type /QUIT and <RETURN>.

On CompuServe, chat takes place in the "CB Simulator" which you can reach by using the *go* command from the menu and typing CB (or, if you don't have CompuServe's Information Manager software, type GO CB). You can choose one of 36 channels to join. To join a channel, type /CHA <CHANNEL NUMBER> and <RETURN>.

AOL's chat area is "The People Connection," which can be reached by using the *keyword* CHAT. The first screen you'll see is called "The Lobby Window." The left side of the window contains four icons: "People," "Rooms," "Center Stage," and "PC Studio." "People" provides information about the people in whatever room you enter. "Rooms" gives a list of the rooms where conversation is currently taking place. "Center Stage" takes you to an online "auditorium" where AOL presents online guests and games. "PC Studio" offers a schedule of "Center Stage" activities and an overall guide to the conversation and topics in each of the rooms.

GEnie's chat area is "ChatLines." You can reach it by typing the *keyword* CHAT. "ChatLines" is part of the "LiveWire" area and is divided into channels that you enter by typing /CHA <CHANNEL NUMBER> and <RETURN>. Information on all the channels is available in Channel 1, the "Welcome Lounge."

Delphi's Chat area is centered in the "Main Conference Area" (type GO GR CONFERENCE). Its subject areas are called "groups." To see a list of available groups when you enter the area, type WHO after the conference prompt. When you've selected a group you want to join, type JOIN <GROUP NAME> or JOIN <GROUP NUMBER> to enter the group. You can create your own conference group by typing JOIN followed by a name that isn't currently on the menu.

25. How do I download a file?

Downloading a file means copying a file from a remote computer onto your own computer. The download command on each of the commercial services may differ slightly depending on the type of computer you use, but in most instances file downloads work as follows:

On America Online, once you locate the file you want, select the file name so that it's highlighted. Then select one of two buttons: DOWNLOAD NOW, or DOWNLOAD LATER. If you choose DOWNLOAD LATER, the file will be added to a list of files, all of which you can download when you're done with your America Online session.

On CompuServe, if you're browsing a library list (using CompuServe's Information Manager), you can highlight a file you want and select the RETRIEVE button to download it immediately. If you want to download it later, select the box next to the file name, then select YES when you leave the forum and a window appears that says DOWNLOAD MARKED FILES? (If you don't have Information Manager, type DOWN and <RETURN> at the prompt following the file description.)

On Delphi, after you read a file description in the file or "database" area, there are four commands available—NEXT, DOWN, XM, and LIST. Type DOWN and <RETURN> to download the file.

On GEnie, after you've chosen a file to download, select DOWNLOAD A FILE from the "RoundTable library" menu. When you see the prompt ENTER THE DOWNLOAD REQUEST: type the file name and <RETURN>. At the next prompt, which asks you to confirm your download, type D and <RETURN> to download the file. At the next prompt, you'll be asked to choose a download "protocol"; your best choice is z-modem (number 4), so type 4 and <RETURN>.

On the Internet, any file that you retrieve using *FTP* will be stored in a personal directory on your Internet site, often called your "Home" directory. To download the file to your PC, follow the instructions for your site—typing a question mark will usually return a list of available commands.

26. How do I get a picture? How do I look at it?

Pictures are available everywhere on the Net. To get a picture or image, use the same process you would use to download any other file. Most photographs are stored in one of two popular file formats: GIF or JPEG (sometimes called JPG). These file formats are easily recognized by their file-name suffixes—the picture of Microsoft's Bill Gates on the back cover of Net Guide, for example, is a file called gates.gif.

You can view these photos with several free or low-cost programs for your computer. Many of them are available for downloading from the computer system forums and conferences listed in Net Guide. On the Macintosh, for example, the most popular program is GIFConverter, which lets you view both GIF and JPEG files. Look for it in the libraries of the Mac Applications Forum (page 82) on CompuServe, or the Macintosh Graphic Arts & CAD Forum (page 70) on America Online. For DOS machines, a popular converter is VPIC, and for Windows, Paint Shop Pro. Both programs are available in the PC Animation & Graphics Forum (page 70) on America Online, and in many other locations.

27. What if forget what to do? What if I get lost? What if I panic? What if I make a fool of myself?

Don't worry, everybody does. Just ask for help (it's one of the easiest ways to get to know people). Each of the commercial services has an online help area, and the system operators (sysops) on BBSs are (usually) delighted to serve their customers.

On the Internet you can get help in a couple of places. If you've reached an *FTP* site but can't remember how to change directories, just type ? to get a list of *FTP* commands. If you're stumped while at a *telnet* site, type ? or HELP to get assistance. In fact, the question mark can be a useful tool at a prompt during any Internet activity.

If all else fails, call us at 1-800-NET-1133 and we'll get you home....

Part 1

Arts & Entertainment

1

Art & design

Direct from the quattrocentro to Cyberspace. One of the world's greatest art troves will reside, now and in the foreseeable future, online. It can be found in **Rome Reborn: The Vatican Library & Renaissance Culture**. All of the images and text that were displayed at the 1993 exhibit at the Library of Congress have been digitized and relocated to an Internet FTP site. Hundreds of high-quality reproductions in GIF form can be downloaded. CompuServe's **Fine Art Forum** and RelayNet's **Fine Arts** both offer extensive coverage of contemporary art comings and goings.

On the Net

Across the board

Afterwards Coffeehouse Offers working artists and art lovers an area to discuss all the arts, including literature, painting, design, opera, dance, and theater. ✓**AMERICA ONLINE**→*keyword* AFTERWARDS

Artcrit (ML) For anyone interested in the visual arts, discussions cover postmodernism, Marxist and feminist theories, curatorial practices, and other art-related topics. Reviews are encouraged and published biweekly. ✓**INTERNET**→*email* LISTSERV@YORKVM1.BITNET ✍ *Type in message body:* SUB ARTCRIT <YOUR FULL NAME>

Nude by Renoir—from America Online's Mac Graphic Arts & CAD Forum.

Arts BB Discuss movies, books, and art. ✓**PRODIGY**→*jump* ARTS BB

Fine arts

alt.binaries.pictures.fineart.digitized (NG) Distribute your work. ✓**USENET**

Fine Art Forum An artists' area sponsored by *Art Cellar Exchange* magazine, with discussions on artists, galleries, and paintings, as well as a classified ad section. ☺♋ ✓**COMPUSERVE**→*go* FINEART

Fine Arts Discussions of all forms of art, including sculpture, painting, dance, music, and language. ✓**ILINK**→*number* 228

Fine Arts Provides information on galleries and museums, upcoming shows, artists, art collecting, painting, photographic reproductions, sculpture, and auctions. Includes advertisements for shows, artist biographies, and buy and sell ads. ✓**RELAYNET**→*number* 353

rec.arts.fine (NG) For those interested in the fine arts. ✓**USENET**

Online museums

Art Gallery An exhibit of computer graphic art—changes monthly. ✓**PRODIGY**→*jump* ARTS GALLERY

The Earth Art BBS! (BBS) An online art gallery. And the hub for GreenNet and the Sierra Club as well as the home of The International Duck Stamp Print Exchange (an official source of information for limited-edition conservation prints). 803-552-4389 FREE

The OTIS Project "The operative term is stimulate." A library of hundreds of images and animations as well as artist information. Includes photos, ray tracings, zine covers, and video stills. ✓**INTERNET** ...→*ftp* SUNSITE.UNC.EDU →ANONYMOUS/<YOUR EMAIL ADDRESS>→pub/ multimedia/pictures/OTIS ...→*ftp* AQL.GATECH.EDU→ANONYMOUS/<YOUR EMAIL ADDRESS>→pub/OTIS

Rome Reborn: The Vatican Library & Renaissance Culture An indefinite online exhibit of more than 200 of the Vatican library's most precious manuscripts, books, and maps. Includes images of each work and the text captions as displayed at the 1993 exhibit held at the Library of Congress. ✓**INTERNET**→*ftp* SEQ1.LOC. GOV→ANONYMOUS/<YOUR EMAIL ADDRESS>→pub/vatican.exhibit

Smithsonian Online Includes information about the museum's exhibits, a photo library, publication information, and educational supplements on America Online. The Internet site has a Smithsonian catalog available in a hypercard stack as well as GIFs and exhibit information. ✓**AMERICA ONLINE**→*keyword* SMITHSONIAN

The Mona Lisa—from America Online's Mac Graphic Arts & CAD Forum.

✓**INTERNET**→*ftp* SUNSITE.UNC.EDU →ANONYMOUS/<YOUR EMAIL ADDRESS> →pub/multimedia/pictures/smith sonian

Design & architecture

AEC Interest Area For those interested in the use of computers in architecture design and construction, including presentation and production output, project management, and multimedia presentation. Provides a software library where users can upload their work. ✓**AMERICA ONLINE**→*keyword* AEC SIG

Design List (ML) Covers art and architecture and information related to design. Conferences are announced. ✓**INTERNET**→*email* LIST SERV@PSUVM.BITNET ✍ *Type in message body:* SUBSCRIBE DESIGN-L <YOUR FULL NAME>

Design Online-Media Net (BBS) For art directors, graphic artists, and multimedia designers. Provides databases on video, film, art, design, animation, and related fields. 212-242-7685 $50/YEAR

Geodesic (ML) Forum for discussing Buckminster Fuller and his works and philosophies. "If

you're interested in discussing Bucky, or finding out about 8500 ft. high pyramidal cities that float in the ocean and house 1,000,000 people comfortably (2000 sq. ft apartments with 1000 sq. ft. extra patio/garden space), or 1+ mile diameter spherical cities that float in the air *WITHOUT POWER*, then sign up for the list!" ✓**INTERNET**→*email* LISTSERV @UBVM.BITNET ✍ *Type in message body:* SUBSCRIBE GEODESIC <YOUR FULL NAME>

Stuxch-L (ML) Forum for students in art, architecture, and visual and basic design. ✓**INTERNET** →*email* LISTSERV@PSUVM. PSU.EDU ✍ *Type in message body:* SUB STUXCH-L <YOUR FULL NAME>

Ceramics

Clayart (ML) Covers topics related to ceramic arts and pottery. Includes exhibition opportunities, conference information, workshop announcements, and grant information. ✓**INTERNET**→*email* LISTSERV @UKCC.UKY.EDU ✍ *Type in message body:* SUB CLAYART <YOUR FULL NAME>

Graffiti

Graffiti Open discussions about graffiti. ✓**BIX**→*conference* GRAFFITI

Art news

alt.artcom (NG) "An online magazine forum dedicated to the interface of contemporary art and new communication technologies." Includes conference, exhibition, and publication announcements. 🖥 ✓**USENET**

Miscellaneous

The Metropolitan Museum of Art Authentic artist reproductions. 🕹 ✓**COMPUSERVE**→*go* MMA

Authors

Major cyberauthors include Douglas Adams, Katherine Kurtz, Anne McCaffrey, Terry Pratchett, Isaac Asimov, David Eddings, J.R.R. Tolkien, Stephen King, Thomas Pynchon, and Anne Rice. What these writers have in common is a certain relationship to reality and fantasy that is very much at home in Cyberspace. Several of them are noted cyberwanderers who gladly offer their email addresses. But never fear, the traditional English department is well represented too, from Jane Austen to Shakespeare.

On the Net

Classics

Austen-L (ML) Devoted to the works of Jane Austen and her contemporaries—e.g., Fanny Burney, Maria Edgeworth, and Mary Wollstonecraft. ✓INTERNET→email CCMW@MUSICA.MCGILL.CA ✍ *Subscribe by request*

Chaucer (ML) An open forum for discussion of medieval English literature. ✓INTERNET→email LIST SERV@SIUCVMB.SIU.EDU ✍ *Type in message body:* SUB CHAUCER <YOUR FULL NAME>

Chaucernet (ML) Devoted to the works of Geoffrey Chaucer and medieval English literature and culture between 1100 and 1500. Sponsored by the New

Terry Pratchett—downloaded from garfield.catt.ncsu.edu.

Chaucer Society. ✓INTERNET→ *email* LISTSERV@UNLINFO.UNL.EDU ✍ *Type in message body:* SUBSCRIBE CHAUCER <YOUR FULL NAME>

Dartmouth Danté Project Full text of *The Divine Comedy* as well as reviews and commentary from the past (extending back 600 years) and the present. Search the text by a specific line, limit your searches to English or Latin or Italian, and more. ✓INTERNET→*telnet* LIBRARY.DARTMOUTH.EDU→connect dante

The Mark Twain Forum (ML) Scholarly discussion of Mark Twain and his writings. Forum includes conference and publication announcements, queries, etc. ✓INTERNET→*email* LISTSERV@VM1. YORKU.CA ✍ *Type in message body:* SUBSCRIBE TWAIN-L <YOUR FULL NAME>

Milton-L (ML) Forum for those interested in the life and writings of John Milton. ✓INTERNET→*email* MILTON-REQUEST@URVAX.URICH.EDU ✍ *Subscribe by request*

Shaksper (ML) For scholars or anyone interested in Renaissance drama to share research, discuss teaching strategies, announce conferences, and engage in debate about Shakespeare. ✓INTERNET →*email* LISTSERV@UTORONTO.BITNET ✍ *Type in message body:* SUB SHAKSPER <YOUR FULL NAME>

Shakespeare Archive Includes directories for his comedies, tragedies, histories, and poetry. Also stores a Shakespeare glossary. Need a Shakespearean tragedy? Choose among *Othello, Hamlet, Macbeth, King Lear, Romeo and Juliet*...Interested in reading some of his poetry? Get the Sonnets or perhaps "The Rape of Lucrece." ✓INTERNET→*ftp* ETEXT.ARCHIVE. UMICH.EDU→ANONYMOUS/<YOUR EMAIL ADDRESS>→pub/Fiction/ Shakespeare

Twentieth century

alt.fan.tom-robbins (NG) For fans of the novelist Tom Robbins. ✓USENET

alt.fan.wodehouse (NG) Discuss humor writer P. G. Wodehouse and his works. ✓USENET

alt.journalism.gonzo (NG) Discussions about Hunter S. Thompson, his works, and his life. ✓USENET

Hesse-L (ML) An international discussion group for studying the life and literary works of the German author Hermann Hesse. English and German are the primary languages of communication and topics range from critiques to interpretations to publication announcements. ✓INTERNET→*email* LISTSERV@UCSBVM.BITNET ✍ *Type in message body:* SUBSCRIBE HESSE-L <YOUR FULL NAME>

Kundera-List (ML) Forum for discussing the works of Czech writer Milan Kundera. ✓**INTERNET** →*email* KUNDERA-REQUEST@ANAT3D1. ANATOMY.UPENN.EDU ✍*Subscribe by request*

Sci-fi and fantasy

alt.books.anne-rice (NG) Forum for discussing her books, movies, and interviews. Are the vampires homosexual? What's the most recent book in the Vampire Chronicles? ✓**USENET**

alt.books.isaac-asimov (NG) "I just finished reading *FtF*, and I cried three times," writes one subscriber. Newsgroup devoted to Isaac Asimov's works. ✓**USENET**

alt.fan.eddings (NG) Discuss the works of fantasy writer David Eddings. ✓**USENET**

alt.fan.kent-montana (NG) For fans of the Kent Montana series. ✓**USENET**

alt.fan.piers.anthony (NG) Talk magic, gnomes, and dragons in the newsgroup devoted to science-fiction author Piers Anthony. ✓**USENET**

Hatrack River Town Meeting Inspired by the works of fantasy writer Orson Scott Card, this forum covers any topic of interest to its members. Includes adult conversations in the Town Meeting, the Battle School for members under 18, manuscripts of the author's works in progress, and original writings by members. ✓**AMERICA ONLINE**→ *keyword* HATRACK

PKD-List (ML) Discussion of the works and life of science-fiction author Philip K. Dick (1928–1982). ✓**INTERNET**→*email* PKD-LIST-REQUEST@WANG.COM ✍*Subscribe by request*

Douglas Adams

alt.fan.douglas-adams (NG) Discussions related to Douglas Adams and his books. Topics range from great lines in *Life, The Universe* and *Everything* to information about the computer game *The Hitchhiker's Guide to the Galaxy* to Douglas Adams' obsession with the Macintosh. ✓**USENET**

Douglas Adams FanClub For Adams fans. ✓**FIDONET**→*tag* ADAMS

Anne McCaffrey

alt.fan.pern (NG) Discussions about the fictional world of Pern in Anne McCaffrey's novels and short stories. Also covers multi-user simulations of Pern. McCaffrey herself occasionally contributes. ✓**USENET**

Stephen King

Post Sematary For Stephen King fans, a conference to discuss his books, his movies, and the horror genre. ✓**RELAYNET**→ *number* 402

Stephen King Discussion-International Devoted to the works of "the modern master of horror." ✓**FIDONET**→*tag* S_KING

Katherine Kurtz

alt.books.deryni (NG) Discussions about the Deryni universe created by fantasy author Katherine Kurtz. "What do you all think is going to happen to Rhys Michael? Will he fall under the regent's spell?" asks one newsgroup reader. ✓**USENET**

Deryni-L (ML) Discuss Deryni's books. ✓**INTERNET**→*email* MAIL-SERVER@MINTIR.NEW-ORLEANS.LA.US ✍*Type in message body:* SUBSCRIBE DERYNI-L <YOUR FULL NAME>

Terry Pratchett

alt.fan.pratchett (NG) Discuss Terry Pratchett and his work. Pratchett, a cult favorite, writes humorous fantasy-based science-fiction novels. His works include the Discworld series, *The Color of Magic*, and *The Light Fantastic*. ✓**USENET**

The Pratchett Archives Collection of material, including *The Annotated Pratchett*, which offers elaborate explanations on the subtexts and subtleties in his work, GIFs of Terry and his book covers, and a quote file. ✓**INTERNET**→*ftp* FTP. CP.TN.TUDELFT.NL→ANONYMOUS/<YOUR EMAIL ADDRESS>→pub/pratchett

J.R.R. Tolkien

alt.fan.tolkien (NG) Discuss dwarves or perhaps create your own Middle Earth riddle. ✓**USENET**

rec.arts.books.tolkien (NG) Discuss the works of J.R.R. Tolkien, including the Middle Earth series, his scholarly writings, and his poetry and essays. Also covers parodies, criticisms, related authors, and graphical depictions of Middle Earth. ✓**USENET**

Tolkien (ML) Discuss Tolkien. ✓**INTERNET**→*email* LISTSERV@JHUVM. BITNET ✍*Type in message body:* SUB TOLKIEN <YOUR FULL NAME>

TolkLang (ML) For fans of Tolkien's languages Sindarin and Quenya. ✓**INTERNET**→*email* JCB-REQUEST@DCS.EDINBURGH.AC.UK ✍ *Subscribe by request*

Books

Although people worry that the Net means the end of books, in fact the Net offers the most extensive book coverage available anywhere, from thousands of reviews on the commercial services, to *Publishers Weekly* on America Online, to **Books In Print** on CompuServe. What's more, you can follow your search into any of the many online bookstores and place your order. The World, an Internet-access BBS, recently started **The Online Bookstore** to provide the full text of current books, with an offer of a free download of the first two chapters of *The Internet Companion*, by Tracy LaQuey—6,000 downloads were booked in one month!

On the Net

Reviews & lists

alt.books.reviews (NG) For book reviews only. ✓USENET

Book Bestsellers Forum Includes the *Publishers Weekly* lists of current best-sellers, candid reader reviews, and general discussion. ✓AMERICA ONLINE→*keyword* BOOKS

Book Charts Best-seller lists. ✓PRODIGY→*jump* BOOK CHARTS

Book Review Digest Includes

Eighteenth century book—from the multimedia archive at sunsite.unc.edu.

reviews from 80 North American and U.K. periodicals, with full citations and abstracts for 26,000 fiction and nonfiction works. ✓COMPUSERVE→*go* BOOKREVIEW $$

Critic's Choice Movie, book, video, and game reviews. Entertainment news. And contests to win tickets and posters. ✓DELPHI→*go* ENT CRIT

Diehl Book Review A new book reviewed each day. ✓PRODIGY→*jump* DIEHL BOOK REVIEW

Rainbo Electronic Reviews Light reviews on popular books, children's books, cookbooks, computer books, and audio books. ✓GENIE→*keyword* RAINBO $$

Reviews of Almost Anything Everything that can be reviewed: movies, television, restaurants, software, and books. ✓FIDONET→*tag* REVIEWS

Reference help

Books In Print An online version of the standard bookstore reference. Search by subject, date, author, and publisher. You can also order books. 🖰 ✓COMPUSERVE→*go* BOOKS $$

Bookshelf Search a directory listing from the *Books in Print* database of virtually all books published in the U.S.—more than 1 million listings. Includes 40,000 book reviews from *Publishers Weekly*, *Library Journal*, and the *School Library Journal*. ✓GENIE→ *keyword* BOOKSHELF $$

Online bookstores

Barnes & Noble Enter their catalog and you can search categories including $10 and Under and Paperback Bestsellers. 🖰 ✓COMPUSERVE→*go* BN

Books On Tape Rent audio books—unabridged editions. 🖰 ✓COMPUSERVE→*go* BOT ✓PRODIGY→*jump* BOOKS ON TAPE

McGraw-Hill Book Store Computer/electronic/business books. Discounts and worldwide shopping available. 🖰 ✓COMPUSERVE→*go* MH ✓GENIE→*keyword* MHBOOKS

The Online Bookstore Looking for current releases? Read full-text books online or download them for a small fee. 617-739-9753 ✓INTERNET→*telnet* WORLD.STD.COM→OBS ✖*Must have a World account*

Online Bookstore Discounted general-interest and computer books. 🖰 ✓AMERICA ONLINE→*keyword* BOOKSTORE

Wiley ProShop Books for professionals. 🖰 ✓COMPUSERVE→*go* JW

Offline bookstores

Bookstores Lists of bookstores worldwide. ✓INTERNET→*ftp* PIT-MAN AGER.MIT.EDU →ANONYMOUS/<YOUR EMAIL ADDRESS>→pub/usenet/news. answers/ books/stores

Classical music

They have a little joke in the newsgroup rec.musical.
classic that no matter what the movie or TV show is, its score is probably either Pachelbel's Canon or Orff's Carmina Burana. Whether you want to know the name of the soundtrack used in *Platoon*, or you're working on a 14th-century chant manuscript from Venice that contains several mensural credos and you need some secondary material on this repertory, or you need to find out what the function of a scherzo in Bruckner's symphonies is—because you *love* them both slow and allegro moderato—here are the places to go.

On the Net

Across the board

3 B's A classical-music forum with information on the current concert scene and classical-music discography. "3 B's" stands for Beethoven, Bach, and Brahms. √SMARTNET→*tag* 3 B'S

Classical Music A regular column on classical music by Martin Bookspan. √PRODIGY→*jump* CLASSICAL MUSIC

Classm-L (ML) Classical music from all periods discussed. √INTERNET→*email* LISTSERV@BROWNVM. BROWN.EDU ✍*Type in message body:*

L. von Beethoven—from America Online's Mac Graphic Arts & CAD Forum.

SUB CLASSM-L <YOUR FULL NAME>

Mozart Discussions about classical music, recordings, performances, and the arts. √ILINK→ *number 47*

Music/Arts Forum Includes a message board and library for classical music where you'll find material ranging from a list of classical music terms to a discussion about the performances of Beethoven's Ninth Symphony to GIFs of a favorite composer. 😊💬 √COMPUSERVE→*go* MUSICA

Music Bulletin Board Discussions for all musical tastes. Classical-music fans should note those in the classical section. √PRODIGY→*jump* MUSIC BB

rec.music.classical (NG) Covers all periods of classical music. √USENET

rec.music.classical.guitar (NG) Forum for discussing classical music played on the guitar. √USENET

University of Wisconsin–Parkside Music Archive A large assortment of music information including information on buiding a classical CD collection, a classical-music buying guide, a music database program, and an a-to-z archive of artists with their music, inteviews, and GIFs. √INTERNET→*ftp* FTP.UWP.EDU→ANONYMOUS/<YOUR EMAIL ADDRESS>→pub/ music

Performers

rec.music.classical.performing (NG) Offers discussion for performers on all instruments, including those for early music. √USENET

Opera

Opera-L (ML) A list for opera fans. List owners ask, "Are you one of the happy few who know that Wagner called his Leitmotive Grundthemae? Or you can't tell a leitmotiv from a pretzel, and yet you love all sorts of operas?" √INTERNET→*email* MAILSERV@BRFAPE SP.BITNET ✍*Type in message body:* SUBSCRIBE OPERA-L <YOUR FULL NAME>

Early music

Earlym-L (ML) Discussions about medieval, Renaissance, and baroque music, including performers, instruments, song texts, research, and more. √INTERNET→*email* LIST SERV@AEARN.BITNET ✍*Type in message body:* SUB EARLYM-L <YOUR FULL NAME>

Medieval & Renaissance Music (ML) Covers medieval and Renaissance music. √INTERNET→ *email* MED-AND-REN-REQUEST@MAIL BASE.AC.UK ✍*Type in message body:* JOIN MED-AND-REN-MUSIC <YOUR FULL NAME>

Comics & cartoons

It used to be that you had to go to a once-in-a-lifetime convention (in Akron, or Phoe-

nix, or Sacramento) to be among fellow comic-book crazies. Now the convention is constant. Want to know where you can find reprints of "Mary Perkins On Stage?" The question is being asked on **rec.arts. comics.info**. Or get down on Trudeau for a deviation in yesterday's strip? Let it fly on **rec.arts.comics.strips**. Or veg out on Beanworld? Subscribe to the **Gunk'l-'dunk** mailing list. For seriously obsessed cartoon fans and those who've pushed their obsession into a livelihood, the Net offers detailed and deadpan discussion on the lore and minutiae of a variety of international cartoon myths and celebrities. This includes *Ren & Stimpy* on **alt.tv.ren-n-stimpy**, major Disney coverage on RelayNet, and a *Tiny Toon* focus on **alt.tv. tiny-toon**.

On the Net

Animation

3D SIG For sharing information on 3-D illustration techniques, 3-D visualization, animation, and design. ✓**AMERICA ONLINE**→ *keyword* 3DSIG

Ren & Stimpy, downloaded from the archive at garfield.catt.ncsu.edu.

Animation Discussions about animation techniques and forms. ✓**BIX**→*conference* ANIMATION

comp.graphics.animation (NG) For technical details of computer animation. ✓**USENET**

rec.arts.animation (NG) Discussion about animation, with a focus on cartoons. ✓**USENET**

Toons Includes cartoons, animation, anime, comics, and computer animation. ✓**FIDONET**→ *tag* TOONS

TV shows

alt.aeffle.und.pferdle (NG) German TV cartoon characters. ✓**USENET**

alt.tv.ren-n-stimpy (NG) For fans of the cartoon *The Ren & Stimpy Show*. ✓**USENET**

Disney

alt.tv.tiny-toon (NG) For fans of

Tiny Toon Adventures. ✓**USENET**

Disney Covers not only Disney movies and cartoons but also the theme parks and collectibles. ✓**RELAYNET**→*number* 257

Disney-Comics (ML) Discussion of Disney comics. ✓**INTERNET**→ *email* DISNEY-COMICS-REQUEST@STU DENT.DOCS.UU.SE ✍*Subscribe by request*

Disney Conference Everything Disney, including the movies, cartoons, theme parks, resorts, and music. ✓**FIDONET**→*tag* DISNEY

Disney GIFs Disney comics, plus a huge selection of other comic GIFs. ✓**INTERNET**→*ftp* GARFIELD.CATT. NCSU.EDU→ANONYMOUS/<YOUR EMAIL ADDRESS>→pub/disney

Disney Software BBS (BBS) For the support of Disney software products. Includes interesting GIFs and animations. 818-567-4027

rec.arts.disney (NG) Anything Disney—the parks, cartoons, collectibles, rumors, trivia, and more. ✓**USENET**

The Tiny Toon Archive Images, sound files, episode guides, and other *Tiny Toon*-related material. ✓**INTERNET**→*ftp* UTPAPA.PH.UTEXAS. EDU→ANONYMOUS/<YOUR EMAIL ADDRESS>→pub/tta

Furry animals

alt.fan.furry (NG) For fans of furry animals, such as those in Steve Gallacci's book. ✓**USENET**

Anthropomorphic Magazines Talk about fanzines between readers and publishers, including the titles *Yark!, Furversion, Furtherance, and Furnography.* Topics include publication standards, distribution, and printing problems. ✓**FIDONET**→*tag* FUR_MAG

Anthropomorphics Discussions about "funny animals," a subgroup of science fiction that includes fans of Albedo, Fusion, Stinz, and the science-fiction roleplaying game Other Suns. ✓**FIDONET**→*tag* FURRY

Anthropomorphics, the Technical Side The technical side of anthropomorphics, including costuming tricks and design, computer animation tricks, biological discussions, traps, and techniques. ✓**FIDONET**→*tag* FUR_TECH

Anime & manga

Anime Offers conversation, announcements, and ads for fans of Japanese animation. ✓**RELAYNET** →*number* 341

AnimeMUCK An anime-oriented multi-user simulated environment.

Daffy Duck—from America Online's Mac Graphic Arts & CAD Forum.

Take on a character persona and join a new world. ✓**INTERNET**→*telnet* ANIME.TCP.COM 2035

Japanese Animation Conference Although primarily devoted to the Japanese Anime and other styles like manga, it also includes discussions on American cartoons and animation. ✓**FIDONET**→*tag* ANIME

Manga FTP Sites Sites with manga scripts, anime, and GIFs. ✓**INTERNET** ...→*ftp* FTP.WHITE.TORON TO.EDU→ANONYMOUS/<YOUR EMAIL ADDRESS>→pub/anime ...→*ftp* TCP.COM→ANONYMOUS/<YOUR EMAIL ADDRESS>→pub/anime

rec.arts.anime (NG) For fans of anime. ✓**USENET**

ANSI

ANSI-Art Learn how to create and animate ANSI drawings. A forum for sharing and viewing. ✓**ILINK**→*number* 132

Comics

Cartoons Offers weekly contributions from four different cartoonists: Charles Rodrigues of *MacWeek* and freelancers Theresa McCracken, Mike Keefe, and Peter Oakley. Includes sections for your own artwork, and sections for *Toon Talk* and *Dilbert.* ✓**AMERI-**

CA ONLINE→*keyword* CARTOONS

Comic Books Covers not only comic books but newspaper comic strips, animation, and the past, present, and future of all these arts. ✓**RELAYNET**→*number* 175

Comics Everything related to comic books, comic strips, and their adaptations in other media.

✓**FIDONET**→*tag* COMICS ✗*No buying, selling, or trading*

Comics RoundTable Discussions about comic books and their creators, comic strips, collecting, and animated comics. ⊕🗘 ✓**GENIE** →*keyword* COMICS

Comics/Animation Forum Offers news, reviews, and discussion with comic-book and animation greats as well as libraries and message boards such as Newspaper Strips, Adult Comics, Anime Picture Files, and several others. ⊕🗘 ✓**COMPUSERVE**→ *go* COMICS

Comix (ML) For discussing non-mainstream and independent comic books. ✓**INTERNET**→*email* COMIX-REQUEST@WORLD.STD.COM ✍ *Subscribe by request*

rec.arts.comics.misc (NG) For comics discussion that doesn't fit into one of the other comics newsgroups. ✓**USENET**

rec.arts.comics.strips (NG) For discussing comic strips, editorial cartoons, their creators, and any spinoffs (e.g., "I agree totally. 'Outland,' IMO, seems to be a very angry and bitter strip. He's not even trying to be funny anymore"). ✓**USENET**

The Rook's Manor (BBS) Focus on comic books and Advanced Dungeons and Dragons. 609-228-9466 FREE

Books & strips

alt.comics.buffalo-roam (NG) For fans of *Where the Buffaloes Roam*. ✓**USENET**

alt.fan.bugtown (NG) Covers Matt Howarth comics—e.g.,

Lodoss Girl—from America Online's Mac Graphic Arts & CAD Forum.

Savage Henry. ✓**USENET**

Dilbert Follow the follies of Dilbert, a clueless engineer, and his cynical dog, Dogbert, from the syndicated comic strip *Dilbert*. Includes a large selection of GIFs. ✓**AMERICA ONLINE**→*keyword* DILBERT

Gunk'l'dunk (ML) Discussion of *Tales of the Beanworld*, a black-and-white comic published by Eclipse comics. ✓**INTERNET**→*email* JEREMY@STAT.WASHINGTON.EDU ✍ *Subscribe by request*

LSH (ML) For those interested in the *Legion of Super Heroes*. ✓**INTERNET**→*email* VH00+@ANDREW.CMU. EDU ✍*Subscribe by request*

Modesty Blaise (ML) Discussion of Peter O'Donnell's *Modesty Blaise* books and comics. ✓**INTERNET**→*email* MODESTY-BLAISE-REQUEST@ MATH.UIO.NO ✍*Subscribe by request*

Penguinlust For fans of *Bloom County* and *Outland*. "These comic strips blend social commentary and political satire with a warped sense of humor and a skewed outlook on reality, all of which may be reflected in the conference." ✓**ILINK**→*number* 172

rec.arts.comics.xbooks (NG) Covers Marvel mutant books. ✓**USENET**

alt.fan.disney.afternoon (NG) For fans of the syndicated Disney cartoons *Goof Troop, Rescue Rangers, Darkwing Duck, Duck Tales,* and *Tale Spin.* ✓**USENET**

Collecting

The Collector Connection (BBS) All kinds of comic-related material: buying, selling, and trading; news; release dates of new books; reviews; and forums. 708-682-9223 $30/YEAR

Comics for Sale Buying, selling, and trading of comics and comic-character toys. ✓**FIDONET**→*tag* CMX4SALE

rec.arts.comics.marketplace (NG) For sale and wanted listings related to comics. ✓**USENET**

Games

Krazy Kaption Prodigy artists create a cartoon, and members compete to come up with the best caption. ✓**PRODIGY**→*jump* KRAZY KAPTION

News

rec.arts.comics.info (NG) For factual and information postings about comics as well as reasonably detailed reviews. ✓**USENET**

Legion of Net heroes

alt.comics.lnh (NG) For discussing the Legion of Net.Heroes. ✓**USENET**

Star Trek

rec.arts.startrek.misc (NG) Includes the quarterly posting of the *Star Trek* Comics Checklist—a list of *Star Trek* comics with a synopsis of each. ✓**USENET**

Fantasy & mystery

Two mystery genre BBSs were singled out by *Wired* magazine in its BBS System of the

Month column. **Over My Dead Body!** ("It was a dark and stormy byte..."), in Tacoma, Washington, offers a broad range of mystery reviews, book and plot discussions, and event updates on conventions and writers' workshops. Guess who **221B Baker Street**, in Mountain View, California, is concerned with? The BBS maintains one of the larger Holmes databases for Baker Street Irregular events locally, nationally, and internationally. Teens can try Prodigy's **Abel Adventures**, with games and mysteries with daily clues. **Quanta**, an electronic journal of fantasy fiction, available on CompuServe and the Internet, is one of the fastest-growing magazines in the country.

On the Net

Mystery

Arts BB Includes a Mystery Novels section. Writes one contributor: "I just had to recommend A Dark-Adapted Eye...it is wonderful...the most effective mystery is one which lingers after the book is done...this one definitely does that." ✓**PRODIGY**→*jump* ARTS BB→Mystery Novels

Faded Wizard—from America Online's Mac Graphic Arts & CAD Forum.

Literary Forum Discussions about your favorite authors and perhaps your own writing submissions. Includes a message board for mystery and suspense topics and a library for mystery and romance. 🖼️💬 ✓**COMPUSERVE**→*go* LITFORUM

Mystery (ML) For mystery and detective fiction, regardless of the medium. ✓**INTERNET**→*email* MYSTERY-REQUEST@CSD4.CSD.UWM.EDU ✍ *Subscribe by request*

Mystery Covers writers, novels, television shows, plays, and other whodunits. ✓**RELAYNET**→*number* 169

Mystery Fiction All works of mystery, espionage, and related genres. ✓**FIDONET**→*tag* MYSTERY

Over My Dead Body (BBS) A board for mystery writers, readers, and fans. Offers book reviews of new works; calendars of conventions, events, workshops, and book swaps; and a morgue of "dead files." 206-473-4522

Sherlock Holmes

alt.fan.holmes (NG) Offers discussion about Sherlock Holmes novels, both the Arthur Conan Doyle originals and all derivatives. There are regular postings of lists of every Holmes book, comic book, and magazine ever published. ✓**USENET**

Sherlock's Haven (BBS) Includes Sherlockian material and discussions as well as *Star Trek* stuff, sci-fi games, adult areas, etc. 🖼️🔲 516-433-1843 $20/YEAR

221B Baker Street BBS (BBS) A BBS devoted to Sherlock Holmes. Includes databases of Holmes events and materials, club contacts, and books. Play mystery games, read the *Vermissa Daily Herald*, and trade at the Sherlockian Trading Post. 🖼️🔲 💬 415-949-1734 $10/YEAR

Mystery games

Abel Adventures For older kids and adults, a new mystery every month with clues offered daily. 🖼️🔲 ✓**PRODIGY**→*jump* ABEL ADVENTURES

Gargoyle Participate in a mystery party. 🖼️🔲 ✓**PRODIGY**→*jump* MYSTERY

Fantasy

Science Fiction and Fantasy Club A guide to science fiction and fantasy in books, movies, and television. Also offers a literary area for original writings by members. ✓**AMERICA ONLINE**→*keyword* SCIENCE FICTION

Science Fiction and Fantasy

RoundTables Discussions about science fiction, fantasy, horror, and related areas. Includes the Fantasy Literature Trivia Quiz in the first RT. ⊕❖ ✓**GENIE**→*keyword* SFRT

Sci-Fi/Fantasy Forum Includes conferences with sci-fi and fantasy authors, producers, and publishers. There are message boards and libraries for McCaffrey's Pern, Fantasy Literature, and SF/Fantasy TV. ⊕❖ ✓**COMPUSERVE**→*go* SCIFI

Fantasy zines

DargonZine An electronic fantasy-fiction anthology magazine based on the shared world of Dargon. The same site includes issues of its predecessor, FSFnet. ✓**INTERNET**→*ftp* FTP.EFF.ORG→ANONYMOUS/<YOUR EMAIL ADDRESS>→pub/journal/DargonZine

Quanta (ML) An electronic journal of fantasy fiction. The journal can be sent in ascii or postscript format, so specify in your request. CompuServe and the FTP site (one of many) carry archives of Quanta. ✓**COMPUSERVE**→*go* EFFSIG→Zines from the Net ✓**INTERNET**→*ftp* FTP.EFF.ORG→ANONYMOUS/<YOUR EMAIL ADDRESS>→pub/journals/Quanta ...→*email* QUANTA@ANDREW.CMU.EDU ✍*Subscribe by request*

Superguy (ML) Alternate worlds —one for superheroes—and science-fiction universes are developed by subscribers. "Readers are welcome and authors are begged for!" ✓**INTERNET**→*email* LISTSERV@UCF1VM.CC.UCF.EDU ✍*Type in message body:* SUB SUPERGUY <YOUR FULL NAME>

Fantasy GIFs

alt.fan.tolkien (NG) Discuss dwarves or perhaps create your own Middle Earth riddle. ✓**USENET**

rec.arts.books.tolkien (NG) Discuss the works of J.R.R. Tolkien, including the Middle Earth series, his scholarly writings, and his poetry and essays. Also covers parodies, criticisms, related authors, and graphical depictions of Middle Earth. ✓**USENET**

Space City Grafix (BBS) A board for the serious GIF collector, with high-resolution pictures of science-fiction, fantasy, and horror subjects. 708-748-4025 $55/YEAR

Tolkien (ML) Discuss J.R.R. Tolkien's books. ✓**INTERNET**→*email* LIST SERV@JHUVM.HCF.JHU.EDU ✍*Type in message body:* SUB TOLKIEN <YOUR FULL NAME>

TolkLang (ML) For fans of Tolkien's languages Sindarin and Quenya. ✓**INTERNET**→*email* JCB-REQUEST@DCS.EDINBURGH.AC.UK ✍*Subscribe by request*

Fantasy authors

alt.books.deryni (NG) Discussions about the universe created by fantasy author Katherine Kurtz. "What do you all think is going to happen to Rhys Michael? Will he fall under the regent's spell?" asks one newsgroup reader. ✓**USENET**

alt.fan.eddings (NG) Discuss the works of fantasy writer David Eddings. ✓**USENET**

alt.fan.pern (NG) Discussions about the fictional world of Pern in Anne McCaffrey's novels and short stories. Also covers multi-user simulations of Pern. McCaffrey herself occasionally contributes. ✓**USENET**

Deryni-L (ML) Devoted to Ka-therine Kurtz's novels, particularly those set in the Deryni universe. ✓**INTERNET**→*email* MAIL-SERVER@MINTIR.NEW-ORLEANS.LA.US ✍*Type in message body:* SUBSCRIBE DERYNI-L <YOUR FULL NAME>

Hatrack River Town Meeting Inspired by the works of fantasy writer Orson Scott Card, this forum covers any topic of interest to its members. Includes adult conversations in the Town Meeting, the Battle School for members under 18, manuscripts of the author's works in progress, and original writings by members. ✓**AMERICA ONLINE**→*keyword* HATRACK

The horror...

Vampires are a big subject in the Net community, with considerable attention paid to the gender/lust/beauty issues inspired by vampire tales. Look for the newsgroup **alt.vampyres** ("My darling Lestat, I have been waiting for you in Cyberspace for some time now. When will you come to join me?") and the mailing list **Vampyres**. More traditionally, **alt.horror** delves into the archaeology of mid-1950s fright features—for instance, *The Deadly Mantis*, one of the great bug horrors; *X the Unknown*, a glop classic; and *Curse of Frankenstein*, one of the truly scariest films of all time. The gang on **alt.horror** is committed to the genre. Horror isn't just entertainment but "something that was to change my life forever," says one user. The newsgroup rediscovers old films as continuing nightmares.

On the Net

Across the board

alt.horror (NG) Discuss popular horror books and movies, including modern horror and the horror classics. ✓ **USENET**

Arts BB Includes a section devot-

King Kong, downloaded from the CompuServe Showbiz Forum.

ed to horror topics. ✓ **PRODIGY**→ *jump* ARTS BB→Horror

Horror Discuss horror movies, books, etc.—from Bram Stoker to scary horror novels. ✓ **RELAYNET**→ *number* 226

rec.arts.sf.reviews (NG) Reviews and critical discussions of sci-fi, fantasy, and horror works in any medium. ✓ **USENET**

Science Fiction and Fantasy RoundTables Discussions about science fiction, fantasy, horror, and other, related areas. Includes several libraries with GIFs, texts, and articles. Also features writers' workshops. ◉🐾 ✓ **GENIE**→*keyword* SFRT

Space City Grafix (BBS) A board for the serious GIF collector, with high-resolution pictures of science-fiction, fantasy, and horror subjects. 708-748-4025 $55/YEAR

Lore

alt.folklore.ghost-stories (NG) Share scary, weird tales: "I have had some strange occurrences in the past ten years I have lived in my house..." or "Somebody told me that the album is evil..." ✓ **USENET**

alt.vampyres (NG) Discussions of vampire legend. ✓ **USENET**

Vampyres (ML) Forum to discuss vampiric lore, with emphasis on "fluff" postings—original fiction and nonfiction stories or poems about vampires. ✓ **INTERNET**→*email* LISTSERV@GUVM.BITNET ✍ *Type in message body:* SUBSCRIBE VAMPYRES <YOUR FULL NAME>

Books

alt.books.anne-rice (NG) Forum for discussing her books, movies, and interviews. Are the vampires homosexual? What's the most recent book in the Vampire Chronicles? ✓ **USENET**

Post Sematary For Stephen King fans, a conference to discuss his books, his movies, and the horror genre. ✓ **RELAYNET**→*number* 402

Stephen King Discussion-International Devoted to the works of "the modern master of horror," with opinions, information, trivia, movie announcements, and discussions. ✓ **FIDONET** →*tag* S_KING

Games

Call of Cthulhu (ML) A horror-based fantasy role-playing game. ✓ **INTERNET**→*email* JAMES@SL.RFHSM. LON.AC.UK ✍*Subscribe by request*

Humor

Rec.humor.funny is Usenet's daily online humor magazine. RHF is read (in theory) by 200,000 people on Usenet, FidoNet, and GEnie. RHF tries to spare its readers the agony of bad jokes by selecting every day one to three good ones from the dozens that are submitted. Topical jokes are the specialty of the house. RHF is one way a joke can travel around the world the same day. *Warning*: Rules for submission are as complicated as filing a tax return.

On the Net

Jokes & stories

alt.shenanigans (NG) Share practical jokes, pranks, and random humor. ✓USENET

Comedy Share a joke or a funny story. ✓ILINK→*number* 28

Comedy Approach the forum with an open mind, a keen imagination, and, above all, a good sense of humor. ✓SMARTNET→*tag* COMEDY

Comedy BB Trade jokes, discuss comedians. Sections range from Classic Comedy to Monty Python to Just Jokes. ✓PRODIGY→*jump* COMEDY BB

The Comedy Club Jokes, jokes, and anything goes. ✓AMERICA

Bud Abbott and Lou Costello—from CompuServe's Showbiz Forum.

ONLINE→*keyword* COMEDY

Funny Stories and Jokes Jokes and stories—anything funny. ✓FIDONET→*tag* FUNNY

General Quotes and Puns Share your favorites. ✓FIDONET→*tag* QUOTES_2

Punchline Tell your own jokes or collect others. ✓PRODIGY→*jump* PUNCHLINE ✖*"Clean" jokes only*

rec.humor (NG) Exchange all types of jokes—both old and new. ✓USENET

rec.humor.d (NG) Discuss, analyze, and critique the humor in REC.HUMOR.FUNNY and REC.HUMOR. ✓USENET

rec.humor.funny (NG) Read by more than 200,000 people on Usenet, FidoNet, and GEnie (in some form). Only the "best" submissions are posted. Jokes with a high likelihood of offending are encrypted. ✓USENET

TeleJoke RoundTable From puns and limericks to "really nasty humor." Includes the board Funny Software & Files. ✏✎ ✓GENIE→*keyword* JOKE

Kids & family

G-Rated Humor Puns, riddles, jokes, limericks, movies, situation comedies, and funny, true stories. ✓FIDONET→*tag* HUMOR ✖*No adult topics*

Krazy Kaption Prodigy artists supply the cartoon and you supply the caption. ✓PRODIGY→*jump* KRAZY

Laugh G-rated jokes. ✓FIDONET→*tag* LAUGH

Twisted Tales Humor for kids. Laugh as the nouns and adjectives you innocently offered are merged into a prewritten story. ✓PRODIGY →*jump* TWISTED TALES

Obsessions

alt.fan.lemurs (NG) Celebrate the legend and lore of the lemurs. Find out who Nigel the Lemur is, what Lemurs do when the weather turns cold, if it's unusual to dream of Lemurs, if there are Lemurs on *Star Trek*, if Lemurs have appeared in any court cases. Lemur poetry included. ✓USENET

alt.religion.kibology (NG) For worshippers of the Net personality Kibo. ✓USENET

Tasteless culture

alt.binaries.pictures.tasteless (NG) Disgusting pictures. ✓USENET

alt.tasteless (NG) For people with a twisted and sick sense of humor. Descriptions range from

A cartoon with Woody, Siskel & Ebert —from CompuServe's Showbiz Forum.

tasteless sex acts to bodily-function humor. Not everyone's cup of tea. ✓**USENET**

alt.tasteless.jokes (NG) Post and read socially unacceptable humor—including offensive ethnic jokes and scatological stories. ✓**USENET**

alt.tasteless.pictures (NG) More tasteless pictures. ✓**USENET**

British humor

alt.comedy.british (NG) Discuss British humor. ✓**USENET**

alt.fan.monty-python (NG) Discussion of the television shows and movies done by the British comedy troupe Monty Python. ✓**USENET**

Monty Python Conference For all fans of the comedy troupe. Includes information, quotes, and related topics that would interest Python fans. ✓**FIDONET**→*tag* MONTE

Monty Python (MntyPyth) Dedicated to discussing Monty Python and other British humor. ✓**RELAYNET**→*number* 414

Join in

alt.flame (NG) *Scream at and insult each other online*. ✓**USENET**

alt.stupidity (NG) People writing stupid things—sometimes apparently trying to be funny. ✓**USENET**

Brainbender Compete by poking fun at political figures, social trends, and other targets with dry, sarcastic humor. ⊞🖵 ✓**PRODIGY**→*jump* BRAINBENDER

Oracle

rec.humor.oracle (NG/ML) The Usenet Oracle will answer all your questions about life. This list compiles the best of the Oracle responses. ✓**USENET** ✓**INTERNET**→*email* ORACLE-REQUEST@IUVAX.CS.INDI ANA.EDU☞*Subscribe by request*

rec.humor.oracle.d (NG) Comments on advice given by the Usenet oracle. ✓**USENET**

Humor zines

Humus An electronic zine dedicated to humor. ✓**INTERNET**→*ftp* QUARTZ.RUTGERS.EDU→ANONYMOUS/ <YOUR EMAIL ADDRESS>→pub/jour nals/Humus

Random Access Humor An electronic magazine with computer, online, and BBS humor, and irregular features like "The Twit Filter" and "The Grunged Glossary." ✓**INTERNET**→*ftp* UGLYMOUSE. CSS.ITD.UMICH.EDU→ANONYMOUS/ <YOUR EMAIL ADDRESS>→pub/Zines/ RAH

News

Comedy Video Announcements of comedies newly released on video. 🖵 ✓**PRODIGY**→*jump* COMEDY

All that jazz

"Here's a melancholy realization," writes the FAQ editor
of **rec.music.bluenote**, the long-running newsgroup for dedicated jazz and blues lovers. "We have to assume there isn't a next time. For me, there wasn't for Bill Chase, and Lightning Hopkins, and Roy Buchanan. So take that 'job-critical' evening off and see Mal Waldron, or drive 250 miles to see Steven Lacy, or through a tornado warning to see Richard Dobson. Some of the old lions in jazz and blues got their starts in the 1930s and 1940s. Check 'em out now and celebrate while you can." Delphi's **Jazz Society** and Prodigy's **Music Bulletin Board** offer particularly wide-ranging and knowledgeable discussions. The **Jazz Archive** is the best stop for quick updates on jazz happenings.

John Coltrane, downloaded from the Jazz Archive at ftp.njit.edu.

On the Net

Across the board

Jazz Jazz technique, artistic value, and music discussed. ✓**FIDONET**→*tag* JAZZ

Jazz Discussion for anyone interested in jazz. ✓**SMARTNET**→*tag* JAZZ

Jazz Archive Includes the subdirectories /images (pictures of favorite jazz artists), /jazz-primer (beginning to intermediate "how to play jazz," history, theory, and jamming), and /rmb (with reviews of jazz books and lists of jazz clubs, festivals, museums, and record stores). ✓**INTERNET**→*ftp* FTP.NJIT.EDU→ANONYMOUS/<YOUR EMAIL ADDRESS>→pub

Jazz Discussions Covers contemporary and traditional jazz and jazz musicians. ☻🏿 ✓**ILINK**→*number* 98

Jazz Society Jazz, fusion, swing, and Dixieland. ✓**DELPHI**→*go* GR MUS

Music and Performing Arts Forum Includes a section called The Blues and another called Jazz/Big Bands for general discussion. The library also has files on both of these topics. ☻🏿 ✓**COMPUSERVE**→*go* MUSICA

Music Bulletin Board Discussions for all musical tastes. Jazz fans should note the Big Band/Nostalgia, Blues, and Jazz sections. ✓**PRODIGY**→*jump* MUSIC BB

rec.music.bluenote (NG) Discussions of past and present jazz and blues music. ✓**USENET**

Artists

Miles (ML) Discussion of Miles Davis, his sidemen, and jazz in general. ✓**INTERNET**→*email* LIST SERV@HEARN.BITNET ✍ *Type in message body:* SUBSCRIBE MILES <YOUR FULL NAME>

78 only

78-L (ML) Discussion dedicated to music of the pre-LP era and music-related collectibles. For those who enjoy listening to music recorded at or about 78 rpm. ✓**INTERNET**→*email* LISTSERV@COR NELL.EDU ✍ *Type in message body:* SUB 78-L <YOUR FULL NAME>

Charts

Billboard Charts Biweekly update of the Jazz Albums *Billboard* chart. 🖼 ✓**PRODIGY**→*jump* JAZZ CHART

Jazz, new age, world

Jazz, New Age & World Music News, music releases, concert information, and gossip about the jazz world. Participate in occasional conferences with stars from the jazz world. ☻🏿 🖼 ✓**GENIE**→*keyword* MUSIC

Shopping

Justice Records Specializes in recordings by rhythm-and-blues and jazz artists. ☝ ✓**COMPUSERVE**→*go* JR

Literature

Just a few of the full-text titles available (for free) from The Reading Room: *Alice in Wonderland, Anne of Green Gables, Dr. Jekyll and Mr. Hyde, Far From the Madding Crowd,* all of Mark Twain, *The Oedipus Cycle, Paradise Lost, Paradise Regained, Peter Pan, Pride and Prejudice, Red Badge of Courage, The Scarlet Letter, The Scarlet Pimpernel,* all of Shakespeare, *The Song of Hiawatha, Time Machine, War of the Worlds, War Lord of Mars, The Wizard of Oz, Wuthering Heights, A Christmas Carol,* all of Yeats, *Aesop's Fables, The Night Before Christmas, The Legend of Sleepy Hollow,* and *Winnie the Pooh.*

On the Net

Across the board

Afterwards Coffeehouse Offers working artists and art lovers an area to discuss all the arts, including literature, painting, design, opera, dance, and theater. 🖥️💬 ✓**AMERICA ONLINE**→*keyword* AFTERWARDS

Arts BB Discuss movies, books, and more. There are sections for Stephen King fans, romance novels, Rush Limbaugh, science fiction, theater, dance, and comic books, as well as special sections reserved for Prodigy guests.

William Shakespeare, downloaded from sumex-aim.stanford.edu.

✓**PRODIGY**→*jump* ARTS BB

Bookmarks Casual discussion about a variety of genres: mystery, romance, horror, adventure, science, art, children's, cooking, computer books, history, philosophy, and more. ✓**ILINK**→*number* 174

Literary (ML) Literature forum for the discussion of literary styles, criticisms, favorite books and authors, and any other literature-related topic. ✓**INTERNET**→*email* LISTSERV@UCF1VM.CC.UCF.EDU ✍ *Type in message body:* SUB LITERARY <YOUR FULL NAME>

Literary Forum Discussions about your favorite authors and perhaps your own writing submissions. Sections include poetry, controversial topics, comics, humor, fiction, scifi, journalism, and libraries of member submissions. 🖥️💬 ✓**COMPUSERVE**→*go* LITFORUM

rec.arts.books (NG) Book discussions (perhaps the Robin Hood legends or maybe Daniele Steele's latest), reviews, and bookstore information. Periodically includes bookstores by geographical area—

e.g., Manhattan bookstores. ✓**USENET**

Poetry

Haiku Poetry and Prose Original work and quotations of haiku and other forms of disciplined, enlightened writing. ✓**FIDONET**→*tag* HAIKU

Poetry Corner Provides an outlet for your original poems or selections from your favorite poet. ✓**RELAYNET**→*number* 314

Poetry In Motion (BBS) Produces the monthly newsletter *Poetry In Motion,* which is distributed worldwide. 212-666-6927 FREE

rec.arts.poems (NG) For posting your poetry. ✓**USENET**

American literature

Amlit-L (ML) For scholars and students of American literature, discussions, conference and book announcements, and information exchange. ✓**INTERNET**→*email* LISTSERV@UMCVMB.MISSOURI.EDU ✍ *Type in message body:* SUB AMLIT-L <YOUR FULL NAME>

British literature

Modbrits (ML) A forum for scholars, teachers, and students to discuss modern British and Irish literature. Papers, conference and job announcements, reviews, and abstracts are all welcome. ✓**INTERNET**→*email* LISTSERV@KENTVM.KENT.EDU ✍ *Type in message body:* SUBSCRIBE MODBRITS <YOUR FULL NAME>

Reading tastes

alt.mythology (NG) Discussion of mythology. ✓**USENET**

Barrons' BookNotes Barrons publishes online plot summaries and analyses for great works of literature, from the *Aeneid* to *Catch 22* to *Wuthering Heights*. ✓**AMERICA ONLINE**→*keyword* BARRONS

Bodice rippers

RRA-L (ML) "I don't know why publishers feel compelled to do clinch covers. Maybe they think we read these books for the sex scenes. :-) " Enjoy a good romance novel? This list is for those who do and are proud of it. ✓**INTERNET**→ *email* LISTSERV@KENTVM.KENT.EDU ✍ *Type in message body:* SUBSCRIBE RRA-L <YOUR FULL NAME>

Online texts

Athene and InterText Electronic zines (Athene is the predecessor to InterText) devoted to short fiction. The Internet site carries several other journals, such as *ScreamBaby*, *The Undiscovered Country*, *Unplastic News*, and *We Magazine*. ✓**COMPUSERVE**→*go* EFFSIG→Zines from the Net ✓**INTERNET**→*ftp* ETEXT.ARCHIVE.UMICH.EDU→ ANONYMOUS/<YOUR EMAIL ADDRESS>→ pub/Zines

bit.listserv.gutnberg (NG) Discussion about Project Gutenberg. ✓**USENET**

Dartmouth Library Catalog Includes the full-text files of *The Shakespeare Plays*, *The Shakespeare Sonnets*, and *The King James Bible*. Search for a line and see it in context. ✓**INTERNET**→*telnet* LIB.DARTMOUTH.EDU→ select file

The Online Book Initiative (ML) Two mailing lists related to OBI, a volunteer project to put books and reference materials online. One list discusses issues

Piglet from Winnie the Pooh—from the graphics archive at wuarchive.wustl.edu

related to the project; another posts announcements. Subscribe for both at the same address. ✓**INTERNET**→*email* OBI-REQUEST@ WORLD.STD.COM ✍*Subscribe by request*

The Online Book Initiative Whether you're interested in Poe, Yeats, Thoreau, Milton, or any of the other greats, the OBI has the full text of many classics, including *Moby Dick* and *Pride and Prejudice*. ✓**INTERNET**→*ftp* WORLD. STD.COM→ANONYMOUS/<YOUR EMAIL ADDRESS>→obi

Project Gutenberg Full-text versions of the complete works of Shakespeare, *Moby Dick*, *Paradise Lost*, *Roget's Thesaurus*, *The Federalist Papers*, *Peter Pan*, and more. Intends to have 10,000 titles by the year 2000. ✓**INTERNET** …→*ftp* MRCNEXT.CSO.UIUC.EDU→ ANONYMOUS/<YOUR EMAIL ADDRESS>→ pub/etext …→*ftp* QUAKE.THINK. COM→ANONYMOUS/<YOUR EMAIL ADDRESS>→pub/etext …→*wais* proj-gutenberg.src

The Reading Room Full-text electronic editions of books by Mark Twain, H. G. Wells, F. Scott Fitzgerald, and others. ✓**INTERNET**→ *ftp* INFO.UMD.EDU→ANONYMOUS/ <YOUR EMAIL ADDRESS>→info/Read ingRoom/Fiction

---

CYBERNOTES

What English-language authors learned English as a second language?

AUTHOR	FIRST LANGUAGE
Arlen, Michael	Armenian
Asimov, Isaac	Yiddish
Bellow, Saul	Yiddish, French
Brodsky, Joseph	Russian
Codrescu, Andrei	Romanian
Conrad, Joseph	Polish
Dinesen, Isak	Danish
Ishiguro, Kazuo	Japanese
Kerouac, Jack	French
Kingston, Maxine Hong	Cantonese
Koestler, Arthur	Hungarian
Kosinkski, Jerzy	Polish
Nabokov, Vladimir	Russian
Nin, Anais	French
Rand, Ayn	Russian
Stoppard, Tom	Czech

—FAQ number 8, **rec.arts.books**

The movies

Selections range from fanzine to film quarterly to cult groups to helpful reviews and the latest gossip. AOL's **Movies**, GEnie's **Show Biz RoundTable**, and CompuServe's **Hollywood Hotline** are a return to the great age of movie magazines. **Magill's Survey of Cinema**, available through CompuServe, is salvation for any film student. As a cult item, Woody Allen on **alt.fans. woody-allen** is right up there with *The Rocky Horror Picture Show* (**alt.cult-movies.rocky-horror**). Check out what you want to rent tonight in AOL's **Movie News/Reviews**.

Across the board

Arts BB Contains sections for discussing movies, laser discs, and celebrity guest stars. ✓**PRODIGY** →*jump* ARTS BB

Hollywood Hotline A guide to the latest in movies, TV, and recordings, with a trivia quiz and reviews. ✓**COMPUSERVE**→*go* HOLLYWOOD ✓**GENIE**→*keyword* HOTLINE ✓**DELPHI**→*go* ENT HOLL

Hollywood Online Features sneak previews of the hottest new motion pictures, pictures of your favorite stars, cast and production notes, movie talk, multimedia clips, and studio promotional

Robert de Niro in Taxi Driver—*from GEnie's Show Biz RoundTable.*

items. ✓**AMERICA ONLINE**→*keyword* HOLLYWOOD

The Movie BBS (BBS) A large collection of star photos, information about scripts, movies, videos, and movie trivia. 718-939-5462 $45 BIANNUALLY

Movies Includes the Hollywood Online area, movie news, reviews, a weekly list of the top ten movies at the box office, members' reviews in "You're the Critic," a video guide, and a database of video reviews. 🖳 ✓**AMERICA ONLINE**→*keyword* MOVIES

Movies For movie reviews, Hollywood gossip, and discussion about film controversies. ✓**SMART-NET**→ *tag* MOVIES

rec.arts.movies (NG) Devoted to discussions about current and classic films, favorite movies, spoilers, and the Academy Awards. ✓**USENET**

Showbiz Forum Share movie reviews; discuss your favorite plays, celebrities, and TV shows; retrieve lists of network executives. ⊕💬 ✓**COMPUSERVE**→*go* SHOWBIZ

The Show Biz RoundTable

Movie and television discussions. Includes a huge library of movie GIFs and episode guides, trivia, a comics RoundTable, and a bulletin board. Also includes information on home entertainment technology. ⊕💬 ✓**GENIE**→*keyword* SHOWBIZ

Woody Allen

alt.fans.woody-allen (NG) For Woody fans and apologists. "There's a long tradition of total jerks creating great art." And: "Anybody who gets involved with a woman does it with somebody's daughter." ✓**USENET**

007

alt.fan.james-bond (NG) For fans of James Bond movies. ✓**USENET**

Alternative film

Alternative Entertainment Covers the offbeat and unusual in television and movies, especially canceled TV series like *Twin Peaks* (the former name of the conference). ✓**RELAYNET**→*number* 345

Cult movies

alt.cult-movies (NG) Covers favorite cult movies like *The Rocky Horror Picture Show, Plan 9 From Outer Space,* and *Reefer Madness.* ✓**USENET**

alt.cult-movies.rocky-horror (NG) Discussion of *The Rocky Horror Picture Show.* ✓**USENET**

Rocky Horror Fan Echo Information for *Rocky Horror Picture Show* fans, including talk about audience participation at screenings. ✓**FIDONET**→*tag* ROCKY

Monty Python

alt.fan.monty-python (NG) Discussion of the television shows and movies from the British comedy troupe Monty Python. ✓**USENET**

Monty Python Conference For all fans of the comedy troupe. Includes information, quotes, and related topics that would interest Python fans. ✓**FIDONET**→*tag* MONTE

Monty Python (MntyPyth) Monty Python and other British humor. ✓**RELAYNET**→*number* 414

Serious film buffs

Classic Film Messages about pre-1950s classic films and their stars. ✓**FIDONET**→*tag* CLASSIC_FILM

Filmus-L (ML) Discussion of music for films and television. Topics range from reviews of film scores to film-music history and theory to contact information about professionals in the field. ✓**INTERNET**→*email* LISTSERV@IUBVM. UCS.INDIANA.EDU ✍*Type in message body:* SUB FILMUS-L <YOUR FULL NAME>

rec.arts.cinema (NG) A moderated group that provides serious analyses of film. ✓**USENET**

Screen-L (ML) Forum for students and teachers of film and TV to discuss topics ranging from post-post-structuralist theory to the next SCS/UFVA conference. ✓**INTERNET**→*email* LISTSERV@UA1VM. UA.EDU ✍*Type in message body:* SUBSCRIBE SCREEN-L <YOUR FULL NAME>

Reviews

Current Films Reviews and recommendations by Prodigy critics. ✓**PRODIGY**→*jump* CURRENT FILMS

Film and Movie Review Everything about movies, videos, and television, for all ages. ✓**FIDONET**→*tag* FILM

Magill's Survey of Cinema Covers articles on films released since 1902, with plot summaries; discussion of influences; and data on titles, release dates, cast, credits, ratings, running times, and studios. ✓**COMPUSERVE**→*go* MAGILL ✓**PRODIGY**→*jump* MOVIE GUIDE $$

Media Movie reviews and discussions of television, radio, and print media. ✓**ILINK**→*number* 52

Movie Charts A list of the highest-grossing films. ✓**PRODIGY**→*jump* MOVIE CHARTS

Movies Credit List Lists of actors, actresses, dead movie stars, directors, writers, composers, cinematographers, and more. The site also contains plot summaries, goofs, movies, trivia, and titles files. ✓**INTERNET**→*ftp* REFUGE.COLORA DO.EDU→ANONYMOUS/<YOUR EMAIL ADDRESS>→pub/tv+movies/lists

Movie News & Views Column by Leonard Maltin. Includes a weekly and monthly feature story as well as his picks of the week. ✓**PRODIGY**→*jump* MOVIE NEWS

Movie News/Reviews Search at home for the video you want to rent. The Video Reviews Database allows you to search by subject, actor, director, and writer. Hollywood Online offers previews for upcoming movies, a movie-review database, GIFs and sounds, and movie notes. ✓**AMERICA ONLINE**→*keyword* MOVIES

Movie Reviews by Cineman Reviews of new films and home videos, and previews of coming attractions. ✓**DELPHI**→*go* ENT MOV ✓**GENIE**→*keyword* CINEMAN

Oscars Hollywood's Oscar winners. ▦ ✓**PRODIGY**→*jump* OSCARS

rec.arts.movies.reviews (NG) Movie reviews. ✓**USENET**

Reel Poll A survey of Prodigy members' movie likes and dislikes. ✓**PRODIGY**→*jump* REEL POLL

Reviews of Almost Anything Everything that can be reviewed: movies, TV, restaurants, software, and books. ✓**FIDONET**→*tag* REVIEWS

Roger Ebert's Reviews & Features Provides reviews, celebrity interviews, a movie source list, and a feedback section that lets you communicate directly with one half of the *Siskel & Ebert* team. ▦ ✓**COMPUSERVE**→*go* EBERT

Videos

Laser Craze Hundreds of laser videos. ☏ ✓**GENIE**→*keyword* LASER-CRAZE

Movies-By-Modem (BBS) Search a library of VHS tapes and laser discs. ☏ 216-694-5736 FREE

Video Exchange Includes reviews of new releases, product information, plus exchanges of tapes and discs. ✓**RELAYNET**→*number* 292

Videos News and reviews on the recent action, comedy, drama, and kids' video releases; the video charts; and shopping for video equipment. ▦ ☏ ✓**PRODIGY**→*jump* VIDEOS

Walden By Mail Discounted videotapes. ☏ ✓**GENIE**→*keyword* WALDENVID

Music

Music achieves an extra di- mension on the Net. There's a database where you can find classical Indian music ("Try typing 'Ali' or 'Khan' or 'Ravi' or 'Krishna' as a first search," advises the **Indian Classical Music** FAQ editor); a list of all the ska zines around, including *Skactualities, Skankersore,* and *The Ska Flame*; the lyrics to a 1930s jazz tune believed to be lost; or serious conversations on instrument design, psychoacoustics, and plainchant. And, of course, opinions galore: "Youssou N'Dour has gone distinctly downhill," says a user on **alt.exotic-music.**

On the Net

Across the board

Allmusic (ML) Offers discussion of all forms of music. Topics include composition, musicology, jazz, classical, funk, acoustics, and performance. ✓ **INTERNET**→*email* LISTSERV@AUVM.AMERICAN.EDU ✍ *Type in message body:* SUBSCRIBE ALLMUSIC <YOUR FULL NAME>

Music Everything about music. Who cut what album? What are the hot new groups? Who's heard that hot new song? ✓ **FIDONET**→*tag* MUSIC

Music Discuss any type of music,

Mr. Lucky, downloaded from ftp.uwp. edu.

access press releases, and join the swap shop. 🖥 ✓ **BIX**→*conference* MUSIC

Music Covers everything from classical to rock, with discussion of bands, music software, operas, Broadway musicals, and recordings. ✓ **RELAYNET**→*number* 131

Music Covers a full spectrum of music topics, from classical to computer music. ✓ **SMARTNET**→*tag* MUSIC

Music/Arts Forum Covers all areas of music, ballet and dance, and drama. An Upcoming Events section has schedules and previews, and a Learning to Play section brings together teachers, parents, and students. Whatever your musical interest—rap, new age, country, adult, alternative—there are discussion boards and libraries. 🖥 ✓ **COMPUSERVE**→*go* MUSICARTS

Music Bulletin Board Discussion boards for all musical tastes— blues, jazz, country, soul, classic rock, modern rock, metal, rap, and techno, to name but a few. ✓ **PRODIGY**→*jump* MUSIC BB

Music City For those interested in music and the music business. Includes information on MIDI. 🖥 ✓ **DELPHI**→*go* GR MUS

Music Connection BBS (BBS)

Everything about music, including MIDI, soundcard files, and the record industry. Win free CDs, cassettes, and other music prizes daily. 🖥 ☎ 404-370-1994 $35 BIANNUALLY

Music RoundTable News about the latest recording releases, gossip about the stars, a music store, and discussions about performers, their music, and music trends. 🖥 🖨 🖥 ✓ **GENIE**→*keyword* MUSIC

University of Wisconsin– Parkside Music Archive Offers hundreds of pictures of pop stars and album covers, covering everyone from Abba to ZZ Top, with REM and 10,000 Maniacs in between; a classical-music buying guide; discographies for more than 350 artists; lyrics for more than 15,000 songs by more than 1,100 artists; logs of music mailing lists available on the Internet, including lists devoted to individual instruments and bands; and guitar tablatures. ✓ **INTERNET**→*ftp* FTP.UWP. EDU→ANONYMOUS/<YOUR EMAIL ADDRESS>→pub/music

A cappella & barber

Barbershop Harmony Offers contact information and discussion for members of barbershop singing organizations, including SPEBSQSA, the Sweet Adolines, and Harmony, Inc. ✓ **RELAYNET**→ *number* 398

The Bobs (Friends of the Bobs) (ML) For discussing The Bobs, a San Francisco a cappella group. Share anecdotes, reviews, and concert dates. ✓ **INTERNET**→ *email* FOBS-REQUEST@NETCOM.COM ✍ *Subscribe by request*

rec.music.a-capella (NG) For those who enjoy performing or merely listening to a cappella music. Discuss technique, books, recordings, and groups. ✓**USENET**

Drum corps

alt.colorguard (NG) Discuss the color guards (bands, DCI, WGI, etc.). ✓**USENET**

rec.arts.marching.drumcorps (NG) Offers information and discussion on the marching and music of drum and bugle corps, especially members of the Drum Corps International (DCI), the drum corps governing organization. ✓**USENET**

rec.arts.marching.misc (NG) Discussion of marching-related activities. ✓**USENET**

Pre-LP

78-L (ML) Discussion dedicated to music of the pre-LP era and music-related collectibles. For those who enjoy listening to music recorded at or about 78 rpm. ✓**INTERNET**→*email* LISTSERV@COR NELL.EDU ✍ *Type in message body:* SUB 78-L <YOUR FULL NAME>

Country & folk

BGrass-L (ML) Discussion of bluegrass music, including bands, performances, publications, history, and more. ✓**INTERNET**→*email* LISTSERV@UKCC.UKY.EDU ✍ *Type in message body:* SUB BGRASS-L <YOUR FULL NAME>

Country Music For country-music fans. ✓**SMARTNET**→*tag* COUN TRYMUSIC

David Wald's Folk Concert Calendar Offers an online calendar of folk-music concerts, with some other musical styles also

included. ✓**INTERNET** ...→*ftp* THEO RY.LCS.MIT.EDU→ANONYMOUS/<YOUR EMAIL ADDRESS>→pub/wald/concert calendar ...→*email* ARCHIVE-SERVER @THEORY.LCS.MIT.EDU ✍ *Type in message body:* SEND WALD CONCERT-CAL-ENDAR

New American Folk Music Discussion List (ML) Tour schedules, reviews, album release dates for artists such as Mary-Chapin Carpenter, David Wilcox, Shawn Colvin, Don Henry, and others. ✓**INTERNET**→*email* LISTSERV@NYSER NET.ORG ✍ *Type in message body:* SUB-SCRIBE FOLK_MUSIC <YOUR FULL NAME>

Filk

alt.music.filk (NG) Science-fiction song parodies. ✓**USENET**

Science Fiction Fannish Folksongs "Filksongs" are fannish folksongs and parodies, an established tradition among science-fiction fans. ✓**FIDONET**→*tag* FILK

International

alt.exotic-music (NG) Recommendations and discussion about "exotic" music. Topics range from "Does anyone know who Paul Bowles is?" to "Looking for another landmark 60's/70's musician with the same frame of music as Brian Eno." ✓**USENET**

alt.music.ska (NG) A forum for discussing ska music. ✓**USENET**

Indian Classical Music A database of Indian CDs, especially Hindustani music. ✓**INTERNET**→ *wais* indian-classical-music.src

Irtrad-L (ML) Discussion about Irish traditional music. ✓**INTERNET** →*email* LISTSERV@IRLEARN.BITNET ✍ *Type in message body:* SUB IRTRAD-L

<YOUR FULL NAME>

Middle-Eastern Music (ML) For fans of Middle Eastern music. ✓**INTERNET**→*email* MIDDLE-EASTERN-REQUEST@NIC.FUNET.FI ✍*Subscribe by request*

Underground

Update Electronic Music News (ML) Discussions about underground music as well as major-label artists. "Update is also attempting to close the popular music gap, or mass music gap, by bringing to the forefront those artists and aspects of the music industry that are struggling to make their voice heard." ✓**INTER-NET**→*email* LISTSERV@VM.MARIST.EDU ✍ *Type in message body:* SUBSCRIBE UPNEWS <YOUR FULL NAME>

Other info

Musical List of Lists Request the list via email or FTP it. Includes information on dozens of music mailing lists. ✓**INTERNET** ...→*email* MLOL-REQUEST @WARIAT.ORG ...→*ftp* ANONYMOUS/<YOUR EMAIL ADDRESS> CS.UWP.EDU→music/info/mailinglist

rec.music.info (NG) A moderated newsgroup with information about music resources on the Internet: FTP sites, music newsgroups, mailing lists, discographies, concert dates, chart listings, and new releases. ✓**USENET**

Miscellaneous

Funky-Music (ML) For discussing funk music. ✓**INTERNET**→*email* FUNKY-MUSIC-REQUEST@APOLLO.LAP. UPENN.EDU ✍*Subscribe by request*

Top Concerts News on the top-grossing music concerts. ▦ ✓**PRODIGY**→*jump* TOP CONCERTS

Musicians & instruments

Cut back on the costs of sheet music by FTP-ing your favorite guitar music from the

Acoustic Guitar Archive or **The Chords and Tablature** archive—from José Feliciano to Frank Zappa. It's free. For innovative composition software, try CSound from MIT's Medialab, at **cecelia.media.mit. edu**. If you'd rather jam at the The Rusty Nail, take a look at the Open Jam Sessions List with open jamming locations throughout the country, available on most music-related newsgroups.

On the Net

Composition

Music Composition Conference For composers, arrangers, and theorists. ✓**FIDONET**→*tag* MUSIC_COMP_101

---

rec.music.compose (NG) Discussion about notation and composition software, sources of inspiration, getting published, theory, orchestration guides, book reviews, and computer hardware used in composition. ✓**USENET**

Keyboards

Music Alley Online Mixers, synthesizers, keyboards. ⊕ ✓**COMPUSERVE**→*go* MAO

Piporg-L (ML) Discussions about all types of organs. Includes stoplists, job postings, restoration hints. ✓**INTERNET**→*email* LISTSERV@

Maigritte's violin—from wuarchive. wustl.edu.

ALBANY.EDU ✍*Type in message body:* SUB PIPORG-L <YOUR FULL NAME>

Percussion

Drum/Percussion Mailing List (ML) Offers discussion on everything related to percussion instruments. ✓**INTERNET**→*email* DRUM-REQUEST@ELOF.MIT.EDU ✍*Subscribe by request*

---

rec.music.makers.percussion (NG) Discussion about percussion instruments. ✓**USENET**

Strings

Acoustic Guitar Archive Carries the *Acoustic Guitar Digest*, an electronic magazine, and song transcriptions, including "Dixie" by The Band and "Sweet Jane" by the Velvet Underground. ✓**INTERNET**→*ftp* CASBAH.ACNS.NWU.EDU→ANONYMOUS/<YOUR EMAIL ADDRESS>→pub/acoustic-guitar

---

The Bottom Line! (ML) For

electric and acoustic bass players. ✓**INTERNET**→*email* BASS-REQUEST@ UWPLATT. EDU ✍*Subscribe by request*

Guitar Chords and Tablature Guitar tablature and chords for old, electric, and acoustic songs. In the *R* directory, for example, you'll find both REM and the Ramones. ✓**INTERNET**→*ftp* FTP.NEVADA. EDU→ANONYMOUS/<YOUR EMAIL ADDRESS>→ pub/guitar

---

Guitar Topics For players, builders, and technicians. Topics include technique, styles, guitar construction and repair, and amplifiers. ✓**FIDONET**→*tag* GUITAR

Lute (ML) For lute players and lute music researchers. ✓**INTERNET** →*email* LUTE-REQUEST@SUNAPEE.DART MOUTH.EDU ✍*Subscribe by request*

Wind

Bagpipe (ML) Forum for any topic related to bagpipes, as well as other Scottish, Irish, and English instruments. ✓**INTERNET**→*email* BAGPIPE-REQUEST@CS.DARTMOUTH.EDU ✍*Subscribe by request*

Brass (ML) Covers brass musical performance and other small musical ensembles. ✓**INTERNET**→ *email* BRASS-REQUEST@GEOMAG.GLY. FSU.EDU ✍*Subscribe by request*

Klarinet (ML) Forum for clarinet players, students, teachers, and others. Includes old and new repertoire, and lists of performances. ✓**INTERNET**→ *email* LISTSERV @VCCSCENT.BITNET ✍*Type in message body:* SUB KLARINET <YOUR FULL NAME>

Performances

"Enter now into a world of high Art Nouveau, much of the decor a recreation of the art of Joseph Urban, set and costume designer for Florenze Ziegfeld," is how AOL sets the scene for its **Afterwards Coffeehouse**. "The color scheme is of the most delicate resda green and dull gold. A magnificent reproduction of Urban's mural 'Garden of Paradise' greets you as you enter, from the ceiling hangs a five foot circular crystal chandelier, and in the background one can hear the strains of Caruso's Aida." Just a bit overdone perhaps, but the discussion, revolving around professional and campus music, dance, acting, and theater, is some of the most energetic, literate, and down-to-earth this side of backstage.

On the Net

Across the board

Afterwards Coffeehouse Offers working artists and art lovers an area to discuss literature, painting, design, opera, dance, and theater. 🌐 ✓**AMERICA ONLINE** →*keyword* AFTERWARDS

Dance

Ballroom (ML) Discussion of

The great Sarah Bernhardt—downloaded from wuarchive.wustl.edu.

ballroom and swing dancing. Events announced. ✓**INTERNET**→ *email* BALLROOM-REQUEST@ATHENA. MIT.EDU ✍*Subscribe by request:* <YOUR FULL NAME><YOUR EMAIL ADDRESS> <AFFILIATION WITH A BALLROOM DANCE GROUP><ZIP CODE>

The Dance Hall (BBS) Dedicated to participatory dance events. Carries dance-related Usenet and FidoNet echoes. 919-688-0174 FREE

Dance-L (ML) Information exchange between dancers, dancing masters, choreographers, and all interested in folk-dance and traditional dance. ✓**INTERNET**→*email* LISTSERV@HEARN.BITNET ✍*Type in message body:* SUB DANCE-L <YOUR FULL NAME>

rec.arts.dance (NG) Covers all aspects of dance—from classical to swing. ✓**USENET**

rec.folk-dancing (NG/ML) Discussion of folk dancing from around the world, with a focus on America, including square, Cajun, contra, barn, and western square morris. ✓**USENET** ✓**INTERNET**→*email* TJW@UNIX.CIS.PITT.EDU ✍*Subscribe by request*

The theater

Astr-L (ML) Academic discussion of the theater. Run by the American Society for Theatre Research. ✓**INTERNET**→*email* LIST SERV@UIUCVMD.BITNET ✍*Type in message body:* SUBSCRIBE ASTR-L <YOUR FULL NAME>

Musicals (ML) For general discussion of musical theater. Gatewayed with the newsgroup REC.ARTS.THE ATRE. ✓**INTERNET**→*email* MUSICALS-REQUEST@WORLD.STD.COM ✍*Subscribe by request*

Perform (ML) Performance theory and medieval drama. ✓**INTERNET** →*email* LISTSERV@IUBVM.BITNET ✍*Type in message body:* SUB PERFORM <YOUR FULL NAME>

rec.arts.theatre (NG) Discussion of all aspects of stage work and theater, including musical theater. ✓**USENET**

Reed-L (ML) Medieval drama. ✓**INTERNET**→*email* LISTSERV@UTORON TO.BITNET ✍*Type in message body:* SUB REED-L <YOUR FULL NAME> ✖*Must request permission*

Stagecraft (ML) Discussions related to stage work, including sound effects, stage management, set and hall design, and show production. Directing, acting, and specific productions do not fall under the purview of this list. ✓**INTERNET**→*email* STAGECRAFT-REQUEST@JAGUAR.UTAH.EDU ✍*Subscribe by request*

Theatre (ML) Theater discussions with a more chatty and less academic tone. ✓**INTERNET**→*email* LIST SERV@GREARN.BITNET ✍*Type in message body:* SUB THEATRE <YOUR FULL NAME>

Radio shows & stars

"I want to write to Howard Stern and tell him (what a dickhead/how wonderful) he is.

What's his address?" The newsgroup **alt.fan.howard-stern** provides the answer and notes: "Particularly vehement and stupid hate letters are likely to get read on the air." Several talk-radio jocks have recently turned into "talk-PC hosts." Digital versions, or "sound files," of their shows are available on a number of Internet sites—a list of which can be found on **alt.internet.talk-radio**.

Rush Limbaugh—from AOL's Mac Graphic Arts & CAD Forum.

Across the board

rec.radio.broadcasting (NG/ML) All about domestic radio broadcasting: programming, new trends, laws and regulations, pirate radio, and more. ✓USENET ✓INTERNET→ *email* JOURNAL@AIRWAVES. CHI.IL.US ✍*Subscribe by request*

Rush Limbaugh

alt.rush-limbaugh (NG) Discussion about Rush Limbaugh, including transcripts of some of his broadcasts. ✓USENET

Rush Limbaugh/EIB Topics General talk and response to Limbaugh's radio and TV shows. ✓FIDONET→*tag* LIMBAUGH

Howard Stern

alt.fan.howard-stern (NG) For fans of Howard Stern. ✓USENET

Howard Stern Discussion Area Discussion about Stern's show and material. ✓FIDONET→*tag* STERN-SHOW

The Greaseman

alt.fan.greaseman (NG) Discussion about the Greasman's radio show. ✓USENET

NPR

NPR Outreach Online Provides education outreach materials such as teachers' guides, newsletters, and brochures about specific NPR programs as well as press releases, programming updates and schedules, and member-station listings. Transcripts may be ordered online. ✓AMERICA ONLINE→*keyword* NPR

rec.arts.wobegon (NG) Discussion of the radio show *A Prairie Home Companion.* ✓USENET

College programming

alt.fan.tna (NG) For the college radio program *T n A.* ✓USENET

DJs

Beats per Minute (ML) A mailing list for DJs. ✓INTERNET→*email*

BPM-REQUEST@ANDREW.CMU.EDU ✍ *Subscribe by request*

DJ List (ML) Covers topics relevant to college DJs: regulations, station policy, equipment, etc. No music reviews. ✓INTERNET→*email* LISTSERV@VM1.NODAK.EDU ✍*Type in message body:* SUB DJ-L <YOUR FULL NAME>

Pirates

Pirate Radio Discussion Area An area for reports of logged pirate radio broadcasts heard on shortwave bands. ✓FIDONET→*tag* FREE_RADIO

Internet talk radio

alt.internet.talk.radio (NG) Discussions about Carl Malamud's *Internet Talk Radio* program. ✓USENET

U.S. Internet Talk Radio Sites A few of the sites carrying the *Internet Talk Radio* program. ✓INTERNET ...→*ftp* SUNSITE.UNC.EDU →ANONYMOUS/<YOUR EMAIL ADDRESS> →pub/talk-radio ...→*ftp* FTP.ACSU. BUFFALO.EDU→ANONYMOUS/<YOUR EMAIL ADDRESS>→pub/talk-radio ...→*ftp* FTP.UTEXAS.EDU→ANONYMOUS/<YOUR EMAIL ADDRESS>→pub/itr

British radio

AMFM (ML) A monthly posting of news stories concerning the UK radio industry. ✓INTERNET→*email* LISTSERV@ORBITAL.DEMON.CO.UK ✍*Type in message body:* SUBSCRIBE AMFM <YOUR FULL NAME>

Records, tapes & disks

You know that tune that you just can't quite get straight in your head? Sort of sounds

like du-du-du-du, a little country, but a little pop too. Mid-seventies. Could be Hall and Oates, but isn't. C'mon. Somebody. Try the Net. "Hi there," begins a query on the mailing list **InfoCD**. "I am looking for a CD for my friend. He told me that it must be Deep Purple or one of their members. There is a song which is the version of Beethoven's Ninth Symphony. I never heard it. But my friend is sure that this CD exists. Please help."

On the Net

Charts

Billboard Charts Updates of the *Billboard* charts. ▦ ✓**INTERNET**→ *finger* BUCKMR@RPI.EDU ✓**PRODIGY**→ *jump* MUSIC CHARTS

Info & reviews

Compact Disc Echo CD and CD-player discussion; laserdiscs and players are also included. ✓**FIDONET**→*tag* CD_ECHO

InfoCD (ML) Information about CDs and CD players. ✓**INTERNET** →*email* CDREQUEST@CISCO.NOSC.MIL ✎*Subscribe by request*

Music Reviews Music reviews by Terry Atkinson, contributor to *Rolling Stone* and the *Los Angeles*

The first Doors album—downloaded from ftp.uwp.edu.

Times. Includes an index for the past year's reviews. ✓**PRODIGY**→ *jump* MUSIC REVIEWS

New/Upcoming Releases (ML) A read-only list with weekly announcements of new releases from the record labels. ▦ ✓**INTERNET**→*email* NEW-RELEASES-REQUEST@ CS.UWP.EDU ✎*Subscribe by request*

rec.audio.pro (NG) Covers studios, equipment, DJ sound, concert recording, special effects, and other information for audio and recording professionals. ✓**USENET**

rec.music.cd (NG) For information and discussion about CDs. ✓**USENET**

Rmusic-L (ML) Forum for discussions of all types of music. Concert and album reviews, lyrics, and more. ✓**INTERNET**→*email* LISTSERV@ GITVM1.BITNET ✎*Type in message body:* SUB RMUSIC-L <YOUR FULL NAME>

Music shopping

Bose Express Music Offers an online catalog and ordering of

CDs, cassettes, videos, laserdiscs, minidiscs, DCC, music magazines and resource books, and accessories. ☻ ✓**AMERICA ONLINE**→ *keyword* EXPRESS MUSIC ✓**COMPUSERVE** →*go* BEM

Columbia House Join and receive free music! ☻ ✓**COMPU-SERVE**→*go* FREECD

Disaster Area Offers industrial, noise, punk, and other strange or experimental music recordings for sale via email orders. ☻ ✓**INTER-NET**→*email* 088940@DOLUNI1.BITNET

Music Works! Over 30,000 CDs and tapes. ☻ ✓**PRODIGY**→*jump* MUSICWORKS!

Noteworthy Music More than 7,500 discounted CDs. ☻ ✓**GENIE** →*keyword* NOTEWORTHY

Personics Custom Cassettes Create a cassette with songs you choose. Pay by the song. ☻ ✓**COMPUSERVE**→*go* PS

Used Music Server Offers a database of CDs, cassettes, and LPs for sale and trade. ✓**INTERNET**→ *email* USED-MUSIC-SERVER@WANG. COM ✎*Type in subject line:* HELP

Miscellaneous

Soundtracks (ML) Includes discussions comparing new and older soundtracks, information about availability of soundtracks, trading lists to enable members to swap, and publication reviews. ✓**INTER-NET**→*email* SOUNDTRACKS-REQUEST@ IFI.UNIZH.CH ✎*Subscribe by request*

Rock & pop

Rock is going global and multimedia on the Net. Download a picture of the Boss in tight jeans and a sweaty, sleeveless T-shirt; get a True-Type font that was used for the script on Enya's album *Watermark*; or notify other fans about a live broadcast on South Africa's cable station M-net of a Sting concert in Oslo, Norway. Not to mention the avalanche of international rock and pop charts the Net provides weekly from Austria to Australia.

Across the board

RockLink Forum Includes news, reviews, concert schedules, gossip, a Grateful Dead forum, and regular contributions from members of the rock radio industry, musicians, and record companies. 🖥 📞 ✓**AMERICA ONLINE**→*keyword* ROCK-LINK

Rock Music Columnist Lisa Robinson writes on the rock scene. 🖥 ✓**PRODIGY**→*jump* ROCK MUSIC

RockNet Forum Provides news, lists of top albums and tapes, articles, and discussion with members of the record industry. 📞🖥 ✓**COMPUSERVE**→*go* ROCKNET

RockNRoll Discussion of rock music and rock groups. Announcements of upcoming con-

Nevermind by Nirvana—downloaded from ftp.uwp.edu.

certs and events. Chat about songwriting, lyrics, and musical instruments. ✓**ILINK**→*number* 63

Rock Week News from the world of rock music. 🖥 ✓**PRODIGY**→*jump* ROCK WEEK

Progressive

alt.music.progressive (NG) Covers the progressive-rock movement that started in the late '60s and early '70s, with groups like King Crimson, Pink Floyd, Kansas, Rush, and Yes. ✓**USENET**

60's/70's Progressive Rock Music Topics include art rock, psychedelia, and all progressive rock music from the period. ✓**FIDONET**→*tag* 60S_70S_PROGROCK

Rave

alt.rave (NG) Discussion about the rave culture, including the underground dance scene and drug use. ✓**USENET**

Raves Archive Includes an archive of the SFRaves mailing list, important posts about the rave scene in general, and numerous examples of rave flier graphics.

✓**INTERNET**→*ftp* SODA.BERKELEY.EDU→ANONYMOUS/<YOUR EMAIL ADDRESS>→pub/sfraves

Grunge

Grunge-L (ML) Discussion of topics related to the form of music known as grunge rock. Information on tour dates, recording reviews, local scene information, interviews and articles, band gossip, etc. Includes adult language and often perverse humor. ✓**INTERNET**→*email* LISTSERV@UBVM.CC.BUFFALO.EDU ✍ *Type in message body:* GRUNGE-L <YOUR FULL NAME>

Punk

alt.music.alternative (NG) Discussions about alternative-music groups. ✓**USENET**

Punk List (ML) Provides discussion and news on punk and hardcore music, bands, and concerts. ✓**INTERNET**→*email* PUNK-LIST-REQUEST @CPAC.WASHINGTON.EDU ✍*Subscribe by request*

The Beatles

Beatles Archive Carries notes and FAQs from the newsgroup REC.MUSIC.BEATLES, hints on the "Paul Is Dead" rumors, and GIFs. ✓**INTERNET**→*ftp* BOBCAT.BBN.COM→ANONYMOUS/<YOUR EMAIL ADDRESS>→beatles

rec.music.beatles (NG) Forum for discussing the Fab Four. ✓**USENET**

Grateful Dead

Dead Flames (ML) Digest for fans of Grateful Dead music. Gated to the Usenet newsgroup REC.MUSIC.GDEAD. ✓**INTERNET**→*email* DEAD-FLAMES-REQUEST@VIRGINIA.EDU ✍

Subscribe by request

Dead Heads (ML) For Grateful Dead fans, concert announcements, ticket availability and ridesharing information. ✓**INTERNET**→*email* DEAD-HEADS-REQUEST@FUGGLES.ACC.VIRGINIA.EDU ✎*Subscribe by request*

Grateful Dead Forum News, GIFs, lyrics, and discussion. 🖼💬 ✓**AMERICA ONLINE**→*keyword* DEAD

Grateful Dead Archive Includes information on Dead head radio hours, graphics, interviews, tour schedules, tape trees, lyrics, discographies, and set lists from concerts. ✓**INTERNET**→*ftp* GDEAD. BERKELEY.EDU→ANONYMOUS/<YOUR EMAIL ADDRESS>→pub/gdead

Grateful Dead (DAT) (ML) Offers a trading center for Dead tapes and discussion about equipment for digital recording. ✓**INTERNET** *email*→DAT-HEADS-REQUEST@FUGGLES.ACC.VIRGINIA.EDU ✎*Type in subject line:* DAT REQUEST

Grateful Dead (Tape) (ML) Discussion about tape trading and audience taping techniques and equipment. Conversation not limited to the Grateful Dead. ✓**INTERNET** *email*→TAPE-HEADS-REQUEST@FUGGLES. ACC.VIRGINIA.EDU ✎*Type in subject line:* TAPE-HEADS REQUEST

Grateful Dead Topics General discussion about the Dead, with reviews, schedules, rumors, and chat. ✓**FIDONET**→*tag* DEADHEAD

rec.music.gdead (NG) For Deadheads. ✓**USENET**

Kate Bush

Love-Hounds (ML) Discussions about music—primarily Kate Bush's. ✓**INTERNET**→*email* LOVE-HOUNDS-REQUEST@EDDIE.MIT.EDU ✎*Subscribe by request*

rec.music.gaffa (NG) Discuss alternative music, especially Kate Bush's music. ✓**USENET**

U2

U2 (ML) All topics related to the band U2. ✓**INTERNET**→*email* U2-REQUEST@HUB.CS.JMU.EDU ✎*Subscribe by request*

Wire (ML) For U2 fans. ✓**INTERNET**→*email* WIRE-REQUEST@HUB.CS.JMU.EDU ✎*Subscribe by request*

Elvis

alt.elvis.king (NG) Speculate on Elvis's whereabouts. ✓**USENET**

Saint Elvis Echo Official echo of the Church of Elvis and the Committee of Honor to Elect Elvis President in 1996. Sightings, personal encounters, and other news on The King. ✓**FIDONET**→*tag* ST_ELVIS

Enya

alt.music.enya (NG) Discuss Enya and her music. ✓**USENET**

Enya (ML) For Enya fans. ✓**INTERNET**→*email* ENYA-REQUEST@BOULDER.COLORADO.EDU ✎*Subscribe by request*

Prince

alt.music.prince (NG) For discussing Prince and his music. ✓**USENET**

Prince (ML) For Prince fans. ✓**INTERNET**→*email* PRINCE-REQUEST@ICPSR.UMICH.EDU ✎*Subscribe by request*

Group lists

10,000 Maniacs (ML) For 10,000 Maniacs fans. ✓**INTERNET**→*email* 10KM.MANAGER@STOKES.STANFORD.EDU ✎*Subscribe by request*

The Alan Parsons List (ML) For fans of Alan Parsons. ✓**INTERNET**→*email* APP-REQ@BALDRICK.CECER.ARMY.MIL ✎*Subscribe by request*

Alicefan (ML) For fans of Alice Cooper. ✓**INTERNET**→*email* LISTSERV@WKUVX1.BITNET ✎*Type in message body:* SUBSCRIBE ALICEFAN <YOUR FULL NAME>

alt.fan.debbie.gibson (NG) For fans of Debbie Gibson. ✓**USENET**

alt.fan.frank-zappa (NG) For fans of Frank Zappa. ✓**USENET**

Arithmetic (ML) For fans of The Sundays. ✓**INTERNET**→*email* ARITHMETIC-REQUEST@UCLINK.BERKELEY.EDU ✎*Subscribe by request*

The Art of Noise (ML) For fans of The Art of Noise. ✓**INTERNET**→*email* AON-REQUEST@POLYSLO.CALPOLY.EDU ✎*Subscribe by request*

Backstreets (ML) For Bruce Springsteen fans. ✓**INTERNET**→*email* BACKSTREETS-REQUEST@UVAARPA.VIRGINIA.EDU ✎*Subscribe by request*

Black Sabbath (ML) For Black Sabbath fans. ✓**INTERNET**→*email* SABBATH-REQUEST@FA.DISNEY.COM ✎*Subscribe by request*

Blue-Eyed-Pop (ML) For fans of The Sugarcubes. ✓**INTERNET**→*email* LISTSERVER@MORGAN.UCS.MUN.CA ✎*Type in message body:* SUBSCRIBE BLUE-EYED-POP <YOUR FULL NAME>

Blue Oyster Cult/Hawkwind (ML) For Hawkwind and Blue

Oyster Cult fans. ✓**INTERNET**→ *email* BOC-REQUEST@SPCVXA.SPC.EDU ✍*Subscribe by request*

Breaking the Chains (Dokken /Lynch Mob) (ML) For Dokken and Lynch Mob fans. ✓**INTERNET** →*email* KYDEN00@UKPR.UKY.EDU ✍ *Subscribe by request*

Chalkhills (ML) For XTC fans. ✓**INTERNET**→*email* CHALKHILLS-REQUEST@PRESTO.IG.COM ✍*Subscribe by request*

Concrete-Blonde (ML) For fans of Concrete Blonde. ✓**INTERNET**→ *email* CONCRETE-BLONDE-REQUEST@ FERKEL.UCSB.EDU ✍*Subscribe by request*

Crowded House (ML) For Crowded House fans. ✓**INTERNET**→ *email* HOUSE-REQUEST@CASBAH.ACNS. NWU.EDU ✍*Subscribe by request*

The Cure (ML) For Cure fans. ✓**INTERNET**→*email* BABBLE-M-REQUEST @CINDY.ECST.CSUCHICO.EDU ✍*Subscribe by request*

David Bowie (ML) For Bowie fans. ✓**INTERNET**→*email* SPIDERS@ PHOENIX.IMAG.FR ✍*Subscribe by request*

Deborah Harry/Blondie Information Service (ML) For Blondie fans. ✓**INTERNET**→*email* CCGUNTER@VAXA.UWA.OZ.AU ✍*Subscribe by request*

Depeche Mode (ML) For Depeche Mode fans. ✓**INTERNET**→ *email* BONG-REQUEST@COMPAQ.COM ✍*Subscribe by request*

Direct (ML) For Vangelis fans. ✓**INTERNET**→*email* DIRECT-REQUEST@ CTSX.CELTECH.COM ✍*Subscribe by request*

Dire-Straits (ML) For Dire Straits fans. ✓**INTERNET**→*email* DIRE-STRAITS-REQUEST@MERRIMACK.EDU ✍*Subscribe by request*

Duran Duran (ML) For Duran Duran fans. ✓**INTERNET**→*email* TIGER-REQUEST@CS.UNCA.EDU ✍*Subscribe by request*

Elvis Costello (ML) For Elvis Costello fans. ✓**INTERNET**→*email* COSTELLO-REQUEST@GNU.AI.MIT.EDU ✍ *Subscribe by request*

Freaks (ML) Covers Marillion and related rock groups. ✓**INTERNET** →*email* FREAKS-REQUEST@BNF.COM ✍ *Type in message body:* SUBSCRIBE FREAKS <YOUR FULL NAME>

Fuzzy Ramblings (ML) Devoted to Fuzzbox. ✓**INTERNET**→*email* FUZZY-RAMBLINGS-REQUEST@FERKEL. UCSB.EDU ✍*Subscribe by request*

Gary Numan (ML) For Gary Numan fans. ✓**INTERNET**→*email* NUMAN-REQUEST@CS.UWP.EDU ✍*Subscribe by request*

Genesis (The New List) (ML) For Genesis fans. ✓**INTERNET**→ *email* GENESIS-REQUEST@CS.UNCA.EDU ✍*Subscribe by request*

Graham Parker (ML) For Graham Parker fans. ✓**INTERNET**→ *email* PARKER-LIST-REQUEST@CONVEX. COM ✍*Subscribe by request*

Hey-Joe (ML) For Jimi Hendrix fans. ✓**INTERNET**→*email* HEY-JOE-REQUEST@MS.UKY.EDU ✍*Subscribe by request*

Indigo-Girls (ML) For fans of Indigo Girls and related artists. ✓**INTERNET**→*email* INDIGO-GIRLS-REQUEST@CGRG.OHIO-STATE.EDU ✍ *Subscribe by request*

INXS (ML) For Inxs fans. ✓**INTER-NET**→*email* INXS-LIST-REQUEST@IAS TATE.EDU ✍*Subscribe by request*

Jamie-L (ML) For fans of Jamie Notarthomas. ✓**INTERNET**→*email* LISTSERV@CORNELL.EDU ✍ *Type in message body:* SUBSCRIBE JAMIE-L <YOUR FULL NAME>

Jane's Addiction (ML) For fans of Jane's Addiction. ✓**INTERNET**→ *email* JANES-ADDICTION-REQUEST@MS. UKY.EDU ✍ *Subscribe by request*

Jazz Butcher (ML) For Jazz Butcher fans. ✓**INTERNET**→*email* JBC-LIST@PASTURE.ECN.PURDUE.EDU ✍ *Subscribe by request*

Jean-Michel Jarre (ML) For fans of the new-age musician Jean-Michel Jarre. ✓**INTERNET**→*email* JARRE-REQUEST@CS.UWP.EDU ✍*Subscribe by request*

Jethro Tull (ML) For Jethro Tull fans. ✓**INTERNET**→*email* JTULL-REQUEST@REMUS.RUTGERS.EDU ✍*Subscribe by request*

Jump-in-the-River (ML) For fans of Sinead O'Connor. ✓**INTER-NET**→*email* JUMP-IN-THE-RIVER-REQUEST @PRESTO.IG.COM ✍*Subscribe by request*

The Kinks (ML) For Kinks fans. ✓**INTERNET**→*email* OTTEN@QUARK. UMD.EDU ✍*Subscribe by request*

Kissarmy (ML) For KISS fans. ✓**INTERNET**→*email* LISTSERV@WKUVX1. BITNET ✍*Type in message body:* SUBSCRIBE KISSARMY <YOUR FULL NAME>

Kraftwerk (ML) For Kraftwerk fans. ✓**INTERNET**→*email* KRAFTWERK-REQUEST@CS.UWP.EDU ✍*Subscribe by request*

Loureed (ML) For Lou Reed fans.

✓**INTERNET**→*email* LOUREED-REQUEST @CVI.HAHNEMANN.EDU ✍*Subscribe by request*

Madonna (ML) For Madonna fans. ✓**INTERNET**→*email* MADONNA-REQUEST@ATHENA.MIT.EDU ✍*Subscribe by request*

Mariah Carey (ML) For Mariah Carey fans. ✓**INTERNET**→*email* SKUL_LTD@UHURA.CC.ROCHESTER.EDU ✍*Subscribe by request*

Melissa Etheridge (ML) For fans of Melissa Etheridge. ✓**INTERNET**→*email* ETHERIDGE-REQUEST@CND.MCGILL.CA ✍*Subscribe by request*

Moody Blues (ML) For Moody Blues fans. ✓**INTERNET**→*email* LOST-CHORDS-REQUEST@ATHENA.MIT.EDU ✍*Subscribe by request*

Neil Young (Rust) (ML) For Neil Young fans. ✓**INTERNET**→*email* MAJORDOMO@DEATH.CORP.SUN.COM ✍*Type in message body:* SUBSCRIBE RUST

Peter Gabriel/Genesis (ML) For Peter Gabriel fans. ✓**INTERNET**→*email* LISTSERV@LISTSERV.ACNS.NWU.EDU ✍*Type in message body:* SUBSCRIBE GABRIEL <YOUR FULL NAME>

Phish (ML) For Phish fans. ✓**INTERNET**→*email* PHISH-REQUEST@FUGGLES.ACC.VIRGINIA.EDU ✍*Subscribe by request*

Ph7 (ML) For fans of Peter Hammill and related rock groups. ✓**INTERNET**→*email* PH7-REQUEST@BNF.COM ✍*Type in message body:* SUBSCRIBE PH7 <YOUR FULL NAME>

Police (ML) For fans of The Police. ✓**INTERNET**→*email* POLICE-REQUEST@CINDY.ECST.CSUCHICO.EDU ✍*Subscribe by request*

Queen (ML) For Queen fans.

✓**INTERNET**→*email* COM@SPACSUN.RICE.EDU ✍*Type in subject line:* SUBSCRIBE

Queensryche (Screaming in Digital) (ML) For fans of Queensryche. ✓**INTERNET**→*email* QUEENSRYCHE-REQUEST@PILOT.NJIN.NET ✍*Subscribe by request*

rec.music.dylan (NG) For Bob Dylan fans. ✓**USENET**

Robin Lane (ML) For Robin Lane fans. ✓**INTERNET**→*email* ROBIN-LANE-REQUEST@CS.WPI.EDU ✍*Subscribe by request*

Rush (ML) For fans of Rush. ✓**INTERNET**→*email* RUSH-REQUEST@SYRINX.UMD.EDU ✍*Subscribe by request*

Siouxsie & the Banshees (ML) Discuss Siouxsie & The Banshees and its offshoots. ✓**INTERNET**→*email* SIOUXSIE-REQUEST+@ANDREW.CMU.EDU ✍*Subscribe by request*

Sisters of Mercy (ML) For fans of Sisters of Mercy. ✓**INTERNET**→*email* DOMINION-REQUEST@OHM.YORK.AC.UK ✍*Subscribe by request*

Smashing Pumpkins (ML) For Smashing Pumpkins fans. ✓**INTERNET**→*email* LISTSERV@LISTS.COLORADO.EDU ✍*Type in message body:* SUBSCRIBE SMASHING-PUMPKINS <YOUR FULL NAME>

Smiths/Morrissey (ML) For fans of the Smiths and Morrissey. ✓**INTERNET**→*email* SMITHS-REQUEST@LANGMUIR.EECS.BERKELEY.EDU ✍*Subscribe by request*

Smothered Hope (ML) For Smothered Hope fans. ✓**INTERNET**→*email* SMOTHERED-HOPE-REQUEST@ECST.CSUCHICO.EDU ✍*Subscribe by request*

Sonic-Life-L (ML) For Sonic Youth fans. ✓**INTERNET**→*email* LISTSERV@CORNELL.EDU ✍*Type in message body:* SUB SONIC-LIFE-L <YOUR FULL NAME> ✖*Membership determined by owner*

Southside Johnny (ML) For Southside Johnny fans. ✓**INTERNET**→*email* SOUTHSIDE-LIST-REQUEST@CONVEX.COM ✍*Subscribe by request*

Steve Morse and the Dixie Dregs (ML) For fans of Steve Morse and the Dixie Dregs. ✓**INTERNET**→*email* BLICKSTEIN@DREGS.ENET.DEC.COM ✍*Subscribe by request*

Tiffany (ML) For fans of the pop singer Tiffany. ✓**INTERNET**→*email* TIFFANY-REQUEST@NYX.CS.DU.EDU ✍*Subscribe by request*

Todd Rundgren (ML) For Todd Rundgren fans. ✓**INTERNET**→*email* AWIZARD-REQUEST@PLANNING.EBAY.SUN.COM ✍*Subscribe by request*

TOP (ML) For fans of the band Tower of Power. ✓**INTERNET**→*email* TOP-REQUEST@CV.RUU.NL ✍*Subscribe by request*

Tori Amos (ML) For Tori fans. ✓**INTERNET**→*email* REALLY-DEEP-THOUGHTS-REQUEST@GRADIENT.CIS.UPENN.EDU ✍*Subscribe by request*

Undercover (ML) For Rolling Stones fans. ✓**INTERNET**→*email* UNDERCOVER-REQUEST@SNOWHITE.CIS.UOGUELPH.CA ✍*Subscribe by request*

Yello (ML) For Yello fans. ✓**INTERNET**→*email* YELLO-REQUEST@POLYSLO.CALPOLY.EDU ✍*Subscribe by request*

Zeppelin (ML) For Led Zeppelin fans. ✓**INTERNET**→*email* LISTSERV@CORNELL.EDU ✍*Type in message body:* SUB ZEPPELIN-L <YOUR FULL NAME>

Science fiction

Sci-fi is, of course, the Rosetta stone or even the Bible of Cyberspace. Authors like Philip K. Dick, Terry Pratchett, and, certainly, William Gibson were exploring out here long before commercial transportation was available. In many ways, the sci-fi grail is pursued on the Net as painstakingly as scholars plumb the depths of ancient texts and fundamentalists decipher Revelations. Try the mailing lists **SF-Lovers** and **The Highly Imaginative Technology-Science Fiction List**, and the online magazine **Multiversal Party Line Storyboard**.

Across the board

Fantasy&SF All aspects of science fiction and fantasy. ✓ILINK→ *number* 62

Science Fiction For fans of SF and fantasy, including *Star Trek*. ✓BIX→*conference* SF

Science Fiction and Fantasy Club A guide to science fiction and fantasy in books, movies, and TV. Also offers a literary area for original writings by members. ✓AMERICA ONLINE→*keyword* SCIFI

Science Fiction and Fantasy Literature Includes discussion, convention news, and writing and

Arnold Schwarzenegger in T2—from GEnie's Show Biz RoundTable.

publishing. ✓FIDONET→*tag* SF

Science Fiction and Fantasy RoundTables Boards and libraries include Science Fact, The Craft of Writing Science Fiction and Fantasy, and *Star Trek*. Chat with the *Next Generation* crew and writers, check out the Society for Creative Anachronism, or discuss the latest sci-fi novels. ✓GENIE →*keyword* SFRT

Science Fiction and Fantasy SIG Fans, readers, and professional sci-fi authors hold discussions and weekly conferences. Includes databases with *Star Trek* information and GIFs, fanzines, book announcements, and a convention calendar. ✓DELPHI→*go* GR SCI

Sci-Fi Books, movies, authors, and TV shows, except *Star Trek* discussions. ✓RELAYNET→*number* 130

Sci-Fi/Fantasy Forum Includes conferences with sci-fi and fantasy authors, producers, and publishers as well as message boards and li-

braries devoted to McCaffrey's Pern, British SF, *Star Trek*, and more. ✓COMPUSERVE→*go* SCIFI

SF-Lovers (ML) For all topics related to science and fantasy fiction, including books, movies, and conventions. This digest is a compilation of articles from the REC.ARTS.SF newsgroups. The archives include episode guides for TV shows, from *Max Headroom* to *Dr. Who*. ✓INTERNET ...→*ftp* ELBERETH.RUTGERS.EDU→ANONYMOUS/ <YOUR EMAIL ADDRESS>→pub/sfl ...→*email* SF-LOVERS-REQUEST@RUTGERS.EDU ↪*Subscribe by request*

Literature & books

Flights of the Mind More than 400 science-fiction and fantasy titles. ✓GENIE→*keyword* FLIGHTS

rec.arts.sf.reviews (NG) Reviews of SF. ✓USENET ✓INTERNET ...→*ftp* TURBO.BIO.NET→ANONYMOUS/ <YOUR EMAIL ADDRESS>→sf-reviews ...→*wais* sf-reviews.src

rec.arts.sf.written (NG) Discussions about written science fiction. Includes informal reviews, continuity discussions, author comparisons, and new-releases announcements. ✓USENET

Science Fiction Reviews Reviews of science-fiction books by Netters. ✓INTERNET→*ftp* BROLGA.CC. UQ.OZ.AU→ANONYMOUS/<YOUR EMAIL ADDRESS>→pub→sfguide6.tar.Z

Fanzines & fandom

Asimov/Analog Forum Includes editorials from *Isaac Asimov's Science Fiction Magazine* (many by Isaac Asimov himself) and *Analog Science Fiction & Fact* that offer thought-provoking views, wit, and predictions about science and society. ✓**AMERICA ONLINE**→*keyword* ASIMOV

Multiversal Party Line Storyboard The online version of *Intercepted*, a science-fiction fanzine. "Think of a head-on collision between *Dr. Who* and *The Addams Family*, with a short visit from Yog-Soggoth." ✓**FIDONET**→ *tag* INTERCEPTED

PMC-List (ML) Material written by McCaffrey, Acker, and others. ✓**INTERNET** →*email* LISTSERV@LIST SERV.NCSU.EDU ✍*Type in message body:* SUB PMC <YOUR FULL NAME>

rec.arts.sf.announce (NG) Announcements of SF conventions, readings, deaths, honors, administrivia, TV specials, and other sci-fi news. ▦ ✓**USENET**

rec.arts.sf.fandom (NG) For discussing fan activities by sci-fi enthusiasts. ✓**USENET**

rec.arts.sf.marketplace (NG) Personal ads for selling or buying sci-fi-related materials. ✓**USENET**

SciFi Science-fiction discussions. ✓**SMARTNET**→*tag* SCIFI

Science Fiction and Fandom Covers science fiction from a fan's view. ✓**FIDONET**→*tag* SFFAN

SF Convention Running For managers of sci-fi and fantasy conventions. ✓**FIDONET**→*tag* SFCON

Future technology

The Highly Imaginative Technology-Science Fiction List (ML) A forum for discussing potential and sci-fi-only technology. "Have you ever wondered how software can start paranoia? Did your last sci-fi book describe a new

kind of energy-plant?" ✓**INTERNET**→*email* LISTSERV@UFRJ.BITNET ✍ *Type in message body:* SUBSCRIBE HIT <YOUR FULL NAME>

rec.arts.sf.science (NG) Forum for discussing science in relation to science fiction. Can scientists help create new SF universes? ✓**USENET**

Pictures

Space City Grafix (BBS) A board for the serious GIF collector, with high-resolution pictures of science fiction, fantasy, and horror subjects. 708-748-4025 $55/YEAR

Movies & TV

Babylon 5 Fan club and discussion of the television series *Babylon 5*. ✓**FIDONET**→*tag* BABYLON5

rec.arts.sf.movies (NG) Discussion of science-fiction movies that do not have their own REC. ARTS.SF group. ✓**USENET**

rec.arts.sf.tv (NG) Discussion of science fiction on TV. ✓**USENET**

Space 1999 (ML) For fans of the TV show *Space 1999*. ✓**INTERNET** →*email* SPACE-1999-REQUEST@QUACK. SAC.CA.US ✍*Subscribe by request*

Star Wars

rec.arts.sf.starwars (NG) Discussion of *Star Wars* books, movies, and lore. ✓**USENET**

Star Wars Covers the movies, books, comics, games, and action figures. ✓**FIDONET**→*tag* STARWARS

MST3K

alt.tv.mst3k (NG) Discuss *Mystery Science Theater 3000*, a program on Comedy Central. ✓**USENET**

MST3K (ML) For fans of *Mystery Science Theater 3000*. ✓**INTERNET** →*email* RSK@GYNKO.CIRC.UPENN.EDU ✍*Type in subject line:* MST3K

Mystery Science Theater 3000 Discussion about the show and classic bad sci-fi and fantasy movies. ✓**FIDONET**→*tag* MST3K

Mystery Science Theater 3000 FTP Site Organizes and archives both the Satellite of Love and the MST3K mailing lists. ✓**INTERNET**→*ftp* GYNKO.CIRC.UPENN. EDU→ANONYMOUS/<YOUR EMAIL ADDRESS>→pub/rsk/mst3k

Quantum Leap

alt.ql.creative (NG) Discussion and fan-produced fiction, parodies, and art about *Quantum Leap*. ✓**USENET**

Quantum Leap Discussion about the time-travel show. ✓**FIDONET**→*tag* QUANTUMLEAP

Dr. Who

The Doctor's Tardis BBS (BBS) "Looking for *Dr. Who* fans and related info." ▮▮◨ 503-938-5110 FREE

Dr. Who Discussion for *Dr. Who* fans. ✓**RELAYNET**→*number* 216

rec.arts.drwho (NG) Anything related to *Dr. Who*. ✓**USENET**

Red Dwarf

alt.tv.red-dwarf (NG) For fans of the British sci-fi comedy TV show *Red Dwarf*. ✓**USENET**

Red Dwarf Archive Episode guides, scripts, quotes, and reviews. ✓**INTERNET**→*ftp* TOASTER.EE. UBC.CA→ANONYMOUS/<YOUR EMAIL ADDRESS>→pub/red-dwarf

Star Trek

"There will be an important assassination today," said

Spock in "Assignment: Earth," a show aired in April 1968. A few days later Dr. Martin Luther King Jr. was shot and killed, notes Mark Holtz in his monthly list of lists on the **rec.arts. startrek.misc**. The list logs everything from number of attempts to self-destruct, references to Shakespeare, and times the phrase "I'm a doctor, not a…" was uttered (five times: "…bricklayer," "…engineer," "…mechanic," "…escalator," and "…coal miner"). It's the true nitpicker's guide.

On the Net

Across the board

The Flagship Enterprise (BBS) A BBS for Trekkies. 304-754-8554 $10 OPTIONAL

rec.arts.startrek.misc (NG) Covers *Star Trek* in all its generations and media. Vote on the best episodes. Learn of references to *Star Trek* in songs. Get answers to your *Star Trek* questions (e.g., how did Tasha die twice?). Includes periodic postings of several lists: *Star Trek*, *Next Generation*, and *DS-9* episode synopses and trivia; starships by type and episode; actors by episode, and their other roles; the *Star Trek* Comics Checklist; *Star Trek* books on tape; etc. Information on Net sites with *Star*

Trek GIFs and sound files. ✓USE-NET

Science Fiction and Fantasy RoundTables Among the many sci-fi features, a bulletin board and a library are devoted exclusively to *Star Trek*. Star Trek On-Line lets you participate in scheduled real-time chat sessions with cast and crew members of *Star Trek: Next Generation*. And, of course, join *Star Trek* Night weekly chats. ◉🝐 ✓GENIE→*keyword* SFRT

Starbase 1 (BBS) *Star Trek* files, role-playing boards, games, messages, etc. 505-425-1863 FREE

StarLink (BBS) Calls itself "America's premier *Star Trek* board." 502-964-7827 FREE

StarTrek Discussions about any generation of *Star Trek*, regardless of its medium—books, movies, TV. ✓ILINK→*number* 107

Star Trek Open discussion on all *Star Trek* topics: movies, television shows, books, comics, and collectibles. ✓FIDONET→*tag* TREK

Star Trek For *Star Trek* fans of any generation. ✓SMARTNET→*tag* STAR TREK

Star Trek Archive Trivia, parodies, background images from the *Star Trek* movies, the original series, and *Next Generation*. ✓INTERNET→*ftp* FTP.UU.NET→ANONYMOUS/<YOUR EMAIL ADDRESS>→usenet /rec.arts.startrek

Star Trek Club Message boards

Lieutenant Troi, downloaded from CompuServe's Showbiz Forum.

on the original *Star Trek*, *Next Generation*, and *DS-9* as well as a library of text files, graphics, sound files, and some animations. Role-play in the StarFleet Academy section and check club news. ◉🝐 🎴 ✓AMERICA ONLINE →*keyword* STAR TREK

Star Trek Movies and TV Shows Covers it all. ✓FIDONET→ *tag* ALL_TREK

Strek-L (ML) All *Star Trek*-related topics open for discussion. ✓INTERNET→*email* LISTSERV@PCCVM.BITNET ✍ *Type in message body:* SUB STREK-L <YOUR FULL NAME>

NG/DS-9

rec.arts.startrek.current (NG) *Star Trek* gossip, inside jokes, production information, and more. Can't wait till the next episode? Covers upcoming episodes, movies, books. Want to find out when to watch *Next Generation* or *DS-9* in another country? There's a guide here. ✓USENET

Star Trek: Deep Space Nine Conference specifically for the

Commander Worff, a Klingon—from CompuServe's Showbiz Forum.

DS-9 series. Comparisons with other *Trek* series are discouraged, but discussion about technology of the era is accepted. ✓**FIDONET**→*tag* STDSN

Star Trek: The Next Generation For *Next Generation* fans only. Discuss Picard, Riker, other members of the *Enterprise* crew, and NCC-1701D. ✓**FIDONET**→*tag* STTNG

Klingons

Hacker's Unlimited BBS (BBS) Supports the Klingon Assault Group. 216-366-1935 $24/YEAR

Star Trek Klingons Dedicated to the Klingon presence in *Star Trek* movies, television, animation, novels, games, and fan publications. Members of KAG and KLAW welcome! ✓**FIDONET**→*tag* KLINGON

tlhIngan Hol (ML) For those interested in the Klingon language. ✓**INTERNET**→*email* TLHINGAN-HOL-REQUEST@VILLAGE.BOSTON.MA.US ✍*Subscribe by request*

News

rec.arts.startrek.fandom (NG) News about conventions and memorabilia. ✓**USENET**

rec.arts.startrek.info (NG) *Star Trek* press releases; episode credits and synopses; factual articles—not opinion pieces—from newspapers, magazines, and other media; and "reliable" insider information. Periodic notices of conventions. ✓**USENET**

Reviews

rec.arts.startrek.reviews (NG) Reviews of *Star Trek* books, episodes, and films. ✓**USENET**

Trek-Review-L (ML) Share reviews and ratings of *Star Trek* material, including all Trekkie generations, and Trekkie media. This isn't a discussion or a list but rather a forum for thoughtful, critical reviews and commentary. ✓**INTERNET**→*email* LISTSERV@CORNELL.EDU ✍*Type in message body:* SUBSCRIBE TREK-REVIEW-L <YOUR FULL NAME>

Tech

rec.arts.startrek.tech (NG) Ask questions about warp drives, phasers, photon torpedoes, saucer separation, view screens, the holodecks, and other *Star Trek* technology. ✓**USENET**

Star Trek Discuss the concepts and technology of *Star Trek.* ✓**RELAYNET**→*number* 201

Star Trek Technical Discussions Generally known as Tech Fandom. Covers technology in all the *Star Trek* genres. ✓**FIDONET**→*tag* TREKTECH

Trekkie fiction

alt.startrek.creative (NG) A forum for original fiction written by *Star Trek* fans, including stories, poems, timelines, parodies, etc. ✓**USENET**

Star Trek Books/Tech Manuals The *Star Trek* novels, *Star Trek* technical manuals, and comic books. ✓**FIDONET**→*tag* STBOOKS ✖*No spoilers or television-show talk*

Q

alt.fan.q (NG) For fans of the infamous Q of the Q Continuum. "The Qmnipotent Qne holds court here." ✓**USENET**

Games

rec.games.netrek (NG) Discussions about the 16-player *Star Trek* battle-simulation game played via client servers. Regular postings include information on Internet game servers, network leagues, tournament competitions, and game explanations. ✓**USENET**

Stargame (ML) Play the *Star Trek* Role-Playing game. ▣▣ ✓**INTERNET**→*email* LISTSERV@PCCVM.BITNET ✍*Type in message body:* SUB STAR GAME <YOUR FULL NAME>

Other info

TrekNet Conferences for the Starfleet Fan Club organization. ✓CHECK LOCAL BULLETIN BOARDS

Captain Kirk with Tribbles—from CompuServe's Showbiz Forum.

TV shows

Do people sound as stupid talking about television in

Cyberspace as they do talking about last night's shows at the hairdresser's or in the dorm or on the elevator? You decide. They're all here, from *Seinfeld* (**alt.tv.seinfeld**) to the *Simpsons* (**alt.tv.simpsons**) to *M*A*S*H* (**alt.tv.mash**) to *The Rockford Files, Cheers, Twin Peaks, Letterman, L.A. Law, Northern Exposure,* and major coverage of the soaps— and everybody's talkin'. If you're still in need of a fix, try the **Hollywood Hotline** on CompuServe and GEnie for the latest gossip.

David Letterman on the February 1993 cover of Rolling Stone—*from the archive at quartz.rutgers.edu.*

On the Net

Across the board

alt.tv.misc (NG) For discussing your favorite TV show. ✓USENET

rec.arts.tv (NG) Discussion about television, including former and current shows. ✓USENET

Showbiz Forum Share movie reviews; discuss your favorite plays, celebrities, and TV shows; get lists of studio and network executives. 🖥️ ✓COMPUSERVE→*go* SHOWBIZ

Show Biz RoundTable Discussions focusing on stars, genre, and time period. Includes information on home entertainment technology. 🖥️ ✓GENIE→*keyword* SHOWBIZ

Television Contains a weekly list of the top TV news programs, the soap opera summaries, a gossip board, and discussion about favorite shows. Provides access to the Educational TV & Radio Forum with information on TV programming for parents and teachers. ✓AMERICA ONLINE→*keyword* TV

TV and Movie Archive In the /cheers directory, get episode guides, Norm sayings, and trivia; in the /letterman directory, get top-ten lists, a transcript of the last show, or Letterman pictures; in the /startrek directory, find virtually any list you can think of; and there's more—from *Tiny Toons* to *M*A*S*H.* ✓INTERNET→ *ftp* QUARTZ. RUTGERS.EDU→ANONYMOUS/<YOUR EMAIL ADDRESS>→pub/ tv+movies

TV BB Discuss shows and personalities. The board is subdivided into topics such as *Seinfeld,* Children's Television, *Beavis & Butthead,* and *90210,* and includes a section for featured guests. Katie Couric and Seinfeld have been guests. ✓PRODIGY→*jump* TV BB

TV-L (ML) For any TV-related dis-

cussions: soap operas, your favorite show, etc. ✓INTERNET→ *email* LISTSERV@TREARN.BITNET *Type in message body:* SUB TV-L <YOUR FULL NAME>

TV/Movie Group Discuss favorite shows, movies, and actors. Download GIFs of actors and actresses or fiction based on the shows. And participate in live conferences with writers or directors. 🖥️ ✓DELPHI→*go* GR TV

Drama

alt.tv.bh90210 (NG) For *90210* fans. ✓USENET

alt.tv.la-law (NG) For fans of *L.A. Law.* ✓USENET

alt.tv.melrose-place (NG) For fans of *Melrose Place.* ✓USENET

alt.tv.mwc (NG) For fans of *Married With Children.* ✓USENET

alt.tv.northern-exp (NG) For *Northern Exposure* fans. ✓USENET

Fox Network Offers discussion for fans of the Fox Network programs, past and present. The discussion is monitored by representatives of Fox-affiliated television stations. ✓RELAYNET→*number* 362

90210 (ML) For *90210* fans. ✓INTERNET→*email* 90210-REQUEST@ FERKEL.UCSB.EDU *Subscribe by request*

Seinfeld

alt.tv.seinfeld (NG) For *Seinfeld* fans. ✓USENET

Seinfeld (ML) A very active forum for discussing the *Seinfeld* show. ✓INTERNET→*email* SEINFELD-REQUEST@CPAC.WASHINGTON.EDU *Subscribe by request*

The Simpsons

alt.tv.simpsons (NG) For *Simpsons* fans. ✓**USENET**

The Simpsons Archive Credits, bibliographies, episode airing dates and summaries, font packs, lyrics, even postcards. ✓**INTERNET**→*ftp* FTP. CS.WIDENER.EDU→ANONYMOUS/ <YOUR EMAIL ADDRESS>→ pub/simpsons

Not just kids

alt.tv.muppets (NG) Discussion of *The Muppets*, *Fraggle Rock* and *Sesame Street*. ✓**USENET**

Clarissa (ML) Discussion of *Clarissa Explains It All*. ✓**INTERNET** →*email* CLARISSA-REQUEST@FERKEL. UCSB.EDU ✍*Subscribe by request*

Parent's Information Network Provides information about educational programs, including a searchable database of educational TV and radio listings and a calendar of broadcast-related events. ✓**AMERICA ONLINE**→*keyword* PIN

Reruns only

alt.tv.mash (NG) For discussing *M*A*S*H*. ✓**USENET**

alt.tv.rockford-files (NG) For *Rockford* fans. ✓**USENET**

alt.tv.twin-peaks (NG) For those who can't forget *Twin Peaks*. ✓**USENET**

Cheers (ML) For *Cheers* fans. ✓**INTERNET**→*email* CHEERS-REQUEST@ COLORADO.EDU ✍*Subscribe by request*

Soaps

rec.arts.tv.soaps (NG) Updates on the soaps. ✓**USENET**

Soap_Opera Discuss all aspects of TV soaps. ✓**ILINK**→*number* 207

Soap Operas Story recaps and gossip for daytime soaps. ✓**PRODIGY**→*jump* SOAP OPERAS

Soap Operas Offers discussion about daytime and evening soaps. Topics include plot developments, favorite characters, and favorite actors. ✓**RELAYNET**→*number* 348

Soap Opera Summaries Detailed summaries of all the afternoon soaps and a few prime-time soaps, such as *L.A. Law*. Includes a weekly newsmagazine with coverage of casting changes and forecasts, addresses, and information on favorite stars. ✓**COMPUSERVE**→ *go* SOAPS ✓**GENIE**→*keyword* SOAPS

Talks shows

alt.fan.letterman (NG) For fans of David Letterman. ✓**USENET**

Rush Limbaugh/EIB Topics General talk and response to Limbaugh's radio and TV shows. ✓**FIDONET**→*tag* LIMBAUGH

Alternative & British

Alternative Entertainment Covers the unusual in TV and movies, especially canceled series like *Twin Peaks* (the former name of the conference). ✓**RELAYNET**→ *number* 345

alt.tv.prisoner (NG) Discuss the British show *The Prisoner*. ✓**USENET**

rec.arts.tv.uk (NG) Discussions of TV shows in the UK. ✓**USENET**

News programming

CNN Newsroom Online Provided by Turner Educational Systems, Inc. offers the latest news, questions for *CNN Newsroom* guests, an idea exchange, multimedia information, and links to the TV forum Network Earth. ✓**AMERICA ONLINE**→*keyword* CNN

Crime shows

True Crime Covers true-crime books, movies, TV shows, and news. ✓**RELAYNET**→*number* 394

News & reviews

Hollywood Hotline A guide to the latest in movies, TV, and recordings, with a trivia quiz, encyclopedia, celebrity interviews, and reviews. ✓**COMPUSERVE**→*go* HOLLYWOOD ✓**DELPHI**→*go* ENT HOLL ✓**GENIE** →*keyword* HOTLINE

Media Movie reviews and discussions of television, radio, and print media. ✓**ILINK**→*number* 52

Reviews of Almost Anything Everything that can be reviewed: movies, TV, restaurants, software, and books. ✓**FIDONET** →*tag* REVIEWS

Television Nielsen's rating charts, news and views, this week's top shows, and today's programming. ✓**PRODIGY**→*jump* TELEVISION

Satellite TV

rec.video.satellite (NG) Discussions about programming via satellite. ✓**USENET**

Satellite Information about satellite TV technology. ✓**ILINK**→*number* 146

Satellite Television Information on programming, technical issues, scrambling, and video piracy. Uplinked to the GTE Spacenet 3 satellite. ✓**FIDONET**→*tag* TVRO

Part 2

Computers & Software

2

Amiga

Check out Communications Room 10 in GEnie's StarShip Amiga RoundTable for the StarShip 5-MINUTE Weekend Newscast, a unique news service for the Amiga community that offers weekly updates and late-breaking news and is repeated every five minutes on weekend nights. You can read and save the text as it scrolls by, or download back issues from the StarShip library. Regular features include industry news, product reviews, trade-show announcements, and a rumor update.

Art created on an Amiga—from the CompuServe Amiga Arts Forum.

News & support

Amiga Tips and talk on all aspects of the Amiga computer. ✓ILINK→*number* 51

Amiga Everything for Amiga users: software, the operating system, tips, and hardware configurations. ✓RELAYNET→*number* 118

Amiga and Commodore Users Network Eight forums devoted to Commodore and Amiga, with discussions on games, arts, applications, service, and more. Also includes a newsletter. ▣◫ ◉☷ ✓COMPUSERVE→*go* CBMNET

Amiga Exchange Includes vendor support conferences such as AMIGA.COM for commercial developers, AMIGA.DEV for developers, AMIGA.WORLD for *Amiga World* magazine, and AMIGA.VENDORS. ✓BIX→*conference* AMIGA.EXCHANGE

Amiga For Sale Buying and selling of Amiga-related material. ✓FIDONET→*tag* AMIGA_SALE

Amiga International Covers all aspects of Amiga computers, with answers to typical user questions, product reviews, and an information clearinghouse for new Amiga products. ✓FIDONET→*tag* AMIGA

Amiga SIG Offers sections on audio, productivity, games, graphics, communications, video, animation, programming, and demos. ◉☷ ✓DELPHI→ *go* COM AMIGA

Amiga Talk General-interest talk for Amiga owners and operators. ✓FIDONET→*tag* AMIGA_TALK

comp.sys.amiga.announce (NG) Announcements about Amiga computers. ✓USENET

comp.sys.amiga.hardware (NG) Discussions about Amiga computer hardware. ✓USENET

StarShip Amiga RoundTable Includes an online magazine, the StarShip Amiga Survival Kit for Amiga users, games, adult libraries, discussion, and software. ▣◫ ◉☷ ✓GENIE→ *keyword* AMIGA

Software

Amiga Gaming Everything about Amiga games, including tips and tricks, reviews, back doors, game comparisons, and solutions. ✓FIDONET→*tag* AMIGAGAMES

Amiga Public Domain & Requests Discussion of public-domain software for the Amiga. Includes requests for types of programs. Discussions of piracy and illegal actions are banned. ✓FIDONET→*tag* AMIGA_PDREVIEW

comp.sys.amiga.applications (NG) Discussions about applications operating under the Amiga computer system. ✓USENET

comp.sys.amiga.games (NG) Discussions about games for the Commodore Amiga. ✓USENET

Specialties

Amiga CDROM & CDTV Discussion/Sales Focus is on CD equipment and titles for Amiga, including CDROM and CDTV. ✓FIDONET→ *tag* AMIGA_CDROM

Amiga Video/Graphics and Desktop Video Issues related to Amiga Video, including display boards, graphic formats, and software. ✓FIDONET→*tag* AMIGA_VIDEO

comp.sys.amiga.audio (NG) Discussions about audio with the Amiga. ✓USENET

Apples

"As long as a computer is useful to you it is not dead,"

says the **comp.sys.apple2** FAQ editor. The Apple IIe is a capable performer. It runs AppleWorks, a simple-to-use program, and a huge amount of educational software has been written for it. Perhaps more important, according to the **comp.sys. apple2** FAQ editor, "Nothing stops you from learning about every nook and cranny in it." Which is exactly what Apple lovers like to do. Rewrite the operating system, do "cool" hardware hacks, or write a game. Some IBMers are so enchanted with Apple that they emulate one on their DOS machine. Check out the newsgroup **alt.emulators.ibmpc.apple2** for free emulators.

On the Net

Across the board

Apple General discussion about Apple II and Apple GS computers. ✓**RELAYNET**→*number* 219

Apple Discuss Apple computers. ✓**SMARTNET**→ *tag* APPLE

Apple II RoundTable Provides a full range of information on Apple II hardware and software, including discussion; downloadable pro-

Steve Wozniak—downloaded from wuarchive.wustl.edu.

grams, utilities, and games; and help files. 🖳 ✓**GENIE**→*keyword* A2

Apple II SIG Offers discussion, live conferences, information files, programs, and online classes. ✓**DELPHI**→*go* COM APPLE

Apple II/III Forums A set of forums devoted to the Apple II and Apple III family of computers. ✓**COMPUSERVE**→*go* APPLE II/III

Apple II Users Forum Learn more about the Apple II for business, school, or the home. 🖳 ✓**COMPUSERVE**→*go* APPUSER

comp.sys.apple2 (NG) Discussion about Apple II micros. ✓**USE-NET**

comp.sys.apple2.usergroups (NG) Provides a forum and information for administrators and members of Apple II user groups. ✓**USENET**

International Apple Echo Help for Apple II computer users, including the II+, IIe, IIc, IIc+, and IIgs. ✓**FIDONET**→*tag* APPLE

Hardware & systems

Apple Emulators Programs to emulate Apple on IBM compatibles. ✓**INTERNET**→*ftp* WILBUR.STAN FORD.EDU→ANONYMOUS/<YOUR EMAIL ADDRESS>→pub/apple2

Apple II Hardware Forum Offers technical discussions, help, and other information for owners and users of Apple II computers. Includes Apple Computer technical notes. 🖳 ✓**AMERICA ONLINE**→ *keyword* AHW

Apple II Pro RoundTable Offers information and contacts for Apple II programmers and software developers, with help from the staff of the A2-Central newsletter. 🖳 ✓**GENIE**→*keyword* A2PRO

Software

Apple II File Archive Provides a set of utilities and information files for Apple II computers, including emulators. ✓**INTERNET**→ *ftp* WILBUR.STANFORD.EDU→ANONY-MOUS/<YOUR EMAIL ADDRESS>→pub/apple2

Apple II Graphics and Sound Forum Offers news and help with Apple II graphics, music, and sound. Special features include regular contests with free online time as prizes. 🖳 ✓**AMERICA ONLINE**→*keyword* AGR

Apple II Productivity Forum Offers ideas, information, and company support for Apple II productivity software, including AppleWorks, HyperStudio, GraphicWriter III, and Publish IT. Also covers topics ranging from business applications to fonts to accounting and personal finance. ✓**AMERICA ONLINE**→*keyword* APR

comp.binaries.apple2 (NG) Encoded public-domain postings for Apple II machines. ✓**USENET**

Artificial intelligence

Probably the most popular portrayal of an artificial intelligence (AI, for short) is *2001*'s

HAL—a logical, heartless, unemotional machine that can't compute irrational human behavior. But current AI research is well on its way to producing a softer, gentler silicon brain based on fuzzy logic. According to the **comp.ai.fuzzy** newsgroup's FAQ, fuzzy logic "has been extended to handle the concept of partial truth—truth values between 'completely true' and 'completely false.'" Someday, our robots might be able to watch, and understand, *Rashomon*.

Robbie the Robot in The Forbidden Planet—*from CompuServe's Graphics Developers Forum.*

On the Net

Across the board

AI Artificial intelligence, expert systems, hypertext retrieval, and related topics. ✓**ILINK**→*number* 46

AI EXPERT A supplement to *AI Expert* magazine. Direct AI questions to industry and academic leaders and exchange information with other members. ✓**COMPUSERVE**→*go* AIEXPERT

Artificial Intelligence Topics include expert systems, knowledge base design, genetic algorithms, natural language interfaces, and artificial life. ✓**FIDONET** →*tag* AI

comp.ai (NG) General discussion of AI, from book announcements

to discussion questions about techniques. ✓**USENET**

Archives

DartNet A Mac-based neural network simulator with tools for building, editing, training, testing, and examining networks. ✓**INTERNET**→*ftp* FTP.DARTMOUTH.EDU→ANONYMOUS/<YOUR EMAIL ADDRESS>→pub/mac→dartnet.sit.hqx

UCLA Artificial Life Depository Repository of articles, papers, software and other materials of interest to artificial-life researchers. ✓**INTERNET**→*ftp* FTP.COGNET.UCLA.EDU→ANONYMOUS/<YOUR EMAIL ADDRESS>→pub/alife

Neural nets

Artificial Neural Network ANNs are called the "bottom up" approach to developing artificial intelligence. Information here includes resource referrals, code exchange, and problem solving for cognitive and behavioral scientists and other researchers. News comes

from the Usenet newsgroup COMP.AI.NEURAL-NETS and Neuron Digest list. ✓**FIDONET**→*tag* NEURAL_NET

C.N.S. BBS (BBS) Neural-network-related information. 409-589-3338

comp.ai.neural-nets (NG/ML) For people interested in exploring neural networks or neural-network-like structures. ✓**USENET** ✓**INTERNET**→*email* NEURON-REQUEST @CATTELL.PSYCH.UPENN.EDU ✎*Subscribe by request*

Applications

AIL-L (ML) Discussion related to artificial intelligence and law. ✓**INTERNET**→*email* LISTSERV@AUSTIN.ONU.EDU ✎*Type in message body:* SUBSCRIBE AIL-L <YOUR FULL NAME>

AI-Medicine (ML) Devoted to discussing computer-based medical-decision support. ✓**INTERNET**→*email* AI-MEDICINE-REQUEST@MED.STANFORD.EDU ✎*Subscribe by request*

comp.ai.edu (NG) Discussions about AI and education, including intelligent computer-aided instruction. ✓**USENET**

Vision-List (ML) Forum for artificial-intelligence vision researchers. "Anything related to vision and its automation is fair game." ✓**INTERNET**→*email* VISION-LIST-REQUEST@ADS.COM ✎*Subscribe by request*

Fuzzy logic

comp.ai.fuzzy (NG) Discussions of fuzzy-logic applications in AI. ✓**USENET**

Graphics & design

State-of-the-art scanning and graphics abilities have ushered in a new age of altered

reality, where enormous flies hover menacingly over Hollywood Boulevard and a young Clint Eastwood appears to guard JFK in the movies. If you're a closet Zelig and want to insert yourself into the picture (you are there at the Arafat-Rabin handshake, perhaps), check out America Online's **Mac** or **PC Graphics** forums. You'll find guidance on scanning, merging, and manipulating images that will help you create a uniquely personal piece of meta-history.

A fly over a Hollywood street—CompuServe's PC Graphics & Sound Forum.

On the Net

Across the board

Graphics Plus Large-size, high-resolution graphics, starting at 80x600x256 and larger, on a variety of subjects. ✓**COMPUSERVE**→*go* GRAPHPLUS

Graphics Support SIG Contains graphics programs, help files, and special sections for animation, multimedia, and technical discussion of high-end video. ✓**DELPHI**→ *go* COM GRAPHICS

Legend Graphics (BBS) Contains a variety of computer art: 3-D animations, ray tracings and renderings, and original scans, including adult images. 909-689-9229 $10/MONTH

Macintosh Graphics, Multimedia & CAD Forum Animation, GIFs, QuickTime movies, commercial demos, and MacPaint. ✓**AMERICA ONLINE**→*keyword* MGR

PC Animation & Graphics Forum Offers discussion on all areas of computer art, with regular conferences on graphics, multimedia, CAD, computer artists, and animation, plus vendor support. ✓**AMERICA ONLINE**→*keyword* PGR

CAD/CAM

AEC Interest Area for Building Professionals Provides aid to professionals in architecture, engineering, and construction, with ideas, tips, and techniques for professionals and students interested in the use of computers and computer design in building and construction. ✓**AMERICA ONLINE**→ *keyword* AEC SIG

alt.cad (NG) Discussion of computer-aided design. ✓**USENET**

CAD Conference on computer-aided design and applications. ✓**BIX**→CAD

CAD Covers CAD programs and design. ✓**RELAYNET**→*number* 212

CAD Discussions about video and graphic support, and CAD products. ✓**SMARTNET**→*tag* CAD

CADD Computer-aided design and drafting, particularly AUTO-CAD and VersaCAD. ✓**ILINK**→ *number* 97

CADD/CAM/CAE Vendor Forum Managed by the League for Engineering Automation Productivity (LEAP), the forum includes vendor support and information on computer-aided design, manufacturing, and engineering hardware and software. ✓**COMPUSERVE**→*go* CADDVEN

Comp-U-Ease (BBS) This board specializes in engineering and CAD files. 408-286-8332 FREE

Vtcad-L (ML) Discussions related to CAD: CAD networking, CAD applications, etc. ✓**INTERNET**→*email* LISTSERV@VTVM2.CC.VT.EDU ✍ *Type in message body:* SUB VTCAD-L <YOUR FULL NAME>

Computer art

3D SIG For sharing information on 3-D illustration techniques, 3-D visualization, animation, and design. ⊕🖰 ✓**AMERICA ONLINE**→*keyword* 3DSIG

---

alt.binaries.pictures.fine-art. graphics (NG) For posting original artwork created using computer programs. ✓**USENET**

---

alt.binaries.pictures.fractals (NG) Contains computer art that was generated using algorithms. ✓**USENET**

Computer Art Forum Focuses on images created by or generated on a computer with a paint program. The file libraries contain thousands of GIFs ranging from animals to science fiction. ✓**COMPUSERVE**→*go* COMART

Fractal Images List (ML) Devoted to fractal images. ✓**INTERNET**→*email* LISTSERV@GITVM1.BITNET ✍ *Type in message body:* SUBSCRIBE FRAC-L <YOUR FULL NAME>

Online Graphics Discussion about all types of high-resolution online graphics, comparing features, advantages, and disadvantages. ✓**FIDONET**→*tag* ONLINE_GRAPHICS

File sites

Picture Archive Contains a large number of decoding and encoding programs for viewing or posting binary files as well as a list of pictures-related stuff on the net. ✓**INTERNET**→*ftp* BONGO.CC.UTEXAS.EDU→ANONYMOUS/<YOUR EMAIL ADDRESS>→gifstuff

---

SIGGRAPH Information Online Provides SIGGRAPH information, including previews of upcoming conference programs and conference archives. ✓**INTERNET** ...→*ftp* SIGGRAPH.ORG→ANONYMOUS/<YOUR EMAIL ADDRESS> ...→*email* archive-server@siggraph.org ✍ *Type in subject line:* SEND INDEX

Fine art & photos

BayView Graphics BBS (BBS) Includes 16- and 24-bit high-end graphic images, in both GIF and TIFF formats, ANSI art, FLI animations, and utilities. 510-799-6456 FREE

Fine Arts Forum Includes specialty libraries with GIFs of paintings by Michelangelo, Renoir, Degas, and Van Gogh. ✓**COMPUSERVE**→*go* FINEARTS

Graphics Gallery Forum An online collection of photos from organizations like the Smithsonian Institution, NASA, and the USDA National Agricultural Library. There are also photos of famous, and less-famous, American sites. ✓**COMPUSERVE**→*go* GALLERY

GIFs

The Gallery An online portrait area of regular participants in America Online's People Connection. You can send your photo into the Gallery for free scanning and uploading. ✓**AMERICA ONLINE**→*keyword* GALLERY

Graphics Corner GIF images ranging from 32-level grays to 256 colors, covering a full range of subjects. ✓**COMPUSERVE**→*go* CORNER

Just GIFs! (BBS) "The place for serious image collectors! Pets to space to celebrity nudes!" 718-939-1824 ✱ *Only 9,600 bps* $25 OPTIONAL

Quick Pictures Forum Medium- and low-resolution GIF graphics, with all files less than 20K in size and 16 colors or fewer. ✓**COMPUSERVE**→*go* QPICS

Tools

alt.binaries.pictures.utilities (NG) For posting source or binary code for picture-related software. ✓**USENET**

---

comp.graphics (NG) For discussing image formats, animation, and image processing. ✓**USENET**

Graphic Display Offers information on creating and displaying computer images. ✓**BIX**→*conference* GRAPHIC.DISP

Graphics Support Forum Advice, discussion, and hardware- and software-support information on graphics in desktop publishing, computer graphics presentation, scanners and digitizers, GIF encoders/decoders, video boards, and paint programs. ✓**COMPUSERVE**→*go* GRAPHSUPPORT

Graphics Vendor Forum Online manufacturers' support for graphics hardware and software products. ✓**COMPUSERVE**→*go* GRAPHVEN

Computer music & sound

If you're a musician on the Net, playing alone doesn't mean playing solo anymore—

you could be part of a brass quartet, a jazz combo, a rock 'n' roll band, or even a symphony orchestra (as the entire string section). Scattered around the globe, the participants in **NetJam** are collaborating on new compositions by recording and exchanging files based on the Musical Instrument Digital Interface (MIDI) standard. Bar by bar, they can build a song that might someday make someone say, "It's got a good beat and you can dance to it."

On the Net

Across the board

Electronic Music (ML) Covers electronic-music-related topics, including synthesis methods, algorithmic composition, MIDI troubleshooting, event announcements, and more. ✓ **INTERNET**→ *email* LISTSERV@AUVM.BITNET ✍ *Type in message body:* SUBSCRIBE EMUSIC-L <YOUR FULL NAME>

Macintosh Music and Sound Forum Offers news and discussion on creating music and designing sound with the Macintosh. Special features include awards of free online time to the top uploaders as well as random conference attendees and message posters. ●🖤 ✓ **AMERICA ONLINE**→ *keyword* MMS

Digitized notes—downloaded from CompuServe's Quick Pictures Forum.

MIDI & Computer Musicians RoundTable Support for MIDI and computer-based musicians. ●🖤 ✓ **GENIE**→*keyword* MIDI

The Musician's BBS (BBS) Devoted to music, computer music, MIDI, and more. 216-639-9508 FREE

PC Music & Sound Forum Includes ready-to-play music and sound-effect files for almost any add-on sound board (for example, Sound Blaster) and sound software packages. Also offers MIDI files and help to professional and amateur musicians. ●🖤 ✓ **AMERICA ONLINE**→*keyword* PMU

Sight & Sound Forum Offers information, discussion, and files on digital sound, and music sampling; plus multimedia, GIF, animation, and other images accompanied by sound and music. ●🖤 ✓ **COMPUSERVE**→*go* SOUND

Composers/musicians

MIDI/Music Forum Recording and playing music with computers using synthesizers, samplers, and other MIDI tools. The MIDI magazine *Live Sound!* is in LIBRARY 9.

●🖤 ✓ **COMPUSERVE**→*go* MIDIFORUM

NetJam (ML) Musicians collaborate with each other on compositions by exchanging MIDI and other music files. Participants can add music and send the revised files back as part of an email jam session. Music and scores are documented and archived. Most collaborations take place via email, but a recently introduced wide-area MIDI network has added real-time jamming. ✓ **INTERNET**→ *email* NETJAM-REQUEST@XCF.BERKELEY.EDU ✍*Subscribe by request*

NetJam Archive Contains archives of jams, music-notation files, and information on the NetJam music collaboration. ✓ **INTERNET**→*ftp* XCF.BERKELEY.EDU→ANONYMOUS/<YOUR EMAIL ADDRESS>

MIDI

Electric Midiland (BBS) Specializes in MIDI, demos, and software, along with IBM shareware programs. 606-324-3917 $20/YEAR

MIDI-NET International MIDI Conference Discussion about MIDI, computer music, and synthesizers. ✓ **FIDONET**→*tag* MIDI-NET

Sound & speech

Sound Site Newsletter An electronic publication with information on digitized sounds and various sound formats for computers, mostly personal computers. ✓ **INTERNET**→*ftp* SOUND.USACH.CL→ANONYMOUS/<YOUR EMAIL ADDRESS> →pub/Sound/Newsletters

Computer news

Larry Magid's PC column on Prodigy finds comfort in news of a technophobia generation gap. In a recent Dell Computer survey, 90 percent of teenagers found computers "fun to use," while only 74 percent of adults agreed. And a hefty 23 percent of adults said they are "ill-at-ease using a computer," compared with 7 percent of teens. "With all the complaints you hear about today's kids," Magid wrote, "and all the fears that they, and America, will fall behind economically and technologically, it's nice to see one area where they are ahead of their parents."

On the Net

News & help

comp.misc (NG) General, broad-interest posts about computers, the computer industry, and computer information on the Internet. ✓USENET

Computer America Offers information and discussion about the weekly radio talk show *Computer America*. Users can correspond with host Craig Crossman, a nationally syndicated computer columnist. 🖵 ✓AMERICA ONLINE→*keyword* COMPUTER AMERICA

Computer Basics A glossary and guide to personal computing. ✓PRODIGY→*jump* COMPUTER BASICS

Ziff editors on the PBS show Computer Chronicles—*from ZiffNet Editorial Forum (via CompuServe).*

Computer Law Offers information on legal issues affecting computers and technology. ✓AMERICA ONLINE→*keyword* COMPUTER LAW

comp.society.cu-digest A digest of messages on the sharing of computer information and other Cyberspace issues. ✓USENET ✓RELAYNET→*number* 412

Larry Magid on PCs Computer news and expert advice. 🖵 ✓PRODIGY→*jump* LARRY MAGID ON PCS

Magazines

BBS Caller's Digest Offers information, subscriptions, a question-and-answer exchange, and contact with the staff of the digest. 🖵 ✓RELAYNET→*number* 334

Byte Magazine Full-text of *Byte* magazine. Each year is its own conference—e.g., byte.94. 🖵 ✓BIX→*conference* BYTE

Windows Magazine The online version of *Windows* magazine. Includes chat with the staff. 🖵 ✓AMERICA ONLINE→*keyword* WINMAG ✖*Not available for Mac users* ✓BIX→*conference* WINMAG

Ziffnet Computer Forums Offers a set of forums with information, files, and an exchange with the editors and staff of Ziff computer magazines, including *PC Magazine, PCWeek, Windows Sources, Computer Shopper, MacUser,* and *MacWeek.* 🖵 ✓COMPUSERVE→*go* ZNT $2.50/MONTH

Stories & opinions

alt.amateur-comp (NG) Discussion about topics in the *Amateur Computerist Newsletter.* ✓USENET

alt.folklore.computers (NG) Stories and anecdotes about computers. ✓USENET

alt.religion.computers (NG) Discuss the merits or failings of particular computer systems. ✓USENET

Databases

Computer & Electronics News-Center Search for articles, abstracts, or product announcements from a database of computer journals and government reports. 🖵 ✓GENIE→*keyword* COMPUTERS $$

Computer Database Plus A database of full-text articles from magazines, newspapers, and journals, including *Byte, PC Magazine, MacUser, PC Week, Digital Review,* and *PC World.* Search by subject, company name, product, publication, or date. 🖵 ✓COMPUSERVE→*go* COMPDB $$

NewsBytes News Network A database of articles from a computer news service with eight U.S. and international bureaus. 🖵 ✓AMERICA ONLINE→*keyword* NEWSBYTES ✓COMPUSERVE→*go* ZNT:NEWSBYTES ✓GENIE→*keyword* NEWSBYTES ✓BIX→*conference* NEWSBYTES

Science & engineering

Renowned among systems engineers as authoritative (and among laymen as indeci-

pherable), **The Cybernetics and Systems** mailing list can offer flames that link pique with professional courtesy: "May I ask for clarification of your comments....I know of nothing that prevents a system without 'internal representation' of the environment from being a priori 'not intelligent,' and rather like the implications that arise from not being dependent on such a thing to create intelligence. Disliking the elliptical nature of email but interested in starting a dialogue, I am, Paul Pangaro, Ph.D."

On the Net

Professionals

comp.org.ieee (NG) Issues and announcements about the IEEE. ✓**USENET**

EETNet A set of forums for electronic engineers and companies, sponsored by *Electronic Engineering Times* newspaper. Includes Profession Forum, Japan Forum, and Engineering Forum. ✓**COMPUSERVE**→*go* EETNET

ETHCSE List (ML) Ethical issues relating to professional software engineering discussed. ✓**INTERNET**→ *email* LISTSERV@UTKVM1.UTK.EDU ✍ *Type in message body:* SUBSCRIBE ETHCSE-L <YOUR FULL NAME>

ENIAC, the first computer—from CompuServe's Graphics Gallery.

Ethics List (ML) Discussions involving ethical issues and computing—from who owns information to who's responsible for program failures. ✓**INTERNET**→*email* LISTSERV@MARIST.BITNET ✍ *Type in message body:* SUBSCRIBE ETHICS-L <YOUR FULL NAME>

IEEE-L (ML) Forum for all IEEE students, members, engineers, and interested others to discuss curriculum, fundraisers, and more. ✓**INTERNET**→*email* LISTSERV@BINGVMB.CC.BINGHAMTON.EDU ✍ *Type in message body:* SUBSCRIBE IEEE-L <YOUR FULL NAME>

Research

Adv-Info (ML) Discussions of the latest advances in computing. ✓**INTERNET**→*email* LISTSERV@UTFSM.BITNET ✍ *Type in message body:* SUB ADV-INFO

comp.doc.techreports (NG) Offers posts about more than 70 FTP sites with collections of computer-science technical reports. ✓**USENET**

Computer Science Paper Bibliography List of articles from several computer journals.

✓**INTERNET**→*ftp* CAYUGA.CS.ROCHESTER.EDU→ANONYMOUS/<YOUR EMAIL ADDRESS>→pub→papers.lst

The Cybernetics and Systems Mailing List (ML) Offers discussion for those interested in systems science, cybernetics, general systems theory, complex systems theory, information theory, and more. ✓**INTERNET**→*email* LISTSERV@BINGVMB.CC.BINGHAMPTON.EDU ✍ *Type in message body:* SUB CYBSYS-L <YOUR FULL NAME>

Machine Learning Databases Offers access and information on data sets and domain theories that evaluate machine-learning algorithms. ✓**INTERNET**→*ftp* ICS.UCI.EDU→ANONYMOUS/<YOUR EMAIL ADDRESS>→pub/machine-learning-databases

Hardware

Chips Discussions about semiconductor technology. ✓**BIX**→*conference* CHIPS

comp.arch (NG) Discussion about computer architecture. ✓**USENET**

comp.lsi (NG) Forum for discussing large-scale integrated circuits. ✓**USENET**

Industrial Computing Society An independent users association that works with the Instrument Society of America to promote the use of computer technology in manufacturing industries. ✓**AMERICA ONLINE**→*keyword* MBS

Computer shopping

With the shelf life and pricing of new computers continually dropping, used machines

are becoming ever more popular among savvy online shoppers. Why pay top dollar, they ask, for a product that may be discounted 20% or more three months after purchase? The best place to comparison-shop for used PCs and peripherals is the **Boston Computer Exchange** on Delphi. Their frequently updated index features ask, offer, and buy prices for equipment made by a variety of vendors.

On the Net

News & info

Computer Directory Provides manufacturers' information and addresses, specifications, compatibility information, and pricing for more than 69,000 computer products from more than 8,500 manufacturers. Products covered include hardware, software, peripherals, and telecommunications equipment. ✓**COMPUSERVE**→*go* COMPDIR $$

CR Computers *Consumer Reports* articles on computers. ✓**PRODIGY**→*jump* CR COMPUTERS

Executives Online Direct contact with computer-industry leaders, including Borland's Philippe Kahn, Dell's Michael Dell, and Microsoft's Mike Maples. ✓**COMPUSERVE**→*go* ZNT:EXEC $2.50/MONTH

Computer shoppers—downloaded from CompuServe's Graphics Plus Forum.

Vendors

Digital Equipment Corporation's Newsletter (ML) For users at educational and research institutions, a monthly newsletter with brief product announcements, special program and services listings, new installations and innovations from Digital's education and science customers, and more. ▦ ✓**INTERNET**→*email* LISTSERV@UBVM. CC.BUFFALO.EDU ✍*Type in message body:* SUB DECNEWS <YOUR FULL NAME>

Hardware Vendors A directory of hardware forums on CompuServe, with support from major manufacturers and vendors. There are forums devoted to Dell, Hewlett-Packard, Intel, Compaq, CompuAdd, Epson, Canon, Logitech, and Hayes, among others. ●⟲ ✓**COMPUSERVE**→*go* HARDWARE

Lotus Hosted by Lotus, Inc., this conference provides support and discussion for all the company's products. ✓**RELAYNET**→*number* 165

Mac Industry Connection Of-

fers support and contact with Macintosh software publishers and manufacturers, including Aldus, Claris, Letraset, Global Village Communication, Radius, Quark, Supermac, and the Voyager Company. ✓**AMERICA ONLINE**→*keyword* INDUSTRY

Microsoft RoundTable Support for Microsoft products. Includes libraries of documentation and utilities and the Microsoft KnowledgeBase, a database of information on all Microsoft products. ●⟲ ✓**GENIE**→*keyword* MICROSOFT

Novell NetWire Information and support for all Novell products, with press releases, compatibility reports, a technical bulletin database, and events announcements from Novell. ▦ ✓**COMPUSERVE** →*go* NOVELL

PC Industry Connection MS-DOS software publishers represented include Shiva, Mustang Software, Claris, Broderbund, Asymetrix, Pixar, and Farallon. ✓**AMERICA ONLINE**→*keyword* INDUSTRY

Product Support RoundTables Offers individual roundtables for major software and equipment makers, including Borland, ChipSoft, CE Software, Forth, Hayes, Microsoft, WordPerfect, Autodesk, Freesoft, and TimeWorks. ●⟲ ✓**GENIE**→*keyword* PCSUPPORT

Software Vendors A directory of software forums on CompuServe, with support from major manufacturers and vendors. There are forums sponsored by or devoted to Adobe, Claris, Userland, Novell, Lotus, Fox, and Borland, among others. ✓**COMPUSERVE**→*go* SOFTWARE

Support On Site (SOS) Online
Technical-support database for leading PC applications from companies including Aldus, Borland, Microsoft, Quarterdeck, WordPerfect, Lotus, and Symantec. The database includes tech notes, proprietary information from support staffs, newsletters, and software. 🖼 ✓**COMPUSERVE**→*go* ONSITE

Vendor FTP Site
Offers archive files for major computer-industry companies, including Microsoft, ClariNet, Morning Star, Bristol, Prentice Hall, and Forth. ✓**INTERNET**→*ftp* FTP.UU.NET→ANONYMOUS/<YOUR EMAIL ADDRESS>→vendor

Vendors
Provides direct vendor support from those companies that do not have their own RelayNet conferences. ✓**RELAYNET**→*number* 166

Outside support

Doctor DeBug's Laboratory
Information, help, and humor from Dr. Debug for all types of computers, operating systems, and languages. ✓**FIDONET**→*tag* DR_DEBUG

MS-Word
Discussion and support for Microsoft Word processing software. ✓**ILINK**→*number* 125

PCMCIA
The Personal Computer Memory Card International Association (PCMCIA) is a nonprofit trade association that sets standards for PC cards. Go here to get more information about joining the association. ✓**COMPUSERVE**→*go* PCVENF

Shopping

Boston Computer Exchange
Brokers the buying and selling of used computer equipment. Search their database for equipment. 📟 ✓**DELPHI**→*go* SHOP BOS

Compusale
Buy, sell, and trade computers and computer products. 📟 ✓**FIDONET**→*tag* COMPUSALE

Computer Express
An online store with Apple, IBM, Mac, and Amiga software—more than 2,000 titles. 📟 ✓**COMPUSERVE**→*go* CE ✓**DELPHI**→*go* SHOP COMPU ✓**AMERICA ONLINE**→*keyword* COMPUTER EXPRESS

Dalco Computer Electronics
PC hardware and supplies. 📟 ✓**COMPUSERVE**→*go* DA

Direct Micro
Microcomputer supplies and accessories. 📟 ✓**GENIE**→*keyword* DIRECTMICRO

MacWarehouse
Macintosh hardware, software, and accessories. 📟 ✓**COMPUSERVE**→*go* MW

Mac Zone/PC Zone
PC and Macintosh equipment. 📟 ✓**COMPUSERVE**→*go* MZ

MicroWarehouse
Hardware, software, and accessories for PCs. 📟 ✓**COMPUSERVE**→*go* MCW

Mission Control Software
Entertainment and education software and CD-ROM titles. 📟 ✓**COMPUSERVE**→*go* MCS

Omni Technics
Computer peripherals and electronics, including software files for downloading. 📟 ✓**GENIE**→*keyword* OMNI

PC Catalog
Mail-order PC products. 📟 ✓**COMPUSERVE**→*go* PCA

CYBERNOTES

Abbreviations & Acronyms Useful in Email & Chat

IMHO: In My Humble Opinion
OTOH: On the Other Hand
ROTF: Rolling On The Floor
BTW: By the Way
ROFL: Rolling on Floor Laughing
ROFLWTIME: Rolling on Floor Laughing With Tears in My Eyes
LOL: Laughing Out Loud
AFK: Away From Keyboard
BAK: Back at Keyboard
GA: Go Ahead
L8r: Later
GMTA: Great Minds Think Alike
NIFOC: Nude in Front of Computer

Shareware Depot
Offers bulk packs of shareware programs, with monthly specials. 📟 ✓**COMPUSERVE**→*go* SD ✓**PRODIGY**→*jump* SHAREWARE DEPOT

Softdisk Publishing
Software by subscription. 📟 ✓**COMPUSERVE**→*go* SP ✓**PRODIGY**→*jump* SOFTDISK

The Software Club
For $10 a year and the cost of download time, commercial software for PC, Amiga, and ST. 📟 ✓**GENIE**→*keyword* SOFTCLUB

Ziff Buyers Market
Choose from more than 10,000 computer products available directly from more than 130 companies. 📟 ✓**COMPUSERVE**→*go* BMC

Hacking & security

Evidently computer users are still appallingly ignorant about computer security despite

the media hubbub surrounding scares like the Michelangelo virus. A user in GEnie's **Virus and Security RT** relayed this comment, overheard at a large international company: "Oh, we have lots of viruses on our computers. But you don't need to worry about them. We just ignore them and eventually they go away. But it is important to save your files to the hard disk. They only affect floppy disks, not the hard disks."

Across the board

McAfee Virus Help Forum Sponsored by McAfee Associates, the forum tells you how to detect and remove computer viruses, with advice from virus experts from around the world. Also offers a message section and library moderated by the National Computer Security Association. ⊕🖫 ✓**COMPUSERVE**→*go* VIRUSFORUM

National Computer Security Association Offers discussion and files on computer viruses, encryption, data-center security, and other issues. ✓**COMPUSERVE**→ *go* NCSA

NIST Computer Security BBS (BBS) Sponsored by the National Institute of Standards and Tech-

"What the hell…?!"—from America Online's PC Graphics & Sound Forum.

nology; provides information for protecting data and computer systems. Includes NIST online publications and newsletters, and virus reviews. ☎ 301-948-5140 FREE

Pirating/Hacks/Trojan/Virus Alerts An open message area to alert personal-computer users to software threats. ✓**FIDONET**→*tag* DIRTY_DOZEN

Virus and Security Round-Table Includes vendor support, conferences, shareware, the Virus-L mailing list, and related news. ⊕🖫 ✓**GENIE**→*keyword* VSRT

Hackers & crackers

alt.crackers (NG) Forum for crackers. ✓**USENET**

alt.hackers (NG) For reporting on hacking projects—every posting must mention a hack in it. To post, you must figure out the moderator's address. Hack away. ✓**USENET**

Computer Underground Digest Archives Offers files about

computer security, frauds, hacking, network legislation, and underground hackers groups, including Germany's Chaos Computer Club. ✓**INTERNET**→*ftp* KRA GAR.EFF.ORG→ANONYMOUS/<YOUR EMAIL ADDRESS>→pub/cud

Protection

alt.security (NG) Covers computer security issues as well as car security, alarm systems, etc. ✓**USENET**

CERT Security Advisories (ML) Advisories about security-related topics issued by the Computer Emergency Response Team, a national organization that assists computer-system operators. ✓**INTERNET** …→*email* CERT-ADVISORY-REQUEST@CERT.ORG ✍*Subscribe by request* …→*wais* cert-advisories.src

comp.security.misc (NG) For the discussion of computer security, especially relating to UNIX operating systems. ✓**USENET**

Computer Emergency Response Team Papers covering computer and networking security and an archive of security alerts. ✓**INTERNET**→*ftp* CERT.ORG→ANONY-MOUS/<YOUR EMAIL ADDRESS>→pub

Data Protection Covers viruses, trojan horses, and other data-destroying programs, with discussion on how to protect against them. ✓**RELAYNET**→*number* 255

The Funny Farm (BBS) Focuses on virus protection. 405-233-7474 FREE

Mac-Security (ML) For Mac users interested in computer security. Includes discussions on viruses, security applications, and network security. ✓**INTERNET**→*email* MAJORDOMO@NDA.COM ✍ *Type in message body:* SUBSCRIBE MAC-SECURITY

Security Conference about computer security issues, including alerts about viruses, trojan horses, worms, and bugs. ✓**BIX**→*conference* SECURITY

Viruses & worms

comp.virus (NG/ML) Discuss computer viruses, protection software, and related topics. ✓**USENET** ✓**INTERNET**→*email* LISTSERV@LEHIGH.EDU ✍ *Type in message body:* SUB VIRUS-L <YOUR FULL NAME>

Valert-L (ML) For virus alerts and warnings only. ✓**INTERNET**→*email* LISTSERV@LEHIGH.EDU ✍ *Type in message body:* SUB VALERT-L <YOUR FULL NAME>

Virus Discussions and warning information on computer viruses, trojan horses, and many other destructive programs. ✓**ILINK**→*number 45*

Virus Discussion about computer viruses. ✓**SMARTNET**→*tag* VIRUS

Virus Info Center Provides assistance to the Macintosh virus and antivirus community, with information on the latest virus or trojan horse, and updates to popular commercial, shareware, and freeware antivirus tools. ✓**AMERICA ONLINE**→*keyword* VIRUS

Virus Information Conference How to detect and remove computer viruses, with methods, tools, and announcements of newly discovered strains. ✓**FIDONET**

→*tag* VIRUS_INFO

*****Virus Questions** Information and safeguards. ✓**PRODIGY**→*jump* VIRUS

VMVirus (ML) Forum for discussing VM, MVS, and VSE viruses and worms. ✓**INTERNET**→ *email* LISTSERV@PCCVM.BITNET ✍ *Type in message body:* SUB VMVIRUS <YOUR FULL NAME>

Privacy

alt.security.pgp (NG) Offers discussion on PGP (Pretty Good Privacy), a public data-encryption package available on the Internet. ✓**USENET**

alt.security.ripem (NG) Offers discussion on RIPEM, a program for public-key mail encryption officially sanctioned by Public Key Partners Inc., the company that owns patents on public keys. ✓**USENET**

comp.risks (NG) A moderated digest with discussion about the public risks from computers and users. ✓**USENET**

comp.society.cu-digest (NG) *The Computer Underground Digest.* ✓**USENET**

Cypherpunk (ML) Discuss technological defenses for privacy in the digital domain. ✓**INTERNET**→ *email* CYPHERPUNKS-REQUEST@TOAD.COM ✍*Subscribe by request*

Public-Key Distribution A companion to the Public Keys echo, where users can enter and gather keys. ✓**FIDONET**→*tag* PKEY_DROP

Public-Key Encryption and Distribution Forum for technical

discussions about public-key privacy and programs. ✓**FIDONET**→*tag* PUBLIC_ KEYS

sci.crypt (NG) Technical and theoretical discussions about cryptography. ✓**USENET**

IBM PCs, DOS & OS/2

"When you purchase a new computer, ask the vendor to install OS/2 2.0, and to offer

credit for dropping DOS and Windows," advises Timothy F. Sipples, FAQ editor at **comp.os.os2.misc**, aiding IBM in its struggle against Microsoft's DOS and Windows. Sipples' list of Big Blue support action includes "Write an outstanding piece of shareware," and "Wear OS/2 pins, shirts, buttons." On the other hand, if you feel like *you're* the one who needs support, there are forums that provide technical help to OS/2 users—some with IBM technicians on board. Then again, if you're sporting a DOS button, you'll find a list of great freeware in "The Ultimate Guide to MS-DOS Archive Files," available on **comp. archives.msdos.d**, such as WordPerfect Password Decryption (freeware)—"the best password cracker for encrypted WordPerfect files."

On the Net

Across the board

IBM European Users Forum Information on IBM PCs and compatibles for European users. ✓ **COMPUSERVE**→*go* IBMEUROPE

A 486 chip—from America Online's PC Graphics & Sound Forum.

IBM Exchange Includes areas devoted to the PS/2 series (IBM.PS), the OS/2 operating system (IBM.OS2), IBM vendors (IBM.VENDORS), products from Microsoft (MICROSOFT), an index to all files in the IBM Exchange (IBM.LISTINGS), and several others. ✓ **BIX**→*conference* IBM.EXCHANGE

IBM File Finder A searchable database of all the IBM-related files available on Compuserve. Criteria available for searches include name, file type, keyword, submission date, forum name, extension, or submitter's user ID. ✓ **COMPUSERVE**→*go* IBMFF

IBM National Support Center BBS (BBS) A user-groups database and newsletter exchange. 919-517-0001

IBM PC Users Network A set of special-interest forums for users of IBM PCs and compatibles, covering all hardware and software issues. ✓ **COMPUSERVE**→*go* IBMNET

IBM RoundTable Covers IBM-

related hardware and software issues, including clones. The software library includes thousands of programs and utilities. ▣ ◉ ✓ **GENIE**→*keyword* IBMPC

PC Compatibles/IBM SIG Full range of discussions, files, and conferences on the IBM PC/AT and compatible computers. Sponsored by *PCM*, a magazine for users of Tandy personal computers. ◉ ✓ **DELPHI**→*go* COM PC

Hardware

Build-a-PC Information on building and upgrading the PC/AT/386 at home. ✓ **ILINK**→*number* 145

comp.sys.ibm.pc.digest (NG) Discussions about the venerable IBM PC, PC-XT, and PC-AT. ✓ **USENET**

comp.sys.ibm.pc.hardware (NG) Hardware discussions related to the IBM PC. ✓ **USENET**

comp.sys.ibm.pc.misc (NG) General discussion about the IBM PC. ✓ **USENET**

comp.sys.intel (NG) General discussion about Intel systems and parts. ✓ **USENET**

IBM Offers technical data and product-release announcements about the IBM PC. ✓ **RELAYNET**→*number* 160

IBM Includes hardware and software information and new-product announcements. ✓ **SMARTNET**→

tag IBM

IBM PC Company IBM advertisements for their PCs, peripherals, and other products. ✓**PRODIGY** → *jump* IBM PC COMPANY

MS-DOS Forum Keep up-to-date with the news from Microsoft. Includes discussions about software and hardware issues, as well as libraries with demos, diagnostic programs, and archives of past discussions. ⊕🕄 ✓**COMPUSERVE**→*go* MSDOS

comp.archives.msdos.d (NG) Discussions and questions about material at MS-DOS FTP archives on the Net. See also COMP.ARCHIVES. MSDOS.ANNOUNCE. ✓**USENET**

PCtech-L (ML) Support-exchange for users of MS-DOS PCs. ✓**INTERNET**→*email* LISTSERV@TREARN. BITNET ✍ *Type in message body:* SUB PCTECH-L <YOUR FULL NAME>

PS/1 Club Support club for IBM PS/1 owners. ✓**PRODIGY**→*jump* PS/1 CLUB

Tech Discussions about IBM computers. ✓**ILINK**→*number* 3

Technical Offers discussion about PC technical issues, focusing on IBM and IBM-clone computers. ✓**RELAYNET**→*number* 106

386 Users (ML) Discussions related to Intel 80386, including reviews, rumors, and hardware and software questions. ✓**INTERNET**→*email* 386USERS-REQUEST@UDEL. EDU ✍*Subscribe by request*

Clones

Bull User's Group Conference Forum for owners and users of Bull and Zenith PCs. ✓**FIDONET**

→*tag* BULL

Tandy Model 1000 Personal Computer Users Conference User group discussing hardware upgrades, software compatibility, and other issues, with input from Radio Shack representatives. ✓**FIDONET**→*tag* MOD1000

Tandy Model 2000 Echomail Conference Discussion about the discontinued MS-DOS computer. ✓**FIDONET**→*tag* TAND2000

MS-DOS

comp.os.msdos.misc (NG) Covers issues related to MS-DOS machines. ✓**USENET**

DOS Offers help, teaching, and support to DOS users. Managed by a professional staff. Features include freeware and shareware files and utilities, discussion of DOS alternatives, and DOS news and updates. ✓**AMERICA ONLINE**→*keyword* DOS

DOS Includes discussion on all MS-DOS and PC-DOS issues, including settings, options, utilities, optimization, and troubleshooting. ✓**RELAYNET**→*number* 383

DOS 6.0 For discussion about DOS 6.0. ✓**SMARTNET**→*tag* DOS 6.0

DOS Shareware and Freeware Repository Large collections of shareware and freeware for MS-DOS. ✓**INTERNET** ...→*ftp* OAK. OAKLAND.EDU→ANONYMOUS/<YOUR EMAIL ADDRESS>→pub/msdos ...→*ftp* GARBO.UWASA.FI→ANONYMOUS/<YOUR EMAIL ADDRESS>→pub/msdos

DOS6 Conference on MS-DOS 6.0. ✓**ILINK**→*number* 179

DOSTips DOS help, particularly

with batch files. Information on major shareware and commercial DOS utilities. ✓**ILINK**→*number* 112

Multitasking Discussions on memory managers, DOS extenders, and multitasking software. ✓**ILINK**→*number* 24

OS/2

comp.binaries.os2 (NG) Binary programs for OS/2 systems. ✓**USENET**

comp.os.os2.announce (NG) Announcements related to OS/2. ✓**USENET**

comp.os.os2.apps (NG) Discussions related to applications under OS/2. ✓**USENET**

IBM OS/2 User Forum Hardware and software information for owners and users of OS/2. ⊕🕄 ✓**COMPUSERVE**→*go* OS2USER

Networking and OS/2 Technical talk about networking computers using OS/2. ✓**FIDONET**→*tag* OS2LAN

OS2 (ML) A weekly digest of questions and answers and articles from various OS/2 newsgroups. Topics range from system versions to communications issues to software packages. ✓**INTERNET**→*email* LISTSERV@CC1.KULEUVEN.AC.BE ✍*Type in message body:* SUBSCRIBE OS2 <YOUR FULL NAME>

OS2 Discussion of the IBM OS/2 operating system. ✓**ILINK**→*number* 67

OS/2 Covers all versions of OS/2, applications that run under the system, development of new applications, and updates to OS/2. ✓**RELAYNET**→*number* 296

OS/2 Discussion about all versions of OS/2. ✓**SMARTNET**→*tag* OS/2

OS/2 Conference The operating system and related topics. ✓**FIDONET**→*tag* OS2

OS/2 Hardware Hardware issues in using OS/2, including device drivers, hardware compatibility, installation, and performance. ✓**FIDONET**→*tag* OS2HW

OS2-l (ML) Discussion of any OS/2 issue, including programming, user queries, OS/2 2.0, and more. ✓**INTERNET**→*email* LISTSERV@FRORS12.BITNET 🖎 *Type in message body:* SUB OS2-L <YOUR FULL NAME>

OS/2 RoundTable Information on the operating system and compatible products. Includes a software library and support from IBM employees and software vendors. ⊕💬 ✓**GENIE**→*keyword* OS/2

OS/2 User Groups & Promotion User group information, promotions, product announcements, and news. ✓**FIDONET**→*tag* TEAMOS2

Software

comp.binaries.ibm.pc (NG) Binary-only postings for MS-DOS machines. ✓**USENET**

comp.binaries.ibm.pc.d (NG) Discussions about the binary-only postings in COMP.BINARIES.IBM.PC. ✓**USENET**

IBM Applications Forum Covers all types of applications available for IBM and compatible personal computers. ✓**COMPUSERVE**→*go* IBMAPP

IBM Connections An online catalog of new systems and software;

IBM news; and the PS/1 Users Club. ☻ ✓**PRODIGY**→*jump* IBM CONNECTIONS

PC Applications Forum Offers help and information on all types of PC applications, shareware files, and regularly scheduled conferences on different types of applications, including word processors and spreadsheets. Includes a staff of experienced PC users. ✓**AMERICA ONLINE**→*keyword* PAP

Word-PC (ML) Discuss all aspects of Microsoft Word for the PC. ✓**INTERNET**→ *email* MAILSERV@UFO BIL.UNI-FORST. GWDG.DE 🖎 *Type in message body:* SUBSCRIBE WORD-PC <YOUR FULL NAME>

News, sales, support

IBM Product Support Round-Table IBM hardware and software vendors answer customer questions, regularly announce new products, and release bug reports and notes. ⊕💬 ✓**GENIE**→*keyword* IBMSUPPORT

misc.forsale.computers.pc-clone (NG) Listings for items for the IBM PC or compatibles. ☻ ✓**USENET**

PCsupt-L (ML) An IBM PC user group where subscribers—including technical professionals—will discuss topics ranging from viruses and vaccines to system upgrades to equipment quality to software evaluation. ✓**INTERNET**→*email* LIST SERV@YALEVM.BITNET 🖎 *Type in message body:* SUBSCRIBE PCSUPT-L <YOUR FULL NAME>

PC User Groups Information for members of PC user groups and people interested in joining them. ✓**FIDONET**→*tag* PCUG

Macintosh

Looking for a hot new game, a useful utility, or a dramat-ic typeface for your Macintosh? The Net offers thousands of "try before you buy" shareware programs that you can download and test, at prices usually much cheaper (sometimes free!) than those of commercial software. Some of the best shareware and freeware files are in the **Mac Shareware 500** library on America Online, the Info-Mac archives at **sumex-aim.stanford.edu** on the Internet, and the **Mac Shareware Emporium** library in CompuServe's Macintosh New Users and Help Forum. Favorites available everywhere include ZTerm, a communications package; Compact Pro, a compression utility; and Covert Action, a submarine war game.

On the Net

Across the board

Apple Macintosh Forums A group of forums for the Mac, covering personal productivity, arts, entertainment, new users, communication, HyperCard, vendors, the new Newton, and developers. ✓**COMPUSERVE**→*go* MACINTOSH

Berkeley Macintosh User Group Provides a clearinghouse

Powerbooks—from ZiffNet: Executives Online Forum, through CompuServe.

of information for both members of BMUG and anyone else interested in graphical-user-interface computers, including the Mac. ✓**AMERICA ONLINE**→*keyword* BMUG

comp.sys.mac.misc (NG) General discussions about the Apple Macintosh. ✓**USENET**

GE-MUG RoundTable For Mac users. Discussions about Mac software and hardware, weekly conferences, and a library with thousands of downloadable files. ▦▤ ◉💬 ✓**GENIE**→*keyword* MAC

Macintosh ICONtact Offers opinions, advice, humor, programs, information files, and conferences on all subjects related to the Mac. ✓**DELPHI**→*go* COM MAC

Macintosh New Users and Help Forum Get all your questions answered, whether you're a novice or a long time Mac user. The libraries include hundreds of useful utility programs and files from the Mac Shareware Emporium book. ✓**COMPUSERVE**→*go* MACNEW→MACHELP

Hardware

comp.sys.mac.hardware (NG)

Macintosh hardware issues and discussions. ✓**USENET**

comp.sys.mac.portables (NG) Discussion for those interested in laptop Macintoshes. ✓**USENET**

Macintosh Hardware Everything about Mac hardware. ✓**FIDONET**→*tag* MACHW

Macintosh Hardware Forum Information on everything from CPUs to peripherals, made by every manufacturer, including Apple. ✓**COMPUSERVE**→*go* MACHW

Macintosh Hardware Forum Includes technical support, help for new users, system software, utilities, announcements from Apple, information on third-party products, and general Mac news. ✓**AMERICA ONLINE**→*keyword* MHW

Software

comp.binaries.mac (NG) For Macintosh freeware and shareware. ✓**USENET**

comp.sys.mac.apps (NG) For discussions of Macintosh applications. ✓**USENET**

HyperCard (ML) "Anything and everything about HyperCard." ✓**INTERNET**→*email* LISTSERV@MSU.EDU ✍*Type in message body:* SUBSCRIBE HYPERCRD <YOUR FULL NAME>

HyperCard Covers both the use of HyperCard stacks and building your own stack using Hypertalk. Areas include learning HyperCard, Hypertalk programming, reviews of stacks and HyperCard books, and a business exchange. ✓**AMERICA ONLINE**→*keyword* MHC

Mac Applications Forum Covers word processors, databases, spreadsheets, personal information managers, and graphics programs. ⊕🕹 ✓**COMPUSERVE**→*go* MACAP

Macintosh Operating Systems Forum Offers downloads of System 7 and related files, help with installation, hints and tips, plus discussion on new and old generations of system software. ✓**AMERICA ONLINE**→*keyword* MOS

Macintosh Software All types. ✓**FIDONET**→*tag* MACSW

Macintosh System Software Forum How to use Systems 6.0 and 7, with extensions, control panels, and other accessories to customize your Mac. ✓**COMPUSERVE**→*go* MACSYS

Mac Shareware 500 Based on the best-selling book by the same title, the forum offers a library of all 500 shareware files, message boards, and discussions with shareware authors. ✓**AMERICA ONLINE**→*keyword* MAC500

Sumex-AIM (ML) Sumex is perhaps *the* repository for Macintosh programs and utilities, with thousands of shareware and freeware files and demos. The daily Info-Mac newsletter (usually 100K or larger) offers updates and reviews of new files in the archive. ✓**INTERNET** ...→*email* INFO-MAC-REQUEST@ SUMEX-AIM.STANFORD.EDU ✍*Subscribe by request* ✖*Email sent only to relays* ...→*ftp* SUMEX-AIM.STANFORD.EDU →ANONYMOUS/<YOUR EMAIL ADDRESS> →info mac/digest

Fun

comp.sys.mac.games (NG) Discussions of games on the Macintosh. ✓**USENET**

Macintosh Entertainment and

Education Reviews of games, education, and children's programs for the Mac. ✓**FIDONET**→*tag* MAC_ GAMES

Macintosh Entertainment Forum Games and other pleasures on the Macintosh, from both a hardware and a software angle. ⊕🕹 ✓**COMPUSERVE**→*go* MACFUN

Specialties

Macintosh Business Forum Offers discussion on using the Mac for business, including software packages for accounting, project management, presentations, spreadsheets, and tax preparation. ✓**AMERICA ONLINE**→*keyword* MBS

Macintosh Communications Forum How to communicate with the Macintosh: hardware, software, BBSs, fax machines, LANs, and more. ⊕🕹 ✓**COMPUSERVE**→*go* MACCOMM

PUMA* A series of FidoNet conferences sponsored by the Power User's Macintosh Association (PUMA). Discussion on everything Macintosh, with echoes on games, classifieds, graphics, programming, multimedia, and more. ✓**FIDONET**→*tag* PUMA*

News, support, sales

comp.sys.mac.announce (NG) Important notices for Macintosh users. ✓**USENET**

comp.sys.mac.digest (NG) Discussion about Apple Macintosh information—no program-specific discussions. ✓**USENET**

Mac Exchange Includes technical information about the Mac (MAC.HACK), Macintosh news (MAC.NEWS), listings of Mac hard-

ware and software (MAC.PRODUCTS), fun with the Macintosh (MAC. SANDBOX), and information from Apple (MAC.APPLE). ✓**BIX**→*conference* MAC. EXCHANGE

Macintosh For Sale/Wanted Noncommercial ads for Mac and NeXT equipment, hardware, and software. ✓**FIDONET**→*tag* MACFSALE ✖*No commercial advertising*

Macintosh Product Support RoundTable Technical support from Macintosh hardware and software vendors. ⊕🕹 ✓**GENIE**→ *keyword* MAC-PS

MacUser Forum Information, reviews, and utilities from the editorial staff of *MacUser*. ✓**COMPUSERVE**→*go* ZMC:MACUSER $2.50/ MONTH

MacWEEK Forum Information exchange, tips, and files from the editors and staff of *MacWEEK*. ✓**COMPUSERVE**→*go* ZMC:MACWEEK $2.50/MONTH

Macworld Online Provides articles and reviews from current and past issues, contact with editors and staff, and a software library. ▦ ✓**AMERICA ONLINE**→*keyword* MACWORLD

misc.forsale.computers.mac (NG) Listings for Apple Mac items. 🖐 ✓**USENET**

Rosenthal on Mac Macintosh news and expert advice by Steve Rosenthal. ✓**PRODIGY**→*jump* ROSENTHAL ON MAC

Tidbits (ML) A weekly report on the microcomputer industry, especially Apple Macintosh news. ✓**INTERNET**→*email* LISTSERV@RICEVM1. RICE.EDU ✍*Type in message body:* SUB TIDBITS <YOUR FULL NAME>

Multimedia

If you still don't know what the heck multimedia is, you
could do worse than by
starting with the **Multimedia** conference on BIX
where you'll find serious discussion about the true nature of the beast. Steve
Rosenthal also covers the
wider theoretical issues of
multimedia for Prodigy.
Smartnet provides good
practical advice for actually
using multimedia in the one
theater where the application has really been successful: corporate meetings and
presentations. **CD-Roms** on
ILink offers a knowledgeable hardware discussion.

Mount St. Helen, as rendered for a multimedia application—from CompuServe's Multimedia Forum.

Across the board

alt.binaries.multimedia (NG)
Sound, text, and graphics files.
✓**USENET**

comp.multimedia (NG) Discussion about hardware and software,
on all platforms. ✓**USENET**

comp.sys.amiga.multimedia
(NG) Covers issues related to using
Amiga computers for creating
multimedia projects. ✓**USENET**

Digital Publishing RoundTable
Multimedia discussion on GEnie,
covering hardware, software, and
creative issues, takes place on the
Multimedia bulletin board. ✓**GE-
NIE**→*keyword* DIGIPUB

House of Sound A file site with
multimedia programs, utilities,
and demonstrations. ✓**INTERNET**
→*ftp* SOUND.USACH.CL→ANONYMOUS/
<YOUR EMAIL ADDRESS>→pub

Megamedia Multimedia BBS
(BBS) File collection and information includes video for Windows,
MPC and MPC files, and a sales
section of CD titles. 408-428-9901
FREE

MPC (Multimedia for Personal Computers) Hardware
and software for multimedia.
✓**FIDONET**→*tag* MPC

Multimedia Computer-generated sights and sounds. ✓**BIX**→*conference* MULTIMEDIA

Multimedia Steve Rosenthal
reports on multimedia in his regularly featured column. ✓**PRODIGY**→
jump MULTIMEDIA

Multimedia For discussions
about slide shows and presentations. ✓**SMARTNET**→*tag* MULTIMEDIA

Multimedia Forum Sponsored
by the Multimedia Computing
Corporation, provides an information exchange and files on audio,
video, animation, music, hypertext, and multimedia hardware
issues. Covers all platforms,
including the Macintosh, Amiga,
Windows, DOS, and OS/2.
✓**COMPUSERVE**→*go* MULTIMEDIA

Sight & Sound Forum Offers
information, discussion, and files
on digital sound and music sampling; as well as multimedia, GIF,
animation, and other images
accompanied by sound and music.
✓**COMPUSERVE**→*go* SOUND

Tempra Multimedia (BBS) An
all-multimedia BBS (a few exceptions). 908-493-0139

CD-ROM

alt.cd-rom (NG/ML) Covers any
CD-ROM topic, from recorders
to suppliers. ✓**USENET** ✓**INTERNET**→
email LISTSERV@UCCVMA.UCOP.EDU ✉
Type in message body: SUBSCRIBE
CDROM-L <YOUR FULL NAME>

**CD ROM Discussion and
Information** General chat about
CD ROM and laser optic technology. ✓**FIDONET**→*tag* CDROM

CDROM Forum The latest information on CD-ROM technology
and products. ⊕💬 ✓**COMPUSERVE**
→*go* CDROM

CD-ROMS Discussion of CD-
ROM players and new disks.
✓**ILINK**→*number* 159

Kodak CD Forum Provides
information and files for Kodak
CD products and technology,
including a CD-ROM drive compatibility guide, news on Kodak's
Shoebox Software for the Mac-

intosh, and related products. 🖥️💬
✓**COMPUSERVE**→*go* KODAK

Technology

bit.listserv.cdromlan (NG/ML)
Covers the use of CD-ROM products on local-area or wide-area networks. ✓**USENET** ✓**INTERNET**→*email* LISTSERV@IDBSU.IDBSU.EDU ✉
Type in message body: SUBSCRIBE CDROMLAN <YOUR FULL NAME>

CD ROM Provides for the exchange of technical information on CD-ROM, including software and hardware setup and operation. For-sale ads may be placed only once per week per item. ✓**RELAY-NET**→*number* 377

Opt-Proc (ML) Discussions of optical computing, optical information processing, and holography. ✓**INTERNET**→*email* LISTSERV@VM. TAU.AC.IL ✉ *Type in message body:* SUBSCRIBE OPT-PROC <YOUR FULL NAME>

Video Special Interest Area For those with an interest in using video on the Mac. You may upload samples of your work to a software library. ✓**AMERICA ONLINE**→*keyword* VIDEO SIG

Education

Media-L (ML) Discussion of educational communications and technology issues for media-services professionals. ✓**INTERNET**→*email* LISTSERV@BINGVMB.BITNET ✉ *Type in message body:* SUBSCRIBE MEDIA-L <YOUR FULL NAME>

The Multimedia Exchange Oriented toward teachers and education, this forum provides examples of multimedia, tools for teachers to build their own multimedia databases, and an idea exchange with the Smithsonian's

National Demonstration Library. ✓**AMERICA ONLINE** →*keyword* MULTI-MEDIA

Creation

CDPub (ML) Dedicated to the discussion of CD-ROM publishing, especially desktop CD-ROM publishing systems. ✓**INTERNET**→*email* MAIL-SERVER@KNEX.VIA.MIND.ORG ✉ *Type in message body:* SUBSCRIBE CDPUB <YOUR FULL NAME>

Image-L (ML) Forum for discussing image processing and related issues, especially video compression. ✓**INTERNET**→*email* LISTSERV@TREARN.BITNET ✉ *Type in message body:* SUB IMAGE-L <YOUR FULL NAME>

Mmos2-L (ML) For programmers, multimedia designers, computer musicians, animators, and others interested in multimedia programming on IBM's OS/2. ✓**INTERNET**→*email* MAIL-SERVER@KNEX.VIA.MIND. ORG ✉ *Type in message body:* SUBSCRIBE MMOS2-L <YOUR FULL NAME>

Products

CD ROM Discussions about massive optical disk storage through CD-ROM drives and WORM. ✓**SMARTNET**→*tag* CD ROM

CD ROM Titles & Hardware for Sale Buying, selling, and trading CD-ROMS and the equipment to use them. ✓**FIDONET**→*tag* CDROM_SALE

Hyperami (ML) Informal discussion of hypermedia products, such as AmigaVision, PILOT, Thinker, and the user's hypermedia projects. ✓**INTERNET**→*email* LISTSERV@ARCHIVE.OIT.UNC.EDU ✉ *Type in message body:* SUBSCRIBE HYPERAMI <YOUR FULL NAME>

CYBERNOTES

What is multimedia?

"According to [Microsoft founder] Bill Gates we have to have something that is called 'Multimedia' which has such an amorphous definition that he cannot fail to hit it no matter how badly he aims. Multimedia is too broad a term to focus. It is another buzzword like 'AI.' [artificial intelligence]. Every AI element that becomes real takes on a different name.... There is 'presentation multimedia,' which helps make things like business presentations effective. There is 'entertainment multimedia,' which has several subdivisions. There is 'broadcast multimedia'—sound and audio and 'style' with a goal usually to entertain. There is 'arcade multimedia.' There is 'Epcot Center multimedia'...."

—from **BIX's Multimedia**

Multimedia Vendors Forum Support and information from companies making multimedia hardware and software. 🖥️💬
✓**COMPUSERVE**→*go* MULTIVENDOR

PC alternatives

There are universal feelings shared by owners of orphan computers, machines that

have been discontinued by their manufacturers—abandonment, anger, fear, and a special longing for contact. "I am very fond of my IPC ...," Jeff Broido posted on GEnie's **TI & Orphans RoundTable** about his Hewlett-Packard Integral Personal Computer. "The only thing is that there's very little software available, commercial or otherwise, and now that H-P has dropped support, there's not likely to be much more written. Is there anyone out there who even knows what this lovely little system is? Do I hear an echo?"

On the Net

Sales, help, support

Boston Computer Society Forum Offers an online guide to the world's largest organization of computer users, with areas for nearly every possible computer or computer-related activity. ✓**AMERICA ONLINE**→*keyword* BCS

PC Preview Computer product news. ✓**PRODIGY**→*jump* PC PREVIEW

PC Quirks Offbeat computer news. ✓**PRODIGY**→*jump* PC QUIRKS

Personal Computer News Columns on personal computing.

A personal computer—downloaded from CompuServe's Atari Arts Forum.

✓**GENIE**→*keyword* PCNEWS

User Group Forum Provides assistance to leaders of Apple and PC user groups on the creation, management, and satisfaction of running a user group. ✓**AMERICA ONLINE**→*keyword* UGC

Atari

Atari Archive Offers a selection of files for Atari computers, excepting the Amiga. ✓**INTERNET**→*ftp* ATARI.ARCHIVE.UMICH.EDU→ANONYMOUS/<YOUR EMAIL ADDRESS>→ atari

Atari 8-bit Computers General talk about Atari 8 computers. ✓**FIDONET**→*tag* ATARI

Atari 8-Bit RoundTable Support from the Atari Corp. as well as GEnie experts for users of Atari 8-bit Computers. Includes a bulletin board and a software library with thousands of downloadable files. ✓**GENIE**→*keyword* ATARI8

Atari ST Discussion for all types of Atari STs, including the Mega

STs and TTs. No 8-bit discussion. ✓**FIDONET**→*tag* ATARI_ST

Atari-ST RoundTable For Atari ST users of all levels of expertise. Includes technical support as well as libraries of downloadable utilities, games, and other shareware. Regular online meetings. ✓**GENIE**→*keyword* ST

Atari Users Network A set of forums for owners and users of Atari computers, including the 8-bit, the ST, and the hand-held Atari Portfolio. ✓**COMPUSERVE**→*go* ATARINET

comp.sys.atari.8bit (NG) Discussion about 8-bit Atari micros. ✓**USENET**

comp.sys.atari.st (NG) A techinically-oriented newsgroup that offers discussion about the 16- and 32-bit Atari computers, including the Atari 520ST, 1040ST, Mega ST, STe, STacy, Mega STe, and TT. ✓**USENET**

Commodore

Commodore Computer Conference Technical discussions about Commodore 8-bit computers. ✓**FIDONET**→*tag* CBM

Commodore Flagship Round-Table For all 8-bit Commodore users. Includes bulletin boards for discussions about Commodore computing, and thousands of programs for the C-64 and C-128. ✓**GENIE**→*keyword* CBM

Commodore SIG A general-interest group covering all topics important to owners and users of Commodore computers. ✓**DELPHI**→*go* COM COM

comp.sys.cbm (NG) Discussion about Commodore microcomputers. ✓**USENET**

Tandy

comp.sys.tandy (NG) Discussion about Tandy computers. ✓**USENET**

Hardware Support Forum Offers information on Tandy equipment, a hardware reference guide, computing newsletters, and special conferences on different manufacturers' computers. ✓**AMERICA ONLINE**→*keyword* PHW

Tandy PC SIG Offers a full range of file libraries, conferences, and message sections for users of Tandy computers, including the Model 1000, 1200, 1400, 2000, 3000, and 4000. Sponsored by *PCM* magazine. ✓**DELPHI**→*go* COM TANDY

Tandy RoundTable For users of Tandy computers: software, support, and discussions. ✓**GENIE**→*keyword* TANDY

Tandy Users Network A set of forums for Tandy computer products: the Color Computer, LDOS/ TRSDOS6, Model 100/Portables, OS-9, Tandy Professional, and the Tandy Corporation Newsletter. ✓**COMPUSERVE**→*go* TANDYNET

Other brands

AT&T Forum for discussing AT&T computer equipment and software. ✓**SMARTNET**→*tag* AT&T

AT&T PC Support Advice and support for all models of AT&T PCs, plus Xerox 6060 and Olivetti M24 PCs. ✓**FIDONET**→*tag* AT&T

comp.sys.att (NG) Offers technical information and support for the 3B2 series of AT&T personal computers. ✓**USENET**

Computer Club Forum A home for users of computers no longer supported by specific manufacturers, including Actrix, Adam, Amstrad, Apricot, Eagle, Kaypro, Ohio Scientific, Panasonic, Sanyo, Timex/Sinclair, and the Victor 9000. ✓**COMPUSERVE**→*go* CLUB

PCBuild (ML) Discussions about upgrading and building your own PC as well as hardware and vendor issues. ✓**INTERNET**→*email* LISTSERV@ TSCVM.TRENTON.EDU ✍*Type in message body:* SUB PCBUILD <YOUR FULL NAME>

Texas Instruments Forum Information and support for TI computers. ✓**COMPUSERVE**→*go* TIFORUM

Texas Instruments Topics Covers the TI-99/4A computer and clones. ✓**FIDONET**→*tag* TI-ECHO

TI & Orphans RoundTable For owners of the TI-99/4A computer and other orphan computers. Includes discussions, a huge software library, and regular conferences. ✓**GENIE**→*keyword* TI

Laptops & handhelds

comp.sys.laptops (NG) General discussion about laptop computers. ✓**USENET**

LapTop Discussions about the business applications and systems operations of laptop computers. ✓**SMARTNET**→*tag* LAPTOP

Laptop Computers Discussions about portable DESC computers, including luggables like the Compaq Portable; DESC laptops, notebooks, and palmtops; and software for these machines. ✓**FIDONET**→*tag* LAPTOP

Laptop Computers Discusses all types of portable computers, including laptops, notebooks, palmtops, and hand-held devices. Includes answers from manufacturers and some advertising. ✓**RE-LAYNET**→*number* 129

The Laptops RoundTable Share tips, information, and programs for laptop computers. Includes a library of thousands of programs and files and a bulletin board system divided into categories. ✓**GENIE**→*keyword* LAPTOPS

Palmtop Forum Information and support for owners of the smallest computers, including how to interface with desktop systems and how to use palmtops for telecommunications. ✓**COMPUSERVE**→*go* PALMTOP

Palmtop SIG For Mac and PC users interested in handheld computer systems. Features a software library, message boards, and product announcements. ✓**AMERICA ONLINE**→*keyword* PALMTOP

Pen Technology Forum Information on pen-based computer products, including discussion with the editors of *Pen Magazine* in the PenWorld section. ✓**COMPUSERVE**→*go* PENFORUM

Portfolio RoundTable Support, information, software, and discussions related to the Atari Portfolio palmtop computer. ✓**GENIE**→ *keyword* PORTFOLIO

Programming

The highest compliment paid to a programmer is, "She writes clean code." If you want to tidy up your lines, take a class at **Programmer U** on America Online. It offers introductory, intermediate, and advanced classes in C and Pascal for AOL members, covering Apple II, Macintosh, and PC-compatible computers. The classes include live online conferences with the instructor, weekly programming assignments, and an area for students to post questions and receive help.

On the Net

Across the board

BASIC Forum Information and customer support for Microsoft's BASIC, QuickBasic, and Visual Basic program-development software. ✓**COMPUSERVE**→*go* MSBASIC

comp.lang* (NG) Usenet offers dozens of newsgroups on computer languages, including COMP.LANG. C, COMP.LANG.FORTRAN, COMP.LANG. LISP, COMP.LANG.MODULA2, COMP. LANG.PASCAL, and COMP.LANG.SCHEME. ✓**USENET**

comp.programming (NG) Programming issues that transcend languages and OSs. ✓**USENET**

comp.sources* (NG) Usenet offers several newsgroups devoted exclusively to offering source code for specific computer systems— e.g., COMP.SOURCES.AMIGA and COMP. SOURCES.MAC. ✓**USENET**

Computer Language Forum Source code, programs, and articles from *Computer Language Magazine.* 🖳 ✓**COMPUSERVE**→*go* CLMFORUM

Dr. Dobb's Journal Electronic version of the magazine, with information on computer languages, tools, utilities, algorithms, and programming techniques. Also allows uploads of article submissions. 🖳 ✓**COMPUSERVE**→*go* DDJ

East Coast Programmers A worldwide conference that originated for East Coast programmers. Covers C, Pascal, Assembler, BASIC, RPG, and others. ✓**FIDO-NET**→*tag* ECPROG

PC Development Forum Provides help and information for everyone from beginning programmers to professional developers. Covers Windows, BASIC, and a variety of computer languages. ✓**AMERICA ONLINE**→*keyword* PDV

Programmers Exchange Includes more than 30 conferences ranging from a conference on the ADA language (ADA) to discussions about the C++ programming language (C.PLUS.PLUS) to a conference on programming and graphics (GRAPHIC.PGMS) to a UNIX conference (UNIX). ✓**BIX**→PROGRAMMERS

Programming General discussions of programming, covering all computer languages and skill lev-

els. ✓**ILINK**→*number* 54

Tools & code

alt.lang.basic (NG) For discussing the BASIC language. ✓**USENET**

alt.sources.d (NG) For discussing source code posted in ALT.SOURCES ✓**USENET**

alt.sources (NG) For posting source code. ✓**USENET**

comp.compilers (NG/ML) Covers compilers in particular and programming-language design and implementation in general. Topics include language-optimization techniques, language-design issues, and new compilers. ✓**USENET** ✓**INTERNET**→*email* LISTSERV@AMERI CAN.EDU ✍ *Type in message body:* SUBSCRIBE COMPIL-L <YOUR FULL NAME>

Programming Includes discussion of all types of programming languages. ✓**RELAYNET**→*number* 110

Protocol (ML) Forum for discussing computer protocols from encodings during file transfer to networking protocols to file formats. ✓**INTERNET**→*email* LISTSERV@ VMD.CSO.UIUC.EDU ✍ *Type in message body:* SUBSCRIBE PROTOCOL <YOUR FULL NAME>

Professionals

Programmer U Offers online classes in programming for all types of computers. Cosponsored by the Apple II, Macintosh, and PC Developer forums. 🖳🐾 ✓**AMERICA ONLINE**→*keyword* ADV

Programmers Distribution Network General discussion for programmers, with information about the PDN. ✓**FIDONET**→*tag* PDNECHO

Shareware & freeware

Shareware authors are the sunny optimists of the computer world—giving away valu-

able software in the hopes that someone, someday, might pay for it. But how to calculate an expected registration rate? In CompuServe's **Association of Shareware Professionals Forum**, George Abbott suggested the following formula: $R=(((3.5 \times NV)+(1.8 \times NX)+(1.05 \times NB)) \times M)/XF$. R is registrations per month. The other variables cover disks sent to ASP vendors, disks sent to non-ASP vendors, uploads to BBSs, and months in distribution. XF (the X factor) is the change left in an author's pocket after a night of barhopping.

On the Net

Across the board

ASP/Shareware Forum Files and information from the Association of Shareware Professionals, which allows you to download and try programs before purchase. ⊕🖾 ✓**COMPUSERVE**→*go* ASPFORUM

Public Domain/Shareware/ Commercial Chatter Catchall discussion for software not covered in other FidoNet echoes. ✓**FIDONET** →*tag* PDREVIEW

The Roadhouse BBS (BBS) Carries a list of BBSs that belong to the Association of Shareware Pro-

Shareware everywhere—from CompuServe's Computer Art Forum.

fessionals, plus hundreds of shareware titles. 317-784-2147

Shareware Shareware information, support, discussions, and reviews. ✓**ILINK**→*number* 79

Experts

Association of Shareware Professionals (ASP) Messages about the ASP and its members, including announcements for new members and new releases of the ASP catalog. Also serves as a contact area for shareware writers, vendors, and BBSs that carry shareware. ✓**FIDONET** →*tag* ASP

SharewareIssue A forum for those who wish to debate on the "advanced" issues of shareware. ✓**ILINK**→*number* 170

Shareware Products Discussion Forum Program reviews; discussion of the ethical issues of shareware, and source information for the free publication *The Hack Report*. ✓**FIDONET** →*tag* SHAREWRE

Shareware Programs Offers discussion about shareware programs offered on BBSs, plus help

on writing and distributing new products. ✓**RELAYNET**→*number* 156

Games

Computer Game Design RoundTable Boards and libraries devoted to game design. Categories range from Talk to the Designers to So You Wanna Be a Game Designer! ⊕🖾 ✓**GENIE**→*keyword* JCGD

Public Brand Software Arcade Forum A shareware library with hundreds of downloadable games and hobby programs, plus programs for use in the home, education, and math. 🎮🖾 ✓**COMPUSERVE**→*go* ZNT:PBSARCADE $2.50/ MONTH ✖*DOS and Windows*

Platforms

Amiga Public Domain & Requests Reviews and discussion of shareware and other public-domain software for the Amiga. Discussions of piracy and illegal actions are banned. ✓**FIDONET**→*tag* AMIGA_PDREVIEW

IBM PC RoundTable Among the many features in this RoundTable are the games in Library 7. For instance, escape from a WWII German dungeon in Wolfenstein 3-D and attempt to defeat Hitler! 🖾 ⊕🖾 ✓**GENIE**→*keyword* IBMPC

Mac Shareware 500 Based on the best-selling book by the same title, the forum offers a library of 500 shareware files, message boards, and discussions. ✓**AMERICA ONLINE**→*keyword* MAC500

Software users

While the gearheads in the computer industry rush ahead
into the brave new world of
Pentium, PowerPC, Tali-
gent, and WindowsNT, the
rest of us are struggling to
make prosaic (but expen-
sive) word-processing and
spreadsheet programs im-
prove our workaday lives. If
your questions tend to the
practical—such as "How do
I change the page margin in
Microsoft Word?"—try the
Software Center on America Online or the **Microsoft
Word Forum** on Compu-
Serve. The online support
staff treats new users and experts alike—gently.

*Impression of a software user—from
CompuServe's Photography Forum.*

On the Net

Across the board

Computer BB Ask any computer-related question, from the does-
this-program-have-that-feature
variety to the what-kind-of-hard-
ware-do-I-need type. ✓**PRODIGY**→
jump COMPUTER BB

File Search Lets users post their
requests for hard-to-find files or
descriptions of what they want a
file to accomplish. Responses offer
specific file names and advice on
where to find the file. Also
includes programs written by hobbyist programmers to fill the
requests. ✓**RELAYNET**→*number* 271

Microtutor Supplies tutorials for
popular software like Windows,

Lotus 1-2-3, and WordPerfect.
✓**PRODIGY**→*jump* MICROTUTOR

Software Center Offers company support and help areas for Mac,
DOS, Amiga, and Apple II software packages. ✓**AMERICA ONLINE**
→*keyword* SOFTWARE

Word processors

Microsoft Word Echo For both
PC and Macintosh users of the
word processor—tips, tricks, and
directions. Also includes Word for
Windows. ✓**FIDONET**→*tag* MS_WORD

Microsoft Word Forum For
everyone using Word for Windows, Macintosh, DOS, or OS/2.
✓**COMPUSERVE**→*go* MSWORD

WordPerfect Users Forum
Support for users of WordPerfect
software on all platforms.
✓**COMPUSERVE**→*go* WPUSERS

WordStar Discuss problems and
projects with other users of the
word-processing program Word-
Star. ✓**ILINK**→*number* 186

Word Processor Information
about word-processing programs.
✓**BIX**→WORD.PROCESSOR

Wordstar Offers discussion on
WordStar. ✓**RELAYNET**→*number* 312

**WordStar International Users
Forum** Covers use of WordStar
with both DOS and Windows.
✓**FIDONET**→ *tag* WORDSTAR

Spreadsheets

comp.apps.spreadsheets (NG)
For discussing spreadsheet applica-
tions on all different platforms.
✓**USENET**

Spreadsheets Discussions of
popular spreadsheet programs
such as Quattro, Excel, Multiplan,
Plan Perfect, and Lotus 1-2-3.
✓**ILINK**→*number* 60

Spreadsheets Includes discussions of all major spreadsheet
packages, including Lotus, Excel,
and Quattro Pro. ✓**RELAYNET**→
number 127

Databases

comp.databases (NG) General
discussion about database management. ✓**USENET**

Database Offers general discussion and review of major database
products like DBase and Paradox.
✓**RELAYNET**→*number* 121

Database RoundTable Discussion and assistance with all the
major PC database products.
✓**GENIE**→*keyword* DBMS

UNIX

Mike Ruble generated an overwhelming response recently when he asked in CompuServe's **UNIX Forum** for an editor that was more "user-friendly" than VI, which he labeled, with some understatement, "less than desirable." F. E. (Fred) Potts, quoting **Toshiba Forum** sysop Jim Roher, agreed: "It's about as intuitive to the average human as a tuba to a tortoise." Pete Holsberg was more sanguine. "People who hate [VI] at first come to appreciate it in time," he wrote. Whereas Greg Dinning raved, "When you know it, you fly, baby, and the world is yours." Learn how to fly on GEnie's **UNIX Round-Table**.

On the Net

Across the board

comp.unix.large (NG) Forum for discussing UNIX on mainframes. ✓**USENET**

comp.unix.misc (NG) General UNIX discussions that don't fit under another newsgroup. ✓**USENET**

UNIX Covers the operating system and all platforms, plus porting, utilities, connectivity, mail readers, tool kits, communications, and UNIX-related software.

Screen of a (UNIX-based) NeXT—downloaded from wuarchive.wustl.edu

✓**RELAYNET**→*number* 174

UNIX Covers all UNIX-related topics of interest. ✓**SMARTNET**→*tag* UNIX

UNIX Forum Discuss UNIX issues and exchange code with other users. ⊛💬 ✓**COMPUSERVE**→*go* UNIXFORUM

UNIX RoundTable For those interested in or using UNIX. Bulletin boards for all levels, from learning UNIX to setting up a system. Includes a software library and weekly conferences. ⊛💬 ✓**GENIE**→*keyword* UNIX

UNIX clones

AIX-L (ML) Discussion of the AIX operating system. ✓**INTERNET**→*email* LISTSERV@PUCC.PRINCETON.EDU ✍ *Type in message body:* SUBSCRIBE AIX-L <YOUR FULL NAME>

comp.os.linux (NG) Covers the free UNIX clone for the 386/486 Linux systems. ✓**USENET**

comp.unix.aix (NG/ML) Discussion of IBM's version of UNIX, mostly focusing on the RS6000 platform. ✓**USENET** ✓**INTERNET**→*email* LISTSERV@PUCC.PRINCETON.EDU ✍ *Type in message body:* SUB AIXNEWS <YOUR FULL NAME> ✖ *Can't post directly to list; post through newsgroup*

comp.unix.amiga (NG) Covers Minix, SYSV4, and other UNIX-related things on the Amiga. ✓**USENET**

comp.unix.aux (NG) Discussions about Apple II's version of UNIX. ✓**USENET**

comp.unix.bsd (NG) Discussion of Berkeley's UNIX. ✓**USENET**

comp.unix.dos-under-unix (NG) Forum for discussing running MS-DOS under UNIX. ✓**USENET**

Experts

comp.unix.programmer (NG) For those programming under UNIX. ✓**USENET**

comp.unix.wizards (NG) For in-depth discussion of advanced UNIX topics. ✓**USENET**

mod.std.unix (NG/ML) Forum for discussing UNIX standards. ✓**USENET** ✓**INTERNET**→*email* STD-UNIX-REQUEST@UUNET.UU.NET ✍*Subscribe by request*

UNIX Help with the UNIX operating system. ✓**ILINK**→*number* 41

Unix Booklist Information about UNIX and C books and how to find them. ✓**INTERNET**→*ftp* FTP.RAHUL.NET→ANONYMOUS/<YOUR EMAIL ADDRESS>→pub/mitch/YABL→yabl.Z

Windows

It's a true-life rescue show for Windows users. Victims with frozen systems are re-animated by Microsoft technical-support people on CompuServe's **MS Windows Forum**. "I'm not sure if you're getting this, I'm getting another error message," is a typical near-death scream. When the customer's heartbeat is back, the MS people sign off with a pleasant "Thank you for using Microsoft products." But sometimes they also whisper a sigh of relief: "Glad we nailed it."

Bill Gates, president of Microsoft—from CompuServe's Quick Pictures Forum.

Across the board

comp.os.ms-windows* (NG) Groups covering applications, programming, MicroSoft announcements, and discussions. ✓**USENET**

The Information Exchange for Windows Provides full-text version of *Windows Magazine* (winmag), and forums for all levels and interests. ✓**BIX**→*conference* WIX

Microsoft Windows User discussions and support. ✓**FIDONET**→*tag* WINDOWS

MSC-Windows Covers Microsoft Windows products. ✓**SMARTNET**→*tag* MSC-WINDOWS

Windows For all Windows issues. ✓**ILINK**→*number* 55

Windows Covers Microsoft Windows and related software. ✓**RELAYNET**→*number* 144

Windows Covers Windows 3.0. ✓**SMARTNET** →*tag* WINDOWS

Windows RoundTable Get technical help and shareware; talk to application developers. ⬛⬛⬛ ⊕💬 ✓**GENIE**→ *keyword* WINDOWS

WindowsNovice For the new Windows user. ✓**SMARTNET**→*tag* WINDOWSNOVICE

Win3-L (ML) Discuss Microsoft Windows and related issues. ✓**INTERNET**→*email* LISTSERV@UICVM. BITNET ✍*Type in message body:* SUB WIN3-L <YOUR FULL NAME>

Applications

comp.binaries.ms-windows (NG) Binary programs for Microsoft Windows. ✓**USENET**

Vendor support

Microsoft Windows Extensions Forum Technical assistance with Microsoft development tools. ✓**COMPUSERVE** → *go* WINEXT

Microsoft Windows Forum Offers support by Microsoft technicians. ⊕💬 ✓**COMPUSERVE**→ *go* MSWIN

Power Windows (BBS) Staffed by experts in Windows, OS/2, and MIDI. 205-881-8619 ✱*DOS only* FREE

Windows Forum Help from experienced Windows users and vendor support. ✓**AMERICA ONLINE** →*keyword* WINDOWS

Windows Vendor Forums Support from vendors. ✓**COMPUSERVE**→*go* WINVEN

Windows NT

Windows-NT Focuses on technical issues related to Windows NT. ✓**ILINK**→*number* 226

Programming

Winappdev Discussions about Windows programming languages. ✓**ILINK** →*number* 55

Windows API For Windows programmers. ✓**SMARTNET**→*tag* WINDOWS API

Windows Basic Discussions about BASIC for Windows. ✓**RELAYNET**→*number* 366

Entertainment

Windows Fun Forum Games, screen savers, and graphics. ⊕💬 ✓**COMPUSERVE**→*go* WINFUN

Shareware libraries

Public Brand Software Applications Forum Hundreds of applications, utilities, and programming tools. ✓**COMPUSERVE**→ *go* ZNT:PBS $2.50/MONTH

Workstations

Once solely an instrument for elite engineers manipulating custom software, the com-

puter workstation is now a trendy must-have item for the status-seeking power user. Earlier generations of workstations offered dull exterior designs that bespoke serious UNIX purposes. The updated '90s models have bright colors, jazzy names, and (best of all) games with full-motion video. Silicon Graphics' new Indy runs DOS, Mac, and UNIX software inside a sparkle-painted CPU case shaped like a deconstructivist wedge, with a built-in video camera perched atop the monitor for face-to-face conferences. See the **comp.sys.sgi** newsgroups for the latest Indy updates.

Artist's impression of a workstation— from wuarchive.wustl.edu.

On the Net

Sun

comp.org.sug (NG) Discussion about and for the Sun User's Group. ✓**USENET**

comp.sys.sun* (NG) A series of newsgroups, including one with announcements from Sun and one that functions as a marketplace for buying and selling hardware and applications, as well as a group for general discussion about Sun systems. ✓**USENET**

SunFlash (ML) A news service for users of Sun Microsystems computers. ✓**INTERNET**→*email* INFO-SUN FLASH@SUNVICE.EAST.SUN.COM ✍ *Type in subject line:* INFO *Type in message body:* INFO

Sun-Nets (ML) List concerned with Sun networking issues—bugs to protocols. ✓**INTERNET**→*email* SUN-NETS-REQUEST@UMIACS.UMD.EDU ✍ *Subscribe by request*

NeXT

comp.sys.next* (NG) NeXT newsgroups include COMP.SYS.NEXT. ANNOUNCEMENTS, COMP.SYS.NEXT. HARDWARE, and COMP.SYS.NEXT.MARKET-PLACE. ✓**USENET**

NeXT-L (ML) Forum for discussing NeXT computers. ✓**INTER-NET**→*email* LISTSERV@ANTIGONE.COM ✍ *Type in message body:* SUBSCRIBE NEXT-L <YOUR FULL NAME>

Next-Managers (ML) Forum for NeXT system managers to troubleshoot and exchange securi-

ty-related information in time-critical situations. Check other sources first before asking the question! ✓**INTERNET**→*email* NEXT-MANAGERS-REQUEST@STOLAF.EDU ✍ *Subscribe by request*

Other systems

Apollo (ML) Share Apollo computer experiences. ✓**INTERNET**→ *email* APOLLO-REQUEST@UMIX.CC. UMICH.EDU ✍ *Type in message body:* SUBSCRIBE APOLLO <YOUR FULL NAME>

comp.sys.apollo (NG) Discussions about Apollo computers. ✓**USENET**

comp.sys.dec (NG) Discussion about DEC computer systems. ✓**USENET**

comp.sys.hp (NG) Covers workstations manufactured by Hewlett-Packard and running the HP-UX operating system. The primary focus is on the HP series 700 workstations. ✓**USENET**

comp.sys.sgi* (NG) Includes Silicon Graphics–oriented newsgroups covering applications, hardware, graphics, and bugs, and general discussion. ✓**USENET**

HP-UX File Site Offers a library of publicly available software from the InterWorks User Group for the HP-UX operating system, plus UNIX software used on Hewlett Packard workstations. ✓**INTERNET**→ →*ftp* IWORKS.ECN.UIOWA.EDU→ANONY-MOUS/<YOUR EMAIL ADDRESS>→comp. hp

Part 3

Telecommuni-cations

&

Electronics

3

Amateur radio

Some people say the Net is just another kind of ham ra-dio. Others say pshaw, the Net is all things to all people, while ham radio is beauty and poetry and for a truly dedicated bunch. Certainly, though, the Net is a great source of new information for the amateur-radio community. CompuServe's **HamNet Forum** lets you into that community. FidoNet's **Amateur Radio Technology Conference** offers top technical coverage of ham operator issues. And **rec.radio.amateur.misc** provides detailed FAQs for anyone who has any questions at all about anything to do with amateur radio.

QSL card from Radio RSA—from GEnie's Radio & Electronics RoundTable.

On the Net

Across the spectrum

Amateur Radio Conference Discussion on all facets of amateur and shortwave radio, including wanted and for-sale ads. ✓**FIDONET** →*tag* AMATEUR_RADIO

Amateur Radio File Announcements and File Requests Messages about new files and bulletins available on select ham-radio bulletin boards—useful for locating files on amateur radio, shortwave, and radio scanners. ✓**FIDONET**→*tag* HAM_REQ

Amateur Radio Packet Echo

Discussion about packet and other digital amateur-radio formats. ✓**FIDONET**→*tag* PACKET

Database of Tennessee (BBS) An amateur-radio information and support board. 901-749-5224 FREE

Dots-N-Dashes (BBS) Support for amateur radio as well as general BBS forums. 315-642-1220 FREE

Grapes-L (ML) Discussions with members of the Georgia Radio Amateur Packet Enthusiasts Society. ✓**INTERNET**→*email* LISTSERV@ KNUTH.MTSU.EDU ✍*Type in message body:* SUBSCRIBE GRAPES-L <YOUR FULL NAME>

HamNet (Ham Radio) Forum Offers contact with others interested in amateur radio and shortwave listening. ⊛☺ ✓**COMPUSERVE** →*go* HAMNET

HamRadio Forum for discussing ham radios and shortwave communications. ✓**SMARTNET**→*tag* HAMRADIO

Radio & Electronics Round-Table For recreational radio interests, including amateur radio, shortwave and scanner listening,

CB, etc. ⊛☺ ✓**GENIE**→*keyword* RADIO

rec.radio.amateur.misc (NG/ML) For all ham-radio topics not covered in the other newsgroups —i.e., contesting and information on becoming a ham. ✓**USENET** ✓**INTERNET**→*email* INFO-HAMS-REQUEST@UCSD.EDU ✍*Subscribe by request*

rec.radio.amateur.packet (NG/ML) For discussions relating to packet radio. ✓**USENET** ✓**INTERNET**→*email* PACKET-RADIO-REQUEST@ UCSD.EDU ✍*Subscribe by request*

rec.radio.amateur.policy (NG) Discuss rules, regulations, legalities, and policies surrounding amateur radio. ✓**USENET** ✓**INTERNET** →*email* HAM-POLICY-REQUEST@UCSD. EDU ✍*Subscribe by request*

rec.radio.info (NG) Informational messages from all REC.RADIO groups. Includes daily solar propagation, bulletins, ARRL bulletins, and FAQs. ✓**USENET**

Ham

Amateur (Ham) Radio Technology Conference Technical aspects of radio, DXing, towers, antennas, radio software, shack design, and equipment modifications. ✓**FIDONET**→*tag* HAM_TECH

Amateur Radio Interest General-interest talk for licensed amateur radio operators and those interested in ham radio. ✓**FIDONET**→*tag* HAM

The American Radio Relay League Includes files on how to get your AR license, FCC exam schedule info, a list of ham-related BBSs, an overview of packet radio, and much more. ✓**INTERNET**→

email INFO@ARRL.ORG

Callsign Servers Search by call, last name, ZIP code or city. ✓**INTERNET** ...→*telnet* CALLSIGN.CS. BUFFALO.EDU 2000 ...→*telnet* HAM. NJIT.EDU 2000

Ham Covers discussions of ham-radio equipment, troubleshooting, and trends, with announcements of upcoming ham-radio festivals. ✓**RELAYNET**→*number* 115

Ham Radio Discussions include computing, digital electronics, and amateur radio. ✓**BIX**→*conference* HAM.RADIO

HamRadio Discuss all aspects of running a ham station. For all amateur radio enthusiasts. ✓**ILINK** →*number* 42

Ham Radio Club Offers features including the American Radio Relay League, the organization that supports and represents the world of amateur radio; information on ham radio, shortwave radio, and scanning; an "Ask the Expert" area; and a swap-and-sell board for equipment. ✓**AMERICA ONLINE**→*keyword* HAM RADIO

The Ham Radio Emporium (BBS) Devoted to ham-radio information and discussions. 918-272-4327 $20 OPTIONAL

Ham Radio FTP Site Site includes the Elmer List, information on regulations and commercial radio's, SWL and scanner material, FAQs, and software. ✓**INTERNET**→ *ftp* FTP.CS.BUFFALO.EDU→ANONYMOUS/ <YOUR EMAIL ADDRESS>→pub/ham-radio

Pipeline (BBS) Some 800 HAM-related files. 502-651-2556 FREE

Equipment

Ham Radio Equipment Sale, Swap and Buy Classified ads for all types of ham-radio equipment offered by ham enthusiasts. ✓**FIDONET**→*tag* HAM_SALE

Hobby Shop Discussions by model builders, ham-radio enthusiasts, and other hobbyists. Share ideas and product information. 🖼️ ✓**DELPHI**→*go* GR HOBBY

rec.radio.swap (NG) For all who have radio equipment, test gear, or computer equipment that hams might be interested in. Post if you have something. Post if you want something. ✓**USENET**

CB & scanner

alt.radio.scanner (NG) Scanner discussions. ✓**USENET**

Scanner & Frequency Discussion Information for people who use scanner receivers. ✓**FIDONET**→ *tag* SCANRADIO

Scanners/SWL Offers discussion about radio monitoring, exchanging frequencies, logging shortwave transmissions, and equipment. ✓**RELAYNET**→*number* 309

rec.radio.cb (NG) Forum for discussing the Citizens' Band radio service. ✓**USENET**

Shortwave

Pirate Radio An area for reports of logged pirate radio broadcasts heard on shortwave bands. ✓**FIDONET**→*tag* FREE_RADIO

rec.radio.shortwave (NG) For those interested in international broadcasting on the HF bands.

CYBERNOTES

"Way back when, before there was a Usenet, the Internet hosted a mailing list for hams, called (appropriately enough) INFO-HAMS. When the Usenet software was created, and Net news as we now know it was developed, a newsgroup was created for hams: net.ham-radio. As the Net grew, another corresponding mailing list was created as well: net.ham-radio.packet....

"Since one of hams' favorite pastimes is swapping gear, it was natural for hams to post messages about equipment for sale to INFO-HAMS/rec.ham-radio. This ran afoul of SIMITEL20's no-commercial-use restriction, and after some argument, a group was created specifically for messages like that: rec.ham-radio.swap."

—from **rec.radio.ama-teur.misc**

✓**USENET**

Shortwave Listeners Conference Tips and instructions on shortwave radio, scanners, satellites, and monitoring broadcast stations at long range. ✓**FIDONET**→ *tag* SHORTWAVE

BBS & Net info

While Net Guide offers the big picture, there are also In-

ternet, Usenet, and FidoNet guides; BBS lists; how-to hints; new-user news; and **E-Mail Etiquette** from the folks at Prodigy. Among their hints: "Don't Shout. Know Your Recipient. Don't Cry Wolf. Be Respectful. Use Cute Symbols Sparingly. Don't Be Pushy. Use Common English." It sounds a bit like the Boy Scout creed ("Be courteous, kind, and obedient..."), save for a final command, "Remember Oliver North." As Ollie learned, email can bite you back.

Al Gore, father of the electronic highway– from CompuServe's Photography Forum.

On the Net

Across the Net

alt.online-service (NG) Discussions about large commercial services and the Internet. ✓**USENET**

Netissues Information and debate about topics important to all computer networks and bulletin boards: for example, how networks function, network policies, problems, government attempts at BBS licensing, and attempts by the Baby Bells to redefine BBSs as businesses for billing. ✓**FIDONET**→ *tag* NETWORK-ISSUES-CONF

Not CI$ Hints for using commercial database systems. ✓**SMARTNET** →*tag* NOT CI$

NREN (ML) Discussions about the National Research and Educational Network. ✓**INTERNET**→*email* NREN-DISCUSS-REQUEST@PSI.COM ✍ *Subscribe by request*

Othernets Information and discussion about networks other than FidoNet, including Alternet, SigNet, EggNet, RBBS-NET, as well as special subject BBS networks for Macintosh computers and *Star Trek*. ✓**FIDONET**→*tag* OTH ERNETS

Internet issues

alt.internet.services (NG) Dedicated to describing services available on the Internet. ✓**USENET**

alt.irc (NG) Devoted to discussing Internet Relay Chat, where users can chat in real time with others around the world. ✓**USENET**

Com-Priv (ML) Focused on issues relating to commercialization of the Internet. ✓**INTERNET** ...→*email* COM-PRIV-REQUEST@UU.PSI.COM ✍ *Subscribe by request* ...→*ftp* UU.PSI.

COM→ANONYMOUS/<YOUR EMAIL ADDRESS>→archive/com-priv

Internet General-interest discussion for novices and non-experts on using the Internet. ✓**FIDONET**→ *tag* INTERNET

Internet Topics range from FTP sites to managing the Internet to how-to questions. ◉💬 ✓**BIX**→*conference* INTERNET

Internet RoundTable Introductory tutorials for navigating the Internet, technical discussions about setting up networks, and information on a variety of Internet resources. ◉💬 ✓**GENIE**→ *keyword* INTERNET-RT $$

Internet Services List A list of Internet services with brief descriptions. Also known as the Yanoff List. ✓**INTERNET** ...→*ftp* CSD4.CSD.UWM.EDU→ANONYMOUS/ <YOUR EMAIL ADDRESS>→pub→inet. services.txt ...→*email* BBSLIST@ AUG3.AUGSBURG.EDU ...→*wais* internet_services

Internet Special Interest Group Offers information, help files, discussion, and connections to Usenet newsgroups and Internet services, including FTP, telnet, and gopher. ✓**DELPHI**→*go* INTERNET $3.00/MONTH

Usenet

news.announce.newusers (NG) Introductory explanations to Usenet. ✓**USENET**

Usenet Frequently Asked Questions Contains FAQ postings from Usenet newsgroups. Delete periods when searching. ✓**INTERNET**→*ftp* RTFM.MIT.EDU→ ANONYMOUS/<YOUR EMAIL ADDRESS>→ pub/usenet

UUNET Archives An archive of Usenet news and free source code and software. ✓**INTERNET** ...→*ftp* FTP.UU.NET→ANONYMOUS/<YOUR EMAIL ADDRESS> ...→*wais* uunet.src

Internet how-to

The Hitchhikers Guide to the Internet An Internet introduction for new users. ✓**INTERNET**→*ftp* FTP.EFF.ORG→ANONYMOUS/<YOUR EMAIL ADDRESS>→pub/internet-info

How to ftp For information on how to use the Internet file-transfer program for remote login. ✓**INTERNET**→*ftp* FTP.SURA.NET→ANONY-MOUS/<YOUR EMAIL ADDRESS>→pub/nic/network.service.guides→how.to.ftp.guide

How to telnet For information on how to use telnet for remote login. ✓**INTERNET**→*ftp* FTP.SURA.NET→ANONYMOUS/<YOUR EMAIL ADDRESS>→pub/nic/network.service.guides→how.to.telnet.guide

Hytel-L (ML) Includes announcements of new versions of the HYTELNET program. ✓**INTERNET**→*email* LISTSERV@KENTVM.KENT.EDU ✍ *Type in message body:* SUB HYTEL-L <YOUR FULL NAME>

The MaasInfo Package How-to information on the Internet as well as lists and bibliographies of network resources. ✓**INTERNET**→*ftp* FTP.UNT.EDU→ANONYMOUS/<YOUR EMAIL ADDRESS>→articles/maas→Maas*

NNSC Internet Resource Guide A database of Internet services organized by type—e.g., library catalogs, networks, data archives, and more. Descriptions include what it is, who can use it, and how to get there. ✓**INTERNET** ...→*wais* internet-resource-guide.

SRC ...→*ftp* NNSC.NSF.NET→ANONY-MOUS/<YOUR EMAIL ADDRESS>→resource-guide ...→*email* RESOURCE-GUIDE-REQUEST@NNSC.NSF.NET

University of Maryland Information Database Information on numerous Internet topics. ✓**INTERNET**→*telnet* INFO.UMD.EDU→INFO/<NONE>

The White Pages Project A directory of individuals, their organizations, and their email addresses. ✓**INTERNET**→*telnet* WP.PSI.NET→FRED/<NONE>

Zen and the Art of the Internet Popular book introducing the Internet—from "netiquette" to FTPing. ✓**INTERNET** ...→*ftp* FTP.CS.WIDENER.EDU→ANONYMOUS/<YOUR EMAIL ADDRESS>→pub/zen

Experts & newbies

Ann-Lots (ML) For experienced Netters and researchers willing to share "worthy" finds, the more specialized the better. Archives include lists of experts in technical fields, online services, specialized FAQs, etc. ✓**INTERNET**→*email* LISTSERV@VM1.NODAK.EDU ✍ *Type in message body:* SUB ANN-LOTS <YOUR FULL NAME>

Help-Net (ML) For novice and experienced Netters. Forum for discussing problems with utilities and software related to the Internet and Bitnet networks. Information for the beginning Netter—e.g., where to find other helpful files—is also available. ✓**INTERNET**→*email* LISTSERV@TEMPLEVM.BITNET ✍ *Type in message body:* SUB HELP-NET <YOUR FULL NAME>

New User's Questions Just what the name implies. ✓**INTERNET**→*ftp* NIC.MERIT.EDU→ANONYMOUS/

<YOUR EMAIL ADDRESS>→documents/fyi→fyi04.txt

News

Network Information Services Announcements List (ML) The source for network information-services announcements. ✓**INTERNET**→*email* LISTSERV@CERF.NET ✍ *Type in message body:* SUBSCRIBE <YOUR EMAIL ADDRESS> NIS

Networkers Journal A monthly column about the Net covering telecommunications news, the commercial services, and network trends. ▦ ✓**GENIE**→*keyword* BOWEN

news.announce.important (NG) General announcements of interest to all Usenet readers. ✓**USENET**

Online Resources Mailing List (ML) Where people announce commercial and fee-charged services on the Internet. ✓**INTERNET** →*email* ONLINE-REQUEST@UUNET.CA ✍ *Subscribe by request*

HPCWire Offers news and information on the Internet. For those doing or interested in supercomputing, there are a research register, a job bank, newsletters, software, and a supercomputing journal. ✓**INTERNET**→*telnet* HPCWIRE.ANS. NET→HPCWIRE/<NONE>

Email

E-Mail Etiquette A report describing the dos and don'ts of electronic communication. ✓**PRODIGY** →*jump* E-MAIL ETIQUETTE

Finding College E-mail Addresses Guide to using whitepages servers at many colleges and universities. ✓**INTERNET**→*wais* college-email.src

Internet Mail Guide Description of how to address email traveling between small, corporate, and dominant networks. ✓**INTERNET**→*ftp* SURA.NET→ANONYMOUS/ <YOUR EMAIL ADDRESS>→pub/nic →internetwork-mail-guide

Mailing lists

The List of Lists Lists of newsgroups, mailing lists, and other lists of electronic discussions. ✓**INTERNET**→*ftp* FTP.NISC.SRI.COM→ ANONYMOUS/<YOUR EMAIL ADDRESS>→ netinfo→interest-groups

List of Mailing Lists (ML) A list that sends a notice when "the list of lists" has been updated. ✓**INTERNET**→*email* INTEREST-GROUPS-REQUEST @NISC.SRI.COM ✍*Subscribe by request*

New-List (ML) Announcements of new mailing lists. ✓**INTERNET**→ *email* LISTSERV@VM1.NODAK.EDU ✍ *Type in message body:* SUB NEW-LIST <YOUR FULL NAME>

Across the boards

alt.bbs (NG) General discussion about BBS operation and use, covering technical issues, regulations, and services. ✓**USENET**

BBS Conference covering dial-up bulletin-board systems. ◉💬 ✓**BIX** →*conference* BBS

BBS Forum Offers information for sysops and BBS callers, including software and BBS lists. ✓**DELPHI** →*go* COM BBS

Boardwatch Magazine Online (BBS) A "guide to online information services and electronic Bulletin Boards." Chronicles BBS community news and lists BBSs. Also carries *USA Today, Newsbytes*, and a variety of online magazines. ▦ 303-973-4222

Bulletin Board System RoundTable Includes complete BBS packages, utilities, online games, and discussion boards related to operating a BBS. ⊞⊟ ◉💬 ✓**GENIE**→*keyword* BBS

CallersDigest For sharing articles about BBS systems, offline readers, shareware, and other BBS-related topics. ✓**SMARTNET**→*tag* CALLERSDIGEST

comp.bbs.misc (NG) Covers all aspects of computer bulletin-board systems. ✓**USENET**

IBM Bulletin Board Forum Bulletin-board information and software for IBM PCs and compatibles. ◉💬 ✓**COMPUSERVE**→*go* IBMBBS

BBS ads & lists

alt.bbs.ads (NG) Offers an area for system operators to post advertisements for their boards. ✓**USENET**

alt.bbs.lists (NG) Offers lists of bulletin boards around the world, organized by area code, subject, and type of computer system. Requests for BBS lists and discussion should be directed to ALT. BBS.LISTS.D. ✓**USENET**

BBS Ads Offers ads provided by BBSs about themselves. ✓**RELAYNET**→*number* 143

BBS owners

BBS-L (ML) Discussions about how to start, use, and maintain a BBS. Includes topics such as networking, software, utilities, etc. ✓**INTERNET**→*email* LISTSERV@SAUPM 00.BITNET ✍ *Type in message body:* SUBSCRIBE BBS-L <YOUR FULL NAME>

Female Sysops Discussion area for female BBS sysops to talk about any issue. ✓**FIDONET**→*tag* FEMALE_SYSOP

Telephone Industry Watchdog Conference Covers regulatory and tariff information important to the BBS community. ✓**FIDONET**→*tag* PHONES

Big boards

Yesterday's hobby has become today's big business—
albeit still often run out of somebody's basement. Many boards boast more downloads per file than CompuServe, serve a growing number of international callers, carry more adult-only entertainment than many exclusively adult boards, and are often a first stop for shareware. There's the squeaky-clean **CRS Online** with its "no sex" and no-telnetting-until-you're-18 rules to **Rusty-n-Edie's** with its no-rules, anything-goes attitude (they've been busted by the police for it once already) to the biggest BBS and shareware haven in the world—**Exec-PC**. The trend toward local access numbers makes many of these boards accessible to a national audience.

On the Net

Aquila BBS (BBS) Chicago's biggest bulletin-board system, with conferences from Usenet, FidoNet, Annex, RelayNet, ILink, and Racenet as well as online articles from publications such as *USA Today*, *Boardwatch* magazine, the *PC-Catalog*, and *The New York Times*. The large file selection includes a significant Windows and OS/2 presence, and yearly subscribers are provided with an

Exec-PC sysop Bob Mahoney—downloaded from Exec-PC.

Internet email address. ▦ ▦◧ ◉💬 708-820-8344 $55–$75/YEAR

Channel 1 (BBS) A large file selection, thousands of conferences from networks such as SmartNet, lLink, RelayNet and Usenet, more than 100 interactive games, horoscopes, an extensive shareware library, computer-industry news, daily stock and mutual-fund closings, and an Internet email address. ▦ ▦◧ ◉💬 617-354-3230/617-354-5776 $22.50 QUARTERLY

CRS Online (BBS) Includes more than 5,000 conferences from numerous networks including Usenet, FidoNet, RelayNet, and QuebecNet—an all-French network of conferences. The BBS also subscribes to many Internet mailing lists that are available as conferences and offers full Internet access. Carries Reuter and UPI news, the Canadian and American stock-market results, and a huge file selection. No adult (i.e., sexually oriented) conferences or files. ▦ ✪ ▦◧ ◉💬 416-213-6002/416-213-

6003 ✖*FTP and telnet are restricted to those over 18, and there are download and online-time restrictions and additional fees for full Internet access* $130/YEAR

Eye Contact (BBS) Huge gay men's BBS (30,000 calls per month) with a large library, chat, conferences, and a very explicit matchmaking database. "If you're looking for sex, there are lots of cute horny guys looking for the same thing." There are also forums ranging from politics to sports. More than 1,000 local-access numbers. ▦◧ ◉💬 415-255-5972 0.06/MIN. IN SAN FRANCISCO; 0.20/MIN. ELSEWHERE IN THE U.S.; $10 STARTUP FEE

Event Horizons (BBS) Nationally recognized for its immense GIF selection, the board also supports an active gaming section, adult party lines ("900 Playmates"), short color movies, and shareware. ▦◧ ◉💬 503-697-5100 $12/HR

Exec-PC (BBS) The largest BBS in the world, with a phenomenal file area that serves as one of the country's most significant repositories of new shareware and freeware. Huge base of financial and investment information, active conferences, searchable vendor catalogs, stock reports, electronic magazines, GIFs (including adult), and games. ▦ ▦◧ ◉💬 414-789-4210 $75/YEAR

THe GaRBaGe DuMP (BBS) A huge collection of adult files, real-time adult chat, a dating registry, and more. Local-access calling in more than 500 cities. To get a local-access number, call the voice number: 505-294-4980. ▦◧ ◉💬 505-294-5675/505-294-0803 $2/ HOUR

The Invention Factory (BBS)

Thousands of conferences from Usenet, a large shareware library, Internet email access, adult GIFs, and games, games, and more games. ⊞▣ ◎⚇ 212-274-8110 $45 QUARTERLY

MindVox (BBS) This large BBS with full Internet access and Usenet feeds has access to more than 10 MUDs, dozens of online games, its own forums for *Wired*, *Mondo*, Cyberspace, Women Online, and more. ⊞▣ ◎⚇ 212-989-4141 ✓**INTERNET**→*telnet* MINDVOX.PHANTOM.COM→GUEST/<NONE> $10–$15/MONTH

The Nashville Exchange (BBS) Classifieds, notes to Nashville's mayor, files and conferences, a travel center, *USA Today*, and *Boardwatch Magazine*. ▦ ◎⚇ 615-383-0727/615-383-0119 $20 QUARTERLY

Odyssey (BBS) Created entirely for adults! Large adult-images collection, adult chat, a matchmaker database, private gay sections, scheduled parties, horoscopes, airline reservations, shareware, multiuser games, *USA Today*, Newsbytes, and other general-interest conferences. For local-access numbers, voice call 818-358-0936. ▦ ⊕ ⊞▣ ◎⚇ 818-358-6968 ✖*Adults only* $24/MONTH FOR 15 HOURS ONLINE TIME; $4.80/HR. AFTER 15 HOURS

PC-Ohio (BBS) Huge file selection and access to more than 1,500 conferences, including adult live-chat areas. Consistently recognized as one of the best BBSs in America. ⊞▣ ◎⚇ 216-381-3320 $52/YEAR

ProStar BBS (BBS) Home of the MajorNet, a BBS conference network. Also features a huge file selection, New York Stock Exchange closings, an Internet email

address, and lots of games. ⊞▣ ◎⚇ 206-941-0317 $0.50/HR.

Rusty-n-Edie's (BBS) A big board promising no censorship, no rules, and no hassle. Includes a huge adult library, more than 20 regularly contributing authors of erotic text, and thousands of shareware programs. Europeans are frequent callers; there are more callers from London than from Youngstown—home of Rusty-n-Edie's. ⊞▣ ◎⚇ 216-726-2620/216-726-3584 $69/YEAR

Software Creations BBS Carries some conferences from FidoNet and RelayNet, but its claim to fame lies in its dedication to shareware. *Boardwatch* readers voted it the best BBS in America in 1993. ⊞▣ ◎⚇ 508-368-7139 $45/YEAR

Texas Talk (BBS) Oriented to adult entertainment, with such live-chat areas as the Lambda Connection and The Wild Thing. Also features Connex, a biorhythm/matchmaking service; a large game selection; a file library; and an online book-and-magazine store where you can read *Peter Pan* or the latest edition of *Boardwatch Magazine* online. ⊞▣ ◎⚇ 214-497-9100 $18/MONTH

The WELL (BBS) Besides a wide range of conferences of its own—Amnesty International, Firearms, Zines, The Future, Jewish, Therapy, Tibet, True Confessions, Beatles, Design, and Best of the WELL, to name but a few—the WELL's full Internet access and Usenet feeds (not to mention its place in Cyberspace history) make it extremely popular. ▦ ⊞▣ ◎⚇ 415-332-6106 ✓**INTERNET**→*telnet* WELL.SF.CA.US→GUEST/<NONE> $15/MONTH AND $2–$3/HR.

The West Side (BBS) Besides a

large collection of files, an online shopping mall, *USA Today* and other online publications, and message conferences, the board also organizes monthly social events and charity benefits in the Los Angeles area. ⊕ ⊞▣ ◎⚇ 213-933-4050/213-277-9724 $38/QUARTERLY

The World (BBS) Provides Usenet, the Online Book Initiative (a repository of books and other textual information), MUDS, hundreds of conferences, and Internet access. ▦ ⊕ ⊞▣ ◎⚇ 617-739-9753 ✓**INTERNET**→*telnet* WORLD.STD.COM →GUEST/<NONE> $20/MONTH FOR 20 HOURS AND $1/HR. AFTER 20 HOURS

Home tech

Still unable to stop that VCR from flashing "12:00?"

Then you're definitely unprepared for a simultaneous interface of your new laser/compact-disc player with the computer, audio, cable, and television systems. Let the Net help you catch up fast—CompuServe's **Consumer Electronics Forum**, GEnie's **Consumer Electronics RoundTable**, and Fidonet **Home Electronics and Appliances** echo offer tips for novices. And if you're a home-tech junkie already bored with DAT, try America Online's **Gadget Guru**—you'll get an insider's scoop on the next generation of digital toys.

Video and audio discs—from CompuServe's Graphics Gallery.

On the Net

Across the board

Adv-Elo (ML) Discussion of the latest advances in electronics. Send the command "Index" to receive a list of archived files. ✓**INTERNET** →*email* LISTSERV@UTFSM.BITNET ✉ *Type in message body:* SUB ADV-ELO <YOUR FULL NAME>

Consumer Electronics Forum Provides information, reviews, and product announcements on VCRs, answering machines, portable stereos, CD players, and other consumer electronic products. Online conferences feature representatives from major manu-

facturers like Sony. ⊕☯ ✓**COMPUSERVE** →*go* CEFORUM

Consumer Electronics RoundTable For those interested in consumer electronics, the RT has files, programs, and discussion boards covering all related topics. ⊕☯ ✓**GENIE**→*keyword* CE

Electronics Discussions of all general home and consumer electronics. ✓**ILINK**→*number* 50

Home Electronics and Appliances Discussions about all kinds of electronic equipment for the home. Conversation sometimes strays into theoretical electronic discussions. ✓**FIDONET**→*tag* ELECTRONICS

HomeTheatre Covers all aspects of home audio and video. ✓**SMARTNET**→*tag* HOMETHEATRE

Info-High-Audio (ML) Devoted to exchanging tips and information about modifying high-end audio equipment. Topics include vacuum-tube electronics, turntables, speakers, room treatments, and more. ✓**INTERNET**→*email* INFO-HIGH-AUDIO-REQUEST@CSD4.CSD.UWM.EDU ✉*Subscribe by request*

✖*Subscribe only if you don't have Usenet access to* REC.AUDIO.HIGH-END

Z Best Discount electronics. 🏷 ✓**COMPUSERVE**→*go* ZBEST

Toys & gadgets

Gadget Guru Offers information and updates on the newest and latest consumer products on the market. Reports are drawn from contacts with industry leaders, distributors, retailers, and trade shows. ✓**AMERICA ONLINE**→*keyword* ELECTRONICS

Gadgets Covers all kinds of new gadgets, where to find them, what makes them interesting, and how to use them. ✓**RELAYNET**→*number* 211

Hewlett Packard Calculator BBS Hewlett Packard support and hints for calculator customers. ✓**INTERNET**→*telnet* HPCVBBS.CV.HP.COM→NEW/<NONE>

Wirewrap Offers contacts for electronics enthusiasts, engineers, and hobbyists. Topics include advice on wire-wrapping circuit boards, where to find chips, and designing with micro-controller chips. ✓**RELAYNET**→*number* 299

CTV

Broadcast Technology Covers audio and video technology used in broadcasting. ✓**RELAYNET**→*number* 323

HDTV (High Definition Television) Provides information and discussion about HDTV, the wide-screen, very-high-resolution television system currently under development. ✓**RELAYNET**→*number* 311

rec.video.cable-tv (NG) Discussion about the technical and regulatory issues involved with cable TV. ✓**USENET**

Satellite Covers equipment, the use of satellite receivers, and legal restraints. ✓**RELAYNET**→*number* 187

Satellite Television Information for dish owners: programming, technical issues, scrambling, and video piracy. Uplinked to the GTE Spacenet 3 satellite. ✓**FIDONET**→*tag* TVRO

Audiophiles

Audio Audiophile discussions on choosing "high-end" audio. ✓**ILINK**→*number* 29

Audio Offers a focus on home audio, including the latest news, reviews, and some advertisements from retail and individual sellers of equipment. The emphasis is on high-end audio equipment and recording. ✓**RELAYNET**→*number* 322

Audio-L (ML) Covers all topics related to audio, from theory to application to equipment. ✓**INTERNET**→*email* LISTSERV@VMTECMEX.BITNET ✍ *Type in message body:* SUBSCRIBE AUDIO-L <YOUR FULL NAME>

Compact Disc Echo Music compact discs and CD players discussion; laserdiscs and their players are also included. ✓**FIDONET**→*tag* CD_ECHO

rec.audio (NG) Offers information and advice on home audio equipment, including stereo systems, wiring, creating a listening room, home acoustics, and recording at home. ✓**USENET**

rec.audio.high-end (NG) Offers

discussion for stereophiles and serious music lovers interested in the subtleties of expensive audio equipment, especially the nuances of audio inaudible to the untrained ear. ✓**USENET**

Videophiles

The Laser's Edge Laserdiscs and laserdisc equipment. 💿 ✓**COMPU-SERVE**→*go* LE

The Photo Forum See Video & Film Making for discussions and images. ✓**DELPHI**→*go* GR PHOTO

rec.video (NG) Provides discussion on video cameras and related equipment, and a monthly survey of mail-order houses that carry such equipment. ✓**USENET**

Video Discussions of VCRs, camcorders, and other video technology. ✓**ILINK**→*number* 88

Video Exchange Offers discussion about consumer video products in both tape and disc formats. Includes reviews of new products, and exchanges of tapes and disks. ✓**RELAYNET** →*number* 292

Video Making! Covers camcorders, VCRs, desktop video production, genlocks, computerized edit controllers, and other equipment. ✓**FIDONET**→*tag* VIDEO

Videos News on the recent action, comedy, drama, and kids' video releases as well as reviews, the video charts, and shopping for video equipment. ▦ 💿 ✓**PRODIGY**→*jump* VIDEOS

VideoTech (ML) Discuss cable TV, video-disc technology, teletext, home satellites, stereo TV, and other related topics. ✓**INTERNET**→*email* LISTSERV@UIUCVMD.BITNET

✍ *Type in message body:* SUB I-VIDTEK <YOUR FULL NAME>

Vidpro-L (ML) Forum to discuss video production, operations, equipment, and related topics. ✓**INTERNET**→*email* LISTSERV@UXA.ECN.BGU.EDU ✍ *Type in message body:* SUBSCRIBE VIDPRO-L <YOUR FULL NAME>

Cyberspace groups

The vision of what Cyberspace could be has largely been articulated by the Electronic

Frontier Foundation (EFF), started by former cowboy and Grateful Dead lyricist John Perry Barlow and the founder of Lotus Development Corporation, Mitch Kapor. Not only has the EFF dedicated itself to propounding this vision, but it has become the main voice in Washington for a sensible, humane, and democratic communications policy. As part of its mission, EFF offers numerous online resources, including news on **comp.org.eff.news**, discussion on **comp.org.eff.talk**, and archives on **Electronic Frontier Foundation**.

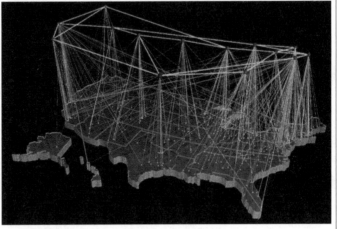

The Net—downloaded from ftp.eff.org.

EFF

comp.org.eff.news (NG) News from the Electronic Frontier Foundation. ✓ **USENET**

comp.org.eff.talk (NG) An unmoderated group that discusses the activities and goals of the EFF. ✓ **USENET**

Elec-Frontier Forum for discussing the legal issues related to telecomputing and Cyberspace, issues being monitored and defined by the Electronic Frontier Foundation. ✓ **SMARTNET**→*tag* ELEC-FRONTIER

Electronic Frontier Foundation The AOL and CompuServe forums provide information and message boards for discussing EFF activities and computer-related policy issues. The Internet site includes information about the foundation, the Computer and Academic Freedom Archives, electronic journals and magazines, and legal material related to computers and networks. ⊛💬 ✓ **AMERICA ONLINE**→*keyword* EFF ⊛💬 ✓ **COMPUSERVE**→*go* EFFSIG ✓ **INTERNET**→*ftp* FTP. EFF.ORG→ANONYMOUS/<YOUR EMAIL ADDRESS>→pub

Electronic Frontier Foundation Offers a meeting place for those interested in the EFF and its work, bridged with Usenet news on the organization. ✓ **RELAYNET**→*number* 357

Hard- & software

Computer Professionals for Social Responsibility A public-interest alliance of computer scientists and others interested in the impact of computer technology on society. It consists of 21 chapters based throughout the U.S., with a national office in Palo Alto, California. Email for more information and a membership application. ✓ **INTERNET**→*email* CPSR@CLSI. STANFORD.EDU

The Free Software Foundation An archive of free UNIX-based software and the Free Software Foundation's position papers. ✓ **INTERNET**→*ftp* PREP.AI.MIT.EDU →ANONYMOUS/<YOUR EMAIL ADDRESS> →pub/gnu

The League for Programming Freedom Organization opposes software patents and interface copyrights. Includes position papers and legal information about important cases. ✓ **INTERNET** →*ftp* PREP.AI.MIT.EDU→ANONYMOUS/ <YOUR EMAIL ADDRESS>→pub/lpf

Networks

comp.org.fidonet (NG) Official news from the FidoNet Association. ✓**USENET**

Internet Society Information from the international professional organization created to promote the use of the Internet for research and scholarly communication. Provides a forum for debate and recommendation of technical standards and procedures for the Internet. ✓**INTERNET**→*email* ISOC@ NRI.RESTON.VA.US

News

The Arachnet Electronic Journal of Virtual Culture (ML) Devoted to the topic of computer-mediated human experiences such as email, conferences, and global connectivity. Five- to 20-page articles may be submitted for review and possible publication. ✓**INTERNET**→*email* LISTSERV@ACADVM1.UOT TAWA.CA ✍*Type in message body:* SUB ARACHNET <YOUR FULL NAME>

CyberSpace and Virtual Reality News about Cyberspace and virtual reality. ✓**FIDONET**→*tag* CYBER

Cyberspace Vanguard (ML) An electronic zine covering Cyberspace, sci-fi, and fantasy worlds. ✓**INTERNET**→*email* CN577@CLEVE LAND.FREENET.EDU ✍*Subscribe by request*

Voices from the Net (ML) An electronic magazine of interviews and essays that present the "voices" of people around the network, especially the odd corners of Cyberspace. The FTP site contains both ASCII text and Macintosh HyperCard versions of the journal. ✓**INTERNET** ...→*email* VOICES-

REQUEST@ANDY.BGSU.EDU ✍*Type in subject line:* VOICES FROM THE NET *Type in message body:* SUBSCRIBE ...→*ftp* AQL.GATECH.EDU→ANONY-MOUS/<YOUR EMAIL ADDRESS>→pub/ Zines

Cyber-hangouts

MindVox (BBS) "MindVox is a celebration of possibilities. Jack In, Rock Out and Feed your Head!" Welcome to MindVox. While new, MindVox quickly became a hip Cyberspace hangout. Includes full Internet access, thousands of Usenet newsgroups, and its own forums (e.g., Bandwidth, Cyberpunk, Mondo, Women-Online, and Psychedelic). 🖥 🖴 ☎ 212-989-4141/212-989-1550 ✓**INTERNET**→ *telnet* MINDVOX.PHANTOM.COM→ GUEST/<NONE> $$

The WELL (BBS) "People come here to build and maintain relationships with interesting people," reads the introductory screen. Mention the virtual communities of Cyberspace and someone inevitably brings up the WELL. In fact, one could say, it's where it all began. With Internet access and Usenet feeds, it's not isolated, but its own forums—from Info Age to Fringes of Reason to Sexuality— attract a devoted following among WELL regulars. 🖥 🖴 ☎ 415-332-6106 ✓**INTERNET**→*telnet* WELL.SF. CA.US GUEST/<NONE> $$

The World (BBS) Besides a full Internet connection, Usenet newsgroups, and its own forums, the World offers a number of special services, including electronic newspapers and the Online Book Initiative, where users can pay a small fee to read online or download recent releases. 🖥 🌐 🖴 ☎ 617-739-9753 ✓**INTERNET**→*telnet* WORLD.STD.COM→NEW/<NONE> $$

Data communications

America Online's Mac Communications Forum has the right attitude about modems and

computers. It is particularly concerned with the *what*—as in "What can electronic communications do for me?"—versus the *how*, which historically tends to dominate online discussions. But while content outstrips process, there is still hardware and software to buy and support. Try the **Hayes RoundTable** on GEnie and Fidonet's **Communications**.

On the Net

Across the board

Communications Topics include technical discussions of communications software, BBS software, phone equipment, modems and protocols, and fax machines and software. Features a beginner's introduction, COMM Echo Tech. ✓ **FIDONET**→*tag* COMM

Communications Covers modems and communications software in general terms without focusing on specific platforms. ✓ **RELAYNET**→ *number* 109

comp.dcom.modems (NG) Information about data-communication hardware and software. ✓ **USE-NET**

IBM Communications Forum Everything about telecommunications on IBM PCs and compatibles. ⊕🎦 ✓ **COMPUSERVE**→*go* IBM-COM

Electronic Frontier Foundation slogan—from ftp.eff.org.

Info-Nets (ML) Discussions focus on networks, inter-network connectivity, and ISDN. ✓ **INTERNET**→ *email* INFO-NETS-REQUEST@THINK.COM ✉*Subscribe by request*

Macintosh Communications Forum How to communicate with the Macintosh: hardware, software, BBSs, fax machines, LANs, ISDN, and more. ⊕🎦 ✓ **COMPUSERVE**→*go* MACCOMM

Macintosh Communications Forum Covers fax technology, computer bulletin boards, communications bulletin boards, ISDN, networking, and support for Mac modem users. ⊕🎦 ✓ **AMERICA ONLINE**→*keyword* MCM

Modem News Conversation for and about the online magazine *Modem News*, hosted by the publisher. ✓ **RELAYNET**→*number* 290

Networks Conference about information networks. ✓ **BIX**→*conference* NETWORKS

PC Telecommunications & Networking Forum Covers fax technology, computer bulletin boards, networking, ISDN, company support, and more. ⊕🎦 ✓ **AMERICA ONLINE** →*keyword* PTC

Software

International Windows Communication Software Discussion and support for communications software written for Windows. ✓ **FIDONET**→*tag* WINCOMM

Mentor Technologies Courses on using CompuServe and popular software packages. ⊕ ⊕🎦 ✓ **COMPUSERVE**→*go* MN

Equipment

Hayes RoundTable Technical support and information provided by Hayes. ✓ **GENIE**→*keyword* HAYES

High Speed Modems Setting up and running high-speed modems from all makers. Includes product announcements from manufacturers, modem specification sheets, and other information. ✓ **FIDONET**→*tag* HS_MODEMS ✖*Ads discouraged*

Modems/Modem Support Covers modems, problems, and solutions; also offers vendor support. ✓ **RELAYNET**→*number* 228

Modem Vendor Forum Support from selected modem manufacturers, with help files, programs, and patches. ⊕🎦 ✓ **COMPU-SERVE**→*go* MODEMVENDOR

Wireless Covers wireless messaging and data transmission using radio for mobile data terminals, pagers, cellular modems, and radio-controlled local area networks. ✓ **RELAYNET**→*number* 338

Desktop publishing

From its earliest PageMaker days, the desktop-publishing (DTP) revolution, by whose

tenets this book was wholly created, has been supported by the exchange of information, tools, and ideas on the Net. From real-time chats with DTP avatar Roger Black on CompuServe's **Desktop Publishing Forum** to shareware *Star Trek* fonts on GEnie's **Design to Print RoundTable**, the Net is part classroom, part design studio. Serious DTP crunchers should try **Prepress/Print** on RelayNet for news of the battle between Quark guerrillas and conventional forces printers.

On the Net

Across the board

comp.text (NG) Offers discussions about the display and printing of text on computers, including in word-processing, desktop-publishing, technical-publishing, and electronic-publishing formats. ✓**USENET**

Digital Publishing Round-Table For writers interested in publishing in electronic media. Includes a bulletin board to converse with others in the publishing industry, a library of articles on the subject, online magazines and newsletters, and software. 🖥 👁‍🗨💬 ✓**GENIE**→*keyword* DIGIPUB

Laser Publishing Includes type-

Desktop-published church bulletin—from CompuServe's Desktop Publishing Forum.

setting, graphic arts (traditional and computerized), design, hardware and software, PostScript issues, and multimedia publishing. ✓**FIDONET**→*tag* LASERPUB

Publish (ML) Forum focusing on the role of computers in publishing. Covers topics such as image processing, document management, magazine publishing, and more. ✓**INTERNET**→*email* PUBLISH-REQUEST@CHRON.COM ✉*Subscribe by request*

Seybold Newsletters and Seminars Online information, conference updates, and subscription forms for the Seybold computer-industry newsletters *Digital Media—A Seybold Report, Seybold Report on Desktop Publishing,* and *Seybold Report on Publishing Systems.* 🖥 ✓**COMPUSERVE**→*go* ZNT:SEY BOLD $2.50/MONTH

DTP

comp.text.desktop (NG) Covers technology and techniques of desktop publishing. ✓**USENET**

Design to Print RoundTable Discussions and information exchange for graphic designers, printers, and desktop publishers. The libraries include hundreds of fonts, clip art, and utilities for most applications. 👁‍🗨💬 ✓**GENIE**→ *keyword* DTP

Desktop Discuss fonts, printers, and DTP software. ✓**SMARTNET**→ *tag* DESKTOP

Desktop Publishing Support for DOS and Windows DTP products: Ventura Publisher, Aldus PageMaker, Power Up! Express Publisher, PFS: First Publisher, and more. Discussions and questions range from novice to expert, with special focus on DTP applications for the business and private sectors. ✓**FIDONET**→*tag* DTP

Desktop Publishing Desktop-publishing-related discussions. ✓**BIX**→DESKTOP.PUB

Desktop Publishing Covers software packages used in DTP, including Ventura Publisher and PageMaker, plus the hardware required. ✓**RELAYNET**→*number* 107

Desktop Publishing Forum Information and tools for DTP, including a classified-ads section; messages on hardware, layout, design, and printing; and libraries containing fonts, utilities, demos, reviews, "publication quality" templates, photos, line art, and more. ⊛💬 ✓**COMPUSERVE**→*go* DTPFORUM

Desktop Publishing SIG Offers discussion, program demos, templates, and information for Mac and PC desktop publishing. ⊛💬 ✓**DELPHI**→*go* COM DESK

DTP Vendor Forum Information and updates from select DTP vendors providing support. ⊛💬 ✓**COMPUSERVE**→*go* DTPVENDOR

Infinite Perspective (BBS) Provides a list of other boards with a desktop-publishing focus. 301-924-0398

Macintosh Desktop Publishing/Word Processing Forum Covers all aspects of Macintosh desktop publishing and word processing, including related topics such as text handlers and outliners, fonts, printers, desktop presentations, and PostScript programming. Also includes service-bureau information and vendor support. ⊛💬 ✓**AMERICA ONLINE**→*keyword* MDP

Prepress/Print Covers the latest news in the prepress and printing industries, especially as they relate to the use of DTP with high-end publishing technology. ✓**RELAYNET**→*number* 371

Electronic publishing

Electronic Publishing All discussions about writing, distribution, and reading of publications using only computers. Topics include current and future technologies, tools such as Hypertext, and the requirements for improvement of electronic publications. ✓**FIDONET**→*tag* E_PUB

Information Retrieval List (ML) All information-retrieval topics are open for discussion, including electronic books, cybernetics, full-text retrieval, statistical techniques, library science, hypertext, and hypermedia. ✓**INTERNET**→ *email* LISTSERV@UCCVMA.BITNET ✍ *Type in message body:* SUB IR-L <YOUR FULL NAME>

Vpiej-L (ML) Discuss electronic-publishing issues related to scholarly electronic journals. Topics range from PostScript to hardware considerations. ✓**INTERNET**→*email* LISTSERV@VTVM1.CC.VT.EDU ✍ *Type in message body:* SUB VPIEJ-L <YOUR FULL NAME>

Tex

comp.text.tex (NG) Covers the TeX and LaTeX computer text systems and macros. ✓**USENET**

TexMaG (ML) Monthly magazine published by the Harvey Mudd College mathematics department. ✓**INTERNET**→*email* LISTSERV@BYUAD MIN.BITNET ✍ *Type in message body:* SUBSCRIBE TEXMAG-L <YOUR FULL NAME>

Tex-Pubs (ML) TeX-related publications, including *TeXhax Digest*, *UKTex*, and *TeXMaG*. ✓**INTERNET**→ *email* LISTSERV@SHSU.BITNET ✍ *Type in message body:* SUBSCRIBE TEX-PUBS <YOUR FULL NAME>

Hypertext

alt.hypertext (NG) Discussion of Hypertext. ✓**USENET**

The Electronic Zone (BBS) Dedicated to Hypertext, with discussions, files, and news. 412-349-3504

Hypertext Forum for Hypertext users as well as programmers. ✓**SMARTNET**→*tag* HYPERTEXT

Software & languages

comp.lang.postscript (NG) Offers information on the Postscript computer language for displaying and printing text. ✓**USENET**

Corel Information about Corel Draw, the drawing and illustration program. ✓**ILINK**→*number* 180

Pagemaker (ML) For DTPers using PageMaker on a Mac or PC. ✓**INTERNET**→*email* LISTSERV@INDYCMS. IUPUI.EDU ✍ *Type in message body:* SUBSCRIBE PAGEMKR <YOUR FULL NAME>

PostScript RoundTable Discuss all issues and uses of Adobe's page-description language. Includes free fonts, shareware, advice, and more. ⊛💬 ✓**GENIE**→*keyword* PSRT

Soft Logik RoundTable Technical support for Soft Logik products for the Atari ST and the Commodore Amiga. Also includes information on page design, clip art, and other computer graphics. ⊛💬 ✓**GENIE**→*keyword* SOFTLOGIK

Fonts

Bitstream RoundTable Support for Bitstream fonts and other products. Technical support provided Monday through Friday. ⊛💬 ✓**GENIE**→*keyword* BITSTREAM

comp.fonts (NG) Discussion on typefaces and fonts available for several computer platforms, including Macintosh, MS-DOS, Unix, Sun, and NeXT. Covers font history, design, vendors, shareware, formats, and output. ✓**USENET**

Tools

Scanners Conference for discussing scanners. ✓**SMARTNET**→*tag* SCANNERS

Free-Nets

Free-Nets are electronic towns that are popping up

across the country. They have post offices, where (you guessed it) you collect and send your email; courthouses, where you can access Supreme Court decisions as soon as they're released; public squares, where you can debate the issues of the day; recreation centers for playing games; and health centers with medical information. The **Cleveland Free-Net**—more a major metropolis than a mere town—has a selection to rival the big boards and commercial services. Almost all the Free-Nets offer local information, some carry the Usenet newsgroups and IRC channels, and all have the Freedom Shrine, where the texts of important U.S. historical documents are stored electronically. See you downtown.

On the Net

Big Sky Telegraph Located in Montana. Includes *Newsweek* classroom guides, and business and education support. ◉❈ 406-683-7680 ✓**INTERNET**→*telnet* BIGSKY. BIGSKY.DILLON.MT.US→BBS/<NONE> $50/YEAR (FOR FULL INTERNET ACCESS AND SOME EXTRAS)

Buffalo Free-Net Located in Buffalo, New York. Features a Western New York Information Center as well as the more traditional library, town hall, special-interest groups, computing center, etc. ▦ ▦▯ ◉❈ 716-645-6128 ✓**INTERNET**→*telnet* FREENET.BUFFALO.EDU→ FREEPORT/<NONE>

The Cleveland Free-Net The original and granddaddy-of-them-all Free-Net, with offerings on an incredible range of subjects from scouting to chess to IRC to information about the city of Brecksville. Located in Cleveland, Ohio. ▦ ▦▯ ◉❈ 216-368-3888 ✓**INTERNET** ...→*telnet* FREENET-IN-A.CWRU.EDU→ 2/<NONE> ...→*telnet* FREENET-IN-B. CWRU.EDU→2/<NONE> ...→*telnet* FREENET-IN-C.CWRU.EDU→2/<NONE> ...→*telnet* HELA.INS.CWRU.EDU→2/ <NONE>

Columbia Online Information Network (COIN) Located in Columbia, Missouri, with all the regular Free-Net features. ▦ ◉❈ 314-884-7000 ✓**INTERNET**→ *telnet* BIG CAT.MISSOURI.EDU→GUEST/<NONE>

Denver Free-Net The arts building provides information on the Denver Chamber Orchestra. The hospital lists support groups for AIDS and Alzheimer's patients. There's also a senior support area, a chatting area in the public square, and more. ▦ ▦▯ ◉❈ 303-270-4865 ✓**INTERNET**→*telnet* FREENET. HSC.COLORADO.EDU→ GUEST/<NONE>

Heartland Free-Net Located in Peoria, Illinois. Includes a home-and-garden center, science-and-technology center, teen center, and senior center. ▦ ▦▯ ◉❈ 309-674-1100 ✓**INTERNET**→*telnet* HEARTLAND. BRADLEY.EDU→BBGUEST/<NONE>

Lorain County Free-Net A smaller Free-Net located in Elyria, Ohio, with IRC, a finance-and-tax center, and more. ▦ ▦▯ ◉❈ 216-366-9721 ✓**INTERNET**→*telnet* FREENET. LORAIN.OBERLIN.EDU→GUEST/ <NONE>

National Capital Free-Net Located in Ottawa, Canada. Includes a policy center, social services center, and education center. ▦ ▦▯ ◉❈ 613-780-3733 ✓**INTERNET**→*telnet* FREENET.CARLETON.CA→GUEST/<NONE>

Tallahassee Free-Net Visit the house of worship or the agricultural center. ◉❈ 904-488-5056 ✓**INTERNET**→*telnet* FREENET.FSU. EDU→VISITOR/<NONE>

Traverse City Free-Net Visit College Corner, the computer center, or the always-active public-discussions area. ◉❈ ✓**INTERNET**→ *telnet* LEO.NMC.EDU→VISITOR/<NONE>

Tri-State Online Based in Cincinnati. Features all the traditional areas. ▦ ▦▯ ◉❈ 513-579-1990 ✓**INTERNET**→*telnet* CBOS.UC.EDU→ CBOS/VISITOR/9999

Victoria Free-Net Located in British Columbia, Canada, Victoria has become known for its storehouse of environmental information. ◉❈ 604-595-2300 ✓**INTER-NET**→*telnet* FREENET.VICTORIA.BC.CA→ GUEST/<NONE>

Youngstown Free-Net Located in Youngstown, Ohio, this Free-Net community includes *USA Today* Headline News and an animal hospital. ▦ ▦▯ ◉❈ 216-742-3072 ✓**INTERNET**→*telnet* YFN.YSU. EDU→VISITOR/<NONE>

Telephony

"Get Moscow on the phone!" prompts a multitude of questions in the modern, con-

nected office. Do you want voice or data transfer? An ISDN or fiber-optic line? A video or audio-only connection? How about a cellular link? Before you answer, check your email. The **Telecom**, **Cellular**, and **ISDN** mailing lists will keep you fully informed on the telecommunications world. But they won't help you with the most frequent phone question in any office: "Where's the number for the pizza place?"

On the Net

Across the Net

comp.dcom.telecom (NG) The Telecommunications Digest, a moderated discussion about all types of telephone issues, including technology, business, and public policy. ✓ **USENET**

Human-Nets (ML) Topics relating to a worldwide computer-and-telecommunications network. Discussions range from mere speculations about technology to discussions about state-of-the-art equipment. ✓ **INTERNET**→*email* HUMAN-NETS-REQUEST@ARAMIS. RUTGERS.EDU ✍*Subscribe by request*

Phones Covers subjects that include the telephone industry, new phone technology, ISDN, wiring, 800 and 900 numbers, bulletin

John Malkovich in In the Line of Fire —*from AOL's Hollywood Online.*

board systems, rates, nostalgia, and new services. ✓ **RELAYNET**→ *number* 227

Telecom (ML) Discuss telecommunications technology. Topics range from the telephone system to modems. ✓ **INTERNET** ...→*email* TELECOM-REQUEST@EECS.NWU.EDU ✍ *Subscribe by request* ...→*ftp* LCS.MIT. EDU→ANONYMOUS/<YOUR EMAIL ADDRESS>→telecom-archives

Telecommunications Forum Discussion about telecommunication services and products, including long-distance service issues and First Amendment rights. ⊛💬 ✓ **COMPUSERVE**→*go* TELECO

Telecommute A conference on telecommunications. ✓ **ILINK**→ *number* 161

Technologies

Cellular (ML) Discussion of cellular phones and technology, including related technology such as

telco. ✓ **INTERNET**→*email* MAIL-SERVER@YNGBLD.GWINNETT.COM ✍*Type in message body:* SUBSCRIBE CELLULAR

Cellular Telephone Discussions Questions and answers about general use and technical issues related to cellular phones. ✓ **FIDONET**→*tag* CELLULAR

ISDN (ML) Covers all ISDN-related topics for both data and voice, including protocols, services, applications, etc. ✓ **INTERNET**→ *email* ISDN-REQUEST@TEKNOLOGI. AGDERFORSKNING.NO ✍*Subscribe by request*

Telecommunications Technology Focuses on hardware and design issues related to telephone and network systems. ⊛💬 ✓ **BIX**→ TELECOMM.TECH

Touchton (ML) Forum for discussing touch tone or voice-response technology. ✓ **INTERNET**→ *email* LISTSERV@SJSUVM1.SJSU.EDU ✍ *Type in message body:* SUBSCRIBE TOUCHTON <YOUR FULL NAME>

Services

Donnelley 900 A directory of 900 numbers for information on sports, music, entertainment, business news, automobiles, medical emergencies, and more. ✓ **GENIE**→ *keyword* DONNELLEY

Telephone Services Features information on calling-card plans and long-distance telephone services, and *Consumer Reports* articles on telephones. ⊕ ✓ **PRODIGY**→ *jump* TELEPHONE SERVICES

Part 4

Nations,

Cultures &

Religions

4

African-Americans

Af-Ams are using the Net as a forum on race issues and as a medium for exploring

broader cultural questions. A frequent theme in **soc. culture.african.american** is the nature of the distinction between race and culture. The mailing lists African American Student Network (**AASNet-L**) and **ASA-L** offer real-world "coping" advice, for instance, on "unintentional" racist remarks: "Should I have said more? Called up the ACLU or Jesse or what? It really caught me off guard and I didn't know what to say. Comments are welcome."

Malcolm X—downloaded from CompuServe's Quick Picture Forum.

On the Net

Across the board

Black Issues Offers a public forum on race issues, with an emphasis on meaningful dialogue between parties. Open to all users. ✓**RELAYNET**→*number* 384

The Blacknet (BBS) Devoted to bringing black/African information to the black community. Carries Afronet, FidoNet echoes, and K12net echoes. 718-602-0943 $29.95/YEAR

Issues Forum An area for the free exchange of opinion and debate. See the African Americans bulletin board and library, where you can get the *Black Student's Guide to Colleges*, discussion on black writers, and a file of black-

oriented FTP sites or BBSs. 🖵🗨 ✓**COMPUSERVE**→*go* ISSUES

soc.culture.african.american (NG) Devoted to discussions of African-American issues. ✓**USENET**

U-People BBS (BBS) Dedicated to collecting, preserving and distributing genealogical information in general, and African-American history and genealogy in particular. Also carries FidoNet conferences, lists of other black-oriented BBSs, a file on CompuServe sources for African-American information, a narrative of black military service in the U.S., and census figures of interest to the black community. 606-268-0801 FREE

Immortal words

I Have A Dream Text of Martin Luther King's "I Have a Dream" speech. ✓**INTERNET**→*ftp* QUARTZ. RUTGERS.EDU→ANONYMOUS/<YOUR EMAIL ADDRESS>→pub/etext/misc→

I_Have_a_Dream.z ✓**COMPUSERVE** →*go* ISSUES→African Amer Issues Library →DREAM.TXT

Research

AFAM-L (ML) For those involved with African-American research. ✓**INTERNET**→*email* LISTSERV@MIZZOU1. MISSOURI.EDU ✍ *Type in message body:* SUBSCRIBE AFAM-L <YOUR FULL NAME>

Students

AASNet-L (ML) African-American students exchange poetry, chat about their studies and lives, and discuss racism. ✓**INTERNET**→*email* LISTSERV @UHUPVM1.BITNET ✍ *Type in message body:* SUBSCRIBE AASNET-L <YOUR FULL NAME>

ASA-L (ML) Forum for members of the African Students Association. ✓**INTERNET**→*email* LISTSERV@ TAMVM1.TAMU.EDU ✍ *Type in message body:* SUBSCRIBE ASA-L <YOUR FULL NAME>

Indigenous cultures

Net discussion of anthropology and cultures clearly divides between scholarship and

advocacy. There's a major cache of documents at the **CoombsPapers Social Sciences Research Data Bank**, one of the biggest collections of its kind anywhere. Anthropological and archaeological interests are covered in depth on several mailing lists. But academic poise and disinterest quickly give way to personal passions and inevitable flames when the subject is living culture. Native American issues are some of the touchiest on the Net.

Plenty Coups of the Crow Tribe—from CompuServe's Graphics Gallery Forum.

On the Net

Across the board

The CoombsPapers Social Sciences Research Data Bank A huge repository of social-science documents including the Aboriginal Studies Electronic Data Archives and the Thai-Yunnan Archives. (Many of the archives available can also be searched through WAIS.) ✓**INTERNET** ...→*ftp* COOMBS.ANU.EDU.AU→ANONYMOUS/ <YOUR EMAIL ADDRESS>→**coombs papers** ...→*ftp* FTP.UU.NET→ANONY-MOUS/<YOUR EMAIL ADDRESS>→doc/ papers/coombspapers

Anthropology

Anthro-L (ML) Discussions of techniques and several fields of research in anthropology, includ-ing computation in anthropology, Anglo-Saxon cemeteries, and political economy, to name but a few. ✓**INTERNET**→*email* LISTSERV@ UBVM.BITNET ✍ *Type in message body:* SUBSCRIBE ANTHRO-L <YOUR FULL NAME>

Human Biology Interest Group Discussion List (ML) Covers biological anthropology, adaptation, biological race, skeletal biology, and much more. ✓**INTER-NET**→ *email* HUMBIO-REQUEST@ ACC.FAU.EDU ✍ *Type in message body:* SUBSCRIBE HUMBIO-L <YOUR FULL NAME>

sci.anthropology (NG) For those involved with or interested in studying mankind. ✓**USENET**

Shaker (ML) Discuss the history, culture, and beliefs of the Shakers. ✓**INTERNET**→ *email* LISTSERV@UKCC. UKY.EDU ✍ *Type in message body:* SUB-SCRIBE SHAKER <YOUR FULL NAME>

Archaeology

Arch-L (ML) Issues related to archaeological research, excava-tions, etc. Post announcements for conferences and jobs. Requests for information, papers, and publica-tions. ✓**INTERNET**→*email* LISTSERV@ DGOGWDG1.BITNET ✍ *Type in message body:* ARCH-L <YOUR FULL NAME>

sci.archaeology (NG) For those interested in archaeology. ✓**USENET**

Indigenous peoples

alt.native (NG) Covers all topics related to American Indians. ✓**USENET**

The Igloo Station (BBS) Focused on issues related to American Indians and other indigenous peo-ples. Includes news, excerpts from speeches, policy reports, and dis-cussion. ▦ 514-632-5556 FREE

Indian Affairs Native American/ American Indian topics, including news, archaeology, anthropology, art, language, religion, and history. ✓**FIDONET**→*tag* INDIAN_AFFAIRS

Nat-Lang (ML) Forum for ex-changing information about the languages of indigenous peoples. ✓**INTERNET**→*email* LISTSERV@TAMVM1. TAMU.EDU ✍ *Type in message body:* SUBSCRIBE NAT-LANG <YOUR FULL NAME>

NoAmNative Native Americans from different tribes and Indian nations exchange knowledge and share cultural experiences. ✓**SMART-NET**→*tag* NOAMNATIVE

soc.culture.native (NG/ML) Forum for discussing the cultures and lives of indigenous peoples. ▦ ✓**USENET** ✓**INTERNET**→ *email* LIST SERV@TAMVM1.TAMU.EDU ✍ *Type in message body:* SUBSCRIBE NATCHAT <YOUR FULL NAME>

Asia & the Pacific Rim

Bit.listserv.seasia-I offers a point of view on Southeast Asia not found in the greater-U.S.

mass media. For instance, a recent report found that "after eighteen years under communism and without war, Vietnam has literally turned into a decadent hub where the sex, drug, and gambling industries are booming." The report says that Dien Bien Phu, France's Waterloo in Vietnam, is now the center of Hanoi's drug industry, and that Vietnam is becoming one of the world's important drug nexuses. Somebody should tell *The New York Times*.

On the Net

Across the board

Asia Connected to Asian countries, a forum for general discussions. ✓**SMARTNET**→ASIA

Asia/North America/Europe Chat General chat for all topics related to Asia and Asian culture. English as well as other languages with English translation are allowed. ✓**FIDONET**→*tag* ASIAN_LINK

bit.listserv.seasia-I (NG) For those interested in Southeast Asia. ✓**USENET** ✓**INTERNET**→*email* LISTSERV @MSU.EDU ✍ *Type in message body:* SUB SEASIA-L <YOUR FULL NAME>

Pacific (ML) For those interested in the Pacific Ocean, its islands

U.S. boats in Thailand—downloaded from wuarchive.wustl.edu.

and people. Topics range from the economy to culture to the ocean itself. ✓**INTERNET**→*email* LISTSERV@ BRUFPB.BITNET ✍ *Type in message body:* SUBSCRIBE PACIFIC <YOUR FULL NAME> <SPECIFIC INTERESTS> SET PACIFIC REPRO

soc.culture.asean (NG) Forum for discussing the countries of Southeast Asia. ✓**USENET**

Asian countries

alt.culture.indonesia (NG) Indonesian culture, news, and related topics. Listings in both Javanese and English. 🖳 ✓**USENET**

alt.culture.kerala (NG) Discussions of the Keralite culture and Malayalam language. ✓**USENET**

MISG-L (ML) A forum, conducted mostly in Bahasa Malaysia, to discuss Malaysian affairs and Islam. ✓**INTERNET**→*email* LISTSERV@PSUVM. PSU.EDU ✍ *Type in message body:* SUBSCRIBE MISG-L <YOUR FULL NAME> <YOUR MAJOR> <YOUR UNIVERSITY>

soc.culture.filipino (NG) Discussion about all aspects of Filipino culture. ✓**USENET**

soc.culture.korean (NG) For discussing Korean culture. ✓**USENET**

soc.culture.malaysia (NG) For discussing Malaysian society and happenings. ✓**USENET**

soc.culture.singapore (NG) Forum about the history, culture, and politics in Singapore. ✓**USENET**

soc.culture.thai (NG) Forum for discussing Thailand. ✓**USENET**

soc.culture.vietnamese (NG) Forum for discussing Vietnamese culture. ✓**USENET**

Thai-Yunnan Project Data on languages, customs, and country interrelations in Southeast Asia. Newsletters related to the project, HyperCard stacks from the Thai-Yunnan Bibliography, and research notes are available at the FTP site, and as a WAIS database. ✓**INTERNET** ...→*wais* ANU-Thai-Yunnan.src ...→*ftp* COOMBS.ANU.EDU.AU ANONYMOUS/<YOUR EMAIL ADDRESS>→ coombspapers/coombsarchives/ thai-yunnan-project

Australia/New Zealand

Down_Under Exchange ideas and cultural viewpoints with members in Australia and New Zealand. ✓**LINK**→*number* 178

soc.culture.australian (NG) Covers Australian culture, society, history, and happenings. ✓**USENET**

soc.culture.new-zealand (NG) Discussions of topics related to New Zealand. ✓**USENET**

The Balkans

Soldiers on the Net can only kill with words. On alt.current-events.bosnia, for example,

a typical posting goes like this: "Well, lets see who is attacking me: 1. Mark 'Wish I was Russian and my name is Khubayev' Hubey (a Turk); 2. Ms. Serdar 'The world needs to know of peace-loving Turkish genocide' Argich (a Turkish net-pest with the Serb last name); 3. Lavor 'Don't tell me anything bad about my Croatia because I was there in May' Dujmovic (a Croat); and last but not least: 4. Mike 'My primary concern are the Bosnian Muslims' Sells (only God knows of what background)." Try the mailing list **Mak-Talk** for seething developments in Macedonia.

Bosnian child—from CompuServe's Reuters NewsPictures Forum.

On the Net

Bosnia-Herzegovina

alt.current-events.bosnia (NG) Discussion of the situation in Bosnia. ✓**USENET**

soc.culture.bosnia-herzgvna (NG) For those interested in the people of Bosnia. ✓**USENET**

Croatia

Croatian-News (ML) News from and related to Croatia. If you would like to receive the news in Croatian as well, indicate that in your request. ▣ ✓**INTERNET**→*email* CROATIAN-NEWS-REQUEST@ANDREW. CMU.EDU ✍*Subscribe by request:* <YOUR COUNTRY><YOUR FULL NAME> <YOUR EMAIL ADDRESS>

Cromed-L (ML) Organized to inform and to seek assistance from the international community regarding events in Croatia. ✓**INTERNET**→*email* LISTSERV@AEARN. BITNET ✍*Type in message body:* SUB CROMED-L <YOUR FULL NAME>

Cro-News (ML) For news from a number of different media sources coming from Croatia. ▣ ✓**INTER-NET**→*email* CRO-NEWS-REQUEST@ MEDPHYS.UCL.AC.UK ✍*Subscribe by request*

Cro-Views (ML) Discussions related to Croatia and other for-mer Yugoslav republics. ✓**INTERNET** →*email* JOE@MULLARA.MET.UNIMELB. EDU.AU ✍*Subscribe by request*

soc.culture.croatia (NG) Forum for discussing life in Croatia. ✓**USENET**

Macedonia

alt.news.macedonia (NG) Fo-rum for discussing news in Mace-donia. ✓**USENET**

Mak-News (ML) News as it develops from and about the Republic of Macedonia. ▣ ✓**IN-TERNET**→*email* LISTSERV@UTS.EDU.AU ✍ *Type in message body:* SUBSCRIBE MAK-NEWS <YOUR FULL NAME>

Mak-Talk (ML) For discussing events in Macedonia. ✓**INTERNET**→ *email* LISTSERV@UTS.EDU.AU ✍*Type in message body:* SUBSCRIBE MAK-TALK <YOUR FULL NAME>

Serbia

Serbian-American Online Information Exchange (BBS) Information on the events in for-mer Yugoslavia, including text files and GIFs. 708-581-1735 FREE

Slovenia

RokPress (ML) News from Slovenia although articles from Croatian, Serbian, Bosnian, and Macedonian sources are also post-ed. ▣ ✓**INTERNET**→*email* ROK PRESS@IJS.SI ✍*Subscribe by request*

Former Yugoslavia

soc.culture.yugoslavia (NG) Forum for discussing the former Yugoslavia and its people. ✓**USENET**

British Isles

If you're a homesick Brit or an inveterate anglophile, there's a bar stool for you on CompuServe's **UK Forum**. Also on CompuServe you'll surely want to check out the latest cricket, snooker, rugby, and football scores on **UK Sports Clips**, then wander over to the **UK Newspaper Library**—an online version of the library in a good club—and settle back with *The Independent* and the *Financial Times*. On the mailing list **Celtic-L**, the talk is deep and Irish (with good travel advice).

Princess Di—downloaded from CompuServe's UK Forum.

Britain

alt.politics.british (NG) Discussions about British politics. ✓**USENET**

Modbrits (ML) A forum for scholars, teachers, and students to discuss modern British and Irish literature. Papers, conference and job announcements, reviews, and abstracts are all welcome. ✓**INTERNET**→*email* LISTSERV@KENTVM.KENT. EDU ✍ *Type in message body:* SUBSCRIBE MODBRITS <YOUR FULL NAME>

soc.culture.british (NG) For discussing British culture and news, specifically political and social commentary. ✓**USENET**

UK Forum Cultural and social topics such as politics, television, business, and travel information. In Rovers Return Pub, members engage in the sort of frank discussions one finds in British pubs. 🖼️ ✓**COMPUSERVE**→ *go* UKFORUM

Ireland & Scotland

Celtic-L (ML) For discussing Celtic culture, especially Irish politics. ✓**INTERNET**→*email* LISTSERV@IRLEARN. BITNET ✍ *Type in message body:* SUB CELTIC-L <YOUR FULL NAME>

Gaelic List (ML) Multi-disciplinary discussions in Scottish, Gaelic, Irish, and Manx. ✓**INTERNET**→*email* LISTSERV@IRLEARN.UCD.IE ✍ *Type in message body:* SUB GAELIC-L <YOUR FULL NAME>

Ireland Offers information for anyone interested in Ireland, including conversations with members on Irish boards connected to RelayNet. ✓**RELAYNET**→*number* 393

IRL-POL (ML) For discussing current Irish politics as directly relevant to the Republic. ✓**INTERNET**→ *email* LISTSERV@IRLEARN. BITNET ✍*Type in message body:* SUBSCRIBE IRL-POL <YOUR FULL NAME>

Irtrad-L (ML) Discussion about Irish traditional music. ✓**INTERNET** →*email* LISTSERV@IRLEARN. BITNET ✍ *Type in message body:* SUB IRTRAD-L <YOUR FULL NAME>

soc.culture.celtic (NG) Forum for discussing Celtic culture. ✓**USENET**

Wales

Welsh-L (ML) Forum for discussing present-day Welsh culture and politics as well as the Welsh language. Practice the Welsh language! English, however, may be used. ✓**INTERNET**→*email* LISTSERV@ IRLEARN.UCD.IE ✍ *Type in message body:* SUBSCRIBE WELSH-L <YOUR FULL NAME>

News

UK News Clips Offers full-text stories from Reuters in a variety of categories—finance, politics, and economic news. 🖼️ ✓**COMPUSERVE** →*go* UKNEWS

UK Newspaper Library Includes articles from the *Independent*, the *Daily Telegraph*, *The European*, *Today*, *The Financial Times*, *The Guardian*, and *The Observer*. Searchable by name, word, or phrase. 🖼️ ✓**COMPUSERVE** →*go* UKPAPERS $$

UK Sports Clips Contains full-text Reuters sports stories on cricket, snooker, track and field, rugby, and football (what Americans call soccer). 🖼️ ✓**COMPUSERVE** →*go* UKSPORTS

UK Weather Offers short-term weather reports for 12 English, Scottish, Welsh, and Northern Irish cities, with both high- and low-resolution maps. 🖼️ ✓**COMPUSERVE**→*go* UKWEATHER

Greater China

Keeping up with China is not easy, but the Net offers

several ways. Try the mailing list **Hong Kong News**. Or better yet, just ask your question. For instance, on **soc.culture.taiwan**: "I now find myself considering the possibility of returning to Taiwan (for the first time since landing in North America over 20 years ago) for some months to properly learn the language. The questions are: What schools are available in Taiwan that specialize in teaching illiterates such as myself? And what are the applications procedures? Please email hints, points, etc.…"

Tiananmen Square crackdown—from wuarchive.wustl.edu.

On the Net

Across the board

Chinese Covers Chinese-language versions of popular software packages, as well as all areas of Chinese culture: language, travel, food, history, martial arts, medicine, aphorisms, inventions, music, religions, education, and current events. ✓**RELAYNET**→*number* 315

The Chinese Community Information Center Includes the Hong Kong Bill of Rights, U.S. immigration information, a collection of Chinese classics, and Chinese software. ✓**INTERNET**→*ftp* IFCSS.ORG→ ANONYMOUS/<YOUR EMAIL ADDRESS>

soc.culture.china (NG) Forum focusing on China and the Chinese people. ✓**USENET**

soc.culture.hongkong (NG) A meeting place for those with an interest in Hong Kong. ✓**USENET**

soc.culture.taiwan (NG) Discussion about Taiwan. ✓**USENET**

Chinese studies

China Discussion on academic topics related to Chinese studies. ✓**INTERNET**→*email* LISTSERV@PUCC. PRINCETON.EDU ✍ *Type in message body:* SUBSCRIBE CHINA <YOUR FULL NAME>

The Chinese Poem Discussion List (ML) For Chinese poetry and related discussion. ✓**INTERNET**→ *email* LISTSERV@UBVM.CC.BUFFALO.EDU ✍ *Type in message body:* SUB CHPOEM-L <YOUR FULL NAME>

Chinese text

alt.chinese.text (NG) Covers any topic as long as postings are made in Chinese text. The FAQ (in English) lists several downloadable programs on the Net that allow you to read and write Chinese. ✓**USENET**

News & pictures

The CND Chinese Magazine Network (ML) A weekly electronic magazine published in Chinese. ✓**INTERNET**→*email* LIST SERV@UGA.CC.UGA.EDU ✍ *Type in message body:* SUB CCMAN-L <YOUR FULL NAME>

CND-Global (ML) Daily news digest about China. 🖳 ✓**INTERNET** →*email* LISTSERV@ASUACAD.BITNET ✍ *Type in message body:* SUB CHINA-NN <YOUR FULL NAME>

Hong Kong News (ML) Primarily clippings from major news wires about China, Taiwan, and Hong Kong—from the pro-democracy movement in China to the stock market in Hong Kong. 🖳 ✓**INTERNET**→*email* REQUEST@AHK CUS.ORG ✍*Subscribe by request*

LYTX (ML) A monthly Chinese electronic journal with articles on topics of general interest, science and technology, literature, and Chinese students. Previous stories: "An Introduction to Zhong Gong," and "Life: Car Repairing." ✓**INTER-NET**→*email* LISTSERV@VM1.MCGILL.CA ✍ *Type in message body:* SUBSCRIBE LYTX <YOUR FULL NAME>

Hong Kong Pictures Archive Currently the archive has an HK pop-star collection, a scenic collection, a comics collection, and a miscellaneous area. The site also carries a more limited China photo archive in the directory pub/china/gif. ✓**INTERNET**→*ftp* ASIA.LCS. MIT.EDU→FTP/<YOUR EMAIL ADDRESS>→ pub/hongkong/hkpa

Politics

talk.politics.china (NG) Debate over political issues relating to China. ✓**USENET**

The CIS & the Baltics

The Commonwealth of Independent States, a.k.a. the former Soviet Union and the new-

ly independent states of Lithuania, Latvia, and Estonia—the Baltics—is 007 stuff for Net surfers. The Internet's **Soviet Archives**, for instance, provides information that was once closed to the public, including top-secret material on the Cuban Missile Crisis. Relax and take a nice, long walk down the memory lane of the Cold War. If your Russian is beyond nyet you can talk to other Russian speakers on the newsgroup **alt. uu.lang.russian.misc**. And the newsgroup **soc.culture. baltics** will keep you up-to-date on the bright new future that's unfolding along the Baltic Sea.

On the Net

Former USSR

soc.culture.soviet (NG) Discuss cultures and events in the nations of the former USSR. ✓**USENET**

Soviet Archives Information from opened Soviet archives about living conditions in the former Soviet Union, Chernobyl, the Cuban Missile Crisis, and more. You can even get a GIF of Gorby. ✓**INTERNET**→*ftp* SEQ1.LOC.GOV→ ANONYMOUS/<YOUR EMAIL ADDRESS>→ pub/soviet.archive

Boris Yeltsin—downloaded from wuarchive.wustl.edu.

Suearn-L (ML) A list focused on issues relevant to computer networking in the former Soviet Union. Topics range from equipment compatibility to directions on reaching sites. ✓**INTERNET**→ *email* LISTSERV@UBVM.CC.BUFFALO.EDU ✍ *Type in message body:* SUB SUEARN-L <YOUR FULL NAME>

talk.politics.soviet (NG) Discussion of domestic and foreign former Soviet politics, as well as current Russian politics. ✓**USENET**

Russia

alt.uu.lang.russian.misc (NG) For Russian-language discussions. ✓**USENET**

Info-Russ (ML) Informal communication within the Russian-speaking community. ✓**INTERNET**→*email* INFO-RUSS-REQUEST@SMARTY.ECE.JHU. EDU ✍*Subscribe by request:* <YOUR FULL NAME><YOUR EMAIL ADDRESS>

k12.lang.russian (NG) For teachers, students, and others interested in conversing in and discussing the Russian language. ✓**USENET**

The Manor BBS! (BBS) BBS that supports both Russian and English. 908-493-3936 FREE

Relcom Dozens of Russian-language newsgroups devoted to a variety of business-related topics such as RELCOM.COMMERCE.ESTATE, RELCOM.COMMERCE.STOCKS, and RELCOM.COMMERCE.JOBS as well as other topics such as the occult, humor, and politics. ✓**USENET**

Russian Studies Archive Includes Russian poetry, Russian translations of Shakespeare, texts of recent referenda, software, and GIFs. ✓**INTERNET**→*ftp* SUNSITE.UNC. EDU→ANONYMOUS/<YOUR EMAIL ADDRESS>→pub/academic/russian-studies

Ukraine

soc.culture.ukranian (NG) For discussions about the politics (especially relations with Russia), history, and current happenings in the Ukraine. ✓**USENET**

The Baltics

Balt-L (ML) Devoted to furthering communications with Lithuania, Latvia, and Estonia. People with specific technical skills or interest in the Baltics are encouraged to join. ✓**INTERNET**→ *email* LISTSERV @UBVM. CC.BUFFALO.EDU ✍*Type in message body:* SUB BALT-L <YOUR FULL NAME>

soc.culture.baltics (NG) For those interested in the people and events in the Baltic states. ✓**USENET**

Eastern Europe

We used to have to depend on *The New York Times* **for** news of Eastern Europe. Now we know what the *Times* doesn't, from detailed coverage of the Polish economy on the mailing list **E-Europe** to the latest rumors in Budapest as told on the **Hungarian Discussion List** to the myriad subtleties of ethnic divisions revealed on the newsgroups **soc.culture.romanian** and **soc.culture.bulgaria**. Not to mention the great recipes!

Across the board

E-Europe (ML) For those interested in business in and the economies of Central and Eastern Europe as well as those of the Commonwealth of Independent States. ✓**INTERNET**→*email* LISTSERV@PUCC. PRINCETON.EDU ✉ *Type in message body:* SUB E-EUROPE <YOUR FULL NAME>

Mideur-L (ML) Middle European discussion list. ✓**INTERNET**→*email* LISTSERV@UBVM.BITNET ✉ *Type in message body:* SUBSCRIBE MIDEUR-L <YOUR FULL NAME>

misc.news.east-europe.rferl (NG/ML) Reports from Radio Free Europe and Radio Liberty. ▦ ✓**USENET** ✓**INTERNET**→*email* LISTSERV @UBVM.CC.BUFFALO.EDU ✉ *Type in message body:* SUB RFERL-L <YOUR FULL NAME>

Prague—downloaded from CompuServe's Travel Forum.

Bulgaria & Romania

Romanians (ML) For discussion, news, and information on Romania. Conducted in Romanian. ▦ ✓**INTERNET**→*email* MIHAI@ SEP.STANFORD.EDU ✉ *Subscribe by request*

soc.culture.bulgaria (NG) Covers a range of Bulgarian-related topics—from recipes to politics to literature to embassy numbers. Most messages written in Bulgarian. ✓**USENET**

soc.culture.romanian (NG) Discussion of Romania and the Moldavian people. Many messages in Romanian. ✓**USENET**

Czech Republic

soc.culture.czecho-slovak (NG) Discussion about the Bohemian, Slovakian, Moravian, and Silesian culture and lifestyle. ✓**USENET**

Hungary

Hungarian Discussion List (ML) An English-language forum for those interested in Hungarian issues. ✓**INTERNET**→*email* LISTSERV@ GWUVM.BITNET ✉ *Type in message*

body: SUBSCRIBE HUNGARY <YOUR FULL NAME>

soc.culture.magyar (NG) Discussion of the Hungarian people and their culture. ✓**USENET**

Poland

Pigulka (ML) News from Poland in English. ▦ ✓**INTERNET**→*email* ZIELINSKI@ACFCLUSTER.NYU.EDU ✉ *Subscribe by request*

Poland and Polish Related Topics Conversations in both Polish and English about Poland and Poles living overseas. ✓**FIDONET**→*tag* POLISH

Poland-L (ML) Dedicated to discussions of Polish culture and events within Poland and abroad. ✓**INTERNET**→*email* LISTSERV@UBVM.BIT NET ✉ *Type in message body:* SUBSCRIBE POLAND-L <YOUR FULL NAME>

Polish Archive News, press reviews, and humor about and from Poland and the Polish abroad. ▦ ✓**INTERNET**→*ftp* MTHVAX.CS.MIAMI. EDU→ANONYMOUS/<YOUR EMAIL ADDRESS>→pub/poland

soc.culture.polish (NG) Polish culture, history, and politcs discussed, often in the Polish language. ✓**USENET**

Slovenia

RokPress (ML) News from Slovenia, although articles from Croatian, Serbian, Bosnian, and Macedonian sources are also posted. ▦ ✓**INTERNET**→*email* ROKPRESS@IJS.SI ✉ *Subscribe by request*

Slovak-L (ML) Discuss Slovak culture. ✓**INTERNET**→*email* LIST SERV@UBVM.BITNET ✉ *Type in message body:* SUB SLOVAK-L <YOUR FULL NAME>

Europe & its cultures

This is the place for homesick Europeans and for that large population of Continental-

philes—Italophiles, Francophiles, Deutschephiles, Iberiaphiles, etc. Discussions range from expat tax issues, to current political crises, to the technical issues of a multilingual Cyberspace. For example, the FAQ editor in **soc.culture.greek** advises: "For those using Windows 3.1, a Classical Greek font is in the works at Monotype. From what I'm told, it will be a PS font but not TrueType. I suggested to them that they create also a Latin font that would have macrons. I think this would make a very marketable classical package. In the meantime, how do Windows users solve the macron problem? I'm using the circumflex vowels in the extended C as a sort of makeshift solution."

On the Net

Across the board

alt.politics.ec (NG) Discussions about EC politics. ✓ **USENET**

alt.politics.europe.misc (NG) For discussing European politics. ✓ **USENET**

EEC Discussions concerning the

Venice—downloaded from CompuServe's Travel Forum.

European Economic Community of nations, including social and financial topics. ✓ **ILINK**→*number* 182

Europe Covers politics, economics, and culture in Europe, with special emphasis on the former Soviet Union and Eastern Europe. Among the topics are history, languages, literature, and business opportunities. ✓ **RELAYNET**→*number* 352

Germany & Europe RoundTable Specific areas for several European countries, with strong emphasis on Germany. Discussions range from the political to the gastronomical. 🖥 🍺 ☕ ✓ **GENIE**→*keyword* EUROPE

soc.culture.europe (NG) Discussion about all aspects of European society. ✓ **USENET**

Austria & Germany

alt.culture.austrian (NG) Discussion of Austrian culture, history, tourist sites, and more. ✓ **USENET**

German Computer Library

An area for German-speaking CompuServe members to discuss common interests—sports, politics, games, travel, and computers. ☕ ✓ **COMPUSERVE**→*go* GERNET

German Chat with users in Germany. Many messages "auf Deutsch." ✓ **ILINK**→*number* 166

German & Yiddish Language Provides a forum for conversation, and practice, in German and Yiddish for native speakers, teachers, and students. ✓ **RELAYNET**→*number* 289

Great German Gifts Products made in Germany, switzerland, and Austria. Products range from Black Forest wooden clocks to hand-crafted bier steins. 🍺 ✓ **GENIE**→*keyword* GERMAN

Lowengrube Mailbox (BBS) German-language BBS. 915-550-5122 FREE

soc.culture.german (NG) German history, culture, and current-event discussions. ✓ **USENET**

France

Francais Based in Quebec, Canada, this includes general chat and discussions in French. ✓ **FIDONET**→*tag* FRANCAIS ✖ *Users must use the full ASCII character set (chars 32 to 152) to promote clarity when writing French*

France Chat with users in France. Many messages in the French language. ✓ **ILINK**→*number* 56

France Conversation in French only. ✓**SMARTNET**→*tag* FRANCE

French Language Offers conversation in French for anyone interested in joining. ✓**RELAYNET**→*number* 306

soc.culture.french (NG) For cultural, political, and travel-related discussions about France. ✓**USENET**

Greece

Greek Converse about ancient and modern Greek culture. ✓**ILINK**→*number* 175

soc.culture.greek (NG/ML) Discussions of Greek society and culture. ✓**USENET** ✓**INTERNET**→*email* SOC-CULTURE-GREEK-REQUEST@CS.WISC.EDU ✍*Subscribe by request*

Italy

alt.politics.italy (NG) Discuss Italian politics. ✓**USENET**

Langit (ML) For those interested in Italian culture and language, from the food to the politics. Students of Italian are encouraged to join. ✓**INTERNET**→*email* LISTSERV@ICINECA.BITNET ✍*Type in message body:* SUBSCRIBE LANGIT <YOUR FULL NAME>

soc.culture.italian (NG) Italian history and culture discussions. ✓**USENET**

The Netherlands

Dutch Chats with users in the Netherlands. Many messages in the Dutch language. ✓**ILINK**→*number* 206

Neder-L (ML) Forum for studying the Dutch language and literature. ✓**INTERNET**→*email* LISTSERV@

NIC.SURFNET.NL ✍*Type in message body:* SUB NEDER-L <YOUR FULL NAME>

soc.culture.netherlands (NG) Forum for discussing the Dutch, in both the Netherlands and Belgium. ✓**USENET**

Portugal

International Portuguese Language Echo General-interest topics for Portuguese speakers from around the world—in Europe, Brazil, North America, and Asia. ✓**FIDONET**→*tag* PORTUGUES

soc.culture.portuguese (NG) Forum for discussing the people and culture of Portugal. ✓**USENET**

Scandinavia

Scandinavia Converse with users from Norway and Sweden on all subjects. ✓**ILINK**→*number* 156

Spain

Espanol Communicate in Spanish about Spanish culture and other topics. ✓**ILINK**→*number* 189

soc.culture.spain (NG) Forum for discussing life in Spain. ✓**USENET**

Spanish Genealogy Questions and answers about Spanish surnames and genealogical research, moderated by a researcher from Automated Archives, the preeminent research authority in the field. ✓**FIDONET**→*tag* SPANISH. GEN

Spanish Language Offers conversation for all Spanish-speakers and those interested in learning the language. ✓**RELAYNET**→*number* 307

CYBERNOTES

BZT Nummer, bitte!

"The German phone system is operated by the German Telecom, a state-owned company. There are no private long distance or local phone companies. Every phone, fax or modem you connect to a phone line needs to be approved by the German Telecom.

"Approved appliances have a special sticker with a BZT number on the back. You may own any phone but you may not connect it to the public system unless it has a BZT number. You may not own radios or cordless phones which are not approved.

"Cordless phones are a real problem. In Germany, cordless phones operate on different frequencies than in most other countries. The frequencies many foreign countries use are used by others (police, emergencies, radio, TV...).

"Therefore, use only approved cordless phones!!!

"OR THEY WILL GET YOU!!!"

—from the FAQ of **soc.culture.german**

Japan

GEnie offers some of the best coverage of Japan, includ-ing a connection to Japan's number-one online service, **PC-VAN**. Started in 1986 by the NEC Corporation, **PC-VAN** offers news, shopping, real-time chat, and access to a variety of commercial and professional databases. Using Kanji, **PC-VAN** is perfect for Japanese who want news from home, and non-Japanese who want to practice language skills. GEnie's **Japan RoundTable** —in English and Kanji— covers an almost unlimited number of subjects of interest to Japanese, Nipponophiles, and those with a more casual interest. Popular subjects include traveling in Japan, learning Japanese, getting jobs in Japan, along with Japanese food, movies, music, and extensive coverage of Kanji software. There is no extra GEnie charge for accessing the **Japan Round-Table**.

On the Net

Across the board

Japan Conference Includes discussions about language, culture, food, current events, music, travel, and history. ✓**RELAYNET**→*number* 273

A Japanese temple—downloaded from the BBS Howard's Notebook

Japanese Economic Newswire Plus Full-text articles from specialized industry newsletters—information on companies, products, markets, and legislation. 🖳 ✓**COMPUSERVE**→*go* IQUEST→**2507** $$

Japan RoundTable Exchange information about traveling or getting a job in Japan, learn Japanese, discuss Japanese movies, music, or manga, download Kanji software, and more. 🖳 ✿ ☺🦃 ✓**GENIE**→*keyword* JAPAN

PC-VAN Gateway Connect with Japan's leading commercial online service—more than half a million users, 140+ interest groups and services (newspapers, databases, and shopping), and links to local bulletin boards throughout several Japanese cities. 🖳 ✿ 🔳 ☺🦃 ✓**GENIE**→*keyword* PC-VAN $$

soc.culture.japan (NG) For discussion of Japan and Japanese culture. Information on movies, food, travel, current events, jobs, and more. ✓**USENET**

Language

Japanese/English Language Educational echo using both languages, with a variety of topics.

Use by pen pals, students, and teachers is encouraged. ✓**FIDONET**→ *tag* NIHON_GO

JTIT (ML) Forum for teachers and media professionals to exchange information on teaching Japanese. Topics include interactive video, learning a second language, and more. A database of conference information includes job and grant opportunities, software, and bibliographies. ✓**INTERNET**→*email* LISTSERV@PSUVM.PSU.EDU 🔖 *Type in message body:* SUB JTIT-L <YOUR FULL NAME>

sci.lang.japan (NG/ML) Discussions about the Japanese language. ✓**USENET** ✓**INTERNET**→*email* LISTSERV @MITVMA.BITNET 🔖 *Type in message body:* SUB NIHONGO <YOUR FULL NAME>

Food & culture

J-Food-L (ML) For those interested in Japanese food and culture. Created at Kinki University in Japan. ✓**INTERNET**→*email* LISTSERV@ UBVM.BITNET 🔖 *Type in message body:* SUB J-FOOD-L <YOUR FULL NAME>

Jpop (ML) Forum for discussing Japanese popular music. ✓**INTERNET** →*email* JPOP-REQUEST@FERKEL.UCSB. EDU 🔖 *Subscribe by request*

More manga

Hayao Miyazaki (ML) For fans of the works of Hayao Miyazaki. Includes discussion of alternative/progressive manga and anime. ✓**INTERNET**→*email* LISTSERV@BROWN VM.BROWN.EDU 🔖 *Type in message body:* SUBSCRIBE NAUSICAA <YOUR EMAIL ADDRESS><YOUR FULL NAME>

rec.arts.manga (NG) Discussions and news about manga, Japanese comics. ✓**USENET**

Jewish culture

The vast array of Jewish discussions and Jewish issues on the Net include many familiar voices. For instance, Rabbi Martin Levin's letter to his daughter Ilana on CompuServe's **Religion Forum**: "...if your friends are primarily the students you happen to meet in class or at a fraternity party or in the local cafeteria, the chances are you will meet a real nice, bright, good looking guy, who will ask you out, and you will accept very innocently, and see again, and like very much, and one day start asking yourself, 'How in Heaven's Name will I tell my Dad about Chris?' And I know you will truly love Chris. But you won't be at peace with yourself, and you won't feel whole. And you won't transmit this legacy, this identity, and all the joy and meaning that goes with it to the next generation."

On the Net

Across the board

Ethics and Religion Forum The Other Religions bulletin board usually has several topics running on Judaism and Jewish life—from Conservative Judaism to Jewish singles. The Judaism

Rabbi Kanduri—downloaded from the sunsite.unc.edu archive.

Library includes Hebrew Review applications, sermons, and calendar software. ☁✔ ✓**AMERICA ON-LINE**→*keyword* RELIGION

IL-Board (ML) General-interest Israeli list. Topics range from the Israeli Internet to general information about Israel to pen-pal searches. ✓**INTERNET**→*email* LISTSERV@VM. TAU.AC.IL ✍ *Type in message body:* SUBSCRIBE IL-BOARD <YOUR FULL NAME>

IL-Talk (ML) Debate and discussion about any topic relating to Jews or Israel. ✓**INTERNET**→*email* LISTSERV@VM.TAU.AC.IL ✍ *Type in message body:* SUBSCRIBE IL-TALK <YOUR FULL NAME>

Jewish Archive Documents about Israel and the Middle East, including the Israeli 'Declaration of Independence,' articles about the PLO, GIFs, a collection of Divrei Torah, archives of Jewish-interest mailing lists, and Hebrew computing software. ✓**INTERNET**→ *ftp* NYSERNET.ORG→ANONYMOUS/ <YOUR EMAIL ADDRESS>→israel

Jewish Discussions The Torah, traditions, and Jewish culture are topics for discussion. ✓**FIDONET** →*tag* JUDAICA

JewishNet Carries reading lists on Judaism, archives of Jewish-related texts, and information on Jewish-interest mailing lists and Usenet newsgroups. Located at Hebrew University in Israel. ✓**INTERNET**→*telnet* VMS.HUJI.AC.IL→ JEWISHNET/<NONE>

KESHERnet A FidoNet-based BBS network with echoes on international Jewish issues, including religious discussions, genealogy, education, matchmaking, Hebrew, and news items. ✓CHECK LOCAL BULLETIN BOARDS

L'Chaim BBS (BBS) A Jewish BBS that carries Jewish magazines, Hebrew programs, including word-processor applications, and Jewish-interest message boards. 718-756-7201 FREE

Religion & Philosophy Round Table Includes the two categories Diaspora & Beyond for Orthodox Jewish Issues and Liberal Judaism Issues. In the former, for instance, topics include anti-Semitism, kosher food, Hebrew, the events in New York City's Crown Heights, and religious teachings. ☁✔ ✓**GENIE**→*keyword* RELIGION

Religion Forum See the Judaism bulletin board for discussions. The Judaism library has a large selection of files, including excerpts from *Maus II: A Survivor's Tale*, Hebrew typefaces, Jewish calendars, conference transcripts, Divrei Torah, Jewish clip art, and HyperCard Torah Hebrew grammar tutors. ☁✔ ✓**COMPUSERVE**→ *go* RELIGION

RESHETnet A worldwide bulletin-board network with conferences such as R_Silhova (general chit-chat), R_Toldot (Jewish genealogy), R_Torah (Bible study), R_Noar (for kids, teens, and young adults), and R_N (for Jews in 12-step programs). For general information, contact the CITY PEOPLE BBS at 212-255-6656. ✓CHECK LOCAL BULLETIN BOARDS

soc.culture.jewish (NG) For discussions concerning Judaism and Jewish culture, including discussions about the various movements, debates over *halacha*, Torah interpretations, etc. ✓USENET

Judaism

Baltuva (ML) Covering issues of concern to observant Jews. ✓INTERNET→*email* LISTSERV@ VM1.MCGILL.CA ✎*Type in message body:* SUBSCRIBE BALTUVA <YOUR FULL NAME>

Ioudaios (ML) Ioudaious, meaning "Jew" in Greek, is a forum for discussing first-century Judaism, particularly the works of Philo of Alexandria and Flavius Josephus. The ability to read classical Greek and a background in first-century Judaism are helpful. ✓INTERNET→ *email* LISTSERV@ YORKVM1.BITNET ✎ *Type in message body:* SUBSCRIBE IOUDAIOS <YOUR FULL NAME>

Kol-Isha (ML) Halachic questions and issues concerning women's roles in Judaism. ✓INTERNET→*email* LISTSERV@ISRAEL.NYSERNET.ORG ✎*Type in message body:* SUB KOL-ISHA <YOUR FULL NAME>

Scrolls from the Dead Sea Exhibition An online exhibition with images of 12 scrolls, interpretion and contextual background, analysis about their significance, and a full glossary of references.

✓INTERNET→*ftp* SEQ1.LOC.GOV→ ANONYMOUS/<YOUR EMAIL ADDRESS>→ pub/deadsea.scrolls. exhibit

Shalom Chit Chat Messianic Judaism. ✓FIDONET→*tag* SHALOM

The Tanach Includes full text of *The Torah*, *The Prophets*, and *The Writings* in three separate files. ✓INTERNET→*ftp* ARCHIVE.UMICH. EDU→ANONYMOUS/<YOUR EMAIL ADDRESS>→mirrors/msdos/foreign_lang/hebrew

Theological Network Discussion topics and databases include studies in Judaism (e.g., download a Jewish time line) and Hebrew Bible studies (individual files for parts of the Old Testament). ✓DELPHI→*go* GR THEO

Judaic studies

Judaica (ML) For anything related to Judaic studies—electronic texts, databases, applications, methodology, research. ✓INTERNET →*email* LISTSERV@VM.TAU.AC.IL ✎*Type in message body:* SUBSCRIBE JUDAICA <YOUR FULL NAME>

Divrei Torah

A Byte of Torah (ML) Divrei Torah. ✓INTERNET→*email* LISTSERV@ ISRAEL.NYSERNET.ORG ✎*Type in message body:* SUB BYTETORAH <YOUR FULL NAME>

Oxford (ML) Divrei Torah. ✓INTERNET→ *email* LISTSERV@ISRAEL. NYSERNET.ORG ✎ *Type in message body:* SUB OXFORD-JUDAISM <YOUR FULL NAME>

Language & culture

German & Yiddish Language Provides a forum for conversation, and practice, in German and

Yiddish for native speakers, teachers, and students. ✓RELAYNET→ *number* 289

Jewish Genealogy General information on research, surnames and families through worldwide help, sources, and contacts. ✓FIDONET→ *tag* JEWISHGEN

Mendele (ML) Discussion of Yiddish literature and language. English and Yiddish are acceptable languages. ✓INTERNET→*email* LIST SERV@YALEVM.YCC.YALE.EDU ✎*Type in message body:* SUB MENDELE <YOUR FULL NAME>

Politics & news

clari.news.group.jews (NG) News of interest to the Jewish community. ▦ ✓USENET

PJML (ML) A place for sharing information on a variety of Jewish concerns, aimed at "inspiring us to move forward and build a better world. We come from many traditions but identify ourselves as 'progressive.'" The Palestinian question often dominates the discussion. ✓INTERNET→*email* LISTSERV@ UTXVM.CC.UTEXAS.EDU ✎*Type in message body:* SUB PJML <YOUR FULL NAME>

Computing

Jewishnt (ML) The Global Jewish Information Network Project covers all topics related to establishing a network that will provide worlwide electronic mail capabilities, Jewish directories and nameservers, access to Jewish databases, newspapers and conferences, libraries, and a Jewish electronic university. ✓INTERNET→ *email* LISTSERV@BGUVM.BGU.AC.IL ✎ *Type in message body:* SUBSCRIBE JEWISHNT <YOUR FULL NAME>

Latin & Caribbean

Most of what's on the Net about Latin America and the Caribbean is at least partially,

and in most cases entirely, in Spanish (**soc.culture.brazil** and **Bras-Net** are generally in Portuguese). Delphi's gateway to Latin America takes you to networks in Argentina and Uruguay. **Delphi/Miami** provides a variety of English-language Delphi services in Spanish. The mailing list **Carecon** is one of the most up-to-date sources on Caribbean economic news. The newsgroup **soc.culture.mexican** is a veritable national magazine, offering news, travel info, recipes, and broad cultural discussions.

On the Net

Across the board

Cread (ML) Discussions covering all aspects of Latin America and the Caribbean. ✓**INTERNET**→*email* LISTSERV@ YORKVM1.BITNET ✍ *Type in message body:* SUBSCRIBE CREAD <YOUR FULL NAME>

Caribbean

Carecon (ML) Forum for discussing the Caribbean economy. ✓**INTERNET**→*email* LISTSERV@YORKVM1.BITNET ✍ *Type in message body:* SUBSCRIBE CARECON <YOUR FULL NAME>

soc.culture.caribbean (NG) Forum for discussing life in the Caribbean. ✓**USENET**

Fidel Castro—downloaded from America Online's PC Graphics Forum.

Latin America

alt.culture.argentina (NG) Forum for discussing Argentinian culture, history, music, food, and other relevant topics. ✓**USENET**

Bras-Net (ML) No specific topics covered. List is for Brazilians and is conducted in Portuguese. ✓**INTERNET**→*email* BRAS-NET-REQUEST@CS. COLUMBIA.EDU ✍*Subscribe by request*

Delphi/Argentina and Delphi/Uruguay A Delphi gateway to Spanish-language networks in Argentina and Uruguay. The networks carry groups and clubs, regional announcements, entertainment features, a shopping center, and more. Connect with Delphi/Uruguay through Delphi/Argentina. 🖳 ⊕ ⊚💬 ✓**DELPHI**→*go* DEL ARG→gateway ✖*Separate password required* $$

Peru (ML) Discussion of Peruvian culture and other issues. ✓**INTERNET**→*email* OWNER-PERU@CS.SFSU.EDU ✍*Subscribe by request*

soc.culture.brazil (NG) General discussion about Brazil. ✓**USENET**

soc.culture.latin-america (NG) For discussing Latin America. ✓**USENET**

soc.culture.mexican (NG) For discussing Mexican culture, history, society, language, and tourism. Archived information from this newsgroup is at the FTP site. Topics include a statistical overview of Mexico, travel information, the origin of the term *gringo*, recipes for tortillas, reading lists, and Internet access in Mexico. ✓**USENET** ✓**INTERNET**→*ftp* ISUMVS.IASTATE.EDU→ ANONYMOUS/<YOUR EMAIL ADDRESS>→ a1$rjs.mexico

soc.culture.peru (NG) All about Peru and its people. ✓**USENET**

soc.culture.venezuela (NG) Covers Venezuelan issues. ✓**USENET**

U.S.

Delphi/Miami Offers the Spanish version of many Delphi services. Also includes information from many Miami-based businesses. 🖳 ⊕ ⊚💬 ✓**DELPHI**→*go* DEL MIA ✖*Separate password required* $$

Issues Forum See the Hispanic Issues bulletin board and library for information and discussion related to Hispanics in the U.S. ⊚💬 ✓**COMPUSERVE**→*go* ISSUES

MCLR (ML) Devoted to research on and by the Latino community in the Midwest and to promoting Latino scholarship. ✓**INTERNET**→*email* LISTSERV@MSU.BITNET ✍*Type in message body:* SUB MCLR-L <YOUR FULL NAME>

Middle East & Turkey

Along with West Bank real-estate speculators, you too might have had some idea that a

peace breakthrough was imminent if only you'd had your ear to the Net. Try **soc.culture.arabic** and **talk. politics.mideast** for up-to-the-minute rumors, nuance, and, of course, emotional and tendentious debate. **soc.culture.iranian** is on top of developments in Iran before the U.S. media too.

On the Net

Across the board

MiddleEast Discussion of political topics related to the Middle East. ✓ILINK→*number* 162

Middle-Eastern Music (ML) For music fans. ✓INTERNET→*email* MIDDLE-EASTERN-REQUEST@NIC.FUNET.FI ✍ *Subscribe by request*

PCarab-L (ML) Forum for discussing Arabization tools for the PC. ✓INTERNET→*email* LISTSERV@ SAKFU00.BITNET ✍ *Type in message body:* SUB PCARAB-L <YOUR FULL NAME>

soc.culture.arabic (NG) Discussions of Arabic culture and Israeli and Arab politics. ✓USENET

talk.politics.mideast (NG) Includes discussions of the Arab-Israeli and the Turkish-Armenian conflicts, the PLO, and other Mideast political issues. ✓USENET

Iran

Iran Archive Includes pictures,

The handshake—from AOL's Smithsonian Online.

recipes, and biographies. Download classical and comical Persian poetry, speeches by famous Iranians, samples of Persian music, and lists of Persian bookstores and publications. ✓INTERNET→*ftp* TEHRAN.STANFORD.EDU→ANONYMOUS/ <YOUR EMAIL ADDRESS>→Iran_Lib

soc.culture.iranian (NG) A discussion of issues related to Iranian culture and politics. ▦ ✓USENET

Lebanon

Lebanon Archive Need a map of Lebanon or a list of Lebanese restaurants in London or a copy of the Arabic alphabet? Includes texts (from poetry to bibliographies), images, and sound files related to Lebanon. ✓INTERNET→*ftp* LIASUN3. EPFL.CH→ANONYMOUS/<YOUR EMAIL ADDRESS>→users/choueiry

soc.culture.lebanon (NG) For discussing Lebanon and the Lebanese culture, from politics to food. ▦ ✓USENET

Palestinians

Palestine-Net (ML) Forum for Palestinians and other Arabs. All topics are permitted. ✓INTERNET→ *email* DOLEH@MCS.KENT.EDU ✍*Subscribe by request*

Saudi Arabia

Saudi Cultural discussions about Saudi Arabia and the Middle East. Communicate directly with users in the Middle East. ✓ILINK→*number* 152

Turkey

Borsa-L (ML) Discussions and information about the Turkish stock exchange. ✓INTERNET→*email* LISTSERV@TREARN.BITNET ✍*Type in message body:* SUB BORSA-L <YOUR FULL NAME>

Politika (ML) For discussing Turkish politics. ✓INTERNET→*email* LISTSERV@TRITU.BITNET ✍*Type in message body:* SUB POLITIKA <YOUR FULL NAME>

soc.culture.turkish (NG) Discussion of Turkish politics, culture, history, news, literature, travel, and related topics. ▦ ✓USENET

Trknws-L (ML) Turkish news. ▦ ✓INTERNET→*email* LISTSERV@USCVM. EDU ✍*Type in message body:* SUB TRKNWS-L <YOUR FULL NAME>

Turkish Electronic List (ML) Open to all discussions in Turkish. ✓INTERNET→*email* LISTSERV@USCVM. BITNET ✍*Type in message body:* SUB TEL <YOUR FULL NAME>

Religion

Religion is one of *the* major subjects on the Net—from scholarly and philosophical discussions about the testaments in Greek in the **NT-Greek** mailing list to college-dorm-like rap sessions on the mailing list **Obj-Rel** to forums for Catholics of wavering faith to the innumerable combative BBSs devoted to the fundamentalist cause, like FidoNet's **International Bible Conference**. Of course, the Net is helping to usher religion into a new cyberfellowship with **Online Bible** and a host of other electronic sacred texts. And, for sure, there's a full-text version of the *Kama Sutra*: "If within the cave of her thighs..."

On the Net

Across the board

Belief-L (ML) All beliefs—ethical, moral, religious, and ideological—discussed. Sometimes discussion is less than serious. ✓**INTERNET**→*email* LISTSERV@BROWNVM.BROWN.EDU ✍*Type in message body:* SUBSCRIBE BELIEF-L <YOUR FULL NAME>

Comparative Religious Writings Includes discussion about sacred texts in all religions, especially the similarities among them. ✓**RELAYNET**→*number* 278

The Contents List (ML) Devoted

Buddha—downloaded from the sun-site.unc.edu archive.

to covering religious-studies-related publications. The list will attempt to post a table of contents, price information, and abstracts for newly released works. Not a discussion forum. ✓**INTERNET** →*email* LISTSERV@ACADVM1.UOTTAWA. CA ✍*Type in message body:* SUBSCRIBE CONTENTS <YOUR FULL NAME>

Ethics and Religion Forum The boards cover a variety of beliefs, including Christianity, Zen, paganism, New Age philosophy, and ethics. Includes a searchable Bible, texts of sermons, GIFs, Jewish-calendar software, and even an attempt to define the "Buddhist Ethics of Cyberspace." ●🗨 ✓**AMERICA ONLINE**→*keyword* RELIGION

Obj-Rel (ML) A self-description reads, "Once one leaves the college dorm, those late night discussions about religion and the nature of the universe are rather hard to come by..." Topics include religion and government, epistemology, creationism versus evolution, and

the existence of God or gods. ✓**INTERNET**→*email* LISTSERV@EMUVM1.CC. EMORY.EDU ✍*Type in message body:* SUBSCRIBE OBJ-REL <YOUR FULL NAME>

Religion Discussions on religious issues. ✓**ILINK**→*number* 59

Religion Offers discussion and debate about religions and religious issues. ✓**RELAYNET**→*number* 176

Religion BB Board subsections range from Anglican to Roman Catholic to Wicca. ✓**PRODIGY**→*jump* RELIGION BB

Religion Forum Offers theological discussions and other information on all organized religions. ●🗨 ✓**COMPUSERVE**→*go* RELIGION

Religion & Philosophy Round-Table For anyone interested in religion, regardless of religious background. Includes an area for religious news, and a religious IQ test, conferences, and a library of religious files. ▦ ●🗨 ✓**GENIE**→*keyword* RELIGION

Review-L (ML) Full-text reviews and book notes published in the *Religious Studies Publications Journal* as well as those THE CONTENTS LIST receives from other publications. ✓**INTERNET**→*email* LISTSERV@ACADVM1.UOTTAWA.CA ✍*Type in message body:* SUB REVIEW-L <YOUR FULL NAME>

Theological Network Discussions related to religion, theology, and metaphysics. Includes relevant software and news as well as several databases, including databases for the clergy, Hebrew Bible studies, meditation and spirituality, and New Testament studies. ▦ ●🗨 ✓**DELPHI**→*go* GR THEO

Episcopalians

Episcopal (ML) For Christians in the Anglican Communion and interested others. ✓**INTERNET**→ *email* LISTSERV@AMERICAN.EDU ✍ *Type in message body:* SUBSCRIBE ANGLICAN <YOUR FULL NAME>

Episcopal Echo An area for Episcopalians and other members of the Anglican Communion to gather and discuss "everything from renegade bishops to swinging incense." Open to all. ✓**FIDONET**→ *tag* EPISCOPAL

Bible studies

AIBI-L (ML) Covers issues related to the computerized analysis of biblical and related texts. ✓**INTERNET**→*email* LISTSERV@ACADVM1.UOTTAWA.CA ✍ *Type in message body:* SUB AIBI-L <YOUR FULL NAME>

The Bible Translations of the bible in English, Finnish, German, Greek, Hebrew, Latin, Swahili, Latin, and Turkish. ✓**INTERNET**→*ftp* NIC.FUNET.FI→ANONYMOUS/<YOUR EMAIL ADDRESS>→pub/doc/bible

Bible News Read-only news for Bible-believing Christians—no discussion. ✓**FIDONET**→*tag* BIBLE _NEWS

Bible Studies Offers conversation based on exploring the Bible, and other religious discussion. ✓**RELAYNET**→*number* 333

Bible, Wholly Bible Serious Bible study, not chat or fellowship. Points must be backed up by references to scripture. Doctrinal discussions face "the Bible test," which "should not be confused with the pseudo Christian, three god cult echos or any other cults or 'denominations' of the RCC."

✓**FIDONET**→*tag* HOLY_BIBLE

International Bible Conference Bible conversations among fundamental Bible believers. ✓**FIDONET**→*tag* BIBLE

King James Bible A full-text King James Bible—missing only the Apocrypha. ✓**INTERNET** ...→*ftp* MRCNEXT.CSO.UIUC.EDU→ANONYMOUS/<YOUR EMAIL ADDRESS>→pub/etext/etext92→bible10.txt ...→*wais* bible.src ✖*Available at the WAIS site 9 a.m. to 9 p.m. EST*

NT-Greek (ML) Scholarly discussions about the Greek New Testament. Working knowledge of biblical Greek assumed. ✓**INTERNET**→*email* NT-GREEK-REQUEST@VIRGINIA.EDU ✍ *Type in message body:* SUB NT-GREEK <YOUR FULL NAME>

Online Bible Freeware with several different English translations of the Bible as well as Greek and Hebrew texts, Spanish and French versions, textual notes, and Scofield's reference Bible. ✓**INTERNET**→*ftp* WUARCHIVE.WUSTL.EDU →ANONYMOUS/<YOUR EMAIL ADDRESS> →doc/bible ✖*Available in both Mac and IBM-PC formats*

Open Bible Conference A vehicle for seeking biblical truth, with a focus on the history and culture of the Bible through investigation of the scholarly credentials and methods of researchers. ✓**FIDONET**→*tag* OPEN_BIBLE

OT-Hebrew (ML) For those involved in the scholarly study of the Hebrew Old Testament. Knowledge of biblical Hebrew and Aramaic expected. ✓**INTERNET** →*email* OT-HEBREW-REQUEST@VIRGINIA.EDU ✍ *Type in message body:* SUB OT-HEBREW <YOUR FULL NAME>

Catholicism

Amercath (ML) Discussion of the history of American Catholicism. Students, researchers, and others can exchange information, share papers, announce conferences, etc. ✓**INTERNET**→*email* LISTSERV@UKCC.UKY.EDU ✍ *Type in message body:* SUB AMERCATH <YOUR FULL NAME>

Catholic (ML) Forum for Catholics to discuss their faith. ✓**INTERNET**→*email* LISTSERV@AMERICAN.EDU ✍ *Type in message body:* SUBSCRIBE CATHOLIC <YOUR FULL NAME>

The New Catholic Doctrine (ML) For discussions of orthodox Catholic theology. ✓**INTERNET**→ *email* CATHOLIC-REQUEST@SARTO.GAITHERSBURG.MD.US ✍*Subscribe by request*

Rome Reborn: The Vatican Library & Renaissance Culture An indefinite online exhibit of more than 200 of the Vatican library's most precious manuscripts, books, and maps. Includes images of each work and the text captions as displayed at the 1993 exhibit held at the Library of Congress. ✓**INTERNET**→*ftp* SEQ1.LOC.GOV→ANONYMOUS/<YOUR EMAIL ADDRESS>→pub/vatican.exhibit

The WAY, The TRUTH, The LIFE (BBS) "Catholic spirituality in a changing world. Dialogue. Daily meditations. Worldwide Marian messages." Includes in the resource directory a listing of more than 500 Christian boards worldwide. 315-392-2368 FREE

Missionaries

Missionary Newsletter Conference A read-only area for letters from missionaries—no discussions. ✓**FIDONET**→*tag* MISSIONS

Christianity

bit.listserv.christia (NG/ML) Discussions on practical Christian life. ✓USENET ✓INTERNET→*email* LISTSERV@FINHUTC.BITNET ✍ *Type in message body:* SUB CHRISTIA <YOUR FULL NAME>

Elenchus (ML) Covers discussions of the literature and thought of Christianity during the period 100 to 500 A.D., including gnosticism, monasticism, early translations of the Scriptures, the history of exegesis, theological developments from the Apologists to the fall of the Western Empire, and more. ✓INTERNET→*email* LISTSERV@ ACADVM1.UOTTAWA.CA ✍ *Type in message body:* SUB ELENCHUS <YOUR FULL NAME>

Inter-Varsity Christian Fellowship (ML) Discussion forum for all affiliated with or interested in Inter-Varsity, a multidenominational Christian group. ✓INTERNET →*email* LISTSERV@UBVM.BITNET ✍ *Type in message body:* SUB IVCF-L <YOUR FULL NAME>

Little Flock BBS (BBS) "Dedicated to the Spread of the Kingdom Message of Our Lord Jesus Christ," reads the opening greeting. Choose to operate in English, French, German, Spanish, Portuguese, or Austrian. 409-769-6880 FREE

Liturgy (ML) An academic forum for discussing Christian liturgy of any historic period or tradition. ✓INTERNET→*email* MAILBASE@MAIL BASE.AC.UK ✍ *Type in message body:* SUBSCRIBE LITURGY <YOUR FULL NAME>

The Promised Land BBS (BBS) A Christian BBS with numerous religious conferences, files, etc. 718-562-1946 FREE

soc.religion.christian (NG) Covers Christianity and related topics. ✓USENET

Vision (ML) For Christian discussions of visions, prophecies, and spiritual gifts—"to seek their significance in the spirit of truth." ✓INTERNET→*email* PRUSS@MATH. UBC.CA ✍ *Subscribe by request*

Eastern religions

ANU Asian Religions Bibliography A searchable database of bibliographic references to documents about Asian religions, especially Buddhism. ✓INTERNET→*wais* ANU-Asian-Religions.src

Baha'i General information and discussion on Baha'i, "the Divine Art of Living." Teachings, principles, and guidelines of the faith are covered. ✓FIDONET→*tag* BAHAI

bit.listserv.hindu-d (NG/ML) Forum for discussing Hindu doctrines as applicable to daily life. Political and cultural discussions are also welcome. ✓USENET ✓INTERNET→*email* LISTSERV@ARIZVM1.CCIT. ARIZONA.EDU ✍ *Type in message body:* SUB HINDU-D <YOUR FULL NAME>

Buddha-L (ML) Scholarly discussion of Buddhism, including history, philosophy, literature, and more. Issues related to teaching Buddhist studies as well as notices of employment opportunities are within the scope of this list, proselytizing is not. ✓INTERNET→*email* LISTSERV@ULKYVM.LOUISVILLE.EDU ✍ *Type in message body:* SUBSCRIBE BUDDHA-L <YOUR FULL NAME>

Buddhist Philosophy and Practice A discussion involving all schools of thought on Buddhist theory, philosophy, and practice. ✓FIDONET→*tag* DHARMA

The CoombsPapers Social Sciences Research Data Bank A huge respository of Asian religion documents including a collection of sermons by 20th century Zen masters, poetry by monks in Malaysia, and a bibliography of French books on Sufism. ✓INTERNET ...→*ftp* COOMBS.ANU.EDU.AU→ ANONYMOUS/<YOUR EMAIL ADDRESS> →coombspapers ...→*ftp* FTP.UU.NET →ANONYMOUS/<YOUR EMAIL ADDRESS> →doc/papers/coombspapers

The Kama Sutra Full text of the *Love Teachings of Kama Sutra*. ✓**INTERNET**→*ftp* FTP.SUNET.SE→ANONY-MOUS/<YOUR EMAIL ADDRESS>→ pub/etext/misc→kamasut.txt

---

Non-violence and Vegetarianism Messages focused on Ahimsa, the Buddhist principle of nonviolence in word, thought, or action toward any sentient being. Also includes discussions of the ethics of vegetarianism. ✓**FIDONET** →*tag* AHIMSA

---

soc.religion.bahai (NG) Forum for discussing the tenets and history of the Baha'i faith. ✓**USENET**

---

soc.religion.eastern (NG) Discussions of eastern religions. ✓**USENET**

Islam

Islam On Line (BBS) A religious BBS dedicated to education about Islam. 912-929-1073 FREE

The Koran The "Quake" site divides the Koran into 114 individual chapters while the "Princeton" site provides it as a single document. It is a searchable database via a WAIS server. ✓**INTERNET** ...→*ftp* QUAKE.THINK.COM→ANONY-MOUS/<YOUR EMAIL ADDRESS>→ pub/etext/koran ...→*ftp* PRINCE TON.EDU→ANONYMOUS/<YOUR EMAIL ADDRESS>→pub→Quran.tar.Z ...→*wais* Quran.src

---

soc.religion.islam (NG) Discussions related to Islam. ✓**USENET**

Mormonism

The Book of Mormon Full text of the Book of Mormon at the FTP sites and a searchable database via WAIS. ✓**INTERNET** ...→*ftp* INFO.UMD.EDU→ANONYMOUS/<YOUR

EMAIL ADDRESS>→info/Reading Room/Mormon ...→*ftp* MRCNEXT. CSO.UIUC.EDU→ANONYMOUS/<YOUR EMAIL ADDRESS>→etext/etext91→mor mon13.txt ...→*wais* Book_of_Mor mon.src

---

LDS (ML) A forum for members of The Church of Jesus Christ of Latter-day Saints. ✓**INTERNET**→ *email* LDS-REQUEST@DECWRL.DEC.COM ✍*Subscribe by request*

Mormon Discuss the Church of Jesus Christ of Latter-day Saints. ✓**FIDONET**→*tag* DENVERNET

Mormon Texts Includes the *Doctrine, Covenants* and *Pearl of Great Price*. ✓**INTERNET** →*ftp* OAK. OAKLAND.EDU→ANONYMOUS/<YOUR EMAIL ADDRESS>→pub/msdos/mor mon

Quakers

soc.religion.quaker (NG) Forum for discussing the Religious Society of Friends. ✓**USENET**

Religious debate

alt.messianic (NG) Intense, often flame-degenerating religious discussion. ✓**USENET**

Religion Debate Discussions and arguments about religion, religious beliefs, and religious practices. Skeptics usually move their messages here after becoming too noisy on the atheist echo. Welcomes all debate, positive and negative, on religious indoctrination. ✓**FIDONET**→*tag* HOLYSMOKE

---

talk.origins (NG) Evolutionism-versus-creationism discussion. Read postings on the Vedic literature, Darwinism, etc. ✓**USENET**

---

talk.religion.misc (NG) For

debating ethics, morals, and religious beliefs. ✓**USENET**

Sects

alt.religion.scientology (NG) Discussion of Scientology, not just for supporters. ✓**USENET**

Osho/Sannyas Discussion about Osho, a.k.a. the Bhagwan Shree Rajneesh, and the *sannyas* experience. ✓**FIDONET**→*tag* OSHO

Shaker (ML) Discuss the history, culture, and beliefs of the Shakers. ✓**INTERNET**→*email* LISTSERV@UKCC. UKY.EDU ✍*Type in message body:* SUB-SCRIBE SHAKER <YOUR FULL NAME>

Swedenborgian Ideas The teachings of Emanuel Swedenborg (1688–1772), the philosopher who believed the Lord called him to revitalize Christianity with new ideas. ✓**FIDONET**→*tag* SWEDENBORG

Urantial (ML) Discuss *The Urantia Book*. Both scientific and theological perspectives are welcome. List is very chatty. ✓**INTERNET**→ *email* LISTSERV@UAFSYSB.BITNET ✍*Type in message body:* SUB URANTIAL <YOUR FULL NAME>

Unitarianism

UUS-L (ML) Forum for those interested in Unitarian Universalism. ✓**INTERNET**→ *email* LISTSERV@UBVM. CC.BUFFALO.EDU ✍*Type in message body:* SUB UUS-L <YOUR FULL NAME>

Other info

The Electric Mystic's Guide A listing of Internet-accessible sacred texts. ✓**INTERNET**→*ftp* COOMBS.ANU. EDU.AU→ANONYMOUS/<YOUR EMAIL ADDRESS>→coombspapers/otherar chives/soc-science-directories→reli-gious-e-texts-93dirctry.txt

Southwest Asia

Discussion on the Net about the subcontinent comes in three parts: politics, in the form of position papers, manifestos, and flames (try **soc.culture.indian** and **soc.culture.tamil**); culture, from the Dravidian languages (Tamil, Malayalam, and Kannada) to critiques of British bias in the *Encyclopaedia Brittanica*; and travel, a subject that commands tremendous passion. Recent advice from **alt.culture.karnataka**: "There are different opinions on traveling by air in India. Unless urgent the general consensus would be to avoid it."

Streetlife in India—downloaded from CompuServe's Graphics Corner Forum

On the Net

News

misc.news.southasia (NG) News on events in the Indian subcontinent. ▦ ✓**USENET**

India & Pakistan

alt.culture.karnataka (NG) Culture and language of the Indian state of Karnataka. ✓**USENET**

alt.culture.us.asian-indian (NG) For Asian Indians in the U.S. and Canada. Exchange news, recipes, and ideas. ▦ ✓**USENET**

alt.politics.india.communist (NG) For discussing communist parties in India. ✓**USENET**

alt.politics.india.progressive (NG) For progressive political discussions about India. ✓**USENET**

India (ML) An open, secular forum for expressing opinions about India, the Indian community, religious beliefs, and ideologies. Includes Indian news. ✓**INTERNET**→ *email* LISTSERV@UKCC.UKY.EDU ✎ *Type in message body:* SUBSCRIBE INDIA-D <YOUR FULL NAME>

The Indian News Network (ML) Discussion list for people from the Indian subcontinent. ✓**INTERNET**→*email* LISTSERV@UTAR LVM1.UTA.EDU ✎ *Type in message body:* SUBSCRIBE INDIA-L <YOUR FULL NAME>

Indology (ML) For academics interested in the study of classical India. Topics range from Indo-European philology and grammar to the exchange of e-texts. ✓**INTERNET**→*email* LISTSERV@LIVERPOOL.AC.UK ✎ *Type in message body:* SUB INDOLO GY <YOUR FULL NAME>

Khush (ML) For discussing the South Asian gay cultural experience. ✓**INTERNET**→*email* KHUSH-REQUEST@LONGHORN.TC.CORNELL.EDU ✎ *Subscribe by request:* <YOUR FULL NAME> <YOUR EMAIL ADDRESS>

Pakistan (ML) News from Pakistan. Includes Radio Pakistan News, Rupee exchange rates, tax and travel information, and more. ✓**INTERNET**→*email* LISTSERV@ASUVM. INRE.ASU.EDU ✎ *Type in message body:* SUB PAKISTAN <YOUR FULL NAME>

soc.culture.indian (NG) General discussions about India. ✓**USENET**

soc.culture.indian.telugu (NG) Discussion about the culture of the Telugu people of India. ✓**USENET**

soc.culture.pakistan (NG) Discussion of Pakistani culture, history, and politics. ✓**USENET**

Other nations

soc.culture.afghanistan (NG) Discussion of Afghan society. ✓**USENET**

soc.culture.bangladesh (NG) Discussion about issues related to Bangladesh. ✓**USENET**

soc.culture.nepal (NG) Discussion about Nepal. ✓**USENET**

soc.culture.sri-lanka (NG) Forum for discussing events in and the people of Sri Lanka. ✓**USENET**

soc.culture.tamil (NG) Covers the culture of the Tamil people. ✓**USENET**

Indian music

Indian Classical Music A database of Indian CDs, especially Hindustani music. ✓**INTERNET**→ *wais* indian-classical-music.src

rec.music.indian.classical (NG) Discussion about Hindustani and Carnatic Indian classical music. ✓**USENET**

World politics & cultures

In its short history, the Net has already played a dramatic political role: It was the one

constant and reliable source of information when the Eastern Bloc and Soviet Union collapsed. The Net's worldwide political coverage continues to be among the most thorough and detailed reporting on international events. The Institute for Global Communications (IGC) provides some of the most extensive computer networking on International Issues. Try its **PeaceNet** and **ConflictNet** for coverage of human rights, disarmament, and conflict-resolution techniques.

African woman—downloaded from CompuServe's Photography Forum.

On the Net

War & peace

Activ-L (ML) Devoted to discussions and news about peace, democracy, freedom, and justice. Amnesty International frequently posts bulletins. 🖳 ✓**INTERNET**→ *email* LISTSERV@MIZZOU1.MISSOURI.EDU 🖎 *Type in message body:* SUBSCRIBE ACTIV-L <YOUR FULL NAME>

alt.war (NG) Discussion of war. ✓**USENET**

Arms-L (ML) Commentary on policy issues related to peace, war, the arms race, national security, etc. ✓**INTERNET**→*email* LISTSERV@ BUACCA.BU.EDU 🖎 *Type in message body:* SUB ARMS-L <YOUR FULL NAME>

Disarm-L (ML) Discussions of military and political strategy, peace activism, disarmament issues, superpower interventions, Third World exploitation, etc. ✓**INTERNET**→*email* LISTSERV@ALBNY VM1.BITNET 🖎 *Type in message body:* SUBSCRIBE DISARM-L <YOUR FULL NAME>

Geo-Political International Relations Offers multilevel discussions about politics, religion, and other issues affecting international relations in areas like the Middle East. ✓**RELAYNET**→*number* 304

Global Observer A column about global relations and other cultures. ✓**PRODIGY**→*jump* GLOBAL VIEW

NATO Public Information Includes NATO fact sheets, the NATO handbook, speeches, press releases, and information on fellowship programs. ✓**INTERNET**→*ftp* BYRD.MU.WVNET.EDU→ANONYMOUS/ <YOUR EMAIL ADDRESS>→pub/history/ military/nato

PeaceNet/ConflictNet/Eco-Net PeaceNet serves peace and social-justice advocates worldwide in areas of human rights, disarmament, and international relations. Includes groups such as Greenpeace, the World Federalist Association and SANE/Freeze. ConflictNet serves those working for conflict resolution. Includes guidelines for choosing a neutral party, sample case development, extensive bibliographies, legislative updates, and newsletters. For a catalog of conferences from both networks, as well as for brochures and price information, FTP to their site. To sign up, send an email request. 🖳 ✓**INTERNET** ...→*email* SUPPORT@IGC.ORG ...→*ftp* IGC.ORG→ANONYMOUS/<YOUR EMAIL ADDRESS> $$

soc.politics.arms-d (NG) Discussion about arms control. ✓**USE-NET**

wars.n.history A mixture of news and discussion about world conflicts and history. Topics include active wars, history, trivia, and problem areas. ▨ ✓**BIX**→*conference* wars.n.history

World At Risk Uncensored news and views about world issues and influence groups, including conspiracy theories, the Trilateral Commission, imperialism, the environment, and political philosophies. ✓**FIDONET**→*tag* W_NEWS

World Talk Conference & United Nations News Includes official information from the UN: Proceedings of the General Assembly, UN Press Releases, UNICEF news flashes, global environmental news, announcements from the World Health Organization and other UN organizations, and articles from the UN magazine *World Perspectives*. ✓**FIDONET**→*tag* WORLDTK

Africa

Africa-L (ML) General discussion about African issues. ✓**INTERNET**→*email* LISTSERV@VTVM2.CC.VT.EDU ✍ *Type in message body:* SUBSCRIBE AFRICA-L <YOUR FULL NAME>

Africana (ML) Forum for discussing information technology and Africa. ✓**INTERNET**→*email* LIST SERV@WMVM1.BITNET ✍ *Type in message body:* SUBSCRIBE AFRICANA <YOUR FULL NAME>

Algnews (ML) Algerian news in French. ▨ ✓**INTERNET**→*email* LIST SERV@GWUVM.GWU.EDU ✍ *Type in message body:* SUBSCRIBE ALGNEWS <YOUR FULL NAME>

soc.culture.african (NG) Discussion about Africa and African cultures. ✓**USENET**

Swahili-L (ML) Discussions con-

ducted in Swahili. ✓**INTERNET**→*email* KUNTZ@MACC.WISC.EDU ✍ *Type in message body:* SUBSCRIBE SWAHILI-L <YOUR FULL NAME>

Tunisnet (ML) The Tunisia Network. ✓**INTERNET**→*email* LISTSERV@PSUVM.PSU.EDU ✍ *Type in message body:* SUBSCRIBE TUNISNET <YOUR FULL NAME>

U.S. and Africa Inter-continent Discussion General talk about issues affecting Africans and Americans. ✓**FIDONET**→*tag* USASA

Languages & folklore

alt.folklore.urban (NG) Discussion of urban legends, beliefs, and alleged facts of all types. Are there workers entombed in the Hoover Dam? What's in a Twinkie? Did a kid receive a death certificate when she sent back a defective Cabbage Patch doll? ✓**USENET**

Folklore (ML) Discuss folklore. ✓**INTERNET**→*email* LISTSERV@TAMVM1. BITNET ✍ *Type in message body:* SUB FOLKLORE <YOUR FULL NAME>

Foreign Language Forum Language conferences, including an Esperanto board; a job bank for translators, teachers, and students; and professional information. The libraries are crammed with resources (e.g., the Slavic library has Cyrillic fonts, texts in Russian, and much more). ▨✇ ✓**COMPU-SERVE**→*go* FLEFO

Interntl For those interested in conversing in a language other than English. ✓**SMARTNET**→*tag* INTERNTL

Languages and Cultures Study and practice other languages and learn about other cultures, including Spanish, German,

French, and Asian languages. ▨✇ ✓**DELPHI**→*go* GR FOR

Ortrad-L (ML) An interdisciplinary forum for studying oral traditions. Topics range from African oral traditions to the *Odyssey's* oral tradition. ✓**INTERNET**→*email* LISTSERV @MIZZOU1.MISSOURI.EDU ✍ *Type in message body:* SUB ORTRAD-L <YOUR FULL NAME>

rec.folk-dancing (NG) Discussions about folk dances, dancers, and dancing. ✓**USENET**

Wordnet Translation Services Documents and messages in any of more than 100 languages can be translated. ✓**DELPHI**→*go* MAI TRAN $$

Esperanto

Esperanto (ML) Discussions about Esperanto, the movement, publications, and more. Use of the Esperanto language is encouraged. ✓**INTERNET**→*email* ESPERANTO-REQUEST@LLL-CRG.LLNL.GOV ✍*Subscribe by request*

Esperanto BBS (BBS) Devoted to the language Esperanto. 416-731-2667

Esper-L (ML) Forum for discussing the Esperanto language. Free Esperanto lessons are offered. ✓**INTERNET**→*email* LISTSERV@TREARN. BITNET ✍ *Type in message body:* SUB ESPER-L <YOUR FULL NAME>

soc.culture.esperanto (NG) Discussion about the international language Esperanto. ✓**USENET**

Miscellaneous

Migra-List (ML) Covers international migration. ✓**INTERNET**→*email* MIGRA-LIST-REQUEST@CC.UTAH. EDU ✍*Subscribe by request*

Part 5

Business & Finance

5

Business news

Online business news is rapidly expanding, from pricey Dow Jones News Retrieval,

available via GEnie, with its searchable full-text editions of *The Wall Street Journal*, *Business Week*, *Fortune*, and *Forbes*, to economical **Business Headlines** on Prodigy or **UPI Business News** on Delphi for a quick update, to the popular **Hoover's Handbooks Company Profiles** on AOL for the rundown before a sales call or job interview. Try Delphi's **PR Newswire** for a corporate spin on the news.

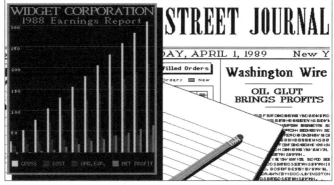

The Wall Street Journal—*from AOL's Macintosh Graphic Arts & CAD Forum.*

On the Net

Across the board

Business Database Plus Offers search and retrieval of full-text articles in more than 450 business and trade publications. ✓**COMPUSERVE**→*go* BUSDB $$

Business Headlines Current business news. 🖳 ✓**PRODIGY**→*jump* BUSINESS HEADLINES

The Business Wire Provides press releases, articles, and other business information. 🖳 ✓**COMPUSERVE**→*go* TBW

Dow Jones News Retrieval Service Searchable full-text articles from newspapers nationwide (e.g., *The Wall Street Journal* from January 1984 to today), the *Congressional Quarterly*, McGraw-Hill publications such as *Aviation Week* and *BYTE*, *Business Week*,

Forbes, *Fortune*, etc. Stock quotes and market reports, transcripts of *Wall $treet Week*, commodities quotes, extracts from Standard & Poor's, Media General, and much more. 🖳 ✓**GENIE**→*keyword* DOW-JONES $$

Economy Headlines U.S. and world economic news. 🖳 ✓**PRODIGY**→*jump* ECONOMY HEADLINES

UPI Business News Articles available from four news categories: general business, Wall Street, commodities reports, and market indexes. Select a single article or a range of articles. 🖳 ✓**DELPHI**→*go* BUS UPI

Company news

Company News Search by company or industry. 🖳 ✓**PRODIGY**→*jump* COMPANY NEWS

Company Screening Allows you to search the Disclosure II database for companies that meet certain criteria: growth rates, book values, financial ratios, etc. ✓**COM-**

PUSERVE→*go* COSCREEN $$

Corporate Affiliations gives profiles and references for most large U.S. public companies and their affiliates, including companies from the New York and American stock exchanges and the OTC markets. ✓**COMPUSERVE**→*go* AFFILIATIONS $$

Disclosure II A searchable database with company news compiled from the 10K reports and other information for public companies registered with the Securities and Exchange Commission. ✓**COMPUSERVE**→*go* DISCLOSURE $$

Dun & Bradstreet Offers thousands of company profiles, part of the Microsoft Small Business Center. ✓**AMERICA ONLINE**→*keyword* MSBC

Executive Desk Register of Public Corporations Search a database of "address book" company information—i.e., name, address, CEO and CFO names, telephone, ticker symbol, and exchange affiliation—by area or any of the above information. ✓**DELPHI**→*go* BUS REG

Hoover's Handbooks Company Profiles

The *Hoover's Handbook* database offers the most comprehensive and best-written profiles of public and private companies around the world available anywhere. Presented in an accessible and lively format, it includes all the nitty-gritty info—name, age, salary of top officers, plus phone, fax, address, and available sales and P&L data, for instance— that you're always desperately looking for. *Hoover's Handbook*'s publisher, The Reference Press, Inc., founded in 1990 by legendary Texas entrepreneur Gary Hoover, adds new companies to the database everyday. ✓**AMERICA ONLINE**→*keyword* COMPANY

PR Newswire

Press releases from thousands of companies, including many from the entertainment world, within minutes of their release. ✓**DELPHI**→*go* BUS PR

Thomas Companies & Products Online

Offers two databases: Thomas Register Online, with company information for almost 150,000 U.S. and Canadian manufacturers and service firms; and Thomas New Industrial Products, with technical information on new products from U.S. as well as some non-U.S. manufacturers and sellers. ✓**COMPUSERVE**→*go* THOMAS $$

Thomas Register of North American Manufacturers

Search for companies by product and products by company. Records include brief descriptions of the company including address information and a listing of its products and services. ✓**GENIE**→

keyword TREGISTER $$

TRW Business Profiles

Offers credit and business information on 13 million organizations, with credit histories, financial information and ratios, business size, ownership, tax liens, judgments and bankruptcies, and more. ✓**COMPUSERVE**→*go* TRWREPORT ✓**GENIE**→ *keyword* TRWPROFILES

Int'l companies

D&B Canadian Company Profiles

Search more than 300,000 companies for number of employees, SIC code, addresses, and telephone numbers. ✓**GENIE**→ *keyword* D&BCANADA $$

D&B European Company Profiles

Search more than 1.9 million companies for number of employees, SIC code, addresses, and telephone numbers. ✓**GENIE**→ *keyword* D&BEUROPE $$

D&B International Company Profiles

Search more than 3 million companies worldwide—not including the U.S. and Canada— for number of employees, SIC code, addresses, and telephone numbers. ✓**GENIE**→*keyword* D&BINTL $$

European Company Library

Directory and financial information for more than 2 million European companies, from a variety of business sources. ✓**COMPUSERVE**→*go* EUROLIB $$

Company analysis

Company Analyzer

Lets you enter a company name, ticker symbol, or CUSIP number to get a full range of financial information from a variety of financial services. The service builds a cus-

tomized menu of services with appropriate information: income statements, balance sheets, and ownership information. ✓**COMPUSERVE**→*go* ANALYZER

S&P Online

Provides Standard & Poor's Corporation recent information on 5,600 companies. Also includes S&P Master List, with buy recommendations, and S&P Investment Ideas, for stocks that S&P expects will outperform the market over the next 12 months. ✓**COMPUSERVE**→*go* S&P $$

Research

Corporate Affiliates Research Center

Search this database for information on company affiliates and relationships between companies. ✓**GENIE**→*keyword* AFFILIATES $$

D&B Dun's Market Identifiers

Offers searchable directories of three Dun & Bradstreet databases: D&B-Dun's Market Identifiers, D&B-Canadian Dun's Market Identifiers, and D&B-International Dun's Market Identifiers. ✓**COMPUSERVE**→*go* DUNS $$

D&B U.S. Business Locator

Search 8.7 million companies for number of employees, SIC code, addresses, and telephone numbers. ✓**COMPUSERVE**→*go* DYP ✓**GENIE**→ *keyword* D&BLOCATOR $$

Investext

Full-text company and industry research reports from the past two years. ✓**COMPUSERVE**→*go* INVTEXT $$

Trade Names Database

Search a database of more than 280,000 consumer brand names and owners. Records may include product description and distributor information. ✓**GENIE**→*keyword* TRADE-NAMES $$

Consulting & home office

The work-at-home dream goes hand in hand with a PC and a modem. Appropriately,

then, the Net offers a wide menu of information and services for anyone trying to get down to work in his or her den. Indeed, the biggest problem of working at home—loneliness—is nearly solved by the opportunities to chat with and complain to other people trying to do just what you're trying to do. The **Working from Home Forum** on CompuServe offers straightforward guidance on setting up, from software to tax issues. FidoNet's **Home Office** is a bit more chatty. You can talk about inertia and procrastination. If your home business involves computers, try **Consultants** on BIX and the newsgroup **alt.computer.consultants**.

Exasperated home worker—from AOL's Macintosh Graphic Arts & CAD forum.

On the Net

Consultants

Consulting A management-and-technology-consultants discussion area that includes starting and running a consulting business, developing clients, and networking. ✓**FIDONET**→*tag* CONSULTING ✖*Not a help area*

Consults Covers topics of interest to consultants. ✓**SMARTNET**→*tag* CONSULTS

Home office

CR Home Office *Consumer Reports* articles about home-office products. ✓**PRODIGY**→*jump* CR HOME OFFICE

Home Business A column from *Home Office Computing.* ✓**PRODIGY**→*jump* HOME BUSINESS

Home Office Running your own business or just plain working at home. Includes tax advice, networking, home-office stories, business-development ideas, and other advice. ✓**FIDONET**→*tag* HOME_OFFICE

Home Office BB For those interested in a home business. ✓**PRODIGY**→*jump* HOME OFFICE BB

Home/Office Small Business RoundTable For small-business owners, including those based at home. Topics cover financing, managing, marketing, and planning. ⊞ ☻ ✓**GENIE**→*keyword* HOSB

Office.at.Home Information on how to set up and run an office out of your home. ✓**BIX**→*conference* OFFICE.AT.HOME

Small Business Work at Home Offers advice and tips on taxes, equipment, marketing, and starting up a home business. ✓**RELAYNET**→*number* 170

WorkAtHome For those who work in their own homes, discussion about taxes, office design, and related topics. ✓**SMARTNET**→*tag* WORKATHOME

Working From Home Forum Gives people who work at home news, software, tips on home-office management, legal and tax information, marketing advice, and other resources. ☻ ✓**COMPUSERVE**→*go* WORK

Computer consultants

alt.computer.consultants (NG) Forum for computer consultants. ✓**USENET**

Computer Consultant's Forum Sponsored by the Independent Computer Consultants Association. Provides contacts and news for consultants, client tips, technical updates, and vendor contacts. ☻ ✓**COMPUSERVE**→*go* CONSULT

Consultants Discussions about computer consulting and contractors. ✓**BIX**→*conference* CONSULTANTS

PC Consultants Forum to discuss hardware, software, and technical writing. ✓**FIDONET**→*tag* PC_CONSULT

The economy

If you liked Ross Perot's "giant sucking sound," you'll love **alt.politics.economics**. "You should read any intro econ book," lectures a NAF-TA enthusiast "Freedom of trade has never, I repeat never, lowered a country's wealth." "You should read an economics book beyond the introductory level," replies an ever-ready-to-pounce protectionist. "It is completely possible that a country may lose by free trade." Before you jump in, back up your arguments with data from Prodigy's **Economic Indicators** area.

Data

Economic Indicators Check the current status of U.S. economic indicators. ▦ ✓**PRODIGY**→*jump* ECONOMIC INDICATORS

Emerging economies

Economy (ML) Focused on the economy and economic problems of less-developed countries. ✓**INTERNET**→*email* LISTSERV@TECMTYVM. MTY.ITESM.MX ✉ *Type in message body:* SUBSCRIBE ECONOMY <YOUR FULL NAME>

E-Europe (ML) For academics, researchers, and businessmen worldwide who are interested in the economies of Central and Eastern Europe and the CIS. ✓**INTER-**

John Kenneth Galbraith—from Compu-Serve's Reuters News Pictures Forum.

NET→*email* LISTSERV@PUCC.PRINCETON. EDU ✉ *Type in message body:* SUB E-EUROPE <YOUR FULL NAME>

Politics

alt.politics.economics (NG) Discuss the relationship between politics and economics. ✓**USENET**

Pol-Econ (ML) Forum for discussing topics within a political-economic framework. Includes tables of contents from relevant periodicals, conference announcements, calls for papers, etc. ✓**INTERNET**→*email* LISTSERV@SHSU.BIT NET ✉ *Type in message body:* SUB-SCRIBE POL-ECON <YOUR FULL NAME>

Research

Corryfee (ML) Information exchange for those doing research in the fields of economics,econometrics, and management. ✓**INTER-NET**→*email* LISTSERV@HASARA11.BITNET ✉ *Type in message body:* SUBSCRIBE CORRYFEE <YOUR FULL NAME>

Current Economic Issues Issues facing the U.S. and Canada. ✓**FIDONET**→*tag* ECONOMY_NOW

Economics Discussion of economic issues, including both policy and theory debates. ✓**ILINK**→ *number* 195

Femecon-L (ML) Information and professional support for female economists. ✓**INTERNET**→ *email* LISTSERV@BUCKNELL.EDU ✉ *Type in message body:* SUB FEMECON-L <YOUR FULL NAME>

sci.econ (NG) General discussions on economics, for professional and student economists. ✓**USENET**

sci.econ.research (NG) Offers discussion and contacts for current academic research in economics. ✓**USENET**

U.S.

Economic Bulletin Board (BBS) Includes press releases from the Bureau of Economic Analysis, the Federal Reserve (daily quotes on Treasury notes), and the Bureau of Labor Statistics as well as items such as a file with full contact information on trade opportunities collected by the U.S. Foreign and Commercial Service and the Treasury's Daily Statement. 202-482-2584/202-482-3870 $$

Cendata Government Information Offers bureau data on manufacturing, housing starts, population, agriculture, and more. Also includes latest press releases from the Census Bureau. ✓**COM-PUSERVE**→*go* CENDATA

Kimberly (BBS) National financial data and forecasts, securities-auction results, bank directories, Federal Reserve information, and online publications such as the *Fedgazette*. Also includes money facts and consumer-finance statistics. 612-340-2489 FREE

The markets

Journalist Joel Kurtzman calls the 1987 stock-market crash "adventures in Cyberspace" in his 1993 book *The Death of Money: How the Electronic Economy Has Destabilized the World Markets and Created Financial Chaos*. Kurtzman notes that despite trillions in losses, few people were irreparably harmed. If he's right, then CompuServe's **Current Quotes**, Prodigy's **Quote Check**, and Delphi's **Stock Quotes** aren't giving individual investors a daily dose of reality; they're only offering them a shot at virtual profit and loss.

On the Net

Quotes

About Quotes Information about using Quote Track and Quote Check. ✓**PRODIGY**→*jump* ABOUT QUOTES

Basic Quotes Gives delayed quotes for stocks, indexes, mutual funds, options, and exchange rates. Each quote has volume, high, low, and most-recent-trade information, plus an indication of current news on an issue. Allows retrieval of up to 20 quotes in a single session. ▦ ✓**COMPUSERVE**→ *go* BASICQUOTES

Citibank's Global Report Updated around the clock, the Report is a primary source for large com-

Edison's stock-market ticker—from CompuServe's Graphics Gallery Forum.

panies worldwide. Includes real-time exchange rates, spot commodity prices, and market and industry news, with six months of news on publicly held companies. ▦ ✓**COMPUSERVE**→*go* GLOREP $$

Credit Rates Provides current benchmark credit ratings, including the prime rate, the fed funds rate, and rates for federal T-bills, U.S. Treasury notes, and U.S. bonds. ✓**PRODIGY**→*jump* CREDIT RATES

Current Market Snapshot Presents key indicators for an up-to-the-minute market report, including highs, lows, and latest for the Dow Jones 30, the S&P 500, and the NASDAQ composite indexes. Also includes current currency and precious-metal prices. ▦ ✓**COMPU-SERVE**→*go* SNAPSHOT $$

Current Quotes Current market quotes, subject to a 15-minute delay. ▦ ✓**COMPUSERVE**→*go* QUOTE $$

Dow Jones Averages Reports

from the N.Y. Stock Exchange, updated every 30 minutes. ▦ ✓**DELPHI**→*go* BUS DOW

MarketPulse Includes the Dow Jones industrial average, market composite indexes, and snapshots of the most active stocks and biggest movers. ▦ ✓**DELPHI**→*go* BUS MARKET $$

Quote Check Quick stock quotes, subject to a 15-minute delay. ▦ ✓**PRODIGY**→*jump* QUOTE CHECK

Quote Configuration Customize Quote Track and Quote Check. ✓**PRODIGY**→*jump* QUOTE CONFIGURATION

Stock Quotes Prices (opening, closing, high, low) for more than 9,000 stocks, options, and mutual funds. ▦ ✓**DELPHI**→*go* BUS STO $$

Historical data

Highlights—Previous Day Analyzes the most recent trading day for the NYSE, Amex, and OTC market, with most-active stocks, largest gainers and losers, and more. ▦ ✓**COMPUSERVE**→*go* MARKET $$

Historical Stock Information Free historical stock information. ✓**INTERNET**→*ftp* DG-RTP.DG.COM→ ANONYMOUS/<YOUR EMAIL ADDRESS>→ pub/misc.invest

Issue Pricing History Provides 12 years of historical prices by day, week, or month for a given security. ▦ ✓**COMPUSERVE**→*go* PRICES $$

Multiple Issues—1 Day Gives volume, close/average, high/ask, low/bid, and CUSIP numbers for issues on a given day. ▦ ✓**COMPU-SERVE**→*go* QSHEET $$

Financial Markets Business & Finance

Price/Volume Graph Provides a chart showing price/volume graphs over a requested period of days, weeks, or months. 🖥 ✓**COMPUSERVE**→*go* TREND ✖*Requires CompuServe Information Manager for display* $$

Pricing Statistics Offers snapshots of price and volume performance of a requested issue over a given period. 🖥 ✓**COMPUSERVE**→*go* PRISTATS $$

UK Historical Quotes Daily price information for U.K. equities and market indexes. 🖥 ✓**COMPUSERVE**→*go* UKPRICE $$

Commodities

Commodity Markets Provided by MJK Associates, the database contains the open, high, low, settling, and cash prices of futures contracts, along with volume and open interest for every trading day over the past 12 years. Covers the U.S., Canadian, and select global exchanges that have significant futures-trading volume. Also includes composite prices from the Commodity Research Bureau. ✓**COMPUSERVE**→*go* COMMODITIES

Commodity Pricing Holds pricing histories, with performance by day, week, or month for each contract (or the contract nearest delivery). Displays open, high, low, and settling prices along with volume and open interest. Also holds aggregated volume and open interest for all contracts for each commodity, along with cash market price for the commodity. ✓**COMPUSERVE**→*go* CPRICE

Commodity Quotes Commodities quotes from the major world commoditites exchanges, available with a 15-minute delay. 🖥 ✓**DEL-**

PHI→*go* BUS COM $$

Commodity Symbol Lookup The commodity group listing includes foods, grains, metals, petroleum, fibers, financial, currencies, and indexes. Also has active contracts, access symbols, exchange where traded, and commodity descriptions. 🖥 ✓**COMPUSERVE**→*go* CSYMBOL

Background

Financial & Commodity News International and domestic commodities prices as well as commodities quotations, analyses of Wall Street activity, Standard & Poors, and Value Line indices. 🖥 ✓**DELPHI**→*go* BUS FIN $$

I/B/E/S Earnings Estimates The Institutional Broker's Estimate System, which includes annual and long-term company forecasts from more than 2,500 analysts at 130 brokerages and research firms. 🖥 ✓**COMPUSERVE** →*go* IBES $$

Index Symbol Lookup Gives the ticker and CUSIP number for all indexes in the MicroQuote II database, categorized into groups that include market/industry indexes, bonds/yields, exchange rates, volumes, and advances and declines. 🖥 ✓**COMPUSERVE**→*go* INDICATORS

List Bonds for Company Displays all active bonds for a designated company. ✓**COMPUSERVE**→*go* BONDS $$

Options Profile Lists all options currently trading on a given common stock or market index, with all relevant price information. ✓**COMPUSERVE**→*go* OPRICE $$

CYBERNOTES

"bandwidth n. 1. Used by hackers (in a generalization of its technical meaning) as the volume of information per unit time that a computer, person, or transmission medium can handle. 'Those are amazing graphics, but I missed some of the detail--not enough bandwidth, I guess.' Compare {low-bandwidth}. 2. Attention span. 3. On Usenet, a measure of network capacity that is often wasted by people complaining about how items posted by others are a waste of bandwidth."

—from the **Jargon File, ver.3.0.0**, Eric Raymond, ed. (eric@snark.thyrsus.com)

Stock Market Information Offers daily market reports, archived for historical data for the major markets, including the New York Stock Exchange and the American Stock Exchange. ✓**INTERNET**→*telnet* RAHUL.NET →GUEST/GUEST→market report ✖*VT100, Ansi, or another terminal emulator*

UK Issue Lookup Provides ability to look up stock exchange daily official list numbers for the U.K. exchanges. 🖥 ✓**COMPUSERVE**→*go* SEDOL

Financial planning

On the Net, you don't need basso-voiced financial advisers to help you make money the

old-fashioned way—you can earn it yourself. In fact, the options are so numerous that some people find themselves spending all their time online building and rebuilding their nest egg. You can analyze a loan in GEnie's **Loan Calculator**, apply for a credit card in Prodigy's **Banks Online**, and research zero-coupon bonds in America Online's **Your Money** area. Where balance sheets go, the taxman follows—the IRS offers electronic filing via its **Information Reporting Project BBS**.

On the Net

Across the board

Financial Financial news and advice. 🖥 ✓**BIX**→*conference* FINANCIAL

Financial General discussions of stocks, bonds, and investments, plus software useful to these topics. ✓**RELAYNET**→*number* 133

Kiplinger's Library Choose from several categories of articles on personal financial management. ✓**PRODIGY**→*jump* KIPLINGER'S LIBRARY

Kiplinger's Magazine Personal-finance info and advice. ✓**PRODIGY** →*jump* KIPLINGER'S MAGAZINE

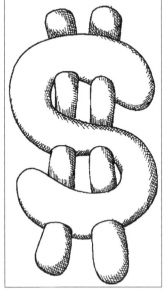

Inflated Dollar—from America Online's Mac Graphic Arts & CAD Forum.

Money Talk BB Discuss business, finance, and investments. ✓**PRODIGY**→*jump* MONEY TALK BB

News/Finance Forum includes national, international, sports, weather, feature, and business news—separated for your convenience. *USA Today* is also available. Stock-market quotes, the Microsoft Small Business Center, with invaluable resources for small businesses, the Ernst & Young Business Series, market news, and much more. 🖥 🖨 ®❤ ✓**AMERICA ONLINE**→*keyword* FINANCE

Worth *Worth* magazine online. ✓**AMERICA ONLINE**→*keyword* WORTH

Your Money Pull a file on "tax-exempt securities" or "zero-coupon

bonds." Set financial goals and get advice on how to meet those goals. Perhaps win a free financial analysis by AOL's financial-planning expert. ✓**AMERICA ONLINE**→*keyword* YOUR MONEY

Personal portfolio

Calculating Personal Finances Offers products that let you determine your net worth and create a loan-amortization schedule. ✓**COMPUSERVE**→*go* FINTOL

Return Analysis Service that helps you calculate annualized returns for your securities. ✓**COMPUSERVE**→*go* RETURN $$

Banking

Banks Online Apply for a credit card with Citibank or Discover. Bank online with Barnett, Peoples Bank, and many others. ✓**PRODIGY** →*jump* BANKS ONLINE

CR Banking & Loans Banking-related articles from the magazine *Consumer Reports*. 🖥 ✓**PRODIGY**→*jump* CR BANKING & LOANS

Heady on Banking News and advice from Robert Heady in his regularly featured column. 🖥 ✓**PRODIGY**→*jump* HEADY

Loan Calculator A program that helps you analyze your loan. One of its features creates a monthly-payment schedule based on information you input, such as loan amount, interest rate, and period. ✓**GENIE**→*keyword* LOAN

Consumer news

ConsumerAfair Discuss and review products and dealers. ✓**SMARTNET**→*tag* CONSUMERAFAIR

ConsumerIssues Discussions of personal experiences with vendors, mail-order companies, technical-support departments, etc. Consumer tips. ✓**ILINK**→*number* 119

Consumer Reports Full-text articles from *Consumer Reports*. 🖾 ✓**PRODIGY**→*jump* CR ✓**COMPUSERVE** →*go* CONSUMER $$

misc.consumers (NG) Discussions related to consumer interests and product reviews. ✓**USENET**

Taxes & disclosures

Annual Wage Reporting BBS (BBS) Employers can file W-2s and W-3s, and leave messages for the IRS or Social Security Administration. 410-965-1133 FREE

Block on Taxes Tax tips from Julian Block. ✓**PRODIGY**→*jump* BLOCK ON TAXES

Edgar Make or get complete SEC filings. ✓**COMPUSERVE**→*go* EDG $$ ✗*Special CompuServe software required*

Federal Taxation (ML) Discussion, from both academic and practical perspectives, of federal-taxation issues. ✓**INTERNET**→*email* LISTSERV@SHSU.BITNET ✍*Type in message body:* SUBSCRIBE FEDTAX-L <YOUR FULL NAME>

H&R Block The income-tax people. ✆ ✓**COMPUSERVE**→*go* HRB

Information Reporting Project BBS (BBS) For filing 1042S tax returns. Includes material relevant

to electronic filing. 304-263-2749 FREE

misc.taxes (NG) Discussions about tax laws. ✓**USENET**

Tax&Finance Covers tax-related issues. ✓**SMARTNET**→TAX&FINANCE

Taxes and Accounting Offers a forum for tax and accounting practitioners and government officials. Online experts—including representatives from IRS Taxpayer Services during the tax season— answer questions. ✓**RELAYNET**→ *number* 400

Tax Forum Offers answers to tax questions, software and tax guides, and online help from a tax accountant. ✆✍ ✓**AMERICA ONLINE** →*keyword* GOTAX

1040 BBS (BBS) An Internal Revenue Service board with electronic-filing information, forms, and bulletins. 202-927-4180 FREE

Electronic billing

CheckFree Pay your bills in just minutes each month without the use of checks. ✆ ✓**GENIE**→*keyword* CHECKFREE

Checkfree Corporation Electronic-payment service. ✆ ✓**COMPUSERVE**→*go* CF

Checkfree Software Support Conference Support for Checkfree software, which allows you to pay your bills electronically via the Federal Reserve System. ✓**FIDONET** →*tag* CHEKFREE

Software

ChipSoft RoundTable Support for users of ChipSoft products, which include the TurboTax series,

ChipLink, Payroll Toolbox, Client Organizer, and Tally Ho! ✆✍ ✓**GENIE**→*keyword* CHIPSOFT

Pers_Finance Information on personal financial software packages. Also covers tax-preparation software. ✓**ILINK**→*number* 209

Quicken For users of the financial-management program Quicken to share ideas. ✓**SMARTNET**→*tag* QUICKEN

Quicken Software Help Information on using the money-management software. ✓**FIDONET**→*tag* QUICKEN

Investments

"Is the end near for MedPhone???" asked a message on

Prodigy's **Money Talk** that got the author into quite a bit of trouble last year. He concluded: "This company appears to be a fraud. Probably will cease operations soon." MedPhone's stock dropped 50 percent and the company sued. On the other hand, when financial expert William Donoghue goofed on a stock pick, amateur investors flamed him to shreds. "I don't know Mr. Donoghue from Jack the Ripper, but it sure seems that some serious inconsistencies arise almost every time he puts his fingers to the keyboard," wrote one subscriber. "Do your homework," is the admonishment on many of these boards and newsgroups, "or you may receive a gentle barb or two."

On the Net

Across the board

Exec-PC (BBS) Probably the largest BBS in the world. Huge base of financial and investment information, and a large selection of shareware. 414-789-4210 $75/YEAR

Invest Topics range from financial programming to investment information to financial assistance.

New York, the world's financial heart—from CompuServe's Photography Forum.

✓**SMARTNET**→*tag* INVEST

Investors' Forum Features market-trends discussions, downloadable investment software, and conferences with money managers, brokers, and individual investors. ✓**COMPUSERVE**→*go* INVFORUM

Investor's Network Discuss investment strategies; use the library for financial decisions. ✓**AMERICA ONLINE**→*keyword* INVESTING

Investors RoundTable Ask investment questions, share ideas, discuss market theories with other investors, and download software, demos, and text files. Includes Charles Schwab brokerage services. ✓**GENIE**→*keyword* INVEST

misc.invest (NG) A forum for beginners to get advice on investing, discount brokers, retirement plans, zero-coupon bonds, and more. ✓**USENET**

The Wall Street Connection (BBS) Covers investing, financial issues, and small business. 808-521-4356 $30/YEAR

Brokers

Charles Schwab Brokerage Services Open an account and get a 10 percent commission discount off the Schwab rate. ✓**GENIE** →*keyword* SCHWAB

Dreyfus Corp. Service for those interested in investing in mutual funds. ✓**COMPUSERVE**→*go* DR

E*Trade, America's Electronic Brokerage An online brokerage service provided by Trade*Plus. ✓**COMPUSERVE**→*go* ETRADE

Max Ule Discount Brokerage Brokerage with financial information. ✓**COMPUSERVE**→*go* TKR

PCFN Account Discount brokerage service. ✓**PRODIGY**→*jump* PCFN ACCOUNT

Quick Way Online brokerage service from the discount broker Quick & Reilly. ✓**COMPUSERVE**→*go* QWK $$

Spear Rees & Company An online investment and brokerage service. ✓**COMPUSERVE**→*go* SPEAR $$

The TradePlus Gateway Follow the major exchange indices. Trade online with the Quick & Reilly brokerage firm. Use a portfolio-management system to keep your records up to date. ✓**AMERICA ONLINE**→*keyword* STOCKS→tradeplus gateway

Resources

Detailed Issue Examination Allows retrieval of trading status, recent price, dividends, risk measures, and capitalization for a single issue, along with stock, bond, and option historical data. ✓**COMPUSERVE**→*go* EXAMINE $$

Dividends, Splits, Bond Interest A database with stock, bond, and mutual-fund distributions information. ✓**COMPUSERVE**→*go* DIVIDENDS $$

DJSA Bulletin (BBS) Information on investments, financial services, mutual funds, and insurance. 305-572-3456 FREE

FundWatch Online A mutual-fund database provided by *Money Magazine* that allows screening and reporting on more than 1,900 professionally managed investments. ✓**COMPUSERVE**→*go* MONEY-MAG

The Investment Analy$t Stock quotes, detailed stock-performance analysis, and stock screening. Access company fact sheets and news articles, Zack earning estimates, and more. 📖 ✓**GENIE**→*keyword* ANALY$T $$

Investor's Glossary Investment terms defined. ✓**PRODIGY**→*jump* INVESTOR'S GLOSSARY

InvesText Reports on companies and industries by financial analysts from leading brokerages and research organizations. Reports include information such as sales and earning forecasts, market-share projections, etc. ✓**COMPUSERVE**→*go* IQUEST→2784 $$

Money Fund Report from Donoghue Updates by News-a-tron on the top 50 money funds. Reports include government-only money funds, tax-free money funds, and general-purpose money

funds. ✓**DELPHI**→*go* BUS MON $$

Portfolio Valuation Finds values of previously created portfolios for dates you select, and displays unrealized gains and losses. Uses continuously updated market prices. ✓**COMPUSERVE**→*go* PORT $$

Quote Track Investors create one or two portfolios with up to 15 securities each and receive updated stock prices and trading-volume figures every 15 minutes. 📖 ✓**PRODIGY**→*jump* QUOTE TRACK

Strategic Investor Premium investment information and analysis. Gives performance, expenses and asset composition, capital distributions, dividend yield, turnover ratio, and other statistics for more than 2,500 mutual funds. ✓**PRODIGY**→*jump* STRATEGIC INVESTOR $$

Trendvest Ratings and Portfolio Analysis Provides an investment-management system, client portfolio analysis, and Trendvest Ratings. ✓**DELPHI**→*go* BUS TRE $$

Twentieth Century Mutual Funds Offers mutual-fund investments. ✓**COMPUSERVE**→*go* TC

Publications

CR Investments Investment-related articles from *Consumer Reports*. ✓**PRODIGY**→*jump* CR INVESTMENTS

Futures Focus A weekly online newsletter for futures traders, published by News-a-tron. 📖 ✓**COMPUSERVE**→*go* ACI $$

Investment Digest Brendan Boyd's investment column. Boyd is both a syndicated newspaper

columnist who writes on financial issues and a book author. ✓**PRODIGY**→*jump* INVESTMENT DIGEST

Recommendations

Futures Focus Trading recommendations provided by the News-a-tron Corporation. ✓**DELPHI**→*go* BUS FUT $$

Independent Investors Research, Inc. Provides earnings forecasts and investment recommendations. ✓**COMPUSERVE**→*go* IIR

National Association of Investors Corporation Forum Educates long-term investors in finding quality companies and buying stocks at good prices. Members share portfolio-management information, software, and tips. 📖💬 ✓**COMPUSERVE**→*go* NAIC

Security Objective Services Publishes two newsletters. *Wall Street S.O.S.* analyzes technical trading patterns, while *Current Recommendations* follows trade-reversal offers, new trade orders, and all trade orders within the last 20 trading days. 📖 ✓**DELPHI**→*go* BUS SOS ✓**GENIE**→*keyword* SOS

Stock Market General talk about investment strategies, stock tips, mutual-fund advice, and other stock topics. 📖 ✓**FIDONET**→*tag* STOCK_MARKET

Wall Street Edge Investment recommendations and forecasts by experts offered daily. ✓**PRODIGY**→*jump* WALL STREET EDGE $$

Miscellaneous

International Investor's Forum Discussions about using personal computers to aid investors. ✓**FIDONET**→*tag* INVEST

Job search

Corporate downsizing and restricted hiring make the '90s
employment market a difficult place for established middle managers and recent college grads alike. The Net gives both baby boomers and baby busters a leg up on the competition, however, with career counseling, résumé assistance, and job listings. For example, FidoNet's **Forty Plus Job Transition Group** helps RIF'ed boomers with job placement and local support-group contacts. Twentysomethings can turn to Prodigy's **Job Market 2000** to find out how to position themselves, careerwise, for the next century. Members of both generations who want to angle for a job on the Net, or just impress the world with their experience, education, and personal interests, can post a CV in **misc.jobs.resumes**.

On the Net

Across the board

Employment and Jobs Conference All employment-related issues, including résumés and positions open. Sister conference of Job & Employment Offerings. ✓**FIDONET**→*tag* JOBS

Job Bank Offers both help-

Checking the Help Wanted ads—from CompuServe's Quick Pictures Forum.

wanted and position-wanted ads. Also includes résumé assistance and help with working at home. ✓**RELAYNET**→*number* 150

Job Market 2000 A report on the job market at the approach of the 21st century. ✓**PRODIGY**→*jump* JOB MARKET 2000

Want ads

E-Span A searchable database with employment ads. Updated twice weekly. ✓**COMPUSERVE**→*go* ESPAN ✓**GENIE**→*keyword* ESPAN

Job & Employment Offerings Postings by individuals and companies with positions open. ✓**FIDONET**→*tag* JOBS-NOW ✗*Strict and detailed conference rules. Read them before posting*

The Job Listing Area Offers three services for job hunters or employers: the E-Span employment database, with nationwide listings in several job fields; the Help Wanted-USA employment database for professionals, with nationwide listings collected from private consultants; and the Classifieds Bulletin Board, with ads

posted by other AOL members. ✓**AMERICA ONLINE**→*keyword* JOBS

Job Opportunities Job openings for those seeking them, and discussions about the job market. ✓**FIDONET**→*tag* EMPLOY

misc.jobs.contract (NG) Listings for contract work and general discussions of contracting. ✓**USENET**

misc.jobs.offered (NG) Job postings by individuals or companies—not for posting résumés or for discussions. ✓**USENET**

misc.jobs.offered.entry (NG) Entry-level positions posted. ✓**USENET**

misc.jobs.resumes (NG) For posting résumés only—not for discussion. ✓**USENET**

People's Electronic Exchange (BBS) Job listings in all fields in a classified format. 908-685-0948 $$

Poindexter Online (BBS) Employment ads and classifieds. 609-486-1983 $10 QUARTERLY

Career advice

Career Center Provides a professional job-counseling and guidance service, with examples of résumés and cover letters, and databases devoted to employment agencies, employer contacts, and occupational profiles. ✓**AMERICA ONLINE**→*keyword* CAREER

Careers Job-related discussions—locating a position, preparing a résumé, job interviews. Also state and national job listings. ✓**ILINK**→*number* 137

Careers BB Discuss jobs and careers. ✓**PRODIGY**→*jump* CAREERS BB

Dr. Job A weekly column covering career and employment issues—office politics to career moves. ✓GENIE→*keyword* DR.JOB

Forty Plus Job Transition Group A group of nonprofit organizations that provide job-placement and professional-growth support to their members. Local affiliates can be found in the calendar section of *The Wall Street Journal's National Business Employment Weekly.* Members include managers, executives and other professionals. ✓FIDONET→*tag* 40_PLUS_INFO

JobPlace (ML) Information exchange for career educators, job-search trainers, and interested others. Focus is on self-directed job-search training and job placement. ✓INTERNET→*email* LISTSERV@UKCC. UKY.EDU ✍*Type in message body:* SUB JOBPLACE <YOUR FULL NAME>

Motivation Offers discussion on a variety of self-help motivational techniques, including those of Dale Carnegie, Og Mandino, W. Clement Stone, and Zig Zeigler. ✓RELAYNET→*number* 374

Federal jobs

EMPLOY (ML) Offers information sharing, contacts, and leads on job opportunities in the federal government. ✓INTERNET→*email* EMPLOY-REQUEST@OTI.DISA.MIL ✍*Subscribe by request*

Federal Jobs (ML) Carries copies of the electronic postings of federal job openings, generally oriented toward current federal employees. ✓INTERNET→*email* LISTSERV@ DARTCMS1.DARTMOUTH.EDU ✍*Type in message body:* SUB FEDJOBS <YOUR FULL NAME>

Feds Provides a discussion area for federal employees and contractors, covering all issues. ✓RELAYNET →*number* 403

PayPerNet (BBS) Title 5 information. 202-606-2675/202-606-1876 FREE

POSH and FJOBS BBSs (BBS) The Federal Job Opportunity Board provides agency recruitment notices, a job database, and a message board for posting résumés and job notices. The Policy Operations and Staff Headquarters offers staffing, veteran, and affirmative-action information and recruitment. 912-757-3100 FREE

Regional

ba.jobs.offered (NG) Job postings for the San Francisco Bay Area. ✓USENET

Federal Job Information Center–Chicago Region BBS (BBS) Job postings, descriptions, and the SF-171 application form. 313-226-4423 FREE

Federal Jobs Board-NJ/ Philadelphia Region (BBS) Job-related conferences and federal job listings and information. 215-580-2216 FREE

FJobs BBS-Atlanta Region (BBS) Job listings for federal offices in the Georgia area. 404-730-2370 FREE

LA Online (BBS) Job listings for all fields in the Los Angeles area, especially freelance computer programming. 310-372-4050

ne.jobs (NG) Job postings for all fields in the northeastern United States. ✓USENET

CYBERNOTES

"My husband and I have struggled together through college. In April of 1994, we will be joyously graduating with respective bachelor degrees. We are young and childless. While not being tied down may seem great, it opens up so many possibilities that it really is frightening! This means that we will be conducting dual job searches with no real boundaries. Please help us set up a plan. We are both completely supportive of each other, and open to moving wherever our careers take us. But with less than 8 mos. to graduation, we are not sure what to do first. For instance, do we decide where we'd like to live then worry about finding jobs once we get there? Or do we go wherever we find jobs? How do we conduct long-distance job searches? Should we concentrate on finding a job for one, then the other look for a job once we move? As you can see, we need HELP!!!!"

—from America Online's **Career Center**

Managing & marketing

If you're the boss (or you plan to be someday), the Net can help you run your business

and reach new customers. CompuServe's **PR and Marketing Forum** includes professional hints on improving your company's image from the Public Relations Society of America. **TQM** on RelayNet provides a brief on the Total Quality Management methods used by Japan's corporate winners. Managers of firms that are already spiffy in appearance and efficient in operation might find that the **Intudm-L** mailing list can pump up a nascent brainstorm with its updates of the latest research on intuition and decision making in business.

On the Net

Across the board

alt.business.misc (NG) General discussions about managing your business, including how to start a business. ✓**USENET**

BizyNet Conferences on international trade, investors, home business, and employment. Member BBSs are those seriously committed to business discussions. Run from the BIZynet BBS. 619-283-1721/619-283-9956 ✓CHECK LOCAL BULLETIN BOARDS

Business Resource Directory

Impression of a manager—from CompuServe's Quick Pictures Forum.

Search the database to locate products, services, contractors, freelancers, associations, agencies, and other resources. Inquire about adding your business to the directory. ✓**GENIE**→*keyword* DIRECTORY $$

IQuest Business Management InfoCenter Lets you search a variety of IQuest databases for information on management research, marketing, and company news. ▦ ✓**COMPUSERVE** →*go* IQBUSINESS $$

Mac Business Forum Offers discussion on using the Macintosh for business, including software packages for accounting, presentations, spreadsheets, project management, and tax preparation. ◉♨ ✓**AMERICA ONLINE**→*keyword* MBS

Marketing/Management Research Center Offers access to nine databases with full-text and index references for business, man-

agement, and technical magazines; market- and industry-research reports; and company news releases. Databases come from ABI/ INFORM, Findex, McGraw-Hill, Infomat, FINIS, Industry Data Sources, PTS MARS, PTS New Product Announcements, and PTS PROMT. ✓**COMPUSERVE**→*go* MGMTRC $$

Quality Advice on how to bring quality to your business. ✓**ILINK**→ *number* 151

Translation Services Documents and messages in any of more than 100 languages can be translated into English. ✓**DELPHI**→ *go* MAI TRAN $$

Management issues

Business Travel Column on executive travel. ✓**PRODIGY**→*jump* BUSINESS TRAVEL

Businessware Reviews for top-selling business software. ✓**PRODIGY**→*jump* BUSINESSWARE

Disability and Job Accommodation Issues An international forum that discusses disability issues affecting employment. ✓**FIDONET**→*tag* ACCOMMODATION

Intudm-L (ML) For discussing research on the use of intuition in decision making. ✓**INTERNET**→ *email* LISTSERV@UTEPVM.EP.UTEXAS.EDU ⤷*Type in message body:* SUBSCRIBE INTUDM-L <YOUR FULL NAME>

IOOB-L (ML) Discussions related to industrial/organizational psychology and organizational behavior. ✓**INTERNET**→*email* LISTSERV@UGA. BITNET ✍*Type in message body:* SUB IOOB-L <YOUR FULL NAME>

Safeware Computer Insurance High-tech equipment insurance. 🖳 ✓**COMPUSERVE**→*go* SAF ✓**GENIE**→*keyword* SAFEWARE

Strategies for Business Provides a resource for business owners and managers, hosted by the staff of Attard Communications, a publishing and small-business consulting firm. Includes a weekly online column, marketing news, and legal and tax guides. ✓**AMERICA ONLINE**→*keyword* BUSINESS-KNOWHOW

TQM Offers discussion on Total Quality Management of business, including topics like statistical quality control, Hoshin planning, leadership and empowerment of workers, and quality function deployment. ✓**RELAYNET**→*number* 410

Trdev-L (ML) Information exchange relating to human-resource development. Includes conference notices, research, discussion of policy practices, etc. ✓**INTERNET**→ *email* LISTSERV@PSUVM.PSU.EDU ✍*Type in message body:* SUBSCRIBE TRDEV-L <YOUR FULL NAME>

Marketing

alt.business.multi-level (NG) For those interested in multi-level marketing. ✓**USENET**

Biz*File Search for company names, addresses, phone numbers, and yellow-pages information for more than 10 million U.S. and Canadian businesses. ✓**COMPUSERVE**→*go* BIZFILE $$

"Delight The Customer" (BBS) Focuses on customer-service issues, training, and information for telemarketing professionals. Also includes a jobs database and a list of BBSs with a business and professional focus. 517-797-3740 $57/YEAR

Market-L (ML) For marketers who want to discuss marketing-related topics. ✓**INTERNET**→*email* LISTSERV@UCF 1VM.CC.UCF.EDU ✍*Type in message body:* SUB MARKET-L <YOUR FULL NAME>

PR and Marketing Forum Offers information and contacts for all areas of PR, marketing, and corporate communications, including public affairs, social services, computer use, financial institutions, and government. Also provides information on the Public Relations Society of America (PRSA). 🖳🗨 ✓**COMPUSERVE**→*go* PRSIG

Advertising

Ad Campaigns Offers examination and critique of ad campaigns in all media: television, radio, billboards, magazines, and other print media. Other topics include agency practices and ethics; the mechanics of ad campaigns; effectiveness; and favorite ads. ✓**RELAYNET** →*number* 361

ADCON Network (BBS) Specializes in advertising, consulting, programming, and consumer information. 913-271-7107 FREE

Advertising Provides an area for exchange of hardware, software, ideas, and business topics between professionals in advertising, design, and marketing. ✓**AMERICA ONLINE** →*keyword* MBS

Location, location...

Someday soon, no doubt, your PC will be your broker. Sitting in New York, you'll be able
to take a virtual visit to the house of your dreams in Sausalito. Meanwhile, AOL does a pretty good job of offering national listings on **Real Estate Online,** and **RealPix**, a BBS, provides full-color photo displays of homes for sale. The newsgroup **misc.invest.real-estate** offers a long-term look at property investments. When you're ready to take the plunge, Delphi's **Mortgage Calculator** is nifty.

Real estate in New York—from CompuServe's Photography Forum.

Across the board

CR Real Estate *Consumer Reports* articles about real-estate-related topics. ✓**PRODIGY**→*jump* CR REAL ESTATE

Home & Real Estate Round-Table Discussions range from redecorating to landscaping to getting a mortgage. Includes a library of information as well as GIFs of homes and decorating projects. ✓**GENIE**→*keyword* HOME

Real Buying, selling, and renting real estate, with information on mortgages, leases, management, and more. ✓**FIDONET**→*tag* REAL

Real_Estate Discuss the buying and selling of property, as well as the use of computers to run a realty business. ✓**ILINK**→*number* 78

RealEstate Hints and guidelines for selling property. ✓**SMARTNET**→ *tag* REALESTATE

Real Estate Online Offers home-buying tips, mortgage guides, listings throughout the U.S., an "Ask Our Broker" board, and contributions from best-selling real-estate author Peter G. Miller. ✓**AMERICA ONLINE**→*keyword* REAL ESTATE

RealPix (BBS) Real-estate-oriented, with full-color pictures of listings. 702-566-6840 FREE

Assistance

Bruss on Real Estate A regular column written by a real-estate expert. ✓**PRODIGY**→*jump* BRUSS ON REAL ESTATE

The Homefinder Service Relocation service. ✓**COMPUSERVE**→ *go* HF

Neighborhood Report Pro-

vides summary demographic data for every U.S. ZIP code, including population, race, and age data; income distribution; housing information; and occupations of neighborhood residents. ✓**COMPUSERVE**→*go* NEIGHBORHOOD $$

Specialties

alt.co-ops (NG) Discuss cooperatives. ✓**USENET**

misc.invest.real-estate (NG) General discussion about property investments. ✓**USENET**

Mortgages

Mortgage Calculator Determine the term, interest rate, principal, or payments on a loan by entering three of the four variables. ✓**DELPHI**→*go* BUS MOR

Mortgages Mortgage information and rates. ✓**PRODIGY**→*jump* MORTGAGES

Small business

The Net offers a veritable MBA correspondence school for entrepreneurs. ILink's Small

Business will take you from concept through to financing your idea, setting up shop, and making your first sale. The newsgroup **misc. entrepreneur** is a good place to share and learn from war stories. **Ernst & Young Business Series** on AOL offers easy access to business reference materials. CompuServe's **Entrepreneurs Small Business Forum** provides feedback for both high fliers ("I am interested in starting an airline. I have the financing as well as Airstream 31s and 41s lined up"), and the more down-to-earth. ("Can anyone give me information on the manufacturing of socks?"). The Small Business Administration (**SBA Online**) is ready to guide you through the process of funding your dream.

Small businesses on a street in Detroit—from CompuServe's Graphics Gallery Forum.

On the Net

Across the board

Air Force Small Business RoundTable For small businesses trying to do business with the Air Force. Information about marketing and performing contracts for the Air Force and the Department of Defense. Includes reference materials, facts, tips, suggestions, and discussions. ✓**GENIE**→*keyword* AFSB3

The American Dream (BBS) Post your "business card" and become part of the board's business database. Need a florist, carpenter, or printer? See who else has posted a card. Use "remind me" to keep appointments. Oh, and you can also check your biorhythms. 606-342-6447 FREE

The Central Information Exchange (BBS) Includes a business directory, real-estate listings, and more. 212-234-5818 $39 QUARTERLY

Delight the Customer (BBS) Focuses on customer-service issues, training, and information for telemarketing professionals. Also includes a jobs database and a list of BBSs with a business and professional focus. 517-797-3740

Ernst & Young Business Se-

ries Offers articles about starting and managing your own business. ✓**AMERICA ONLINE**→*keyword* FINANCE

The Microsoft Small Business Center Articles and information for the small-business owner from the American Institute for Small Business, the American Management Association, the Cobb Group, Dun & Bradstreet, *Home-Office Computing*, Microsoft Corporation, *Nation's Business*, Heizer Software, the Small Business Administration, the U.S. Chamber of Commerce, and more. Arranged by topics such as international business, legal issues, marketing/advertising, women in business, etc. ✓**AMERICA ONLINE**→*keyword* MSBC

Money Talk BB Discuss business, finance, and investments. ✓**PRODIGY**→*jump* MONEY TALK BB

SBA Online (BBS) Information on a wide range of occupations, schedules of seminars and training programs offered all over the country, and a huge library of downloadable files covering information about grants, loans, résumé writing, and more. 800-697-4636 FREE

Small Business Get help on how to start and run a small-business enterprise from people who have done it successfully. ✓**ILINK**→*number* 65

Entrepreneurs

Business How to start and operate a business. ✓**FIDONET**→*tag* BUSINESS ✖*No advertising*

Business Forum Economic news, a consultants' database, business software, and discussion groups of interest to entrepreneurs. 🖥️💬 🔲 ✓**DELPHI**→*go* GR BUS

CEO Compete to rise to the top of your industry. 🎮 ✓**PRODIGY**→*jump* CEO

Creativity and Creative Problem Solving (ML) Forum for discussing topics such as creativity and new-product development, creativity in an organizational setting, computer-assisted creativity, and more. ✓**INTERNET**→*email* LIST SERV@NIC.SURFNET.NL ✎*Type in message body:* SUBSCRIBE CREA-CPS <YOUR FULL NAME>

Entrepreneur Conference For those who own their own business, the self-employed, and those who want to be. Coverage includes money-making ideas, legal matters, and other topics. ✓**FIDO-NET**→*tag* ENTREPRENEUR ✖*No multilevel marketing discussions*

Entrepreneur Magazine Shop for guides with information on specific small businesses. 🛒 ✓**COMPUSERVE**→*go* ENT

Entrepreneur's Small Business Forum An information and resource center sponsored by Entrepreneur Groups, the publishers of *Entrepreneur Magazine*, covering business start ups and entrepreneurial development. 🖥️💬 ✓**COMPUSERVE**→*go* USEN

misc.entrepreneurs (NG) Discussions about operating a business. ✓**USENET**

Strictly Business! BBS (BBS) An information exchange service for entrepreneurs. Also carries how-to information. 614-538-9250 FREE

Assistance

BusinessAdm Assistance and information for small businesses. ✓**SMARTNET**→*tag* BUSINESSADM

Business Incorporating Guide How to incorporate nationwide. 🛒 ✓**COMPUSERVE**→*go* INC

FEBBS Federal Highway Electronic Bulletin Board (BBS) Includes contract and procurement conferences, transportation-policy information, safety and system applications, and open discussions about the FHA. 202-366-3764

Navy Online Automation System (BBS) Includes information on Navy contracts for outside contractors and on computer security. 804-445-1121/804-445-1627 FREE

Reminder Enter information about an important event and GEnie mails you a reminder on the date of your choice. ✓**GENIE**→*keyword* REMINDER

Networking, research

Business Demographics Helps businesses analyze their markets, with reports tailored to geographical units. ✓**COMPUSERVE**→*go* BUSDEM $$

Commerce Business Daily Online database with the full text of U.S. Commerce Department publications, including all significant federal contracts, requests for proposals, and other government-contract data. ✓**COMPUSERVE**→*go* COMBUS ✓**GENIE**→*keyword* CBD $$

Phone*File Holds names, addresses, and phone numbers for more than 75 million U.S. households, searchable by name and address, surname, or telephone number. ✓**COMPUSERVE**→*go* PHONE-FILE $$

Sartre Collection (BBS) A free-access conference for executives looking for work and networking contacts; also includes Wealth-builders. 407-881-0358 FREE

SUPERSITE Provides demographic information from CACI on general demographics, market potential, and retail-sales potential. Reports can be generated on the entire U.S., states, counties, TV markets, Census tracts, ZIP codes, and other geographical areas. ✓**COMPUSERVE**→*go* SUPERSITE $$

Products

Executive Stamper Order rubber stamps, engraved gifts. 🛒 ✓**COMPUSERVE**→*go* EX

Penny Wise Office Products Brand-name low-price office products. 🛒 ✓**COMPUSERVE**→*go* PW ✓**GENIE**→*keyword* PENNYWISE

Part 6

Games,

Sports &

the Outdoors

6

Baseball

"You're a manager, in a crucial game. In the bottom of the 9th your team is ahead by a run, the home team is batting. Your ace closer messes it up and loads the bases with no one out. Now the juicy part..." The debates of the Hot Stove League, once confined to those winter days between seasons, have moved online to **rec.sport.baseball** and become a year-round activity. If you want to discuss situations, the eternal questions (who was better— Williams or DiMaggio?), the current pennant races, or the latest major-league trade, here's the place for it.

On the Net

Across the board

The Dugout Devoted specifically to baseball—news, chat, collectibles, stats, etc. There's also a Fantasy Baseball League, Simulation Baseball, a sports library, a sports news service, regular live conferences (The Bullpen, for example), as well as the Online Baseball Card Forum. 🖿 🎴 🎮 ✓**AMERICA ONLINE**→*keyword* GRANDSTAND→dugout

Internet Baseball Archive Includes simulated baseball software, major-league schedules, GIFs of the team logos, playing rules, major- and minor-league stats, and ticket information. 🎴

Pitching practice—from America Online's Graphic Arts & CAD Forum.

✓**INTERNET**→*ftp* EUCALYPTUS.CC. SWARTHMORE.EDU→ANONYMOUS/ <YOUR EMAIL ADDRESS>→baseball

Major League Baseball Discussion, facts, opinions, stats, and questions about the major leagues. ✓**FIDONET**→*tag* ML-BASEBALL

rec.sport.baseball (NG) Discussion with emphasis on the major leagues. ✓**USENET**

News

Baseball Coverage News, scores, schedules, and stats. 🖿 ✓**PRODIGY**→*jump* BASEBALL COVERAGE

Baseball Odds Who's favored to win tonight's game? Get the odds. 🖿 ✓**PRODIGY**→*jump* BASEBALL ODDS

Baseball Talk Prodigy's online baseball column written by ESPN's Peter Gammons. ✓**PRODIGY**→*jump* BASEBALL TALK

Teams

alt.sports.baseball.atlanta-

braves (NG) Dedicated to the Atlanta Braves. ✓**USENET**

Athletics (ML) Oakland A's discussion group. ✓**INTERNET**→*email* ATHLETICS-REQUEST@MAREDSOUS. ENG.SUN. COM ✉*Subscribe by request*

Bosox Mailing List (ML) Red Sox fans discuss the Sox. ✓**INTERNET**→*email* BOSOX-REQUEST@WORLD. STD.COM ✉*Subscribe by request*

Jays (ML) For Toronto Blue Jays fans. 🖿 ✓**INTERNET**→*email* JAYS-RE QUEST@HIVNET.UBC.CA ✉*Subscribe by request*

Mets (ML) A forum for Mets fans. ✓**INTERNET**→*email* METS-REQUEST@ ASD.COM ✉*Subscribe by request*

Pirates (ML) For fans of the Pittsburgh Pirates. ✓**INTERNET**→ *email* PIRATES-REQUEST@CATS.UCSC.EDU ✉*Subscribe by request*

San Francisco Giants (ML) Discussion about the San Francisco Giants. ✓**INTERNET**→*email* GIANTS-REQUEST@MEDRAUT.APPLE.COM ✉*Subscribe by request*

Twins (ML) For baseball fans in Minnesota. ✓**INTERNET**→*email* FANS@TWINS.CORP.SUN.COM ✉*Subscribe by request*

Minor leagues

Minor League Baseball (ML) Discussions about issues affecting the minor leagues as well as schedules, franchise changes, stats, and collectibles. 🖿 ✓**INTERNET**→*email* MINORS-REQUEST@MEDRAUT.APPLE.COM ✉*Subscribe by request*

rec.sport.baseball.college (NG) Discussions of collegiate baseball. ✓**USENET**

Card & board games

Unimpressed with the hundreds of razzle-dazzle shoot-'em-up games available for the

computer, some people still like to face opponents over a card table. To serve this constituency, Usenet offers strategy debates and electronic kibitzing on **rec.games.backgammon**, **rec.games.bridge**, and **alt.games.tiddlywinks**. And busy traditionalists who like to play at their leisure can find an outlet in America Online's **Play-By-Mail & Strategy Gaming Area**, where email replaces snail mail as the vehicle of choice for moves. Their winning combinations are described in **rec.games.pbm**.

Van Gogh's Night Café—*from gaurung.mcgill.edu.ca.*

and exchange hints on board games that do not have their own REC.GAMES group—e.g., Scrabble, Monopoly, Risk, the fantasy game Talisman, and military- and historic-simulation board games. ✓ **USENET**

rec.games.board.ce (NG) Discussion about the game Cosmic Encounter. ✓ **USENET**

rec.games.bridge (NG) Describe a play problem, recap an auction, and discuss the game of bridge in general. ✓ **USENET**

rec.games.diplomacy (NG/ML) Discussion of the board game Diplomacy, where players are pitted against each other in a battle of wits and negotiations. ✓ **USENET** ✓ **INTERNET**→*email* LISTSERV@MITVMA.MIT.EDU ✍ *Type in message body:* SUBSCRIBE DIPL-L <YOUR FULL NAME>

rec.games.go (NG) Discussion of Go, a two-player strategy game. ✓ **USENET**

Info & design

Game Designer's Forum Forum for game designers and fans

interested in game design, with two sections: computer and non-computer games. Share ideas and learn more about game design. ⊕💭 ✓ **AMERICA ONLINE**→*keyword* GAME DESIGN

GameBase A database with detailed information about noncomputer games and gaming companies. ✓ **AMERICA ONLINE**→*keyword* GAMEBASE

Play by mail

Play-By-Mail Games Forum Covers all kinds of commercial games, with some companies sponsoring CompuServe-only versions of their games. Talk about them online, or play via email and the message boards with others in the forum. Articles from several play-by-mail game magazines are available in library 14. 💭 ▦ ✓ **COMPUSERVE**→*go* PBMGAMES

Play-By-Mail & Strategy Gaming Area Lets you play games online using electronic mail and bulletin boards. Even if you have a busy schedule, you need only a short amount of time each week to send mail, plan moves, and react to your opponents. Play-by-mail includes sports games, war games, adventure games, and more. ▦ ✓ **AMERICA ONLINE**→*keyword* PBM

rec.games.pbm (NG) Discussions about a number of play-by-mail games—both ordinary mail and electronic—including Galaxy, Legends, and Duelmasters. ✓ **USE-NET**

On the Net

On the table

alt.games.tiddlywinks (NG) For fans of the game tiddlywinks. ✓ **USENET**

Board and Logic Games Includes computer simulations of classics such as Othello, Reversi, and Lunar Lander as well as the strategy game Aliens or multiplayer FlipIt. ▦ ✓ **DELPHI**→*go* ENT BOA

rec.games.backgammon (NG) Discussion devoted to backgammon. ✓ **USENET**

rec.games.board (NG) Discuss

Chess

The 36 MHz Mephisto Vancouver 68030 can be beaten—
if your USCF rating is 2,449 or better. In other words, if you're among the top twenty ranked men or the top four women you have fighting odds against the Mephisto. Anyone else hasn't much of a prayer. If you're looking for an honest challenge, find a machine that plays at least 300 points above your rating, recommends the newsgroup **rec. games.chess**.

On the Net

Across the board

alt.chess.ics (NG) Discussion about the Internet Chess Server. Check this group for server locations on the Net. ✓**USENET**

Chess Play traditional or Chinese chess, one-on-one or in a tournament. Or discuss the games. ⊞▣ ☜✧ ✓**BIX**→*conference* CHESS

Chess Besides move-by-move coverage of major international chess matches (with animated display and analysis), there's a tutorial for beginners, games, and discussion. ⊞▣ ✓**PRODIGY**→*jump* CHESS

ChessBoard (BBS) Provides listings of chess clubs and tournaments in the Chicago area, game files from national and international tournaments, message areas, tournaments, and chess software files. ⊞▣ 312-784-3019 FREE

A chessboard—from CompuServe's Graphics Plus Forum.

Chess Forum Play others in games of electronic postal chess. Includes U.S. Chess Federation ratings, chess news, and worldwide tournament updates. ☜✧ ⊞▣ ✓**COMPUSERVE**→*go* CHESSFORUM

Chess Hotline BBS (BBS) Includes correspondence chess play, chess data files, and Chessmaster's Corner for advice. ⊞▣ 310-634-8549 FREE

International Chess Users— from the novice to the grandmaster—debate chess topics and participate in individual, tournament, and play-by-mail chess games. ⊞▣ ✓**FIDONET**→*tag* CHESS

Rob Roy BBS (BBS) A huge selection of chess files, echoes, and message boards. Also carries hundreds of computer games and ham radio files. ⊞▣ 203-596-1443 FREE

Chess play

Chess Play online chess games, participate in tournaments, keep track with the scoreboard, or read their online instructions. ⊞▣ ✓**GENIE**→*keyword* CHESS

Chess Play chess through the message boards. ⊞▣ ✓**RELAYNET**→ *number* 232

Match talk

Chess Discuss strategies, tournament chess, and "postcard chess." ✓**ILINK**→*number* 84

Chess-L (ML) For discussing chess and organizing tournaments. ✓**INTERNET**→*email* LISTSERV@GREARN. BITNET ✍ *Type in message body:* SUB CHESS-L <YOUR FULL NAME>

rec.games.chess (NG/ML) Includes information about network chess games, chess foundations, ratings, and chess-playing software, as well as a forum for chess-related discussions. ✓**USENET** ✓**INTERNET**→*email* CHESSNEWS-REQUEST@ TSSI.COM ✍ *Subscribe by request:* <YOUR EMAIL ADDRESS>

Shogi-L (ML) Discussions and strategizing about Shogi, a chess-like game popular in Japan. ✓**INTERNET**→*email* LISTSERV@TECH NION.BITNET ✍ *Type in message body:* SUB SHOGI-L <YOUR FULL NAME>

Downloads

Photon Chess Traditional chess pieces fire laser guns, beam spitters, and more. Available for downloading. ⊞▣ ✓**GENIE**→*keyword* WINDOWS→software library→ photon.zip ✱*DOS only*

UChess Download this sophisticated chess game, which allows you to play against the computer or to watch the computer play itself. The Amiga software library has many other chess games. ⊞▣ ✓**GENIE**→*keyword* STARSHIP→library →Uchess217.LHA ✱*Amiga only*

Cycling

America Online's BikeNet leads the pack of cycling ser-
vices online. Sponsored by
four leading national bicycle
organizations—the Bicycle
Federation of America,
BikeCentennial, the International Mountain Bicy-
cling Association, and the
113-year-old League of
American Wheelmen—it's
one of AOL's most-visited
areas. There are central message sections covering bike
tours, racing, advocacy,
equipment, and classified
ads; the four sponsors also
offer their own message
board and libraries. A regularly scheduled Monday-
night conference (10 p.m.
Eastern time) discusses current issues important to the
bicycle community, with
guest speakers and topics
suggested by members. See
the General Topics board
for a schedule.

On the Net

Across the board

Bicycle Archives Includes files
on bike-locker vendors, travel-
ogues, bike-lights information,
articles on how to paint a bike, the
Bike Manager software program,
and much more. ✓**INTERNET**→*ftp*
UGLE.UNIT.NO→ANONYMOUS/<YOUR
EMAIL ADDRESS>→local/biking

*Biker—downloaded from America On-
line's BikeNet.*

Bicycles Provides information
and help to bike riders, with tips
on equipment, riding technique,
and upcoming events. ✓**RELAYNET**
→*number* 185

Bicycling Discussion for bicyclists of all types. Information on
equipment, repair tips, riding and
training, and races and tours.
✓**ILINK**→*number* 232

**Bicycling and Human-Pow-
ered Vehicles** Bicycle and other
human-powered-vehicle riding,
racing, commuting, touring,
repairs, and new technology.
✓**FIDONET**→*tag* BIKENET

BikeNet Offers biking and racing
guides, articles from bike periodi-
cals, and forums for the four
BikeNet sponsors: BikeCenten-
nial, the Bicycle Federation of
America, the International Moun-
tain Bicycling Association, and the
League of American Wheelmen.
⊕ ✓**AMERICA ONLINE**→*keyword*
BIKENET

Spoked Wheel Includes racing
information plus news and views
of bicycling by competitive and
recreational cyclists. ⊕ ✓**AMERI-**

CA ONLINE→*keyword* GRANDSTAND→
Spoked Wheel

On the road

rec.bicycles.racing (NG) Race
results, racing techniques, rules,
and organizations. ✓**USENET**

rec.bicycles.rides (NG) Discussions about tours and training or
commuting routes. ✓**USENET**

Sales & discussion

rec.bicycles.marketplace (NG)
Postings by those looking for or
wanting to sell bicycle equipment.
Includes equipment reviews and
names of businesses selling bicycle
components. ✓**USENET**

rec.bicycles.misc (NG) General
riding techniques, rider physiolo-
gy, injuries and treatment, diets,
and other cycling topics. ✓**USENET**

rec.bicycles.soc (NG) Discuss
cycling transportation, laws, conduct of riders and drivers, road
hazards, and sociopaths. ✓**USENET**

Technology

HPV list (ML) Discuss the design,
construction, and operation of
human-powered vehicles. ✓**INTER-
NET**→*email* LISTSERV@SONOMA.EDU ✍
Type in message body: SUBSCRIBE HPV
<YOUR FULL NAME>

rec.bicycles.tech (NG) Discuss
the engineering, construction, and
repair of bicycles and ancillary
equipment. ✓**USENET**

Tandem (ML) Forum for tandem
bicyclists. "A place to carry on
about tandems..." ✓**INTERNET**→
email LISTSERV@HOBBES.UCSD.EDU ✍
Type in message body: SUB TANDEM
<YOUR FULL NAME>

Fantasy role-playing

It all started with *Dungeons & Dragons*, the fantasy role-playing game that developed

split personalities in millions of nerdy, socially inept teenagers. Inevitably, these teenagers became nerdy, socially inept college students and introduced their obsessions and fantasy characters to the Net. The *D&D* role-playing game and its many variants are discussed on **rec.games.frp.dnd**. GEnie's **TSR Online RoundTable** offers information from the company that invented the game and its commercial spin-offs. America Online's **Role-Playing Games Forum** provides its own fantasy games, where you can play live online against other members.

Man on Pegasus—from lajkonik.cyf-kr.edu.pl.

On the Net

Across the board

Computer RPGs and Adventure Games General discussion, reviews, hints, and support for role-playing- and adventure-game computer software. ✓**FIDONET**→*tag* CRPGS

Gaming College Learn about role-playing games. ☻💬 ✓**BIX**→ *conference* GAMING.COLLEGE

GMAST-L (ML) Covers all role-playing games and their design. ✓**INTERNET**→*email* LISTSERV@UTCVM. BITNET ✍ *Type in message body:* SUB

GMAST-L <YOUR FULL NAME>

rec.games.frp.advocacy (NG) Defend or trash various role-playing games. ✓**USENET**

rec.games.frp.announce (NG) Announcements, not discussions, relating to role-playing games. Announce new games, conventions, and events. ✓**USENET**

rec.games.frp.marketplace (NG) Buy and sell role-playing-game materials. 📧 ✓**USENET**

rec.games.frp.misc (NG) Covers all fantasy role-playing not covered in the other FRP newsgroups. Topics include role-playing advice, product reviews, scenario ideas, gaming anecdotes, live-action role-playing and other related topics. ✓**USENET**

Roleplay Conference for playing role-playing games via messages. ▦ ✓**ILINK**→*number* 158

Role Playing Games Includes discussion about all types of role-playing games: fantasy, board, war, and science-fiction. ✓**FIDONET**→*tag* RECFRP

Role-Playing Games Discuss role-playing games. ✓**RELAYNET**→ *number* 138

Role-Playing Games Forum Discuss, play, and gather information on all board, paper, and text role-playing games. ☻💬 ▦ ✓**COMPUSERVE** →*go* RPGAMES

Game makers

The Illuminati BBS (BBS) Sponsored by Steve Jackson Games; offers files and discussion about their products, role-playing games in general, and cyberpunk culture. 512-447-4449

TSR Online RoundTable Includes *Dragon* magazine online, *AD&D Forgotten Realms* Headquarters, *Advanced Dungeons & Dragons* Support Center, Marvel Superheroes Support Center, TSR Books: Sample Chapters, etc. ☻💬 ✓**GENIE**→*keyword* TSR

Live-action

alt.games.frp.live-action (NG) Discussions about live-action role-playing. ✓**USENET**

Pyramid BBS (BBS) A gaming bulletin board with an entire area dedicated to live-action role-playing and discussion. Includes an area for the Interactive Literature Foundation. ▒▒▒ 703-912-9878 FREE

Ravenloft Mailing List (ML) For those interested in TSR's *Ravenloft* fantasy world and doomful things in general. ✓INTERNET →*email* RL-REQUEST@UMCC.UMICH.EDU ✍Subscribe by request

Online

Free-Form Gaming Forum Provides information and discussion areas for all interested in role-playing games, interactive play, and creative development. You may visit as yourself or "in character." ▒▒ ✓AMERICA ONLINE→*keyword* RDI

The Realms Fantasy role-playing games. ▒▒ ✓BIX→*conference* THE. REALMS

Role-Playing Games Forum Offers daily live role-playing games for every taste, with new games added regularly. Schedules and descriptions are posted for every game available. ▒▒ ✓AMERICA ONLINE →*keyword* RPG

Smasher Land BBS (BBS) Message bases, files, and utilities for AD&D, GURPS, Shadowrun, Fantasy Hero, Traveller, and other RPGs. Also provides a variety of online games. ▒▒ 614-593-8359

Dungeons & Dragons

AD&D Archive at Stanford Contains the UCR Guildsman, varous versions of the net spellbooks, character sheets, hex graph paper, Alpha's Spells, the Elf's Gamebook, the Net Monster Manual, the MU Spell List, the Spell Description Language, and

WATSFIC Tournament, as well as organized *Advanced Dungeons & Dragons* game material from REC. GAMES.FRP.DND. ✓INTERNET→*ftp* GREY HAWK.STANFORD.EDU→ANONYMOUS/ <YOUR EMAIL ADDRESS>→D_D

ADND-L (ML) All aspects of the *Dungeons & Dragons* and *Advanced Dungeons & Dragons* games covered, including new spells, new monsters, and more. ✓INTERNET→ *email* LISTSERV@PUCC.BITNET ✍*Type in message body:* SUB ADND-L <YOUR FULL NAME>

Advanced Dungeons and Dragons Despite the *Advanced Dungeons & Dragons* label, the discussions also cover the *Dungeons & Dragons* RPG, as well as novels and other material based on TSR's fantasy worlds. ▒▒ ✓FIDONET→*tag* AD&D

Dungeons & Dragons Discussion A discussion area for the D&D RPG. Players discuss ideas, experiences, and strategies. This is a discussion-only companion to the AD&D FidoNet conference. ✓FIDONET→*tag* DND ✗*No game playing*

rec.games.frp.dnd (NG) For discussions about the official rules in the *Dungeons & Dragons* and *Advanced Dungeons & Dragons* games. Topics include character classes, races, monsters, magic spells, and other powers. ✓USENET

Miscellaneous

alt.games.torg (NG/ML) Discussions about the Infiniverse and the fantasy role-playing game Torg. ✓USENET ✓INTERNET→*email* TORG-REQUEST@MORTICIA.CNNS.UNT.EDU ✍ *Type in subject line:* SUBSCRIBE <YOUR FULL NAME>

alt.pub.dragons-inn (NG)

Chronicles the activities and ongoing adventures of characters in the Dragon Inn pub and the City of Generica. Role-playing becomes more story telling, not gaming. Introduce your character and get involved. The stories are involved and complicated. The FAQ and archives of all that has transpired at the Inn and in Generica— indexed by subject—are available at the FTP site. ✓USENET ✓INTERNET→*ftp* NETCOM.COM→ANONYMOUS/<YOUR EMAIL ADDRESS>→pub/ mrhyde/APDI

GemStone III One of the key social arenas on GEnie. Enter, as whatever character you choose, the world of Kulthea. Interact in real time with other players as you seek treasure and glory, and fight to stay alive. Haggle over prices in the marketplace, react to and puzzle over the mysteries that emerge as the game develops, and, of course, use your character's strengths and powers against others. ▒▒ ✓GENIE→*keyword* GS3

Neverwinter Nights Software for an online version of *Advanced Dungeons & Dragons Forgotten Realms* adventure, created by TSR, Inc., is available from AOL. Rule books, bulletin boards, a chat lounge, and a software library are also available. ▒▒ ▒▒ ✓AMERICA ONLINE→ *keyword* ADD ✗*PC only*

rec.games.frp.cyber (NG) For discussion of several kinds of cyberpunk-related games and topics. ✓USENET

rec.games.moria (NG) Discussions about this game of wizards, spells, dragons, and monsters. Includes information on where to find the program on the Net. ✓USENET

Field, stream & outdoors

The outdoor community has a slightly uneasy relationship with the Net. The Cavers

mailing list, for instance, would prefer to be regarded as semiprivate. If too many people know where the good caves are, they aren't good caves anymore. And **rec.backcountry** proclaims that information is not a substitute for skill, while the NRA on **info.firearms** debates the merits of establishing email access. Men who shoot guns don't play with computers. On the other hand, many of the outdoors-related FAQs are nearly poetic. Try, for example, the FAQ on **rec.boats.paddle**: "It is difficult to find in life any event which so effectually condenses intense nervous sensations into the shortest possible space of time as does the work of shooting, or running an immense rapid. There is no toil, no heartbreaking labour about it, but as much coolness, dexterity, and skill as man can throw into the work of hand, eye, and head."

On the Net

Across the board

Camping Covers summer sports,

Saltwater—from CompuServe's Graphics Plus Forum.

including information on canoe trips, fishing, and more. ✓**SMART-NET**→*tag* CAMPING

Great Outdoors Covers every outdoor activity, including hiking, mountain climbing, fishing, swimming, and camping. ✓**RELAYNET**→*number* 193

Outdoor Forum Covers all aspects of camping, climbing, hiking, hunting, fishing, cycling, sailing, and winter sports. The NRA manages the firearm section. ◉🏃 ✓**COMPUSERVE**→*go* OUTDOORFORUM

Outdoor News Clips Full-text stories from AP, UPI, and Reuters on outdoor activities. ▦ ✓**COMPUSERVE**→*go* OUTNEWS

Outdoors For the best places to camp, turn to the Camping topic;

rock climbing, the Belay Ledge topic; hunting, the Hunting topic; etc. ◉🏃 ✓**BIX**→*conference* OUTDOORS

Outdoors Discuss outdoor-activities. ✓**ILINK**→*number* 101

Bird-watching

Birdcntr (ML) A clearinghouse for transcribed birding hotlines in the Central United States (Ohio, Ind., Mich.). One of the three hotlines operating under the auspices of the National Birding Hotline Cooperative. ✓**INTERNET**→*email* LISTSERV@ARIZVM1.CCIT.ARIZONA.EDU ✍ *Type in message body:* SUB BIRDCNTR <YOUR FULL NAME>

Birdeast (ML) A clearinghouse for transcribed birding hotlines in the East. ✓**INTERNET**→*email* LISTSERV@ARIZVM1.CCIT.ARIZONA.EDU ✍

Type in message body: SUB BIRDEAST <YOUR FULL NAME>

Birdwest (ML) A clearinghouse for transcribed birding hotlines in the West (N.M., Ariz., Calif.). ✓**INTERNET**→*email* LISTSERV@ARIZVM1. CCIT.ARIZONA.EDU ✍*Type in message body:* SUB BIRDWEST <YOUR FULL NAME>

rec.birds (NG) From "How can we help the injured finch?" to news from the Audubon Society to bird-watching discussions. ✓**USENET**

Boating & fishing

Boating General boating discussion. ✓**FIDONET**→*tag* BOATING

Boating Join the BIX Yacht Club, peruse the ads in the For Sale topic, discuss maintenance techniques in the Workshop, and explore computer applications and navigation in the Computers and Boating topic. ⊛☺ ✓**BIX**→*conference* BOATING

Boating Covers any boating topic. ✓**RELAYNET**→*number* 213

Fishing Discussions Conference for all types of fishermen—saltwater, fresh, and ice—and their big-fish stories. ✓**FIDONET**→*tag* FISHING

Maritime All issues connected with the sea, including vessels, sea sports, fishing, oceanography, and transportation. ✓**ILINK**→*number* 202

rec.boats (NG) For hobbyists interested in boating—from racing to maintenance topics. ✓**USENET**

rec.boats.paddle (NG) Discuss whitewater sports and experiences, including canoeing, kayaking, and rafting. ✓**USENET**

rec.outdoors.fishing (NG) Covers all aspects of fishing—from Florida fly-fishing to plastic worms. ✓**USENET**

rec.sport.rowing (NG) For rowers or those interested in the sport. ✓**USENET**

Sailing General information for sailors. ✓**FIDONET**→*tag* SAILING

Sailing Forum Offers discussion on all aspects of sailing, with visits and advice from sailing celebrities and experts. ⊛☺ ✓**COMPUSERVE**→*go* SAILING

Yacht-L (ML) Discuss yachting, design, technique, racing, and amateur boat building. ✓**INTERNET** →*email* LISTSERV@GREARN.BITNET ✍ *Type in message body:* SUB YACHT-L <YOUR FULL NAME>

Caving

Cavers (ML) For anyone interested in caving. Moderator wishes to keep the list exclusive and has threatened to discontinue service if subscriptions grow too quickly. ✓**INTERNET**→*email* CAVERS-REQUEST@ M2C.ORG ✍*Subscribe by request:* <YOUR FULL NAME> <YOUR EMAIL ADDRESS> <GEOGRAPHIC LOCATION> <CAVING EXPERIENCES>

Caving Includes information on the National Speleological Society, cave protection, the science of speleology, cave sporting, and cave rescues. ✓**RELAYNET**→*number* 401

Spelunker's Forum Discussions about caving. ✓**FIDONET**→*tag* CAVERS

Climbing

Mount-L (ML) Forum for mountaineers. ✓**INTERNET**→*email* LIST

SERV@TRMETU.BITNET ✍*Type in message body:* SUB MOUNT-L <YOUR FULL NAME>

rec.climbing (NG) Offers discussion and information on climbing around the world, techniques, competitions, and more. ✓**USENET**

Field hockey

rec.sport.hockey.field (NG) Discussion about field hockey. ✓**USENET**

Hunting & firearms

Firearms Covers the use of firearms in sport, hunting, collecting, and self-protection. ✓**RELAYNET**→*number* 205

Firearms (ML) Discussion group for sportsmen to discuss hunting, firearms safety, legal issues, maintenance suggestions, and other related issues—not gun control. ✓**INTERNET**→*email* LISTSERV@UTAR LVM1.BITNET ✍*Type in message body:* SUBSCRIBE FIREARMS <YOUR FULL NAME>

Firearms Technical Discussion Technical discussions for shooters, from novice to expert. Topics include hunting and self-defense. Political discussion should be kept to the Right to Keep and Bear Arms conference. ✓**FIDONET**→*tag* FIREARMS ✖*No political discussions*

Guns Technical information about handguns and firearms, particularly aimed at gun collectors. ✓**ILINK**→*number* 133

info.firearms (NG) NRA issues dominate the mostly political discussion. ✓**USENET**

rec.guns (NG) For discussion of shooting sports, training and safety, issues of defense, weaponry such as bows and knives, non-commercial announcements of firearms and accessories, and information but not debate on legislation. ✓**USENET**

rec.hunting (NG) Discussions about hunting—deer scents, tree stands, pickups, 7mm rem or 300 win mag, etc. ✓**USENET**

ShootingSport Conference for discussing shooting sports. ✓**SMARTNET**→*tag* SHOOTINGSPORT

Riding & archery

alt.archery (NG) Archery-related discussions and information. ✓**USENET**

Equine-L (ML) For horse enthusiasts and riders. ✓**INTERNET**→*email* LISTSERV@PCCVM.BITNET ✍*Type in message body:* SUBSCRIBE EQUINE-L <YOUR FULL NAME>

Horse Discussion Discussions of horses and horsemanship: all breeds and all riding styles. ✓**FIDONET**→*tag* EQUUS

rec.equestrian (NG/ML) Horse enthusiasts of all disciplines and levels of experience are welcome. ✓**USENET** ✓**INTERNET**→*email* EQUESTRIANS-REQUEST@WORLD.STD.COM ✍*Subscribe by request*

Scuba diving

rec.scuba (NG/ML) For discussion of scuba diving, snorkeling, dive travel, and other underwater activities. ✓**USENET** ✓**INTERNET**→*email* LISTSERV@BROWNVM.BROWN.EDU ✍*Type in message body:* SUB SCUBA-D <YOUR FULL NAME>

Scuba Forum for discussing scuba and diving. ✓**SMARTNET**→*tag* SCUBA

Scuba Diving For novices, sport divers, and professionals, including equipment reviews, dive training, favorite dive sites, and travel. ✓**FIDONET**→*tag* SCUBA

Scuba Forum Run by experienced divers; covers everything from scuba instruction and certification to careers in diving. @💬 ✓**COMPUSERVE** →*go* DIVING

Scuba Forum Includes information and commentary on general diving, dive instruction, dive medicine, still and video diving photography, and specialties like wreck, cavern, and cave diving. Also covers dive destinations around the world. @💬 ✓**AMERICA ONLINE**→*keyword* SCUBA

Scuba RoundTable Libraries of equipment reviews, dive sites, and accident reports. Bulletin boards with more than 50 categories for discussing, say, your last dive or "hanging around a dive shop on a rainy Saturday afternoon." @💬 ✓**GENIE**→*keyword* SCUBA

Scuba-L (ML) All scuba-related discussions or information welcome. From articles on the best places to dive to discussion about the newest technologies. ✓**INTERNET**→*email* LISTSERV@BROWNVM.BITNET ✍*Type in message body:* SUB SCUBA-L <YOUR FULL NAME>

Skating & skiing

rec.skate (NG) For discussions of all kinds of skating, including in-line (Rollerblading), speed skating, figure skating, and skating-skiing. ✓**USENET**

rec.skiing (NG) For anyone interested in snow skiing. ✓**USENET**

Ski Center Includes ski conditions and weather forecasts for slopes across the country, a ski-resort guide, and an inn directory. ✓**PRODIGY**→*jump* SKI CENTER

Skiing Covers everything from downhill to cross-country to snowboarding. Topics include reviews of equipment and resorts, opinions, stories, and tips on improving skills. ✓**RELAYNET**→*number* 415

Surfing & swimming

alt.surfing (NG) For discussing surfing. ✓**USENET**

rec.sport.swimming (NG) Discussion about training and swimming competitions. ✓**USENET**

rec.windsurfing (NG) For discussions of windsurfing. ✓**USENET**

Swim-L (ML) Any swimming-related topic open for discussion. ✓**INTERNET**→*email* LISTSERV@UAF SYSB.UARK.EDU ✍*Type in message body:* SUB SWIM-L <YOUR FULL NAME>

Wilderness survival

rec.backcountry (NG) Offers information on staying alive and having fun in backcountry areas, with postings on travel conditions, dealing with wild animals and plants, and more. ✓**USENET**

SurvNet General Discussion For exchanging information for wilderness survival. ✓**FIDONET**→*tag* SURVIVAL_ORIENTED

Wilderness Travel Covers wilderness fundamentals, including backpacking, camping, hiking, and mountaineering. Equipment recommendations and personal experiences are among the message topics. ✓**FIDONET**→*tag* WILDRNSS

Football

Sheer volume alone makes rec.sport.football.pro a must-
read for fans—more than
6,000 messages per month
are posted during the season. This past season, for
example, there were posts
about a poll of non-U.S.
Usenet football fans to determine their favorite team
(49ers), and an update on
an NFL computer ranking
devised at Cal Tech's Jet
Propulsion Laboratory ("I
had the spread going 9-2
picking winners with a
14.66 RMS deviation").
And there's always a flame
war going between fans of
rival teams ("The Bears will
CRUSH the Packers on
Sunday—I guarantee it!").

*The Buffalo Bills' Jim Kelly—down-
loaded from wuarchive.wustl.edu.*

On the Net

Across the board

50-Yard Line Contains a simulation football game, fantasy football, a Pro Picks contest, a library,
and the year's NFL schedule.
✓ **AMERICA ONLINE**→*key-
word* GRANDSTAND→50-Yard Line

Football An area with NFL odds,
schedules, draft news, statistics, a
regular Football Talk column,
Canadian and arena football news,
College football statistics and
schedules, and a fantasy football
league. ✓ **PRODIGY**→*jump*
FOOTBALL

National Football League
Friendly talk about the gridiron,
including facts and figures, opinions, questions, and commentary.
✓ **FIDONET**→*tag* NFL

rec.sport.football.college
(NG) Discussion of college football. ✓ **USENET**

rec.sport.football.misc (NG)
For any football topics, including
fantasy football leagues. ✓ **USENET**

rec.sport.football.pro (NG)
Forum for discussing professional
football. ✓ **USENET**

Football games

Fantasy Football Provides
online football statistics within
hours of the game's conclusion for
use in offline fantasy football
games. Also sells the Fantasy
Football League Software needed

to set up your own league. ✓ **PRODIGY**→*jump* FANTASY FOOTBALL

Fantasy Football Pool The big
winner wins $20 worth of GEnie
online time! Start by choosing a
16-player team and earn points
according to the real-life performance of your players in that
week's games. ✓ **GENIE**→*keyword* FOOTBALL

QB1 As you watch a televised
football game, predict the quarterback's next move, the referee's call,
etc., and gain points if you're
right. (You'll be competing against
others playing in bars and restaurants across the country.) At the
same time, chat live with other
GEnie players about the game.
✓ **GENIE**→*keyword* QB1

RFL & RBL Dedicated to fantasy
baseball and football sports leagues
—RelayNet Football League and
RelayNet Baseball League.
✓ **RELAYNET**→*number* 194

The Sports Forum Offers fantasy football leagues for members.
✓ **COMPUSERVE**→*go* FANS

Teams

**alt.sports.football.mn-
vikings** (NG) For fans of the
Minnesota Vikings. ✓ **USENET**

**alt.sports.football.pro.wash-
redskins** (NG) For fans of the
Washington Redskins. ✓ **USENET**

Miscellaneous

clari.sports.football (NG) UPI
football news. ✓ **USENET**

rec.sport.football.canadian
(NG) All about Canadian-rules
football. ✓ **USENET**

Hockey

Ask any hockey fan and he'll tell you: Hockey just doesn't get enough media coverage. Not true on the Net! In the middle of a baseball pennant race, when hockey is nowhere to be seen in the papers, hockey trade rumors fly, past defeats are re-hashed, and lineups are debated to death on the Internet team lists and the very active **Hockey-L**. And there is no shortage of hard news: Prodigy's **Hockey Coverage** features team schedules and the odds on tonight's games, and the newsgroup **rec. sport.hockey** lists more stats than any fan could possibly digest.

On the Net

Across the board

Blue Line Provides a fantasy hockey league, general hockey discussions, and a hockey library. ▦ ◉◗ ✓**AMERICA ONLINE**→*keyword* GRANDSTAND→Blue Line

---

Hockey Coverage Hockey news, team schedules and game reports, scores, odds, standings, and statistics. ▦ ✓**PRODIGY**→*jump* HOCKEY COVERAGE

North American Hockey Everything about ice hockey in North America and the world, including the NHL, minor leagues like the AHL and IHL, college hockey, other world leagues, and

A Detroit Red Wings goalie—from CompuServe's Quick Picture Forum.

the Olympics. ✓**FIDONET**→*tag* HOCKEY

---

rec.sport.hockey (NG) For discussions and news about the NHL, minor leagues, and college hockey teams. Includes schedule, trade, award, rule, and ownership information. ✓**USENET**

Leagues

AHL Newsletter (ML) News about the American Hockey League. ▦ ✓**INTERNET**→*email* AHL-NEWS-REQUEST@ANDREW.CMU.EDU ✍ *Subscribe by request*

ECHL Newsletter (ML) News about the Eastern Conference Hockey League. ▦ ✓**INTERNET**→ *email* ECHL-NEWS-REQUEST@ANDREW. CMU.EDU ✍*Subscribe by request*

Hockey-L (ML) Collegiate ice hockey discussions, scores, team information, schedules, etc. For discussion (L) or news only (D). ✓**INTERNET**→*email* LISTSERV@MAINE. MAINE.EDU ✍*Type in message body:* SUBSCRIBE HOCKEY-L OR D> <YOUR FULL NAME> <COLLEGE TEAMS OF INTEREST>

Teams

Boston Bruins (ML) For Bruins fans. ✓**INTERNET**→*email* BRUINS-REQUEST@CS.USASK.CA ✍*Subscribe by request*

Buffalo Sabres (ML) For Sabres fans. ✓**INTERNET** →*email* SABRES-REQUEST@POTTER.CSH.RIT.EDU ✍ *Subscribe by request*

Los Angeles Kings (ML) For fans of the Kings. ✓**INTERNET**→ *email* KINGS-REQUEST@CS.STANFORD. EDU ✍*Subscribe by request*

The Olympic Hockey Discussion List (ML) Covers Olympic hockey news and discussion. ✓**INTERNET**→*email* LISTSERV@MAINE. MAINE.EDU ✍*Type in message body:* SUBSCRIBE OLYMPUCK <YOUR FULL NAME> <YOUR FAVORITE COUNTRIES>

Philadelphia Flyers (ML) For Flyers fans. ✓**INTERNET**→*email* SETH @HOS1CAD.ATT.COM ✍*Subscribe by request*

San Jose Sharks (ML) Discussion about the San Jose Sharks. ✓**INTERNET**→*email* SHARKS-BYTES-REQUEST@MEDRAUT.APPLE.COM ✍ *Subscribe by request*

St. Louis Blues (ML) For St. Louis Blues fans. ✓**INTERNET**→ *email* JCA2@CEC1.WUSTL.EDU ✍ *Subscribe by request*

Vancouver Canucks (ML) For Canucks fans. ✓**INTERNET**→*email* BOEY@SFU.CA ✍*Subscribe by request*

Fantasy leagues

RBL & RHL Offers discussion about fantasy basketball and hockey leagues on RelayNet. ▦ ✓**RELAYNET**→*number* 344

Online games

Games are like a parallel universe on the Net, into which

residents of our space-time reality can disappear, never to be seen again. Many of them were last sighted entering an Internet MUD (multi-user dungeon) or MUSE (multi-user social environment), where players explore, and even alter, virtual worlds described on screen. Try the Internet's **Cyberion City** as an introduction. Others were lost in more familiar diversions offered by Prodigy's **Game Center**, America Online's **Online Gaming Forums**, GEnie's **Multiplayer Games RoundTable,** and CompuServe's **Games Menu**. Each has a range of trivia, adventure, combat, and sports games.

On the Net

Across the board

The Entertainment Center Offers multiplayer games with color graphics, including space combat and popular board games. Download games and meet fellow players from around the world. ▥ ✓COMPUSERVE→*go* ECENTER ✖*DOS only*

Game Center Access all the games on Prodigy from this main menu as well as related areas such as News (articles collected about

Ischade of the Bard Guild—from CompuServe's Role Playing Games Forum.

games), Poll (a Prodigy member survey of favorite games), and the Game Club (bulletin boards about specific types of games). ▦ ▥ ✓PRODIGY→*jump* GAME CENTER

Games Menu Offers access to a menu of CompuServe's basic games, including Hangman, Classic Adventure, Enhanced Adventure, CastleQuest, and BlackDragon. Also provides access to the rest of CompuServe's gaming areas and forums. ▥ ✓COMPUSERVE→*go* GAMES

Inter-BBS Games Discussions about games that can be played over the FidoNet network, including the games Barren Realms, Dwarz, and Tradewars. The general information includes league announcements and discussion. ✓FIDONET→ *tag* INTER_BBS_GAMES

Online Games Talk, help, and release notices for new games and updates. ✓FIDONET→*tag* ON_LINE_

GAMES

Online Gaming Forums Forums for role-playing games, free-form gaming, play-by-mail games, and war-gaming; a gaming information exchange; commercial-game-company support; and areas to discuss the games and share strategies. ▥ ◉? ✓AMERICA ONLINE→*keyword* GAMING

Prime Time BBS (BBS) Offers a variety of games, including backgammon, Yahtzee, Forbidden Lands, Sub-Striker, poker, and solitaire. ▥ 818-982-7271 FREE

Sierra Online A commercial service network devoted almost entirely to gaming. Log on to TSN and enter the environment of ImagiNation, where you can shop at the mall or go to the post office to pick up your email or stop at the telephone booth for online chatting. But where you are most likely to hang out is in one of the gaming sections: Sierra Land includes Graffiti for creating and animating works of art, Rocket Quiz for math competitions, Boogers for competing in a Reversi-style game, Red Baron for flight simulation, as well as Paintball and MiniGolf; in Clubhouse you can choose from a large selection of the computerized versions of traditional card and board games; LarryLand is for adults only and features several casino-style games (and adult conversation); and the popular MedievaLand is where the player assumes the role of a character he or she has created and embarks on adventures in the game Shadow of Yserbius—adventures that can last anywhere from days to months. For trial membership, contact Sierra by voice: 1-800-SIERRA-1. ◉ ▥ ◉? ✓THE SIERRA NETWORK

✖ *DOS only* DIFFERENT RATES

MUDS

alt.mud (NG) Includes MUD lists and requests for MUD information. ✓ USENET

Cyberion City One of the most popular and extensive socially oriented MUSEs on the Internet. A simulated 24th-century space colony where text descriptions and simple commands create and continually alter the environment. ▦ ◕❞ ✓ INTERNET→*telnet* MICHAEL.AI.MIT.EDU →GUEST/<NONE>

InfernoMOO Travel to Dante's *Inferno* or a MOO (MUD Object Oriented) based on the classic. Stumble into pits, play darts in the basement of the Blues Hotel, or wander around Hollywood Hell while passages from the *Inferno* appear and you socialize with the other inhabitants. ◕❞ ▦ ✓ INTERNET→*telnet* 129.238.20.32 2001

rec.games.mud.admin (NG) Offers guidance on creating and maintaining all types of multi-user games. ✓ USENET

rec.games.mud.announce (NG) Notices when MUDs open, close, or move. ✓ USENET

rec.games.mud.misc (NG) General-interest posts about MUD playing. ✓ USENET

rec.games.mud.tiny (NG) Discuss tiny MUDs, including MUSHs (multi-user shared hallucination), MUSEs, and MOOs, which are socially oriented multi-user environments. ✓ USENET

The Totally Unofficial List of Internet Muds (ML) Provides email updates of a list of Internet-

based MUDs. ✓ INTERNET→*email* MUDLIST@GLIA.BIOSTR.WASHINGTON.EDU ✍ *Type in subject line:* MUD LIST

Multiplayer

The Multi-Player Games Forum Get hints, discuss strategies, and meet other players from CompuServe's online multi player games, including British Legends, Island of Kesmai, You Guessed It, MegaWars, and Sniper. ▦ ✓ COMPUSERVE→*go* MPGAMES

Multiplayer Games Round-Table Features support, training, and discussion for all of GEnie's multi-player games, including A-Maze-ing, Air Warrior, Dragon's Gate, Federation II, Gemstone III, MultiPlayer Battletech, Stellar Emperor, and Stellar Warrior. ◕❞ ▦ ✓ GENIE→*keyword* MPGRT

The Multiple Choice The games offered includes trivia, word jumbles, achievement-test challenges, and personality profiles. For all ages. ▦ ✓ COMPUSERVE→*go* TMC

rec.games.corewar (NG) Discussion group about the game Core War, a seminal Internet game, where players write computer programs that battle each other for possession of the host machine. Includes information on Core War locations around the Net. ✓ USENET

rec.games.empire (NG) Discussion of the multi-user strategy game Empire. Includes Internet addresses for ongoing and new Empire games, which can have hundreds of participants. ✓ USENET

Sports Games Features sports-related games, some of which last an entire season, others a single online session. ▦ ✓ PRODIGY→

jump SPORTS GAMES

TradeWars Forum for discussing Trade Wars–style games. For players, utility authors, and sysops. ✓ RELAYNET→*number* 396

TW2002-L (ML) For discussing the "finer points" of the game Trade Wars 2002. ▦ ✓ INTERNET→ *email* LISTSERV@FERRIS.BITNET ✍ *Type in message body:* SUB TW2002-L <YOUR FULL NAME>

Adventure & strategy

Adventure Games Adventure and role-playing games including Colossal Cave and the French game Aventure—en Français. ▦ ✓ DELPHI→*go* ENT ADV

Diplomacy Devoted to the online game Diplomacy. ✓ RELAYNET →*number* 191

Diplomacy Discussion about the popular online game of strategy. ✓ SMARTNET→*tag* DIPLOMACY

First Internet Backgammon Server Play a game of backgammon online, watch other players, or engage in live conversation. ▦ ◕❞ ✓ INTERNET→*telnet* OUZO. ROG.RWTH-AACHEN.DE 8765→GUEST/ <CHOOSE YOUR OWN PASSWORD>

GO List (ML) Discussion forum and meeting place for those interested in the game Go. ✓ INTERNET →*email* MAILSERV@SMVAX.BITNET ✍ *Type in message body:* SUBSCRIBE GO-L <YOUR FULL NAME>

Internet GO Server Play a live game of Go, watch others play, or chat. ▦ ◕❞ ✓ INTERNET …→*telnet* HELLSPARK.WHARTON.UPENN.EDU 6969→GUEST/<NONE> …→*telnet* FLAMINGO.PASTEUR.FR 6969→GUEST/ <NONE>

PC & video games

If you're addicted to Flight Simulator but still can't get your F-16 to straighten up and

fly right, there's only one thing left to do. Cheat. CompuServe's **Electronic Gamer Archives** offers "walkthroughs" (in school they called them cheat sheets) of some of the most popular games made for personal computers, Nintendo, and Sega. More upright citizens can maintain their integrity and still pick up a hint or two from other players in GEnie's **Games RoundTable**. America Online's **GameBase** puts you in touch with the companies that make and sell the hottest new home video products.

Flight-simulation game—from CompuServe's Graphics Corner.

On the Net

Across the board

Apple II Games Forum Offers anything and everything about games for Apple Computers, plus Nintendo, Genesis, Turbo-Grafix 16, Sega, and more. Includes news and industry updates. ⚅💬 ▦
✓**AMERICA ONLINE**→*keyword* AGM

Chips & Bits Order software for adventure, role-playing, simulation, sports, war, and other games. ☂ ✓**GENIE**→*keyword* CHIPS

Digital Games (ML) A digest devoted to reviewing all types of computer and video games,

including those for the portable market. ✓**INTERNET**→*email* DIGITAL-GAMES-REQUEST@DIGITAL-GAMES.INTU ITIVE.COM ✍*Subscribe by request*

The Electronic Gamer Archives Offers reviews and walk-throughs (detailed, step-by-step solutions) for popular computer and cartridge games. ✓**COM-PUSERVE**→*go* TEG

Games Discuss commercial, shareware, video, and other games. ✓**RELAYNET**→*number* 134

Games BB Discuss games of all sorts. Topics include sci-fi games, arcade games, and flight simulators. ✓**PRODIGY**→*jump* GAMES BB

Game SIG Offers hints, reviews, product information, and discussion on all types of computer games, including Delphi's online role-playing and adventure games.

Among the group's topics are adventure, action/ arcade, sports, strategy/war, D&D, and board games. ▦▣ ⚅💬 ✓**DELPHI**→*go* GR GAME

Gaming Information Exchange Offers a forum for discussion and debate on gaming topics. Covers creation of new games, opinions on a new or existing gaming systems, a convention calendar, and game-rules questions. ✓**AMERICA ONLINE**→*keyword* GIX

rec.games.design (NG) Discuss game design of both computer and traditional games. ✓**USENET**

Computer

comp.sys.ibm.pc.games (NG) Offers discussion on games made for the IBM PC and compatible machines, including those using

MS-DOS, OS/2, and Windows operating systems. Covers new games, game companies, hints and spoilers, sales and trading, and help. ✓**USENET**

comp.sys.mac.games (NG) Discussions about computer games for the Apple Macintosh. ✓**USENET**

Game Publishers Forum Product demos, program updates, new releases, and news from selected publishers of computer games for all types of computers. ◉✿ ✓**COMPUSERVE**→*go* GAMPUB

Games List (ML) Discussions of computer games—any system. ✓**INTERNET**→*email* LISTSERV@BROWN VM.EDU ✍*Type in message body:* SUBSCRIBE GAMES-L <YOUR FULL NAME>

Games RoundTable by Scorpia Exchange hints, discuss strategy, download game-manual supplements, or leave suggestions for the game creators on the bulletin board. Covers adventure, action/arcade, sports, strategy/war, role-playing, and board games. ◉✿ ✓**GENIE**→*keyword* SCORPIA

Gameware Reviews for top-selling game software. ✓**PRODIGY**→*jump* GAMEWARE

Gaming Discuss all types of computer games. ✓**ILINK**→*number* 120

International Personal Computer Gaming Game discussions for PCs. Owners of Macs and Amigas are encouraged to use games forums for their machines to cut down traffic in this conference. ✓**FIDONET**→*tag* GAMING

PC Games Archive A major file site of public-domain games for IBM PCs and compatible machines. ✓**INTERNET**→*ftp* RISC.UA.EDU →ANONYMOUS/<YOUR EMAIL ADDRESS> →pub/games/pc

PC Games Forum Covers adventure games, arcade games, simulations, and all other types of computer games. Includes reviews and announcements. ⊞◨ ◉✿ ✓**AMERICA ONLINE**→*keyword* PGM

Sierra Online Computer games and accessories. ◔ ✓**COMPUSERVE** →*go* SI

Strategic Wargames Discuss your favorite computer war games —from strategies in Harpoon to tactics in Falcon 3. ✓**RELAYNET**→ *number* 409

ZiffNet Public Brand Software Arcade Forum A shareware library with hundreds of downloadable games and hobby programs, plus programs for use in the home, education, engineering, and math. ⊞◨ ✓**COMPUSERVE**→*go* ZNT: PBSARCADE ✖*DOS and Windows* $2.50/MONTH

Home video

alt.games.lynx (NG) Discuss games played with the Atari Lynx. ✓**USENET**

alt.games.video.classic (NG) Discuss the classics of video games, from Space Invaders to Pacman. ✓**USENET**

GameBase GameBase is an online game company and product database for use by gaming companies, game distributors, and the game buyers and players on America Online. Offers information on new editions of products, and the latest games and most recent inventories of the online game companies. Does not cover computer games. ▦ ✓**AMERICA ONLINE**→*keyword* GAMEBASE

The Gamers Forum Meet other computer gamers, discuss your favorite games, and keep up with the latest news, tips, and reviews, including information on Nintendo and other cartridge games. Several gaming magazines, such as *The Electronic Gamer*, *Strategy Plus*, and *Zapp!*, are archived in libraries 15 and 16. ◉✿ ▦ ✓**COMPUSERVE** →*go* GAMERS

Nintendo Covers all video games from Genesis to GameBoy. ✓**RELAYNET**→*number* 259

rec.games.video (NG) All aspects of non-arcade video games open for discussion. ⊞◨ ✓**USENET**

rec.games.video.misc (NG) General discussion about home video games. ✓**USENET**

rec.games.video.nintendo (NG) Discuss Nintendo and Super Nintendo. ✓**USENET**

rec.games.video.sega (NG) For general discussions of the Sega Genesis video games, including Air Diver, Arnold Palmer Golf, Fantasia, Sonic the Hedgehog, and Thunder Force III. ✓**USENET**

Videogame System Discussion Systems covered include the Sega Genesis, Sega Master System, Nintendo, NES GameBoy, Sega Game Gear, NEC TurboGrafx, NEC TurboExpress, Atari Lynx, and the Neo Geo machines. Includes reviews, hints, new-game announcements, and industry-development news. ✓**FIDONET**→*tag* VID_GAME

World of Video Games Along

Artist's rendering of a GameBoy—from America Online's PC Graphics Forum.

with general discussions about Nintendo, Genesis and other video game makers, participate in live conferences with industry experts and software writers. ▦ ◉♋ ✓**DELPHI**→*go* GR WORLD

Flight simulators

Air Warrior A GEnie favorite! Choose a MiG 15, a B-17G Flying Fortress, or a Yak9D, and enter enemy territory—the enemy being another player. ▦ ✓**GENIE**→*keyword* AIR ✘ *Requires downloading the front end to play*

Flight Simulation Forum Discussions about civilian, space, combat, and air-traffic-control simulations. Includes playing tips, software critiques, and "fly-ins" with other members. ▦ ◉♋ ✓**COMPUSERVE**→*go* FSFORUM

Flight Simulator (ML) Discussion topics range from hardware and software questions to product reviews to rumors. ✓**INTERNET** →*email* FLIGHT-SIM-REQUEST@GROVE. IUP.EDU ✉*Subscribe by request*

Flight Simulator Reviews Reviews, bug fixes and notices, screen snapshots, and other related infor-

mation. ✓**INTERNET**→*ftp* RASCAL.ICS. UTEXAS.EDU→ANONYMOUS/<YOUR EMAIL ADDRESS>→misc/av/simulator-folder

Flight Simulators All aspects of simulators discussed, including hardware, games, tips, new products, and multiplayer flying via modem. ✓**FIDONET**→*tag* FS

Flight Simulators For users of serious flight simulators, including Microsoft Flight Simulator and Flight Sim: ATP. All aspects of computer flying are open for discussion. ✓**RELAYNET**→*number* 355

rec.aviation.simulators (NG) Devoted to air- and spacecraft-simulation discussions, including game-related simulators. ✓**USENET**

Interactive fiction

Interactive Fiction Archive For those interested in developing author-adventure games—an archive of software, source code, binaries, and games. ▦ ✓**INTERNET**→ *ftp* WUARCHIVE.WUSTL.EDU→ ANONYMOUS/<YOUR EMAIL ADDRESS>→ mirrors/if-archive

Interactive Role-Playing Games Interactive role-playing games that are not fantasy-oriented. ▦ ✓**BIX**→*conference* D.HORI-ZONS

rec.games.int-fiction (NG) Discussions about interactive fiction games, ranging from the early classics such as the Colossal Cave Adventure to modern and non-text IF games. ✓**USENET**

Walkthrough Solution Files Solution files for many interactive fiction games. ✓**INTERNET**→*ftp* FTP.UU.NET→ANONYMOUS/<YOUR EMAIL ADDRESS>→pub/games/solutions

Modem-to-modem

Modemable Games Games that can be played user-to-user via modem, with information on tournaments. ✓**FIDONET**→*tag* MDM GAMES

The Modem Games Forum Meet other members who own modem-capable games, play head-to-head, and download dozens of one-on-one modem programs from the library. ▦ ◉♋ ✓**COM-PUSERVE**→*go* MODEMGAMES

Modem Games SIG Meet prospective opponents, discuss games, or organize a tournament. Games offered include ChessNet, Tele-cards (for gin rummy, cribbage and crazy eights), and several war-simulation/strategy games. ▦ ◉♋ ✓**DELPHI**→*go* ENT MODEM

The Modem-To-Modem Challenge Board Find opponents for your modem games using the MTM Board. Among the popular games covered are Armor Alley, Flight Simulator, Super Tetris, and Battle Chess. ▦ ✓**COMPUSERVE** →*go* MTMCHALLENGE

Arcade

Arcade Game Discussions Hints, tips, and reviews about arcade games, both the original and home versions. ✓**FIDONET**→*tag* ARCADE

rec.games.pinball (NG) Discussions about the game of pinball. ✓**USENET**

rec.games.video.arcade (NG) Dedicated to discussion about the maintenance, support, playing, and preservation of arcade video games. ✓**USENET**

Rotisserie baseball

First, name your team. Anything goes, like the Glimmer Kids, or the Bay City Bombers.

Next, start drafting your dream team of four pitchers and ten batters. Oh, and if you start Dwight Gooden, and five minutes before the game his real-life manager decides not to start him, it's a tough break for you, but these things happen. Finally, guess how many points your team will score that week. On GEnie's **Fantasy Baseball League** they'll do all the scoring for you. And every week and season they reward a successful Glimmer Kids or Mack's Monkeys manager with as much as $100 in free online time. CompuServe gives its top players prizes that range from team jackets to free trips to spring training.

On the Net

Baseball Manager Games are based on statistics gathered from real major-league games. Everybody starts with an imaginary budget of $18 million to build a team. Play for a full season or a third of a season. ✓ **PRODIGY**→ *jump* BASEBALL MANAGER $$

Computer Sports World (BBS) Offers access to a database of baseball statistics compatible with most fantasy and Rotisserie programs to help you manage your offline teams. Also provides widespread statistical coverage of all sports teams for a different price. 800-321-5562 $225/SEASON

Fantasy Baseball Pool Play a weekly version of Rotisserie baseball. Draft a team of new players each week, track their statistics, and add up the results—the winners receive free online time. ✓ **GENIE**→*keyword* BASEBALL

The Grandstand The Grandstand Fantasy Baseball League for AOL players is accompanied by newsletters, stats and standings, and more. ✓ **AMERICA ONLINE**→*keyword* GRANDSTAND→dugout

The Neon-Sign Baseball Statistics League (ML) A head-to-head Rotisserie league pitting fan against fan as each tries to assemble the best team of major-league players. ✓ **INTERNET**→*email* LIST SERV@SBCCVM.BITNET ✍ *Type in message body:* SUB STATLG-L <YOUR FULL NAME>

RFL & RBL Dedicated to fantasy baseball and football sports leagues—RelayNet Football League and RelayNet Baseball League. ✓ **RELAYNET**→*number* 194

The Sports Pages (BBS) Join a fantasy sports league or play in the Jack Nicklaus & Links Pro tournaments. 718-761-9513 FREE

The Sports Forum Offers season-long fantasy baseball leagues based on the original Rotisserie League baseball competition. End-of-the-season prizes awarded to winners. ✓ **COMPUSERVE**→*go* FANS

The USA Today Sports Center (BBS) Offers a comprehensive database of sports statistics to support your offline Rotisserie league as well as its own international fantasy baseball game (daily and weekly competitions). Provides the option of receiving a season of hassle-free downloads of the player statistics required to manage a team. Local access numbers available. 919-855-3491 $$

Batting practice—from America Online's Graphic Arts & CAD Forum.

Sports omnibus

There's talk and there's action. America Online's The Grandstand, GEnie's **Sports RoundTable**, CompuServe's **Sports Forum**, and Prodigy's **Sports** area are online versions of sports radio call-in shows, where everyone wants to fire the coach and trade the quarterback. Serious black belts discuss technique in the **rec.martial-arts** newsgroup. **The Dead Runners Society** mailing list offers training tips for marathoners. And the newsgroup **rec.sport.disc** reviews individual and team Frisbee games—disc golf, freestyle, and ultimate.

The Utah Jazz's Karl Malone—from CompuServe's Photography Forum.

On the Net

Across the board

The Grandstand A complete sports forum with sections devoted to baseball, football, basketball, hockey, boxing/wrestling, auto racing, and cycling. Another section is open to discussions of "other sports." There's a library, a news service, an arena for trading and discussing sports cards and collectibles, and much more. 🖥️ 📼 💬 ✓**AMERICA ONLINE**→*keyword* GRANDSTAND

Sports General chat about events on the field; baseball-card discussions are discouraged. ✓**FIDONET**→ *tag* SPORTS

Sports Converse about national and regional football, baseball, hockey, and basketball. ✓**ILINK**→ *number* 73

Sports Covers major spectator sports that are in season from a fan's perspective, including baseball, football, hockey, racing, basketball, and soccer. Also includes discussion on upcoming sports events. ✓**RELAYNET**→*number* 108

Sports Anything related to sports is open for discussion. Discuss the New England Patriots, the U.S. Open, or perhaps a specific brand of shin guards. ✓**SMARTNET**→*tag* SPORTS

Sports An elaborate offering of sports information and entertainment. Explore a particular sport (golf, skiing, soccer, football, etc.) or a particular type of activity (e.g., schedules, news, statistics). From the Sports menu, you can move to the Sports Play BB for participatory-sports discussions (e.g, shooting sports, running, hockey) or to the Sports BB for spectator-sports discussions (e.g., hockey-pro, college football, golf). If you're interested in news, there's Sports Highlights, featuring today's top stories, International Sports for sporting news from around the world, and a Sports News option for virtually every sport (e.g., basketball, auto racing, horse racing). Looking for schedules? See Sports Schedules (either on the specific sport's menu or the generic Sports Schedules menu. Are statistics your thing? Go to Soccer Statistics, Bowling Statistics, Skiing Statistics, etc. And if, say, basketball's got you hooked, then jump to Basketball Coverage, which carries stats for each team in the NBA, news, odds, scores, and schedules. There's also Sports Games, featuring Pick the Nightly Winners, Baseball Manager, and Prodigy Golf Tour. 🖥️ 🎮 📼 ✓**PRODIGY**→*jump* SPORTS

The Sports Forum Covers major-league baseball, NFL football, the NBA, NHL hockey, all the college sports, and the Olympics. Also offers fantasy baseball and football leagues for members. 🖥️ 📼 💬 ✓**COMPUSERVE**→*go* FANS

Sports RoundTable Sports news and statistics, sports gossip, a sports magazine, and libraries of information and software (e.g., the stretching FAQ or fantasy-football-league stats). The bulletin board carries discussion on numerous sports topics. 🖥️ 💬 ✓**GENIE** →*keyword* SPORTS

Basketball

rec.sport.basketball.college

(NG) Discussions about collegiate basketball. ✓**USENET**

rec.sport.basketball.misc (NG) General discussion about basketball. ✓**USENET**

rec.sport.basketball.pro (NG) Discussion about professional basketball—from last night's game to the latest trade rumors. ✓**USENET**

Collegiate sports

NCAA Collegiate Sports Network Provides news releases, current statistics, and national polls for college sports, including football, basketball, baseball, and softball in Divisions I, II, and III. 🖥 ✓**COMPUSERVE**→*go* NCAA

Cricket

Cricket (ML) Includes score sheets of first-class matches as well as tour itineraries. ✓**INTERNET**→*email* LISTSERV@VM1.NODAK.EDU ✍ *Type in message body:* SUB CRICKET <YOUR FULL NAME>

rec.sport.cricket (NG) Discussion about cricket. ✓**USENET**

rec.sport.cricket.scores (NG) Cricket scores from matches around the globe. ✓**USENET**

Fantasy leagues

RBL & RHL Offers discussion about fantasy basketball and hockey leagues on RelayNet. ✓**RELAYNET** →*number* 344

The Sports Pages BBS (BBS) Join a fantasy sports league or play in the Jack Nicklaus & Links Pro tournaments. There's also sports stats, news, and discussion. 🖥 📠 718-761-9513 FREE

Golf

Austads Golf Golf equipment and supplies. 🖨 ✓**PRODIGY**→*jump* AUSTADS GOLF

Golf-L (ML) All golf-related topics open for discussion. ✓**INTERNET**→ *email* LISTSERV@UBVM.CC.BUFFALO.EDU ✍ *Type in message body:* SUBSCRIBE GOLF-L <YOUR FULL NAME>

Prodigy Network Golf Challenge others to an online game of golf. 🖼 ✓**PRODIGY**→*jump* NETWORK GOLF ✖*IBM compatibles only* $$

rec.sport.golf (NG) Forum for discussing all aspects of golf—as a spectator and player. ✓**USENET**

Flying objects

Balloon (ML) Forum for balloonists when they're not in the air. ✓**INTERNET**→*email* BALLOON-REQUEST @LUT.AC.UK ✍*Subscribe by request*

rec.juggling (NG) Jugglers share tricks and technique tips. ✓**USENET**

rec.kites (NG) Discussions about kites and kiting—from fighter kites to kiting tricks. ✓**USENET**

Laser tag & paintball

alt.sport.lasertag (NG) Discussions about the game of laser tag. ✓**USENET**

rec.sport.paintball (NG) For discussing the game paintball. ✓**USENET**

Martial arts

Martial Arts Theory and Practice Focuses on the spirit of conflict and violence avoidance inherent in the martial arts.

✓**FIDONET**→*tag* EMPTY_HAND

rec.martial-arts (NG) Discuss various martial arts forms. ✓**USENET**

rec.sport.fencing (NG) Discussions about fencing. ✓**USENET**

Motor sports

alt.autos.karting (NG) For discussing the motor sport and hobby karting. ✓**USENET**

Auto Racing All types of car racing, with focus on drag racing, the Winston Cup, the Busch Grand National, and the World of Outlaws. ✓**FIDONET**→*tag* AUTORACE

Motor Sports Forum Offers news and information about car racing worldwide, with driver biographies, schedules, and racetrack information. 🖥 📷 ✓**COMPUSERVE**→*go* RACING

Motorsports Includes discussion of all types of motor racing, fan news, and upcoming events. ✓**RELAYNET**→*number* 135

rec.autos.sport (NG) For both participants and spectators of legal, organized auto competitions. ✓**USENET**

Olympics

Olympics Search for medalists by year, sport, or country. Also includes archives of information on the 1992 Olympics. 🖥 ✓**PRODIGY**→*jump* OLYMPICS

Running

The Dead Runners Society (ML) For runners of all levels and interests. Discussions range from meditation to marathon training in a relaxed, informal manner. ✓**INTERNET**→*email* LISTSERV@DARTCMS 1.DARTMOUTH.EDU ✍ *Type in message body:* SUB DRS <YOUR FULL NAME>

rec.running (NG) Includes discussion about marathoning, running injuries, training guides, nutrition, race schedules, the weather, and running clubs. A beginners' FAQ with advice for aspiring runners is regularly posted to the newsgroup. ✓**USENET**

Running and Being Offers a meeting place for runners and joggers, with training tips, encouragement, lists of upcoming races by region, and discussion of other aerobic activities. ✓**RELAYNET**→ *number* 264

Running and Related Issues Information on competitive and recreational running, for runners and non-runners, with nutrition updates, race announcements, and training tips. ✓**FIDONET**→*tag* RUNNING

T & F (ML) A track-and-field mailing list; for information contact Charlie Mahler at this address. ✓**INTERNET**→*email* LISTPROC@GAC.EDU ✍ *Type in message body:* SUBSCRIBE T-AND-F <YOUR FULL NAME>

Skates & boards

alt.skate-board (NG) "Wahoo. I just did a varial kick-flip and I'm happy." Discuss all aspects of skateboarding and share your successes with other skateboard enthusiasts. ✓**USENET**

rec.skate (NG) For discussions of all kinds of skating, including inline (Rollerblading), speed skating, figure skating, and skating-skiing. ✓**USENET**

Sports news

Associated Press Sports Wire The very latest scores, news, and league leaders in baseball, basketball, football, hockey, soccer, golf, and tennis, plus updates on the Olympics, college sports, and more. ▦ ✓**COMPUSERVE**→*go* AP-SPORTS $$

Other Sports Offers news, scores, and reports on sports including golf, tennis, and boxing. ▦ ✓**AMERICA ONLINE**→*keyword* TENNIS

The Sports Network Up-to-the-minute sports coverage on every major sports event as it happens. ▦ ✓**GENIE**→*keyword* SPORTS-NEWS

UK Sports Clips Contains full-text Reuters sports stories on cricket, snooker, track and field, rugby, and football (what Americans call soccer). ▦ ✓**COMPUSERVE** →*go* UKSPORTS

UPI Sports Sports news and statistics, including coverage of less publicized sports such as bowling and cycling. ▦ ✓**DELPHI**→*go* NEW SPO

Wrestling

Pro Wrestling Covers business and fan news on pro wrestling, for insiders, fans, and people who want to find out about the sport. ✓**RELAYNET**→*number* 379

rec.sport.pro-wrestling Discussions about professional wrestling. ✓**USENET**

Other sports

alt.sport.bowling (NG) Discussions about bowling. ✓**USENET**

alt.sport.bungee (NG) For discussing bungee jumping. ✓**USENET**

alt.sport.darts (NG) Discussions about the game of darts. ✓**USENET**

alt.sport.pool (NG) Discussions about the game of pool—from cue care to tournament recaps. ✓**USENET**

rec.sport.disc (NG/ML) Discussion of disc-based sports, such as Frisbee, ultimate, or disc golf. ✓**USENET** ✓**INTERNET**→*email* ULTIMATE-REQUEST@DOE.CARLETON.CA ✍ *Subscribe by request*

rec.sport.football.australian (NG) Discussion of Australian football. ✓**USENET**

rec.sport.misc (NG) General discussions about spectator sports. Boxing, anyone? ✓**USENET**

rec.sport.rugby (NG) Discuss the game of rugby. ✓**USENET**

rec.sport.soccer (NG) For discussing soccer. ✓**USENET**

rec.sport.table-tennis (NG) For discussing table tennis. ✓**USENET**

rec.sport.tennis (NG) A forum for tennis discussions. ✓**USENET**

rec.sport.triathlon (NG) A forum for discussing all aspects of multi-event sports. ✓**USENET**

rec.sport.volleyball (NG) Discuss techniques, rules, tournaments, and any other volleyball-related subject. ✓**USENET**

Miscellaneous

Schaap on Sports Column by Dick Schaap on the world of sports. ▦ ✓**PRODIGY**→*jump* SCHAAP

Part 7

Mind & Body

7

AIDS

Support and information. AOL's Gay & Lesbian Forum conducts regular meetings for HIV-positive members. **AIDS Memorial BBS Quilt** offers discussion around the Names Quilt Project. The information that's available is vast and timely. **CAIN (Computerized AIDS Information Network)** offers background for aggressive treatment. **CCML AIDS Articles** on CompuServe brings you up-to-date with full-text articles from the medical press. The **FDA Electronic Bulletin Board** reports on the latest drug testings and approvals.

On the Net

Across the board

AIDS Discussion of AIDS, its impact on society, and possible cures. ✓ILINK→*number* 205

AIDS Open and informative discussions about AIDS. ✓SMARTNET →AIDS

AIDS/ARC Discussion of AIDS/ARC/HIV information, for all audiences. ✓FIDONET→*tag* AIDS/ARC

AIDS-HIV Discussion Views and data on AIDS and HIV infection. Name-calling and derogatory remarks are not tolerated by the moderators. ✓FIDONET→*tag* AIDS_HIV

The Names Quilt Project—from CompuServe's Graphics Gallery Forum.

CAIN (Computerized AIDS Information Network) General HIV information and health-agency recommendations. Includes lists of treatment centers and hotlines, medical-journal articles and abstracts, a forum for discussion, as well as databases of information on financial, educational, organizational, and other relevant resources. ✓DELPHI→*go* REF CAIN

Gay & Lesbian Forum Includes a support group for those testing HIV-positive that meets weekly as well as a library of information. ✓AMERICA ONLINE→*keyword* GAY→HIV/AIDS Information

HIV/AIDS Information BBS (BBS) AIDS news and statistics, FidoNet conferences, an AIDS library, and a list of BBSs with AIDS sections. 714-248-2836

HIV/ARC/AIDS Offers public discussion about treatments, progress in research, and questions and answers on AIDS. ✓RELAYNET →*number* 347

The Recovery Room BBS (BBS) Conferences related to addictions and 12-step recovery programs as well as AIDS/HIV-support conferences and online chat support. 713-242-9674 FREE

sci.med.aids (NG) Information and discussion about AIDS treatments, the pathology/biology of HIV, and prevention. ✓USENET

Reference and data

AIDS HyperCard Stacks This HyperCard directory carries three AIDS stacks, including AIDS.SIT.HQX, which features a mortality clock tracking AIDS deaths; AIDSACADEMICCOURSE7.02.CPT.HQX, which documents AIDS issues in a black-and-white photo album; and AIDSSTACK.CPT.HQX, which provides information on AIDS. ✓INTERNET→*ftp* FTP. SUNET.SE→ANONYMOUS/<YOUR EMAIL ADDRESS>→pub/mac/misc/medical/hypercard

CCML AIDS Articles Offers a medical library with full-text articles from the medical press, including the *New England Journal of Medicine*, *Science*, and *Nature*. ✓COMPUSERVE→*go* CCMLAIDS $$

FDA Electronic Bulletin Board (BBS) FDA congressional testimony and speeches, reports on drug approvals, a magazine index to FDA stories, consumer information, and sections on AIDS. When dialing the BBS, log in with "bbs." 301-594-6849/301-594-6850 ✓INTERNET →*telnet* FDABBS.FDA.GOV→BBS/<NONE>

Miscellaneous

AIDS Memorial BBS Quilt An ongoing message version of the Names Quilt Project. ✓FIDONET→*tag* BBS_QUILT

Call 911!!

Disasters of all kind, from Hurricane Andrew to the World
Trade Center bombing to the carnage in Waco, to blood and guts wherever they spill, get some of their most intense—and detailed—coverage online. Paramedics and other first responders and uniformed services, as well as "citizen heroes," gather on the emergency-response newsgroups, forums, clubs, and BBSs. It's major-league reality programming.

On the Net

Across the board

Careers BB EMS professionals discuss work, pay, employment opportunities, and educational requirements while professionals and nonprofessionals share real-life stories and tips in the Medical/ Veterinary section. ✓**PRODIGY**→*jump* CAREERS BB

Emergency General discussion for EMS crews, fire fighters, police, and other public-safety officers. ✓**ILINK**→*number* 199

Emergency Medical Services General discussions about Emergency Medical Services. ✓**FIDONET** → *tag* EMS

The Emergency Response Club In the Tips and Techniques area, emergency-service professionals share the tricks they've learned in the field. The Open Forum is a

Hurricane Andrew approaches—from CompuServe's Graphics Corner Forum.

question-answer forum for professionals. The Medical Journal Library keeps the latest abstracts of professional articles. And in The Police Station, law-enforcement professionals share their experiences and answer safety questions from the public. ⊛🖳 ✓**AMERICA ONLINE**→*keyword* EMERGENCY

EMS Emergency Medical Services Conference. ✓**SMARTNET**→*tag* EMS

Fire and Emergency Medical Topics General discussion about fires, SCUBA, EMS, hazardous materials, and other emergency topics. ✓**FIDONET**→*tag* FIRENET

Fire/EMS Run by EMS employees—a conference for anyone interested in the EMS professions. ✓**RELAYNET**→*number* 239

Medical RoundTable Topics range from computer simulation in EMS training to fire-department paramedics/EMTs to trauma junkies. ⊛🖳 ✓**GENIE**→*keyword* MEDICAL

Safetynet Libraries, conference areas, and message boards on safety-related issues. Includes fire services, prevention and investigation, and emergency medical services. ⊛🖳 ✓**COMPUSERVE**→*go* SAFETYNET

Safety Professional's Forum Includes topics such as industrial hygiene and fire, chemical, and radiation safety. ✓**FIDONET**→*tag* SAFETY

Search & Rescue Discussions related to search and rescue. ✓**FIDONET**→*tag* SAR

911 systems

Emergency Communications Covers all aspects of 911 systems and other public-safety communications for police, fire, and EMS units, including dispatch training, equipment, and operations. ✓**RELAYNET**→*number* 381

EmergNet A network of emergency-services-related echoes. ✓CHECK LOCAL BULLETIN BOARDS

misc.emerg-services (NG) Discussions about 911 and E911 systems, Computer Aided Dispatch systems, radio and telephone systems, operating methods and procedures, and other aspects of communications operations in public-safety fields. Both professionals and citizens welcome. ✓**USENET** ✓**FIDONET**→*tag* ECOMNET

Other info

SafetyNet This national net covers safety in the public and private arenas. A list of BBSs carrying SafetyNet conferences can be found on the Safety Connection BBS at 503-744-1716. ✓CHECK LOCAL BULLETIN BOARDS

Fitness & nutrition

The formula for ideal body weight and tone is a combination of how-to, support, and

information. Trade recipes on ILink's **WeightControl**, get together with other people with eating disorders on the newsgroup **alt.support.diet**, and find out about fitness programs on the newsgroup **misc.fitness**. CompuServe's **Health and Fitness Forum** offers extensive news about nutrition and fitness. FidoNet's **Muscle and Fitness** is strong on weight-training programs and diet information.

Morning run—downloaded from CompuServe's Photography Forum.

On the Net

Across the board

Fit List (ML) Information exchange about exercise, diet, and wellness. ✓**INTERNET**→*email* LIST SERV@ETSUADMN.BITNET ✍ *Type in message body:* SUB FIT-L <YOUR FULL NAME>

Health and Fitness Provides information on weight-loss programs, fitness, and general health. ✓**RELAYNET**→*number* 267

Health and Fitness Forum Offers health news and support groups that deal with nutrition, exercise, and fitness as well as several other health issues. ☻📟 ▦ ✓**COMPUSERVE**→*go* GOODHEALTH

Dieting

alt.support.diet (NG) Support and information forum for those trying to lose weight or change

their diet. ✓**USENET**

Dieting Discussions about healthy diets, weight gain, and weight loss. ✓**FIDONET**→*tag* DIETING

Diets and Dieting Support group for issues related to dieting, including exercise. ✓**FIDONET**→*tag* DIETS ✖*No recipes*

OAsis for Compulsive Overeaters Eating-disorders discussion, especially about compulsive eating, plus information on the Overeaters Anonymous 12-step program. ✓**FIDONET**→*tag* OASIS

WeightControl Trade recipes and exchange experiences on dieting. ✓**ILINK**→*number* 183

Fitness

Athletics Discussion of fitness, diet, and exercise. ✓**ILINK**→*number* 136

CR Exercise & Recreation *Consumer Reports* articles on exercise and sports. ▦ ✓**PRODIGY**→*jump* CR EXERCISE & REC

misc.fitness (NG) Discussions

about physical fitness and exercise. ✓**USENET**

Muscle and Fitness Weight-training, nutrition, and fitness information. ✓**FIDONET**→*tag* MUSCLE

Large stature

alt.support.big-folks (NG) Support group for larger people. ✓**USENET**

Nutrition

CR Diet & Nutrition Articles from *Consumer Reports* on nutrition. ▦ ✓**PRODIGY**→*jump* CR DIET & NUTRITION

Nutrition Information and hints on diet and nutrition. ✓**FIDONET**→*tag* NUTRITION

sci.med.nutrition (NG) Discussion about the physiological impacts of diet. ✓**USENET**

Vitamins

Vitamin Express Vitamins and health- and skin-care products. ⊖ ✓**PRODIGY**→*jump* VITAMIN EXPRESS

Health & Illness

The Net is about information, which, for patients and their families, means empowerment. The information and data that used to belong exclusively to "the doctor" are now more and more available from online databases and support groups. **Physician Data Query** on CompuServe offers databases from the National Cancer Institute. The **Diabetes Forum** on CompuServe provides both info and contacts. **The National Alliance for the Mentally Ill** on AOL brings you up-to-date on the latest research. The newsgroup **alt.suicide. holiday** takes you the final step.

On the Net

Across the board

Ask a Nurse Discuss health issues with nurses. If posting about sensitive subjects, you're encouraged to use an alias. ✓**FIDO-NET**→*tag* ASK_ A_NURSE

Ask the Doctor General health discussions for laypeople and physicians. ✓**FIDONET**→*tag* ASK_ THE_DOCTOR

Better Health and Medical Forum For both consumers and health professionals interested in health. Provides a database of documents on prevention, diseases,

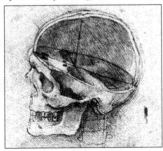
Human skull—downloaded from biome.bio.dfo.ca.

tests, medications, technologies, and health reform as well as message boards for exchanging health-related information and asking questions. Boards range from Lifestyles & Wellness to Patients' Rights. ◉ ✓**AMERICA ONLINE**→ *keyword* HEALTH

Grand Rounds Medical Information Medical and health information for laymen. ✓**FIDONET**→*tag* GRAND_ROUNDS

Health Talk with health professionals about any health-care or medical issue. ✓**ILINK**→*number* 72

Health and Fitness Forum Offers health news and support groups that deal with nutrition, exercise, fitness, mental health, emotional and family health, food, the elderly, substance abuse, environmental hazards, and alternative health care. ◉ ▦ ✓**COMPUSERVE** →*go* GOODHEALTH

Health & Lifestyles BB Bulletin board covering general health-related topics and issues. Topics include the Women's Health Initiative, Diet, Holistic Medicine,

Exercise, and Parenting. ✓**PRODIGY** →*jump* HEALTH BB

Medical Includes coverage of new medical techniques, current health issues, the use of computers in medicine, and general information. Hosted by a pair of M.D.'s who offer bulletins for non–medical professionals. ✓**RELAYNET**→ *number* 111

Medical For anyone interested in medicine. Physicians and medical professionals participate in the discussions. ✓**SMARTNET**→*tag* MEDICAL

Medical Support BB Members discuss medical issues. ✓**PRODIGY** →*jump* MEDICAL SUPPORT BB

Survivor A support group for people coping with serious illness, especially cancer, leukemia, blood and bone-marrow disorders, and immune-system damage. Information includes pediatric oncology and hematology, book reviews, event notices, and personal testimonies. ✓**FIDONET**→*tag* SURVIVOR

Cancer

alt.support.cancer (NG) Support forum for those dealing with cancer. ✓**USENET**

Cancer Forum Offers cancer information and support for cancer patients and their loved ones. The support staff includes forum members and the Kansas City Cancer Hotline. ◉ ✓**COM-PUSERVE**→*go* CANCER

Cancer Recovery Offers peer-group discussion for recovering cancer victims and others looking for information on fighting the disease. ✓**RELAYNET**→*number* 342

Cancer Survivors Support-group discussions on surviving cancer for patients, family, and friends. ✓**FIDONET**→*tag* CARCINOMA

Physician Data Query Offers four databases from the National Cancer Institute, with articles for laypeople on types of cancer, treatment, and prognoses; current cancer information for health-care providers; a directory of doctors, organizations, and treatment centers; and a treatment-protocol database. ✓**COMPUSERVE**→*go* PDQ $$

Caregivers

Care Giver Information, help, ideas, and support for people faced unexpectedly with the need to care for an impaired patient. ✓**FIDONET**→*tag* CARE_GIVER

Deafness

American Sign Language General talk for the deaf who use American Sign Language as their first language. ✓**FIDONET**→*tag* ASL

Conference for the Deaf and Hard of Hearing Information on all types of hearing impairment and assistive devices: the ADA, TDD/TTs, organizations, and communication modes. ✓**FIDONET**→*tag* SILENTTALK

Silent PC Provides the hearing-impaired with discussion on computer services available to them and other issues affecting their daily life. ✓**RELAYNET**→*number* 406

Diabetes

Diabetes Discussion and Support A conference for diabetics on controlling the disease. ✓**FIDONET**→*tag* DIABETES

Diabetes Forum Offers infor-

mation and contacts for anyone interested in diabetes, hypoglycemia, and related autoimmune disorders. Topics include diet and exercise, and medication. ⊕💬 ✓**COMPUSERVE**→*go* DIABETES

Diabetic (ML) A discussion group for diabetics. ✓**INTERNET**→*email* LISTSERV@PCCVM.BITNET ✍ *Type in message body:* SUBSCRIBE DIABETIC <YOUR FULL NAME>

Drugs

Electronic Media Venture Marijuana Information Information on use of medicinal marijuana for a variety of conditions, including AIDS, arthritis, eye diseases, multiple sclerosis, drug dependency, epilepsy, and the side effects of cancer chemotherapy. ✓**FIDONET**→*tag* NORML

Pharmacy Offers discussion for pharmacists, other medical professionals, and consumers. Topics include drug costs, usage, therapy, and pharmaceutical practices. The host is a registered pharmacist. ✓**RELAYNET**→ *number* 359

Health news

Health News Daily coverage of health-related news. 🖩 ✓**PRODIGY** →*jump* HEALTH NEWS

MEDNEWS (ML) A weekly newsletter containing AIDS statistics, FDA bulletins, the latest news from the Centers for Disease Control, medical news from the U.N. etc. ✓**INTERNET**→*email* LISTSERV @ASUACAD.BITNET ✍ *Type in message body:* SUBSCRIBE MEDNEWS <YOUR FULL NAME>

Mental illness

alt.angst (NG) Share your anxi-

eties. ✓**USENET**

alt.suicide.holiday For those exploring the concept and techniques of suicide as well as for those looking for emotional support. ✓**USENET**

Issues in Mental Health Provides question-and-answer areas, conferences, and information for mental-health professionals and laypeople about parenting, the stresses of day-to-day life, relationships, divorce, and separation. ⊕💬 ✓**AMERICA ONLINE** →*keyword* IMH

Mental Health Support group dealing with depression, schizophrenia, phobias, and other illnesses. ✓**FIDONET**→*tag* MENTAL_HEALTH

Multiple Personality Disorder Support For individuals with MPD and their families. Pseudonyms are allowed. ✓**FIDONET**→*tag* M_P_D

The National Alliance for the Mentally Ill A searchable database of articles on disorders and illnesses (e.g., panic and obsessive-compulsive disorders), medicine, and the latest research. Also features bulletin boards for discussing mental illness. 🖩 ⊕💬 ✓**AMERICA ONLINE**→*keyword* NAMI

Phobias A support groups for people with phobias and others wanting to know more about them. ✓**RELAYNET**→*number* 317

Psychology Discussions of human psychology and behavior. All interested parties are welcome. ✓**ILINK**→*number* 121

Psychology Offers discussion about psychological treatment in a nontechnical manner, with information on books, theories, and personal development. ✓**RELAYNET** →*number* 351

Public Psychology Support Discussion for the general public, especially those who don't understand "psychobabble." ✓**FIDONET**→ *tag* PUBLIC_PSYCH

Singleness in Purpose—Multiple Personality Disorder Support group for patients and loved ones dealing with MPD. ✓**FIDONET** →*tag* SIP_MPD

Walkers-in-Darkness (ML) For sufferers from depression and/or bipolar disorders, and affected friends. ✓**INTERNET**→*email* WALKERS-REQUEST@WORLD.STD.COM ✍*Subscribe by request*

Other illnesses

alt.med.cfs (NG) Chronic-fatigue-syndrome information and support. ✓**USENET**

Autism (ML) Devoted to discussions about the developmentally disabled; teachers encouraged to participate. ✓**INTERNET**→*email* LIST SERV@SJUVM.BITNET ✍*Type in message body:* SUB AUTISM <YOUR FULL NAME>

Cerebral Palsy Support group for those affected by CP. ✓**FIDO-NET**→*tag* CPALSY

International Post-Polio Survivors Information on post-polio sequalae syndrome (PPS), a medical condition that causes the unexpected return of polio symptoms to those who were originally stricken and survived the epidemics of the 1940s and 1950s. ✓**FIDONET**→*tag* POST_POLIO

LymeNet-L (ML) A newsletter that chronicles developments relat-

ing to Lyme disease, including treatments and research. ✓**INTERNET**→*email* LISTSERV@LEHIGH.EDU ✍*Type in message body:* SUBSCRIBE LYMENET-L <YOUR FULL NAME>

Muscular Dystrophy Conference For people with MD, their families, friends, and medical professionals treating them. ✓**FIDONET** →*tag* MDYSTROPHY

NORD Services/Rare Diseases Database Provides information on AIDS research, handicapped education, and digestive diseases. Also offers networking support for those with orphan disorders as well as access to biomedical literature. ✓**COMPUSERVE**→*go* NORD

Rare Diseases A way to meet others who share your condition. ✓**FIDONET**→*tag* RARE_CONDITION

Stroke-L (ML) General and scientific discussions about strokes. ✓**INTERNET**→*email* LISTSERV@UKCC. UKY.EDU ✍*Type in message body:* SUB STROKE-L <YOUR FULL NAME>

Witsendo (ML) Forum for discussing endometriosis, especially coping and its treatment. Also serves as a clearinghouse of information. "The list is primarily dedicated to the women who suffer from this painful and often demoralizing disease, therefore any information should be expressed in lay terms..." ✓**INTERNET**→*email* LISTSERV@DARTCSM1.DARTMOUTH.EDU ✍ *Type in message body:* SUB WITSENDO <YOUR FULL NAME>

Reference

Consumer Medicine A database of more than 3 million summarized articles in English relating to human medicine. Enter a topic

and get articles with the latest research and information. ✓**GENIE** →*keyword* MEDICINE $$

CR Health *Consumer Reports* articles on health-related topics. 🖳 ✓**PRODIGY**→*jump* CR HEALTH

FDA Electronic Bulletin Board (BBS) FDA congressional testimony and speeches, reports on drug approvals, a magazine index to FDA stories, consumer information, and sections on veterinary medicine and AIDS. Log in when dialing the BBS with "bbs." 301-594-6849/301-594-6850 ✓**INTERNET**→ *telnet* FDABBS.FDA.GOV→BBS/<NONE> ✖*Modem parameters 7E1 only* FREE

Health Database Plus Provides full-text articles from consumer and professional publications, including *Psychology Today, Food and Nutrition,* the *New England Journal of Medicine, Health,* and *RN.* More than 127,000 full-text articles on health, fitness, and nutrition. 🖳 ✓**COMPUSERVE**→*go* HLTDB $$

Health Topics A library of health-related articles on timely topics. 🖳 ✓**PRODIGY**→*jump* HEALTH TOPICS

HealthNet An online medical reference library with a newsletter dedicated to advances in medicine and a collection of information on prescription drugs, eye care, diseases and disorders, sports medicine, and symptoms. 🖳 ✓**COMPU-SERVE**→*go* HNT ✓**DELPHI**→*go* REF HEALTH

IQuest Medical InfoCenter Provides database access for information on research, pharmaceutical news, medical practices, and allied health studies. ✓**COMPUSERVE** →*go* IQMEDICINE $$

Physically disabled

From support groups to the politics of the disabled to rehabilitation and lifestyle issues,

coverage of disability-related topics has grown rapidly on the Net. The **DisABILI-TIES Forum** on Compu-Serve includes support for families. The **Handicapped News BBS** offers detailed service info. GEnie's **Disabilities RoundTable** concentrates on rights and public policy. FidoNet's **Spinal Cord Injuries** is a comprehensive discussion of all SCI topics. **Handicap** on ILink has info on adaptable software.

Wheelchair users—downloaded from CompuServe's Photography Forum.

leisure, and technology. Visit the "Equal Access Cafe" to exchange ideas. 🖼️🎮 ✓**GENIE**→*keyword* ABLE

Handicapped News BBS (BBS) Provides more than 50 conferences on handicapped-related services, and a list of other BBSs with a handicapped focus. 203-926-6168

WIDNet—Disability Network Includes a database of disability-related materials and links with community and government disability groups. 🖥️ 🖼️🎮 ✓**DELPHI**→*go* GR WID

Technologies

Adaptive Technologies Conference for professionals with physical disabilities. ✓**BIX**→*conference* ADAPTIVE.TECH

Handicap A contact and support area for the physically disabled. Information on computer software and hardware and other means of aiding the handicapped. ✓**ILINK**→*number* 86

Independent Living Confer-

ence Information for the disabled who want to live alone. Discussions about personal-care attendants, independent-living centers, and adaptive technology. Also carries information for families and friends. ✓**FIDONET**→*tag* ILC

L-HCAP (ML) Discussions about technology for the handicapped. Topics include relevant computer hardware and software, adaptive devices, meetings and conferences, suppliers, and more. ✓**INTERNET**→ *email* LISTSERV@NDSUVM1.BITNET ✍ *Type in message body:* SUB L-HCAP <YOUR FULL NAME>

News & discussions

Disability News General-interest information for the disabled, their families, and professionals who work with them. Includes news, resources, and referrals. 🖥️ ✓**FIDONET**→*tag* ABLENEWS

Disabled Offers support discussions, help with problems, and technical/hardware news for the disabled. ✓**RELAYNET**→*number* 146

Disabled Discussions about assistance for the handicapped and disabled. ✓**SMARTNET**→*tag* DISABLED

disABLED Users Information Exchange Information, help, and support for the disabled community. ✓**FIDONET**→*tag* ABLED

misc.handicap (NG) Discuss issues related to the physically and mentally handicapped. Includes medical, educational, legal, and technological aids. ✓**USENET**

On the Net

Across the board

ADAnet A network of conferences on FidoNet devoted to disability topics. ✓CHECK LOCAL BULLETIN BOARDS

Disabilities Forum Offers information, communications, and support for the disabled community, including parents and professionals. 🖼️🎮 ✓**COMPUSERVE**→*go* DISABILITIES

DisABILITIES Forum Offers information for individuals with a disability, caregivers, and health professionals. 🖼️🎮 ✓**AMERICA ON-LINE**→*keyword* DISABILITIES

Disabilities RoundTable Covers rights, resources, laws, employment information, education,

Recovery & abuse

The Net mirrors the huge upsurge nationwide in 12-step and other recovery programs.

Promises a Recovery BBS, **The Diner BBS**, and the FidoNet **12 Steps Discussion** are support groups for people involved with a program. The newsgroup **alt.support** offers online support discussion and materials for a wide range of "personal recovery" issues. FidoNet's **Survivors of Ritual Abuse** covers an area of increasing controversy. **Victims of False Accusations of Abuse**, also on FidoNet, was started in response to what is perceived as an epidemic of false charges. The newsgroup **alt.abuse.recovery** deals with all types of relationships. And, if you still think you're in pretty decent shape, there's always RelayNet's **Computer Addicts**.

On the Net

Across the board

12 Steps Discussion Discuss experiences with 12-step self-help programs. ✓**FIDONET**→*tag* 12_STEPS

Addict-L (ML) Academic discussion of addictions, less focused on particular addictions than on the phenomenon—e.g., etiology of addictions, 12-step programs, and articles on addictions. ✓**INTERNET**→

O.D. victim at rock concert—from CompuServe's Photography Forum.

email LISTSERV@KENTVM.KENT.EDU ✍ *Type in message body:* SUB ADDICT-L <YOUR FULL NAME>

alt.support (NG) A newsgroup where you can ask for or offer support without restrictions on the type of problem. ✓**USENET**

Better Health and Medical Forum Features mental-health and addictions libraries with articles and information on mental health, stress management, and smoking, as well as chemical dependencies. ⊕📇 ✓**AMERICA ONLINE** →*keyword* HEALTH

Dawn Cove Abbey (BBS) Features both PathNet (e.g., Self Help, Depression, SmokeFree, and Eating Disorders) and RecoverNet conferences. Home of the 24 HR CRISIS/DISTRESS HelpLine Conference. Very New Age-y. ⊞▫ ⊕📇 902-742-3399

The Diner (BBS) Intended "to provide a safe place for all people who are working 12-step programs to talk about their issues." Carries RecoverNet and local conferences.

908-418-4354 FREE

Health & Fitness Forum Includes bulletin boards and libraries on abuse issues and 12-step programs. 📇 ⊕📇 ✓**COMPUSERVE**→ *go* HEALTH

Promises a Recovery BBS (BBS) Online support for those involved with 12-step recovery programs. Both local and national conferences carried. "If you feel that you have a problem with alcohol, drugs, compulsive overeating, or other compulsive behaviors, you've come to the right place." 615-385-9421 FREE

Public Forum NonProfit Connection Includes discussion of 12-step programs as well as a library that includes a list of recovery-oriented BBSs. 📇 ✓**GENIE**→ *keyword* PF

RecoverNet Conferences include Al-Anon, Alcoholics Anonymous, Cocaine Anonymous, The 12 Traditions, Narcotics Anonymous, Over Eaters Anonymous, Sex in Sobriety, Sponsorship, Youth in Recovery, and Survivors. ✓CHECK LOCAL BULLETIN BOARDS

Recovery A self-help area for those recovering from drug, alcohol, or other addictions. Users may log in under a pseudonym. ✓ILINK→*number* 108

Recovery Offers open discussion about addiction and recovery, and includes participants and nonparticipants in 12-step programs. Not affiliated with any recovery program. ✓**RELAYNET**→*number* 172

Recovery (International 12-Step Oriented) Discussion and support for members of 12-step programs and others who are interested in them. ✓**FIDONET**→*tag* RECOVERY

The Recovery Room BBS (BBS) Conferences related to addictions and 12-step recovery programs as well as AIDS/HIV-support conferences. ☎ 713-242-9674 FREE

Alcoholism

ACOA (Adult Children of Alcoholics) Provides a meeting area and discussion forum for people dealing with family alcoholism. ✓**RELAYNET**→*number* 316

Adult Children of Alcoholics Follows the 12-step program, with help for anyone raised in an alcoholic or dysfunctional family. ✓**FIDONET**→*tag* SIP_ACA

Alcohol (ML) Forum for discussing alcohol abuse. Psychologists, medical professionals, and students encouraged to participate. ✓**INTERNET**→*email* LISTSERV@LMUACAD.BITNET ✍ *Type in message body:* SUB ALCOHOL <YOUR FULL NAME>

Alcoholism & Recovery Sharing area for participants in Alcoholics Anonymous 12-step program. ✓**FIDONET**→*tag* SIP_AA

Abusive relationships

alt.abuse.recovery (NG) For those recovering from abusive relationships. ✓**USENET**

Child Abuse Information and Recovery Discussions for those who were sexually, physically, or emotionally abused as children, and for those trying to stop abuse, including recovering child abusers. ✓**FIDONET**→*tag* CHILD_ABUSE

Family Violence Discussions about battered and abused spouses and children and dysfunctional families. ✓**FIDONET**→*tag* BATTERED

Stopping the Cycle of Child Abuse Support group for people who were abused as children. ✓**FIDONET**→*tag* PLEASE ✖ *Recovering child abusers cannot participate*

Survivors A conference for people who were victims of child abuse and others with special interest in the topic. ✓**ILINK**→*number* 211

Survivors of Ritual Abuse A support area. ✓**FIDONET**→*tag* SRA

Victims of False Accusations of Abuse Discussion about false charges of child abuse, spouse abuse, and other accusations often levied during child-custody disputes. ✓**FIDONET**→*tag* VFALSAC

Codependency

alt.recovery.codependency (NG) Discussions about codependency. ✓**USENET**

Computer addictions

Computer Addicts A meeting area for people addicted to computers. ✓**RELAYNET**→*number* 321

Drug abuse

Narcotics Anonymous For members of NA programs and those who want to stop using drugs. ✓**FIDONET**→*tag* SIP_NA

Substance Abuse Forum For mobilizing teachers, parents, and communities on drug prevention. ☎ ✓**AMERICA ONLINE**→*keyword* SUBSTANCE ABUSE

Sex addiction

12-Step Recovery from Sexual Addiction For people suffering from addiction to sex. ✓**FIDONET**→*tag* SIP_SAA

Sexual abuse

SOI (Survivors of Incest) Includes a discussion of incest issues, help with anger, lessons on dealing with day-to-day life, and guidelines for protecting children. ✓**RELAYNET**→*number* 260

Survivors of Incest and Childhood Sexual Abuse Support group and recovery program for victims of childhood abuse. ✓**FIDONET**→*tag* SIP_INCEST

Twelve Step Discussion for Survivors of Incest Support for incest and other sex-abuse survivors. ✓**FIDONET**→*tag* SIP_SURVIVOR

Smoking

No-Smoking Discussion about smoking. ✓**RELAYNET**→*number* 266

Smoke-Free (ML) Support for people recovering from addiction to cigarettes as well as those thinking about quitting. ✓**INTERNET**→*email* LISTSERV@RA.MSSTATE.EDU ✍ *Type in message body:* SUB SMOKE-FREE <YOUR FULL NAME>

Tobacco Quitters Information for people trying to quit and support for those who have, with attitude reinforcement, technique advice, and philosophy sharing. ✓**FIDONET**→*tag* QUIT_SMOKE

Part 8

Home, Hobbies & Shopping

8

Animals & pets

Animals as pets, animals as companions, animals as a cause: The Net's wide-ranging

coverage of the animal kingdom includes most cultures, ideologies, and species. FidoNet's **Ferret Forum** offers info and advocacy (ferret rights). If your passion is tropical fish, try Smartnet's **FishNet**. There are numerous sites for bird people, including FidoNet's **Bird Info Network**. The newsgroup **rec.pets.cats** covers all breeds. The mailing list **Golden** (for retriever) is extensive and expert. Animal-rights issues are covered in many locations. FidoNet's **Animal Rights Conference** can be heart-wrenching.

Puppy—downloaded from CompuServe's Graphics Plus Forum.

On the Net

Across the board

Animals Share animals-as-companions stories. ✓**FIDONET**→*tag* ANIMALS

Maggie-Mae's Pet-Net & Co. RoundTable Information for lovers of both pets and wild animals. Categories range from Ask the Vet to Elephants to Kids 'n Pets. Users can also take the Pet Owners Survey and quizzes, acquire images from Maggie Mae's Picture Gallery, or share pet-training techniques. ☜☞ ✓**GENIE**→ *keyword* PET

Pet Care Club Hosted by a pair of veterinarians. Provides care hints and information about dogs, cats, reptiles, birds, and other animals. Other online experts include professional breeders, informed pet owners and staff veterinarians from universities and private practices around the country. Also offers pet-nutrition news, funny pet stories, and animal-politics debate. ☜☞ ✓**AMERICA ONLINE**→ *keyword* PET CARE

Pets Features separate categories for cats, dogs, and horses with other animals falling under the "other.animals" category. Health (that is, pet health) is also its own category. ☜☞ ✓**BIX**→*conference* PETS

Pets Discussions among pet owners about animal health problems, training and feeding, and animal psychology. ✓**ILINK**→*number* 61

Pets Offers advice on pets and pet problems, including unusual animals like ferrets and snakes. Some advice available from veterinarians. ✓**RELAYNET**→*number* 152

Pets Discussions for pet lovers. ✓**SMARTNET**→*tag* PETS

Pets/Animal Forum Provides information and help with all types of pets, from behavior issues to veterinarian questions to anecdotes. ☜☞ ✓**COMPUSERVE**→*go* PETS

Pets BB Discussions for pet lovers. Topics include exotic pets, barnyard pets, reptiles, and pet adoption. ✓**PRODIGY**→*jump* PETS BB

rec.pets (NG) General discussion of pets and their care. ✓**USENET**

Animal rights

Animal Rights Includes discussions and article reprints on animal-rights issues affecting both domesticated and wild animals. ✓**RELAYNET**→*number* 340

Animal Rights Conference Open to every aspect of animal rights, pro and con. Conversations are often emotional, but personal attacks and flames are discouraged. Look for the Rules File ANIM_ RTS.RUL for guidance. ✓**FIDONET** →*tag* ANIMAL_RIGHTS

AR-Alerts (ML) Forum for posting important information about animal-rights issues. Encourages communication between animal-rights groups and activists. ✓**INTERNET**→*email* LISTSERV@NY.NEAVS.COM ✍ *Type in message body:* SUBSCRIBE AR-ALERTS <YOUR FULL NAME>

Humane Society of the United States Forum Covers—apart from topics regarding the humane education of children—wildlife protection, pet care, and animal experimentation. ☺💬 ✓**COMPU-SERVE**→*go* HSUS

talk.politics.animals (NG) Debate and discussion about animal rights. ✓**USENET**

Aquaria

alt.aquaria (NG) Hobbyist discussions about aquaria-related topics. Articles are often cross-posted with REC.AQUARIA. ✓**USENET**

Aqua-L (ML) Forum for discussions about rearing aquatic species. Topics include problems and solutions rearing aquatic larvae, commercial-aquatic-systems design and operation, genetics, sex reversal and hormonal manipulation, the aqua-business. ✓**INTERNET**→ *email* LISTSERV@VM.UOGUELPH.CA ✍ *Type in message body:* SUB AQUA-L

<YOUR FULL NAME>

Aquaria Fish Forums News and information about the health and care of marine life, as well as discussion with hobbyists and professionals. ☺💬 ✓**COMPUSERVE**→*go* FISHFORUMS

Aquarium Offers a variety of topics for aquarium hobbyists, covering all types of marine life, equipment discussions, and advice from professionals. ✓**RELAYNET**→ *number* 343

Fishkeeping Covers all aspects of keeping fish, salt- or freshwater. Topics range from installing tanks to aid for experienced aquarists. ✓**FIDONET**→*tag* AQUARIUM

FishNet Discussion about raising tropical fish. ✓**SMARTNET**→*tag* FISH NET

rec.aquaria (NG) Hobbyist discussions about aquaria-related topics. Articles are often cross-posted with ALT.AQUARIA. ✓**USENET**

sci.aquaria (NG) For scientific discussions about fish, including taxonomy, plant biology, and ecology. ✓**USENET**

Birds

Bird Info Network Discussions on the breeding and raising of exotic birds, with a full range of conferences devoted to medical care, feeding, legal issues, wild birds, and specific breeds like parrots and cockatiels. ✓**FIDONET**→*tag* BIN_*

Bird Info Network (BBS) Discuss raising, breeding, and taming exotic birds. Carries BirdNet, Usenet, and FidoNet conferences. 🖥️☺💬 303-423-9775/303-581-9100

Captive Propagation of Birds Discussions about birdkeeping, especially breeding and raising nondomesticated birds in captivity. ✓**FIDONET**→*tag* AVICULTURE

Exotic Birds All bird-related topics: keeping them as pets, bird-watching, and natural histories of species. ✓**FIDONET**→*tag* EXOTIC_BIRDS

Parrots/Hookbill Conference Covers jungle birds like macaws, conures, cockatoos, and cockatiels. ✓**FIDONET**→*tag* PARROTS

rec.pets.birds (NG) For discussing the hobby of keeping birds. ✓**USENET**

Camels

Camel-L (ML) A forum for discussing camel research. ✓**INTERNET** →*email* LISTSERV@SAKFU00.BITNET ✍ *Type in message body:* SUB CAMEL-L <YOUR FULL NAME>

Cats

Cat Conference Anecdotes and tips on cat care and feeding. ✓**FIDONET**→*tag* KATTY_KORNER

Feline-L (ML) Forum for discussing cats. ✓**INTERNET**→*email* LISTSERV@PCCVM.BITNET ✍ *Type in message body:* SUBSCRIBE FELINE-L <YOUR FULL NAME>

rec.pets.cats (NG) Discuss cat training, breeding, habits, care, and any other cat-related subject. ✓**USENET**

Dogs

Canine-L (ML) Active list covering all matters of interest to dogs and their owners. ✓**INTERNET**→ *email* LISTSERV@PSUVM.BITNET ✍ *Type in message body:* SUB CANINE-L <YOUR

FULL NAME>

Dog Lovers' Discussions Open discussion about man's best friend, with stories, veterinary discussions, news, and dog-lover socializing. ✓**FIDONET**→*tag* DOGHOUSE

Golden (ML) Discussions for golden retriever devotees, including breeding, training techniques, show information, bragging, and more. ✓**INTERNET**→*email* LISTSERV@ HOBBES.UCSD.EDU ✍ *Type in message body:* SUBSCRIBE GOLDEN <YOUR FULL NAME>

Herders (ML) For those interested in herding issues. ✓**INTERNET**→ *email* HERDERS-REQUEST@MCNC.ORG ✍ *Subscribe by request*

Obedience (ML) For those interested in dog obedience, primarily the AKC and UKC trials. ✓**INTERNET**→*email* OBEDREQ@REEPICHEEP. GCN.UOKNOR.EDU ✍*Subscribe by request*

Police Dogs Discuss breeding, raising, training, and using police dogs. ✓**FIDONET**→*tag* K9DOGS

rec.pets.dogs (NG) Discussions about specific breeds, training, showing, care, and other dog-related topics. ✓**USENET**

Ferrets

Ferret Forum An area for posts from members of the International Ferret News Service (IFNS), with discussions of interest to ferret owners, ferret fanciers, and those who want to learn more about them. Topics include husbandry, breeding, shows, and lobbying for legislation in those areas where ferrets are not welcomed as pets. ✓**FIDONET**→*tag* FERRET_FORUM

Cat—downloaded from CompuServe's Graphics Plus Forum.

Ferrets (ML) "A group of people interested in ferrets, Mustela Putorius Furo, as pets. All aspects of ferrets are discussed: advocacy, funny stories, health, training, ferret frolics (parties) and so on." ✓**INTERNET**→*email* FERRET-REQUEST@ FERRET.OCUNIX.ON.CA ✍*Subscribe by request*

Horses

Equine-L (ML) Covers all facets of horse ownership, management, and related subjects. ✓**INTERNET**→ *email* LISTSERV@PCCVM.BITNET ✍*Type in message body:* SUB EQUINE-L <YOUR FULL NAME>

Horse Discussion Discussions of horses and horsemanship: all breeds and all riding styles. ✓**FIDONET**→*tag* EQUUS

Snakes 'n' stuff

Herp-Net/Satronics TBBS (BBS) Discuss fish, snakes, and all reptile- and amphibian-related topics. Includes a general message area, a library of files, a database of local herpetology societies, and a calendar of events. Besides Herp-Net, the board features several spe-

cial-interest groups such as a Mac user group, a writers' forum, and an Esperanto area. 215-698-1905/215-464-3562

rec.pets.herp (NG) Interested in snakes? If so, this forum is for you. ✓**USENET**

Reptile, Amphibian, and Exotic Pets For discussing exotic pets. ✓**FIDONET**→*tag* CHAMELEON

Pet health

Petcare Guide Articles on pet behavior and health written for the non veterinarian. ▦ ✓**PRODIGY** → *jump* PETCARE GUIDE

Pet supplies

Petworks Professional pet supplies. ⊕ ✓**COMPUSERVE**→*go* PT ✓**PRODIGY**→*jump* PETWORKS

The vet

Animal Medicine Doc Don Thomson, D.V.M., helps answer questions on sicknesses and cures for all breeds. ✓**FIDONET**→*tag* ANI MED

Petline on Petcare A regularly featured column on caring for your pets, written by a veterinarian. ✓**PRODIGY**→*jump* PETLINE QUESTIONS

Veterinary Information Network Includes more than 600 member veterinarians. Provides general-practice vets with regular contact with more than 150 specialists in all veterinary disciplines, including cardiology, neurology, surgery, and radiology, as well as exotic-animal and exotic-bird experts. ✓**AMERICA ONLINE**→*keyword* VIN ✖*Must request access* $30/ MONTH

Arts & crafts

Writes a subscriber to the Woodwork mailing list: "I am headed to some dumpsters at the 5 & 57 & 55 interchange in Southern CA where a great deal of refuse is discarded. Mostly shoring that is broken, and some concrete forms. Major elevated freeway construction in progress. Plywood, 2x4s, 4x4s, 4x6s, and 12x12s; quite literally by the ton. If I had a bandsaw and plane, I might start a small business rescuing this stuff." Need we say more?

Across the board

Arts & Crafts Discussions Discusses designing and making all types of arts and crafts. Topics include woodworking, needlepoint, quilting and blocking, knitting, cross-stitching, crueling, pattern-making, seasonal gifts, and sewing kids' clothes. Also includes questions on where to buy supplies, both locally and via mail order. ✓**FIDONET**→*tag* ARTS_CRAFTS

Crafts BB Topics include quilting, stained glass, and woodworking. ✓**PRODIGY**→*jump* CRAFTS BB

Crafts Forum Offers ideas and techniqes for knitting, stitching, woodworking, quilting, sewing, painting, and other crafts. The libraries include downloadable craft patterns. ●💬 ✓**COMPUSERVE**

Quilting—downloaded from Compu-Serve's Graphics Gallery Forum.

→*go* CRAFTS

Handicrafts A conference for arts and crafts of all sorts. ✓**ILINK** →*number* 201

Fiber arts

Craft & Needlework Hobbies Discussion and pointers about favorite craft hobbies. ✓**FIDONET**→ *tag* CRAFTING

Hobby RoundTable Databases of information as well as message boards on many hobbies, including fiber arts. ●💬 ✓**GENIE** →*keyword* HOBBY

Quilt List (ML) Very active list for discussing quilting. Store and pattern recommendations, questions, and hints are all welcome. ✓**INTERNET**→*email* LISTSERV@CORNELL.EDU ✍ *Type in message body:* SUBSCRIBE QUILT <YOUR FULL NAME>

rec.crafts.textiles (NG) Forum for discussing sewing, weaving, knitting, and other fiber arts. ✓**USENET**

Stitches Offers discussion on sewing, knitting, crocheting, and other needlework. ✓**RELAYNET**→ *number* 424

Kids crafts

Make It! Each month a new project with illustrated step-by-step instructions that demonstrate how to make a specific craft. Previous projects and different levels are also available. ✓**PRODIGY**→ *jump* MAKE IT

Woodworking

rec.woodworking (NG) For discussions related to woodworking. ✓**USENET**

Woodwork (ML) Discuss woodworking techniques, tools, and projects. Open to hobbyists as well as professionals. ✓**INTERNET**→*email* LISTSERV@IPFWVM.BITNET ✍ *Type in message body:* SUB WOODWORK <YOUR FULL NAME>

Miscellaneous

Clayart (ML) Covers topics related to ceramic arts and pottery. Includes exhibition opportunities, conference information, workshop announcements, grant information, and more. ✓**INTERNET**→*email* LISTSERV@UKCC.UKY.EDU ✍ *Type in message body:* SUB CLAYART <YOUR FULL NAME>

Origami-L (ML) Discussions about the art of origami. Bibliographies, folding techniques, computer representations of folds, and more are welcome. ✓**INTERNET**→ *email* ORIGAMI-L-REQUEST@NSTN.NS. CA ✍ *Type in message body:* SUBSCRIBE ORIGAMI-L

rec.crafts.metalworking (NG) Covers all aspects of metal crafting. ✓**USENET**

Collectibles & hobbies

HO Trains, Charles and Diana commemorative stamps, Angie Dickinson posters (also Barbara Eden, Tina Louise, and Alyssa Milano), any good celebrity nudes, baseball cards, Swatch watches (**Watch Out On-line**), 78s, clocks, coins, horse models, dollhouses, etceteras (truly). Just find your passion. Or try **rec.collecting** if you're looking for new things to get hooked on.

On the Net

Across the board

The Exchange Features Collector's Corner, which greets AOL'ers with the note "If you like to collect stamps, comic books, model railroad cars, antiques, records, sport cards; then post here," and the Hobbies Board, where you can discuss kiting, fine scale modeling, fencing, greyhound racing, railroads, and other hobbies. ✓**AMERICA ONLINE**→*keyword* EXCHANGE

Hobbies BB Topics range from ham radio to model making to outdoor activities. ✓ **PRODIGY**→ *jump* HOBBIES BB

Hobby RoundTable Databases of information and bulletin boards divided into separate hobby categories, from dollhouse miniatures to radio controlled models to needle and fiber arts. 🖼✓**GENIE**→ *keyword* HOBBY

Hobby Shop Discussions by model builders, ham-radio enthu-

Misprint of a 24-cent stamp—downloaded from the sunsite.unc.edu.

siasts, and other hobbyists. Share ideas and extra product information. 🖼✓**DELPHI**→*go* GR HOBBY

Antiques

rec.antiques (NG) Discussions about collecting antiques and vintage items—from where to find them to how much they're worth. ✓**USENET**

Collectibles

alt.collecting.autographs (NG) Discussion about collecting autographs. ✓**USENET**

Coin Collection Catalog A Lotus 1-2-3 catalog program for coin collecting. ✓**INTERNET**→*ftp* FTP.WUSTL.EDU→ANONYMOUS/<YOUR EMAIL ADDRESS>→systems/ibmpc/msdos/lotus123→123_coin.zip

Collectibles For those interested in stamps, dolls, coins, cards, and other collectibles. ✓**SMARTNET**→*tag* COLLECTIBLES

Collectibles Forum Offers pricing and trading information, dis-

cussion, and professional contacts for collectors of stamps, coins, baseball cards, and other items. 🖼✓**COMPUSERVE**→ *go* COLLECT

Collecting BB Trading, buying, and selling are permitted. Areas include Art/Antiques, Baseball Cards, Cottages, Precious Moments, Stamps, and Teddy Bears. ✓**PRODIGY**→*jump* COLLECTING BB

Collectors Discuss collection of just about anything—comic books, antiques, stamps, etc. ✓**ILINK**→*number* 141

Doll Houses List (ML) Devoted to discussing dollhouses, including constructing and playing. ✓**INTERNET**→*email* LISTSERV@FERRIS.BITNET ✍ *Type in message body:* SUB DOLLH-L <YOUR FULL NAME>

Hobbies Covers collecting everything from baseball cards to antiques to rare coins. Also includes tips on getting started, financial guides to collecting, and announcements of upcoming events. ✓**RELAYNET**→*number* 153

Postcard (ML) For all with an interest in postcards—collecting, exchanging, discussing their history, etc. ✓**INTERNET**→*email* LISTSERV@IDBSU.BITNET ✍*Type in message body:* SUB POSTCARD <YOUR FULL NAME>

rec.collecting (NG) Collectors talk. "My friend is a very serious collector of Karen Carpenter memorabilia."…"I saw an ad for Kirk, Spock, etc. action figures by Playmates in a Penny's catalog."…I have a complete set or whatever of stamps commemorating the wedding of Charles and Diana. Does anyone have any idea if this is worth anything now that the marriage is kaput?" ✓**USENET**

78-L (ML) Discussion dedicated to music of the pre-LP era and music-related collectibles. For those who enjoy listening to music recorded at or about 78 rpm. ✓**INTERNET**→*email* LISTSERV@COR NELL.EDU ✍*Type in message body:* SUB 78-L <YOUR FULL NAME>

Watch Out On-Line (BBS) Located on the Home Office BBS, a service for Swatch-watch traders and collectors worldwide. Comprehensive Swatch-watch information including current market prices and graphics. 908-647-2202 $19.95 QUARTERLY

Hobby store

Master Hobbies Online hobby store with more than 55,000 items. 👜 ✓**GENIE**→*keyword* HOBBYSTORE

Models

alt.models (NG) Discussion about model building and collecting for those who don't get REC. MODELS.SCALES. ✓**USENET**

Model Aviation Forum For hobbyists interested in rockets, planes, cars, and boats. Topics range from Sport Rocketry to RC —radio controlled—Cars. Libraries include software and GIFs. 👁🗨 ✓**COMPUSERVE**→*go* MODELNET

Model-Horse (ML) Discussion for all ages of the model-horse hobby. ✓**INTERNET**→*email* MODEL-HORSE-REQUEST@XZCAT.COM ✍*Subscribe by request*

Radio Controlled Models All

types: boats, cars, planes, helicopters, and other aircraft. Participants have a yearly meeting to discuss their projects. ✓**FIDONET**→ *tag* RCM

RCModeling Discussions of radio-controlled modeling. The building and operation of radio-controlled cars, boats, and planes. ✓**ILINK**→*number* 116

rec.models.rc (NG) For hobbyists interested in radio-controlled models. ✓**USENET**

rec.models.rockets (NG) For those devoted to model rockets. ✓**USENET**

rec.models.scales (NG) A hobbyist forum for discussing the construction and collecting of all types of models. ✓**USENET**

Railroads

ModelRR Conference for model-railroading hobbyists. ✓**SMARTNET** →*tag* MODELRR

Railfans, Train Watching, and Prototype Railroads General conference on railroad news, excursions, and product reviews. Model railroaders should use the TRAINS echo. ✓**FIDONET**→*tag* RAILFANS

Railroad (ML) All railroad-related topics considered, both real and models. ✓**INTERNET**→*email* LIST SERV@CUNYVM.CUNY.EDU ✍*Type in message body:* SUB RAILROAD <YOUR FULL NAME>

rec.models.railroad (NG) For model railroaders. Discuss scales, associations, books, and other topics. ✓**USENET**

rec.railroad (NG) For fans of real trains. ✓**USENET**

TrainNet Forum A forum for model railroaders and fans of real trains, with contacts for railroad historical societies, magazines, hobby shops, GIFs, and news. 👁🗨 ✓**COMPUSERVE**→*go* TRAINNET

Trains The National Model Railroading and Railfanning conference—covers trains, railroads, and models. ✓**FIDONET**→*tag* TRAINS

Stamps

Stamp & Cover Collectors Discussion for hobbyists. ✓**FIDO-NET**→*tag* STAMPS

Stamp Collection Inventory System A Windows shareware program for organizing stamp collections. ✓**INTERNET**→*ftp* RIGEL.ACS. OAKLAND.DU→ANONYMOUS/<YOUR EMAIL ADDRESS>→pub/msdos/win dows3→stampb.zip

Stamps (ML) For those interested in stamps and related items. ✓**IN-TERNET**→*email* LISTSERV@CUNYVM. CUNY.EDU ✍*Type in message body:* SUB STAMPS <YOUR FULL NAME>

Trading cards

Baseball Card Conference The official support forum for Grand Slam Baseball Card Manager. Subjects include card collections, collection software, card listings, sales, and trades. ✓**FIDONET**→*tag* BB-CARDS

rec.collecting.cards (NG) Discussions about card collecting—sports and non-sports. ✓**USENET**

Trading Cards Offers discussion for anyone collecting sports and non-sports bubblegum cards. Includes buying, selling, and trading of cards, plus card news. ✓**RELAYNET**→*number* 202

Family & senior life

Parents who need support, help, advice, information, or just another parent to talk to

(which is all parents) have all kinds of opportunities on the Net. AOL's **Parents' Information Network** wants to be a combination parents' magazine, community center, play group, and database. GEnie's **The Family and Personal Growth RoundTable** covers all varieties of family relationships. Preschoolers are the focus of **Parenting** on BIX. The newsgroups **alt.child-support** and **alt.dads-rights** are clearinghouses of information on custody issues.

Kids—downloaded from CompuServe's Photography Forum.

Across the board

The Family and Personal Growth RoundTable Covers all aspects of family life, relationships, and personal growth. Includes private boards for kids and teens, and discussions about adult relationships and sexuality (for both married couples and singles). Also covers issues from parenting to wedding planning with real-time weekly conferences for parents, teens, singles, and the whole family. ⊛💬 ✓**GENIE**→*keyword* FAMILY

Home Life BB Members discuss home and living. Topics include Home Organization, Parenting Practices, Stay-At-Home Parents, and Playful Parents. The "Other" topic has become home to couples without children. ✓**PRODIGY**→*jump* HOMELIFE BB

misc.kids (NG) Discussions about pregnancy, child rearing, and parental concerns. ✓**USENET**

Parenting "A caring and supportive atmosphere where we can share the experiences, the joys, and the problems that go with raising children." Topics include Prenatal, School, and the Wonder Years. ⊛💬 ✓**BIX**→*conference* PARENTING

Parents A conference about raising children in today's world for parents, grandparents, and potential parents. ✓**FIDONET**→*tag* PARENTS

Parents Discussions of issues of parenting such as birth, childrearing, and child psychology. ✓**ILINK**→*number* 87

Parents Offers general-interest conversation among parents, including problem-solving and better-parenting tips. ✓**RELAYNET**→*number* 192

Parents Open discussion about raising children. ✓**SMARTNET**→*tag* PARENTS

Parents' Information Network Offers the Parents' System Map, a parents' guide to resources throughout America Online, a newsstand, contests, a database of kids media, and several forums on children's education. ⊛💬 ▦ ✓**AMERICA ONLINE**→*keyword* PIN

Relationships Family, dating, work, and other relationships discussed. Issues include communication, conflict resolution, and intimacy. ✓**RELAYNET**→*number* 240

Divorce & custody

alt.child-support (NG) Discussions about raising children in a split family, the legalities, and especially fathers' rights. ✓ **USENET**

alt.dads-rights (NG) Discuss the rights of fathers trying to win custody. ✓ **USENET**

Dads Sponsored by the National Congress for Men and Children, a fathers'-rights organization. Discussions include father-child relationships, general parenting issues, role models, and custody or visitation problems from divorce. ✓ **FIDONET**→*tag* DADS

Parent-child

alt.parents-teens (NG) Forum for discussing parent-teenager relationships—from what your children read to how you communicate with them. ✓ **USENET**

alt.support.step-parents (NG) Supportive forum for those dealing with the issues involved in being a stepparent. ✓ **USENET**

Pregnancy, adoption

Adoptees Information Exchange Helps adoptees and birth parents search for their biological relatives. Messages discuss the public and private organizations that help in these searches, and the legislation affecting adoptees, biological parents, and adoptive families. ✓ **FIDONET**→*tag* ADOPTEES

alt.adoption (NG) For those involved with or considering adoption. ✓ **USENET**

Pregnancy and Childbirth Offers practical information about childbirth, pregnancy, postpartum depression, and maternity care. The host is the author of the bestseller *Mind Over Labor*. ✓ **RELAYNET** →*number* 423

Research & advice

CR Kids *Consumer Reports* articles about children's products and services. ▨ ✓ **PRODIGY**→*jump* CR KIDS

Jane Dare's Advice A personal-advice column that appears twice a week. ✓ **PRODIGY**→*jump* JANE DARE

Parenting Center Advice from parenting experts. ✓ **PRODIGY**→ *jump* PARENTING CENTER

Parenting Guide A library of articles relating to parenting. ✓ **PRODIGY**→*jump* PARENTING GUIDE

Seniors

Senior Citizens Provides a discussion area for anyone over 55, with topics that include aging in America and companionship for seniors. ✓ **RELAYNET**→*number* 196

Senior Forum Socialize with other senior citizens on the message boards or explore the databases on genealogy, women, health, and computers. ▨✿ ✓ **DELPHI**→*go* GR SEN

SeniorNet SeniorNet is a nonprofit organization for older adults (55 or over) interested in using computers. The online area includes weekly events, a newsletter, and forums devoted to senior issues ranging from politics to cooking to retirement to grandparenting. ▨✿ ✓ **AMERICA ONLINE** →*keyword* SENIOR

Seniors BB A bulletin board for senior citizens. Talk about your family in "Meet the Family" or join in the discussion in one of the other topics—e.g., Born in the '20s, Senior Living, Retirement, and Leisure. ✓ **PRODIGY**→*jump* SENIORS BB

Miscellaneous

alt.missing-kids (NG) Forum for discussing missing children. ✓ **USENET**

KIDSNET Provides an educational TV and radio database with detailed information on thousands of children's programs on television and radio; a calendar listing events, public-service projects, relevant legislation, international media awards, and more; a bulletin announcing upcoming children's programs; and study guides to supplement educational programming—e.g., one based on the Peter Jennings news special *Prejudice: Answering Children's Questions*, and a chronology poster to accompany the Lincoln television special. ▨ ✓ **AMERICA ONLINE** →*keyword* KIDSNET

Misc (ML) Ask any question. Seek an answer to any problem, family-related or otherwise. Only computer-related issues are not welcome. What is? You may want to get advice on how to fix your child's bicycle or what gift to buy a one-year-old. ✓ **INTERNET**→*email* LISTSERV@TREARN.BITNET ✍ *Type in message body:* SUB MISC <YOUR FULL NAME>

Problem Children Information on controlling and helping children who are underachievers, delinquents, substance abusers, or antisocial. Linked with the ADHD echo. ✓ **FIDONET**→*tag* PROBLEM_CHILD

Twins (ML) Discussion about twins, triplets, etc. Includes parenting issues, adult-twin concerns, and research. ✓ **INTERNET**→*email* OWNER-TWINS@ATHENA.MIT.EDU ✍ *Subscribe by request*

Food, wine & cooking

Foodies, gorgers, expense-account abusers, and restaurant snobs look no further. The

Net is as compulsive about food as you are. There's the **J-Food-L** mailing list for sushi lovers. There's **Omaha Steaks** and **Honey Baked Hams** on CompuServe. With near missionary zeal, the newsgroup **rec.food. cooking** helps cooks from one nation communicate with cooks from another. **Zagat**, the master restaurant rater, has thousands of spots searchable by all desires on CompuServe and Prodigy. There's vegetarianism (**rec. food.veg**), there's **Robert Parker on Wine**, there's cooking lite (**Gourmet Cooking**). And for the rest of us, well, there's the universal newsgroup **alt.mc-donalds.**

Monet's picnic—downloaded from biome.bio.dfo.ca.

On the Net

Across the board

Cooking Class Cooking lessons and recipes. ✓**PRODIGY**→*jump* COOKING CLASS

Cooking Club Offers a cookbook full of recipes for all courses, with wine recommendations; The Cupboard, with news on the latest culinary trends and reviews of cookbooks and cooking software, online cooking classes, and online wine tastings. ✓**AMERICA ONLINE**→ *keyword* COOKING

Cooks Online Swap recipes, exchange cooking tips, and plan menus with other cooks. Also includes restaurant reviews and online visits from cooking experts. ✓**COMPUSERVE**→*go* COOKS

CR Foods Articles from *Consumer Reports* on food. ▦ ✓**PRODIGY**→*jump* CR FOODS

Cuisine Chatter on food and drink. Includes many well-tested recipes. ✓**ILINK**→*number* 74

Cuisine Offers shopping tips, recipes, food advice, and restaurant recommendations. ✓**RELAYNET** →*number* 173

Cuisine For sharing recipes and ideas. Covers all types of cuisine. ✓**SMARTNET**→*tag* CUISINE

Food From gourmet recipes to microwave-cooking tips to eating-healthy advice. ⊕☘ ✓**BIX**→*conference* FOOD

Food & Wine Club An umbrella group for all of Prodigy's food and wine services. Includes access to *Zagat*'s guide, recipes, online classes, wine reviews, and access to the FOOD BB. ✓**PRODIGY**→ *jump* FOOD & WINE CLUB

Food & Wine RoundTable Recipe exchanges, discussions about starting a catering business or writing a cookbook, beer-brewing and wine-tasting advice, kitchen-remodeling information, online cooking classes, and more. ⊕☘ ✓**GENIE**→*keyword* FOOD

Food BB Discuss cooking and fine

dining. ✓**PRODIGY**→*jump* FOOD BB

Foodwine (ML) Discussions about food and its accompaniments between people from a variety of disciplines and professions—marketing, hotel management, communications, cultural anthropology, etc. ✓**INTERNET**→*email* LISTSERV@CMUVM.CSV.CMICH.EDU ✍*Type in message body:* SUBSCRIBE FOODWINE <YOUR FULL NAME>

Mariani on Dining A regularly featured column by John Mariani about where and what to eat. ✓**PRODIGY**→*jump* MARIANI

National Cooking Covers everything about food and cooking, including preparation, and the kitchenware and appliances used. ✓**FIDONET**→*tag* COOKING

Cookbooks

Celebrity Cookbook Provides a searchable database of recipes and diets of the stars. Other offerings include etiquette in Perle Mesta's Party Tips and cooking advice. ✓**AMERICA ONLINE**→*keyword* CELEBRITY COOKBOOK

Cookbook A cookbook in compressed postscript. Organized by main ingredient. ✓**INTERNET**→*ftp* MTHVAX.CS.MIMAI.EDU→ANONYMOUS/<YOUR EMAIL ADDRESS>→recipes→beyond.ps.Z ✖*Must be printed on a postscript printer*

Prodigy Cookbook Recipes for more than 2,500 dishes from the *Los Angeles Times* and Betty Crocker cookbooks. ✓**PRODIGY**→*jump* COOKBOOK

rec.food.cooking (NG) For cooks worldwide to share recipes. ✓**USENET**

rec.food.recipes (NG) Even more recipes. ✓**USENET**

Recipes Recipes searchable by keyword and contents. ✓**INTERNET**→*wais* recipes.src

Usenet Cookbook A huge archive of recipes from the REC.FOOD.COOKING newsgroup. ✓**INTERNET**→*ftp* GATEKEEPER.DEC.COM→ANONYMOUS/<YOUR EMAIL ADDRESS>→pub/recipes

Desserts

Chocolate A meeting place for chocolate lovers. ✓**ILINK**→*number* 115

Gimmee Jimmy's Cookies Homemade gourmet cookies. 🛒 ✓**COMPUSERVE**→*go* GIM ✓**GENIE**→*keyword* COOKIES

Drinks

Cider-List (ML) Covers the brewing of cider. ✓**INTERNET**→*email* CIDER-REQUEST@EXPO.LCS.MIT.EDU ✍*Subscribe by request*

Coffee Anyone??? Order from a selection of the world's finest coffees and teas and other gourmet food items. 🛒 ✓**COMPUSERVE**→*go* COF ✓**DELPHI**→*go* SHOP COFFEE ✓**GENIE**→*keyword* COFFEE

CR Beverages Articles in *Consumer Reports* on beverages. ▦ ✓**PRODIGY**→*jump* CR BEVERAGES

rec.food.drink (NG) Recipes for both alcoholic and nonalcoholic drinks. ✓**USENET**

Gourmet foods

Adventures in Food Gourmet food items for sale. Includes fresh cheese, flavored pasta, and meat

CYBERNOTES

"My favorite recipe for bar-bee-que chicken :)

"Go to nearest Keyfood or cheap supermarket and buy/lift/barter some chicken quarters for about 35-45 cents a pound.

"If chicken seems dead anough to cook, then proceed to purchase some end-of-season charcoal.

"Then stock up on some yummy generic bar-bee-que sauce.

"Boil chicken in pot to kill whatever salmonella germs are alive, and remove.

"Schlep to back yard, scrape rust off grill, and proceed to start charcoal.

"If you haven't been engulfed by flames at this point, take chicken and puncture holes throughout.

"Place chicken on grill. Baste with sauce. Bring good book to read as the grease cathes fire and scorches chicken.

"After chicken is a carbonized lump of flesh, get local yellow pages, look up 'chicken delight' and order the 8 piece special. :)

"Total cost: $ 20. Bon appetit! :)"

—from **MindVox's Food Forum**

and fish. 🍲 ✓COMPUSERVE→*go* AIF

Gourmet Cooking Discussions of light, lean, healthy cooking. ✓FIDONET→ *tag* GOURMET

Honey Baked Hams Shop for gourmet food items, including their "world-famous Honey Baked brand ham." 🍲 ✓COMPUSERVE→*go* HAM

Just Terrific Gifts Includes smoked meats, fish and poultry, gourmet gift baskets, teas, and other gourmet foods. 🍲 ✓GENIE →*keyword* GIFTS

Omaha Steaks Gourmet food. Special buys on corn-fed, Midwestern beef. 🍲 ✓COMPUSERVE→ *go* OS

International cuisine

International Cooking International cooking and recipe conference, in English. ✓FIDONET→*tag* INTERCOOK

J-Food-L (ML) For those interested in Japanese food and culture. Created at Kinki University in Japan. Discussions include Japanese restaurants and cooking in the U.S. ✓INTERNET→*email* LIST SERV@UBVM.BITNET ✍ *Type in message body:* SUB J-FOOD-L <YOUR FULL NAME>

Online Gourmet Classical Italian, American, and French cooking recipes. Select from several categories including vegetarian, desserts, and fish and seafood. ✓DELPHI→*go* REF ONLINE

Restaurants

alt.mcdonalds (NG) Discussions about McDonald's. Seriously! ✓USENET

alt.restaurants (NG) Where everyone's a restaurant critic. ✓USENET

rec.food.restaurant (NG) The official group for amateur restaurant critics. ✓USENET

Zagat Restaurant Survey Thousands of restaurant reviews. Search by name, location, cuisine type, or price. ✓COMPUSERVE→*go* ZAGAT ✓PRODIGY→*jump* ZAGAT GUIDE

Vegetarianism

Non-violence and Vegetarianism Messages focused on Ahimsa, the Buddhist principle of nonviolence in word, thought, or action toward any sentient being. The ethics of vegetarianism are a primary topic. ✓FIDONET→*tag* AHIMSA

rec.food.veg (NG) Discussion group and information exchange for vegetarians. ✓USENET

Vegetarian A conference on issues of interest to vegetarians. Discuss recipes, nutrition, philosophy, and concern for animals. ✓ILINK→*number* 165

Vegetarian Restaurants Contains guides to vegetarian restaurants in Canada, the United States, Europe, and other regions. ✓INTERNET→*ftp* PIT-MANAGER.MIT.EDU →ANONYMOUS/<YOUR EMAIL ADDRESS>→pub/usenet/news.answers. vegetarian/guide

Wine

Bacchus Wine Forum Provides information and contacts for a variety of both wine and homebrewing topics. Includes full-text issues of the newsletter *The*

Informed Enophile and regular online wine-tasting parties with other members. 🍲💬 ✓COMPUSERVE→*go* WINEFORUM

Home Wine Maker's Conference Information on wine kits, recipes, and techniques for the novice as well as the expert. ✓FIDONET→*tag* VIN_MAISON

Parker on Wine A column written by wine expert Robert Parker. ✓PRODIGY→*jump* PARKER

Wine&Beer Conference about tasting and making wines and beers. ✓ILINK→*number* 176

Wine & Dine Online Offers a database of wine ratings and reviews, a restaurant and winery guide, a home-brewing section, and a travel guide. 🍲💬📷 ✓AMERICA ONLINE→*keyword* WINE

Wine, Beer & Spirits BB Topics include beer and wine basics, wine making and equipment, and a Wine Talk Lounge. Wine experts are often Prodigy guests. ✓PRODIGY→*jump* WINE BB

Wines For wine lovers, a forum devoted exclusively to wine topics. ✓SMARTNET→WINES

Miscellaneous

The Chef's Catalog Cookware and kitchen accessories. 🍲 ✓COMPUSERVE→*go* CC

Florida Fruit Shippers Oranges, grapefruit, and tropical fruit. 🍲 ✓COMPUSERVE→*go* FFS

rec.food.historic (NG) From dining etiquette to comparative cuisines from different countries. ✓USENET

Gardening

Cultivate a mango tree, try out the Troy-Bilt lawn vacuum

and shredder, keep a grapefruit tree alive in winter, find out what's killing your jade plant, get some info on mutant gaillardias, or graft a tomato plant onto a potato plant, all on the newsgroup **rec.garden**. Determined to keep a bonsai tree alive? Consult the FAQ on **rec.arts.bonsai**. Want to integrate your technical life with your gardening one? Get the shareware program **The Gardener's Assistant**. For the full menu of gardening interests try the **Gardening Forum** on CompuServe.

On the Net

Across the board

Agriculture Covers agriculture, farming, and gardening topics. ✓**SMARTNET**→AGRICULTURE

The Gardening Message Center Where AOL'ers go to share gardening tips. ✓**AMERICA ONLINE**→*keyword* EXCHANGE→THE GARDENING MESSAGE CENTER

Gardening Archive An archive of information about gardening gathered from postings on Usenet newsgroups and arranged in directories such as Herbs, Bonsai, Lawns, Soil, Ornamentals, and Edibles. ✓**INTERNET**→*ftp* FTP.LYSATOR. LIU.SE→ANONYMOUS/<YOUR EMAIL

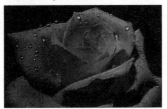

A rose—from America Online's PC Graphics Forum.

ADDRESS>→gardening

Gardening Forum Managed by the National Gardening Association, publishers of the *National Gardening Magazine.* Contains guides to create and care for flower, vegetable, herb, and fruit gardens. Also offers help with houseplants, tools, landscaping, and pest control.  ✓**COMPUSERVE**→*go* GARDENING

Gardens Offers general discussion for home gardening, including the care and growth of vegetables, flowers, bonsai trees, and indoor plants. ✓**RELAYNET**→*number* 386

Gardens & Gardening (ML) From herbs to flowers to vegetables, any topic relating to home gardening is open for discussion. Novices welcome. ✓**INTERNET**→ *email* LISTSERV@UKCC.UKY.EDU ✍*Type in message body:* SUBSCRIBE GARDENS <YOUR FULL NAME>

Home and Garden Not only gardening but lawn care, home maintenance, and other hints. ✓**FIDONET**→*tag* HOME-N-GRDN

Home&Garden Advice on gardening and landscaping. ✓**ILINK**→

number 134

rec.gardens (NG) Where professional and amateur gardeners share tips, stories, and reviews. ✓**USENET**

Victory Garden Includes advice from plant pathologists, horticulturists, and gardeners who are also involved with the *Victory Garden* series on PBS-TV. ✓**PRODIGY** →*jump* VICTORY GARDEN

Bonsai

Bonsai (ML) Discussion of bonsai maintenance and philosophy. ✓**INTERNET**→*email* LISTSERV@CMS. CC.WAYNE.EDU ✍*Type in message body:* SUB BONSAI <YOUR FULL NAME>

rec.arts.bonsai (NG) Discussions about miniature trees and shrubbery. ✓**USENET**

Gardening software

The Gardener's Assistant A shareware program (DOS) that analyzes the information you enter and responds with gardening advice. ✓**INTERNET**→*ftp* WUARCHIVE. WUSTL.EDU→ANONYMOUS/<YOUR EMAIL ADDRESS>→systems/ibmpc/msdos/ database→gardner.zip

Orchids

Orchids (ML) A forum for gardeners raising orchids. ✓**INTERNET**→ *email* MAILSERV@SCU.BITNET ✍*Type in message body:* SUBSCRIBE ORCHIDS

Florist

Flower Stop Flowers and gifts. ✓**COMPUSERVE**→*go* FS

Walter Knoll Florist Plants, flowers, fruits, and balloons. ✓**COMPUSERVE**→*go* WK ✓**GENIE**→ *keyword* KNOLL

Genealogy

"One of the difficult aspects of genealogy—at least for
me—is trying to explain to friends why a grown man should spend countless hours in a musty library or chasing around the country copying inscriptions from tombstones in overgrown cemeteries," says one participant in the CompuServe **Genealogy Forum**. Nevertheless, genealogy has made it big. The **FamilySearch Center**, a Mormon offshoot, supplies much of the genealogy data information on the Net (Mormons believe they can correct ancestral missteps). The other contributor to the genealogy movement is the PC, which has automated searches and made available efficient database programs. Check out shareware genealogy databases on FidoNet's **Genealogy Software**.

On the Net

Across the board

Genealogy Features information on how to begin researching your family history, helpful computer software, and more. ✓**RELAYNET**→ *number* 136

Genealogy and Family History International Discussions about family history anywhere in

Coat of arms—from CompuServe's Genealogy Forum.

the world except the U.S., although information on records of immigration to and from the U.S. is discussed. ✓**FIDONET**→*tag* GENE ALOGY.EUR

Genealogy BB Research your roots. Board topics include surnames, national and state resources, adoption, nationalities, and more. ✓**PRODIGY**→*jump* GENE ALOGY BB

Genealogy Club Offers beginner and advanced classes in genealogy, software, research help, and a surname file area. ⊛✪ ✓**AMERICA ONLINE**→*keyword* ROOTS

Genealogy Forum Want to know how to read or photograph a faded tombstone? Or find a list of foreign genealogical societies? Or search for people with your parent's surnames? Offers answers to these questions, plus contacts with professional and amateur genealogists, programs for PCs, and other research aids. ⊛✪ ✓**COMPUSERVE** →*go* ROOTS

Genealogy & History Round-Table Exchange genealogical information or discuss means of genealogical research, historical periods, software, and new books on historical subjects. ⊛✪ ✓**GENIE**→ *keyword* HISTORY

National Genealogical BBS (BBS) Share findings and discuss family-history research. Sponsored by the National Genealogical Society and includes FidoNet conferences and a list of genealogy BBSs. 703-528-2612

soc.roots (NG/ML) For those tracing their roots. ✓**USENET** ✓**INTERNET** →*email* LISTSERV@VM1.NODAK.EDU ✍ *Type in message body:* SUB ROOTS-L <YOUR FULL NAME>

Data & software

Genealogy Archive Database programs, lists of genealogical societies, magazines and newsletters, cemetery infomation, tips for beginners, and much more. ✓**INTERNET**→*ftp* WOOD.CEBAF.GOV →ANONYMOUS/<YOUR EMAIL ADDRESS> →genealogy

Genealogy Forum: "Who's Got What" (WGW) Ask a question of the WGW database, a directory of where to find family-tree source information. ✓**FIDONET** →*tag* WGW

Genealogy Software Software and hardware for building family trees. Includes reviews, announcements from suppliers, and help. ✓**FIDONET**→*tag* GENSOFT

National Genealogical Conference Data exchange on all aspects of genealogy, including questions, help, software announcements, and research information. ✓**FIDONET**→*tag* GENEALOGY

Homeownership

So you've bought the dream house. Now wake up and smell the mildew, the septic sys-tem, and the gas leaks. And try **This Old House** on Prodigy for sane, calm, and expert advice; **Home & Real Estate RoundTable** on GEnie for its database of home-decorating and -repair info; and **HouseNet**, a BBS run by a husband-and-wife fixer-up team. Alternative energy systems for the home are covered in detail on FidoNet's **Alternative Energy Systems** and **Homemade Power.**

On the Net

Across the board

Cohousing (ML) Discussion of cohousing. ✓**INTERNET**→*email* LIST SERV@UCI.COM ✍ *Type in message body:* SUBSCRIBE COHOUSING-L <YOUR FULL NAME>

Home & Real Estate Round-Table Discussions range from redecorating to landscaping to getting a mortgage. Includes a library of information as well as GIFs of homes and decorating projects. ◉✿ ✓**GENIE**→*keyword* HOME

Homehnts Offers household hints, solutions to problems, and discussion about other home issues. ✓**RELAYNET**→*number* 215

Homelife BB Topics range from marriage to interior decoration. ✓**PRODIGY**→*jump* HOMELIFE BB

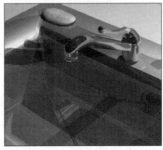

Kitchen sink—from CompuServe's Graphics Developers Forum.

misc.consumers.house (NG) Discussion about maintaining a house, with advice on plumbing, carpentry, and other interior and exterior work. ✓**USENET**

Real Buying, selling, and renting real estate, with information on mortgages, leases, management, and more. ✓**FIDONET**→*tag* REAL

Relocation Network Try the International Relocation Network for advice when moving to a new city. ◉ ✓**COMPUSERVE**→*go* RELO

This Old House A weekly column on home maintenance and repair written by a staff of professional carpenters, electricians, plumbers, civil engineers, and renovation experts. ✓**PRODIGY**→*jump* THIS OLD HOUSE

Handyman

CR Workshop *Consumer Reports* articles on workshop-related products. ▦ ✓**PRODIGY**→*jump* CR WORKSHOP

Handyman Offers tips and advice on do-it-yourself projects in the home, materials to use, and auto repair. ✓**RELAYNET**→*number* 149

Home Repair Do-it-yourself home handyman advice. ✓**FIDONET** →*tag* HOME_REPAIR

HouseNet (BBS) Expert home-repair and remodeling advice, run by a husband-and-wife team of syndicated columnists who cover the home and workshop. 410-745-2037 $25/YEAR

Tools & appliances

alt.locksmithing (NG) For discussions of locksmithing, ranging from picking locks to home security. ✓**USENET**

Andersen Windows For window shopping. ◉ ✓**PRODIGY**→ *jump* ANDERSEN

CR Tools *Consumer Reports* articles on tools. ▦ ✓**PRODIGY**→*jump* CR TOOLS

HomeAppliance Features discussions about repairing home appliances, including buying and selling parts. ✓**SMARTNET**→HOME APPLIANCE

Energy

Home Automation "The home automation boom is just around the corner; join the conference now for a head start." Discussions about wireless remote controls, energy-saving devices, voice control, scheduled controls, and more. ✓**FIDONET**→*tag* HOMEAUT

Kids & teens

Prodigy works for kids. After school, they'll rush to Kid's Games, where there are math quizzes as well as evil forces to battle, or **Kid's Stories**, where reading becomes a participatory activity, or **Make It**, for easy crafting instructions, instead of to the sitcom reruns on TV. For preschoolers, Prodigy has **Sesame Street**; for older kids, **National Geographic** and **Nova**; and for preteen girls, **The Baby-Sitters Club**—interactive stories based on the ubiquitous book series. Older teens move to AOL for real-time chat on **Teen Scene**.

On the Net

Across the board

alt.kids-talk (NG) From aliens to relationships, talk is oriented toward the younger crowd, but there are no age limits. ✓**USENET**

The Baby-Sitters Club For girls ages 7 to 14, BSC offers monthly interactive stories where those participating determine the outcome; advice from author Ann Martin on teen problems; an electronic datebook to keep track of birthdays, homework, and babysitting jobs; a library of articles and tips on babysitting; and other features. ✓**PRODIGY**→*jump* BABYSITTERS $$

The Family and Personal Growth RoundTable Covers all

Teenager—downloaded from Compu-Serve's Graphics Plus Forum.

aspects of family life, relationships, and personal growth. Includes private boards for kids and teens. ✓**GENIE**→*keyword* FAMILY

International Kids Conference Offers users under age 18 a free exchange. Adults are encouraged to give it direction. ✓**FIDONET** →*tag* KIDS

Students' Forum Offers students contact with other students worldwide for general discussion. ✓**COMPUSERVE**→*go* STUFO

Crafts 'n' games

Kid's Games Access a menu of games including Square Off (a

timed math game), Guts (7 minutes for 7 trivia questions in a 7-week tournament), Frantic Guts (even harder than Guts), Mad Madmaze (evil forces threaten your town in this maze adventure game), Twisted Tales (see your prechosen words flowed into a story with hilarious effect), Smart Kids Quiz, FITB (fill in the blanks to solve the puzzle), Boxes (a.k.a. Reversi or Othello), Game Center, Thinker (a challenging online puzzle game), and, of course, the ever-popular Carmen Sandiego (follow Carmen across the globe in mystery capers). ✓**PRODIGY**→*jump* KIDS GAMES

Kid's Stories Features several interactive stories: For Kids By Kids posts kids' responses to topics such as "your most embarrassing moment"; Reading Magic allows the reader to determine the outcome of a story by making choices throughout the story; Story World challenges the reader to write the story's ending, and the best endings are posted; Krazy Kaption seeks the best caption for a weekly cartoon; Punch Lines is always looking for good jokes; Abel Adventures takes the reader on a mystery voyage; and By the Sword is an ongoing adventure in a land of dragons, wizards, and magic. ✓**PRODIGY**→*jump* KIDS STORIES

Make It! Each month a new project with illustrated step-by-step instructions that demonstrate how to make a specific craft. Previous projects and different levels are also available. ✓**PRODIGY**→*jump* MAKE IT

Kid talk

The Club BB Kids meet and talk with peers. This board is accessible to users under the age of 12.

✓**PRODIGY**→*jump* THE CLUB BB

Kids A closed conference for kids. ✓**BIX**→*conference* BIX.KIDS ✖ *No adults*

Pre-Teens Offers conversation and education in BBS skills for anyone under the age of 13. ✓**RELAYNET**→*number* 310

Scouting

International Scouting Conference For young people: meet and discuss scouting with fellow scouts from around the world. ✓**FIDONET**→*tag* SCOUTING

---

rec.scouting (NG) For international discussions about scouting. ✓**USENET**

Scouter Discussions on everything about the Boy Scouts, Girl Scouts, and other scouting organizations worldwide. Includes adult leaders and youth members. ✓**FIDONET**→*tag* INTERNATIONAL

Scouting Offers contacts and discussion for Boy Scouts and Girl Scouts. ✓**RELAYNET**→*number* 247

Scouts-L (ML) For youth-group members, including those in Scout troops, to interact. ✓**INTERNET**→ *email* LISTSERV@TCUBVM.BITNET ✎*Type in message body:* SUBSCRIBE SCOUTS-L <YOUR FULL NAME>

Smart play

National Geographic A new interactive feature each month about the region focused on in the current issue of *National Geographic*. World problems and possible solutions are covered. The Viewpoint area allows you to express an opinion, and Other Features takes you back to previ-

ous destinations. ✓**PRODIGY**→*jump* NATIONAL GEO

NOVA Offers a monthly, interactive science feature, the NOVA Lab and Experiment Archive, where simple science experiments are described. Also features articles. ✓**PRODIGY**→*jump* NOVA

Sesame Street Fun learning for preschoolers. Activities include helping Big Bird find hidden numbers, counting games with the Count, a story section, letters to the child from *Sesame Street* characters, and the ever popular "one of these things is not like the other" challenge. ✓**PRODIGY**→*jump* SESAME STREET

Teen talk

Gayteen Forum for gay teenagers or those questioning their sexuality to communicate, discuss problems, and encourage safe sex. ✓**FIDONET**→*tag* GAYTEEN ✖ *Under 20 only*

International Teenagers By and for teens, with general discussion, review of controversies, and chat ranging from useless to deadly serious. ✓**FIDONET**→*tag* TEEN

Person to Person Often called the Teen SIG, this area serves as a meeting place for young people. ◉♥ ✓**DELPHI**→*go* GR PERS

Teenage Chatter All topics of interest to teenagers. Other generations interested in teen issues are welcome. ✓**FIDONET**→*tag* ECHO_ TEEN

Teens A closed conference just for teens. ✓**BIX**→*conference* BIX.TEENS ✖ *Teens only*

Teens Discussion forum for teens

between 12 and 19 years of age. ✓**RELAYNET**→*number* 142

Teens BB Teens discuss common interests. Only those from 12 to 20 years of age may post on this board. ✓**PRODIGY**→*jump* TEENS BB

Teen Scene A general discussion and conference area for teens, with topics that include likes and dislikes, online pen pals, and opinions about movies, videos, video games, and music. ◉♥ ✓**AMERICA ONLINE**→*keyword* TEEN

TeenTalk Popular forum for teens —no specific topics. ✓**SMARTNET**→ *tag* TEENTALK

Tott Special support group for teens facing a variety of problems, including, drug use, gang involvement, pregnancy, and low self-esteem. Includes peers and adult supporters—handles are used to protect special participants from the Fresno County Juvenile Hall. ✓**FIDONET**→*tag* TOTT ✖*No profanity, racial remarks, name-calling, or gang propaganda*

Young Adult Forum A place to talk about growing up and the problems of youth. For the young and the young-at-heart. ✓**FIDONET** →*tag* YOUNG_ADULT

Miscellaneous

Ask Beth Advice for teenagers and their parents. ✓**PRODIGY**→ *jump* BETH

Kid Video The latest video releases for kids. ✓**PRODIGY**→*jump* KID VIDEO

RHS "Raider" BBS (BBS) Interested in what a high school BBS is like? Check out Richmond High School's board. 615-527-3994 FREE

Photography

Would-be or amateur photographers could take a course, or spend money on trial

and error, or check out the FAQ on **rec.photo**. It's pithy, succinct and just about all you'll have to know. For equipment issues try **Nikon IC** on AOL, the **Photography Forum** on CompuServe, or the **Photo Forum** on Delphi. For technological updates, try the **Photo Conference** on BIX and the mailing list **Stereo Photography**.

On the Net

Cameras For anyone with an interest in photography. ✓ **SMART-NET**→*tag* CAMERAS

Kodak Photography Forum Provides answers to questions about Kodak products, explanations of photographic techniques, online exhibits, chat, and photo aids. ⊕☺ ✓ **AMERICA ONLINE**→*keyword* PHOTOGRAPHY

Nikon IC Information and discussions related to Nikon Electronic Imaging. Areas include Nikon News, Product Information, Tech Support, Developer Services, and a message board. Open to discussions about electronic photography and image processing. ▦ ⊕☺ ✓ **AMERICA ONLINE**→*keyword* NIKON

Photo Conference for photographers. Topics include cameras, composition, camera exchange (for swapping, selling, or buying

Camera—downloaded from Compu-Serve's Graphics Developers Forum.

equipment), digitizing, and a calendar (for event postings). ⊕☺ ✓ **BIX**→*conference* PHOTO

Photo Covers photographic techniques, equipment, film development, and photo news. ✓ **RELAY-NET**→*number* 113

Photo & Video RoundTable For both pro and amateur photographers. Features libraries of photo tips, software, and utility programs as well as the Smithsonian On Line and Kodak On Line. Discuss photography on one of the many bulletin-board topics. ⊕☺ ✓ **GENIE**→*keyword* PHOTO

The Photo Forum Includes databases of information such as Starting Out/Keeping Up and Cameras/Film/Technical as well as the photo databases Portraits & People and Natural Beauty & Animal Life, among others. And

for professionals, there's the Pro's Corner. ⊕☺ ✓ **DELPHI**→*go* GR PHOTO

Photography Forum For professionals and amateurs, with tips and discussion on equipment, techniques, types of film, and examples of photo work. Exchange advice on the 35mm Cameras or the Color Processing boards or explore the Photo Software or Camera & Lenses libraries. ⊕☺ ✓ **COMPUSERVE**→*go* PHOTOFORUM

Photo-L (ML) Discuss any aspect of photography, from photo aesthetics to camera equipment. ✓ **INTERNET**→*email* LISTSERV@BUACCA.BITNET ✍ *Type in message body:* SUB PHOTO-L <YOUR FULL NAME>

Photosig Discuss photography and photographic techniques, film, cameras, and auxiliary equipment. Amateurs and professionals welcome. ✓ **ILINK**→*number* 12

Photosource International Listings of the photo needs of buyers in the publishing and promotion industries, includes deadlines and fees. ✓ **GENIE**→*keyword* PSI

rec.photo (NG) Includes information and discussion on equipment, film, camera settings, and photo subjects. ✓ **USENET**

Stereo Photography (ML) Covers all topics related to stereo or 3-dimensional photography. ✓ **INTERNET**→*email* LISTSERV@CSG.LBL.GOV ✍ *Type in message body:* SUBSCRIBE PHOTO-3D <YOUR FULL NAME>

Shopping & classified

Will the Net become a cybermall? Once thought of as primarily a shopping medium, the commercial Net has so far disappointed many with wild retail fantasies. But each of the commercial services maintains fairly broad shopping services. Perhaps the most successful selling on the Net is user to user (rather than retailer to user) in the classified listings that have been created in specialty markets. Try the newsgroup **misc.forsale.computers** and **rec.bicycles. marketplace** and **rec. games.video.marketplace**. And check out **GarageSale** on SmartNet for the last word in cyberjunk.

On the Net

Classifieds

ADCON Network (BBS) Specializes in advertising, consulting, programming, and consumer information. 🛒 913-271-7107 FREE

Buy-Sell Ads for those interested in selling and those interested in buying. 🛒 ✓ILINK→*number* 48

Classified Ads Buy or sell computers, cars, collectibles, and more. 🛒 ✓GENIE→*keyword* ADS

Classified Advertising An area for all users to advertise for-sale, wanted, or tradable items. 🛒 ✓FIDONET→*tag* CLASSIFIEDS ✗*No*

Shopping mall—downloaded from CompuServe's Graphics Gallery.

commercial ads

Classifieds Read or place your own classified advertisement. 🛒 ✓PRODIGY→*jump* CLASSIFIEDS

Classifieds Sell, find, and trade goods and services with other America Online members. 🛒 ✓AMERICA ONLINE→*keyword* CLASSIFIEDS

Commercial For Sale Message Area Commercial ads placed by businesses—purchases open to anyone. 🛒 ✓FIDONET→*tag* CFORSALE ✗*No personals*

FidoNet Yellow Pages Area for commerical systems to place brief ads—a "legal" conference for commercial advertising. 🛒 ✓FIDONET →*tag* YELLOWPAGES

4$Sale Buy and sell ads from users, primarily of computer equipment and software. Dealers

are allowed, but they may advertise the same products only once each week. 🛒 ✓RELAYNET→*number* 102

ForSale Interested in buying or selling something at a discount? Here's the place. 🛒 ✓SMARTNET→ *tag* FORSALE

GarageSale Post any items, except computer products, that you're interested in selling. Commercial ads are allowed with restrictions. 🛒 ✓SMARTNET→ GARAGESALE

Log On America (BBS) Features a shopping area, a classifieds section, and *USA Today*. 🖥 🛒 ◉▪ 401-739-4100 FREE

Marketplace BB Buy, sell, and trade personal items and rent property. Categories range from comics to computers. 🛒 ✓PRODIGY→*jump* MARKETPLACE BB

misc.forsale (NG) Messages about any and all items that Usenet users are looking to sell. 🛒 ✓USENET

National For Sale Conference for selling personal items only— not for selling your business's products. 🛒 ✓FIDONET→*tag* FORSALE ✗*No commercial ads*

rec.arts.anime.marketplace (NG) For those selling and buying anime videos and other products. 🛒 ✓USENET

rec.arts.comics.marketplace (NG) For-sale and wanted listings related to various kinds of comics. 🐦 ✓**USENET**

rec.arts.sf.marketplace (NG) Personal ads for selling or looking to buy sci-fi-related materials. 🐦 ✓**USENET**

rec.bicycles.marketplace (NG) Postings by those looking for or wanting to sell bicycle equipment. Includes equipment reviews and names of businesses selling bicycle components. 🐦 ✓**USENET**

rec.games.frp.marketplace (NG) Buy and sell role-playing-game materials. 🐦 ✓**USENET**

rec.games.video.marketplace (NG) Video games for sale! 🐦 ✓**USENET**

rec.music.makers.marketplace (NG) Requests range from MIDI equipment to grand pianos. 🐦 ✓**USENET**

rec.music.marketplace (NG) Post here for CDs and tapes. 🐦 ✓**USENET**

rec.travel.marketplace (NG) Postings of tickets and accommodations for those looking to buy or sell. 🐦 ✓**USENET**

Unclassifieds Conference for buying, selling, and swapping whatever you want. 🐦 ✓*BIX→conference* UNCLASSIFIEDS

Computer classifieds

comp.sys.amiga.marketplace (NG) Discussions about where to buy Amiga products. 🐦 ✓**USENET**

comp.sys.apple2.marketplace (NG) For buying and selling products related to the Apple II

system. ✓**USENET**

comp.sys.next.marketplace (NG) Postings about where to buy NeXT hardware and software as well as NeXT-related job announcements. 🐦 ✓**USENET**

misc.forsale.computers* (NG) Several newsgroups (e.g., MISC. FORSALE.COMPUTERS.MAC) devoted to selling used computer equipment. 🐦 ✓**USENET**

Consumer affairs

Consumer Advocate General talk about consumer affairs, boycotts, laws and legislation, and scams or rip-offs. ✓**FIDONET→***tag* C_ADVOCAT

Consumer Report Discussions, pro and con, about products and services, with ideas taken from the consumer press. ✓**FIDONET→***tag* CONSUMER_REPORT ✖*No advertising*

Consumer Reports Full-text articles from *Consumer Reports.* ▤ ✓**AMERICA ONLINE→***keyword* CONSUMER ✓**COMPUSERVE→***go* CONSUMER ✓**PRODIGY→***jump* CR

Consumer Self-Defense and Scam Alert Remedies against scams, con games, and other unethical practices. Helps users learn how to protect themselves and recoup their losses. ✓**FIDONET** →*tag* ANTI_SCAM

TRW Credentials Service Maintain vigilance over your credit. 🐦 ✓**COMPUSERVE→***go* CRE ✓**GENIE→***keyword* TRWCREDIT

Shopping centers

The AOL Products Center Shop in a single area and go through the "checkout" only once

for all AOL products. Bill them to your AOL account or a credit card. 🐦 ✓**AMERICA ONLINE→***keyword* AOL PRODUCTS

Comp-u-Store Online Offers discounts on numerous manufacturers' list prices (and even greater discounts and warranties if you become a member). Shop for more than 250,000 products with brand names from Radio Shack to Rayban. 🐦 ✓**AMERICA ONLINE→** *keyword* COMPUSTORE ✓**DELPHI→***go* SHOP COMP ✓**GENIE→** *keyword* CUS

The Electronic Mall Includes stores such as Barnes & Noble, Brooks Brothers, Lands End, Gimmee Jimmy's Cookies, and Walter Knoll Florist. 🐦 ✓**COMPUSERVE→***go* MALL

GEnie Shopping Mall More than 25 shops and services. 🐦 ✓**GENIE→** *keyword* GENIEMALL

The Prodigy Mall The menu to all Prodigy stores and catalogs. 🐦 ✓**PRODIGY→***jump* PRODIGY MALL

Prodigy Shop Items with the Prodigy logo. 🐦 ✓**PRODIGY→***jump* PRODIGY SHOP

Department stores

JCPenney Apparel, electronics, merchandise, and gift certificates. 🐦 ✓**COMPUSERVE→***go* JCP ✓**GENIE→** *keyword* JCPENNEY

Sears Online department store. 🐦 ✓**COMPUSERVE→***go* SR ✓**PRODIGY** →*jump* SEARS

Shopping clubs

Shoppers Advantage Club Discount shopping club. 🐦 ✓**COMPUSERVE→***go* SAC

Part 9

Lifestyles, Leisure & Travel

9

Amusements & thrills

Roller coasters, pyrotechnics, nootropic drugs, and *MacGyver* just about sums it up.

Certainly, you won't want to miss the **rec.roller-coaster** FAQ, where you'll learn the vocab (*negative G's, positive G's, speed dip,* and *parabolic,* for instance); locate the steepest, highest, fastest, and most demented coaster; and get a scorecard for the wildest/awesomest/scariest coaster. For a treatise on hallucinogenic mushrooms ("If you know or suspect that a tripper is experiencing eyes-open visual hallucinations, you might want to take them to a place where there are no regular geometric patterns"), check out the natural-highs FAQ on **alt. drugs**.

Marijuana leaves—downloaded from ftp.u.washington.edu.

Pyrotechnics

The Big Book of Mischief A compilation of articles from sources such as *The Poor Man's James Bond* and REC.PYROTECHNICS. Also known in certain circles as *The Terrorist's Handbook.* ✓**INTERNET**→*ftp* WORLD.STD.COM→ANONYMOUS/<YOUR EMAIL ADDRESS>→obi/ Mischief→tbbom 13.txt

National Pyrotechnic Echo The art and technique of legal fireworks, including construction and display. Includes information on shows and upcoming events.

✓**FIDONET**→*tag* PYRO

rec.pyrotechnics (NG) For discussion of fireworks and explosives, especially their construction. ✓**USENET**

Recreational drugs

alt.drugs (NG) Offers a guide to "natural highs," including serious discussion of the botanical and chemical background of wild and domesticated plants that can be used in illegal ways. ✓**USENET**

alt.hemp (NG) Discuss hemp and its agricultural and medicinal uses. ✓**USENET**

alt.psychoactives (NG) Share experiences and discuss side effects of nootropic "smart" drugs. ✓**USENET**

alt.rave (NG) Discussion of the rave culture, including the underground dance scene and drug use. ✓**USENET**

Drugs Archive Contains the FAQs from the ALT.DRUGS newsgroup as well as other drug-related files (e.g., how to make cocaine or grow mushrooms). ✓**INTERNET**→*ftp* FTP.U.WASHINGTON.EDU→ANONYMOUS/<YOUR EMAIL ADDRESS>→pub lic/alt.drugs

talk.politics.drugs (NG) Almost entirely devoted to drug-legalization issues. ✓**USENET**

Roller coasters

rec.roller-coaster (NG) Promises to provide everything you need to know to be a coaster fanatic. Review roller coasters, discuss experiences, learn the jargon, and more. ✓**USENET**

Roller Coaster Archive Roller coaster images, descriptions and reviews, and other coaster stuff. ✓**INTERNET**→*ftp* GBORO.ROWAN.EDU→ ANONYMOUS/<YOUR EMAIL ADDRESS>→ pub/Coasters

Automobiles

A middle-aged man in a sports car—in the 1960s, baby boomers laughed when their

fathers made this a cliché of the mid-life crisis. But today's aging boomers, immune to self-consciousness, are setting sales records for a new generation of imported roadsters and fixing up the classic models their dads left in the garage. You can find them on the Net sending pictures of their convertible Miatas (cherry red with black interior) to the **Auto RoundTable** on GEnie, or hunting after parts for their '63 MG on the Internet's **British-Cars** mailing list.

Chevrolet—downloaded from America Online's PC Graphics Forum.

On the Net

Across the board

Auto RoundTable Discussions range from the speed limit to car classics. Includes a software library where you can download a GIF of a favorite car and a program that lets you design your own car. 🔵🎮 ✓**GENIE**→*keyword* AUTO

Automobile Forum Covers all areas of the auto world, including buying and selling, repair, insurance, safety issues, classic cars, and cars of the future. 🔵🎮 ✓**COM-PUSERVE**→*go* CARS

Automotive BB Discuss auto interests and automotive industry issues. ✓**PRODIGY**→*jump* AUTOMOTIVE BB

Autos Topics include Racing for the amateur and professional; Detroit, for discussions about American cars; Models, which covers model cars of all types; and Tech, for engineering and technical discussions. 🔵🎮 ✓**BIX**→*conference* AUTOS

Cars Everything about cars, old and new, including personal gripes. ✓**FIDONET**→*tag* CARS

Cars&Driving Covers anything related to automobiles, RVs, trucks, or motorcycles. ✓**ILINK**→*number* 110

For the Automotive Enthusiast Conversations about everything automotive, from car restoration to auto-racing. ✓**FIDONET**→*tag* AUTOMOTIVE

rec.autos (NG) Discussion on all automotive topics not covered in the other auto newsgroups. Lots of "Hey, does anyone have this problem" inquiries. The REC.AUTOS FAQ lists several other auto mailing lists not covered here. ✓**USENET**

Mobile stereo

MobileStereo Discussions about car stereos. ✓**ILINK**→*number* 200

rec.audio.car (NG) Offers a wide range of discussions about car stereos, including favorite brands, installation, speakers, car acoustics, and custom creations. ✓**USENET**

Auto repair

Auto-Fix Intended to provide honest advice to car owners with questions and repair needs. Car racing is also a frequent topic of discussion. ✓**SMARTNET**→*tag* AUTO-FIX

Last Chance Garage Regular column written by an auto-maintenance-and-repair expert. ✓**PRODIGY**→*jump* LAST CHANCE GARAGE

rec.autos.tech (NG) For discussing the design, construction, diagnosis, and service of automobiles. ✓**USENET**

British cars

British Car Echo Talk about all types of British autos, including repair suggestions, where to find parts, club notices, and show announcements. ✓**FIDONET**→*tag* BRIT_CAR

British-Cars (ML) Forum for discussing British sports cars. Topics include repairing and racing. ✓**INTERNET**→*email* BRITISH-CARS-REQUEST@AUTOX.TEAM.NET ✍*Subscribe by request*

Car companies

Buick Magazine Car information and customer service for Buick owners. ☞ ✓**COMPUSERVE**→*go* BU

Ford Electronic Showroom Information about cars and trucks, as well as a dealer locator. ☞ ✓**COMPUSERVE**→*go* FORD

Lincoln Mercury Electronic Showroom Car information and dealer locator. ☞ ✓**COMPUSERVE**→*go* LM

Hot rods

alt.autos.rod-n-custom (NG) Devoted to the American hobby of customizing and souping up older cars. ✓**USENET**

alt.hotrod (NG/ML) Forum for people interested in high-performance vehicles. ✓**USENET** ✓**INTERNET**→*email* HOTROD-REQUEST@DIXIE.COM ✍*Type in subject line:* SUBSCRIBE <YOUR EMAIL ADDRESS>

rec.autos.rod-n-custom (NG) Offers discussion about high-performance cars, from body modifications to car racing. ✓**USENET**

Listings & quotes

Auto Manufacturers Advertisements and information from a variety of cars manufacturers, including Audi, BMW, Chrysler, Lincoln, Mazda, Volkswagen, and several others. ✓**PRODIGY**→*jump* AUTO MANUFACTURERS

Automobile Information Center Wholesale and retail prices listed from 1978 to the present. Software and videotapes with automobile information are also available. ☞ ✓**COMPUSERVE**→*go* AI

AutoQuot-R Vehicle price quotes and reports on new cars. Search by make, model, or car type. Discounts on repairs and parts available to club members. ☞ ✓**COMPUSERVE**→*go* AQ ✓**GENIE**→*keyword* AUTOQUOT-R

AutoVantage Online New- and used-car information. Includes car shopping guidelines, price guides for both used and new cars, a locator service for discount service centers, rebates, and more. Browse at no cost or become a member. ☞ ✓**AMERICA**

ONLINE→*keyword* AUTO ✓**COMPUSERVE**→*go* ATV ✓**DELPHI**→*go* SHOP AUTO ✓**GENIE**→*keyword* CARS

New Car Showroom A shopping guide that allows comparisons of price, features, and specifications for more than 500 domestic and foreign cars and trucks. Also lets you calculate monthly payments on the vehicle you select. ☞ ✓**COMPUSERVE**→*go* NEW-CAR $$

Models & makes

Honda-L (ML) Discussions cover Honda and Acura automobiles. ✓**INTERNET**→*email* LISTSERV@BROWN VM.BROWN.EDU ✍*Type in message body:* SUBSCRIBE HONDA-L <YOUR FULL NAME>

Land Rovers (ML) For discussing your Land Rover. ✓**INTERNET**→*email* LAND-ROVER-OWNER-REQUEST@STRATUS.COM ✍*Subscribe by request*

Miata (ML) For Mazda Miata owners. ✓**INTERNET**→*email* LISTSERV@JHUNIX.HCF.JHU.EDU ✍*Type in message body:* SUBSCRIBE MIATA <YOUR FULL NAME>

MR-2 (ML) For those interested in Toyota MR-2s. ✓**INTERNET**→*email* MR2-INTEREST-REQUEST@VALIDGH.COM ✍*Subscribe by request*

Porschephiles (ML) Discussion of Porsches. ✓**INTERNET**→*email* PORSCHEPHILES-REQUEST@TTA.COM ✍*Subscribe by request*

Quattro (ML) Discussion about all Audi cars, especially the AWD Quattro models. ✓**INTERNET**→*email* QUATTRO-REQUEST@ARIES.EAST.SUN.COM ✍*Subscribe by request*

rec.autos.vw (NG) For discussing Volkswagen automobiles.

Automobiles Lifestyles, Leisure & Travel

✓**USENET**

RX7Net (ML) For those who own or are interested in RX7 Mazdas. ✓**INTERNET**→*email* RX7CLUB@CBJJN.ATT.COM ✍*Subscribe by request*

Saturn (ML) Discussion about Saturn cars—the good and the bad. ✓**INTERNET**→*email* SATURN-REQUEST@OAR.NET ✍*Subscribe by request*

Toyota (ML) Discussion for Toyota owners and prospective buyers. ✓**INTERNET**→*email* TOYOTA-REQUEST@QUACK.SAC.CA.US ✍*Subscribe by request*

VetteNet (ML) For Corvette owners and enthusiasts. ✓**INTERNET**→*email* VETTES-REQUEST@CHILLER.COM PAQ.COM ✍*Subscribe by request*

Volvo Net (ML) Discussion of Volvo automobiles, especially about those of the last 25 years. ✓**INTERNET**→*email* VOLVO-NET-REQUEST @ME.ROCHESTER.EDU ✍*Subscribe by request*

Old & exotic

Exotic-Cars (ML) Discussion about the world's rarest and most desirable cars. ✓**INTERNET**→*email* EXOTIC-CARS-REQUEST@SOL.ASL.HITACHI.COM ✍*Subscribe by request*

Old Cars Talk about old cars (15 years old or older), parts for them, and stories. ✓**FIDONET**→*tag* OLDCARS

Old Cars Offers discussion on everything about old cars, including finding parts, restoration techniques, car-club shows, auctions, and the vintage-car hobby in general. ✓**RELAYNET**→*number* 331

rec.autos.antique (NG) Forum for discussing older cars, especially parts, auto shows, car care, history, and nostalgia. ✓**USENET**

Worldwide Car Network The Worldwide Car Network is the largest provider of information on the exotic- and collectible-car market. The forum covers everything from nostalgia to driving to parts information for classic and later models of cars, motorcycles, and trucks from around the world. A large percentage of the members are from the United Kingdom and Europe. ✓**COMPUSERVE**→*go* WCN

Reviews

Consumer Reports Auto *Consumer Report* articles on cars. 🖳 ✓**COMPUSERVE**→*go* CSR-7741 ✓**PRODIGY**→*jump* CR AUTOS

Consumer Reports Insurance *Consumer Reports* articles on insurance, including car insurance. 🖳 ✓**PRODIGY**→*jump* CR INSURANCE

1994 Cars Reports on car trends and reviews of the new models. ✓**PRODIGY**→*jump* 1994 CARS

Miscellaneous

The Electric Vehicle Discussion Mailing List (ML) Discussions about the present and future direction of electric vehicles. Not intended as a forum for comparing electric vehicles to other vehicles. ✓**INTERNET**→*email* LISTSERV@ SJSUVM1.SJSU.EDU ✍*Type in message body:* SUBSCRIBE EV <YOUR FULL NAME>

Offroad (ML) Share experiences about 4x4 and off-road adventures or anything related to four-wheeling. ✓**INTERNET**→*email* OFFROAD-REQUEST@AI.GTRI.GATECH.EDU ✍*Subscribe by request*

rec.autos.driving (NG) For

---

sharing driving experiences. ✓**USENET**

Truckers Offers information and discussion for truck drivers and their friends on the road. ✓**RELAYNET**→*number* 418

Chat

Rolling thunder. All over the world, people have found a local number that unites them with like-minded (or not) chatters. The leading global kaffeeklatsch is **IRC** (interactive relay chat), available on the Internet. It's divided into hundreds of specialty channels, ranging from the **news** and the **report** channels, which consistently have had the most up-to-date facts about the many crises in Russia, to sex channels galore, to channels in a multitude of languages, to live cricket reporting from India, to a range of oh-hell-let's-just-talk channels. On most chat connections you can create a "private" space to pursue private interests with selected chat partners.

Real-life chatters—downloaded from CompuServe's Graphics Gallery Forum.

On the Net

Live chat

CB Simulator Chat through the night with CompuServe members on one of the three CB bands— General, Adult I, and Adult II— with dozens of channels on each. Pick a channel, some of which have a focus (e.g., teen only) and others of which are open to virtually any topic. There's also the CB Forum, with bulletin boards and libraries, and the Entertainment Center for live gaming. Check out the special CB club rates for CompuServe online time. ⊞▣

⊕💬 ✓**COMPUSERVE**→*go* CB

Conference Enter one of the live conferences that are hosted by the forums, or join a more general live gab session. ⊕💬 ✓**DELPHI**→*go* CONFERENCE

IRC Channels IRC channels come and go, but some survive to become the daily meeting places of people who enjoy real-time group interaction. Channels range from those focused on life and events in specific places— #ARGENTINA, #FRANCE, #ISRAEL, #NIPPON, #SAIGON, #SLOVENIA, #NYU, #BOSTON—to religion-oriented chat in #CHRIST and #ISLAM to computer-oriented chat in #AMIGA and #MACINTOSH. And, as in the Usenet groups, the topics can be oh-so-specific or sometimes just silly: #ANIME, #BORED, #CRICKET, #GAY-TEEN, #HOTSEX, #LONELY, #ROMANCE, #VAMPIRES, and #WRITERS. ⊕💬 ✓**INTERNET**

LaPub An online party designed to remind you of your corner pub. Meet new friends, kick back with a cold drink, and join the monthly contests. ⊕💬 ✓**AMERICA ONLINE**→ *keyword* LAPUB

LiveWire Chat Lines Chat live with several people or privately with one. Live conferences are regularly scheduled on topics ranging from homework help to the paranormal. This is the place to go for quick answers to questions about GEnie or for companionship at 3 a.m. The RoundTable includes a bulletin board and a gossip column. ⊕💬 ✓**GENIE**→*keyword* CHAT

People Connection Start at The Lobby, where you're announced, greeted by a guide who can answer your questions, and allowed to roam around and just talk with those you meet. Move on, if you want, to one of several event rooms where real-time conversations have been scheduled: Authors Cafe, The Women's Room, Romance Connection, New Member Lounge, etc. Create a private room with someone, perhaps a "special someone," and no one else will know you're there. Go to the Center Stage to join an online gameshow or to attend a panel discussion with celebrity guests. And for more real-live chat you'll find chat rooms in almost all the specific forums. ⊕💬 ✓**AMERICA ONLINE**→*keyword* CHAT

Pen pals

Pen Pals For school children who are looking for pen pals in other parts of the world. ✓**RELAYNET**→ *number* 354

soc.penpals (NG) A group to make friends and pen pals. Readers can post information about themselves, such as their interests and hobbies, and those with similar interests will—hopefully—respond. ✓**USENET**

Cyberpunk

The newsgroup alt.cyberpunk is pretty much the last word in cybermeaning, cyberattitudes, and cyberreferences (not to mention cybersuffixes). For true obsessive arcania check out the *Blade Runner* FAQ in the **Cyberpunk Archive**. "What are Replicants?—Replicants are manufactured organisms designed to carry out work too boring, dangerous, or distasteful for humans." Memorable quotes from the film: "Is this testing whether I'm a replicant or a lesbian?" The mailing list **Future Culture** is a must-subscribe for anyone even faintly curious about technology's future. Virtual reality is covered in all its metaphysical and commercial aspects on **sci.virtual-worlds** and in the **Virtual Reality Archive**.

A cover of Inquisitor—*from AOL's Macintosh Communications Forum.*

On the Net

Cyberpunk culture

alt.cyberpunk (NG) Covers virtual reality, the fiction of writers like William Gibson (*Neuromancer*) and Bruce Sterling, and the convergence of cyberpunk with mainstream culture. ✓**USENET**

alt.cyberpunk.chatsubo (NG) For discussions about prose in a virtual-reality setting. ✓**USENET**

alt.cyberpunk.tech (NG) Discuss the latest techie toys (a.k.a. cutting-edge technology). ✓**USENET**

Cyberpunk Archive FAQs on ALT.CYBERPUNK, *Bladerunner*, and the zine *Future Culture*; Bruce Sterling articles and columns; cyberpunk fiction; and cyberpunk news. ✓**INTERNET**→*ftp* MILTON.U.WASHINGTON.EDU→ANONYMOUS/<YOUR EMAIL ADDRESS>→pub/alt.cyberpunk

Cyberspace Vanguard (ML) An electronic zine dedicated to Cyberspace and sci-fi. ✓**INTERNET**→*email* CN577@CLEVELAND.FREENET.EDU ✍*Subscribe by request*

Future Culture (ML) Discussion covers cyberpunk, virtual reality, raves, Generation X, industrial culture, post-postmodernism, etc. Claims the FAQ, "At one time the members of the list were simultaneously discussing Bell's Theorem and who we would cast in *Neuromancer* if it becomes a movie."

✓**INTERNET**→*email* LISTSERV@UAFSYSB.UARK.EDU ✍*Type in message body:* SUBSCRIBE FUTUREC <YOUR FULL NAME>

Virtual reality

Macintosh Virtual Reality FTP Site Repository for Macintosh-related virtual-reality software and *Wired* magazine articles. ✓**INTERNET**→*ftp* FTP.APPLE.COM→ANONYMOUS/<YOUR EMAIL ADDRESS>→pub/VR

sci.virtual-worlds (NG/ML) Discuss all aspects of virtual reality. ✓**USENET** ✓**INTERNET**→*email* LISTSERV@VMD.CSO.UIUC.EDU ✍*Type in message body:* SUB VIRTU-L <YOUR FULL NAME>

VirtReality Discussions on virtual reality and Cyberspace. ✓**ILINK**→*number* TBA

Virtual Reality Includes general-interest and technical discussions on VR, covering availability of units, development of new technologies, computer software, and how to build and use VR hardware like data gloves. ✓**RELAYNET**→*number* 416

Virtual Reality Archive Includes directories on pglove and raytracing as well as virtual audio files, FAQs from groups such as SCI.VIRTUAL-WORLDS, and vendor press releases. ✓**INTERNET**→*ftp* MILTON.U.WASHINGTON.EDU→ANONYMOUS/<YOUR EMAIL ADDRESS>→pub

Virtual World Conference to discuss virtual reality. Topics include bandwidth, where technology challenges are considered; politics, where government involvement with VR is analyzed; and cyberpunk, for discussing the Cyberspace culture and consciousness. ✓**BIX**→*conference* VIRTUAL.WORLD

Cyberdating

With personal pages, dating services, and singles bars out in Cyberspace, it's pretty

much like the real world— except that cyberdating is 100% safe and you don't have to dress for it. If you hit it off, you can create a private room and do what you will with whomever it is you are doing it with. Of course, there are often men who are "hot-chatting" as women and, no doubt, women doing their share of gender surfing too. AOL's **People Connection** is the place to be, whether you're Collette or Mickey Spillane.

A date—downloaded from America Online's Graphic Arts & CAD Forum.

Across the board

People Connection Start at the lobby, where you're announced, greeted by a guide who can answer your questions, and allowed to roam around and just talk with those you meet. Move on, if you desire, to one of several event rooms where live conversations have been scheduled: Authors Cafe, The Women's Room, Romance Connection, New Member Lounge, and several others. You can also create a private room with someone, perhaps a "special someone," and no one else will know you're there. 🖼🗨
✓**AMERICA ONLINE**→*keyword* PC

Flirting

The Flirt's Nook A place for flirts to engage in their art.
✓**FIDONET**→*tag* FLIRTS NOOK

The Friendship Express (BBS) "Our members include singles, couples, bi's, gays, lesbians, as well as those interested in alternative lifestyles such as leather, Xdress, etc." Members from across North America. 612-566-5726 $1/HOUR

Lovers and Other Strangers Flirt electronically. Includes a G-rated area for teen audiences.
✓**FIDONET**→*tag* LOVELINE

Pursuit Men in pursuit of women with attitude, dreams, and high ideals. ✓**FIDONET**→*tag* PURSUIT

soc.couples (NG) Men and women currently involved in relationships talk to each other. ✓**USENET**

soc.singles (NG) Men and women currently not involved in relationships talk to each other. ✓**USENET**

Matchmaking

THe GaRBaGe DuMP (BBS) One of the "big boards." A huge collection of adult files, real-time adult chat, a dating registry, and much more. Local access calling available in more than 500 cities. To get a local access number, call the voice number: 505-294-4980. 🖼🗨 505-294-5675/505-294-0803 $2/HOUR

Interactive Personals Network (BBS) Personals and matchmaking with user photos. 🗨 612-890-8405 $40/YEAR

KCMatch (BBS) More than 10,000 users in its Date-A-Base. 417-578-4275 FREE

Romance Connection Matchmaking by age or geographical area for all sexual preferences.
✓**AMERICA ONLINE**→*keyword* ROMANCE

What is Net sex?
"Net.sex is about fantasy. If I get hot-n-heavy with someone, I couldn't care less whether the person on the other end of the line was a man pretending to be a woman, a woman pretending to be a man, a man pretending to be a dark elf, a thousand people pretending to be one 350lb women, or (gasp!) actually who they claimed to be. I do care about whether they they can provide, in a stream of bits, an image, a fantasy, that moves my imagination."

"i have a lot of really cool net.friends, some really cool net.flirts ;) and once a net.serious.relationship that maybe got confused into a rl.relationship, and it doesn't work real well i guess if it has to stay net and not translate into an x-y-z space-time right here right now kind of rl thing (...) damnit mice are getting more ergonomic but they're no substitute for a hand to hold..."

—from MindVox's
Sexuality Forum

Relationship talk

alt.polyamory (NG) Discussion about the practice and philosophy behind polyamory—open relationships with multiple partners. ✓**USENET**

alt.romance (NG) Read about what other couples have done for romance or share your own experiences. ✓**USENET**

Close Encounters Discuss dating, sexuality, and other relationship-related topics. ⊛❓ ✓**DELPHI**→*go* GR CLOS ✖*Adults only*

The Family and Personal Growth RoundTable Covers all aspects of family life, relationships, and personal growth. Includes private boards for kids and teens, discussions about adult relationships and sexuality (for both married couples and singles). Also covers issues from parenting to wedding planning. ⊛❓ ✓**GENIE**→*keyword* FAMILY

Human Sexuality Database and Forums Discuss feelings and dating experiences. Includes sections with articles on dating, social skills, etc. Frank sexual questions asked by members and answered by physicians and counselors. A dictionary of sexual terminology is also included. The Gay Alliance sections offer the gay perspective. ⊛❓ ✓**COMPUSERVE**→*go* HUMAN

Relationships Family, dating, work, and other relationships discussed. Issues include communication, conflict resolution, and intimacy. ✓**RELAYNET**→*number* 240

Advice

Singles Column Susan Deitz gives advice to singles in her col-

umn. ✓**PRODIGY**→*jump* SINGLES

Personals

alt.personals (NG) Meet someone on the Nets. ✓**USENET**

alt.personals.ads (NG) People seeking people for companionship. ✓**USENET**

alt.personals.bi (NG) Bisexuals looking for companionship. ✓**USENET**

alt.personals.misc (NG) Another forum to place your personal ad. ✓**USENET**

alt.personals.poly (NG) For people seeking multiple partners. ✓**USENET**

Weddings

Wedding Planner Shareware that helps you organize a wedding. ✓**INTERNET**→*ftp* WUAR CHIVE.WUSTL. EDU→ANONYMOUS/<YOUR EMAIL ADDRESS>→systems/ibmpc/msdos/database→wedplan.zip ✖*DOS only*

Lovers, downloaded from CompuServe's Graphics Gallery Forum.

Fringe culture

Does "fringe culture," from body art (rec.arts.bodyart) to skinheads (alt.skinheads) to

conspiracy theories galore, reflect the true soul of the Net? Only a little lurking will tell. Peak in on the **Deviants** mailing list for varied experiments in living, or try the newsgroup **talk.bizarre** or the mailing list **Weird-L** for a glimpse of the outrageous, disturbing, and, depending on your point of view, genuinely off-putting. And certainly try the netherworld of Kennedy-assassination-conspiracy obsessions, especially the **JFK Assasination Forum** and **alt.conspiracy.jfk** for a real sense of the passions that swirl at the edge of our time and at the center of the Net.

President Kennedy's motorcade through Dallas—from CompuServe's Issues Forum.

On the Net

Across the board

Deviants (ML) "Occasionally disgusting, but not always, it is the home of ranting, experimental reports, news clippings, and other related items. Medical curiosities, cults, paranoia, cling film/Saran wrap, murders, and other phenomena are well in place here." ✓**INTERNET**→*email* DEVIANTS-REQUEST @CSV.WARWICK.AC.UK ✍*Subscribe by request*

Plane of NonConformity (BBS) "Conformity is evil. This BBS has no rules." 701-772-0137 FREE

talk.bizarre (NG) For discussing the outrageous. ✓**USENET**

Weird-L (ML) Welcomes anything strange, particularly short bizarre stories. Looking for the disturbing rather than the humorous. ✓**INTERNET**→*email* LISTSERV@BROWNVM.BITNET ✍*Type in message body:* WEIRD-L <YOUR FULL NAME>

Wunderment Discussions drawing on an eclectic mix of offbeat topics. "We welcome fen, anachronists and anarchists, dystopics and discordians, pagans and peripatetics." ✓**FIDONET**→*tag* WUNDERMENT

Body art

rec.arts.bodyart (NG) Discussions about tattoos and other body decorations. ✓**USENET**

Conspiracy theories

alt.conspiracy (NG) Debate, discuss, and report on conspiracy theories. ✓**USENET**

alt.conspiracy.jfk (NG) Theories about the assassination of JFK. ✓**USENET**

Conspiracy (BBS) Dedicated to news and discussions about conspiracies. 508-478-1714

ConspiracyJFK The latest facts and rumors concerning the JFK assassination. ✓**ILINK**→*number* 212

JFK Assassination Forum Discuss motives, analyze the latest theories, and share information with professional researchers as well as others. Includes extensive libraries of material related to the Kennedy assassination. ⊛💥 ✓**COMPUSERVE**→*go* JFK

JFK Conspiracy Archive Includes a memo by J. Edgar Hoover on a meeting with LBJ, articles, information on the movement to open the JFK files, full texts of two books on the assassination, and book reviews. ✓**INTERNET**→*ftp* PENCIL.CS.MISSOURI.EDU→ANONYMOUS/ <YOUR EMAIL ADDRESS>→ pub/jfk

Skinheads

alt.skinheads (NG) Discussion by members of the skinhead culture and movement. ✓**USENET**

Gay, bi & trans

Where's the party? In America Online's Lambda Lounge.

AOL is the only major commercial service offering a forum devoted to the gay community. Founded in 1991 by the Gays & Lesbians United Electronically (GLUE), the forum offers a map—updated weekly—to all the gay and lesbian discussions peppered throughout AOL. On the Internet, **soc.motss** (members of the same sex) was started in 1983 and now has more than 70,000 readers.

Across the board

Alternative Lifestyles Discuss gay, lesbian, and bisexual lifestyles. ✓**GENIE**→*keyword* CHAT→LIVEWIRE EXCHANGE/ALTERNATIVE LIFESTYLES ✖*By request only*

The Gay and Lesbian Community Forum The entire forum is devoted to the gay community. Conferences include Coming Out Support, HIV+ Support, Gay 12-Step Support, Women's Space & Lambda Lounge, Gender, and Bodybuilding. The message board Heart-to-Heart is filled with personals. National Gay and Lesbian Task Force is a forum with news about the task force's fight for freedom and equality for lesbians and gay men. Includes fact sheets, alerts, and newsletters. The Info Exchange publicizes community and local events. The Gay Map to

At the leather bar—from the soc.motts picture archive at ursa-major.spdcc.com.

America Online lists folders in a variety of forums that carry topics of interest to gays. ✓**AMERICA ONLINE**→*keyword* GAY *or* LESBIAN

Gay-Issues Discussions about gay sexuality and lifestyles. ✓**ILINK** →*number* 169

Gaylink A discussion of homosexual lifestyles. The focus is on nonsexual talk about daily gay life. All callers and all ages allowed. ✓**FIDONET**→*tag* GAYLINK

Graffiti BBS (BBS) Includes discussion, gay news, pictures, chat, and free online classifieds. ▦ ◉📞 404-972-4999 $30/YEAR

Health and Lifestyles BB In the Alternatives section, discussions about gay, lesbian, and bisexual issues. ✓**PRODIGY**→*jump* LIFE STYLES BB

soc.motss (NG) MOTTS, an acronym for "members of the

same sex," is a discussion group open to all gay-related topics except "condemnations and justifications." Issues vary from health to parenting to job security. Heterosexuals are welcome. ✓**USENET**

Gay men

Eye Contact (BBS) Gay men's BBS with more than 1,000 local access numbers. ▤▥ ◉📞 415-255-5972

Mail.Bears (ML) Forum for gay and bisexual men who are bears or enjoy the company of bears. Includes sexually explicit conversation. Women are welcome, but the

---

CYBERNOTES

"There is some controversy over what makes a man a 'bear.' First and foremost is a cuddly demeanor, followed by a cuddly bod. Body or facial fur can be important, since they are some of a bear's identifying characteristics in the wild. Bears have been found with heavy to stocky to medium builds; very slender individuals are generally thought to be some other, closely related species. For the purposes of this list, we encourage the participants in this forum to use their own definition, using this paragraph as a guide."

—from the mailing list **Mail.Bears**

topics are oriented toward gay males. ✓**INTERNET**→*email* BEARS-REQUEST@SPDCC.COM ✍*Subscribe by request*

Lesbians

Lisaben (ML) Discussion of lesbian issues. Men welcome. ✓**INTERNET**→*email* LISABEN-REQUEST@QUEERNET.ORG ✍*Subscribe by request*

Sappho (ML) Lesbian issues. ✓**INTERNET**→*email* SAPPHO-REQUEST@MC.LCS.MIT.EDU ✍*Subscribe by request* ✖ *Women only*

Two Babes (BBS) Includes hundreds of lesbian GIFs. Free ladies' access. 206-885-4236 MEN: $60/YEAR

Bisexuals

Bifem-L (ML) Forum for bisexual women. ✓**INTERNET**→*email* LISTSERV@BROWNVM.BROWN.EDU ✍*Type in message body:* SUBSCRIBE BIFEM-L <YOUR FULL NAME> ✖ *Women only*

Bisexu-L (ML) Discussion of bisexuality and bisexual issues. ✓**INTERNET**→*email* LISTSERV@BROWNVM.BROWN.EDU ✍*Type in message body:* SUBSCRIBE BISEXU-L <YOUR FULL NAME>

Bithry-L (ML) For the theoretical discussion of bisexuality and gender issues. ✓**INTERNET**→*email* LISTSERV@BROWNVM.BROWN.EDU ✍*Type in message body:* SUB BITHRY-L <YOUR FULL NAME>

soc.bi (NG) For the discussion of any issues related to bisexuality. ✓**USENET**

Transsexuals

Cdforum (ML) Devoted to the interests of transvestites, transsexuals, and transgenderists. Suppor-

A wedding—from the soc.motts picture archive at ursa-major.spdcc.com.

tive others welcome. ✓**INTERNET**→*email* CDFORUM-REQUEST@WIZVAX.METHUEN.MA.US ✍*Subscribe by request*

Gender Dysphoria Information and Support A support area for discussions about gender roles: transsexualism, transvestism, cross-dressing, and other topics. Open to all, including behavioral specialists and counselors. Groups and BBSs advertising conferences and other events may post phone numbers and other contact information. ✓**FIDONET**→*tag* GENDER

Tiffany Club of New England (BBS) A support and education board for transgendered and gender-dysphoric people. Includes GIFs and ads. 617-899-3230 $25/YEAR

Transgen (ML) Discussion and support forum devoted to transsexual, transvestite, and transgender issues. ✓**INTERNET**→*email* LISTSERV@BROWNVM.BROWN.EDU ✍*Type in message body:* SUB TRANSGEN <YOUR FULL NAME>

Teens & students

Gay Teenagers Message area where gay teens, or those who think they might be gay, can talk.

Social problems of gay teens and safe-sex promotion are primary topics. ✓**FIDONET**→*tag* GAYTEEN

GayNet (ML) Lesbian and gay concerns on campus. ✓**INTERNET**→*email* MAJORDOMO@QUEERNET.ORG ✍*Type in message body:* SUBSCRIBE GAYNET

Issues Concerning Gays and Lesbians Real-world problems facing homosexuals. This is not a general chat or sexually explicit conference; the focus is on honest interchange and support-group information. ✓**FIDONET**→*tag* ICGAL

Scouts

Eagles (ML) Forum for scouts, scouters, and and former scouts interested in pressuring the BSA to change their homophobic policies. ✓**INTERNET**→*email* EAGLES-REQUEST@FLASH.USC.EDU ✍*Subscribe by request*

Seniors

Gay & Lesbian Senior Issues Topics for gay and lesbian senior citizens. ✓**AMERICA ONLINE**→*keyword* SENIOR

News & resources

Gay & Lesbian Communications (BBS) Covers topics of interest to the gay and lesbian community. 816-561-1186 FREE

Gay and Lesbian Information Bureau (GLIB) (BBS) Sponsored by the Community Educational Services Foundation. ▦ 703-578-4542

Gays/Lesbians News Current news for the gay community, with articles posted from around the world. Replies and discussions of the articles are permitted. ▦

Gay, Lesbian, Bisexual & Transsexual Lifestyles, Leisure & Travel

✓**FIDONET**→*tag* GAYNEWS

GLB News (ML) Informative articles for gay, lesbian, bisexual, transsexual, transgender, and sympathetic persons. Those posting will remain anonymous unless they explicitly request not to do so. 🖳 ✓**INTERNET**→*email* LISTSERV@BROWNVM.BROWN.EDU ✍*Type in message body:* SUB GLB-NEWS <YOUR FULL NAME>

GLINN Multi-Board Super System (BBS) Home of the Gay/Lesbian/International News Network. Also provides adult and gay-adult areas and the KC AIDS InfoLink Database. 📧💬 🖳 414-289-0145 FREE

Regional

ba.motss (NG) For MOTSS in the Bay Area. ✓**USENET**

LA-Members of the Same Sex (ML) Discussion of gay, lesbian, and bisexual issues in the Los Angeles and Southern California area. ✓**INTERNET**→*email* LA-MOTSS-REQUEST@FLASH.USC.EDU ✍*Subscribe by request*

New York Metro Area Gay/Lesbian Conference Discuss subjects concerning gays and lesbians in New York. ✓**FIDONET**→ *tag* METROGAY ✖*Distributed in NY only*

NE-Social-Members of the Same Sex (ML) Socializing-only forum for gays, lesbians, and bisexuals in the northeast corridor. ✓**INTERNET**→*email* NE-SOCIAL-MOTSS-REQUEST@CASTLE.ORG ✍*Subscribe by request*

OH-Members of the Same Sex (ML) Gay, lesbian, and bisexual issues in and affecting the Ohio area. All welcome. ✓**INTERNET**

→*email* OH-MOTSS-REQUEST@CPS.UDAYTON.EDU ✍*Subscribe by request*

UK-Members of the Same Sex (ML) Gay, lesbian, and bisexual discussion group focusing on issues in the United Kingdom. ✓**INTERNET**→*email* UK-MOTSS-REQUEST @PYRA.CO.UK ✍*Subscribe by request*

Professionals

Chorus (ML) Discussions range from repertoire to fundraising to costuming. Members include gay and lesbian artistic directors, singers, chorus leaders, interpreters, and support staff. ✓**INTERNET**→*email* CHORUS-REQUEST@PSYCH.TORONTO.EDU ✍*Subscribe by request*

National Organization of Gay and Lesbian Scientists and Technical Professionals (ML) Network with others. ✓**INTERNET**→*email* NOGLSTP-REQUEST@ELROY.JPL.NASA.GOV ✍*Subscribe by request*

Out in Linguistics (ML) Forum for gay, lesbian, and bisexual linguists and others to communicate, discuss issues, and organize social events for conferences. ✓**INTERNET** →*email* OUTIL-REQUEST@ CSLI.STANFORD.EDU ✍*Subscribe by request*

Socializing

alt.sex.motss (NG) Sexually explicit talk between members of the same sex. ✓**USENET**

The Backroom (BBS) Calls itself "America's largest gay/lesbian computer information service." Coordinates the GayCom network. 📧💬 718-951-8256

Bubba's Place (BBS) For gay, bi, and lesbian singles and couples. 📧💬 206-854-0896 $10 QUARTERLY

Close Encounters Discussions of social and sexual relationships that include gay, lesbian, and bisexual topics. 📧💬 ✓**DELPHI**→*go* GR CLO

Human Sexuality Database and Forums Forums are available for sharing feelings and dating experiences; other sections offer expert advice, as well as articles on dating, social skills, etc. Frank sexual questions asked by members and answered by physicians and counselors—dictionary of sexual terminology also included. The Gay Alliance sections offer the gay perspective. 📧💬 ✓**COMPUSERVE**→*go* HUMAN

Romance Connection Matchmaking by age or geographical area for all sexual preferences. ✓**AMERICA ONLINE**→*keyword* ROMANCE

Bondage and S&M

GL-ASB (ML) Discussion of bondage and S&M topics for gay men and lesbians. ✓**INTERNET**→ *email* MAJORDOMO@QUEERNET.ORG ✍ *Type in message body:* SUBSCRIBE GL-ASB END

Spirituality

Religion Bulletin Board In the Other area, gay and lesbian topics discussed. ✓**PRODIGY**→*jump* RELIGION BB

Voices Discussion of spirituality with a focus on gay, lesbian, and transsexual issues. ✓**FIDONET**→*tag* VOICES

Other sources

S-TEK BBS (BBS) Features a list of BBSs carrying gay/lesbian-related topics as well as AIDS information services. 514-597-2409

Motorcycles

Even the most fanatical hobbyists can find a subject too tiresome; hence this plea

from the moderator of the **Harleys** electronic mailing list: "With this issue the im-moderator asks that a few tired and will-never-be-re-solved topics be brought to an end. I am referring to the Japanese vs. Harley bikes (and reliability) topic which we all have engaged in at bars, campfires, newsgroups, and everywhere else... please try to wrap up these discussions unless you really feel you have something NEW to contribute. You can always email each other DIRECTLY rather than via the digest, if you feel you really must 'convert' some-one."

On the Net

Across the board

International Motorcycle Conference Everything about motorcycles: favorite makers, rac-ing, equipment, and locations. ✓**FIDONET**→*tag* MOTORCYCLE

Motorcycles Offers general con-versation for all motorcyclists. ✓**RELAYNET**→*number* 241

Motorcycling RoundTable For enthusiasts of all ages and skill lev-els. Discussion topics include spe-cific vehicles, clubs, touring, rac-ing, safety, and legislation. Li-

"Born to be wild"—downloaded from cerritos.edu.

braries of GIFs and information also available. ●🕹 ✓**GENIE**→*key-word* MOTO

rec.motorcycles (NG) Forum for discussing motorcycles and related products and laws. ✓**USENET**

The rec.motorcycles Photo Archive Photos of motorcyclists and their bikes. ✓**INTERNET**→*ftp* CERRITOS.EDU→ANONYMOUS <YOUR EMAIL ADDRESS>→dod

Harleys

Harleys (ML) Discussion about the bikes, politics, lifestyles, and other interests of Harley-Davidson motorcycle fans. ✓**INTERNET**→*email* HARLEY-REQUEST@THINKAGE.COM ✍ *Subscribe by request*

rec.motorcycles.harley (NG) Discussion covers all aspects of Harley-Davidson motorcycles. ✓**USENET**

Mechanics

Moto (ML) Devoted to discussing motorcycle-chassis design and construction. ✓**INTERNET**→*email* MOTO.CHASSIS-REQUEST@OCE.ORST.EDU ✍*Subscribe by request*

Two-Strokes (ML) Discussion of two-stroke motorcycle technology, maintenance, and riding. ✓**INTER-NET**→*email* 2STROKES-REQUEST@ MICROUNITY.COM ✍*Subscribe by request*

Racing & off-road

Motor Sports Forum Includes the Motorcycle Racing and Mo-torcycle Topics (from a report on a fall foliage ride to VFR750 perfor-mance reviews) boards and lib-raries. Writes one motorcycle owner, "I have a '93 Fat Boy that I have enjoyed for 5,000 miles this year. However, I sometimes find myself yearning for more perfor-mance and riding comfort..." He's certain to get advice! ●🕹 ✓**COM-PUSERVE**→*go* RACING

rec.motorcycles.dirt (NG) Forum for discussing riding off-the-road motorcycles and ATVs. ✓**USENET**

rec.motorcycles.racing (NG) Discussion of all aspects of racing motorcycles. ✓**USENET**

Regional

ba.motorcycles (NG) Motor-cycles in the San Francisco Bay Area. ✓**USENET**

Wetleather (ML) For discussion, ride reports, socializing, and announcements of upcoming motorcycle events in the greater Pacific Northwest. ✓**INTERNET**→*email* WETLEATHER-REQUEST@FRIGG.ISC-BR.COM ✍*Type in message body:* SUB-SCRIBE WETLEATHER <YOUR FULL NAME>

New Age

Journey to Body Dharma Online, home of DharmaNet International, a BBS that is one of

the leading sources for information on New Age philosophies and lifestyles—from holistic thought to Zen Buddhism. Indeed, the full course load of New Age topics has found a dedicated following across the Net, from astrology to Tarot cards to dream interpretation to biorhythms and alternative healing. Try **New Age** on RelayNet, **New Age Forum** on CompuServe, and **New Age Network** on Delphi. And then, of course, there's always the perennial Jeanne Dixon's **Horoscope** on Prodigy.

Stonehenge—downloaded from CompuServe's UK Forum.

On the Net

Across the board

Body Dharma Online (BBS) "This BBS is dedicated to spreading Dharma, not Dogma." A health- and spirituality-oriented BBS with hundreds of conferences—from Tibetan Buddhism to Natural Healing to Reincarnation. 510-836-4717 FREE

New Age A glossary, history, and explanation of the New Age movement and philosophy as well as direct access to the Health and Lifestyles bulletin board for New Age discussions. ✓**PRODIGY**→*jump* NEW AGE

New Age Offers discussion on

spirituality, the metaphysical, and man's cosmic destiny. ✓**RELAYNET**→ *number* 404

New Age Forum Covers New Age books, science, and health as well as Tarot and astrology, UFOlogy, and pagan and occult beliefs. Download a fortune-telling program, an astrology HyperCard stack, a list of occult BBSs, herbal recipes, or President Clinton's astrology chart. ⊕📁 ✓**COMPUSERVE** →*go* NEWAGE

New Age Network Includes live classes and seminars, an online store, and discussion boards for topics such as astrology, meditation, and alternative healing. ⊕ ⊕📁 ✓**DELPHI**→*go* GR NEW

New Age Open Discussion Offers news on "a transition, a blending of ancient values and new breakthroughs," with the arrival of the New Age. ✓**FIDONET** →*tag* NEW_AGE_ECHO

Seven Ray Institute (BBS) "Quality New Age teaching." Discuss Alice Bailey, Rosicrucianism,

Steiner, astrology, and theosophy. Carries the POD (occult) echoes. 718-380-5750 FREE

talk.religion.newage (NG) For debating and discussing New Age philosophies and religions. ✓**USENET**

Alternative healing

Bodywork & Massage Therapy Forum for professionals and laypeople to discuss the "healing" touch, with discussions on technique, education about the body, and recent developments in the field. ✓**FIDONET**→*tag* BODYWORK

Herbal Delights for Anyone Discuss the use of all legal herbs for a variety of purposes: medicinal, aromatic, aesthetic, and culinary. Whether you make a tea blend, hair rinse, or salad, whether you grow your own or buy them, you are invited. ✓**FIDONET**→*tag* HERBS-N-SUCH

Holistic Thought & Lifestyle Covers the interconnectedness of body, mind, spirit, and planet:

lifestyle as ecosystem, planetary ethics, preventive medicine, and networking for a sustainable future. ✓**FIDONET**→*tag* HOLISTIC

HomeoNet A network of news and conferences relating to homeopathy. For more information or to register, send an email request. Includes a calendar of homeopathic events, a homeopathic bookstore, a clinical database, conferences, and news. 🖳 ☏ ✓**INTERNET**→*email* SUPPORT@IGC.APC. ORG

Homeopathy Provides news, ideas, advice, and anecdotes about homeopathic medicine. Participants include homeopathic physicians, patients, pharmacists, and other health professionals. Also offers service advertisements, seminar news, and product announcements. ✓**RELAYNET**→*number* 335

misc.health.alternative (NG) Covers alternative, complementary, and holistic health care. ✓**USENET**

Traditional Asian Medicine & Bodywork Theories and practices of Asian health care—for lay people and professionals. ✓**FIDONET**→*tag* TCM

Vibrational Healing Techniques discussed include balneology (therapeutic baths), aromatherapy, homeopathy, uropathy, radionics, dowsing, magnets, and crystals. ✓**FIDONET**→*tag* VHEAL

Astrology & Tarot

alt.astrology (NG) For astrologers of all levels of expertise to discuss astrology—not for skeptics. ✓**USENET**

alt.divination (NG) For discussing divination techniques such as Tarot-card reading or I Ching.

✓**USENET**

Astrolog Easy-to-use astrology software with screen graphics, astrology articles, and an ALT.ASTROLOGY archive. ✓**INTERNET** …→*ftp* HILBERT.MATHS.UTAS.EDU.AU→ ANONYMOUS/<YOUR EMAIL ADDRESS>→ pub/astrology …→*ftp* FTP.UU.NET→ ANONYMOUS/<YOUR EMAIL ADDRESS>→ usenet/comp.sources.misc/volume 28/astrolog ✖*PC and UNIX compatible only*

Astrology Offers discussion about users of astrology, the system of beliefs, and how to write a horoscope. ✓**RELAYNET**→*number* 181

Astrology RoundTable Discussions on all aspects of astrology. Answers to your questions from professional astrologers. 🖳 ☏ ✓**GENIE**→*keyword* ASTROLOGY

Astro News & Events Includes the Daily Guides from *American Astrology* magazine for daily sun-sign forecasts, news of upcoming astrological conferences, and information on local and national astrological groups. 🖳 ✓**GENIE**→ *keyword* ASTRO

Astro-Predictions General astrology information—including how to use it, weekly zodiac forecasts, and an explanation of how sex and personality are related to the zodiac. You can also order an extensive personalized natal chart from Delphi's astrologer for an extra fee. ✓**DELPHI**→*go* ENT AST

The Crystal Ball Submit your eye color, hair color, approximate age, and sex to the Tarot reader Cerridwyn for an online reading. ✓**AMERICA ONLINE**→*keyword* CRYSTAL BALL

Horoscope Jeanne Dixon's column. ✓**PRODIGY**→*jump* HOROSCOPE

Biorhythm

Biorhythm Charting Determine your emotional, mental, and physical states, with personalized charts for any month or a series of months. ✓**COMPUSERVE**→*go* BIORHYTHM

Meditation & dreams

alt.dreams (NG) "Hello dreamers! I'd like to tell about a recurring theme in my dreams..." Share your dreams and help interpret others'. ✓**USENET**

alt.dreams.lucid (NG) Exchange stories about your lucid dreaming experiences: describe the "gray area," the emotions, or perhaps the techniques you use to remember your dreams. ✓**USENET**

alt.hypnosis (NG) Discuss hypnotic trances and techniques. ✓**USENET**

alt.meditation (NG) General discussion of meditation, including books on the subject, techniques, and experiences. ✓**USENET**

alt.out-of-body (NG) Discuss meditation and out-of-body experiences. ✓**USENET**

Meditation Covers the practices, techniques, and experiences of meditation, with help for the neophyte. ✓**FIDONET**→*tag* MEDITATION

Mental Power and Stress Management A copyrighted conference of sciences of the mind. Shows how to use hypnosis, self-hypnosis, meditation, and other techniques to reduce stress. ✓**FIDONET**→*tag* STRESS_MGMT

Nudists

From the search for a no-hassle nude beach to propagat-ing nudism as an inclusive philosophy, the Net is here to help. The newsgroup **rec.nude** offers comprehensive coverage of CO (clothing-optional) vacation spots. FidoNet's **Naturist/Nudist** (with much discussion on the differences between the two) also offers an up-to-date CO travel advisory. In general, nudism is a hot BBS subject—from **Dan's Domain**, a clothing-optional BBS where many Netters are NIFOC (nude in front of computer), to **Howard's Notebook**, a BBS devoted to nudism, peace, and justice. AOL's **The Exchange** keeps you current on nude-related court rulings.

Nudists—downloaded from Compu-Serve's Travel Forum.

On the Net

Bare Essence Provides information on clubs and resorts and naturist contact groups. ▦ ✓**DELPHI**→*go* GR CLO→bare ✖*No discussion*

Body Dharma Online (BBS) A health- and spirituality-oriented BBS with more than 200 conferences including REC.NUDE, Naturist, and Baynude, in addition to a Body Culture file area with hypertext programs on the naturist lifestyle. 510-836-4717 FREE

The California RoundTable
Includes several areas of discussion of interest to nudists and naturists, such as the Beaches and Tanning area in California Lifestyles and Attitudes, and the Nude Beaches, Hot Springs, and Resorts area in Sports, Health and Adventure. ⊜🏴 ✓**GENIE**→*keyword* CALIFORNIA

Clothing Optional Digest (ML) The weekly *Clothing Optional Digest*, from skinny-dipping to topless issues for women. ✓**INTERNET**→*email* HENDRY@ETSUADMN. ETSU.EDU ✍*Subscribe by request*

Dan's Domain—A Clothing Optional BBS (BBS) "Wearing clothing is not a requirement of using Dan's Domain." The Naturist area features information on the origins of naturism, news clips relevant to nudism, FAQs, and access to the REC.NUDE newsgroup. ▦ ▦▭ ⊜🏴 201-586-1223

The Exchange The Nudism area covers travel destinations, court rulings, the sex question, beaches, and lifestyle issues. ✓**AMERICA ONLINE**→*keyword* EXCHANGE→other special interests

Hobbies BB See the Outdoor Activities section for topics and discussions that are of interest to nudists and naturists. ✓**PRODIGY**→*jump* HOBBIES BB

Howard's Notebook (BBS) A strong nudist section as well as sections on the environment, peace, politics, and justice. ⊜🏴 816-331-5868

Human Sexuality Forum Bulletin board and library devoted to naturist lifestyles. ⊜🏴 ✓**COMPUSERVE**→*go* HSX100→Naturist Lifestyles

Naturist Lifestyle (Northern California) Naturist and nudist discussion about Northern California. Nude beaches, resorts, and the philosophy of naturism are discussed. ✓**FIDONET**→*tag* BAYNUDE

Naturist/Nudist Information for serious naturists, wannabes, and people curious about the lifestyle. Includes information about clubs, nude beaches, skinny-dipping, family involvement, and more. ✓**FIDONET**→*tag* NATURIST

Nude Is Natural BBS (BBS) "To promote nudism/naturism in all its varied forms." 206-485-6141

Public Forum NonProfit Connection Nude recreation and lifestyle topics are featured in topic 12 of the Making Connections, Locating Resources board. ▦ ✓**GENIE**→*keyword* PF

rec.nude (NG) A forum for views, news, and philosophies relating to the nudist and naturist lifestyle. Also serves as a clearinghouse for information on clothing-optional travel and recreation. Read the FAQ. ✓**USENET**

Paganism & the occult

"Magick is the science and art of causing change to occur in conformity with will,"
according to an essay by Aleister Crowley on **alt. magick**, or, as it is defined on RelayNet's **Magick**, it is the alteration of objective reality through the alteration of subjective reality. RelayNet's **Pagan** offers updates of traditional pagan beliefs and practices for today's world. The BBSs **The Forest Path** and **Inspiration of the Goddess** are also important guides to the world of modern paganism.

"Everything is connected to everything"
—from CompuServe's New Age forum.

On the Net

Paganism

alt.pagan (NG) For the discussion of paganism and witchcraft in various traditions. ✓**USENET**

The Forest Path (BBS) Provides a sub-board for discussion about wicca, pagan, neo-pagan, and thelmic topics. 813-628-4045 FREE

Inspiration of the Goddess (BBS) Alternative-lifestyle, pagan, wicca, and magical-based discussions. Provides psychic readings for a fee. 919-686-4932 FREE

Pagan (ML) Forum for discussing paganism—its philosophies and religious tenets. ✓**INTERNET**→*email* PAGAN-REQUEST@DRYCAS.CLUB.CC.CMU. EDU ✍*Subscribe by request*

Pagan Covers classical paganism, modern adaptations of pagan be-

liefs, earth religions, shamanism, witchcraft, and related topics. Includes mythology, folklore, and superstitions in various cultures. ✓**RELAYNET**→*number* 397

The occult

Dreaming Isle on the Sea of Fate (BBS) Paranormal conferences, an occult library, role-playing games, and a little shopping. 🐾 📠 🌐💬 412-464-0296 FREE

Mysteria (BBS) Features occult/metaphysical topics, the PODS conference (a national network of occult conferences including Pagan Teen, New Magick, I Ching, Gay Pagans, Book of Shadows, Occult Book Review, and many others), NOVANET conferences (another national network of conferences, including Ghostnet, Crystal Work, Pantheon, etc.), and a file area that includes a list of BBSs carrying occult-related topics. 🌐💬 818-353-8891/818-353-8761

The Occult Archive Includes occult files in the subdirectories /crowley, /magick, and /set as well as *A Mage's Guide to the Internet*, which lists Internet resources related to mysticism, the occult, and

fringe beliefs. ✓**INTERNET**→*ftp* QUARTZ.RUTGERS.EDU→ANONYMOUS/ <YOUR EMAIL ADDRESS>→pub/occult

Para_Realm For those interested in the occult. ✓**FIDONET**→*tag* PRRLM

Atheism

alt.atheism (NG) Discussion of atheism. Includes debate, reading recommendations, and topics such as Sunday trading laws, closet atheists, discrimination against atheists, etc. ✓**USENET**

alt.atheism.moderated (NG) Moderated discussion of atheism. ✓**USENET**

Magick

alt.magick (NG) For warlocks, witches, members of secret societies, and those interested in the science of causing change in conformity with will. ✓**USENET**

Magick Covers the alteration of objective reality through the alteration of subjective reality (magick), as well as stage magic. ✓**RELAYNET**→*number* 147

Not-so-evil

alt.evil (NG) A forum for saying "what shouldn't be said," from the tasteless to the depraved to the wacky. ✓**USENET**

alt.satanism (NG) From news about occult shops to the I-hate-Barney (a devil disguised as a dinosaur) newsletter. ✓**USENET**

Sex

Erotic (adj.): Of or arousing sexual feelings or desires

having to do with sexual love; amatory. **Binary erotica** (n.): *Representations rendered in digital form arousing sexual feelings of desire.* Amateur, professional, and stolen, depicting everyone from the couple next door to the new model on the block to this month's centerfold, the world's largest collection of erotic photographs reposes in Cyberspace. Maybe you'll find someone you know.

Botticelli's Venus—downloaded from biome.bio.dfo.ca.

On the Net

Across the board

The Adult Information Exchange (BBS) Matchmaking services and adult GIFs. 📞 407-451-1984 $$

AfterDark Network A network of adult conferences including AF_Personals, AF_Pleasures, AF_Lesbian, AF_Bisexual, AF_Pillow, AF_Fantasy, AF_Blue, AF_Dr_Love, AF_Kinky, and AF_Gay. ✓ CHECK LOCAL BULLETIN BOARDS

alt.sex (NG) Perhaps one of the most controversial groups on the Net. Discuss sexual experiences—the good and the horrible. Share the details of your sex life. ✓ USENET

alt.sex.stories (NG) More people talking about their sex lives. ✓ USENET

alt.sex.stories.d (NG) People still talking about their sex lives. ✓ USENET

alt.sex.wanted (NG) Explicit personals, updates on singles clubs, dating lines, etc. ✓ USENET

Chat Chalet (BBS) "Where new friends meet." 🖥️ 📞 201-791-8850/201-791-6548 $$

Close Encounters Discussions of social and sexual relationships. 📞 ✓ DELPHI→*go* GR CLO

Close Encounters BBS (BBS) Includes interactive (and very active) adult chatting and games. 🖥️ 📞 813-527-2616 FREE

Danse Macabre (BBS) Includes adult, paranormal, and occult conferences (AdultNet, PodNet, DarkNet, and FidoNet). Adult games such as Studs! and Studette! are available. 🖥️ 210-623-1395

The Daze Inn (BBS) Adult and general-interest conferences (Fido-

Net, KinkNet, AdaNet, and Las Vegas Net), the MatchMaker database, adult chat and games, and more. 🖥️ 📞 708-437-8394/708-437-8387 FREE

Fantasy Party Line (BBS) Social events every weekend. Chat, role-play, use the GIF library and matchmaking databases, etc. 📞 713-596-7101 $$

The Honey Dripper (BBS) Includes the MatchMaker database and more than 150 national conferences from KinkNet and FidoNet. 🖥️ 📞 305-220-0369 $$

The Hot Tub Club (BBS) Log on to the following: "Better hurry up and get your clothes off! The Hot Tub is cumming!" Run by Meat Eater and Lusty Linda, the board caters to singles and couples—with a waiting list for single men—and has strict policies regarding the treatment of women. Other than that, anything goes. Receives FidoNet, KinkNet, and other adult conferences. 🖥️ 📞 214-530-8931 $$

Human Sexuality Databank and Forums Frank sexual questions asked by members and answered by physicians and counselors. Includes a dictionary of sexual terminology. The Gay Alliance sections offer the gay perspective. 📞 ✓ COMPUSERVE→*go* HUMAN

Jezebel's Parlour (BBS) An adult BBS with a feminine touch. Includes adult chat, message conferences, matchmaking, adult graphics, and general-interest files. 🖥️ 📞 201-927-2932

KinkNet/Adult Link A BBS network (the second-largest in the country) that caters to an adult audience and features the following rather self-explanatory forums: the extremely popular A_Personal, the S&Mers' haven Desade, the women-only conference Ladies, as well as A_Cunt, A_Erotica, Backroom, Couples, Foot_Fetish, Heavy_Love, Hot_Tub, Mateswap, Orgyroom, Spanky, and Waterbed, to name but a few. ✓CHECK LOCAL BULLETIN BOARDS

NightLife Adult BBS (BBS) An exclusively adult BBS carrying AfterDark, KinkNet, ThrobNet, WildNet, and local adult conferences. Digital advertisements for items such as adult toys, videos, and leather and rubber goods are also featured but the items are not sold directly through the BBS. And, of course, lots of adult GIFs. 🖐 🖥 😋 215-288-9368 FREE

Nix*Pix Denver (BBS) "Home to many hot-blooded yummy Nixxxies who love to share their slithery lurching sexualities with you!" Get very personal online; huge GIF selection, including Nixxxies at play. 303-375-1263 $$

Odessa Nightlife BBS (BBS) Matchmaking service and adult GIFs. 😋 915-550-0633/915-550-0632 $$

Odyssey (BBS) Created entirely for adults. Large adult-images collection, adult chat, a matchmaker database, private gay sections, scheduled parties, horoscopes, and other, more general-interest types of conferences. 🖐 🖥 😋 818-358-6968 ✖Adults only VARYING RATE STRUCTURE

OverExposed BBS (BBS) An adult-entertainment board. 203-627-8088

Pleasure Dome (BBS) A highly popular sexually explicit board

A happy couple—downloaded from alt. binaries.pictures.erotica.

with conferences and live chat. 🖥 😋 804-490-5878

Puss 'N Boots (BBS) Carries several adult networks, including KinkNet, the TransGender Network, FidoNet, and GayNet. Adult games such as Voyeur, Pimp Wars, Strip Poker, Sex Quiz, the Purity Quiz, and others are available. And, of course, the staples of adult boards—live adult chatting and GIFs—are also here. 🖥 😋 214-641-1822

The Queen of Hearts BBS (BBS) Carries KinkNet, ThrobNet, FidoNet, and GayNet conferences. Only their extensive adult GIF selection requires a fee. Take a personality test, play in their X-rated arcade, join the MatchMaker database, and chat with other adults. Also offers non-adult conferences. 🖥 😋 904-789-6843

Rendezvous (BBS) Local conferences through the Pleasure Dome network, including Erotica, Fetishes, and Swinging. Chat and play with other adults. Also check out the Ditzy Graphics selection. 🖥 😋 619-689-2817

S/W Michigan Access BBS (BBS) Adult message conferences, files, and chat. 🖥 😋 616-468-

5026/616-468-4079 $$

T&E in the Gorge (BBS) Huge file selection (adult and others), KinkNet and FidoNet conferences, adult chat, and online games. 🖥 😋 503-386-2903 $$

Tasty Delites (BBS) Carries the KinkNet adult conferences. 518-884-2649

Texas Talk (BBS) Adult entertainment, including live chat on the Lambda Connection and the Wild Thing. Includes Connex, a biorhythm/matchmaking service. 🖥 😋 214-497-9100 $18/MONTH

ThrobNet A popular adult Net with the following message conferences: T_Fantasy, T_SexToys, T_S&M, T_Fetish, T_Lesbian, T_Porno, T_SexTalk, T_Singles, T_Gay, T_Photo, T_SexHelp, T_ThrobMail, T_Women, T_Judi, and Dr_Rude. ✓CHECK LOCAL BULLETIN BOARDS

WildNet Besides some general-interest conferences such as Debate, Norton Utilities, and Rush Limbaugh, WildNet is home to the following adult conferences: XXX Rated Movies, Groaners, Swingers, Fantasy, Catcalls, Adult Humor, SexToys, Wildside Inn, and Women Only. ✓CHECK LOCAL BULLETIN BOARDS

Windup BBS (BBS) "For serious adult erotic experiences" for couples and singles alike. Includes ThrobNet and KinkNet echoes. 😋 718-428-6123 $50/YEAR

Bestiality

alt.sex.bestiality (NG) "Happiness is a warm puppy." Exchange stories about your latest experiences. ✓**USENET**

Zoophilia ("Bestiality") Discussion Social, legal, and personal issues for zoophiles and people interested in the subject. ✓**FIDONET**→*tag* ZOOPHILE ✗*No religious discussions; no sales, trades, or negotiations for pornography*

Bondage

alt.sex.bondage (NG) From the psychology of being confined by your sexual partner to the latest toys to how-to instructions (diagrams sometimes included). ✓**USENET**

GL-ASB (ML) Very active discussion of bondage and S&M topics for gay men and lesbians. Lots of regulars. ✓**INTERNET**→*email* MAJOR DOMO@QUEERNET.ORG ✍*Type in message body:* SUBSCRIBE GL-ASB END

Masturbation

alt.sex.masturbation (NG) Compare habits and masturbation aids. ✓**USENET**

Porn & erotica

alt.sex.movies (NG) Enjoy X-rated movies? Post about porn queens, describe your favorite scenes, and review the latest in triple-X. ✓**USENET**

rec.arts.erotica (NG) Erotic fiction and verse—submit your own work or just enjoy. ✓**USENET**

Sex addiction

12-Step Recovery from Sexual Addiction For people suffering from addiction to sex. ✓**FIDONET**→*tag* SIP_SAA

Sex and the disabled

Disability and Sexuality

Woman on white satin—from CompuServe's Graphics Plus Forum.

Discuss sexuality and the disabled. ✓**FIDONET**→*tag* ADA_SEXUALITY

Sex manual

The Kama Sutra Full text of the *Love Teachings of Kama Sutra.* ✓**INTERNET**→*ftp* FTP.SUNET.SE→ANONYMOUS/<YOUR EMAIL ADDRESS>→pub/etext/misc→kamasut.txt

Sex research

alt.sex.fetish.feet (NG) For those with a foot fetish. ✓**USENET**

Legs (ML) "Discusion sobre piernas de Mujeres." A forum conducted in Spanish for lovers of women's legs. GIFs and discussion. ✓**INTERNET**→*email* LISTSERV@UTFSM.BITNET ✍*Type in message body:* SUBSCRIBE LEGS <YOUR FULL NAME>

ssssTalk (ML) Forum for researchers, clinicians, educators, and students in the field of sexuality to discuss any relevant topic. ✓**INTERNET**→*email* LISTSERV@TAMVM1.TAMU.EDU ✍*Type in message body:* SUB SSSSTALK <YOUR FULL NAME>

Just pictures

alt.binaries.pictures.erotica

(NG) For erotic pictures only. ✓**USENET**

Digital Images (BBS) A graphics BBS with extensive adult areas. GIFs in the 1,024x768 range. Scanning service available. 414-338-9999 FREE

Electric Eye BBS (BBS) A graphics bulletin boad with a large selection of adult GIFs and TIFFs. ▦▫ ◉☋ 212-673-0301

The Gallery of Graphics Giffy Girls, Meet Amanda (nudes of a 20-year-old exotic dancer), Madonna nudes, and more. Vote for the model of the month. See the following databases: R-rated Celebrities, Pugdog's Playground, Thompson Film & Art, Giffy Graphics, Fresh Faces, and Info (for new nudes). ✓**DELPHI**→*go* COM GRAPH $$

Macintosh Graphic Arts & CAD Forum See GIF pin-ups in the GIF Library and the Pin-Up Library in the EPSF/Postscript Library. ✓**AMERICA ONLINE**→*keyword* GRAPHICS

Graphics & Animation Forum See the Faces & Bodies folder in the GIF Images Folder. ✓**AMERICA ONLINE**→*keyword* PGR

Just GIFs! (BBS) "The place for serious image collectors! Pets to space to celebrity nudes!" 718-939-1824 ✖*Only 9,600 bps* $25 OPTIONAL

MacEntertainment Forum See the Glamour Illustrations library. ✓**COMPUSERVE**→*go* MACFUN

The Photo Forum Check out The Nude & Pin-Up Images database. Regularly conducted model-of-the-month poll. ✓**DELPHI**→*go* GR PHOTO

Woman in underwear—from alt.binaries.pictures.erotica.

Photography Forum See the Human Form library, where "a fine image of a young lady, wrapped in a towel" is located. ◉☋ ✓**COMPUSERVE**→*go* PHOTOFORUM

Photography RoundTable Software Library The Body Beautiful library is an R-rated photo gallery. ✓**GENIE**→*keyword* PHOTO

Plain Brown Wrapper A series of libraries with adult pictures. ◉☋ ✓**COMPUSERVE**→*go* QPICS ...→ *go* GRAPHPLUS ...→*go* GALLERY ...→*go* CORNER

The Sex Attic (BBS) Adult GIFs and more adult GIFs. 313-269-6575

Starship Amiga RoundTable Software Library The Play-Bytes library has adult files in Amiga-style LHA and JPG formats. ✓**GENIE**→*keyword* AMIGA

Pictures +

After Hours BBS (BBS) Large collection of adult GIFs and matchmaker service. ▦▫ ◉☋ 512-320-1650/512-320-1679 $0.50/ HOUR

Brooklyn Perverts (BBS) Full-featured adult BBS and member of KinkNet. 908-888-0176 $30/YEAR

Chuck and Ginger's Board
(BBS) Home of the Babe series and Doll series GIFs. 210-523-1560 FREE

Classified Connection BBS
(BBS) Collection of adult files includes Giffy Girls—nude images of the girl next door. ⊞◨ 619-566-7347 $35/YEAR

Compu-Erotica (BBS) Offers adult conferences and pictures (including member GIFs). "If you like your chat hot, you'll love CEBBS!" Women receive free access. ⊞◨ ◉💬 312-902-3599

Date-Line (BBS) Includes photos of users, an adult file library (X-rated pictures), the MatchMaker database, and personals. ◉💬 718-876-7720 FREE

Ebony Shack BBS (BBS) An adult BBS with original scans and animations. 419-241-4600

Gabby's Lounge (BBS) An adults-only board with free scanning. ◉💬 816-887-3480 $2/MONTH ✖ *Signed release form with proof of age required*

THe GaRBaGe DuMP (BBS) One of the "big boards." A huge collection of adult files, real-time adult chat, a dating registry, and more. Local-access calling in more than 500 cities. To get a local-access number, call the voice number: 505-294-4980. ⊞◨ ◉💬 505-294-5675/505-294-0803 $2/HOUR

The Hard Drive (BBS) An exclusively adult board with more than 45 adult message conferences and a huge selection of adult GIFs. ⊞◨ ◉💬 816-763-7058 $15 BIANNUALLY

Isle-Net (BBS) Live erotic chat,

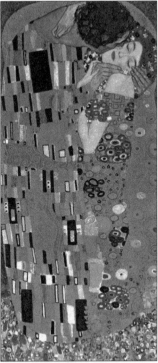

Gustav Klimmt's Kiss—downloaded from alt.binaries.pictures.misc.

GIFs, fantasy forums, and more. ⊞◨ ◉💬 908-320-1650 $45/ YEAR

Kentuckiana Magazines (BBS) Adult images and conferences for both straight and gay users. 812-948-9670 $50/YEAR

The Lambda Zone (BBS) An adult information and entertainment system featuring a a huge selection of graphics. ⊞◨ 312-693-7871 $32/YEAR

The Newton Express (BBS) Largest selection of adult GIFs in the Pa.-N.J.-Del. area. 215-943-6806 $20 QUARTERLY

Rusty-n-Edie's (BBS) A big board with a reputation. Includes a huge adult library and regularly con-

tributing authors of erotic text. They live by the three nos: no censorship, no rules, and no hassle. ⊞◨ ◉💬 216-726-2620 $69/ YEAR

Models

alt.binaries.pictures.super-models (NG) Images of supermodels. ✓**USENET**

alt.supermodels (NG) Talk about the supermodels—their careers, ages, measurements. Announcements of where the models are appearing both in person and in print are posted. ✓**USENET**

Supermodel Pictures Almost exclusively PG-rated pictures of supermodels. ✓**INTERNET**→*ftp* GARFIELD.CATT.NCSU.EDU→ANONYMOUS/ <YOUR EMAIL ADDRESS>→pub/graphics/images/girls

Swimsuit Models Alphabetically arranged images of swimsuit models and the like. All the subdirectories in the GIF directory have images of models. ✓**INTERNET**→*ftp* WUARCHIVE.WUSTL.EDU→ANONYMOUS/<YOUR EMAIL ADDRESS>→gif/s/ swimsuit

Talk about pictures

alt.binaries.pictures.erotica.d (NG) Talk about the pictures on the ALT.BINARIES.PICTURES.EROTICA newsgroup. ✓**USENET**

Other info

comp.bbs.misc (NG) Several hundred BBSs that carry adult GIF files are periodically listed in this forum of general BBS information. ✓**USENET**

Q Continuum BBS (BBS) Carries a list of a adult BBSs. 310-434-0401

Travel guides

Your best chance to get bumped is "Wednesday before Thanksgiving, Sunday after; a couple of days before and after Christmas, ditto with New Year's. Also, Friday afternoons, evenings, and Sunday afternoons and evenings bump a lot," says the **rec.travel.air** newsgroup, which focuses—relentlessly—on the art of obtaining inexpensive airfares. "Getting bumped," occurs when a flight is overbooked. The airline will ask volunteers to take the next flight in exchange for compensation—a free round trip, for example. "It gets even cheaper when you manage to get bumped while using a previous bump ticket."

On the Net

Across the board

The Independent Traveler Includes discussion boards about U.S. and world travel as well as a library of travel-related articles. Among services offered: a list of 800 numbers for airlines and hotels in the U.S., information on European rail passes, and U.S. and foreign tourist-office information. ✓**AMERICA ONLINE**→*keyword* TRAVELER

The Mobil Travel Guide A source for restaurant, lodging, and other travel information for more than 3,300 cities and recreation areas in the U.S. and Canada. ✓**PRODIGY**→*jump* MOBIL TRAVEL

Prodigy Traveler Along with passport information, travel planners, and discounts, this service also offers a travel feature. Past features have included national parks, Florida, and New England. ✓**PRODIGY**→*jump* PRODIGY TRAVELER

rec.travel (NG) Discuss destinations and sites, cost-saving tips, and bureaucratic issues with other travelers. ✓**USENET**

Travel News & Information Services Articles on corporate travel, information on worldwide travel promotions, notices about international events and celebrations, travel alerts, State Dept. advisories, ski-conditions reports (for a minimal fee), travel-industry codes, and essential information for traveling in specific countries. ▦ ✓**DELPHI**→*go* TRAV NEWS

Travel RoundTable Features several bulletin boards ranging from adventure travel to working abroad, plus libraries of information with travel journals, Caribbean travel announcements, and images. ☏ ✓**GENIE**→*keyword* TIS

Media

Adventures in Travel Articles on travel around the world by professional travel writers. Updated twice each month. ✓**COMPUSERVE**→*go* AIT

CR Leisure & Travel Leisure and travel articles from *Consumer Reports*. ✓**PRODIGY**→*jump* CR LEISURE & TRAVEL

Florida

Destination Florida RoundTable Featuring the bulletin boards Walt Disney World, Sea World, Universal Studios, and Discounts/Coupons/Bargains. Also includes the libraries Kennedy Space Center, and Daytona Beach area. ☏ ✓**GENIE**→*keyword* FLORIDA

Disney Conference Everything Disney—including the movies, cartoons, theme parks, resorts, and music. ✓**FIDONET**→*tag* DISNEY

Florida Forum Wealth of material for vacationers, including opportunities to speak with residents about where to stay, dine, and visit. Check out the Disney-

A remainder of the Berlin wall—from AOL's Graphic Arts & CAD Forum.

mania section for Disney World information. ⊛🎭 ✓**COMPUSERVE**→ *go* FLORIDA

West Coast

Left Coast Online! Round-Table Offers travel information, recreation news, and business resources for residents and visitors of Alaska, Washington, Oregon, and California. ⊛🎭 ✓**GENIE**→*keyword* CALIFORNIA

West Coast Travel Provides descriptions, directions, and historical overviews of travel destinations in the western United States. ✓**COMPUSERVE**→*go* WESTCOAST

Skiing

Ski Resort Guide Guide to more than 200 ski resorts. Listed by region, with the best feature of each resort noted (e.g., great nightlife). ✓**PRODIGY**→*jump* SKI RESORT GUIDE

Cross-country

Backroads Descriptions and directions to the scenic roads of America. Stories about journeys, not vehicles, are the focus, especially stories that aren't found in the tour guides. Much of the material is eventually published in the nonprofit volumes *Atlas of Winding and Scenic Backroads*. ✓**FIDONET**→*tag* BACKROADS

U.S. cities

City Guides Members rate the pluses and minuses of U.S. destinations in Prodigy's guides to major U.S. metropolitan destinations. ✓**PRODIGY**→*jump* TRAVEL GUIDES

Worldwide

Adventure Atlas Trips are sug-gested, complete with detailed information, based on your preferences—perhaps you're interested in a safari or vacation in France or a cruise. ✓**GENIE**→*keyword* ATLAS $$

British Travel Agency Online British travel brochures and information on England, Scotland, Wales, and Northern Ireland. ✓**PRODIGY**→*jump* BTA

CIA World Factbook Provides information on the population, politics, and economies of nations. ✓**INTERNET** ...→*wais* world-fact-book.src ...→*ftp* WORLD.STD.COM→ ANONYMOUS/<YOUR EMAIL ADDRESS>→ obi→World.Factbook

Mexico-L (ML) Interested in knowing more about Mexico? Presents the attractions of Mexico—including its cities, customs, and sites. ✓**INTERNET**→*email* LISTSERV@TECMTYVM.BITNET ✍ *Type in message body:* SUBSCRIBE MEXICO-L <YOUR FULL NAME>

rec.travel Library Read a trav-elogue called "Tanzania: The Dangers of Africa" or another titled "2 Wheels, 3 Fins, 4 Brits, and 5 Days in Java." There's a 1993 guidebook to Hong Kong, a "London Theater Trip" travelogue, and a guide to Disneyland. ✓**IN-TERNET**→*ftp* FTP.CC.UMANITOBA.CA→ ANONYMOUS/<YOUR EMAIL ADDRESS> →pub/rec-travel

Travel Talk to other travelers for suggestions on how to make your trip easy and inexpensive. ✓**ILINK**→ *number* 43

Travel Forum packed with information on national and international travel. ✓**SMARTNET**→*tag* TRAVEL

Travel BB Share travel experiences; pick up hints and ideas.

Topics organized into several categories—from adventure travel to Europe to motorcycling to singles travel. ✓**PRODIGY**→*jump* TRAVEL BB

Travel Forum Talk travel. Share experiences, exchange advice, and learn about foreign customs. ⊛🎭 ✓**COMPUSERVE**→*go* TRAVSIG

Travel-L (ML) Discussions of tourism. ✓**INTERNET**→*email* LIST-SERV@TREARN.BITNET ✍ *Type in message body:* SUBSCRIBE TRAVEL-L <YOUR FULL NAME>

Vacation Discuss things to do and places to see on vacation in the U.S. and abroad. ✓**RELAYNET**→ *number* 139

Travel services

You don't have to sit on the other side of the travel agent's desk anymore. Make your

own schedule. Find your own bargains. Do it the way you want to do it. Information is power. Start with **American Airlines—EAASY SABRE,** available through most services. Check out the **Official Airline Guide,** also widely available. For rooms, there's the **ABC Worldwide Hotel Guide** on CompuServe and **The Guide to Hotel Chains** on Delphi. For one of the niftiest navigators try **Bed and Breakfast Guide Online** on AOL.

On the Net

Across the board

Official Airline Guide Airline, hotel, and rental-car reservations. Discount tours and frequent-flier information. Also includes information on the weather, lodging and dining, cruises and discount travel packages, the travel industry, and more. ✓**COMPUSERVE**→*go* OAG ✓**DELPHI**→*go* TRAV AIR→oag ✓**GENIE**→ *keyword* OAG $$

Travelshopper Airline, hotel, and rental-car reservations as well as weather reports, currency exchange rates, flight-operations information, and more. Travelshopper's Low Fare Finder helps you find the lowest fares. ✓**COMPU-SERVE**→*go* WORLDSPAN ✓**DELPHI**→*go* TRAV AIR→travelshopper $$

Scotland—downloaded from CompuServe's Graphics Gallery Forum.

Air travel

Air France Tour booking, info on sights and scenes, chauffeur offers, frequent-flier programs, and schedule information. ✓**COM-PUSERVE**→*go* AF

American Airlines—EAASY SABRE Make reservations with any of 350-plus airlines, 27,000-plus hotels, or 60-plus rental companies. Check and see which planes have departed or arrived. With the free membership (you must give a credit-card number), you'll also get a newsletter. ✓**AMER-ICA ONLINE**→*keyword* SABRE ✓**COM-PUSERVE**→*go* SABRE ✓**DELPHI**→*go* TRAV AIR→eaasy ✓**GENIE**→*keyword* SABRE ✓**PRODIGY**→*jump* EAASY SABRE $$

Bargain Finders International Search by carrier, city, country, or region for discount international airfares and order tickets. ✓**DELPHI** →*go* TRAV AIR→bargain $$

Commercial SABRE Airline discounts and ticket services for subscribing corporate users. Gives direct access to SABRE. ✓**DELPHI**→ *go* TRAV AIR→commercial $$

Lufthansa Inquire about the German airline Lufthansa, get route updates, and reserve tickets. ✓**PRODIGY**→*jump* LUFTHANSA

rec.travel.air (NG) Includes, among general discussions about air travel, a monthly posting of the Airfare FAQ, which describes ways to get cheap flights, including the pluses and minuses of flying by courier, as well as information on student discounts, compassion discounts, special travel agents, senior-citizen fares, family fares, etc. ✓**USENET**

Assorted services

American Express Traveler's checks and gift checks. ✦ ✓**COM-PUSERVE**→*go* AE

Guide to Car Rental Companies Enter the name of the car company you're interested in and receive the company news and promotions. To reserve cars online, you must be a member of the Delphi VIP Club. √**DELPHI**→*go* TRAV CAR

Hospex-L (ML) Dedicated to discussions about hospitality exchanges. Serves as a forum for users of the Hospex database. √**INTERNET**→*email* LISTSERV@PLEARN. BITNET ✍*Type in message body:* SUB HOSPEX-L <YOUR FULL NAME>

rec.travel.marketplace (NG) Buy and sell anything related to travel: tickets, accommodations, luggage, etc. ⊕ √**USENET**

Special Travel Services Purchase travel insurance, confirm a limousine rental in more than 200 cities worldwide, order theater tickets for Broadway or London, request a visa application, get the latest skiing-conditions updates, and use other travel-related services. √**DELPHI**→*go* TRAV SPEC

Ticketmaster On-Line An up-to-date source of information on upcoming events in Chicago. Order theater, concert, and sporting-event tickets. For instance, you can get a listing of all home games for the Cubs, choose the game you're interested in seeing, look at available seating, get directions to the park, and charge your tickets to a credit card. √**AMERICA ONLINE** →*keyword* TICKETMASTER

Tour Packages Looking for the right tour package? Search a database of hundreds of tours by area, tour features, or length of tour. VIP Club members receive tour discounts. √**DELPHI**→*go* TRAV TOUR

Travel Source A store with travel goods. ⊕ √**GENIE**→*keyword* TRAVEL-SOURCE

U.S. State Department Travel Advisories (ML) U.S. State Department travel advisories on safety conditions in foreign countries, including terrorist activities, warfare, political unrest, and other factors of concern. The mailing list sends advisories as the State Department releases them. √**COMPUSERVE**→*go* STATE √**DELPHI**→*go* TRAV NEWS √**INTERNET** ...→*ftp* FTP.STOLAF. EDU→ANONYMOUS/<YOUR EMAIL ADDRESS>→pub/travel-advisories ...→*email* TRAVEL-ADVISORIES-REQUEST @STOLAF.EDU ✍*Subscribe by request*

Visa Advisors A company that tells you what documentation you need to get your visa. Will also assist you, for a fee, in filling out the forms and delivering them to the appropriate embassies or consulates. √**COMPUSERVE**→*go* VISA

Cruises

Cruises Includes a guide to cruises, ship and cruise-line profiles, and CruiSEARCH, which enables you to search by ship name, cruise line, location, month, or number of vacation days. VIP Club members get discounts on all cruises. √**DELPHI**→*go* TRAV CRUIS

Cruise Scan "Lowest prices on cruises." ⊕ √**PRODIGY**→*jump* CRUISE SCAN

Cruise Trek's (BBS) Travel-related forums, games, and software, including information on discounted cruises and tours. ⊞⊡ 802-438-2517 FREE

Hotels & inns

ABC Worldwide Hotel Guide

A comprehensive listing of more than 60,000 hotels worldwide, with location, contact information, accepted credit cards, rates, and facilities. √**COMPUSERVE**→*go* ABC

Bed & Breakfast Guide On-line Includes more than 9,000 bed-and-breakfasts and small inns in the U.S. and Canada. Search by region or name. The information exchange lets you give tips or ask advice about traveling and staying at B&Bs. Innkeeping Dream provides information on starting a B&B. Also vote for the best B&B, exchange recipes, and get industry news. ▦ √**AMERICA ONLINE**→*keyword* B&B

The Guide to Hotel Chains Information on hotels worldwide and, for VIP Club members, reservation assistance and discounts are available. √**DELPHI**→*go* TRAV HOTEL→ guide

Inn Directory A listing of inns and B&Bs. √**PRODIGY**→*jump* INN DIRECTORY

Travel clubs

The Travel Club For $49.95 join TWA's Travel Club, which offers hotel and airline discounts, vacation and tour packages, and other travel-related services. ⊕ √**COMPUSERVE**→*go* TTC

Travelers Advantage "Join for travel discounts." √**PRODIGY**→*jump* TRAVELERS ADVANTAGE

VIP Club Offers discounts on airline tickets, tours, and cruises. Ticket delivery, travel brochures and professional vacation-planning services are also available. √**DELPHI** →*go* TRAV VIP $$

Part 10

Public Affairs, Politics & the Media

10

Civil liberties

In addition to being perhaps the ultimate free speech ve-hicle, the Net is also host to a wide variety of interest groups monitoring, protecting, and discussing civil-liberties issues. The **Civil Liberties Archive** presents the ACLU's positions on the full range of rights challenges. The newsgroup **comp.society-privacy** covers up-to-the-moment technical issues involving privacy. Issues related to encryption, increasingly one of the most sensitive topics on the Net, are covered on Fido-Net's **Public-Key Encryption and Distribution**.

On the Net

Across the board

ACLU On-Line (BBS) A public bulletin board with ACLU news, a case database, files, and a forum on civil liberties. 212-944-0801/212-944-1657 ✖ *Some features limited to members*

alt.society.civil-liberty (NG) Discussion about individual rights, from cannabis rights to the right to keep your social-security number private. ✓**USENET**

Civil Liberties Sponsored by the Arizona Civil Liberties Union, an affiliate of the ACLU, it includes discussion on all issues related to the rights granted by the U.S. Constitution and the Bill of

The Supreme Court—downloaded from CompuServe's Graphics Gallery Forum.

Rights. Commentary about and criticism of the ACLU are welcomed. "It's your right." ✓**FIDONET**→*tag* CIVLIB

Civil Liberties Archive An archive with ACLU positions: campus hate speech, the death penalty, employee rights, lie detectors, reproductive freedom, art censorship, and AIDS; also U.N. covenants on civil rights. ✓**INTERNET**→*ftp* FTP.EFF.ORG→ANONYMOUS/<YOUR EMAIL ADDRESS>→pub/academic/civil-liberty

Censorship

alt.censorship (NG) Discussions about restricting freedoms of speech and the press. ✓**USENET**

IFreedom (ML) Serves as both a registry of censorship challenges in Canada and a forum for discussing censorship and intellectual freedom. ✓**INTERNET**→*email* LISTSERV@SNOOPY.UCIS.DAL.CA ✍ *Type in message body:* SUBSCRIBE IFREEDOM <YOUR NAME>

Privacy & security

alt.privacy (NG) Covers privacy issues in everyday life, including taxpaying, licensing, and the use

of social-security numbers, although many of the postings are related to Net issues. ✓**USENET**

comp.society.privacy (NG) Covers privacy issues affected by computers and technology, including telephone caller-I.D. files, credit records, mailing lists, and social-security numbers that are stored on computers. ✓**USENET**

McAfee Virus Forum Offers discussion and files on computer viruses, encryption, data security, and other issues. ✓**COMPUSERVE**→*go* NCSA

Public-Key Distribution A distribution-only area for entering and gathering public keys. ✓**FIDONET**→*tag* PKEY_DROP

Public-Key Encryption and Distribution Technical discussions about public-key privacy issues and programs. ✓**FIDONET**→*tag* PUBLIC_KEYS

Second Amendment

2nd Amendment Discussion Debate about the right to keep and bear arms as defined in the U.S. Constitution. ✓**FIDONET**→*tag* RTBKA

Gun-News (ML) Discussion about the politics of guns—especially the protection of the second Amendment. Reports on current firearm-related legislation. ✓**INTERNET**→*email* LISTSERV@PCCVM.BITNET ✍ *Type in message body:* SUBSCRIBE GUN-NEWS <YOUR FULL NAME>

talk.politics.guns (NG) While discussion often strays, firearm politics is the focus, including second Amendment issues. Both sides are firing. ✓**USENET**

Civil rights

Human-rights activists can respond to news reports and action appeals from Amnesty International, the East Timor Action Network, and other human-rights organizations in **soc.rights.human**. Gay-rights activists can turn to the huge **Queer Resources Directory** for texts of legislation or the names and telephone numbers of local gay organizations. And disability-rights advocates can dial up the government's **Civil Rights Division BBS** for the full text of the Civil Rights Act and detailed information on enforcement procedures and new rights initiatives.

On the Net

Discrimination

alt.discrimination (NG) Often heated discussions about all types of discrimination. ✓**USENET**

International RACISM Forum Allows people to discuss their feelings, ideas, beliefs, and emotions about racism "without personal contact." ✓**FIDONET**→*tag* VN_RACISM

Gay rights

Act-Up (ML) Interested in gay rights? Discuss the work being done by Act-Up chapters worldwide. ✓**INTERNET**→*email* ACT-UP-REQUEST@WORLD.STD.COM *Subscribe by request*

Martin Luther King Jr.—from America Online's Civil Rights Forum.

alt.politics.homosexuality (NG) Discussion about gay rights, politics and legislation. ✓**USENET**

Gay Issues Disussions about gay/lesbian/bisexual civil rights, bashing, and other related legal or religious issues. ✓**RELAYNET**→*number* 225

Gay Issues Discussion about issues affecting the gay community. ✓**SMARTNET**→*tag* GAY ISSUES

QN (ML) Forum for Queer Nation activists to network and discuss strategy and "how to bring about Queer Liberation." ✓**INTERNET**→*email* MAJORDOMO@QUEERNET.ORG *Type in message body:* SUBSCRIBE QN

Queer Resources Directory Includes contact information for support and activist groups; sections on AIDS; a bibliography of community-interest publications; information on civil rights and domestic partnerships; excerpts from the *GLAAD Newsletter*; every issues of *AIDS Treatment News*; addresses and numbers of elected officials as well as résumés for members of the Clinton Cabinet; transcripts of important legal opinions; and texts of articles on gay issues. ✓**INTERNET**→*ftp* VECTOR.INTERCON.COM→ANONYMOUS/<YOUR EMAIL ADDRESS>→pub/QRD/qrd

Human rights

Human Rights Issues, News, and Concerns Focus on human-rights information and news. Other topics include Amnesty International's Urgent Action notices of human-rights abuses. This is a general conference that is not affiliated with a specific human-rights group. ✓**FIDONET**→*tag* AI_HUM_R

Issues Forum An area for the free exchange of opinion and debate. See the Ethics/Human Rights section. 👁 ✓**COMPUSERVE**→*go* ISSUES

soc.rights.human (NG) Discussion and activism information about human-rights conditions and campaigns. ✓**USENET**

Public policy

Civil Rights Act of 1991 Text of the 1991 civil rights legislation. ✓**INTERNET**→*ftp* FTP.SPIES.COM→ANONYMOUS/<YOUR EMAIL ADDRESS>→Gov/US-Docs→civil91.act

Civil rights Division BBS (BBS) Information on civil-rights enforcement, the Americans With Disabilities Act, and some policy statutes. Provides a message forum. 202-514-6193 FREE

Youth rights

Y-Rights (ML) Forum to discuss youth rights. Adults and young people welcome. ✓**INTERNET**→*email* LISTSERV@SJUVM.BITNET *Type in message body:* SUB Y-RIGHTS <YOUR FULL NAME>

Debate

Get it off your chest. Vent. Spew. Hold forth. C'mon, don't be shy. We want to hear from you. We really, really do! You've got something to say. It's sharp, penetrating, brilliant. Knock'em dead on **Alpha-Omega-Open Forum,** where you can take on anybody about anything. Or rush in with your opinion on the latest news event on **alt.current-events**. And of course try **National Flame!** for the best in gross personal attacks. And when you've gotten it all out of your system and you just want to sit back, try **Mindless Chatter** for a bit of the old babble. What's the point? None at all.

Political debate in Canada—from Com-puServe's Reuters News Pictures Forum.

On the Net

Alpha-Omega-Open Forum An conference unlimited in content and scope, about any subject under the sun, including, but not limited to, science, politics, religion, the paranormal, and history. ✓**FIDONET**→*tag* ALPHA

alt.current-events＊ (NG) Newsgroups occasionally emerge following major events (e.g., ALT.CURRENT-EVENTS.SOMALIA, ALT.CURRENT-EVENTS.BOSNIA, and ALT.CURRENT-EVENTS.FLOOD-OF-93) ✓**USENET**

Bull Moose Tavern A debate and argument area based on Boston's famous Bull Moose Tavern, where the topics range from politics to the benefits of a well-brewed beer. ☜☞ ✓**AMERICA ONLINE**→*keyword* BULL MOOSE

Chaos_Landing A free-form speech area, with topics from the silly to the serious. Open, frank discussions are encouraged on any issue. ✓**FIDONET**→*tag* CHAOS_LANDING

Close-Up BB Discuss current events and controversies. Steady topics include Congress, the White House, and the courts, but the board also covers the topics of the day—e.g., school reform, health-care reform, euthanasia, etc. ✓**PRODIGY** →*jump* CLOSE-UP BB

Coffee_Klatsch Gossip and chat with a household feeling, including not only what goes on at home but world and national events too. ✓**FIDONET**→*tag* COFFEE_KLATSCH

Controversial A no-holds-barred discussion and debate about current events, societal attitudes, and other subjects of controversy. ✓**FIDONET**→*tag* CONTROV

Current Events Discuss the news of the day. Topics range from civil-rights issues to sexual politics to firearms. ☜☞ ✓**BIX**→*conference* CURRENT. EVENTS

Current Events/Debate Covers current social and political issues in an often intense manner. No religious discussions allowed. ✓**RELAYNET**→*number* 103

Debate General debates on a full range of issues: current social and political issues as well as historical and philosophical topics welcome. ✓**FIDONET**→*tag* DEBATE

Issues & Debate Forum Offers debate on controversial topics and current events. A resource center has backup data relating to current discussion topics, archives of past discussions, and articles from the *Truth Seeker* magazine. ☜☞ ✓**AMERICA ONLINE**→*keyword* ISSUES

Issues Forum An area for the free exchange of opinion on current events and social trends. Sections cover peace, politics, individualism, high tech, social issues, men's and women's issues, the handicapped, the paranormal, and youth. ☜☞ ✓**COMPUSERVE**→*go* ISSUES

Mindless Chatter A lighthearted message alternative of utter babbling and nonsense, including jokes, stress relief, and aardvarks. ✓**FIDONET**→*tag* CHATTER

National Flame! An uncensored, no-holds-barred debate area devoted to the flame tradition. Personal attacks, nastiness, obscenities, and insults are allowed—and likely. "It's not for the weak of heart." ✓**FIDONET**→*tag* FLAME

Opinion A general forum for debates on current social issues. ✓**ILINK**→*number* 22

Media industry

Keep up with media takeovers on Delphi's Entertainment News, speculate about the "real" trouble between Loni and Burt on **alt.showbiz. gossip**, get a fan's instant memoir about Letterman's first night on CBS on CompuServe's **Media Industry**. Pros can get full text of trade publications on CompuServe's **Media Newsletters**, while others can subscribe to magazines of their choice on Prodigy's **Magazine Deals**. If you're a broadcaster, check the bulletin board **Public Access Link** for all the paperwork you've got to fill out.

Across the board

Entertainment Includes reviews and light discussion of current books, movies, television, and radio programs. ✓**RELAYNET**→*number 116*

Entertainment News News about the entertainment industry. What's happening on Broadway? In Hollywood? On your favorite soaps? ▦ ✓**DELPHI**→*go* NEW ENT

Hollywood Hotline A guide to the latest in movies, TV, and recordings, with a trivia quiz, encyclopedia, and reviews. ✓**COMPUSERVE**→*go* HOLLYWOOD ✓**DELPHI**→*go* ENT HOLL ✓**GENIE**→*keyword* HOTLINE

Media magician—from the pictures archive at ftp.uwp.edu.

Media Movie reviews and discussions of television, radio, and print media. ✓**ILINK**→*number 52*

Media Newsletters Provides full-text articles from leading broadcasting- and publishing-industry newsletters. ✓**COMPUSERVE**→*go* MEDIANEWS $$

The Show Biz RoundTable Movie and television discussions and a huge library of GIFs. Also includes information and discussions on radio, theater, and home-entertainment technology. ◉♡ ✓**GENIE**→*keyword* SHOWBIZ

Broadcasting

Broadcast Professional Forum Provides publication, association, and convention information for broadcast- and audio-engineering, production, and land-mobile-communications professionals. Libraries for job listings, résumés, and broadcast transcripts. ◉♡ ✓**COMPUSERVE**→*go* BPFORUM

Broadcast Professionals For those considering broadcast ca-

reers. Covers daily issues in broadcasting. ✓**RELAYNET**→*number* 132

Broadcast Radio & Television Discussion of radio and television broadcasting. ✓**FIDONET**→*tag* BROADCAST

Broadcaster's Professional Communications Network (BPCNet) A professional network available via FidoNet or PCRelay, with separate conferences for radio and television broadcasters, engineers, producers, management, and sales people. ✓CHECK LOCAL BULLETIN BOARDS

Public Access Link (BBS) The FCC's board—contains forms, fee schedules, and regulations for broadcast license applicants. 301-725-1072 FREE ✗*Allowed six minutes*

Magazines

Magazine Deals Order a magazine subscription through Publishers Clearing House. ⊕ ✓**PRODIGY** →*jump* MAGAZINE DEALS

Awards

Awards Winners and nominees for a variety of entertainment awards: MTV awards, Daytime Emmys, News & Documentary Emmys, and others. Also includes an award archive. ▦ ✓**PRODIGY** →*jump* AWARDS

Celebrity news

alt.showbiz.gossip (NG) All the dirt on your favorite celebrities. ✓**USENET**

People News Latest news on celebrities. Includes a Guest Spotlight section and celebrity birthday announcements. ▦ ✓**PRODIGY**→ *jump* PEOPLE NEWS

Government info

This is your information. You owned it even before you could get it. Now it's truly free.

Try the **Federal Register Electronic News Delivery** for the minute-by-minute minutiae of the federal government. **FedWorld** is a backlist of White House press releases and also a great source for federal job postings, and your access point to other government BBSs. But don't stop there; there's a river of info flowing from Washington: from the **HUD News and Events BBS** to the **Whistleblower's BBS**—perhaps the only board with a congressman, Gary Condit, for a system operator.

The Mall in Washington D.C.—from CompuServe's Graphics Gallery Forum.

On the Net

Congress

US-Congress-Phone-Fax Phone and fax numbers of congressmen. Search by name. ✓**INTERNET**→*wais* US-Congress-Phone-Fax

Government BBS

Congressional Budget Office BBS (BBS) For an electronic copy of the deficit-reduction report. 202-226-2818 FREE

Federal Deficit Reduction BBS (BBS) Leave anonymous messages on government waste or corruption. Information will be investigated. 202-225-5527 FREE

Federal Register Electronic News Delivery (BBS) Includes summaries of public laws signed by the president, news and announcements, documents placed into the public record, and the tables of contents for the Federal Register, the official book of federal-government activity. Full access to the record is provided on Delphi. ▦ 202-275-0920/202-275-1538 FREE ✓**DELPHI**→*go* REF FED $9/HR

FedWorld (BBS) Links dozens of government BBSs worldwide. Includes archives of White House press releases and speeches as well as job information, foreign news accounts, and government statistics. 703-321-8020 ✓**INTERNET**→*telnet* FEDWORLD.GOV→NEW/<NONE> FREE

Government Printing Office WINDO Online Service (BBS) Information published by a number of government agencies—the State Department, EPA, DOE, etc. 202-512-1387

HUD News and Events BBS (BBS) Surveys of mortgage lending, the HUD secretary's public schedule, testimony, program fact sheets, personnel biographies, and other media-oriented information. 202-708-3563 FREE

Office of Government Ethics BBS (BBS) Covers ethics regulations. Download texts of regulations, information on training sessions, and reports. 202-523-1186 FREE

U.S. Small Business Administration (BBS) Features an overview of SBA programs and information on business-development programs, financial services and loans, government contracting opportunities, legislation and regulations, small-business minority programs as well as small-business statistics and a listing of SBA offices. 800-859-4636/800-697-4636

Research

bit.listserv.govdoc-l (NG/ML) Information on federal depository libraries—Freedom of Information Act issues, electronic dissemination policies of the GPO, etc. Also, a great source of information on where government resources are located on the Net. ✓**USENET** ✓**INTERNET**→*email* LISTSERV@PSUVM. BITNET ✍*Type in message body:* SUB GOVDOC-L <YOUR FULL NAME>

Information USA Based on Matthew Lesko's book *Information USA.* Provides three sections of free or low-cost access to government publications: a general guide to government publications and services, international information from the State Department, and travel information. ✓**COMPUSERVE** →*go* INFOUSA

Journalists & writers

Amateurs, pros, wannabes, has-beens, hacks, geniuses, poets, journalists (gonzo and otherwise), scriptwriters, romance novelists, pornographers, punsters, collaborators, and the disabled. In addition to being the world's largest publisher (publishing perhaps as many words a week as all major U.S. publishing houses issue in a year), the Net is also one of the weirdest writers' parties ever. Try the mailing list **Writers** for a fairly professional tone, or the mailing list **Nerdnosh** for a more romantic one. Would-be script writers should try the mailing list **Scrnwrit**. The newsgroup **rec.arts.erotica**, one of the most popular on the Net, is actually hot.

On the Net

Across the board

AuthorsNet Conferences include AN-Horror Writing, AN-Movies, AN Science Fiction, AN Writers Life, AN E-Publishing, and AN Young Authors. The home board is the Authors' Area Writers' Forum (513-848-4288), which carries a library of files for writers. ✓CHECK LOCAL BULLETIN BOARDS

Literary Forum Discussions about your favorite authors and perhaps your own writing submissions. Sections include poetry, comics, humor, fiction, sci-fi, and

There could be a note for help inside from someone stranded on some deserted island. He must have tossed the bottle in the ocean and it floated over thousands of miles to this beach! I'll bet he's still waiting for someone to rescue him, I could give the note to the Coast Guard and they would be able to find him!
No, I guess not. This bottle is certainly too heavy to float all that way. What else could it be?

Online graphic novel—from Compu-Serve's Computer Art Forum.

journalism. ✓**COMPUSERVE**→*go* LITFORUM

New Writers Discussions about getting started as a writer. Topics include doing research, plotting a story, developing characters, reporting, and getting published. ✓**BIX**→NEW.WRITERS

Sharp-L (ML) Dedicated to bringing together a variety of perspectives and interests relating to the printed word—from discussions of literary theory to the business of publishing. ✓**INTERNET**→ *email* LISTSERV@IUBVM.UCS.INDIANA. EDU ✍ *Type in message body:* SUB-SCRIBE SHARP-L <YOUR FULL NAME>

Writers (ML) Forum for professional and aspiring writers to discuss writing, business issues, and other related topics. ✓**INTERNET**→ *email* LISTSERV@VM1.NODAK.EDU ✍ *Type in message body:* SUB WRITERS <YOUR FULL NAME>

Writers BIX's orginal writers' conference. ✓**BIX**→WRITERS

Writers For professional or amateur writers. Topics covered in-

clude the publishing industry, grammar, writing style, and writing submissions. ✓**ILINK**→*number* 26

Writers Offers discussion of fiction, nonfiction, and poetry for writing professionals, amateurs, and aspiring writers. ✓**RELAYNET**→ *number* 140

Writers Club Provides areas on fiction, nonfiction, poetry, and science fiction, with regularly scheduled workshops and conferences. ✓**AMERICA ONLINE**→*keyword* WRITERS

Writers Group Writers and editors work together in conferences. Includes publishing tips and information resources. ✓**DELPHI**→*go* GR WRITERS

Writers' Ink RoundTable Fiction, nonfiction, poetry, screenwriting, and other writing-related areas. Discuss tax problems, attend live conferences with professional writers, and peruse the libraries, which have hundreds of files and applications for writers. The Writers Bookstore carries books for writers. ✓**GENIE**→*keyword* WRITERS

The Writers Market Forum For writers, artists, songwriters, photographers, poets, illustrators, cartoonists, and other creative professionals. Includes a database of publishers organized by the categories of interest to publishers—match your talent with the right publisher. Also contains a collection of articles written by experts in the field of publishing, a listing of books and magazines for writers, information on Writers Digest Schools, which offer correspondence courses, and a list of associations that offer assistance to creative individuals. ⊕💬 ✓**AMERICA ONLINE**→*keyword* WRITERS MARKET

Writers Talk Advice from professional writers. ✓**BIX**→WRITERS.TALK

Writing Covers the craft and business of writing fiction and nonfiction. ✓**FIDONET**→*tag* WRITING

Editing & usage

alt.usage.english (NG) English usage discussions and advice. Compare word choice, dictionaries, etc. ✓**USENET**

Copyediting-L (ML) For those, especially copy editors, interested in discussing editorial issues, client relations, Internet resources, dictionaries, and more. ✓**INTERNET**→ *email* LISTSERV@CORNELL.EDU ✍ *Type in message body:* SUBSCRIBE COPYEDITING-L <YOUR FULL NAME>

Lexicon Topics include etymology, malapropisms, wordplay, and PEN.N.INK, a general discussion area about words. ⊕💬 ✓**BIX**→LEXICON

Words-L (ML) Forum for discussing the English language. ✓**INTERNET**→*email* LISTSERV@UGA. CC.UGA.EDU ✍*Type in message body:* SUB WORDS-L <YOUR FULL NAME>

Journalism

alt.journalism (NG) Forum for discussing journalism and any issues of interest to journalists (e.g., censorship). ✓**USENET**

alt.journalism.criticism (NG) Forum for debating media coverage of current and historical

events. ✓**USENET**

alt.journalism.gonzo (NG) Discussions about Hunter S. Thompson, his works, and his life. ✓**USENET**

alt.music.journalism (NG) General discussion of issues relating to music journalism. ✓**USENET**

Carr-L (ML) Focused on the use of computers, including online research and graphics, in journalism. ✓**INTERNET**→*email* LISTSERV@ ULKYVM.LOUISIVILLE.EDU ✍*Type in message body:* SUBSCRIBE CARR-L <YOUR FULL NAME>

Journalism A forum to discuss writing and reporting news. ⊕💬 ✓**BIX**→JOURNALISM

Journalism Forum Serves the professional journalist with job listings, freelance contacts, source information, and commentary. For radio, TV, print, and photo/video journalists. ⊕💬 ✓**COMPUSERVE**→*go* JFORUM

Journalism Periodicals Index More than 10,000 citations from the Index to Journalism Periodicals. ✓**INTERNET**→*wais* journalism. periodicals.src

Journet (ML) Covers topics of interest to journalists and journalism educators. ✓**INTERNET**→*email* LISTSERV@QUCDN.QUEENSU.CA ✍SUBSCRIBE JOURNET <YOUR FULL NAME>

Poetry

Poetry Prose Conference dedicated to writing both poetry and prose. Topic areas include Prose Poetry Posts, Talk Poetry, Essay, and the Coffee House for relaxing and dicussing writing with other members. ⊕💬 ✓**BIX**→POETRY. PROSE

CYBERNOTES

"Allow me to out you, Mr Dinn. You are not so different from the viler epicene creatures who compulsively frequent this stagnant pond. While you marginally distinguish yourself from the noxious MID-WESTERN HAG by charitably sparing the assembled audience the signs of your drooling incontinence, your underlying demeanor reveals you as yet another small-minded, resentful nancy-boy. I leave you to seethe and stew in your own juices; the possibility of dialogue between us has long ago exhausted itself."

—from **rec.arts.poem**

The Poetry Workshop (ML) A forum for poets. ✓**INTERNET**→*email* POETRY-REQUEST@GONZAGA.EDU ✍ *Subscribe by request*

rec.arts.poems (NG) For posting your poetry. ✓**USENET**

We Magazine (ML) A poetry zine. ✓**INTERNET** ...→*ftp* ETEXT. ARCHIVE.UMICH.EDU→ANONYMOUS/ <YOUR EMAIL ADDRESS>→pub/Zines/ We_Magazine ...→*email* CF2785@ ALBNYVMS.BITNET ✍*Subscribe by request*

Professionals

Business of Writing Covers all aspects of the writing business.

✓**FIDONET**→*tag* PROWRITE

misc.writing (NG) Forum for discussing agents, manuscripts, writing aids, etc. ✓**USENET**

Professional Writers Conference for professional writers. 🖥️💬 ✓**BIX**→WRITERS.PROS ✗*For professional writers only*

Scrnwrit (ML) Forum for discussing screenwriting for film or TV. Related issues such as agents, and producers are acceptable. ✓**INTERNET**→*email* LISTSERV@TAMVM1. TAMU.EDU ✍️*Type in message body:* SUB SCRNWRIT <YOUR FULL NAME>

Techwr-L (ML) A forum for technical writers to discuss terminology, presentation, and any other related issues. ✓**INTERNET**→*email* LISTSERV@VM1.UCC.OKSTATE.EDU ✍️*Type in message body:* SUBSCRIBE TECHWR-L <YOUR FULL NAME>

Quotations

alt.quotations (NG) For sharing and discussing quotations of all sorts. ✓**USENET**

General Quotes and Puns Share your favorites. ✓**FIDONET**→ *tag* QUOTES_2

Romance & erotica

rec.arts.erotica (NG) Erotic fiction and verse. ✓**USENET**

Romance Writers Exchange RoundTable Devoted to discussing romance fiction. Includes tips, information, and conferences on learning to write women's fiction and romance as well as conferences with published authors. Unpublished writers should visit the Aspiring Authors Lounge. 🖥️💬 ✓**GENIE**→*keyword* ROMANCE

Science fiction

Science Fiction RoundTable 1 Includes the Writing Workshop— a private, by-request-only board where stories are uploaded and critiqued by other members. But sci-fi writing is welcome (and not private) in many of the other categories: write your own *Star Wars* adventure, join the Queens Own Writers Guild, participate in the Fan Fiction Writers Academy, etc. 🖥️💬 ✓**GENIE**→*keyword* SFRT1

Share your writing

alt.prose (NG) For posting original writing. ✓**USENET**

alt.prose.d (NG) Discussions about the work posted in ALT.PROSE. ✓**USENET**

Athene and InterText Devoted to short fiction. *InterText* is a bimonthly zine with a huge Net following (more than 1,000 subscribers). *Athene* preceded *Inter-Text* and is now defunct. ✓**COMPUSERVE**→*go* EFFSIG→Zines from the Net ✓**INTERNET** …→*ftp* ETEXT.AR CHIVE.UMICH.EDU→ANONYMOUS/ <YOUR EMAIL ADDRESS>→pub/Zines …→*ftp* NETWORK.UCSD.EDU→ANONY-MOUS/<YOUR EMAIL ADDRESS>→inter text …→*email* JSNELL@OCF.BERKELEY. EDU ✍️*Subscribe by request*

Collaborative Novel Choose from dozens of novels in progress (e.g., *Muffy and the Skinheads*) and contribute a chapter. ✓**DELPHI**→*go* GR WR COLL

CORE A zine for poetry, essays, and fiction. ✓**INTERNET** …→*ftp* ETEXT.ARCHIVE.UMICH.EDU→ANONY-MOUS/<YOUR EMAIL ADDRESS>→pub/ Zines/Core_Zine …→*email* CORE-JOURNAL@EFF.ORG ✍️*Subscribe by request*

The Fiction Writers Workshop

(ML) A supportive environment for writers to submit their works for criticism as well as to discuss writing itself. ✓**INTERNET**→*email* LISTSERV@ PSUVM.PSU.EDU ✍️*Type in message body:* SUB FICTION <YOUR FULL NAME>

Miscellaneous

The Composition Digest (ML) Forum for writers to discuss computer-related issues—e.g., psychological effects of computer writing, anecdotes, and text-editor design. ✓**INTERNET**→*email* LISTSERV@ULKYVX. BITNET ✍️*Type in message body:* SUB-SCRIBE COMPOS01 <YOUR FULL NAME>

The Computer Art Forum Features a Graphics Novel library and bulletin board. Members share their illustrated stories (often children's stories) with each other—each page is a GIF file in the library. Members are also collaborating on building a graphically illustrated world; weekly live conferences and discussion on the boards keep members up-to-date on the project. 🖥️💬 ✓**COMPUSERVE** →*go* COMART

disABLED Artists Forum A poetry-and-prose outlet for people with disabilities. Readers also discuss how disabilities are portrayed in the media and the arts. ✓**FIDONET**→*tag* ABLED_ART

Nerdnosh (ML) Forum for writers and nerds. "Think of it as a universal camp town meeting in M.F.K. Fisher shades and Jack Kerouac tones. Frivolous, friendly, and informative, in roughly that order." ✓**INTERNET**→*email* MAJORDO MO@SCRUZ.UCSC.EDU ✍️*Type in message body:* SUBSCRIBE NERDNOSH <YOUR FULL NAME>

Law & lawyers

Lawyers discovered the online world years ago through services like **Lexis/Nexis** and **Westlaw**. Of course, lawyers paid (and still pay) dearly for the privilege (you can too by getting your own account and telnetting from the Internet). But there's more competition now, for instance from the **Cornell Law School Server**, or **Project Hermes**, and **Washington and Lee Law Library**. And the big databases are no doubt feeling the pinch. For legal amateurs, grass-roots activists, and cranks there's the mailing list **Rights-L**, and Compu-Serve's **Legal Forum**.

On the Net

Across the board

A Legal Genius (BBS) Includes a huge library of wills, leases, and contracts; outlines for law students; an area where students can post their résumés; and legal-related conferences from several networks. 215-695-9689 FREE

Law Topics include litigation, legislation, law schools, Supreme Court decisions, property issues, and the full texts of cases and decisions. ⊛♋ ✓**BIX**→*conference* LAW

The Law RoundTable Discussions about current legal controversies, libraries of decisions (including Project Hermes texts),

Ruth Bader Ginsburg—from Compu-Serve's Graphics Gallery Forum.

legal software, law-student course outlines, and lawyer referrals. ⊛♋ ✓**GENIE**→*keyword* LAW

Legal Discussion on legal issues, practice problems, judicial practices, and legal software. Open to legal professionals and interested laypersons. ✓**ILINK**→*number* 9

Legal Covers all legal areas, with a focus on computer law. The host introduces current legal issues to readers to stimulate discussion, then offers extensive factual information and position papers on the issues. ✓**RELAYNET**→*number* 119

Legal Discussions about all aspects of the law, particularly issues related to data communications. ✓**SMARTNET**→*tag* LEGAL

Legal Forum Provides information for attorneys, corrections officers, paralegals, and members of the public interested in the law. Topics include copyrights, bankruptcy, law-office software and hardware, polygraph tests, and fingerprinting of children. ⊛♋ ✓**COMPUSERVE**→*go* LAWSIG

Legal Issues Legal professional information, including court deci-

sions, rules, statutes, and journal articles. For judges, attorneys, and the public. ✓**FIDONET**→*tag* LAW

The Legal SIG Legal forum, especially for Mac users. Includes software, court decisions, and a bulletin board for legal discussions. ✓**AMERICA ONLINE**→*keyword* LEGAL SIG

misc.legal (NG) Legal advice for whoever needs it. ✓**USENET**

Washington and Lee Law Library It's a legal treasure trove (that extends beyond legal) with access to information from sites worldwide. ✓**INTERNET** ...→*telnet* LIBERTY.UC.WLU.EDU→LAWLIB/<NONE> ...→*ftp* LIBERTY.UC.WLU.EDU→ANONYMOUS/<YOUR EMAIL ADDRESS>

Copyright law

CNI-Copyright Exchange information about copyright law on the CNI Copyright and Intellectual Property list. ✓**INTERNET**→*email* LISTSERV@CNI.ORG ✍*Type in message body:* SUBSCRIBE CNI-COPYRIGHT <YOUR FULL NAME>

Copyright FAQ Six-part FAQ covering all aspects of copyright law. ✓**INTERNET**→*ftp* CHARON. AMDAHL.COM→ANONYMOUS/<YOUR EMAIL ADDRESS>→pub/misc.legal/ Copyright-FAQ

Copyright Guide for Photographers Photography archive that includes the copyright guide produced by the American Society of Media Photographers. ✓**INTERNET**→*ftp* MOINK.NMSU.EDU→ANONYMOUS/<YOUR EMAIL ADDRESS>→rec. photo

Legal news

clari.news.law* Newspaper

articles relating to a number of legal areas including CLARI.NEWS. LAW.CIVIL, CLARI.NEWS.LAW.CRIME, CLARI.NEWS.LAW.CRIME.SEX, and CLARI. NEWS.LAW.PROFESSION. ✓**USENET**

Supreme court

Project Hermes Complete text of Supreme Court opinions as soon as they are made public. ✓**INTERNET** ...→*wais* supreme-court.src ...→*ftp* FTP.CWRU.EDU→ ANONYMOUS/<YOUR EMAIL ADDRESS>→ hermes ...→*email* AA584.CLEVELAND. FREENET.EDU@CUNYVM ...→*telnet* FREENET-IN-A.CWRU.EDU→VISITOR/ <NONE>→go hermes

Technology & the law

AIL-L (ML) Forum for discussing legal issues related to artificial intelligence. ✓**INTERNET**→*email* LIST SERV@AUSTIN.ONU.EDU ✍ *Type in message body:* SUBSCRIBE AIL-L <YOUR FULL NAME>

Bulletin Board Legal Issues Conferences Case histories, legislation, and other legal issues affecting sysops and bulletin boards. ✓**FIDONET**→*tag* BBSLAW

Law & Technology Professional discussions on technology's effect on the legal system, as well as the legal implications of developing technology. ✓**FIDONET**→*tag* LAW_ TECH

misc.legal.computing (NG) Covers all legal issues related to computers. ✓**USENET**

Reference

Cornell Law School Server Use World Wide Web technology to search and retrieve information from numerous legal texts, including the U.S. Copyright Act,

Supreme Court decisions, and the Uniform Commercial Code. ✓**INTERNET**→*telnet* FATTY.LAW.CORNELL →WWW/<NONE>

Legal Research Center Provides the resources of the following databases: *American Banker* Full Text, Child Abuse and Neglect, Congressional Information Services, Criminal Justice Periodical Index, Legal Resource Index, National Criminal Justice Reference Service, and Tax Notes Today. ✓**COMPUSERVE**→*go* LEGALRC $$

Lexis/Nexis A commercial service used by most law firms, with numerous legal databases. ✓**INTER-NET** ...→*telnet* LEXIS.MDC.ORG ...→*telnet* HERMES.MERIT.EDU ✖*Password needed. Voice call 1-800-543-6862. Requires sophisticated searching techniques* $$

Sidney University Law School FTP Archive A collection of U.S. state laws, speeches, and articles including "The Constitution in Cyberspace," (an analysis of computer law), Thoreau's *Civil Disobedience*, the telecommunications acts, etc. ✓**INTERNET**→*ftp* SULAW.LAW. SU.OZ.AU→ANONYMOUS/<YOUR EMAIL ADDRESS>→pub/law

Westlaw The other big online legal-reference center used by law firms. ✓**INTERNET**→*telnet* HERMES. MERIT.EDU ✖*Password needed. Voice call 1-800-543-6862. Requires sophisticated searching techniques* $$

Miscellaneous

CJUST-L (ML) Devoted to criminal-justice issues. ✓**INTERNET**→ *email* LISTSERV@CUNYVM.CUNY.EDU ✍ *Type in message body:* SUBSCRIBE CJUST-L <YOUR FULL NAME>

Ed Law (ML) Forum for exchanging information about legislation and litigation affecting public education, private education, and colleges and universities. ✓**INTERNET**→ *email* LISTSERV@UKCC.UKY.EDU ✍ *Type in message body:* SUBSCRIBE EDLAW <YOUR FULL NAME>

Hislaw-L (ML) For students and scholars of the history of law. Feudal, common, and canon law are all discussed, upcoming meetings and papers are announced, short scholarly pieces are offered, etc. ✓**INTERNET**→*email* LISTSERV@ ULKYVM.LOUISVILLE.EDU ✍ *Type in message body:* SUB HISLAW-L <YOUR FULL NAME>

Int-Law (ML) For those interested in finding information on foreign and international law or careers in international law. ✓**INTERNET**→ *email* LISTSERV@VM1.SPCS.UMN.EDU ✍ *Type in message body:* SUBSCRIBE INT-LAW <YOUR FULL NAME>

Rights-L (ML) Devoted to discussing an individual's rights and responsibilities, including children's and prisoners' rights. ✓**IN-TERNET**→*email* LISTSERV@AMERICAN. EDU ✍ *Type in message body:* SUB-SCRIBE RIGHTS-L <YOUR FULL NAME>

Other info

The Legal List A continually updated guide to legal resources on the Internet, including addresses for U.S. law schools connected to the Internet, information on pay resources such as Lexis and Westlaw, and other sites and lists. ✓**INTERNET** ...→*ftp* FTP.MIDNIGHT.COM →ANONYMOUS/<YOUR EMAIL ADDRESS> ...→*email* JUSTICE‖LEGAL-LIST-REQUEST @NIC.UNH.EDU ✍ *Type in message body:* SUBSCRIBE <YOUR FULL NAME> <YOUR EMAIL ADDRESS>

Law enforcement

Primarily for police officers and other law enforcement professionals, GEnie's Law

Enforcement Roundtable and **PoliceNet International** on **RoboCop BBS** are also open to curious (or irate) citizens. FidoNet's **Ask A Cop** and **Ask A Cop 2** are eager to develop a dialogue between the police and the public. Cops should try the BBS **Magnum** and FidoNet's **Law Enforcement Officers National Echo,** which are restricted to members of the trade.

On the Net

Across the board

A Law Enforcement Round-Table For those with both a professional and a general interest in law enforcement. Includes the Hitech Unit board for discussing the use of computers to solve and commit crimes, the Uniformed Division board, the Law Enforcement Groups board, the Training Announcements & Ideas library, and the Wanted Persons library. ⊕🕮 ✓*GENIE*→*keyword* ALERT

alt.law-enforcement (NG) Discussion about law enforcement and crimes. ✓**USENET**

Cop Shop (BBS) Law-enforcement-oriented, with FidoNet conferences. ⊕🕮 908-254-8117 FREE

Law Enforcement Officers National Echo Discussion for sworn officers. ✓**FIDONET**→*tag*

Police in action—from CompuServe's Graphics Plus Forum.

POLICE

LawEnforcmnt Features discussions about police science and law enforcement. ✓**SMARTNET**→LAWEN FORCMNT

Magnum (BBS) Law-enforcement-related message bases, files, games, etc. 🕮 ⊕🕮 405-536-5032 FREE

Police Law-enforcement and criminal-justice discussions. ✓**ILINK**→ *number* 90

Police Offers everything about police, in partnership with the EMS/Fire conference. ✓**RELAYNET**→ *number* 243

PoliceNet International A BBS network for those interested in law enforcement. Specific conferences include Firearms, Police, Corrections, Shomrim (for Jewish law-enforcement personnel), Posse (for women involved in relationships with police officers), Job_Search, K-9_Cops (for police K-9 handlers), Blue_Fever (an adult message area), and Swat. ✓CHECK LOCAL BULLETIN BOARDS

RoboCop BBS (BBS) Home of PoliceNet International. Carries law-enforcement conferences and related files. Users are almost exclusively law-enforcement personnel. ⊕🕮 619-299-0351/619-299-0357

K-9

Police Dogs Breeding, raising, training, and using police dogs. ✓**FIDONET**→*tag* K9COPS

Q&A

Ask A Cop An information exchange for law-enforcement professionals and the general public; created to develop a better understanding between the two. ✓**FIDONET**→*tag* ASKACOP

Ask A Cop 2 Covers the same topics as ASK A COP, but includes law enforcers and citizens from Canada and Australia as well as the U.S. ✓**FIDONET**→*tag* ASKACOP2

Law & Order Answers questions about law enforcement, including issues like community policing, crime prevention, and firearms. ✓**FIDONET**→*tag* LAW_&_ ORDER

Miscellaneous

Forensic List (ML) Discussions include the forensic aspects of anthropology, chemistry, odontology, pathology, psychology, toxicology, criminalistics and the use of forensic evidence in court, etc. ✓**INTERNET**→*email* FORENS-REQUEST@ ACC.FAU.EDU ✍*Type in message body:* SUBSCRIBE FORENS-L <YOUR FULL NAME>

The military

Arpanet was the military's precursor to the Internet. But on the Net today it's a bit harder to find military secrets or to launch a nuclear-missile attack, as Matthew Broderick did in *War Games*. What you'll find on Usenet's **sci.military** are military people as well as heavy-fire buffs rehashing battle scenarios or discussing weapons capabilities. AOL's **Military & Vets Club** tackles issues like gays and POWs. The mailing list **Milhst-L** covers military history. "Virtually" be all that you can be.

On patrol—downloaded from wuarchive.wustl.edu

Across the board

Military Open to all topics dealing with the military. ✓**ILINK**→ *number* 229

Military & Vets Club For everyone with an interest in the military. Participants include active-duty personnel, members of the Reserves and National Guard, retired servicemen, veterans, and military dependents. Also offers help to those interested in joining the military, finding a military buddy, or learning about veterans' benefits. Weekly live-talk meetings in the Commanders Conference Room are devoted to current events. ⊕💬 ✓**AMERICA ONLINE**→ *keyword* MILITARY

Military Forum Covers all topics related to the military, with special areas devoted to MIA/POW issues, Vietnam veterans, military hardware, current military news, and "Atomic Vets." 🖳 ⊕💬 ✓**COM-PUSERVE**→*go* MILITARY

Military Issues Borderless military discussions by Netters from numerous nations, including those on active duty, veterans, disabled veterans, and civilians. ✓**FIDONET**→ *tag* MILITARY_PEOPLE

Military RoundTable Forum for discussing the military. Military professionals exchange information while others are welcome to ask questions. Topics include reunions, looking for former military friends, the military of the 1990s, the Canadian armed forces, homosexuality and the U.S. military, sexual harassment in the military, military anecdotes, the military and UFOs, and military wives. ⊕💬 ✓**GENIE**→*keyword* MILITARY

Gays

Queer Resources Directory

The QRD has an extensive collection of military-related materials, including a contact list of queer veterans, transcripts of Senator Sam Nunn's Senate hearings on homosexuals in the military, a Colin Powell article in the *Harvard Gazette*, and ROTC resources. ✓**INTERNET**→*ftp* VECTOR. INTERCON.COM→ANONYMOUS/<YOUR EMAIL ADDRESS>→pub/QRD/qrd

Military history

Byrd Marshall University History FTP Site A large collection of military-history documents and GIFs. For example, the archive carries military-aviation GIFs, the text of the Declaration of Arms, a bibliography for U.S. military planning for WWI, the texts of the German and Japanese surrenders, Vietnam GIFs, and the Senate POW/MIA report. See also the /pub/history/maritime directory. ✓**INTERNET**→*ftp* BYRD.MU. WVNET.EDU→ANONYMOUS/<YOUR EMAIL ADDRESS>→pub/history/mili tary

Milhst-L (ML) For those with a serious interest in military history. Open to discussions about any time period. Social, economic, and political analysis welcome. ✓**INTERNET**→*email* LISTSERV@UKANVM.CC. UKANS.EDU ✍*Type in message body:* SUB MILHST-L <YOUR FULL NAME>

POW/MIA

The Forget-Me-Not POW/MIA BBS (BBS) "Dedicated to the Prisoner of War/MIA issue." Includes articles, biographies, updates on political representatives' actions, and links to computer networks relevant to the MIA issue. 🖳 908-787-8383 FREE

POW/MIA Message Center

Includes discussion about prisoners and missing soldiers from all American wars. Provides information on lobbying of government officials. ✓**RELAYNET**→*number* 164

Support

Military Offers help to military personnel on all issues. ✓**RELAYNET**→*number* 141

Navy Support for active, retired, and reserve members of the Navy, Marine Corps, and Coast Guard. ✓**FIDONET**→*tag* NAVY

Servicemen in Action (SIA) Provides support for families with members in the armed forces during any conflict. ✓**RELAYNET**→*number* 350

Technology

sci.military (NG) For those interested in military technology. Discuss actual or potential conflict scenarios with an emphasis on equipment capabilities. Typical posting: "Matter of fact I don't think you can get to within ASROC range with a good submarine as a foe. He'd nail you with a torp before that." ✓**USENET**

Veterans

In Country For veterans of all conflicts who have received a combat-zone campaign ribbon. ✓**FIDONET**→*tag* IN_COUNTRY

soc.veterans (NG) Discussion about issues relating to military veterans. Lots of information requests and military news. ▦ ✓**USENET**

Veterans Participation by veterans of the U.S. Armed Forces and supported by the Veterans Ad-

The Vietnam Memorial—downloaded from byrd.mu.wvnet.edu.

ministration. ✓**ILINK**→*number* 85 ✖ *Veterans only*

Veterans Discussions about veterans' issues. ✓**RELAYNET**→*number* 163

Veterans BB Topic sub-boards include Air Force, Army, Coast Guard, Marines, Merchant Marines, Navy, cadets, reunions, Korea, and military brats. ✓**PRODIGY**→*jump* VETERANS BB

Vets Conference for veterans. ✓**BIX**→*conference* VETS ✖ *For veterans only*

Vets For veterans to discuss common interests. ✓**SMARTNET**→*tag* VETS

Vietnam Vets International Vietnam Veterans conference. ✓**FIDONET**→*tag* VIETNAM_VETS

War games

Conflict Simulation Games List (ML) Devoted to discussing historical-conflict simulation games, but discussion extends to military history, tactics and strategy, game collecting, club an-

nouncements, and more. ✓**INTERNET**→*email* LISTSERV@VM.UCS.UALBERTA.CA ✎ *Type in message body:* SUB CONSIM-L <YOUR FULL NAME>

Strategic Wargames Discuss your favorite computer war games —strategies in harpoon and tactics in Falcon 3. ✓**RELAYNET**→*number* 409

News services

One of the early visions of the online universe was as a

kind of news service in every pot. With a keystroke we'd all have our real-time headlines; the AP wire would come directly, instead of through a newsroom, to all of us. If information were chicken we'd all be happy now. The AP, Reuters, and UPI are available from one or more of the commercial services. More and more newspapers and magazines arrive online (before they hit the newsstand) every day. What's more, they can be searched by keyword quickly and easily. CompuServe offers several electronic clipping services. Recently **The Geraldo Show** hit AOL—maybe because emoticons like :#< hurt less than a real-life punch in the nose.

Paperboy by E. M. Bannister—from CompuServe's Graphics Gallery Forum.

On the Net

Across the board

ClariNet Over a hundred fee-based newsgroups with newspaper articles and news releases on topics ranging from business products to baseball (e.g., CLARI.BIZ.MARKET, CLARI.CANADA.FEATURES, CLARI.LOCAL. ILLINOIS, CLARI.NEWS.ARTS, and CLARI. SPORTS.TENNIS) ▦ ✓USENET

Dow Jones News/Retrieval
Searchable full-text articles from hundreds of publications such as *The Wall Street Journal*, the *Congressional Quarterly*, and McGraw-Hill publications such as *Aviation Week* and *BYTE, Business Week, Forbes, Fortune*, etc. Stock quotes, transcripts of *Wall $treet Week*, commodities quotes, extracts from Standard & Poor's, and much more. ▦ ✓GENIE→*keyword* DOW-JONES $$

GEnie Newstand Search more than 900 full-text publications, including 12 major U.S. newspapers and hundreds of popular magazines. ▦ ✓GENIE→*keyword* NEWSSTAND $$

News & Finance A forum with more "sections" than your newspaper, including national, international, weather, sports, features, business, cartoons, stock-market charts, elections, and an investors'

network. Also provides access to *USA Today* and *Time* Online. ▦ ✓AMERICA ONLINE→*keyword* NEWS

NewsGrid Provides searchable wire-service reports on business, national, and world news. ▦ ✓COMPUSERVE→*go* NEWSGRID

News Search Enter a term and search news clips from the Comtex News Service for articles you're interested in. ▦ ✓AMERICA ONLINE→*keyword* NEWS SEARCH

Alternative news

News of the US and World An alternative news service that focuses on items overlooked by the "establishment" media. Social, labor, and environmental stories receive emphasis. ▦ ✓FIDONET→ *tag* ANEWS ✖*No conversations*

News with an angle

The Geraldo Show Geraldo goes online. ☻ ▦ ✓AMERICA ONLINE→*keyword* GERALDO

Human Interest News Surprising, shocking, and amusing stories. ▦ ✓DELPHI→*go* NEW HUMAN

National News Federal, regional, and local news. ▦ ✓DELPHI→*go* NEW NAT

NewsLink An updated list of the day's top stories. ▦ ✓AMERICA ONLINE→*keyword* NEWSLINK

Clipping services

Executive News Service An electronic clipping service that lets you create custom folders to capture articles on your chosen topics from the AP, UPI, Reuters, and *Washington Post* wire services. ▦ ✓COMPUSERVE→*go* ENS $$

NewsNet Articles from more than five hundred sources and a clipping service. ▦ ✓**COMPUSERVE**→*go* NN

QuikNews Indicate which type of story you are interested in and GEnie scans news services and then mails relevant stories to you. ▦ ✓**GENIE**→*keyword* QUIKNEWS $$

Magazines

Consumer Reports Full-text articles from *Consumer Reports*. ▦ ✓**PRODIGY**→*jump* CR ✓**COMPUSERVE**→*go* CONSUMER

Magazine Database Plus About 150,000 full-text articles from more than 130 general-interest publications, including *The Nation*, *The Atlantic*, *Consumer's Digest*, and *Popular Mechanics*. Search by subject, time period, publication, and more. ▦ ✓**COMPUSERVE**→*go* MAGDB $$

Time Online Articles are online before the magazine hits the stands, including some that have been cut from the hard-copy version. Back issues are available and can be searched by keyword. Message boards and letters to the editor are also featured. And, of course, you can subscribe online to receive the hard-copy version. ▦ ✓**AMERICA ONLINE**→ *keyword* TIME

Newspapers

Chicago Online *The Chicago Tribune* online includes news, weather, sports headlines, restaurant reviews, and Gene Siskel's movie reviews. In addition, message boards are available for commenting on the news, looking for Chicago information, and speaking out about Chicago happen-

ings. ▦ ✓**AMERICA ONLINE**→*keyword* CHICAGO TRIBUNE

Mercury Center An electronic extension of the *San Jose Mercury News* with current articles, back issues, and more. Each day's edition of the *Mercury News* contains references and guides to material available on Mercury Center. ▦ ✓**AMERICA ONLINE**→*keyword* MERCURY CENTER $$

Newspaper Library Full-text articles from more than 50 U.S. newspapers, ranging from the *Akron Beacon Journal* to the *Wisconsin State Journal & Capital Times*. Major city papers include the *Boston Globe*, *Chicago Tribune*, *Detroit Free Press*, and *Washington Post*. ▦ ✓**COMPUSERVE**→*go* NEWSLIB $$

UK Newspaper Library Includes articles from *The Independent*, the *Daily Telegraph*, *The European*, *Today*, *The Financial Times*, *The Guardian*, and *The Observer*. Searchable by name, word, or phrase. ▦ ✓**COMPUSERVE**→*go* UKPAPERS $$

USA Today An online version of *USA Today*. ✓**AMERICA ONLINE**→*keyword* USATODAY ✓CHECK LOCAL BULLETIN BOARDS

Regional news

AP Online The latest AP news, updated hourly. Categories include the nation, Washington, the world, politics, entertainment, Wall Street, Dow Jones averages, features, sports, science, and health. ▦ ✓**COMPUSERVE**→*go* APO

CNN Newsroom Online Provided by Turner Educational Systems, Inc. Offers news, a forum for asking questions of CNN

Newsroom guests, an idea exchange, and multimedia information. Teachers can order classroom guides to Turner programs. ▦ ✓**AMERICA ONLINE**→*keyword* CNN

misc.news.east-europe.rferl (NG/ML) Reports from Radio Free Europe and Radio Liberty. ▦ ✓**USENET** ✓**INTERNET**→*email* LIST SERV@UBVM.CC.BUFFALO.EDU ✍*Type in message body:* SUB RFERL-L <YOUR FULL NAME>

Newsday Online (BBS) Read today's *Newsday* online and discuss the news on the board's bulletin boards. ▦ 516-454-6959 ✘ *Time limit: 60 minutes/day* FREE

Public Opinion Online A database of public-opinion surveys conducted in the U.S. by major polling firms such as Gallup, Harris, Roper, NBC, etc. ✓**GENIE**→*keyword* POLL $$

Reuters Information Services International and financial wire news service. Reporting 24 hours a day. ▦ ✓**DELPHI**→*go* NEWS REUTER ✓**GENIE**→*keyword* REUTERS

Reuters News Pictures Forum View the photo for tomorrow's front page minutes after it's been taken. Get immediate access to the same photos that major newspapers across the country are getting off the Reuters wire service. ✓**COMPUSERVE**→*go* NEWSPIX

UK News Clips Offers Reuters stories related to the U.K.—finance, politics, and economic news. ▦ ✓**COMPUSERVE**→*go* UKNEWS

United Press International Includes stories about Europe, Asia, and Africa that often don't appear in local newspapers. ▦ ✓**DELPHI**→*go* NEW INT

Politics

All major and not-so-major groups and movements are represented here, from the Democrats and Republicans (**alt.politics.democrats** and **alt.politics.usa.republican**) to the followers of Rush Limbaugh on the newsgroup **alt.rush-limbaugh** and on FidoNet's **Rush Limbaugh/EIB Topics** (Rush is only slightly less a presence on the Net than on radio and television) to the **ACT-UP** mailing list to monarchy revivalists on the newsgroup **alt.revolution. counter**. The Net is also an op-ed page with columnists Jack Germond and Robert Novak on Prodigy. And, of course, Ross Perot is his own cottage industry: there's **alt.politics.perot** for discussion and debate, and the **Perot Archive** for everything he's ever uttered.

On the Net

Across the board

Activ-L (ML) Devoted to discussions about peace, democracy, freedom, and justice. ✓**INTERNET**→ *email* LISTSERV@MIZZOU1.MISSOURI.EDU ✍ *Type in message body:* SUBSCRIBE ACTIV-L <YOUR FULL NAME>

ActNow-L (ML) Discussion group for college activists. ✓**INTERNET**→ *email* LISTSERV@BROWNVM.BITNET ✍

President Bill Clinton—from CompuServe's Graphics Gallery Forum.

Type in message body: SUBSCRIBE ACT NOW-L <YOUR FULL NAME> <YOUR SCHOOL NAME>

ACT-UP (ML) Interested in gay rights? Discuss the work being done by ACT-UP chapters worldwide. ✓**INTERNET**→ *email* ACT-UP-REQUEST@WORLD.STD.COM ✍ *Subscribe by request*

alt.activism (NG) Information and activities for activists. ✓**USENET**

alt.activism.d (NG) For discussing the activities and issues described in ALT.ACTIVISM. ✓**USENET**

alt.politics* (NG) Dozens of newsgroups dedicated to news and discussion about the politics of a certain issue or area—from ALT.POLITICS.CLINTON to ALT.POLITICS.EUROPE. MISC. to ALT.POLITICS.VIETNAMESE. ✓**USENET**

misc.activism.progressive (NG) News for progressive activists. ✓**USENET**

PeaceNet/ConflictNet/EcoNet Serves peace and social-justice advocates worldwide in areas of human rights, disarmament, and international relations. Includes groups such as Greenpeace, the World Federalist Association and SANE/Freeze. News resources from all over the world. For a catalog of conferences from the networks, brochures, and price information, FTP to their site. To sign up, send an email request. 💻 ☺🐾 ✓**INTERNET** ...→*email* SUPPORT@IGC. ORG ...→*ftp* IGC.ORG→ANONYMOUS/ <YOUR EMAIL ADDRESS>

The Pencil FTP Server Information on a slew of causes, from military invasions to the environmental movement (including articles and judicial decisions) to political campaigns. Lists of government telephone numbers as well. ✓**INTERNET**→*ftp* PENCIL.CS.MIS SOURI.EDU→ANONYMOUS/<YOUR EMAIL ADDRESS>→pub/map

Public Forum NonProfit Connection A forum to discuss news, current events, and social issues. Topics are oriented toward problems in government, rights and regulations, current events, and activism. Hundreds of topics are active daily on the bulletin board, and the libraries are stores of information—download the U.S. Congress directory, Rush Limbaugh transcripts, the NAFTA agreement, Clinton speeches, Amnesty International reports, or the search warrant in the WACO debacle. 💻 ☺🐾 ✓**GENIE**→*keyword* PF

Superdemocracy Foundation BBS (BBS) Discussions about democracy and political culture. If you "wish to explore and debate the potentialities of self-government in the electronic age, this is the BBS for you." 305-370-9376 FREE

Anarchists

alt.society.anarchy (NG) Discuss anarchists' lifestyles and beliefs. ✓**USENET**

Conservatism

alt.rush-limbaugh (NG) Discussion about Rush Limbaugh, including transcipts of some of his broadcasts. ✓**USENET**

alt.society.conservatism (NG) For discussions about social, cultural, and political conservatism. ✓**USENET**

Rush Limbaugh/EIB Topics General talk and response to Limbaugh's radio and TV shows. ✓**FIDONET**→*tag* LIMBAUGH

Town Hall (BBS) Conservative political discussion and debate sponsored by *National Review* magazine. Includes a Washington political digest; a Conservative Calendar, listing events nationwide; news; weather and financial statistics; William F. Buckley's Word of the Day; an archive of *National Review*; and an online university. ▨ ☏ 301-262-8610 $20/MONTH

Issues & agendas

alt.politics.reform (NG) Covers discussions about political reform—from the UN to Congress—as well as news from the Clinton White House. ✓**USENET**

Christian Action Line News and listings of "legislative and corporate attacks on traditional family values." No debate, strictly voter and consumer information. ✓**FIDONET**→*tag* C_ACTLINE

Concord Coalition Discuss the

Former president George Bush and Queen Elizabeth—from sunsite.unc.edu.

Concord Coalition, a bipartisan, nonprofit organization devoted to reducing the federal deficit in the United States. It is headed by former Republican senator Warren Rudman and former Democratic senator and presidential candidate Paul Tsongas. ✓**FIDONET**→*tag* CONCORD

Governmental Reform A sister conference to the national PEROT echo, this includes discussions of general political reform "that is so sorely needed to keep this country the greatest on the planet." Topics are limited to nonpartisan, constructive solutions to what's wrong. ✓**FIDONET**→*tag* GOV-REFRM

Health Reform (ML) Forum for discussing health-care reform. ✓**INTERNET**→*email* LISTSERV@UKCC. UKY.EDU ✍ *Type in message body:* SUB HEALTHRE <YOUR FULL NAME>

Libertarianism

alt.politics.libertarian (NG) For the serious discussion of libertarianism. ✓**USENET**

alt.politics.marrou (NG) Discussion about the politics of Andre Marrou and the Libertarian Party. ✓**USENET**

alt.society.sovereign (NG) Topics include the rights of man, taxing and licensing, the legitimacy of the federal government, and defending the individual's rights in the American courts. ✓**USENET**

Libernet (ML) Electronic magazine "for libertarians, classical liberals, objectivists, and anybody else interested in a free market/social tolerance approach to political issues." Carries book reviews, seminar announcements, election results, and articles. ✓**INTERNET**→*email* MAJORDOMO@DARTMOUTH.EDU ✍ *Type in message body:* SUBSCRIBE LIBERNET-BATCH-LIST <YOUR EMAIL ADDRESS>

Libernet-D (ML) Discussion forum for libertarian ideas and "the more philosophical issues related to a free society, such as political strategy." ✓**INTERNET**→*email* MAJORDOMO@DARTMOUTH.EDU ✍ *Type in message body:* SUBSCRIBE

LIBERNET-D-BATCH-LIST <YOUR EMAIL ADDRESS>

Libertarian Politics—Theory and Practice News and information about the Libertarian Party. Includes the party's political philosophy, theory, and activism. Also gives access to the multi-network Libernet facility. ✓**FIDONET**→*tag* LIBERTY

Major parties

alt.politics.democrats (NG) News and announcements about Democratic politicians and policies. 🖾 ✓**USENET**

alt.politics.democrats.d (NG) Discussion about announcements in ALT.POLITICS.DEMOCRATS*. ✓**USENET**

alt.politics.usa.republican (NG) Discussion about Republican Party politics and perspectives. ✓**USENET**

GOP-L (ML) A list to discuss conservative ideas. ✓**INTERNET**→*email* LISTSERV@PCCVM.BITNET 🖾 *Type in message body:* SUBSCRIBE GOP-L <YOUR FULL NAME>

Repub-L (ML) Discuss Republican politics and conservative ideas. ✓**INTERNET**→*email* LISTSERV@MARIST. BITNET 🖾 *Type in message body:* SUB REPUB-L <YOUR FULL NAME>

Monarchists

alt.revolution.counter (NG) Monarchists, conservatives, traditionalists, and others theorize and debate. ✓**USENET**

Peace Corps

bit.org.peace-corps (NG/ML) Discuss the Peace Corps experience with former, current, and

The Capitol—downloaded from CompuServe's Graphics Gallery Forum.

prospective volunteers. Members of other international volunteer organizations welcome to participate. ✓**USENET** ✓**INTERNET**→*email* LISTSERV@CMUVM.CSV.CMICH.EDU 🖾 *Type in message body:* SUBSCRIBE PCORPS-L <YOUR FULL NAME>

Perot

alt.politics.perot (NG) Discussion and debate of United We Stand, America perspectives. Perot schedules and news from conservative organizations are also carried. ✓**USENET**

Perot News from UWSA. ✓**INTERNET**→*email* LISTSERV@MARIST.BITNET 🖾 *Type in message body:* SUBSCRIBE PEROT <YOUR FULL NAME>

Perot Archive Perot speeches, his platform, and a biography. ✓**INTERNET**→*ftp* CCO.CAL.TECH.EDU→ANONYMOUS/<YOUR EMAIL ADDRESS>→pub/bjmccall/perot

Reforming the American Government Discussion about reforming government the Ross Perot way, with information on his volunteers and other groups. ✓**FIDONET**→*tag* PEROT

United We Stand, America Discuss the activities of the

national reform organization founded by Ross Perot. ✓**FIDONET**→*tag* UWSA

Political columns

Capital Connections Karen Feld's column on politics. ✓**PRODIGY**→*jump* CAPITAL CONNECTIONS

Germond on Politics Regularly featured political column by Jack Germond. ✓**PRODIGY**→*jump* GERMOND

Novak on Politics Political opinion—on the conservative side—by Robert Novak. ✓**PRODIGY**→*jump* NOVAK

Valentine Michael Smith's Commentary (ML) Commentary on world events. ✓**INTERNET**→*email* LISTSERV@UCF1VM.CC.UCF.EDU 🖾 *Type in message body:* SUB VAL-L <YOUR FULL NAME>

Political debate

alt.politics.correct (NG) Discussions about political correctness, particularly terminology issues and stereotype discussions. ✓**USENET**

alt.politics.usa.constitution (NG) Covers U.S. constitutional politics. ✓**USENET**

alt.politics.usa.misc (NG) Discussions about politics in the U.S. and news from the White House. ✓**USENET**

Canadian Politics Conference Public-affairs and political issues in Canada. All users and all political viewpoints welcomed. ✓**FIDONET**→*tag* CANPOL

Poli-Phil Express political convictions. ✓**SMARTNET**→*tag* POLI-PHIL

Political Debate Forum Includes numerous political bulletin boards and libraries, including a biography of Hillary. ☜🕿 ✓**COMPUSERVE**→*go* POLITICS

Politics A letters-to-the-editor-style general political discussion. ✓**FIDONET**→*tag* POLITICS

Politics (ML) For serious political discussion. ✓**INTERNET**→*email* LISTSERV@UCF1VM.CC.UCF.EDU ☜ *Type in message body:* SUB POLITICS <YOUR FULL NAME>

Politics Discuss national political issues. ✓**ILINK**→*number* 58

Politics Offers debate on current political and social issues. ✓**RELAYNET**→*number* 178

soc.politics (NG) General discussion about politics and political systems. ✓**USENET**

talk.politics* (NG) Newsgroups dedicated to discussion (often heated) about the politics of specific areas or issues: TALK.POLITICS.MIDEAST, TALK.POLITICS.SPACE, TALK.POLITICS.GUNS, etc. ✓**USENET**

talk.politics.theory (NG) Political debate ranging from libertarianism to the controversy over the "voucher system" for schools.

✓**USENET**

Political media

alt.news-media (NG) Carries White House press releases, schedules, and media-related discussion. ✓**USENET**

alt.politics.media (NG) Discussion about media political coverage and ethics. ✓**USENET**

Resistance

alt.society.resistance (NG) Discussion about all types of social resistance, including resistance against the government and social mores. ✓**USENET**

alt.society.revolution (NG) All types of radical political ideas discussed. ✓**USENET**

The Left

alt.politics.radical-left (NG) Discussion about left-radical political movements and struggles. ✓**USENET**

Progressive News & Views Left-wing progressive news, with cross-posts from the Usenet newsgroup MISC.ACTIVISM.PROGRESSIVE, PeaceNet, and other sources. ✓**FIDONET**→*tag* P_NEWS

The political process

alt.politics.election (NG) Discuss local and state politics. ✓**USENET**

alt.politics.org.misc (NG) White House schedules, press releases, and speeches. ✓**USENET**

Elections Discuss U.S. elections. ✓**BIX**→*conference* ELECTIONS

CYBERNOTES

"The word 'racism' is a powerful weapon for the politically correct left. If a discussion is going badly for them they always have the option of making an accusation of racism, at which point you *must* stop talking ... and defend yourself.

"Naturally the left would like to reserve such a powerful weapon for themselves, even as they advocate ... policies which are explicitly racist (in the usual sense). So they redefine the word 'racism' ... in such a way that the word can only refer to members of empowered classes (i.e., whites). ... If the new definition is accepted you will not be able to accuse members of the protected classes of racism. ... You can point out that some blacks have been known to do unkind things to whites just because they are white. But whatever words you eventually come up with, you will not find one with the resonance and irrational force of *RACISM*."

—from **alt.politics.correct**

The White House

One reason the Internet (or, as they say in Washington, the Information Highway) burst

onto front pages is that Bill Clinton got wired. Indeed, he certainly has enough email addresses. Email to the president, however, is not a helluva sight better than snail mail. Your email gets processed through the cubicles of the Executive Office Building and months from now you get a response—in your mail (that is, U.S. Postal Service) box. While you wait, there's a host of newsgroups, mailing lists, and forums all flooding the Net with info from the White House.

The White House—downloaded from CompuServe's Graphics Gallery Forum.

On the Net

Across the board

The White House Download press releases, briefings, and transcripts of speeches put out by the White House. Voice your opinion by sending email (ready-to-go form—just choose "send") to White House staffers. Responses will arrive via conventional mail, so don't forget to include your home address. ▦ ◉💬 ✓**AMERICA ONLINE** →*keyword* WHITE HOUSE

White House Archives Archives of press releases, speeches, and other materials released from the White House. The CPSR site includes a Clinton biography; the SUNSITE site includes databases of Bush and Clinton speeches, posi-

tion papers, and press releases. ✓**INTERNET** ...→*ftp* FTP.CCO.CALTECH. EDU→ANONYMOUS/<YOUR EMAIL ADDRESS>→pub/bjmccall ...→*ftp* CPSR.ORG→ANONYMOUS/<YOUR EMAIL ADDRESS>→cpsr/clinton ...→*telnet* SUNSITE.UNC.EDU→ POLITICS/<NONE>

The White House Forum Sections range from Mr. President (to which Clinton sometimes replies) to Reinventing Government to Justice/FBI. Also includes libraries of press releases and speeches. ▦ ◉💬 ✓**COMPUSERVE**→*go* WHITEHOUSE

White House RoundTable Official press releases and announcements from the White House, libraries of files, a bulletin board to discuss the news and issues relevant to the administration. Also, send a letter to the president. ◉💬 ✓**GENIE**→*keyword* WHITEHOUSE

Addresses

Al's Email Address The vice president's email address. ✓**INTERNET**→*email* VICE.PRESIDENT@WHITE HOUSE.GOV

Bill's Email Address Send a let-

ter to Bill, but include your snail-mail address—responses are sent conventionally. ✓**AMERICA ONLINE** →*email* CLINTONPZ ✓**COMPUSERVE**→ *email* 75300,3115 ✓**INTERNET**→*email* PRESIDENT@WHITEHOUSE.GOV

Write to Washington Write to the White House (Bill, Hillary, or Al) or to a member of the Cabinet, U.S. House, or U.S. Senate. Your letter will be printed and conventionally mailed. ✓**PRODIGY**→*jump* WRITE TO WASHINGTON $2.50/500 WORDS

The scoreboard

alt.politics.clinton (NG) Discussions about Bill Clinton's presidency. ✓**USENET**

alt.president.clinton (NG) More commentary, debate, and news about the Clinton White House. ✓**USENET**

Press releases

alt.politics.democrats.clinton (NG) Announcements from the Clinton administration. ✓**USENET**

News Media Offers direct feeds of White House press releases, announcements, and transcripts, along with select news commentaries. ✓**RELAYNET**→*number* 426

White House Press Releases Proclamations, press releases, and the official remarks of the president, released by the Executive Office of the President and the Office of the Press Secretary. ✓**FIDONET**→*tag* WHITEHOUSE

Women & gender issues

There's a lot less dogma and a lot more debate in the area of feminism and gender is-sues on the Net than you might think. According to the backgrounder provided by **soc.feminism**, "It turns out that the subject matter of the group has evolved toward a basic assumption of the notion that women deserve equality with men, with the disagreement focused on how best to achieve that. Unfortunately, many of these disagreements overwhelm the group at times...." Men, too, in FidoNet's **Men's Issues** and the newsgroup **soc.men**, grope—quite unsuccessfully —toward consensus.

On the Net

Across the board

Gender Equality Philosophical and political discussions about gender, including subjects like constitutional protections, custody, child support, insurance, professional equality, harassment, and electoral power. ✓**FIDONET**→ *tag* GENDER_EQUALITY

Feminism

alt.feminism (NG) Where feminists and anti-feminists confront each other. ✓**USENET**

Feminism Discussions of women's issues in the social, economic, and political arenas. ✓**ILINK**

Renoir's Young Women Talking— *from uxa.fine-art.index.*

→*number* 135

Feminism Conference for discussing women's-rights issues. ✓**SMARTNET**→*tag* FEMINISM

Feminism and Gender Issues General-interest discussions on feminism and gender. ✓**FIDONET**→ *tag* FEMINISM

Feminist (ML) Owned by the Feminist Task Force of the American Library Association. Covers issues such as sexism in libraries, pornography and censorship in libraries, and racism and ethnic diversity in librarianship. ✓**INTERNET**→*email* LISTSERV@MITVMA.MIT.EDU ✍*Type in message body:* SUB FEMINIST <YOUR FULL NAME>

Femisa (ML) An information exchange for those involved with the areas of feminism, gender,

women and international relations, international political economics, or global politics. Intended to be a forum for exchanging articles, course outlines, job or conference information, and more. ✓**INTERNET**→*email* LISTSERV@ CSF.COLORADO.EDU ✍*Type in message body:* SUB FEMISA <YOUR FULL NAME>

Femrel-L (ML) Covers women and religion and feminist theology. Quite chatty. ✓**INTERNET**→*email* LISTSERV@MIZZOU1.MISSOURI.EDU ✍*Type in message body:* SUB FEMREL-L <YOUR FULL NAME>

Medfem-L Discussion for medieval feminists. ✓**INTERNET**→*email* LISTSERV@UWAVM.U.WASHINGTON.EDU ✍*Type in message body:* SUBSCRIBE MEDFEM-L <YOUR FULL NAME>

soc.feminism (NG/ML) Moderated discussion where feminist issues other than the "validity of feminism" are discussed. Open to both men and women. Topics range from the activities of feminist organizations to the feminist experience to feminist philosophies. ✓**USENET** ✓**INTERNET**→*email* FEMINISM-DIGEST@NCAR.UCAR.EDU ✍*Subscribe by request*

SWIP-L (ML) Discussion of feminist philosophy. ✓**INTERNET**→*email* LISTSERV@CFRVM.CFR.USF.EDU ✍*Type in message body:* SUB SWIP-L <YOUR FULL NAME>

Reproductive rights

Abortion Covers all aspects of abortion and the debate over abortion rights, including religious views, medical opinions, and secular positions. Also includes announcements of pro-choice and pro-life meetings and marches. ✓RELAYNET→*number* 411

alt.abortion.inequity (NG) Where the abortion debate rages. ✓USENET

Christian Perspective Abortion Discussion "Anyone who had been aborted wouldn't be here. If inconvenient babies weren't really alive babies, there would be no need to kill them." ✓FIDONET→*tag* KILLBABY

Reproductive Rights (Choice) Issues Provides support and information about reproductive rights. ✓FIDONET→*tag* REPRO_RIGHTS

talk.abortion (NG) For debating the issues involved with abortion. ✓USENET

Women's forums

Echo (BBS) Features a high percentage of women online, the Women's Action Coalition which hosts a forum, and full Internet access. ▆▆ ◉☺ 212-989-8411 ✓INTERNET→*telnet* ECHONYC.COM $19.95-$52.43/MONTH

Issues Forum See the Women's Issues bulletin board and library. Board topics include feminism, postfeminism, femininity, dieting, and whatever else is of interest. ◉☺ ✓COMPUSERVE→*go* ISSUES

soc.women (NG) Any topic related to women's issues, concerns, or interests. Topics range from child custody to relationships to comfortable shoes. ✓USENET

WIRE The Women's Information Resource and Exchange network.

Call 1-800-210-9999 (voice) for their free starter kit. ✓INTERNET→*email* SUPPORT@WIRE.NET

Women Conference about issues of concern to professional women. ◉☺ ✓BIX→*conference* WOMEN

Women About, and primarily for, women and their concerns. Men are welcome to participate. ✓ILINK→*number* 139

Women Open to all. Topics include equal rights, equal pay, feminism, and lesbianism. ✓RELAYNET→*number* 180

Men's movement

alt.dads-rights (NG) Discuss the rights of fathers, especially those trying to win custody of their children. ✓USENET

Free-L (ML) Discussion regarding a fathers' rights following divorce, in custody disputes, and in child-support arrangements. ✓INTERNET→*email* LISTSERV@INDYCMS.IUPUI.EDU ✍ *Type in message body:* SUB FREE-L <YOUR FULL NAME>

Men's Issues Men's support group. Topics include sexual politics, custody and child support, male spirituality, recovery programs, and the men's movement. ✓FIDONET→*tag* MENS_ ISSUES

Men's Issues Covers a full range of issues, including divorce, child custody, friendships, and being gay. Open to all. ✓RELAYNET→*number* 220

MensNet A forum for men devoted to men's issues. Topics range from fathering to the men's movement to relating to women. ◉☺ ✓DELPHI→*go* GR MEN

Men's Rights/Equality Issues A male viewpoint on equality of men and women and fatherhood. ✓FIDONET→*tag* RIGHTS

soc.men (NG) Issues related to men's concerns or interests. Topics include child support and relationships. Lively debates on both SOC.MEN and SOC.WOMEN when gender issues are hot. ✓USENET

Miscellaneous

talk.rape (NG) For discussing rape (e.g., personal experiences and legal issues). ✓USENET

CYBERNOTES

"Am I imagining things? I don't think I am. I have to say that from what I've seen, this garbage is starting with us, just as it's been done to men regards women, and I'm very annoyed by it. I DON'T want the men I love and care about to start thinking that they have to pop steroids to look like the Official Man(tm) any more than I like my friends (and hell, me too!) being told that we have to starve ourselves and get cancer-causing chemicals injected into our breasts to look like the Official Woman(tm).

"This has got to STOP, and it has got to stop now."

—from **alt.feminism**

Zines

A "zine" is a magazine created for fun and virtually no profit, usually specializing in the bizarre, esoteric, campy, and extreme. Quite often the subject matter involves drugs, politics, and/or science fiction. Although not all zines are electronic (see **FactSheet Five** for print zines), because of cost (no paper, no printing) and audience (you know who), the Net is a natural medium for a zine. Big zines include **Athene** and **InterText** and **DargonZine** and **CTheory**. But certainly check out **Funhouse** and **ScreamBaby**. The newsgroup **alt.zines** is the best introduction and overview.

On the Net

Across the board

Anthropomorphic Magazines Talk about fanzines between readers and publishers, including the titles *Yark!*, *Furversion*, *Furcherance*, and *Furnography*. Topics include publication standards, distribution, and printing problems. ✓**FIDONET**→*tag* FUR_MAG

Arm the Spirit With a focus on armed struggle and militant resistance in the "so-called 'Third World.'" ✓**INTERNET** …→*ftp* ETEXT. ARCHIVE.UMICH.EDU→ANONYMOUS/ <YOUR EMAIL ADDRESS>→pub/Politics/Arm.the.Spirit …→*email* AFO

Cover of the zine Sound—*downloaded from sunsite.unc.edu.*

RUM@MOOSE.SF.CA.US ✍*Subscribe by request*

Armadillo Culture Weirdness, humor, short fiction, music, etc. ✓**INTERNET** …→*ftp* ETEXT.ARCHIVE. UMICH.EDU→ANONYMOUS/<YOUR EMAIL ADDRESS>→pub/Zines/Armadillo.Culture …→*email* SOKAY@ MITRE.ORG ✍*Subscribe by request*

Athene and InterText Devoted to short fiction. *InterText* is a bimonthly zine with a huge Net following. *Athene* preceded *InterText* and is now defunct. ✓**COMPUSERVE** →*go* EFFSIG→Zines from the Net ✓**INTERNET** …→*ftp* ETEXT.ARCHIVE. UMICH.EDU→ANONYMOUS/<YOUR EMAIL ADDRESS>→pub/Zines …→*ftp* NETWORK.UCSD.EDU→ANONYMOUS/ <YOUR EMAIL ADDRESS>→intertext …→*email* JSNELL@OCF.BERKELEY.EDU ✍ *Subscribe by request*

CORE Poetry, essays, and fiction. ✓**INTERNET** …→*ftp* ETEXT. ARCHIVE. UMICH.EDU→ANONYMOUS/<YOUR EMAIL ADDRESS>→pub/Zines/Core_

Zine …→*email* CORE-JOURNAL@ EFF.ORG ✍*Subscribe by request*

CTheory An electronic review of books on theory, technology, and culture. ✓**INTERNET**→*email* LISTSERV @VM1.MCGILL.CA ✍*Type in message body:* SUBSCRIBE CTHEORY <YOUR FULL NAME>

Current Cites A monthly publication of brief annotated citations of articles published in journals ranging from *BYTE* to *Wired* about optical disc technologies, computer networks and networking, information transfer, expert systems and AI, electronic publishing, and hypermedia and multimedia. ✓**INTERNET** …→*ftp* ETEXT. ARCHIVE.UMICH.EDU→ANONYMOUS/ <YOUR EMAIL ADDRESS>→pub/Zines/ CurrentCites …→*email* DROBISON @LIBRARY.BERKELEY.EDU ✍*Subscribe by request*

DargonZine An electronic fantasy-fiction anthology magazine based on the shared world of Dargon. The same site includes issues of its predecessor, *FSFNet*. ✓**INTERNET** …→*ftp* ETEXT.ARCHIVE. UMICH.EDU→ANONYMOUS/<YOUR EMAIL ADDRESS>→pub/Zines/Dargon Zine …→*email* WHITE@DUVM.BITNET ✍*Subscribe by request:* <YOUR FULL NAME> <YOUR EMAIL ADDRESS>

Funhouse "The Cyberzine of degenerate pop culture…Dedicated to whatever happens to be on my mind at the time that I'm writing…Offbeat films, music, literature, and experiences are largely covered." ✓**INTERNET** …→*ftp* ETEXT. ARCHIVE.UMICH.EDU→ANONYMOUS/ <YOUR EMAIL ADDRESS>→ pub/Zines/ Funhouse …→*email* JEFFDOVE@WELL. SF.CA.US ✍*Subscribe by request*

Holy Temple of Mass Consumption Twisted commentary,

satire, humor, and reviews. ✓**INTERNET** ...→*ftp* ETEXT.ARCHIVE.UMICH.EDU→ANONYMOUS/<YOUR EMAIL ADDRESS>→pub/Zines/HToMC ...→*email* SLACK@NCSU.EDU ✍*Subscribe by request*

Mike's Madness Bizarre, tasteless, satirical. ✓**INTERNET**→*ftp* FTP.CIS.UFL.EDU→ANONYMOUS/<YOUR EMAIL ADDRESS>→pub/mikesmad

Multiversal Party Line Storyboard The on-line version of *Intercepted*, a science-fiction fanzine. "Think of a head-on collision between Dr. Who and the Addams Family, with a short visit from Yog-Soggoth added in. A storyboard, of sorts. Talk with Indiana Jones. BE Indiana Jones. Handles encouraged." ✓**FIDONET**→*tag* INTERCEPTED

Quanta Science-fiction and fantasy zine with contributions from both professionals and amateurs. ✓**COMPUSERVE**→*go* EFFSIG→Zines from the Net ✓**INTERNET** ...→*ftp* ETEXT.ARCHIVE.UMICH.EDU→ANONYMOUS/<YOUR EMAIL ADDRESS>→pub/Zines/Quanta ...→*ftp* QUARTZ.RUTGERS.EDU→ANONYMOUS/<YOUR EMAIL ADDRESS>→pub/journals ...→*email* QUANTA+REQUEST-ASCII@ANDREW.CMU.EDU ✍*Subscribe by request*

Random Access Humor An electronic zine with computer, online, and BBS humor, and irregular features like "The Twit Filter" and "The Grunged Glossary." ✓**INTERNET**→*ftp* ETEXT.ARCHIVE.UMICH.EDU→ANONYMOUS/<YOUR EMAIL ADDRESS>→pub/Zines/RAH

ScreamBaby A zine for the deviant subculture, a tour of cyberculture, and lots of weird stuff. ✓**COMPUSERVE**→*go* EFFSIG→ZINES FROM THE NET ✓**INTERNET**→*ftp* ETEXT.ARCHIVE.UMICH.EDU→ANONY-MOUS/<YOUR EMAIL ADDRESS>→pub/Zines/ScreamBaby ...→*email* BLADEX@WIXER.CACTUS.ORG ✍*Subscribe by request*

Screams of Abel Covers the very latest in metal rock music, including group news, festival and concert announcements, reviews, etc. ✓**INTERNET** ...→*ftp* ETEXT.ARCHIVE.UMICH.EDU→ANONYMOUS/<YOUR EMAIL ADDRESS>→pub/Zines/Screams.of.Abel ...→*email* PHIL.POWELL@LAUNCHPAD.UNC.EDU ✍*Subscribe by request*

The Undiscovered Country "Dedicated to the study of literature, life & humanunkind." ✓**INTERNET** ...→*email* CBLANC@POMONA.CLAREMONT.EDU ✍*Subscribe by request* ...→*ftp* ETEXT.ARCHIVE.UMICH.EDU→ANONYMOUS/<YOUR EMAIL ADDRESS>→pub/Zines/The_Undiscovered_Country

Unplastic News An electronic magazine of short stories, blurbs, quotes, songs, and other weirdness. ✓**INTERNET** ...→*ftp* ETEXT.ARCHIVE.UMICH.EDU→ANONYMOUS/<YOUR EMAIL ADDRESS>→pub/Zines/Unplastic_News ...→*email* TIBBETS@HSI.HSI.COM ✍*Subscribe by request*

Voices from the Net An electronic magazine of interviews and essays that present the "voices" of people around the network, especially the odd corners of cyberspace. The AQL.GATECH.EDU FTP site contains both ASCII text and Macintosh Hypercard versions of the journal. ✓**INTERNET** ...→*ftp* ETEXT.ARCHIVE.UMICH.EDU→ANONYMOUS/<YOUR EMAIL ADDRESS>→pub/Zines/Voices ...→*ftp* AQL.GATECH.EDU→ANONYMOUS/<YOUR EMAIL ADDRESS>→pub/Zines ...→*email* VOICES-REQUEST@ANDY.BGSU.EDU ✍*Type in subject line:* VOICES FROM THE NET *Type in message body:* SUBSCRIBE

We Magazine A poetry zine. ✓**INTERNET** ...→*ftp* ETEXT.ARCHIVE.UMICH.EDU→ANONYMOUS/<YOUR EMAIL ADDRESS>→pub/Zines/We_Magazine ...→*email* CF2785@ALBNYVMS.BITNET ✍*Subscribe by request*

Other info

alt.zines (NG) Devoted to discussing and reviewing zines. ✓**USENET**

E-Zine List A list of e-zines with descriptions and address information. Closely follows the ever-changing world of electronic zines. ✓**INTERNET** ...→*email* JOHNL@NETCOM.COM ✍*Subscribe by request* ...→*ftp* ETEXT.ARCHIVE.UMICH.EDU→ANONYMOUS/<YOUR EMAIL ADDRESS>→pub/Zines→e-zine-list

FactSheet Five A clearinghouse of information on both electronic and print zines. ✓**INTERNET** ...→*ftp* QUARTZ.RUTGERS.EDU→ANONYMOUS/<YOUR EMAIL ADDRESS>→pub/journals/misc→factsheet5.gz ...→*ftp* ETEXT.ARCHIVE.UMICH.EDU→ANONYMOUS/<YOUR EMAIL ADDRESS>→pub/Factsheet.Five

San Francisco Zine Publishers Resource Guide For zine publishers in the San Francisco Bay Area. Includes information on retail outlets for zines, printers, and copiers. ✓**INTERNET**→*ftp* FTP.EFF.ORG→ANONYMOUS/<YOUR EMAIL ADDRESS>→pub/journals→EJournal.Directory2.1.Z

Zine Archive Stores back issues of both active and out-of-commission zines, including *Cyberspace Vanguard, Future Culture, Scratch, Purps, High Weirdness, Blooball,* and almost every zine mentioned in these pages. ✓**INTERNET**→*ftp* ETEXT.ARCHIVE.UMICH.EDU→ANONYMOUS/<YOUR EMAIL ADDRESS>→pub/Zines

Part 11

Nature, Science & Technology

11

Aviation

Some of the FAQs on the newsgroup rec.aviation: Are slips with flaps prohibited in Cessnas? What are the alternatives for taking an FAA written examination? I'd like to learn to fly. How do I do it? How much does it cost? How long does it take? What about logging cross-country time? Tell me about DUATS online weather briefings. What about hang-gliding? Ultralights? Can I use my cellular telephone in an airplane? Where can I get a copy of public-domain flight-planning software and other good stuff on the net?

On the Net

Across the board

Aircraft (ML) Discussions about aircraft and helicopters. Air-show announcements welcome. ✓**INTERNET**→*email* LISTSERV@GREARN.BITNET ✍ *Type in message body:* SUB AIRCRAFT <YOUR FULL NAME>

Aviation Plane talk—from aviation exploits to industry news to debate over the latest air disaster. ◉💬 ✓ *BIX*→*conference* AVIATION

Aviation General discussions on flying, airplanes, licensing, air-parks, and equipment. ✓**RELAY-NET**→*number* 122

Aviation Archive Aviation-related material including reviews of flight-simulation software, infor-

An A-2C, downloaded from the CompuServe Aviation Forum.

mation on aircraft specifications, an archive of REC.AVIATION newsgroup postings, and NTSB accident abstracts in /safety. ✓**INTERNET** ...→*ftp* RASCAL.ICS.UTEXAS.EDU→ ANONYMOUS/<YOUR EMAIL ADDRESS>→ misc/av ...→*wais* aeronautics.src

Aviation Club Aviation topics are covered on five message boards: The Line Shack is for those interested in smaller aircraft; The Terminal, the big airliners; Top Gun, military aviation; The Hangar, aircraft maintenance; and The Tower, the latest aviation news. In addition, the Log Book library provides files of information, tips, product demos, and reviews. ◉💬 ▦ ✓**AMERICA ONLINE** →*keyword* AVIATION

Aviation Forum A broad range of aviation-related topics and information, including air-traffic control, weather, balloons, want ads, and personal-computer programs. For instance, look in Library 7 for information on flight schools (learn2.fly) or for an IBM-compatible program based on the FAA's *Pilot's Handbook of Aeronautical Knowledge* (cfi.zip). ◉💬 ✓**COMPUSERVE**→*go* AVSIG

Aviation RoundTable Discus-

sion categories range from Aviation History, Facts, Discussions, Trivia, and Questions to Military Aviation to Fernando's Aviation Clubhouse to Aviation Employment. The libraries of files include Safety, Aviation Entertainment Software, and Late Breaking Aviation News, among others. ▦ ◉💬 ✓**GENIE**→*keyword* AVIATION

Aviation SIG Includes news about aviation and related technologies, flight-safety information, career advice, software, FAA requirements, insurance explanations, learning-to-fly material, and a database of aviation stories called Close Encounters. ▦ ◉💬 ✓**DELPHI** →*go* GR AVI

International Aviation General, commercial, and military aviation discussed, including products and services related to flying. Excludes PC-based simulators/games. ✓**FIDONET**→*tag* AVIATION

rec.aviation.answers (NG) Frequently asked questions about aviation. ✓**USENET**

Airlines

Airline (ML) Prototype subjects discussed for those interested in airlines and civil aircraft. ✓**INTERNET**→*email* LISTSERV@CUNYVM.CUNY. EDU ✍*Type in message body:* SUB AIRLINE <YOUR FULL NAME>

sci.aeronautics.airliners (NG) Discussion about airliner technology. ✓**USENET**

Alternative flight

Hang-Gliding (ML) Discuss hang gliding. ✓**FIDONET**→*tag* HANGLIDE ✓**INTERNET**→*email* HANG-GLIDING-REQUEST@FUGGLES.ACC.VIR GINIA.EDU ✍*Subscribe by request*

rec.aviation.misc (NG) All topics in aviation, but particularly those not covered by the other aviation newsgroups: ultralight planes, balloons, rotorcraft, and skydiving. ✓**USENET**

rec.aviation.soaring (NG) Discussion covers all facets of sailplanes and hang gliders. ✓**USENET**

rec.skydiving (NG) For discussions about skydiving. Includes event notices and reviews, equipment questions, and skill and technique discussions. ✓**USENET**

Skydiving, Parachuting, and Paragliding Open discussion—non-jumpers welcome. ✓**FIDONET→** *tag* SKYDIVE

Ultralight-Flight (ML) Forum for discussing and exchanging information about ultralight aircraft. ✓**INTERNET→***email* ULTRALIGHT-FLIGHT-REQUEST@MS.UKY.EDU ✍*Subscribe by request*

Industry news

rec.aviation.announce (NG) Upcoming events in the aviation community. ▦ ✓**USENET**

rec.aviation.products (NG) Aviation products reviewed and discussed. ✓**USENET**

sci.aeronautics (NG/ML) Devoted to the science of aeronautics and related technology. The mailing list is a moderated version. ✓**USENET** ✓**INTERNET→***email* AERONAUTICS-REQUEST@RASCAL.ICS.UTEXAS.EDU ✍*Type in message body:* SUBSCRIBE AERONAUTICS <YOUR FULL NAME>

Piloting

DUAT Pilot services including weather briefings and flight plan-

Skydivers—downloaded from CompuServe's Photography Forum.

ning. ✓**INTERNET** ...→*telnet* DUAT.CONTEL.COM ...→*telnet* DUATS.CONTEL.COM ✖ *The first address is for certified pilots only; the second is for student pilots*

EMI Aviation Services Allows a pilot to produce cockpit flight logs for trips between points in the 48 contiguous states and Canada. Also offers weather information, time and distance checks, and customized briefing and flight-plan filing. ✓**COMPUSERVE→***go* EMI $$

NWS Aviation Weather Uses the National Oceanographic and Atmospheric Administration "A" weather wire to provide pilots with instant weather forecasts. ▦ ✓**COMPUSERVE→***go* AWX

rec.aviation.ifr (NG) Discussion about flying under Instrument Flight Rules. ✓**USENET**

rec.aviation.owning (NG) Information on owning airplanes. ✓**USENET**

rec.aviation.piloting (NG/ML) Covers issues germane to piloting such as training systems, avionic products, safety issues, historical notes, and relevant laws. ✓**USENET** ✓**INTERNET→***email* AVIATION-REQUEST @MC.LCS.MIT.EDU ✍*Subscribe by request*

rec.aviation.stories (NG) Flight

experiences described. ✓**USENET**

rec.aviation.student (NG) For those learning to fly. ✓**USENET**

Safety

Air Safety Week Regulatory Log Contains summaries of all FAA regulatory actions and some actions established by other agencies. ▦ ✓**COMPUSERVE→***go* IQUEST→ 2572 $$

Aviation Safety Institute A medium for reporting unsafe conditions or acts observed during aviation activities. No attempt to identify those reporting will be made. Also includes safety tips, a newsletter, and safety reports. ✓**COMPUSERVE→***go* ASI

Hobbies

Airplane-Clubs (ML) Devoted to managing and operating an aircraft group. ✓**INTERNET→***email* AIRPLANE-CLUBS-REQUEST@DG-RTP.DG.COM ✍*Subscribe by request*

rec.aviation.homebuilt (NG) Discussion about selecting, designing, building, and restoring aircraft. ✓**USENET**

Military planes

Blackbird (ML) Devoted to discussion of the Blackbird (A-12, YF-12, and SR-71) and U-2 programs, but includes other Lockheed special-project planes. ✓**INTERNET→***email* LISTSERV@HARBOR.ECN.PURDUE.EDU ✍*Type in message body:* SUBSCRIBE SKUNK-WORKS <YOUR FULL NAME>

rec.aviation.military (NG) Military aviation of the past, present, and future discussed. ✓**USENET**

Biology

Just about everyone on RelayNet's Biology conference had a drosophila story or two to share with Karen, the high school junior who wrote, "My genetics class is currently breeding drosophila fruit flies. We are currently at the point where we must separate the virgin fruit flies from the males. The only problem is, how can we tell whether they are females or males? My genetics teacher knows as much about determining fruit fly sex as his puzzled students do." The newsgroup **sci. biotechnology** is another Everyman's biology conference while most of the other lists are populated by the professors.

On the Net

Across the board

Biology Offers discussion about current life-science issues, covering genetics, ecology, biochemistry, bionics, and exobiology. ✓**RELAY-NET**→*number* 195

bionet* (NG) Includes the newsgroups BIONET.BIOLOGY.TROPICAL, BIO NET.CELLBIOL, BIONET.GENOME.CHROMO SOMES, BIONET.JOBS, BIONET.MOLBIO. BIO-MATRIX, BIONET.PLANTS, BIONET.SCI-RESOURCES, BIONET.VIROLOGY, BIONET. WOMEN-IN-BIO, and many others. ✓**USENET**

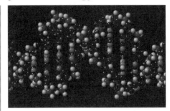

A DNA model—downloaded from CompuServe's Photography Forum.

Humbio-L (ML) Covers biological anthropology, adaptation, biological race, skeletal biology, forensic anthropology, primate biology, and more. ✓**INTERNET**→*email* HUMBIO-REQUEST@ACC.FAU.EDU ✍ *Type in message body:* SUBSCRIBE HUMBIO-L <YOUR FULL NAME>

sci.bio (NG) Forum for discussing biology and related sciences. For the professional as well as the curious who want to know why leaves change color in the fall. ✓**USENET**

Biotechnology

Biotech Briefs A bimonthly electronic version of a publication for those involved with the biotechnology industry. ▦ ✓**INTERNET**→ *telnet* CATICSUF.CSUFRESNO.EDU→ SUPER/<NONE>

sci.bio.technology (NG) For those interested in technology in the biological sciences. Mostly information requests. ✓**USENET**

Evolution

Darwin-L (ML) Dedicated to discussion about the historical sciences, including, but not limited to, evolutionary biology. ✓**INTER-NET**→*email* LISTSERV@UKANAIX.CC.

UKANS.EDU ✍ *Type in message body:* SUBSCRIBE DARWIN-L <YOUR FULL NAME>

Evolutionary Mechanism Theory For scientists to organize against SciCre (creationist) arguments. SciCre-ists are welcomed, with the warning that they "will receive exactly the level of respect that they give here." ✓**FIDONET**→ *tag* EVOLUTION

Molecular & genetics

The Evolution FTP Server Carries the Phylip package, the bibliography of Theoretical Population Genetics, lab preprints, and a population-genetics teaching program. ✓**INTERNET**→*ftp* EVOLUTION.GENET ICS.WASHINGTON.EDU→ANONY-MOUS/<YOUR EMAIL ADDRESS>→pub

Houston Gene Server Includes molecular-biology software, the Protein Information Resource database, and the Protein Data Bank crystallographic entries. ✓**INTERNET** →*ftp* EVOLUTION.BCHS.UH. EDU→ANONYMOUS/<YOUR EMAIL AD-DRESS>→ pub/gene-server

RBMI (ML) For discussions and news about molecular biology. ✓**INTERNET**→*email* LISTSERV@FRORS13. BITNET ✍ *Type in message body:* SUB-SCRIBE RBMI <YOUR FULL NAME>

Miscellaneous

biologists-addresses Email addresses of biologists. ✓**INTERNET** →*wais* biologists.addresses.src

Other info

Biologist Guide to the Internet Biology resources on the Internet. ✓**INTERNET**→*ftp* CASBAH. ACNS.NWU.EDU→ ANONYMOUS/<YOUR EMAIL ADDRESS>→ pub/dicty→biologists.guide.to.internet

Earth sciences

If you're an earthquake connoisseur or you're paranoid, you can stay on top of the latest tremors with the mailing list **Seism-L**, which monitors seismological activity in various parts of the U.S. The newsgroup **ca. earthquakes** specializes in activity around the San Andreas Fault. The newsgroup **Seismd-L** offers discussion about the meaning of the latest data. You might just get the word in time.

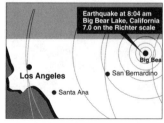

A seismological map—from AOL's Graphic Arts & CAD Forum.

On the Net

Earthquakes

ca.earthquakes (NG) Discussion and news of earthquakes in the California area. ✓**USENET**

Earthquake Information Location, magnitude, and accuracy given for recent earthquakes. ✓**INTERNET**→*finger* QUAKE@GEO PHYS.WASHINGTON.EDU

Seismd-L (NG) Discuss seismology and new data. ✓**INTERNET**→*email* LISTSERV@BINGVMB.CC.BINGHAM TON.EDU *Type in message body:* SUB-SCRIBE SEISMD-L <YOUR FULL NAME>

Seism-L (ML) Data reports on seismological activity. ✓**INTERNET**→*email* LISTSERV@BINGVMB.CC.BINGHAM TON.EDU ✍ *Type in message body:* SUB-SCRIBE SEISM-L <YOUR FULL NAME>

Geology

Computer Oriented Geologi- **cal Society (COGS) Archive** Landsat images, and software for geophysics, mining, hydrology, as well as a list of geological resources available on the Internet. ✓**INTER-NET**→*ftp* CSN.ORG→ANONYMOUS/ <YOUR EMAIL ADDRESS>→ COGS

Geology (ML) For discussing geology-related topics. ✓**INTERNET** →*email* LISTSERV@PTEARN.BITNET ✍ *Type in message body:* SUB GEOLOGY <YOUR FULL NAME>

sci.geo.fluids (NG) Discuss geophysical fluid dynamics. ✓**USENET**

sci.geo.geology (NG) Discussion of the solid earth sciences. ✓**USENET**

USGS Geological Fault Maps A digital database of geological faults in the United States with the mapping software to draw maps from the fault data. ✓**INTERNET**→*ftp* ALUM.WR.USGS.GOV→ANONYMOUS/ <YOUR EMAIL ADDRESS>→pub/map

Volcano (ML) Discuss volcanoes and volcanic activity. ✓**INTERNET**→ *email* LISTSERV@ASUVM.INRE.ASU.EDU ✍ *Type in message body:* SUBSCRIBE VOL CANO <YOUR FULL NAME>

Marine ecology

Bedford Institute of Oceanography Used by marine scientists to exchange scientific data and programs. Files include the Uniforum Atlantic minutes, the BSIM simulation package, spreadsheets and ecological models, and reports from the Department of Fisheries and Oceans. ✓**INTER-NET**→*ftp* BIOME.BIO.DFO.CA→ANONY-MOUS/<YOUR EMAIL ADDRESS>→pub

Deepsea (ML) For deep-sea and hydrothermal-vent biologists working in evolution, ecology, biogeography, paleontology, systematics, phylogenetics, and population genetics. ✓**INTERNET**→*email* LISTSERV@UVVM.UVIC.CA ✍ *Type in message body:* SUB DEEPSEA <YOUR FULL NAME>

Marine-L (ML) Dedicated to discussions of marine-related studies and educational programs as well as email connectivity at sea. Topics range from marine electronic communications to fisheries science to ocean racing to oceania and maritime anthropology. ✓**INTERNET**→ *email* LISTSERV@VM.UOGUELPH.CA ✍ *Type in message body:* SUB MARINE-L <YOUR FULL NAME>

Maritime All issues connected with the sea, including vessels, sea sports, fishing, oceanography, and transportation. ✓**ILINK**→*number* 202

OCEANIC The Ocean Information Center Bulletin Board has specialized information on oceanographic experiments, field trials, and meetings, as well as an extensive address list for researchers in oceanography. ✓**INTER-NET**→*telnet* DELOCN.UDEL.EDU→INFO/ <NONE>

Engineering

Engineering Paradise and Enginet are two strong, pro- fessionally oriented BBSs specializing in a variety of application files, technical discussions, and job info. **Enginet**'s job bank is particularly comprehensive. The **Patent Research Center** on CompuServe and GEnie offers summaries of all patents in engineering fields. **Compendex-Engineering Index** and **NTIS-Government Sponsored Research** on CompuServe are search databases of technical and professional journals.

On the Net

Across the board

Engineering Offers a forum for technical discussions for engineers. ✓**RELAYNET**→*number* 208

Engineering For engineers to discuss the applications they use and share engineering information. Bulletins are also archived and conferences listed. 🖐💬 ✓**BIX** →*conference* ENGINEERING

Engineering Paradise (BBS) Engineering-related files and echoes from several different nets, including FidoNet, TechNet, and MATHNet International. 513-864-1386 FREE

Enginet (BBS) For technical professionals to share resources with associates. Includes engineering

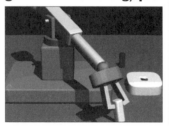

Engineering arm—downloaded from CompuServe's Quick Pictures Forum.

files and a job bank where you can place or search for résumés. 513-858-2688 FREE

Institute of Electrical and Electronics Engineers The national conference of the I.E.E.E. provides information for local members and includes general discussion for the engineering community. ✓**FIDONET**→ *tag* IEEE

sci.engr* (NG) Several newsgroups devoted to technical discussions for engineers: SCI.ENGR, SCI.ENGR.BIOMED, SCI.ENGR.CHEM, SCI. ENGR.CIVIL, SCI.ENGR.CONTROL, SCI. ENGR.MANUFACTURING, and SCI.ENGR. MECH. ✓**USENET**

Mechanical

Mech-L (ML) Covers issues relevant to mechanical engineers, such as software reviews, composite material research, conference announcements, and more. ✓**INTERNET**→*email* LISTSERV@UTARLVM1.UTA. EDU ✍ *Type in message body:* SUB MECH-L <YOUR FULL NAME>

sci.materials (NG) For discussing topics related to materials engineering. ✓**USENET**

Reference

Compendex—Engineering Index A searchable database of article abstracts from a variety of technical journals, professional publications, conference proceedings, and government reports. Topics cover all areas of engineering, including applied physics, pollution controls, fluid flow, food technology, and materials testing. ✓**COMPUSERVE**→*go* COMPENDEX $$

IQuest Engineering InfoCenter Provides database access for information on physics, aerospace, mathematics materials, and engineering research. ✓**COMPUSERVE**→ *go* IQENGINEER $$

NTIS-Government Sponsored Research A database of articles from the National Technical Information Service covering government-sponsored research, development, and engineering reports. ✓**COMPUSERVE**→*go* NTIS $$

Patent Research Center Databases of U.S. patents in the chemical, mechanical, electrical, and design categories; also included are summaries of international patents. ✓**COMPUSERVE**→*go* PATENT ✓**GENIE**→*keyword* PATENTS $$

Students

CCES-L (ML) A forum for Canadian engineering students and others with an interest in engineering. ✓**INTERNET**→*email* LISTSERV@UNB.CA ✍ *Type in message body:* SUBSCRIBE CCES-L <YOUR FULL NAME>

Other info

Computer Plumber (BBS) Provides a list of engineering-related BBSs. 319-337-6723

The environment

In his book *Ecolinking*, the environmentalist Don Rittner envisions a world where "scien-

tists, environmentalists, and concerned citizens around the globe" share ideas and research through the Net. Indeed, the Net is probably the most comprehensive source of current environmental information and news. The **Environmental Forum** on AOL and **Earth Forum** on CompuServe, which provide news, how-to advice, and discussion areas, are just two of the multitude of online environmental offerings that have started over the last few years for a general audience. **EcoNet** is among the leading professional online environment resources.

On the Net

Across the board

AlterNet (BBS) Offers complementary solutions to problems in health care, energy, and the environment. Features Keely Net, a conference on alternative energy, and *Family News*, a gazette of oxygen information and products, as well as health-related information in the *Common Ground* newsletter and *Health Consciousness* magazine. ▦ ⊕ ◉✆ 508-827-5274 FREE

Alternatives BBS (BBS) Main BBS areas include Computers/ Tech, Environment, Health,

Recyclables—downloaded from CompuServe's Graphics Corner Forum.

Politics, Seniors, and Womyn. The Environment area features news, libraries of information (looking for research on nuclear power, the ozone depletion, or toxic materials?), message forums, the Greenpeace online publications, and more. ▦ ⊕✆ 604-430-8080

Earth Forum Provides information and contacts for those interested in solving environmental problems. Message sections and libraries include Wetlands, Eco-Philosophy, Green Business, Energy, and Population. ⊕✆ ✓**COMPUSERVE**→*go* EARTH

Ecology Network Officially affiliated with the Institute for Global Communications (IGC), this forum covers environmental problems and solutions. ▦ ✓**FIDONET**→*tag* ECONET

Environet (the Greenpeace

BBS) (BBS) Issues range from disarmament to ecological concerns. Includes newsletters, bulletins, conferences, and a list of BBSs devoted to environmental topics. ▦ ⊕✆ 415-512-9108/415-512-9120

Environment Discussions about environmental issues. Topics include conservation, action (boycotts, lawsuits, cleanups), Greenpeace, news, information (magazines, newsletters, groups, etc.), and energy. ▦ ⊕✆ ✓**BIX**→ *conference* ENVIRONMENT

Environment Discussions concerning ecology and the environment. Includes scientific, legal, sociopolitical, and economic issues. ✓**ILINK**→*number* 147

Environmental Concerns A free exchange for views and information on the environmental movement. ✓**FIDONET**→*tag* ENVIRO

The Environmental Forum Features bulletin boards on the Biosphere and Mother Earth, and a debate forum called the Water Cooler. News updates from the Environmental News Service are available, and the Litter Free Library has a huge amount of material. ▦ ⊕✆ ✓**AMERICA ON-LINE**→*keyword* EARTH

Environmental Issues A Canadian-based echo with topics ranging from diapers to nuclear power. ✓**FIDONET**→*tag* ENVIRON

Environmental Issues Covers the political, sociological, economic, and educational issues in the environmental debate. Specific environmental topics addressed include recycling, energy issues, wilderness preservation, and pollution. ✓**RELAYNET**→*number* 373

Environment SIG Discussions about any environment-related topic such as recycling, toxic chemicals, and ecological philosophy. Environmental-law newsletters as well as databases of files on population, water, toxic and hazardous substances, minerals and mining, and solid waste are also available. ▦ ◉☘ ✓**DELPHI**→*go* GR ENV

EnvirProtect Forum for discussing issues related to environmental protection. ✓**SMARTNET** →ENVIRPROTECT

Howard's Notebook (BBS) Conferences and information concerned with the environment, peace, politics, and justice issues. Also includes a graphics library. ◉☘ 816-331-5868

The International Environment Conference General debate (no party-political discussions) about environmental issues. ✓**FIDONET**→*tag* GREEN.029

Network Earth Online Communicate with producers and viewers of the Turner Broadcasting weekly environmental magazine program *Network Earth* in live conferences or on the message boards. Download transcripts of the program from the News and Resources section and press releases, book reviews, and background environmental reports from the Resource Library; use the Resource Library to learn which organizations are working on issues you are concerned about; read environmental tips, keep up-

dated on environmental legislation, and monitor your congressman's performance through the League of Conservation Scorecards. ▦ ◉☘ ✓**AMERICA ONLINE**→ *keyword* NETWORK EARTH

Save the Earth BBS (BBS) "Dedicated to bringing you the most controversial info involving the hottest topics in the 90s: recycling and energy conservation." If you're in the neigborhood, the sysop will arrange to have your recyclables picked up; if not, just enjoy the message conferences (GN-Green Tech, Not In My Backyard, EARTH Stuff, etc.), newsletters, environmental alerts, descriptions of endangered species, and more. ▦ ⊞▣ 805-833-1437

Science & Environment BB Relevant topics include the biosphere-atmosphere, green issues, community activism, and pollution. ✓**PRODIGY**→*jump* SCIENCE BB

sci.environment (NG) Discussions about the environment and ecology. ✓**USENET**

Space & Science RoundTable Includes the Environment Library which has loads of files, and topics such as nuclear power, global warming, your lawn and garden, solar and wind electric power, and deforestation in the Environment category. ▦ ◉☘ ✓**GENIE**→*keyword* SPACE

Activism & politics

alt.politics.greens (NG) Discuss environment politics. The list circulates contact names, meeting announcements, and articles. ✓**USENET**

alt.save.the.earth (NG) Forum to discuss the environment and

environmental activist efforts. ✓**USENET**

EcoNet Serves individuals and organizations—the who's who of the environmental movement—working for environmental preservation and sustainability. Issues range from energy policy to environmental education. Includes databases (e.g., California environmental issues, environmental-movement events, and EPA citations), more than 500 conferences, an additional 300 conferences from other networks, an impressive number of environmental newsletters, and news features. For more information, download EcoNet's brochure from the FTP site or register by mail. ▦ ◉☘ ✓**INTERNET** ...→*ftp* IGC.ORG→ANONYMOUS/<YOUR EMAIL ADDRESS> ...→ *email* SUPPORT@IGC.ORG $$

Sierra Club Information on campaigns, events, news, and outings. ▦ ✓**FIDONET**→*tag* SIERRAN

talk.environment (NG) Debate and discussion over environmental issues. ✓**USENET**

Anti-radicals

Sahara Club Discussion Area Pro-business, pro-land-use, pro-gun-rights organization that fights "environmental-radical tactics." ✓**FIDONET**→*tag* SAHARA

Ecology

Coin of the Realm (BBS) Carries a guide to online resources related to conservation and nature. 301-585-6697

Ecology Problems and Potential Solutions What are the problems with the earth's ecology? What can be done about them? A forum for discussing and debating these questions. ✓**FIDONET**→*tag* ECOLOGY

Energy

Carbon Dioxide Information Analysis Center Archive Sponsored by the U.S. Department of Energy. Carries information about atmosphere and climate changes, including data and scientific papers on global warming, and numerous databases of related scientific data (e.g., production of CO_2 from fossil-fuel burning, 1950–89). ✓**INTERNET**→*ftp* CDIAC. ESD.ORNL.GOV→ANONYMOUS/<YOUR EMAIL ADDRESS>→pub

Commission Issuance Posting System (BBS) A bulletin board that contains texts of energy-related regulatory proceedings. 202-208-1397 FREE

Energy List (ML) A newsletter covering all aspects of energy research in Israel. ✓**INTERNET**→ *email* LISTSERV@VM.TAU.AC.IL ✍*Type in message body:* SUB ENERGY-L <YOUR FULL NAME>

Fossil Energy Telenews (BBS) Fossil-energy news releases from the Department of Energy: testing schedules, news releases and speeches by DOE officials, excerpts from *Commerce Business Daily*, and research-and-development reports on fossil fuel issues. ▓ 202-586-6496 FREE

Office of Statistics and Information BBS (BBS) Information on offshore oil and gas operations, including federal offshore statistics, annual reports to Congress, and reports on the Gulf of Mexico and Alaska. 703-787-1181/703-787-1225 FREE

Hazardous waste

CleanUp Information BBS (BBS) Information on groundwater contamination. Includes treatments, EPA newsletters, Federal Register summaries, and a hazardous-waste-collection database. 301-589-8366 FREE

FEMA Hazardous Materials Information (BBS) Chemical databases, FEMA and DOT publications, and technical and educational materials relating to hazardous materials. 708-972-3275 FREE

Gulfline BBS (BBS) Provided by the National Oceanic and Atmospheric Administration. Includes several environmental bulletin boards, a database focused on the Gulf, EPA toxic-release data, and news articles. 601-688-2677/601-688-1065 FREE

Research & news

Institute of Global Communications Archive Includes files about reducing the use of fossil fuels from the Energy and Climate Information Exchange (ECIX), information on environmental tourism, the EcoNet brochure listing EcoNet services, the Green-Disk directory with the *GreenDisk* environmental journal (300 plus pages each issue with employment notices, educational resources, conference announcements, an index of environmental newsletters, and press releases from environmental organizations). ✓**INTERNET**→*ftp* IGC.ORG→ANONYMOUS/<YOUR EMAIL ADDRESS>→pub

Outdoor News Clips Includes full-text stories from the AP and UPI on the environment and outdoor activities. ▓ ✓**COMPUSERVE**→ *go* OUTNEWS $$

The EPA

Environmental Protection Agency's Library A catalog of the library's holdings; includes abstracts. ✓**INTERNET**→*telnet* EPAIBM. RTPNC.EPA.GOV→PUBLIC/<NONE>

OAQPS Technology Transfer Network (BBS) Gateway to several other EPA BBSs (e.g., the AIRS BBS maintains "Airsletters," brochures, air data, technical information, reports, and messages related to air-pollution control). ☏ 919-541-5742 FREE

The Office of Environmental Affairs BBS (BBS) Covers water research, energy facilities, hazardous materials, the National Park Service, land and marine research, urban transportation, and minerals. 202-208-7119 FREE

PPIES/PPIC/ICPIC (BBS) Includes three systems with EPA calendars; pollution-program summaries from the federal, state, and corporate level; publications on waste reduction; ozone information; and chemical and pollutant data. 703-506-1025 FREE

Whole Earth Review

alt.co-evolution (NG) Covers the *Whole Earth Review* and related topics. ✓**USENET**

Miscellaneous

Envbeh-L (ML) Discussion covers environmental behavior. Topics range from the relationship between people and their physical environment to the connection between environmental stress and behavior. ✓**INTERNET**→*email* LIST SERV@VM.POLY.EDU ✍*Type in message body:* SUB ENVBEH-L <YOUR FULL NAME>

Farming

Technology has radically altered nearly everything about farming. It has mechanized the farm, and pushed the farmer into the information age. PCs watch over the pigs in today's barns, and farmers are online for instant weather reports, irrigation schedules, the latest biotechnology developments, and commodities-market news. Indeed, farming is an industry as information-driven as any other, from USDA announcements on **PENpages** to information on grants and research funding on the BBS **Farm Net USA**.

On the Net

Across the board

Advanced Technology Information Network An extensive agricultural service with market news, events, weather, job listings, and safety information. Includes information on trade, exports, and biotechnology. 🖳 ✓ **INTERNET**→*telnet* CATICSUF.CSUFRESNO.EDU→SUPER/ <NONE>

Agriculture Includes news and discussion for farmers, ranchers, trade editors, manufacturers of farm equipment, government professionals, students and teachers, farm suppliers, and other members of the food industry. ✓ **RELAY-NET**→*number* 422

Agriculture Covers agriculture,

A barn—downloaded from America Online's PC Graphics forum.

farming, and gardening topics. ✓ **SMARTNET**→AGRICULTURE

Agricultural Library Forum (ALF) (BBS) GAO reports, as well as agricultural, animal, nutrition, and 4H information. See the subboard on alternative farming systems. 301-504-5496/301-504-6510

alt.agriculture.misc (NG) General discussions about agriculture, farming, etc. ✓ **USENET**

Farm Net USA (BBS) Agricultural newsletters, grants and research funding, lists of members on agricultural-related Senate committees, weather reports, irrigation schedules, water outlook, agricultural software, a calendar of rural events, and *USA Today* online. 805-339-0945 FREE

PENpages USDA announcements, commodity prices, information on small and part-time farms, market news, oatmeal cookie recipes, gardening tips, information on rural life—e.g., family farm life and senior citizens, and the *Horticultural Engineering Newsletter*. ✓ **INTERNET**→*telnet* PSU PEN.PSU.EDU→<STATE ABB.>/<NONE>

Fruit

alt.agriculture.fruit (NG) Discussions run from mail-order fruit trees to planetary healing. ✓ **USENET**

Sustainable

alt.sustainable.agriculture (NG) Forum for discussing issues related to sustainable agriculture. ✓ **USENET**

Sustainable Agriculture News on natural, biologically oriented, low-input regenerative agriculture. Includes gardeners, homeowners, farmers, nurserymen, and other specialists. ✓ **FIDONET**→*tag* SUST_AG

Rural living

H-Rural (ML) For scholars of rural and agricultural history and culture. Discussion encompasses rural people and society throughout human history. ✓ **INTERNET**→ *email* LISTSERV@UICVM.UIC.EDU ✍ *Type in message body:* SUBSCRIBE H-RURAL <YOUR FULL NAME>

Production systems

AG-EXP-L (ML) Covers the use of expert systems in agricultural production and management. ✓ **INTERNET**→*email* LISTSERV@VM1.NODAK.EDU ✍ *Type in message body:* SUB AG-EXP-L <YOUR FULL NAME>

Other info

Agricultural List Describes online resources related to agriculture. ✓ **INTERNET**→*ftp* FTP.SURA.NET→ ANONMYOUS/<YOUR EMAIL ADDRESS>→ pub/nic→agricultural.list

Fringe science

You guessed it. Lights in the sky, lights in the mind, lights after death. Definitely try to contact a UFO with telepathy (**alt.paranet.abduct**). And, if you're at all future-oriented, you'll want to stay up-to-date with developments in the cryonics field. Skeptical about such things? Try the mailing list **Skeptic** and the newsgroup **sci.skeptic**. And don't miss **CUFON** (Computer UFO Network), dedicated to reliable, verifiable info about UFO's, a *Wired* magazine BBS of the month.

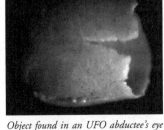

Object found in an UFO abductee's eye —from CompuServe's New Age Forum.

On the Net

Across the board

Alam Al-Mithal (BBS) Enter "the mystical world of similitudes where all physical limitations are removed....Alam Al-Mithal is where you came from and where you shall return to," reads an opening greeting. Conferences and files on the paranormal, UFOs, the occult, and a single world order. 704-732-1852 FREE

alt.paranet.paranormal (NG) Discuss paranormal experiences and theories. ✓**USENET**

alt.paranet.science (NG) A more or less scientific perspective on topics covered on ParaNet. ✓**USENET**

alt.paranormal (NG) Discuss paranormal literature, beliefs, and experiences. ✓**USENET**

Beyond Meeting place for those interested in ghosts, ghoulies, UFOs, aliens, psychic phenomena, and unexplained happenings. All contributions welcome. ✓**ILINK→** *number* 109

Dreaming Isle on the Sea of Fate (BBS) Paranormal conferences, an occult library, role-playing games, and a little shopping. 412-464-0296 FREE

Odyssey Fringe Science Official echo of the Odyssey Fringe Science Research Network. Includes fringe science and Fortean subjects. ✓**FIDONET→** *tag* BAMA

(Out On) The Perimeter Messages on physics, metaphysics, paraphysics, fringe science, and the paranormal—"Between the Cutting Edge and the Lunatic Fringe." ✓**FIDONET→** *tag* PERIMETER

ParaNet A national network of BBSs organized to become an electronic clearinghouse for news and information on the paranormal and fringe sciences. Carries echoes on fringe technology, psychic predictions, skeptical analysis, UFO abductions, and even a research-on-request echo. Some ParaNet conferences are linked with ALT.PARANET* newsgroups. For a list of ParaNet boards, contact the Bay Area Skeptics Board (415-572-0359), which also carries other fringe-science-related echoes besides those from ParaNet, or get the list from the CompuServe UFOlogy library. ✓CHECK LOCAL BULLETIN BOARDS

PSI-NET Covers everything from UFOs to psychic powers. Track urban legends in Rumor Track, monitor Satanic Panic, and share prophecies or alien-abduction experiences. ✓**GENIE→** *keyword* PSI-NET

Speculation "Welcome to 'Speculation,' where ideas flow freely, restrained only by the imagination." Discuss the supernatural, unusual science, the future, and magic. ✓**BIX→** *conference* SPECULATION

Strange & Unexplained Covers, but is not limited to, paranormal events, UFOs, psychic phenomena, natural anomalies, and strange creatures. ✓**RELAYNET→** *number* 279

The Wrong Number (BBS) Discuss UFOs, fringe science, conspiracy theories, TESLA texts, etc. 201-451-3063 FREE

Aliens & UFOs

alt.alien.visitors (NG) Discussions about encounters with aliens, the likelihood of such encounters, and skeptical responses. ✓**USENET**

alt.paranet.abduct (NG) Discuss abductions. ✓**USENET**

alt.paranet.ufo (NG) And even more UFO discussions—very active. ✓**USENET**

CUFON (Computer UFO Network) (BBS) A UFO reporting and information service. 📠 206-776-0382 FREE

MICAP UFO International Conference Up-to-the-minute news and information about UFOs from an international research organization. ✓**FIDONET**→*tag* MICAP_UFO

The MufoNet BBS Network For scientists and other researchers involved in the investigation of unidentified flying objects. The Worldwide Mutual UFO Network is for serious study of UFOs, channeling, dreams, and related subjects. The Mufon BBS (901-785-4943) carries a list of all MufoNet boards. ✓CHECK LOCAL BULLETIN BOARDS

New Age Forum Includes a UFOlogy bulletin board and library. Discuss sightings or download NASA press releases, lists of ParaNet BBSs, GIFs, and UFO conference transcripts. 🖥️💬 ✓**COMPUSERVE**→*go* NEWAGE

Odyssey UFO Reporting UFO reports from the UFOBASE and Official Odyssey sighting forms. ✓**FIDONET**→*tag* SKYWATCH ✖*Odyssey BBS networks only*

UFO Intelligence Network (BBS) Carries MufoNet, FidoNet, and ParaNet conferences as well as a large library of UFO-related files. 416-459-6259

UFO Topics General discussion and news about UFO research and sightings. ✓**FIDONET**→*tag* UFO

Cryonics

Cryonics (ML) All cryonics-related topics covered, from biochemistry of memory to philosophy of identity to legal status of cryonics. ✓**INTERNET**→*email* KQB@WHSCAD1.ATT.COM ✉*Subscribe by request*

sci.cryonics (NG) For anyone interested in cryonics or "who finds the prospect of certain death irritating." ✓**USENET**

Extropians

Extropians (ML) Devoted to the development and discussion of Extropian ideas, including anarchocapitalist politics, cryonics, nanotechnology, and other related ideas. ✓**INTERNET**→*email* EXTROPIANS-REQUEST@GNU.AI.MIT.EDU ✉*Subscribe by request*

Skeptics

alt.paranet.skeptic (NG) Skeptical analysis of paranormal experiences. ✓**USENET**

sci.skeptic (NG) For those skeptical of paranormal experiences. Often includes discussions of scientific evidence for and against astrological hypotheses. ✓**USENET**

Skeptic (ML) A forum to critically discuss paranormal experiences and share papers on the subject. Topics range from the Bermuda Triangle to astrology. ✓**INTERNET**→*email* LISTSERV@YORKVM1.BITNET ✉*Type in message body:* SUB SKEPTIC <YOUR FULL NAME>

Skeptical Inquiry Critical examination of paranormal claims, including psychic powers, UFOs, astrology, Bigfoot, biorhythms, crystals, satanic cults, fire walking, Tarot, and more. Includes book

reviews of related material. ✓**FIDONET**→*tag* SKEPTIC

Math & physics

The cold-fusion debate continues in the newsgroup sci.physics.fusion. "People on all sides of this discussion make misstatements or may lose their cool (including myself in a rather intemperate moment)," writes an emotional scientist. Things are not so heated on other lists, where information exchange, the raison d'être of the Net, is a more academic affair. Typical is a request on **The Computational Chemistry** list from a scientist in Taiwan looking for the "parameters of selenium (Se) for extended Huckel (and charge iterative EH)."

The mathematician Blaise Pascal—from CompuServe's Quick Pictures Forum.

On the Net

Chemistry

Chminf-L (ML) The Chemical Information Sources list covers topics related to chemistry and to finding information about chemical compounds. ✓INTERNET→*email* LISTSERV@IUBVM.UCS.INDIANA.EDU ✍ *Type in message body:* SUBSCRIBE CHMINF-L <YOUR FULL NAME>

The Computational Chemistry List (ML) For computational chemists to exchange information and experience. ✓INTERNET→*email* CHEMISTRY-REQUEST@OSCSUNB.OSC.EDU ✍*Subscribe by request:* <YOUR FULL NAME><YOUR EMAIL ADDRESS><YOUR AFFILIATION>

sci.chem (NG) Forum for discussing chemistry with often not-so-academic inquiries (What happens when I mix this household item with that? How can I painlessly poison someone?). ✓USENET

Mathematics

Com-Alg (ML) Discussion and information exchange among professionals in the field of commutative algebra. ✓INTERNET→*email* LISTSERV@VM1.NODAK.EDU ✍*Type in message body:* SUBSCRIBE COM-ALG <YOUR FULL NAME>

e-Math system American Mathematical Society membership database, employment opportunities, publication ordering, author lists, meeting notices, a directory of journals and newsletters. Provides professional and research information for mathematicians. ✓INTERNET→*telnet* E-MATH.AMS.COM →E-MATH/E-MATH

ILAS-Net (ML) Designed to encourage activities, including publications and meetings, in linear algebra. ✓INTERNET→*email* LISTSERV@TECHNION.TECHNION.AC.IL ✍ *Type in message body:* SUBSCRIBE ILAS-NET <YOUR FULL NAME>

Mathematics Talk about mathematics. The "main" topic area is for general discussion; "symbolic," for symbolic algebra; "teaching," for teaching mathematics; "games," for mathematical games. ●🐝 ✓BIX→ *conference* MATHEMATICS

Science/Math Forum Serves science students and teachers with software and discussion. Includes practice problems for the science and math college boards. ●🐝 ✓COMPUSERVE→ *go* SCIENCE

sci.math (NG) Lots of equations! Emotions run high here. Flame fests are not uncommon. ✓USENET

sci.math.research (NG) Discussions related to current mathematical research. ✓USENET

sci.math.symbolic (NG) Devoted to symbolic math algorithms, applications and issues relevant to symbolic math languages. ✓USENET

sci.stat.math (NG) Offers discussion about statistics from a strictly mathematical approach. ✓USENET

Physics

alt.sci.physics.new-theories (NG) For discussing and suggesting new physics theories. ✓USENET

Physics For physicists and others interested in the subject. ✓FIDONET →*tag* PHYSICS

sci.physics (NG) Covers topics in physics. ✓USENET

sci.physics.fusion (NG) Information and discussion about fusion, especially cold fusion. ✓USENET ✓INTERNET→*email* FUSION-REQUEST@ZORCH.SF-BAY.ORG ✍*Type in message body:* SUB FUSION <YOUR FULL NAME>

Science

Except for public television, general science coverage is notably absent from the American media. The Net fills in a little of the gap. FidoNet's **National Science** offers comprehensive and intelligent conversation about contemporary scientific issues. **PBS's NOVA** is presented on Prodigy with simple science experiments for kids and young adults. **Sciences** on BIX has some good how-things-work discussions. And, never fear, even in Cyberspace there are dinosaurs—on the mailing list **Dinosaur** and CompuServe's **The Dinosaur Forum**.

On the Net

Across the board

alt.folklore.science (NG) Scientific "explanations" and debate over questions such as why car color affects a passenger's comfort or how high a spy satellite orbits. ✓USENET

Beyond Belief A regular column by NOVA. ✓PRODIGY→*jump* BEYOND BELIEF

National Science For general-interest science discussion. ✓FIDO-NET→*tag* SCIENCE

NOVA Offers a monthly, interactive science feature, the NOVA Lab and Experiment Archive,

Albert Einstein—downloaded from wuarchive.wustl.edu

where simple science experiments are described, as well as articles. ✓PRODIGY→*jump* NOVA

Science Includes conversation about current scientific issues and the history of the scientific method. ✓RELAYNET→*number* 183

Science BB A bulletin board for all science-related topics. ✓PRODIGY→*jump* SCIENCE BB

Sciences Includes the "how.n.why" topic for general discussions about science and how things work, as well as other topics, such as "experiments." ⊕🔷 ✓BIX→*conference* SCIENCES

sci.misc (NG) A forum for science discussions without a specific newsgroup. ✓USENET

Dinosaurs

Dinosaur (ML) Discuss dinosaurs and other archosaurs—from the popular press to paleontological theories. ✓INTERNET→*email* DINOSAUR-REQUEST@DONALD.WICHITAKS.NCR.COM ✍*Subscribe by request*

The Dinosaur Forum Devoted to dinosaurs: information, reports on recent discoveries, articles from the popular press, humor, GIFs, notices about museum events, and scientific discussions. ▦ ⊕🔷 ✓COMPUSERVE→*go* DINOFORUM

News & reference

Science News Timely science-related news stories. ▦ ✓PRODIGY→*jump* SCIENCE NEWS

Science education

Science/Math Forum Software and discussion for students and teachers. Specialties include practice problems for the science and math college boards. ⊕🔷 ✓COMPUSERVE→ *go* SCIENCE

Science community

alt.info-science (NG) Science-related information requests (e.g., searching for articles, colleague's email addresses, conference schedules). ✓USENET

Science and Technology Information Service The National Science Foundation bulletin, a guide to programs, program announcements, press releases, and award listings. ✓INTERNET→*telnet* STIS.NSF.GOV→PUBLIC/NEW

Wisenet (ML) A networking forum for women in science, mathematics, and engineering in the Midwest. ✓INTERNET→*email* LISTSERV@UICVM.UIC.EDU ✍*Type in message body:* SUBSCRIBE WISENET <YOUR FULL NAME>

Space & astronomy

The heavens, quite appropriately, are a vast subject in Cyberspace. There is coverage

enough for amateurs and professionals, teachers and students, philosophers and scientists. AOL's **Astronomy Club** is a great place for a novice to start exploring the sky. The newsgroup **sci.astro** is just one of the places you'll find the professional community. From **NASA's Lunar and Planetary Institute** you can download space landscapes. Follow the schedule of national and international events and natural phenomena on CompuServe's **Astronomy Forum**.

A digital image of Neptune, downloaded from ames.arc.nasa.gov.

On the Net

Across the board

Space/Astronomy Forum Connect to the Space and the Astronomy forums. Also access *Sky & Telescope* Online, which features a weekly calendar of astronomical events, news bulletins, and a list of astronomical computing programs available in the Astronomy Forum's library; solar-flare information from the American Sunspot Program; shuttle updates; and Space in the Classroom, a program providing educational resources to teachers. ✓**COMPUSERVE**→*go* SPACE

Astronomy

Advanced Astronomy A low-volume echo for the serious astronomer. Tips for finding hard-to-spot objects, observation reports, and equipment reviews. ✓**FIDONET**→*tag* STARNET ✖*Private distribution; requires moderator approval*

alt.sci.planetary (NG) Discussions about topics in the field of planetary science. ✓**USENET**

Astronomy Discussion forum for amateur and professional astronomers. ✓**BIX**→*conference* ASTRONOMY

Astronomy Postings of coming astronomical events and discussion of astronomical topics. ✓**ILINK**→*number* 57

Astronomy Includes discussion about the stars and stargazing, the physics of astronomy, and current news and events. ✓**RELAYNET**→*number* 188

Astronomy For those interested in the stars and stargazing. ✓**SMARTNET**→*tag* ASTRONOMY

Astronomy Club Hosted by an associate editor for *Sky & Telescope* magazine, the club offers a guide to what's currently "hot" in the skies; a question-and-answer board for novices, instrument tips, graphics of astronomical events, and information on local star-watching clubs. ✓**AMERICA ONLINE**→*keyword* ASTRONOMY

Astronomy Forum Provides contacts and information for both amateur and professional astronomers, with discussions encompassing national and international events and natural phenomena, as well as libraries of GIFs, databases, and software. ✓**COMPUSERVE**→*go* ASTROFORUM

The Event Horizon (BBS) Specializes in astronomy software, data, and images. More than 150 conferences, including Usenet newsgroups. Get information on astronomy clubs and daily solar-system data. Computer-related conferences are also available. 602-780-9217 FREE

sci.astro (NG) Astronomy discussions and information. Postings include the monthly *Electronic Journal of the Astronomical Society of the Atlantic*; ephemerides for asteroids, comets, conjunctions, and encounters; a guide to buying telescopes; and lists of FTP sites with space and astronomy information. ✓ **USENET**

Space Base's Solar Flare Activity Alerts & Reports solar-flare alerts, auroral-activity alerts, geomagnetic-storm and satellite-proton-event warnings, and discussion about all of the sun's activities. ✓ **FIDONET**→*tag* SB-SOLAR_RPT

Astronomy data

Celestial BBS (BBS) Orbital elements from recent *NASA Prediction Bulletins*. Includes documentation and tracking software. 513-427-0674

Minnesota Spacenet (BBS) Includes daily NASA news and information, space-related Fido-Net conferences, launch-date bulletins, lists of astronauts scheduled for flight, etc. 📧 612-920-5566/612-459-0892

NASA/IPAC Extragalactic Database (NED) Abstracts and bibliographies of astronomical research and information on more than 200,000 astronomical objects. Devoted to objects not belonging to the Milky Way galaxy.

Searches provide positions, basic data, and bibliographic references. ✓ **INTERNET**→*telnet* DENVER.IPAC.CAL TECH.EDU→NED/<NONE>

National Space Science Data Center (BBS) Access to several NASA data catalogs and centers, including facilities such as the Astronomical Data Center. The *CANOPUS* newsletter is available. Some of the data is relevant for climatological research. 301-286-9000/301-286-9500 ✓ **INTERNET**→*telnet* NSSDCA.GSFC.NASA.GOV→NODIS/ <NONE>

The Yale Bright Star Catalog Several databases available (e.g., an asteroid database and the Yale Bright Star catalog). Software for using the databases is also available. ✓ **INTERNET**→*ftp* POMONA.CLARE MONT.EDU→ANONYMOUS/<YOUR EMAIL ADDRESS>→yale_bsc

NASA

NASA News Brief descriptions of current events at NASA, including launch schedules. 📧 ✓ **INTERNET** →*finger* NASANEWS@SPACE.MIT.EDU

NASA's Lunar and Planetary Institute Includes a bibliographic database, *The Lunar & Planetary Information Bulletin*, conference notices, journal abstracts, and the image-retrieval-and-processing system, which allows you to display digital images of planets if you have the appropriate software. ✓ **INTERNET**→*telnet* IPI.JSC.NASA.GOV→ LPI/<NONE>

Nasa Spacelink NASA news. Information on the history and future of NASA and spaceflight. Materials for teaching students about spaceflight available. For further information, voice-call 205-544-6531. ✓ **INTERNET**→*telnet*

SPACELINK.MSFC.NASA.GOV→NEWUSER/ NEWUSER

Space Base Nasa News and Press Releases Daily NASA headline news, press releases, and wire excerpts. 📧 ✓ **FIDONET**→*tag* SB-NASA_NEWS ✖ *Read only—no posting*

Space

JPL BBS (BBS) Run by the Jet Propulsion Laboratory. Includes educational guides to space-related topics, GIFs, mission and probe information, NASA/JPL news, space related software, and issues of JPL's magazine, Universe. 818-354-1333 FREE

National Space Society A nonprofit, publicly supported organization promoting space research, exploration, development, and habitat. Its board of governors includes Hugh Downs, Arthur C. Clarke, Jacques Cousteau, John Glenn, Kathy Keeton, Nichelle Nichols, Alan Shepard, and Maria von Braun. ✓ **AMERICA ONLINE**→*keyword* NSS

sci.space (NG) Information and debate on space, space-related research, and space programs. Often includes summaries of *Aviation Week and Space Technology* stories, summaries of Soviet space activities, NASA updates, and listings of FTP sites with astronomy data. ✓ **USENET**

sci.space.news (NG) Space-related news and announcements. 📧 ✓ **USENET**

sci.space.shuttle (NG) Discussion and news about the space shuttle and the STS program. 📧 ✓ **USENET**

SEDSNEWS (ML) News items, press releases, shuttle status reports, and other space-related bulletins. 🖳 ✓**INTERNET**→*email* LIST SERV@TAMVM1.BITNET ✍*Type in message body:* SUBSCRIBE SEDSNEWS <YOUR FULL NAME>

Space Conference about space exploration and development. ◉🗨 ✓**BIX**→*conference* SPACE

Space Space and astronomy, with particular attention to spaceflight, probes, and the shuttle missions. Includes reports direct from NASA. ✓**ILINK**→*number* 49

Space Archive A treasure chest of space information. News and images from space missions, lists of frequently asked questions about astronomy and the space program, databases on constellations, information on corporations working on space projects, a list of earth-orbiting satellites, and much more. ✓**INTERNET**→*ftp* AMES.ARC. NASA.GOV→ANONYMOUS/<YOUR EMAIL ADDRESS>→pub/SPACE

Space Base Discussion and Q&A Discussion about the four read-only Space Base echoes. ✓**FIDONET**→*tag* SB-QUESTIONS

Space Base Technical News & Deep Space Probe Reports Daily shuttle status reports, and status and mission reports from Galileo, Magellan, Ulysses, the Hubble Space Telescope, and the GRO. 🖳 ✓**FIDONET**→*tag* SB-NASA_ TECH ✖*Read only—no posting*

Space Base's Rest of the World In Space News items from the European Space Agency, NASDA Japan, the Commonwealth of Independent States, China, Australia, Canada, and more. 🖳 ✓**FIDONET**→*tag* SB-

WORLD_NWS

Space Base's Electronic Space Related Newsletters Includes publications like *Spacenews, APS What's New, Amset Ham Sat News,* and *Jonathan's Space Report.* 🖳 ✓**FIDONET**→*tag* SB-E/N/L ✖*Read only—no posting*

Space Development Conference Focuses on the settlement, exploration, and development of space, with discussions on technology, politics, and industrial issues. ✓**FIDONET**→*tag* SPACE ✖*No discussions about ham communications, extraterrestrials, UFOs, paranormal phenomena, or future mutant humans*

Space Forum Offers news and discussion for anyone interested in space exploration, travel, colonization, research and development, and other activities. Includes regular postings of NASA press releases. 🖳 ◉🗨 ✓**COMPUSERVE**→*go* SPACEFORUM

Space & Science RoundTable General discussions about space, astrononomy, space pioneering, and related subjects. Includes space news and libraries of information. 🖳 ◉🗨 ✓**GENIE**→*keyword* SPACERT

SpaceMet Curriculum-planning information, information on NASA, and a bulletin board to communicate with other science teachers as well as a section noting events and meetings in the northeastern U.S. ✓**INTERNET**→*telnet* SPACEMET.PHAST.UMASS.EDU→ GUEST/<YOUR FIRST NAME>

talk.politics.space (NG) Debate over the politics influencing space exploration. ✓**USENET**

Space technology

Amateur Satellite Tracking Discussion and Information Includes *NORAD Satellite Elements Weekly* and *Satellite Activity Bulletin,* with general discussion on satellite tracking. ✓**FIDONET** →*tag* SB-SAT_TRACK

Space-IL (ML) Forum for discussing space technologies in Israel. ✓**INTERNET**→*email* LISTSERV@ TAUNIVM.BITNET ✍*Type in message body:* SUB SPACE-IL <YOUR FULL NAME>

Space-Tech (ML) Discussion of space topics, including esoteric propulsion technologies, starflight, orbital-debris removal, etc. ✓**INTERNET**→*email* SPACE-TECH-REQUESTS @CS.CMU.EDU ✍*Subscribe by request*

The Hubble

Observational Astronomy Among the topics are astrophotography, observing techniques, telescope building, and tips and hints. Regular reports from the Hubble Space Telescope are also posted. ✓**FIDONET**→*tag* ASTRONOMY

sci.astro.hubble (NG) Hubble Space Telescope data and reports. ✓**USENET**

Space Telescope Science Institute Information about the Hubble Space Telescope and the institute. Instrument reports, data, grant information, FAQ lists, software, etc. ✓**INTERNET**→*ftp* STSCI.EDU →ANONYMOUS/<YOUR EMAIL ADDRESS>

Reference

Space & Science Information Center Reference materials including *Grolier's Encyclopedia,* weather maps, and the *Planetary Report KB.* ✓**GENIE**→*keyword* SPACE

Technology & society

One of the most important recent contributions to the discussion of technology and its

effect on society is in the low-tech form of a magazine. Published out of San Francisco, *Wired* magazine, the brainchild of techno-visionary Louis Rossetto, has achieved much of its renown on the Net, from extreme praise to radical ridicule. Now, however, with the advent of the newsgroup **alt.wired** and the **Wired Forum** on America Online, *Wired* is no longer just a print medium, it's an official cybervoice. Also try **Computer Underground Digest** for the kind of coverage of technology issues that doesn't make it into the mass media. For a more technical emphasis, try the **Science & Technology Conference** on FidoNet.

On the Net

Across the board

comp.society (NG) Discussion about the impact of technology on society and general explanations of how technology works. ✓ **USENET**

Technology "Devoted to discussing and studying new technologies and the impact caused by these technologies." ⊚🐝 ✓ **BIX**→ *conference* TECHNOLOGY

Bladerunner, *the cult movie for technophiles—from Howard's Notebook BBS*

Ethics & policy

comp.society.development (NG) Forum for discussing computer technology in developing countries. ✓ **USENET**

Computer Underground Digest A weekly electronic journal dedicated to computer and Cyberspace issues—especially the legal, ethical, and social issues related to computer communication. Besides the locations listed, it is available in several areas on each of the major commercial services and on many BBSs. ✓ **RELAYNET**→ *number* 412 ✓ **USENET**→COMP.SOCIETY.CU-DIGEST ✓ **INTERNET**→ *ftp* FTP.EFF.ORG→ANONYMOUS/<YOUR EMAIL ADDRESS>→pub/cud/cud ...→*email* TK0JUT2@MVS.CSO.NIU.EDU *Type in subject line:* SUB CUD <YOUR FULL NAME>

Science & Technology Conference Debate facts and public policy related to science and technology. ✓ **FIDONET**→*tag* SCI&TECH

Techno-Ethics Covers the legal and ethical issues raised by the use of current and developing technologies. ✓ **RELAYNET**→*number* 382

New technologies

alt.clearing.technology (NG) Ostensibly a forum for postings about technological development but pretty much anything goes— religion, marijuana legalization, rape, sexuality, etc. ✓ **USENET**

comp.society.futures (NG) Forum for discussing technology and the future. ✓ **USENET**

sci.nanotech (NG) For discussing self-reproducing molecular-scale machines. ✓ **USENET**

Sci-Tech Discussions of all relevant topics related to science, technology, and engineering. ✓ **ILINK**→*number* 100

The information age

alt.wired (NG) Rave and rant about *Wired* magazine. ✓ **USENET**

Shothc-L (ML) Researchers discuss the information age, computing and society, etc. ✓ **INTERNET**→ *email* LISTSERV@SIVM.BITNET ✍ *Type in message body:* SUBSCRIBE SHOTHC-L <YOUR FULL NAME>

Wired Archive An archive of *Wired* articles. ✓ **INTERNET**→*ftp* FTP.APPLE.COM→ANONYMOUS/<YOUR EMAIL ADDRESS>→pub/VR/Wired

Wired Forum Discuss *Wired*— the magazine covering the information age and its technology. Read articles from back issues and preview upcoming issues. ▦ ✓ **AMERICA ONLINE**→*keyword* WIRED

The weather

You *do* need a weatherman. Check out AOL's Weather, which has one of the best weather maps this side of *USA Today*. Professionals in the weather business should try the mailing list **WX-talk** for events and job listings. **Cumulus Archive** offers some astounding images for downloading. Get real-time images from **FAX/Satellite Services BBS.**

On the Net

Across the board

sci.geo.meteorology (NG) Covers meteorology and related subjects. ✓ **USENET**

Weather Check out the Hurricane Center, color weather maps, and weather news. 🖥 📡 ✓ **AMERICA ONLINE**→*keyword* WEATHER

Weather Offers discussion of weather from a scientific viewpoint. ✓ **RELAYNET**→*number* 254

WX-Talk (ML) For general weather discussions and talk. Also carries event notifications, job announcements, and administrative messages. ✓ **INTERNET**→*email* LIST SERV@VMD.CSO.UIUC.EDU ✍ *Type in message body:* SUB WX-TALK <YOUR FULL NAME>

Images

Cumulus Archive Image files from the METOSTAT 4 and METOSTAT 3 satellites—both infrared and visible—updated

Lightning strikes—downloaded from wuarchive.wustl.edu.

daily. The directory /calmet includes software and documents for computer-aided learning in meteorology. ✓ **INTERNET**→*ftp* CUMULUS.MET.ED.AC.UK→ANONYMOUS/<YOUR EMAIL ADDRESS>→images

FAX/Satellite Services BBS (BBS) Provides real-time NOAA, GOES, and METEOSAT weather satellite images. 619-224-3853 $25/YEAR

Weather-Image Archive Surface maps, satellite images for several U.S. regions, weather-radar maps, and other GIFs and PICT files, including hurricane images. ✓ **INTERNET**→*ftp* FTP.COLORADO.EDU→ ANONYMOUS/<YOUR EMAIL ADDRESS> →pub/weather-images

Weather data

EMI Non-graphic Map Shows National Weather Service measures of precipitation around the U.S., with a numerical display of intensity. For a fee, maps can be sent directly to a fax machine. ✓ **COMPUSERVE**→*go* AERORAD

NCAR Data Support Section Server Access catalogs, documentation, programs, and data files for meteorological research—many of the data files are available only on request and for a fee. It's suggested you start with the README file. ✓ **INTERNET**→*ftp* NCARDATA.UCAR.EDU →ANONYMOUS/<YOUR EMAIL ADDRESS> ✖ *Fee charged for some services*

Weather forecasts

NASA Weather Reports Weather reports and forecasts for NASA launch dates. ✓ **INTERNET**→ *ftp* AMES.ARC.NASA.GOV→ANONYMOUS/<YOUR EMAIL ADDRESS>→pub/ SPACE/WEATHER

Weather Continually updated weather forecasts and statistics for locations all over the world by Accu-Weather. 🖥 ✓ **DELPHI**→*go* NEW WEA

Weather Includes information for the U.S. from the National Weather Service and Accu-Weather—forecasts, maps, and current conditions. 🖥 ✓ **COMPUSERVE**→*go* WEATHER

Weather Interested in the weather in Dublin, Ireland, or perhaps Manhattan? Weather reports and maps from all over the world, including ski conditions. ✓ **PRODIGY**→*jump* WEATHER

Weather Underground Sites U.S. and Canadian weather forecasts, ski conditions, earthquake reports, severe-weather reports, hurricane advisories, and weather conditions in some international cities. 🖥 ✓ **INTERNET** ...→*telnet* DOWNWIND.SPRL.UMICH.EDU 3000 ...→*telnet* MEASUN.NRRC.NCSU.EDU 3000 ...→*telnet* WIND.ATMOS.UAH. EDU 3000 ...→*telnet* UCSU.COLORADO. EDU 3000

Part 12

Schools, Reference & Higher Learning

12

Colleges

Add Cyberspace to the ever-more-competitive, I-need-an-
edge world of college admissions. You can file an application through the **Rensselaer Polytechnic Institute RoundTable** on GEnie or study for your SATs with **College Board Online** on AOL. Search for the right school using **Peterson's College Database** on CompuServe and then roam the college lists and newsgroups looking for the inside scoop on the schools of your choice. When you're on campus, academics, fraternities, the SGA, and even roommate whining have a voice on the Internet.

On the Net

College-bound

College Board Online Provides a handbook with descriptions of more than 3,100 colleges, a question-and-answer area, testing information, financial-aid guides, and a store offering college-prep materials from SAT software to college guide-books. ✓**AMERICA ONLINE**→*keyword* COLLEGE BOARD

Peterson's College Database Offers descriptions of more than 4,000 U.S. and Canadian colleges that grant degrees. Enter your criteria and see your choices. ✓**COMPUSERVE**→*go* PETERSON

Peterson's Connexion Educa-

Stanford University—from Compu-Serve's Graphics Corner Forum

tional and career information. 🖨 ✓**COMPUSERVE**→*go* PBX

Rensselaer Polytechnic Institute RoundTable Get information on the curriculum, student life, and application process at RPI. Includes bulletin boards for communicating with admissions staff, and an alumni area. File your application online! 🖨💬 ✓**GENIE**→*keyword* RPI

College life

alt.flame.roommate (NG) Roommate-from-hell stories. ✓**USENET**

alt.folklore.college (NG) Share college stories and rumors. ✓**USENET**

International House A gathering place for students from all nations, based on the independent off-campus residential halls found at many colleges. The online dining hall features a different language—and a different menu—nightly. There are also cultural shops, libraries, and HyperCard Esperanto lessons. 🖨💬 ✓**AMERICA ONLINE**→*keyword* INTERNATIONAL

soc.college (NG) Covers discussions about getting into college, colleges, and collegiate activities. ✓**USENET**

Undergraduate Discussions about college life for the pre-college crowd. ✓**SMARTNET**→*tag* UNDERGRADUATE

Student body

Non Traditional Student For the adult returning to college. Includes topics like cost, scheduling, prior credit, study habits, and competing with younger students. ✓**FIDONET**→*tag* NON_TRAD_ STU

Sigma-Nu (ML) For members of the Sigma Nu fraternity around the country. ✓**INTERNET**→*email* LISTSERV@ HEARN.CC.VT.EDU ✍ *Type in message body:* SUB SIGMA-NU <YOUR FULL NAME>

Sinfonia (ML) Forum for brothers of Phi Mu Alpha Sinfonia, the men's professional fraternity in music. ✓**INTERNET**→*email* LISTSERV@ASUVM.INRE.ASU.EDU ✍ *Type in message body:* SUB SINFONIA <YOUR FULL NAME> ✖ *Brothers only*

Thetaxi (ML) Forum for brothers in the Theta Xi fraternity. ✓**INTERNET**→*email* LISTSERV@GITVM1.GATECH.EDU ✍ *Type in message body:* SUB THETAXI <YOUR FULL NAME>

Campus politics

ActNow-L (ML) Discussion group for college activists. ✓**INTERNET**→*email* LISTSERV@BROWNVM.BITNET ✍ *Type in message body:* SUBSCRIBE ACTNOW-L <YOUR FULL NAME> <SCHOOL NAME>

SGANet (ML) For members of student government associations at colleges and universities world-

Colleges Schools, Reference, & Higher Learning

wide to discuss issues. **✓INTERNET→** *email* LISTSERV@VTVM1.BITNET ✍ *Type in message body:* SUBSCRIBE SGANET <YOUR ORGANIZATION'S FULL NAME>

Majors & minors

Screen-L (ML) Forum for students and teachers of film and television. Topics range from post-post-structuralist theory to the next SCS/UFVA conference. **✓INTERNET→***email* LISTSERV@UA TVM. UA.EDU ✍ *Type in message body:* SUBSCRIBE SCREEN-L <YOUR FULL NAME>

Snurse-L (ML) Forum for nursing students to discuss nursing, network with other students, and share health information. **✓INTERNET→** *email* LISTSERV@UBVM.CC.BUFFA LO.EDU ✍ *Type in message body:* SUB SNURSE-L <YOUR FULL NAME>

Stuxch-L (ML) Forum for students in art, architecture, and visual and basic design. **✓INTERNET→***email* LISTSERV@PSUVM.PSU.EDU ✍ *Type in message body:* SUB STUXCH-L <YOUR FULL NAME>

Graduate studies

Dissertation Abstracts Offers information on all doctoral dissertations submitted at accredited U.S. institutions since 1861, along with selected masters' theses and dissertations from many Canadian and foreign schools. Also offers abstracts for all dissertations added to the database since July 1980. **✓COMPUSERVE→***go* DISSERTATION $$

Grad-Adv (ML) Serves as a meeting area for those advising undergraduates about graduate school; collects electronic information about graduate schools; endeavors to create a database of electronic information about graduate schools. **✓INTERNET→***email* LIST-SERV@LISTSERV.ACS.UNC.EDU ✍ *Type in message body:* SUBSCRIBE GRAD-ADV <YOUR FULL NAME>

Lawsch-L (ML) Forum for law students to interact with other law students and applicants. **✓INTERNET →***email* LISTSERV@AUVM.BITNET ✍ *Type in message body:* SUB LAWSCH-L <YOUR FULL NAME>

Legal Forum Includes law-school rankings, exam-taking strategies, and law-exam questions. Libraries and boards for paralegals, Supreme Court decisions, software, and even cyberlaw. 🕮 **✓COMPUSERVE →***go* LAWSIG

MBA-L (ML) Information and news about MBA programs for students, faculty, and administrators. **✓INTERNET→***email* LISTSERV@ VM.MARIST.EDU ✍ *Type in message body:* SUBSCRIBE MBA-L <YOUR FULL NAME>

Medstu-L (ML) Forum for medical students worldwide. **✓INTERNET →***email* LISTSERV@UNMVMA.UNM.EDU ✍ *Type in message body:* SUB MEDSTU-L <YOUR FULL NAME>

Met-Stud (ML) Forum for meteorology students. Topics range from scholarship and program information to meteorology-related questions. **✓INTERNET→***email* DENNIS@ METW3.MET.FU-BERLIN.DE ✍*Subscribe by request*

PsycGrad (ML) A forum for psychology graduate students. **✓IN-TERNET→***email* LISTSERV@ACADVM1. UOTTAWA.CA ✍ *Type in message body:* SUB PSYCGRAD <YOUR FULL NAME>

Psygrd-J (ML) Professional-level psychology articles published by graduate students. **✓INTERNET→** *email* LISTSERV@ACADVM1.UOTTAWA.CA ✍ *Type in message body:* SUB PSYGRD-J <YOUR FULL NAME>

soc.college.grad (NG) For grad-school students. Covers general issues related to life as a grad student. **✓USENET**

soc.college.gradinfo (NG) Provides information about graduate schools. **✓USENET**

Scholarships

College Aide Sources for Higher Education (CASHE) A scholarship database with listings on undergraduate and graduate scholarships, fellowships, loans, internships, and work study programs. **✓GENIE→***keyword* CASHE $$

Federal Information Exchange Up-to-date listings of federal education and research programs, scholarships, fellowships, available funding, and other information. Access to three services: Federal Opportunities, the Minority On-Line Information Service (MOLIS), and Higher Education Opportunities for Minorities & Women. 800-783-3349 **✓INTERNET →***telnet* FEDIX.FIE.COM→NEW/YOUR EMAIL ADDRESS

Academic freedom

alt.comp.acad-freedom.news (NG) A moderated discussion about academic freedom and privacy issues at colleges and universities. Includes documented violations of privacy, especially of email and censorship of Usenet groups. **✓USENET**

alt.comp.acad-freedom.talk (NG) An unmoderated discussion of the same issues covered in ALT.COMP.ACAD-FREEDOM.NEWS. **✓USENET**

European history

"Daily I listen to the news surrounding the coming down of the Berlin Wall. I find myself

sitting and watching the television reports with tears in my eyes. I had, like many of my friends, never thought I would see this happen in my lifetime..." And so the mailing list **9NOV89-L** began, leaving behind an archive of first reactions to "the event," raw files of shock and joy. Four years later the list is still in business, chronicling the birth pains of a new Europe, from outbreaks of terrorism to the new German ZIP codes.

On the Net

By period

Ancien-L (ML) Debate forum related to the ancient history of the Mediterranean. ✓**INTERNET**→*email* LISTSERV@ULKYVM.LOUISVILLE.EDU ✍ *Type in message body:* SUB ANCIEN-L <YOUR FULL NAME>

Ficino (ML) Covers the Renaissance and Reformation. ✓**INTERNET**→*email* LISTSERV@UTORONTO.BITNET ✍ *Type in message body:* SUB FICINO <YOUR FULL NAME>

9NOV89-L (ML) Named after the date the Berlin Wall came down. Topics include recent developments in Europe and the CIS. ✓**INTERNET**→*email* LISTSERV@DBO TUI11.BITNET ✍ *Type in message body:* SUB 9NOV89-L <YOUR FULL NAME>

Winston Churchill—from Compu-Serve's Quick Pictures Forum.

Renais-L (ML) Forum for scholars of the Renaissance. Papers, announcements, and queries are welcome. ✓**INTERNET**→*email* LISTSERV@ULKYVM.LOUISVILLE.EDU ✍ *Type in message body:* SUB RENAIS-L <YOUR FULL NAME>

By country

Dutch History Archive Includes historical texts, many of which are relevant to Dutch history. ✓**INTERNET**→*ftp* TYR.LET.RUG.NL→ANONYMOUS/<YOUR EMAIL ADDRESS>→pub/gheta

Espora-L (ML) Forum for discussing the history of the Iberian Peninsula to the present. Postings in English, Spanish, Portuguese, and Catalan are welcome. ✓**INTERNET**→*email* LISTSERV@UKANVM.BITNET ✍ *Type in message body:* SUB ESPORA-L <YOUR FULL NAME>

FranceHS (ML) An interdisciplinary list focusing on the historical study of France. ✓**INTERNET**→*email* LISTSERV@UWAVM.U.WASHINGTON.EDU ✍ *Type in message body:* SUBSCRIBE FRANCEHS <YOUR FULL NAME>

Habsburg (ML) Covers Austrian history since 1500. ✓**INTERNET**→*email* LISTSERV@VM.CC.PURDUE.EDU ✍ *Type in message body:* SUBSCRIBE HABSBURG <YOUR FULL NAME>

Albion-L (ML) Discussions related to Irish and British history, all time periods. ✓**INTERNET**→*email* LISTSERV@UCSBVM.BITNET ✍ *Type in message body:* SUBSCRIBE ALBION-L <YOUR FULL NAME>

Ansax-L (ML) Discussion about Anglo-Saxon history and related subjects. ✓**INTERNET**→*email* LISTSERV@WVNVM.BITNET ✍ *Type in message body:* SUB ANSAX-L <YOUR FULL NAME>

Victoria-L (ML) Very active forum focusing on all aspects of 19th-century Britain. For students of history, literature, politics, and art, and interested others. ✓**INTERNET**→*email* LISTSERV@IUBVM.UCS.INDIANA.EDU ✍ *Type in message body:* SUB VICTORIA <YOUR FULL NAME>

Immortal words

The Magna Carta/The Rights of Man Download the full-text, electronic versions of the Magna Carta and the Rights of Man. ✓**INTERNET** ...→*ftp* BYRD.MU.WVNET.EDU→ANONYMOUS/<YOUR EMAIL ADDRESS>→pub/history/political ...→*telnet* FREENET.VICTORIA.BC.CA→GUEST/<NONE>→Library and Information Services/Online Modern History Review/Library of Historical Documents

Geo- & demography

Borders, going up and coming down, often simultaneously, may be the central drama

of our time. The balance of power is measured by wealth, ethnicity, age, and temperament, nation by nation, region by region, enclave by enclave. Indeed, demographic and geographic data are the warheads of the post–Cold War era. **CENDATA**, offered by the Census Bureau on CompuServe, and the **CIA World Map Database**, an FTP site, are invaluable tools for configuring this new world.

On the Net

Demographic data

Census-BEA Electronic Forum (BBS) Includes 1990 Census information, housing statistics, trade data, country business policies, state economic ratings, population estimates, and more. Also offers forums based on specific business interests. 301-763-7554 FREE

CompuServe Demographics Databases Features a menu of several databases of demographic information: Business Demographics breaks down businesses by size and geographical unit; Cendata offers data on manufacturing, housing starts, population, and agriculture, as well as press releases from the Census Bureau; Neighborhood Report provides demographic data by ZIP code; and Supersite uses demographic data to determine market and

A map of L.A.—from AOL's Macintosh Graphic Arts & CAD Forum.

retail-sales potential for as large an area as the U.S. or as small as a ZIP-code region. ✓ **COMPUSERVE**→ *go* DEMOGRAPHICS ✖ *Extra costs for some databases*

Geography

CIA World Map Database Map data includes coastlines, rivers, lakes, international political boundaries, and U.S. state boundaries. A map-drawing program and source code are also available. ✓ **INTERNET**→ *ftp* HANAUMA.STANFORD. EDU→ANONYMOUS/<YOUR EMAIL ADDRESS>→ pub/World_Map

COGS Archive Information on mapping, GIS, remote sensing, and geology. Also carries a list of resources on the Internet (INTERNET.RESOURCES.EARTH.SCI). ✓ **INTERNET** →*ftp* CSN.ORG→ANONYMOUS/<YOUR EMAIL ADDRESS>→ COGS

Geograph (ML) General discussions about geographical issues for those with relevant skills or interests. Based in Helsinki, Finland.

✓ **INTERNET**→*email* LISTSERV@SEARN. BITNET ✍ *Type in message body:* SUBSCRIBE GEOGRAPH <YOUR FULL NAME>

Geographic Name Server Enter a city name in the U.S. and its latitude, longitude, elevation, population, and ZIP code are returned. ✓ **INTERNET**→*telnet* MARTINI. EECS. UMICH.EDU 3000→•?/<NONE>

Ingrafx (ML) Covers theories of graphic representations, graphics in animation, the relationship between graphics in academia and in the popular media, and cartography. ✓ **INTERNET**→*email* LISTSERV@ PSUVM.PSU.EDU ✍ *Type in message body:* SUB INGRAFX <YOUR FULL NAME>

Mapping Information on geography, navigation, surveying, cartography, and geodesy. ✓ **FIDONET**→ *tag* MAPPING

USGS Geological Fault Maps A digital database of geological faults in the U.S. and mapping software. ✓ **INTERNET**→*ftp* ALUM.WR. USGS.GOV→ANONYMOUS/<YOUR EMAIL ADDRESS>→pub/maps

GIS software

bit.listserv.uigis-l (NG/ML) Covers GIS user interfaces. ✓ **USENET** ✓ **INTERNET**→ LISTSERV@ UBVM.BITNET ✍ *Type in message body:* SUBSCRIBE UIGIS-L <YOUR FULL NAME>

comp.infosystems.gis (NG/ML) Covers issues relating to GIS. ✓ **USENET** ✓ **INTERNET**→*email* LIST SERV@UBVM.CC.BUFFALO.EDU ✍ *Type in message body:* SUBSCRIBE GIS-L <YOUR FULL NAME>

History

Revisionism!!! The Holocaust. Vietnam. Pearl Harbor. The Depression. The Civil War. The Kennedy (and Lincoln) assassinations. Did any of this really happen? Many people on the newsgroup **alt.revisionism** generally believe not. The revisers haunt other newsgroups as well. On the mailing lists **History** and **Holocaust** and **WWII-L** and the newsgroups **alt.war.vietnam** and **soc.history**, the revisers stand ready to pounce on anyone who doesn't have a body in hand. Check out the **Baby Boomers Club** on AOL while it's still nostalgia (soon it will be history). For professionals, **Modern History Review** tracks endowments, scholarships, and grants.

On the Net

Across the board

History Discussions about world history and historical writing. ✓**ILINK**→*number* 138

History Includes serious, often academic discussions about historical events and their impact today. ✓**RELAYNET**→*number* 137

History (ML) For any history-related discussions. ✓**INTERNET**→

General Robert E. Lee—downloaded from wuarchive.wustl.edu.

email LISTSERV@UBVM.CC.BUFFALO.EDU ✍ *Type in message body:* SUBSCRIBE HISTORY <YOUR FULL NAME>

History Topics in Spanish With wide distribution in Spain and Spanish America, this echo exchanges information on a wide variety of topics. Spanish language use is encouraged, but English is allowed for those not fully confident with written Spanish. ✓**FIDONET**→*tag* HISTORIA

International History General discussions ranging across the subject of history, including events, impacts, causes, and intrepretation. All views and participants are welcome. ✓**FIDONET**→*tag* HISTORY

Modern History Review Includes articles—often the full text of Ph.D. dissertations, book reviews, a library of historical documents (e.g., the Articles of Confederation, the Paris Treaty of 1783, the Gettysburg Address, the Monroe Doctrine, and the Jap-

anese Surrender in WWII), information on endowments, scholarships, and grants, a directory of professional historians, and moderated and unmoderated discussion about history. 604-595-2300 ✓**INTERNET**→*telnet* FREENET.VICTORIA. BC.CA→GUEST/<NONE> →go history

soc.history (NG) A general forum for discussing history. ✓**USENET**

American history

alt.war.civil.usa (NG) Discussion of the United States Civil War. ✓**USENET**

Baby Boomers Club A club for anyone born between 1946 and 1969—the generation that grew up with the mass of high technology and scientific development. Discussions cover historic events, old TV shows and movies, and the sounds of the '60s, '70s, and '80s. ✓**AMERICA ONLINE**→*keyword* BABY BOOMERS

Civil War The causes and effects of the Civil War, with "a little education, a little fun." ✓FIDONET→*tag* CIVIL_WAR

H-AmStdy (ML) Covers all topics and disciplines related to American studies. ✓INTERNET→*email* LISTSERV@UICVM.CC.UIC.EDU ✍ *Type in message body:* SUBSCRIBE H-AMSTDY <YOUR FULL NAME>

H-CivWar (ML) For historians and teachers to discuss the Civil War, teaching methods, and new research. ✓INTERNET→*email* LISTSERV@UICVM.CC.UIC.EDU ✍ *Type in message body:* SUBSCRIBE H-CIVWAR <YOUR FULL NAME>

Nat-1492 (ML) Discussion covers the Columbus voyage to the Americas and its consequences. ✓INTERNET→*email* LISTSERV@TAMVM1.TAMU.EDU ✍ *Type in message body:* SUBSCRIBE NAT-1492 <YOUR FULL NAME>

Pioneer Journals and Diaries Entries from original diaries and journals of the pioneers on the American frontier. You're invited to submit similar entries from your own ancestors' documents. ✓FIDONET→*tag* PIONEER

Chinese history

Emedch-L (ML) Discussion covering Chinese history between the Han and the Tang dynasties (third through sixth centuries A.D.) ✓INTERNET→*email* LISTSERV@USCVM.BITNET ✍ *Type in message body:* SUB EMEDCH-L <YOUR FULL NAME>

Russia, USSR, CIS

RusHist (ML) Covers Russian history from the reign of Ivan III to the end of the Romanov dynasty. ✓INTERNET→*email* LISTSERV@VM.USC.EDU ✍ *Type in message body:* SUB

RUSHIST <YOUR FULL NAME>

Sovhist (ML) Any topic in Soviet history is open for discussion—from the 1917 revolution to the 1991 breakup. ✓INTERNET→*email* LISTSERV@VM.USC.EDU ✍ *Type in message body:* SUB SOVHIST <YOUR FULL NAME>

Soviet Archives Information from opened Soviet archives about living conditions in the former Soviet Union, Chernobyl, the Cuban Missile Crisis, and more. You can even get a GIF of Gorby. ✓AMERICA ONLINE→*keyword* SOVIET ✓INTERNET→*ftp* SEQ1.LOC.GOV <ANONYMOUS/<YOUR EMAIL ADDRESS>→pub/soviet.archive

The classical world

sci.classics (NG) Forum for discussing classical history, languages, art, etc. ✓USENET

World War II

Holocaust (ML) Topics include the Holocaust, anti-Semitism, Jewish history in the 1930s and 1940s, and closely related topics in German, diplomatic, and WWII history. Scholarly discussion about the topics as well as about teaching these subjects. ✓INTERNET→*email* LISTSERV@UICVM.UIC.EDU ✍ *Type in message body:* SUB HOLOCAUS <YOUR FULL NAME>

Holocaust Archive Files An index of files—actual files are retrievable from the same address—relating to the Holocaust. Files include accounts of time at Auschwitz, the story of Kurt Gerstein, bibliographic sources, biographies of Nazi war criminals, diary notes from an Auschwitz doctor, and writings by Elie Weisel. ✓INTERNET→*email* LIST-

SERV@ONEB.ALMANAC.BC.CA ✍ *Type in message body:* INDEX HOLOCAUST

World War II Bibliography Online bibliography for World War II books. ✓INTERNET→*ftp* SEQ1.LOC.GOV→ANONYMOUS/<YOUR EMAIL ADDRESS>→Library.of.Congress /research.guides/humanities.soc.sci →WWII.hist.biblio

WWII-L (ML) Forum for World War II veterans to discuss politics, history, technology, and any other topic of interest. ✓INTERNET→*email* LISTSERV@UBVM.CC.BUFFALO.EDU ✍ *Type in message body:* SUBSCRIBE WWII-L <YOUR FULL NAME>

The Vietnam War

alt.war.vietnam (NG) Discussion of the Vietnam War. ✓USENET

Vwar-L (ML) For anyone interested in the Vietnam War. ✓INTERNET→*email* LISTSERV@UBVM.CC.BUFFALO.EDU ✍ *Type in message body:* SUB VWAR-L <YOUR FULL NAME>

Diplomatic history

H-Diplo (ML) For scholars and teachers of diplomatic history and international relations to discuss new research and books, share teaching tips, and report on resources available on the Net. ✓INTERNET→*email* LISTSERV@UICVM.CC.UIC.EDU ✍ *Type in message body:* SUBSCRIBE H-DIPLO <YOUR FULL NAME>

Historical archives

Byrd Marshall University History FTP Site With directories on diplomatic history, women's history, maritime history, politics and government, and ethnicity history—to name a few—the archive is a great source for historical material, including the text of the Monroe Doctrine, a timeline of history, syllabuses for U.S.-history courses, letters from Ngo Dinh Diem to Eisenhower and Kennedy, and the text of the infamous "White Paper." Get a GIF of the Vietnam memorial, a M.A. thesis on U.S. military planning for WWI, or a copy of Maya Angelou's poem read at the Clinton Inaugural. ✓**INTERNET**→*ftp* BYRD. MU.WVNET.EDU→ANONYMOUS/<YOUR EMAIL ADDRESS>→pub/history

Mississippi State History Archives A collection of materials on the Vietnam War as well as materials on subjects ranging from medieval studies to the American Indian movement to African and Asian history. The directory /newsletter holds the National Council of History's Education newsletter. ✓**INTERNET**→ *ftp* RA.MSSTATE.EDU→ANONYMOUS/ <YOUR EMAIL ADDRESS>→docs/history

The University of Kansas Server for Historians Easy-to-follow menu system (via telnet) takes you to history sites all over the world. Read online a brief biography of Marie Curie or the full text of John Stuart Mill's *The Subjection of Women* or the memoirs of William Hulme (in the Australian-history archive); access a Dutch-history database in the Netherlands; connect with the Library of Congress Information Server; have the Jefferson Inaugural speech or the Mayflower Compact emailed to you; and get information on new Internet history resources and exhibitions. The FTP site holds articles ranging from "The Great Marriage Hunt: Finding a Wife in Fifteenth Century England" to "The Coming of Age: The Role of the Helicopter in the Vietnam War", syllabuses, extensive bibliographies,

and shareware. ✓**INTERNET** ...→*telnet* UKANAIX.CC.UKANS.EDU→HISTORY/ <NONE> ...→*ftp* UKANAIX.CC.UKANS. EDU→ANONYMOUS/<YOUR EMAIL ADDRESS>→pub/history

Historical theory

Cliology (ML) For the theoretical discussion of history. ✓**INTERNET** →*email* LISTSERV@MSU.EDU ✍ *Type in message body:* SUBSCRIBE CLIOLOGY <YOUR FULL NAME>

Sochist (ML) Forum to discuss three aspects of the "new social history": emphasis on quantitative information, an interdisciplinarian perspective, and inclusion of groups that have traditionally been ignored (such as women, children, labor, etc.). ✓**INTERNET**→*email* LIST SERV@VM.USC.EDU ✍ *Type in message body:* SUBSCRIBE SOCHIST <YOUR FULL NAME>

World-L (ML) Theory, methodology, and strategy for teaching world history from a non-Eurocentric perspective. ✓**INTERNET** →*email* LISTSERV@UBVM.CC.BUFFALO. EDU ✍ *Type in message body:* SUB WORLD-L <YOUR FULL NAME>

Revisionists

alt.revisionism (NG) Many of the postings relate to the history of the Holocaust—with some disputing that it even happened. Discussion often degenerates into flamefests. ✓**USENET**

What if'ers

alt.history.what-if (NG) Discussions about what would have happened if certain historical events were somehow altered (e.g., "If only the south had Mustard gas at Gettysburg"). ✓**USENET**

Miscellaneous

C18-L (ML) Discussion forum for those interested in the 18th century. ✓**INTERNET**→*email* LISTSERV@ PSUVM.BITNET ✍ *Type in message body:* SUBSCRIBE C18-L <YOUR FULL NAME>

Emhist-L (ML) Discussions about early modern history. ✓**INTERNET**→ *email* LISTSERV@RUTVM1.BITNET ✍ *Type in message body:* SUB EMHIST-L <YOUR FULL NAME>

General Ethnology and History Discussion List (ML) Covers topics relevant to both ethnology and history—e.g., anthropology of museums, missionary photography, and more. ✓**INTERNET** →*email* LISTSERV@NIC.SUFNET.N1 ✍ *Type in message body:* SUB ETHNOHIS <YOUR FULL NAME>

Hislaw-L (ML) For students and scholars of the history of law. Feudal, common, and canon law are all discussed, meetings and upcoming papers are announced, scholarly pieces are offered, etc. ✓**INTERNET**→*email* LISTSERV@ULKYVM. LOUISVILLE.EDU ✍ *Type in message body:* SUB HISLAW-L <YOUR FULL NAME>

H-Urban (ML) A forum for scholars of urban history to share research and materials, discuss methods of analysis, announce papers and conferences, note job opportunities and fellowships, and more. Archived files include bibliographies, book reviews, teaching materials, computer software, etc. ✓**INTERNET**→ *email* LISTSERV@UICVM. UIC.EDU ✍ *Type in message body:* SUBSCRIBE H-URBAN <YOUR FULL NAME>

MedSci (ML) Discussions of medieval and Renaissance science. ✓**INTERNET**→*email* LISTSERV@BROWN VM.BROWN.EDU ✍ *Type in message body:* SUB MEDSCI-L <YOUR FULL NAME>

Libraries

From Cyberspace, you can swoop down into the great libraries of the world. These include the Library of Congress, the New York Public Library, Harvard University, Oxford University, and the Boston Library Consortium —the libraries of Boston College, Boston University, Brandeis, MIT, Northeastern, Tufts, Wellesley, and UMass. For seekers of wisdom and for research drudges the Net is where the Holy Grail can be found. Try **Hytelnet** or **CARL** on the Internet and the **Dante Project** at **Dartmouth Library Catalog**.

On the Net

Catalogs & more

Boston Library Consortium Includes the libraries of BC, BU, Brandeis, MIT, Northeastern University, Tufts, Wellesley, UMass/Boston, and UMass/Amherst as well as the Boston Public Library and the State Library of Massachusetts. ✓**INTERNET**→*telnet* BLC. LRC.NORTHEASTERN.EDU→BLC/<NONE>

CARL (Colorado Association of Research Libraries) A catalog of almost every academic library in Colorado (as well as access to libraries nationwide). Indexes of school programs, book reviews, facts about Denver, an environmental-education database, an online encyclopedia, mag-

The Library of Congress—downloaded from CompuServe's Graphics Gallery.

azine and newspaper databases, and a service to search the Internet Resource Guide. Luxury features (i.e., the encylopedia) are limited to those with a Colorado library card. ✓**INTERNET**→*telnet* PAC.CARL. ORG→PAC/<NONE>

comp.internet.library (NG) Discussions and announcements about electronic libraries. ✓**USENET**

Dartmouth Library Catalog Besides access to Dartmouth's library catalog, the full-text files of the Shakespeare plays, The Shakespeare sonnets, Dante's writings, and The King James Bible. ✓**INTERNET**→*telnet* LIB.DARTMOUTH.EDU

Harvard University Connect to Harvard's library catalog. ✓**INTERNET**→*telnet* HOLLIS.HARVARD.EDU→HOLLIS/<NONE>

Library of Congress Access from the Internet to its catalogs as well as information about the library, exhibits, and federal legislation. On AOL, view the exhibits, get information on the library, and learn about ongoing projects. ✓**AMERICA ONLINE**→ *keyword* LIBRARY

✓**INTERNET**→*telnet* LOCIS.LOC.GOV

New York Public Library Search the catalogs of the New York Public Libraries. ✓**INTERNET**→ *telnet* NYPLGATE.NYPL.ORG→NYPL/ <NONE>

Oxford University Search the libraries of Oxford University ✓**INTERNET**→*telnet* LIBRARY.OX.AC.UK

Other sources

Billy Baron's List Provides a standard description for all electronic library systems listed in the St. George Directory, including addresses and log-on and log-off instructions. ✓**INTERNET**→*ftp* FTP. UTDALLAS.EDU→ANONYMOUS/<YOUR EMAIL ADDRESS>→pub/staff/billy /libguide

Hytelnet Servers Access Internet addresses and information on libraries all over the world. Choose from hundreds of libraries and get the telnet address, log-on information, and instructions on how to use the system. Hytelnet also offers information on databases and other Internet resources. ✓**INTER-NET** ...→*telnet* ACCESS.USASK.CA→HYTELNET/<NONE> ...→*telnet* INFO. CCIT.ARIZONA.EDU→HYTELNET/<NONE> ...→*telnet* LAGUNA.EPCC.EDU→LI BRARY/<NONE> ...→*telnet* LIBRARY. ADELAIDE.EDU.AU→ACCESS/<NONE>

The St. George Directory An extensive list of libraries and databases on the Internet, organized by location and cost of use (if any). Includes information on BBSs and on campus-wide information systems. ✓**INTERNET** ...→*ftp* NIC.CERF. NET→ANONYMOUS/<YOUR EMAIL AD-DRESS>→internet/resources/library _catalog ...→*ftp* ARIEL.UNM.EDU→ANONYMOUS/<YOUR EMAIL ADDRESS>→library→internet.library

Philosophy

From the witches-do-not-exist proposition being debated in **sci.logic** to the "new ways of thinking" on the mailing list **FNORD-L** to Ayn Rand being discussed everywhere else, the discussion groups are a philosopher manqué's dream (although, to be honest, not all dreamers have done their homework, and discussions often quickly disintegrate into all-out wars and insult matches). Besides these discussion groups, professional philosophers can get grant notices, information on where to get specific philosophy texts, and APA newsletters on the **APA Bulletin Board**. And they may participate in more educated discourse on **L-Hume** or **The Hegel Society**.

On the Net

Across the board

American Philosophical Association Bulletin Board Conference information, APA newsletters, news about other philosophical societies, a "white pages" service, bibliographies, discussion groups, and more. Listings of grants, fellowships, and academic positions. ✓**INTERNET**→*telnet* ATL.CALSTATE.EDU→APA/<YOUR EMAIL ADDRESS>

Fnord-L (ML) The New Ways of

Larent de La Hyre's Laban Seeking His Idols—*from uxa.ecn.bgu.edu.*

Thinking list covers the gamut of philosophical discussions in an often less-than-academic approach (vulgarity is not uncommon). ✓**INTERNET**→*email* LISTSERV@UVBM.CC.BUFFALO.EDU ✍ *Type in message body:* SUBSCRIBE FNORD-L <YOUR FULL NAME>

History of the Philosophy of Science Discussion List (ML) Information exchange—including job and conference announcements, course syllabi, queries, and ideas—covering a broad range of perspectives and periods. Topics include the philosophy of science from antiquity to the 20th century, the history of logic and mathematics, social and institutional history, and more. ✓**INTERNET**→*email* LISTSERV@UKCC.UKY.EDU ✍ *Type in message body:* SUB HOPOS-L <YOUR FULL NAME>

Noble Savage Philosophers (ML) Open to all philosophical topics and issues, from the pragmatic to the bizarre. ✓**INTERNET**→*email* LISTSERV@RPIECS.BITNET ✍ *Type in message body:* SUBSCRIBE NSP-L <YOUR FULL NAME>

Philos-L (ML) For philosophers by nature or profession in the United

Kingdom. ✓**INTERNET**→*email* LISTSERV@LIVERPOOL.AC.UK ✍ *Type in message body:* SUBSCRIBE PHILOS-L <YOUR FULL NAME>

Philosop (ML) Works in progress, conference advertisements, job opportunities, newsletters, and other items related, in a broad sense, to academic philosophy. ✓**INTERNET**→*email* LISTSERV@VM1.YORKU.CA ✍ *Type in message body:* SUBSCRIBE PHILOSOP <YOUR FULL NAME>

Philosophy All philosophical topics, including metaphysics, epistemology, and ethics. ✓**FIDONET**→*tag* PHIL

Philosophy Discussions of classical and current philosophical issues. ✓**ILINK**→*number* 71

Philosophy Covers classical and modern philosophers, along with current philosophical issues. ✓**RELAYNET**→*number* 179

sci.philosophy.tech (NG) Intended for the academic discussion of the philosophy of science, mathematics, logic, and language, or any technical-style philosophy, but in reality a forum for all philosophy discussions. ✓**USENET**

talk.philosophy.misc (NG) A free-for-all philosophy-discussion forum. ✓**USENET**

Consciousness

comp.ai.philosophy (NG) Discussion relating to consciousness with respect to computers, humans, and animals. ✓**USENET**

Ethics

Biomed-L (ML) Discussion of biomedical ethics, from the right to die to abortion to suicide to drug legalization. Philosophical, religious, political, and sometimes personal perspectives welcome. ✓**INTERNET**→*email* LISTSERV@VM1. NODAK.EDU ✍*Type in message body:* SUBSCRIBE BIOMED-L <YOUR FULL NAME>

Logic

sci.logic (NG) For all aspects of—and debate about—logic, including philosophy and mathematics. ✓**USENET**

Objectivism

alt.philosophy.objectivism (NG) Philosophy popularized by Ayn Rand. ✓**USENET**

Ayn Rand Philosophy (ML) Discussion of objectivist philosophy and reviews of Rand's work. ✓**INTERNET**→*email* LISTSERV@IUBVM. UCS.INDIANA.EDU ✍*Type in message body:* SUBSCRIBE AYN-RAND <YOUR FULL NAME>

Objectivism Information on the Ayn Rand founded philosophy. ✓**FIDONET**→*tag* OBJECTIV

Feminist philosophy

SWIP-L (ML) Discussion of feminist philosophy. ✓**INTERNET**→*email* LISTSERV@CFRVM.CFR.USF.EDU ✍*Type in message body:* SUB SWIP-L <YOUR FULL NAME>

Traditions

Academic Philosophy The empiricist tradition; no New Age or Eastern mysticism. ✓**FIDONET**→*tag* PLATOS_ACADEMY

alt.individualism (NG) Discuss philosophies in which individual rights are dominant. ✓**USENET**

Geodesic (ML) Forum for discus-sing Buckminister Fuller and his works and philosophies. "If you're interested in discussing Bucky, learning more about him, or finding out about 8500 ft. high pyramidal cities that float in the ocean and house 1,000,000 people comfortably (2000 sq. ft apartments with 1000 sq. ft. extra patio/garden space), or 1+ mile diameter spherical cities that FLOAT IN THE AIR *WITHOUT POWER*, then sign up for the list!" ✓**INTERNET**→*email* LISTSERV@UBVM. BITNET ✍*Type in message body:* SUBSCRIBE GEODESIC <YOUR FULL NAME>

Hegel Society (ML) For discussing Hegel's philosophy. ✓**INTERNET**→*email* LISTSERV@VILLVM.BITNET ✍*Type in message body:* SUBSCRIBE HEGEL <YOUR FULL NAME>

Hume-L (ML) Discussion about the philosophy and writings of David Hume. ✓**INTERNET**→*email* LISTSERV@WMVM1.CC.WM.EDU ✍*Type in message body:* SUBSCRIBE HUME-L <YOUR FULL NAME>

Kurt Goedel Society (ML) For members and those interested in the activities of the Kurt Goedel Society. ✓**INTERNET**→*email* KGS@ LOGIC.TUWIEN.AC.AT ✍*Subscribe by request*

Non Serviam (ML) Newsletter that subscribes to the philosophy of insurrection, particularly that of Max Stirner, author of *Der Einzige und Sein Eigentum*. Forum for both amateur and professional philosophers. ✓**INTERNET**→*email* SOLAN@MATH.UIO.NO ✍*Subscribe by request*

sci.philosophy.meta (NG) For metaphysical philosophy discussions. Topics include holism, metaethics, consciousness, chaos theory, and Ayn Rand. ✓**USENET**

CYBERNOTES

"Well, then, if you're an ambitious logician, try your hand at describing the anaphoric construction (and finding the indirect quotation) in this example:

"John didn't catch a fish, and he didn't eat it."

"This is piss easy: quantify over concepts, and define the relation of things falling under (singular or natural kind) concepts. Then proceed to say that there is no object X falling under the concept of fish, such that John caught X, or John ate X. (Note that this analysis works for unicorns just as well.) As for the scope of indirect quotation, it is implicit in the intentional aspect of John's sporting and alimentary failure, since to catch X is to succeed in seeking that X comes in one's possession. Again, all of this is exceedingly well known from intensional logic."

—from **sci.philoso-phy.tech**

Reference

One of the most frequently asked questions on the Net, regardless of whether you're on a literature mailing list or a religion newsgroup, is "Where can I get *Books in Print*?" Answer: CompuServe's **Books in Print** or GEnie's **Bookshelf**. Across the Net there are numerous other standard references, from **Roget's Thesaurus** on CompuServe to the **CIA World Factbook** on the Internet to **Compton's Encyclopedia** on AOL to the **NYNEX Northeast Access** phone book on Delphi.

On the Net

Almanacs

CIA World Factbook Provides data on the nations of the world—e.g., population, politics, economies. Search the WAIS database or download country chapters. ✓**INTERNET** ...→*wais* world-factbook.src ...→*ftp* WORLD.STD.COM→ANONYMOUS <YOUR EMAIL ADDRESS>→pub/library/reference/world

Dictionaries

Roget's Thesaurus Need a synonym? Search the WAIS database or download the entire text. ✓**COMPUSERVE**→*go* STUFO→Library→Roget2.ZIP ✓**INTERNET** ...→*ftp* MCRNEXT.CSO.UIUC.EDU→ANONYMOUS <YOUR EMAIL ADDRESS>→pub/etext/etext91→roget13a.txt ...→*wais* roget-thesaurus.src

Webster's Dictionary Server Easy-to-use online dictionary. ✓**INTERNET**→*telnet* CHEM.UCSD.EDU→WEBSTER/<NONE>

Directories

Books in Print An online version of the standard bookstore reference. 💲 ✓**COMPUSERVE**→*go* BOOKS $$

NYNEX Northeast Access Search for a company telephone number. Covers Conn., Maine, Mass., N.H., N.Y., R.I., and Vt. Information is updated quarterly. ✓**DELPHI**→*go* REF NYNEX

Phone*File Holds names, addresses, and phone numbers for more than 75 million U.S. households, searchable by name and address, surname, or phone number. ✓**COMPUSERVE**→*go* PHONEFILE $$

Zipcode Guide 1993 A list of postal ZIP codes for the U.S. ✓**INTERNET** ...→*ftp* OES.ORST.EDU→ANONYMOUS/<YOUR EMAIL ADDRESS>→pub/almanac/misc→zipcode.p2 ...→*wais* zipcodes.src

Encyclopedias

Academic American Encyclopedia An online edition of Grolier's encyclopedia, with more than 33,000 entries. ✓**COMPUSERVE**→*go* ENCYCLOPEDIA ✓**DELPHI**→*go* REF GROL ✓**PRODIGY**→*jump* ENCYCLOPEDIA

Compton's Encyclopedia Includes more than 63,000 index entries. ✓**AMERICA ONLINE**→*keyword* ENCYCLOPEDIA

Kussmaul Encyclopedia An online encyclopedia. ✓**DELPHI**→*go* REF KUSS

Media databases

Bookshelf Search a directory listing from the *Books in Print* database of virtually all books published in the U.S. More than 1 million books are listed. Includes 40,000 book reviews from *Publishers Weekly*, *Library Journal*, and the *School Library Journal*. ✓**GENIE**→*keyword* BOOKSHELF $$

Computer & Electronics NewsCenter Search for articles, abstracts, or product announcements from a database of computer journals and government reports. 🖳 ✓**GENIE**→*keyword* COMPUTERS $$

The Dialog Database Center More than 400 databases, including the *Los Angeles Times*, *New England Journal of Medicine*, *Peterson's College Database*, and *TRW Business Credit Profiles*. ✓**GENIE**→*keyword* DIALOG $$

IQuest Provides access to 850 databases from Dialog, BRS, NewsNet, Data-Star, ORBIT, Pergamon Financial Data Services, H.W. Wilson, FT Information Online, G. CamL-Europeenne De Donnees, Questel, and VU/TEXT. ✓**COMPUSERVE**→*go* IQUEST $$

Librarian Searchline Associates, an online research service, will search more than 3,000 regional trade journals, magazines, newspapers, and directories on any topic you request and will email you the results. ✓**DELPHI**→*go* REF LIB $$

Reference Center Information on almost any topic. Searches several databases by subject. ✓**GENIE**→*keyword* REF CENTER $$

Schooling

The explosion in home study for both children and adults is supported and inspired by

what's on the Net. AOL's **Interactive Education Services** is a model for continuing education in a technologically adapting world. No more borrowed offices and classrooms. Instead, take what you want when you want: online lectures, daily message-board and email support, and private libraries of supplementary materials. The **Academic Assistance Center**, also on AOL, is designed to help students with their "real" classes. This includes tutoring sessions for all major academic subjects, private sessions by appointment, and message boards that provide help at all hours.

At school—downloaded from AOL's Graphic Arts & CAD Forum.

On the Net

Across the board

Apple Classrooms of Tomorrow Provides information on Apple Classrooms of Tomorrow (ACOT), a long-term research project sponsored by Apple Computer that explores the effect of interactive computer technologies on education; offers The Bering Bridge, an international link between children and teachers in the USA and the CIS; provides a software library of lessons and educational programs; and promotes the Hyperstudio Network,

which supports hypermedia learning applications—order the applications, download demos, and discuss the products. ✓ **AMERICA ONLINE**→*keyword* AED

Education Covers all aspects of modern education. ✓ **RELAYNET**→ *number* 320

Education and Related Discussions General discussion about private and public education. ✓ **FIDONET**→*tag* EDUCATION

Education BB Regular topics include Adult Education, Curriculum, Gifted & Talented, Home Schooling, Preschool, and Reform. ✓ **PRODIGY**→*jump* EDUCATION BB

Education Forum Provides contacts and information for teachers, parents, students, and other edu-

cation professionals. Among the topics are the use of computers in the schools, home education, and multimedia applications. Libraries carry ERIC digests, reading lists, and standardized-test preparation materials. 🖼💬 ✓ **COMPUSERVE**→*go* EDFORUM

Education RoundTable Boards for teachers, home-schooling parents, students, and librarians. Learn about conferences, get help on the SATs, find a pen pal, or discuss education policy. Includes a library of software. 💬 ✓ **GENIE**→ *keyword* ERT

The Empire Internet Schoolhouse The Assembly Hall offers discussion boards for educators; the Library & Internet Reference Tools section gives access to ERIC databases, the Daily Report Card News Service, the U.S. Federal

Register, the Library of Congress, and CNN classroom guides; the Academic Wings section includes world news, dictionaries, and Shakespearean texts. It is broken down into traditional school subjects—foreign languages, for instance. And you can also read and post to the Kidlink lists or get information on the Kidlink 94 project. Furthermore, there are sections for career-guidance and school-reform issues. ✓ **INTER-NET**→*telnet* NYSERNET.ORG→EMPIRE/ <NONE>

misc.education (NG) Discussions about education in general, from "Is it possible to teach algebra to a 6-year-old?" to the merits of memorization. ✓ **USENET**

Sendit (BBS) Easy-to-use system features more than 200 K12Net conferences, local education-related conferences (Nodak), the Kidlink mailing lists, a pen-pals area, and links with university card catalogues and the NASA Spacelink system. The Online Discovery section carries weekly lesson plans on topics such as astronomy. The Electronic Classroom section offers resource guides (e.g., CNN guides), education newsletters, and Internet Classroom projects. 701-237-3383 ✓ **INTERNET**→*telnet* SENDIT.NODAK.EDU→BBS/SENDIT2ME FREE

The Society of Dead Teachers (ML) A free-ranging discussion of education. ✓ **INTERNET**→*email* LIST SERV@IUBVM.BITNET ✍ *Type in message body:* SUB DTS-L <YOUR FULL NAME>

Adult literacy

Adult Literacy Forum Offers networking for literacy workers, ideas, and resources to teach adult new readers. There is also a master

calendar of adult-literacy conferences. ☺✍ ✓ **AMERICA ONLINE**→ *keyword* READ

Digital education

ACSOFT-L (ML) Discussions about using software (simulations, hypermedia, drills, etc.) in academic environments, from courseware development to faculty acceptance to available resources and more. ✓ **INTERNET**→*email* LIST SERV@WUVMD.BITNET ✍ *Type in message body:* SUB ACSOFT-L <YOUR FULL NAME>

Ednet (ML) Discussion concerning the educational potential of the Internet, especially for those in the five-college area in Massachusetts. Includes topics relevant to K–12 educators as well as those in higher education. ✓ **INTERNET**→ *email* LISTSERV@NIC.UMASS.EDU ✍*Type in message body:* SUBSCRIBE EDNET <YOUR FULL NAME>

MBU-L (ML) Megabyte University —forum for planning "electronic universities" of the future. ✓ **INTERNET**→*email* LISTSERV@TTUVM1.BITNET ✍ *Type in message body:* SUBSCRIBE MBU-L <YOUR FULL NAME>

The Multimedia Exchange
Oriented toward teachers and education. Provides examples of multimedia, tools for teachers to build their own multimedia databases, and an idea exchange with the Smithsonian's National Demonstration Library, a leader in the field of interactive video. ✓ **AMER-ICA ONLINE**→*keyword* MULTIMEDIA

Newedu-L (ML) "What are the new paradigms in education and how can they be implemented?" The mailing list considers issues such as artificial intelligence, independent learning, effects of tech-

nology, etc. ✓ **INTERNET**→*email* LIST SERV@VM.USC.EDU ✍ *Type in message body:* SUBSCRIBE NEWEDU-L <YOUR FULL NAME>

Distance education

alt.education.bangkok (NG) Information about the Bangkok distance-education project. ✓ **USE-NET**

alt.education.distance (NG) Discussion about distance education, including educational resources on the Net. ✓ **USENET**

DEOS-L (ML) Intended to disseminate information and requests about distance education as well as promote communication among distance educators. Sponsored by the American Center for the Study of Distance Education. ✓ **INTERNET** →*email* LISTSERV@PSUVM.PSU.EDU ✍ *Type in message body:* SUBSCRIBE DEOS-L <YOUR FULL NAME>

Edista (ML) A forum for discussing distance education; sponsored by the University of Santiago (Chile). ✓ **INTERNET**→ *email* LISTSERV@USACHVM1.BITNET ✍ *Type in message body:* SUBSCRIBE EDISTA <YOUR FULL NAME>

Diversity

Divers-L (ML) Devoted to bringing diverse ethnic perspectives to academic needs and programs— e.g., lectures, exhibits, etc. ✓ **INTER-NET**→*email* LISTSERV@PSUVM.PSU.EDU ✍ *Type in message body:* SUBSCRIBE DIVERS-L <YOUR FULL NAME>

Online access

Computer Assisted Learning Center (CALC) An online college for students of all ages. Take courses conducted in real time on a variety of subjects with professional educators from around the nation. Grades and certificates are given and students may study toward a degree at Edison State College. ⊕💬 ✓**GENIE**→*keyword* CALC

Electronic University Network Offers college courses for credit that can be used toward associate, bachelor, or graduate degrees. Provides free mini-courses to familiarize AOL members with taking online classes. 💬 ✓**AMERICA ONLINE**→*keyword* EUN

Interactive Education Services Learn basic Japanese or study the Arab-Israeli conflict. Register for nonaccredited online courses in the summer, fall, winter, or spring. New course selections are offered each semester and run for about eight weeks. Each class offers live lectures, daily message-board support, and libraries of materials. ⊕💬 ✓**AMERICA ONLINE**→ *keyword* IES $20/CLASS

University of Phoenix Accredited business-degree programs online. ✓**COMPUSERVE**→*go* UP

Research

ASCD Online Provides resources for teachers and the public about the Association for Supervision and Curriculum Development, a nonprofit, nonpartisan international organization devoted to improving schools, early childhood education, and student achievement. Resources include a catalog of their books and audio- and videotapes. ✓**AMERICA ONLINE**→*keyword* ASCD

AskERIC Send a question about education—from lesson plans to student discipline—and the ERIC

Karel Appel's Questioning Child— *from CompuServe's Student's Forum.*

staff will respond within 48 hours. ✓**INTERNET**→*email* ASKERIC@ERICIR. SYR.EDU

Educational Research Forum Sponsored by the American Educational Research Association, the forum allows researchers and educators to discuss and share the latest research news. Discussions range from distance education to teaching methods. ⊕💬 ▦ ✓**COMPUSERVE**→*go* EDRESEARCH

The Educator's Center Enter a topic on subjects ranging from child abuse to teaching aids, and a number of databases are searched, including those of the U.S. Department of Education, the American Psychological Association, Ulrich's Periodicals, and the University of Leeds. ✓**GENIE**→*keyword* EDUCATORS $$

ERIC AOL offers information about ERIC (including a number of ways to access it on the Internet), while CompuServe provides the two ERIC databases—

Resources in Education and the Current Index to Journals in Education, which includes article abstracts from more than 750 professional journals. The FTP site offers hundreds of ERIC digests on topics such as Spelling, The Only Child, and Student Financial Aid and Women, while the telnet site is a searchable database of articles. ✓**AMERICA ONLINE** ...→*keyword* ERIC ✓**COMPUSERVE**→*go* ERIC $$ ✓**INTERNET**→*ftp* NIC.SURA.NET →ANONYMOUS/<YOUR EMAIL ADDRESS> →pub/databases/ERIC ...→*telnet* SKLIB. USASK.CA→SONIA/<NONE>→ 4/1

IQuest Education InfoCenter Provides access to databases with information on education theory, research, testing, and vocational education. ✓**COMPUSERVE**→*go* IQEDUCATION $$

JTE-L (ML) Electronic version of the scholarly print publication the *Journal of Technology Education.* ✓**INTERNET**→*email* LISTSERV@VTVM1. CC.VT.EDU ✎*Type in message body:* SUBSCRIBE JTE-L <YOUR FULL NAME>

NEA Public Forum Sponsored by the National Education Association and open to teachers, parents, and students. Offers news releases from NEA headquarters, an attorney-referral program, a message board, The Daily Report Card—an eight-page online newsletter on current education news —and fact sheets outlining current debates in education. AOL offers a special membership arrangement that allows for unlimited access to this forum with no hourly charges, while regular rates apply to all other AOL services. ⊕💬 ▦ ✓**AMERICA ONLINE**→*keyword* NEA PUBLIC

The Teachers' Newsstand Includes current articles from leading education journals, such as the *American School Board Journal* and the *Education News Summary*. Also includes an Educational Magazines database, with information on more than 300 related journals, magazines, and newsletters. 🖼 ✓**AMERICA ONLINE** →*keyword* TNEWS

Special needs

alt.education.disabled (NG) Discussions about the learning experiences of the disabled. ✓**USENET**

IBM Special Needs Forum Offers information on all aspects of special education, including K–12, adult literacy, bilingual education, vocational education, and the use of IBM computers in these areas. 💬 ✓**COMPUSERVE**→*go* IBMSPECIAL

Special Education Topics Created for parents, it also includes handicapped adults, educators, and anyone else interested in the issues. ✓**FIDONET**→*tag* SPECIAL_ED

Women

Educom-W (ML) Forum for discussing education and technology issues of interest to women. ✓**INTERNET**→*email* LISTSERV@BITNIC. EDCOM.ORG ✍ *Type in message body:* SUB EDUCOM-W <YOUR FULL NAME>

Fist (ML) Devoted to discussion of science, technology, and feminism. Topics range from critiques of science and the development of a feminist science to how feminists teach science. ✓**INTERNET**→*email* LISTSERV@DAWN.HAMPSHIRE.EDU ✍ *Type in message body:* SUB FIST <YOUR FULL NAME>

Gifted children

Tag-L (ML) A forum to discuss programs for gifted and talented children. Issues to be discussed are resources, research, etc. ✓**INTERNET** →*email* LISTSERV@NDSUVM1.BITNET ✍ *Type in message body:* SUBSCRIBE TAG-L <YOUR FULL NAME>

Home schooling

Bloomunit BBS for Homeschool Families (BBS) Family-oriented home-schooling information. Features a library of educational shareware. 407-687-8712 FREE

Home-Ed (ML) "Welcomes everyone interested in educating their children at home, whatever the reasons." Topics include curricula-based home schooling, the "unschooling" approach, and others. ✓**INTERNET**→*email* HOME-ED-REQUEST @WORLD.STD.COM ✍*Subscribe by request*

HomeEducation Discussion about all aspects of home education. ✓**SMARTNET**→*tag* HOMEEDUCATION

Home Schooling Provides contacts and references for families interested in, or participating in, home schooling. Topics include where to find materials and which books to use. ✓**RELAYNET**→*number* 332

Homeschooling Support Curricula, questions, and answers about teaching your children at home. ✓**FIDONET**→*tag* HOMESCHL

Kids & computers

misc.kids.computer (NG) Forums for discussing the use of computers by children and resources on the Net. ✓**USENET**

Kids networks

CNEDUC-L (ML) Designed to encourage children to use the networks. ✓**INTERNET**→*email* LISTSERV@ TAMVM1.TAMU.EDU ✍*Type in message body:* SUBSCRIBE CNEDUC-L <YOUR FULL NAME>

The Electronic Schoolhouse In this forum, a teacher and her class can connect with a class in another state to work on projects together and share information; a student can connect with a pen pal from another country via the Global Links board; the Schoolhouse Calendar lists upcoming events, projects, and classroom connections; the Home Schools board assists parents schooling their children at home with ongoing curricula, teaching methods, and religious home-schooling discussions; and the Intergenerational Links board hooks up students with senior citizens for history and other discussions. ☺💬 ✓**AMERICA ONLINE**→*keyword* ESH

FrEdMail Network A network of BBSs run by K–12 schools. Designed to promote learning, reading, and writing skills in students and facilitate the exchange of ideas and materials between teachers. Workshop announcements, job postings, and education legislation are posted for teachers. The network is also sponsoring (for a fee) Usenet-style education newsgroups. Write to the email address for information about a local FrEdMail board near you or dial up one of the following boards: 501-569-3268/909-986-9890/215-233-0240 ✓**INTERNET**→ *email* FRED@ACME.FRED.ORG ✓CHECK LOCAL BULLETIN BOARDS

Kidlink (ML) News about the various Kidlink Internet projects and

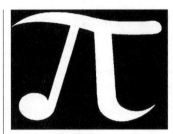

3.14159265—from CompuServe's Science/Math Education Forum.

discussion lists and how to subscribe to them. Kidlink sponsors annual projects (Kidforum) and general discussion lists (Kidcafe) in which children 10 to 15 years old participate. Other lists are geared toward the parent or educator. ✓**INTERNET**→*email* LISTSERV@VM1. NODAK.EDU ✍*Type in message body:* SUB KIDLINK <YOUR FULL NAME>

K12Net (NG) Dozens of conferences from K12Net, the worldwide network of school-based BBSs. Students and teachers practice a foreign language, discuss homework and lesson plans, and chat. Includes K12.ED.MATH, K12.ED. LANG.ART, and K12.LANG.RUSSIAN. Available both as newsgroups (with Usenet groups) and BBS conferences. ✓CHECK LOCAL BULLETIN BOARDS ✓**USENET**

Kids resources

CNN Newsroom Online Continually updated news provided by Turner Educational Systems, Inc. Teachers can order classroom guides for Turner programs. The CNN Teacher Exchange is a meeting place for teachers; for younger AOL members, CNN Under 21 is a place to discuss the news; the Newroom Lesson & Resource Exchange offers files ranging from images of the world's flags to a report on endangered species. ▦ ✓**AMERICA ONLINE**→*keyword* CNN

Educational TV & Radio Forum Provides an educational TV-and-radio database with detailed information on thousands of children's programs on television and radio; a calendar listing events, public-service projects, relevant legislation, international media awards and more; a bulletin announcing upcoming children's programs; and study guides to supplement educational programming—e.g., one based on the Peter Jennings news special *Prejudice: Answering Children's Questions,* and a chronology poster to accompany the Lincoln television special. ▦ ✓**AMERICA ONLINE** →*keyword* KIDSNET

The Learning Adventure Computer Club Fun, educational software at a discount. 🖱 ✓**PRODIGY**→ *jump* LEARNING ADVENTURE

National Geographic A new interactive feature each month about the region focused on in the current issue of *National Geographic.* World problems and possible solutions are covered. The Viewpoint area allows you to express an opinion, and Other Features takes you back to previous destinations. ✓**PRODIGY**→*jump* NATIONAL GEOGRAPHIC

National Geographic Online Sponsored by the National Geographic Society, it offers articles from *National Geographic, Traveler,* and *World* magazines; information on the National Geographic Kids Network—a science curriculum for grades 4 through 6; the Geographic Store; a Geographic Television library that includes teacher resource guides for NG specials (e.g., *Voices of Leningrad and Bali, Masterpiece of the Gods*) and a chat forum to discuss the specials; and the Geography Education Program, which includes the Talk About Geography Teaching bulletin board and libraries of articles, curriculum resources, and teaching materials. 📠 ⊕ ⊕💬 ✓**AMERICA ONLINE** →*keyword* GEOGRAPHIC

National Public Radio Outreach Provides educational guides such as "The Prejudice Puzzle," which explores the impact of prejudice on young people; newsletters; and brochures about specific NPR programs as well as press releases, programming updates and schedules, and member-station listings. 📠 ✓**AMERICA ONLINE** →*keyword* NPR

Schoolware A description of topselling education software. ✓**PRODIGY**→*jump* SCHOOLWARE

Software Central's Educational BBS (BBS) Carries educational shareware for children, adults, and teachers. 508-537-5148 FREE

Students

Academic Assistance Center An umbrella forum for all the AOL student services. Offers students of all ages help with homework, study skills, and exam preparation. For live chat with teachers, attend the Homework Help sessions scheduled a couple of times a night (sometimes for specific subjects and other times for any subject) or post on the subject-specific boards, including Geometry and Russian and Business Management. If you need an immediate live session with a teacher, use the Teacher Pager (*keyword* TEACHER PAGER), and AOL will try to set one up. For help with research papers, post on one of the Online Research Service boards. The Study Skills

The Lecture, *by Berthe Morisot— downloaded from uxa.ecn.bgu.edu.*

Service (*keyword* STUDY) offers 24 lessons on improving those skills, and the Exam Prep Center (*keyword* EXAM PREP) provides sample tests on a of variety subjects and study sessions during midterms and finals. Barrons' Booknotes (*keyword* BARRONS)—online plot summaries and analyses for great works of literature, from the *Aeneid* to *Catch 22* to *Wuthering Heights*—and Kids Online (*keyword* KOOL) can also be accessed from this forum. ⊕💬 ✓**AMERICA ONLINE**→*keyword* HOMEWORK

Newton For teachers, students, and scientists. Features AskA Scientist message boards; forums for teachers with information on experiments, field trips, videos, and books; the Kidsphere mailing list, where students can engage in talk with other students; a hobbies exchange; and private sections reserved for specific schools. 708-2352-8241 ✓**INTERNET**→*telnet* NEWTON.DEP.ANL.GOV→BBS/<NONE>

Science/Math Education Forum Serves science students and educators with software and discussion. Specialties include practice problems for the science and math college boards. ⊕💬 ✓**COMPUSERVE**→*go* SCIENCE

Students' Forum Student-to-student discussion about a range of subjects. Boards for all ages and

libraries of software, including geography or *Alice in Wonderland* games, clip art, and typing tutors. ⊞📱 ⊕💬 ✓**COMPUSERVE**→*go* STUFO

Theories

The Learning List (ML) Forum for discussing how to improve the learning process for children. The philosophy here is that "humans as a species have an innate ability to learn, and that current methods of 'teaching,' 'education,' and 'schooling' serve primarily to thwart or diminish that ability." ✓**INTERNET**→*email* LEARNING-REQUEST @SEA.EAST.SUN.COM ✍*Subscribe by request*

Teachers

By, for, and generally all about teachers. From depart-ment chairmen (**Chairs-L**) to teaching assistants (**T-Assist**), from federal education policy initiatives (**The Education Policy Analysis Forum**) to politically correct teaching methods (**World-L**), the Net is one of the largest info banks and kaffeeklatsches for teachers of all affinities and passions. Try **Teachers' Information Network** on AOL for some of the broadest coverage of the profession.

Across the board

Community Colleges (ML) Discussion group for administration, staff, and faculty at two-year colleges. ✓**INTERNET**→*email* LISTSERV@ UKCC.UKY.EDU ✍ *Type in message body:* SUB COMMCOLL <YOUR FULL NAME>

The Education Policy Analysis Forum (ML) For educators to discuss and share their ideas. Includes analysis of major policy decisions, journal abstracts, job and conference announcements, policy papers, and more. ✓**INTERNET**→ *email* LISTSERV@ASUACAD.BITNET ✍ *Type in message body:* SUBSCRIBE EDPOLYAN <YOUR FULL NAME>

Educator For discussing issues of interest to educators. ✓**FIDONET**→ *tag* EDUCATOR

The professor—downloaded from CompuServe's Student Forum

STLHE-L (ML) Discussions about teaching and learning in higher education in Canada. Includes the Society of Teaching and Learning in Higher Education newsletter. ✓**INTERNET**→*email* LISTSERV@UNB.BIT NET ✍ *Type in message body:* SUB STLHE-L <YOUR FULL NAME>

Teachers' Forum Includes weekly live conferences—up to six a week—for teachers, parents, and others interested in education on issues like merit pay, children at risk, and team teaching. Special sections are devoted to computers in the schools and parent-teacher contact. ⊕💬 ✓**AMERICA ONLINE**→ *keyword* TTALK

Teachers' Information Network Includes news items from teachers' magazines, a resource question area with answers from education experts, a multimedia area, an idea exchange, an electronic schoolhouse, online seminars, and access to the other educational forums on AOL. Check out the Convention Center for notices of upcoming conferences, take a class at Teacher's University, where teachers teach teachers, and explore the Lesson Plan libraries, where you can get materials from a college-level critical-thinking course or an elementary-school music lesson plan. 🖳 ⊕💬 ✓**AMERICA ONLINE**→ *keyword* TIN

Administrators

Chairs-L (ML) Covers the issues and difficulties faced by department chairs in academic institutions, from personnel matters to tenure. ✓**INTERNET**→*email* CHAIRS-REQUEST@ACC.FAU.EDU ✍ *Type in message body:* SUBSCRIBE CHAIRS-L <YOUR FULL NAME>

Finaid-L (ML) Information exchange among college administrators involved with financial-aid issues. Policies, professional practices, and job positions are also covered. ✓**INTERNET**→*email* LIST SERV@PSUVM.BITNET ✍ *Type in message body:* SUB FINAID-L <YOUR FULL NAME>

Advisers

ACADV (ML) Discussion group for academic advisers at colleges and universities. ✓**INTERNET**→*email* LISTSERV@NDSUVM1.BITNET ✍ *Type in message body:* SUB ACADV <YOUR FULL NAME>

Arts

Facxch-L (ML) Discussions for college educators in art, architecture, and design. ✓**INTERNET**→ *email* LISTSERV@PSUVM.PSU.EDU ✍ *Type in message body:* SUB FACXCH-L <YOUR FULL NAME>

Humanities

Crewrt-L (ML) Forum for discussing the teaching of creative writing at colleges and universities, including classroom strategies, its role in the curriculum, the history of creative-writing programs, etc. Members often share their own writing. ✓**INTERNET**→*email* LIST SERV@UMCVMB.MISSOURI.EDU ✍ *Type in message body:* SUB CREWRT-L <YOUR FULL NAME>

Scolt (ML) For those interested in foreign-language education. ✓**INTERNET**→*email* LISTSERV@CATFISH. VALDOSTA.PEACHNET.EDU ✍ *Type in message body:* SUBSCRIBE SCOLT <YOUR FULL NAME>

Slart-L (ML) For educators interested in second-language acquisition. Share advice and research, submit papers for constructive criticism, or discuss any issue relevant to language acquisition. ✓**INTERNET**→*email* LISTSERV@CUNYVM. CUNY.EDU ✍ *Type in message body:* SUBSCRIBE SLART-L <YOUR FULL NAME>

Math & sciences

Environmental Studies List (ML) Information exchange about environmental-studies programs, including discussions about curriculum and the balance between various academic fields within ES programs. ✓**INTERNET**→*email* LIST SERV@BROWNVM.BITNET ✍ *Type in message body:* SUB ENVST-L <YOUR FULL NAME>

Phys-L (ML) For college physics teachers. Topics include using the networks to teach courses, innovative laboratory experiments, etc. ✓**INTERNET**→*email* LISTSERV@UWF. BITNET ✍ *Type in message body:* SUB-SCRIBE PHYS-L <YOUR FULL NAME>

Software and Aids for Teaching of Mathematics Software, newsletters, reprints, and other material to assist math teachers. ✓**INTERNET**→ *ftp* WUARCHIVE.WUSTL. EDU→ANONYMOUS/<YOUR EMAIL ADDRESS>→edu/math

Professional

Jesse (ML) Forum for discussing the teaching of library and information science. Topics range from curricula to methodology to computing as a research tool. ✓**INTER-NET**→*email* LISTSERV@ARIZVM1.CCIT. ARIZONA.EDU ✍ *Type in message body:* SUBSCRIBE JESSE <YOUR FULL NAME>

Journet (ML) Covers topics of interest to journalists and journalism educators. ✓**INTERNET**→*email* LIST SERV@QUCDN.BITNET ✍ *Type in message body:* SUBSCRIBE JOURNET <YOUR FULL NAME>

Social sciences

PSRT-L (ML) For political scientists and educators to share research and teaching techniques, discuss the trends in the discipline of political science, and post job and conference announcements. ✓**INTERNET**→*email* LISTSERV@UMCVMB. BITNET ✍ *Type in message body:* SUB PSRT-L <YOUR FULL NAME>

TIPS (ML) Information and idea exchange about teaching in the psychological sciences. Conference announcements are also welcome. ✓**INTERNET**→*email* LISTSERV@FRE.FSU. UMD.EDU ✍ *Type in message body:* SUBSCRIBE TIPS <YOUR FULL NAME>

Wmst-L (ML) Forum for discussing women's-studies issues, including teaching and researching. Conferences may be publicized, papers announced or requested, curriculum proposals and bibliographies shared, etc. ✓**INTERNET**→*email* LISTSERV@UMDD. UMD.EDU ✍ *Type in message body:*

SUBSCRIBE WMST-L <YOUR FULL NAME>

World-L (ML) Theory, methodology, and strategy for teaching world history from a non-Eurocentric perspective. ✓**INTERNET**→ *email* LISTSERV@UBVM.CC.BUFFALO.EDU ✍ *Type in message body:* SUB WORLD-L <YOUR FULL NAME>

Teaching assistants

T-Assist (ML) Chatty forum for university teaching assistants to discuss their roles as teachers and students. Topics range from teaching methods to balancing the roles of student and teacher. ✓**INTERNET** →*email* LISTSERV@UNMVMA.UNM.EDU ✍ *Type in message body:* SUB T-ASSIST <YOUR FULL NAME>

CYBERNOTES

"My first class starts in an hour. I've got a clean white shirt with a color illustration of a purple dog baying under a helix sun, and the inscription 'Mad Dog.' I've got fresh course outlines with only a few typos. I haven't got my text, because the plant people can't find three boxes of my stuff they stored in February. But I hear the overture, the curtain's about to go up, I shall be brilliant. They'll love me. Or maybe I'll just cope--good wishes to all the rest of you..."

—from **Crewrt-L**

Appendices

Netted!

A selection of the best, funniest, worst, sexiest...

Absolutely do not miss

Cyberion City ✓INTERNET→*telnet* MICHAEL.AI.MIT.EDU→GUEST/<NONE>

The Internet Hunt (alt.internet.services) (NG) ✓USENET

Project Gutenberg ✓INTERNET ...→*ftp* MRCNEXT.CSO.UIUC.EDU→ ANONYMOUS/<YOUR EMAIL ADDRESS>→ pub/etext ...→*ftp* QUAKE.THINK.COM →ANONYMOUS/<YOUR EMAIL ADDRESS> →pub/etext ...→*wais* proj-gutenberg.src

University of Wisconsin-Parkside Music Archive ✓INTERNET→*ftp* FTP.UWP.EDU→ANONYMOUS/<YOUR EMAIL ADDRESS>→pub/ music

Best board for women

Echo (BBS) ⊞◨ ☺☹ 212-989-8411 ✓INTERNET→*telnet* ECHONYC.COM $19.95–$52.43/MONTH

The best FAQs

alt.hemp (NG) ✓USENET ✓INTERNET→*ftp* RTFM.MIT.EDU→ANONYMOUS/<YOUR EMAIL ADDRESS>→pub/ usenet/alt.hemp

alt.sex (NG) ✓USENET ✓INTERNET →*ftp* RTFM.MIT.EDU→ANONYMOUS/ <YOUR EMAIL ADDRESS>→pub/usenet/ alt-sex

rec.arts.startrek * (NG) ✓USE-NET ✓INTERNET→*ftp* RTFM.MIT.EDU→ ANONYMOUS/<YOUR EMAIL ADDRESS>→ pub/usenet/rec.arts.startrek.misc

Better than *Penthouse*

alt.binaries.pictures.erotica (NG) ✓USENET

Electric Eye BBS (BBS) ⊞◨ ☺☹ 212-673-0301

Better than *The New York Times*

Executive News Service ▦ ✓COMPUSERVE→*go* ENS $$

Internet Relay Chat (IRC) Especially #report and #discuss. ☺☹ ✓INTERNET

Usenet (NG) ✓USENET

Better than Howard Stern

alt.flame (NG) ✓USENET

Uprooted Netters' haven

Prodigy Refugees Forum An AOL forum for those who've left Prodigy. Find your former Prodigy buddies and learn about AOL. ☺☹ ✓AMERICA ONLINE→*keyword* PRODIGY

Positively the grossest

alt.binaries.pictures.tasteless (NG) ✓USENET

ROFL: Roll on floor laughing

alt.alien.visitors (NG) ✓USENET

The hardest list to unsubscribe from

Hong Kong News (ML) ▦ ✓INTERNET→*email* REQUEST@AHKCUS. ORG ✍*Subscribe by request*

The hottest hackers' hangout

MindVox (BBS) 212-989-1550/212-989-4141 ✓INTERNET→*telnet* MINDVOX. PHANTOM.COM→GUEST/<NONE>

Kelly's favorite

alt.fan.lemurs (NG) ✓USENET

Popular newsgroups

alt.atheism (NG) ✓USENET

alt.binaries.pictures.erotica (NG) ✓USENET

alt.folklore.urban (NG) ✓USENET

alt.sex.stories (NG) ✓USENET

misc.kids (NG) ✓USENET

rec.arts.movies (NG) ✓USENET

rec.arts.tv.soaps (NG) ✓USENET

Netted

soc.culture.indian (NG) ✓USENET

soc.motss (NG) ✓USENET

soc.singles (NG) ✓USENET

The most popular spots on the commercial services

America Online

BikeNet ✓AMERICA ONLINE→*keyword* BIKENET

The Grateful Dead Forum 🖳 ◉💬 ✓AMERICA ONLINE→*keyword* DEAD

Time Online ✓AMERICA ONLINE→*keyword* TIME

BIX

Amiga Exchange ✓BIX→*conference* AMIGA.EXCHANGE

Internet ✓BIX→*conference* INTERNET

Newsbytes News Network 🖳 ✓BIX→*conference* NEWSBYTES

CompuServe

Desktop Publishing Forum ◉💬 ✓COMPUSERVE→*go* DTPFORUM

Executive News Service 🖳 ✓COMPUSERVE→*go* ENS $$

Human Sexuality Database and Forums ◉💬 ✓COMPUSERVE →*go* HUMAN

Delphi

Close Encounters ◉💬 ✓DELPHI →*go* GR CLO

The Gallery of Graphics ✓DELPHI→*go* COM GRAPH $2/HOUR

Internet Services 🖳 ⊞◻ ◉💬 ✓DELPHI→*go* INTERNET

GEnie

LiveWire Chat Lines ◉💬 ✓GE-

NIE→*keyword* CHAT

Multiplayer Games Round-Table ⊞◻ ✓GENIE→*keyword* MPGRT

Science Fiction and Fantasy RoundTables ◉💬 ✓GENIE→*keyword* SFRT

Prodigy

Games BB ⊞◻ ✓PRODIGY→*jump* GAMES BB

Health and Lifestyles BB ✓PRODIGY→*jump* LIFESTYLES BB

Teens BB ✓PRODIGY→*jump* TEENS BB

Monster FTP sites

The Bloom-Picayune FTP Server at MIT ✓INTERNET→*ftp* RTFM.MIT.EDU→ANONYMOUS/<YOUR EMAIL ADDRESS>

The Gatekeeper Archives ✓INTERNET→*ftp* GATEKEEPER.DEC.COM →ANONYMOUS/<YOUR EMAIL ADDRESS>

Library of Congress Archives ✓INTERNET→*ftp* SEQ1.LOC.GOV→ ANONYMOUS/<YOUR EMAIL ADDRESS>

Mississippi State Archives ✓INTERNET→*ftp* RA.MSSTATE.EDU→ ANONYMOUS/<YOUR EMAIL ADDRESS>

Netcom FTP Server ✓INTERNET→*ftp* FTP.NETCOM.COM→ANONYMOUS/<YOUR EMAIL ADDRESS>

The Oak Software Repository ✓INTERNET→*ftp* OAK.OAKLAND.EDU→ANONYMOUS/<YOUR EMAIL ADDRESS>

Princeton University's FTP Server ✓INTERNET→*ftp* PRINCETON.EDU→ANONYMOUS/<YOUR EMAIL ADDRESS>

Rutgers University's FTP Archives ✓INTERNET→*ftp* QUARTZ.RUTGERS.EDU→ANONYMOUS/<YOUR EMAIL ADDRESS>

Stanford's Macintosh Archives ✓INTERNET→*ftp* SUMEX-AIM.STANFORD.EDU→ANONYMOUS/<YOUR EMAIL ADDRESS>

Sunsite's FTP Server ✓INTERNET →*ftp* SUNSITE.UNC.EDU→ANONYMOUS/<YOUR EMAIL ADDRESS>

The Typhoon FTP Server at Berkeley ✓INTERNET→*ftp* OCF.BERKELEY.EDU→ANONYMOUS/<YOUR EMAIL ADDRESS>

University of Michigan's Electronic Texts Archive ✓INTERNET→*ftp* ETEXT.ARCHIVE.UMICH.EDU→ANONYMOUS/<YOUR EMAIL ADDRESS>

University of Michigan's Software Archives ✓INTERNET →*ftp* ARCHIVE.UMICH.EDU→ANONYMOUS/<YOUR EMAIL ADDRESS>

UUNET Archives ✓INTERNET→*ftp* FTP.UU.NET→ANONYMOUS/<YOUR EMAIL ADDRESS>

Washington University's Archives ✓INTERNET→*ftp* WUARCHIVE.WUSTL.EDU→ANONYMOUS/<YOUR EMAIL ADDRESS>

Favorite finger sites

Billboard Chart Includes U.S. Top Pop Singles, U.S. Top Pop Albums, Top Adult Contemporary Singles, Top Rhythm and Blues Singles, Top Modern Rock Tracks, and the #1 Rap Single. ✓INTERNET→*finger* BUCKMR@RPI.EDU

Daily Summary of Solar Geophysical Activity Daily solar- and geophysical-activity statistics and summaries. ✓**INTERNET**→ *finger* DAILY@XI.ULETH.CA

Daily Updates The phase of the moon, number of days until Christmas, birthdays in history, sports schedules, music lyrics, and more. ✓**INTERNET**→*finger* COPI@ODD-JOB.UCHICAGO.EDU

Earthquake Information Recent earthquake statistics. ✓**INTER-NET**→*finger* QUAKE@GEOPHYS.WASH-INGTON.EDU

NASA News Information on happenings at NASA. ✓**INTERNET** →*finger* NASANEWS@SPACE.MIT.EDU

Nielsen Ratings Interested in what TV show received the best ratings last week? Get the latest Nielsen ratings. ✓**INTERNET**→*finger* NORMG@HALCYON.HALCYON.COM

Soda Machine Check on the status of the drinks in the soda machine. Seriously. ✓**INTERNET**→ *finger* DRINK@DRINK.CSH.RIT.EDU

Star Trek Quotes Get your daily fix of *Star Trek* quotes. ✓**IN-TERNET**→*finger* FRANKLIN@UG.CS.DAL.CA

Tropical Storm Forecast Find out about the status of hurricanes and tropical storms. ✓**INTERNET** →*finger* FORECAST@TYPHOON.ATMOS.COLOSTATE.EDU

Archie

ANS Server ✓**INTERNET**→*telnet* ARCHIE.ANS.NET→ARCHIE/<NONE>

Australian Server ✓**INTERNET**→ *telnet* ARCHIE.FUNET.FI→ARCHIE/ <NONE>

Austrian Server ✓**INTERNET**→ *telnet* ARCHIE.EDVZ.UNI-LINZ.AC.AT→

ARCHIE/<NONE>

Canadian Server ✓**INTERNET**→ *telnet* ARCHIE.UQAM.CA→ARCHIE/ <NONE>

Finnish Server ✓**INTERNET**→*telnet* ARCHIE.FUNET.FI→ARCHIE/<NONE>

German Server ✓**INTERNET**→ *telnet* ARCHIE.TH-DARMSTADT.DE→ ARCHIE/<NONE>

Italian Server ✓**INTERNET**→*telnet* ARCHIE.UNIPI.IT→ARCHIE/<NONE>

Japanese Server ✓**INTERNET**→ *telnet* ARCHIE.KUIS.KYOTO-U.AC.JP→ ARCHIE/<NONE>

Korean Server ✓**INTERNET**→*telnet* ARCHIE.KR→ARCHIE/<NONE>

New Zealand Server ✓**INTER-NET**→ *telnet* ARCHIE.NZ→ARCHIE/ <NONE>

Rutgers Server ✓**INTERNET**→*telnet* ARCHIE.RUTGERS.EDU→ARCHIE/ <NONE>

Spanish Server ✓**INTERNET**→*telnet* ARCHIE.REDIRIS.ES→ARCHIE/ <NONE>

SURAnet Server ✓**INTERNET**→ *telnet* ARCHIE.SURA.NET→ARCHIE/ <NONE>

Swedish Server ✓**INTERNET**→ *telnet* ARCHIE.LUTH.SE→ARCHIE/ <NONE>

Swiss Server ✓**INTERNET**→*telnet* ARCHIE.SWITCH.CH→ARCHIE/<NONE>

Taiwanese Server ✓**INTERNET**→ *telnet* ARCHIE.NCU.EDU.TW→ARCHIE/ <NONE>

United Kingdom Server ✓**IN-TERNET**→*telnet* ARCHIE.DOC.IC.AC.UK

→ARCHIE/<NONE>

University of Nebraska Server ✓**INTERNET**→*telnet* ARCHIE.UNL.EDU→ARCHIE/<NONE>

Gopher

Australian Gopher ✓**INTERNET** → *telnet* INFO.ANU.EDU.AU→INFO/ <NONE>

Ecuadorian Gopher ✓**INTERNET** →*telnet* ECNET.EC→GOPHER/<NONE>

European Gopher ✓**INTERNET** → *telnet* GOPHER.EBONE.NET→GO-PHER/<NONE>

Japanese Gopher ✓**INTERNET**→ *telnet* GAN.NCC.GO.JP→GOPHER/ <NONE>

Michigan State University Gopher ✓**INTERNET**→*telnet* GO-PHER.MSU.EDU→GOPHER/<NONE>

South American Gopher ✓**IN-TERNET**→*telnet* TOLTEN.PUC.CL→ GOPHER/<NONE>

Sunsite Gopher ✓**INTERNET**→ *telnet* SUNSITE.UNC.EDU→GOPHER/ <NONE>

Swedish Gopher ✓**INTERNET**→ *telnet* GOPHER.CHALMERS.SE→GOPHER/ <NONE>

University of Illinois Gopher ✓**INTERNET**→*telnet* UX1.CSO.UIUC. EDU→GOPHER/<NONE>

University of Iowa Gopher ✓**INTERNET**→*telnet* PANDA.UIOWA.EDU →VT-100/<NONE>

University of Michigan Gopher ✓**INTERNET**→*telnet* CONSUL-TANT.MICRO.UMN.EDU→GOPHER/ <NONE>

Netted

Virginia University Gopher
✓**INTERNET**→*telnet* GOPHER.VIRGINIA.
EDU→GWIS/<NONE>

WAIS

Finnish WAIS Server ✓**INTERNET**
→*telnet* ARCHIE.FUNET.FI→WAIS/
WAIS/SWAIS

Quake WAIS Server ✓**INTERNET**
→*telnet* QUAKE.THINK.COM→WAIS/
<NONE>

Sunsite WAIS Server ✓**INTER-
NET**→*telnet* SUNSITE.UNC.EDU→SWAIS/
<NONE>

WWW

Finnish WWW Server ✓**INTER-
NET**→*telnet* INFO.FUNET.FI→WWW/
<NONE>

**New Jersey Institute of Tech-
nology WWW Server** ✓**INTER-
NET**→*telnet* WWW.NJIT.EDU→WWW/
<NONE>

Swiss WWW Server ✓**INTERNET**
→*telnet* INFO.CERN.CH→<NONE>/
<NONE>

**University of Kansas WWW
Server** ✓**INTERNET**→*telnet* UKANAIX.
CC.UKANS.EDU→WWW/<NONE>

Archie, Gopher, WAIS, and WWW information

Archie Information Directions
for using Archie. ✓**INTERNET**→
email FILESERV@SHSU.EDU ✍*Type in
message body:* SEND ME MAASINFO.
ARCHIE

comp.infosystems.gopher
(NG) Discussion and information

about gopher servers. The gopher
FAQ is frequently posted. ✓**USENET**

comp.infosystems.wais (NG)
Discussion and information about
using *WAIS* servers and clients.
WAIS FAQ is often posted.
✓**USENET**

comp.infosystems.www (NG)
Information, notices, and discussions about World Wide Web
servers and hypertext. ✓**USENET**

**Navigating the Internet:
Tools for Discovery** ✓**INTERNET**
→*email* LISTSERV@BITNIC.EDUCOM.EDU
✍*Type in message body:* GET INTERNET
UPDEGR_D CCNEWS F=MAIL

WAIS Discussion Discuss Wide
Area Information Servers. ✓**INTER-
NET**→*email* WAIS-DISCUSSION-REQUEST
@THINK.COM ✍*Subscribe by request*

More offline reading

Magazines

BBS Caller's Digest	*Net Guide*
Boardwatch Magazine	*Online Access*
Mondo	*Wired*

Books

Cruising Online by Lawrence J. Magid (1994)

Internet Basics by Steve Lambert and Walter Howe (1993)

The Internet Companion: A Beginner's Guide to Global Networking
by Tracy LaQuey and Jeanne C. Ryer (1992)

The Whole Internet: User's Guide and Catalog by Ed Krol (1992)

FidoNet BBSs

A selection of FidoNet BBSs in the United States and Canada by area code

United States

201

Hackers Guild BBS
546-0391
The Laboratory
342-5659
Third Stone From the Sun
666-7873
The Unconscious BBS
573-0556
The Wall
831-9562

202

The Baobab
296-9790
Cockpit!
728-0055
The CyberChurch BBS
269-2547
Europa BBS
588-0465
Powderhorn
562-8239

203

Alice's Restaurant
488-1115
HAL 9000
934-8432
Hippocampus BBS
484-4621
New England
949-0375
The Pipeline
878-5879

205

Batteries Included
264-8000
Cyclone
974-5123
Gulf Coast Net
666-0932
The Motherboard BBS
851-0503
The Timelords BBS
881-5657

206

The Budget Board
271-8613
Cornerstone
362-4283
Electric Eye
696-2851
The Looking Glass
535-8917
The Total Access Board
472-9611

207

Bangor ROS
942-7803
OCI Online Communications
990-3511

208

Boise Access BBS
331-1413
Future Times BBS
368-0365
Horizon BBS I
375-4073
The Idaho Root Cellar

362-1441
Mountain Echo's BBS
345-1446

209

The Anti Mystics BBS
431-1921
Bermuda Triangle
299-3899
Dark Side of the Moon
447-5515
Scream of the Butterfly
222-6879
Stingray!
434-4215

210

Brave New World
415-4366
Pretzel Logic
497-4552
Rampant Griffin
494-1142
The Ranger Station
672-2219
Revelation
341-1293

212

The Beginner's BBS
397-1576
BlueDog BBS
594-4425
City People BBS
255-6656
The Electric Eye BBS
477-0683
Thunderdome BBS
567-2509

FidoNet BBSs

213

Alex's Place
937-8734
Expiring Mind
874-9484
Hooray 4 Hollywood
653-7508
The Think Tank
464-4614
Zone One
653-4970

214

Critical Mass
617-0617
Lazarus
416-2797
Nibbles & Bytes
231-3841
Wanderland
258-1037
Wildfire
613-7795

215

Anterra Network
675-8239
Cyberdrome
923-8026
Ivy Garden
644-5314
Proteus BBS
743-8779
Threshold BBS
942-3874

216

Buggie Works
225-6130
The Forbidden Zone
228-7372
Infinite Earth BBS
848-0273
Night * Watch BBS
261-8552
The Pentagon
493-3522

217

CybreTransfre
384-4234
Lucid Dream
344-7773
Night Shift
431-4999
The Rift
522-1937
Tequila Sunset
355-9233

218

The Basement BBS
626-1109
The Board Not Taken
729-7026
Information Central
729-7072
Latenite's at the Lake
739-5752
NorthStar BBS
749-8809

219

Granny's Place
663-2349
The Great Beyond
233-8854
Mars' Hill
289-4641
Midwest Express
273-8789
Walden Pond
665-8767

301

Deaf New World
587-2278
The Moonrise BBS
593-9609
The Relative Connection
762-6813
The Shoreline BBS
946-2771
Tools for Knowledgeworkers
585-6697

302

Andromeda BBS
284-3178
The Hourglass BBS
678-1613
The Nut House
674-5496
Space Station Alpha
653-1458
TenderFeet's BBS
492-0701

303

Denver Area Net
779-4253
The Dinosaur Board
652-3595
Down To Earth BBS
530-0331
Sun Mountain BBS
665-6922
-=The Other Side=-
979-5376

304

The Black Hole BBS
727-5711
The Final Frontier
748-1377
The Hangout
296-3579
House of Pancakes
594-9169
Midnight Madness!
599-9308

305

Gammatown
572-7060
The Information Exchange
321-8235
The Jungle BBS
755-5872
Trek Land
370-0374
The Wild Thing
587-3496

307

Big Horn BBS
587-2510
The Enterprise
237-0800
Fascinations
382-6851
Ragged Edge
265-0612
Rocky Mountain Rendezvous
638-8506

308

Central CC
389-6495
Mid Plains CC
532-8306
The Panhandle Connection
487-5505
Towne Crier Systems
487-5390

309

Altered Paradise
681-9643
Ancient Mariner
755-5910
Data Stream
688-7713
Hacker's World
672-4427
Outer Chamber
692-7471

310

The Learning Curve BBS
371-0007
One World
372-0987
Paul Revere Network: Los Angeles
837-7818
The Q Continuum BBS
434-0401
The Spiders Web
416-9901

312

Chicago South
702-2119
Crossroads
587-8756
I CAN!
736-7434
OnLine ReSource
631-7393
Space_Oddity
477-0716

313

The Heart of the Sun
738-1068
The Razor's Edge
293-0879
SLiPPED DiSK
546-5950
The Tool Box
247-0094
What's ON
644-2444

314

The B.S. Box
427-4230
The Dataline
884-5167
Fido's Puppy
521-8197
The Gathering BBS
839-2978
Modem Madness Rehab Center
343-9556

315

Aether and Neither
451-5592
AirTime Network
768-8317
The Motherboard BBS
673-9415
Odyssey BBS
336-3297
Storm Watch BBS
445-5643

316

Fawnetta
721-1005
Jack Daniels Drinkers
265-1012
Kansas Konnektion
342-3967
Land of Awes
269-3172
The Panther
942-1975

317

Graffiti on the BBS Wall
448-2842
The Lightning Rod
449-4871
The mdbs Connection
447-6685
Portable Hole
575-6426
Software Zone
342-2094

318

The DarkSide of Telecomm
925-1104
Down In Da'Bayou
938-5166
L!nking R!ngs
449-4824
Lunatic Labs BBS
227-0575
My Secret Garden BBS
865-4503

319

Aardvark's Aquarium
438-1921
Devil's Fork
324-4211
Icarus
337-9878
Searchlight City
391-0658
Visionary
927-4474

FidoNet BBSs

401

The 95th Floor
941-7851
Art of the Possible
421-2218
Cerebral Babylon
435-3576
Connections BBS
658-3465
The Parthenon
823-8859

402

Another Boring BBS
397-5088
Church Chatters BBS
593-8863
Larry's Hot Tub
571-4316
The Legend BBS
438-2433
Ready Room: The Next Generation
691-0946

404

Afterburner BBS
531-0093
The Lion's Den BBS
536-3455
Phoenix StarFighter BBS
869-3410
Software Monster
967-6473
Son of Monster
967-2200

405

The Bat Cave
920-1162
Ironsides BBS
226-7126
Majik Shoppe BBS
482-2536
Monty Python's Flying BBS
524-3006
Strawberry Fields
943-5126

406

Beaverhead BBS
683-4809
The Big Sky BBS
542-3622
Montana Net
423-5433
Mountain Valley BBS
496-2047
Pioneer Telegraph
232-4602

407

Cornerstone BBS
770-2004
The Door
682-3732
Generic BBS
380-7680
Imajika
238-1415
Trap Door
382-6035

408

Communication_Breakdown
297-8383
Driven_Element
267-2335
The GasPump BBS
223-2949
Genesis Division
238-4213
The Zone BBS
720-1152

409

The Hacker's Forum
447-2277
Heartbreak Hotel
762-2842
Hermes BBS
823-4442
The Neutral Zone
532-1231
The Source!
776-1311

410

261-Elsewhere
252-5518
The Keeping Room
276-0658
The North Star
974-9305
Outside the Wall
665-1855
Pooh's Corner
327-9263

412

The Lair
771-9218
Mabel's Mansion
981-3151
Project Aurora
962-1590
Transwarp
824-8443
Wayfarer's Inn
821-0552

413

The Axis BBS
586-7993
NiteFire BBS
737-2100
The Owls Domain
527-7487
SpaceMet Great Falls
863-3703
The Village BBS
584-3065

414

The Anonymous BBS
251-2580
The Castle
327-5085
The Gray Alternative
452-2977
Modern Pastimes
384-1701
Sanctuary
426-3715

415

Autodesk Global Village
289-2270
The Lost Realms
550-2498
The Oracle BBS
365-4819
Run of The Mill BBS
343-5160
Valley of the Wind
341-5986

417

The Fire-BBS!
831-7171
Hard Rock BBS
887-7005
The Outer Realms
863-0041
Shadow BBS
864-6371
Short Circuit
753-5025

419

The Arena BBS
636-7197
Blizz's Ozz
865-7470
The Country Club BBS
843-5801
Dry Dock
353-0452
Grendel's Lair BBS
523-3818

501

The Chicken Coop
273-9257
Freedom One
932-7932
The Looking Glass
750-3284
The Lost Domain
931-3236
Techno-Distortion Elite! BBS
327-8814

502

Friendship Factory
867-1800
The Sandcastle
943-8111
ToolBox BBS
942-1111
The Underground
351-2728
The Wild Side BBS
439-0576

503

Event Horizons BBS
697-5100
Hardware Wars
646-4853
Information Anxiety
635-4386
The Universal Joint
240-1943
Up All Night BBS
472-9329

504

The Bird's Eye BBS
643-1119
Curtain Call
857-8009
The Flying Dutchman
649-7101
The Naquin Express
594-5087
The Shark Bite BBS
868-9751

505

Cavern of Cyborg
268-1669
The Cellar Door
763-1795
The Colosseum BBS
784-3275
Leisure Time
434-6940
Whole Enchilada Net
523-2811

507

The Eagles Talon
285-9639
The Heritage BBS
437-1342
The North Castle
281-9886
Outer Dominions
252-8284
South Minnesota Net
281-9886

508

Blue box BBS
829-3475
Cul De Sac
429-8385
King Davids Spaceship
756-1442
The Lighthouse
892-8857
The Smorgasbord
580-5806

509

In The Meantime
966-3828
Moonlight Delight
664-0692
We Be Games n' Stuff
545-4249
Wirehaired Terrier Opus BBS
448-4774
The Wishing Well
375-0507

510

Alpha and Omega
278-0297
Down Under
790-3432
Party Warehouse
256-9809
Screaming Electron
935-6888
Walden Puddle
795-7660

FidoNet BBSs

512

Digital Passageway
850-7866
Electronic Horizons
292-1863
The Hall Closet
836-3635
The SeaHorse
994-9643
Thin Ice BBS
939-7572

513

Access!
244-2255
The Arena
252-8891
Shareboard
231-8278
White Room
533-0949
Wolverine Lair
422-9652

515

Alternatives
285-1190
Fog Line BBS
964-7937
Ground Zero
292-5979
The Harkkonnen Empire
221-9859
Oasis in the Digital Desert
432-4472

516

The Far Side BBS
588-3175
The Last Place on Earth
243-1949
Long Island Network
731-1094
The Midnight Star BBS
371-0539
The Monitor BBS
546-8731

517

BabbleNet
321-9652
Classroom Earth
797-2737
The Ghetto
263-3590
Programmers Attic
655-3347
Weasel's Workshop
627-4461

518

Adirondack Net
761-0869
The Boondocks
483-3348
The Frontline
782-1244
The Liquid Sky
883-5326
Other Worlds
583-9291

601

Berserker
362-9958
Cell Block
992-5567
The Land of the Lost
467-0801
Sid's Play Toy
932-4157
Underworld
825-9392

602

Borrowed Time
257-4370
The Living Dead BBS
493-7557
The Ranch
780-9180
Rare Readers BBS
756-2855
The Sleep Robber BBS
985-1088

603

Alter-Net
524-9010
The Big Queue
429-2419
Cape Retreat
672-8123
The Firing Line
898-1314
The Hobby Center
279-9028

605

The Cosmopolitan BBS
226-0641
Silver Bullet's Lounge
343-0755
Sonny's Garage
232-3170
The Time Portal
348-4113
The Voyager BBS
232-4648

606

Ohio River Net
836-1267
Peace Connection BBS
439-1734
The Razor's Edge
873-6637
U-People
268-0801
The ZOO
586-7508

607

Hidden Agenda
786-0775
The Money Pit
797-3392
Pax Tharkas
749-3689
The Projects
723-6141
The Sanatorium!
648-8565

608

The Iconoclast
246-9660
The Other Woman
654-7678
The Parody BBS
277-8597
The Razor's Edge
238-6317
Rosie's BBS
784-4679

609

Cyclops BBS
742-8223
The Inferno
886-6818
Maple Shade Opus
482-8604
The Shore Connection
971-2937
Vulcanian BBS
645-7080

612

Fire Opal
822-4812
Offhook BBS
929-0127
Slackers Palace
884-0575
Smart Stuff BBS
926-3843
Terraboard
721-8967

614

The Archive
447-2352
Colossus
885-9829
Marduk
841-0355
Monolith
279-9970
The Unknown BBS
264-1912

615

Chatline
821-5751
Inner Circle
479-3686
Skynet
265-4260
Society of Independent People
493-9826
Voltage Drop
332-2637

616

Channel 1
895-9677
Fireside
323-0585
Marriage Bed BBS
467-4550
Rogue River
361-8267
The TimeWarp
327-1595

617

Bionic Dog
964-8069
Frazzle's Free For All
789-5840
Hacknet
942-1298
Starbase: Boston
739-9246
Tom's BBS
698-8734

618

Bold Truth BBS
937-3962
The Emerald Keep
394-0065
The Free World
746-9176
Mental Vortex
529-3486
The 90th Meridian
692-2169

619

The Box
421-7807
The Fully Involved BBS
256-7885
The Surf Shack BBS
967-6017
Trade Winds
271-9969
The Wave of the Future BBS
390-7217

701

Buffalo Chip BBS
251-1903
City Lites BBS
746-6010
The Gamer's Guild
852-9435
Gamma World
727-9811
Text BBS
239-6048

702

Desert Frenzy BBS
453-7948
Eclipse BBS
651-8536
The Rebel BBS
435-0786
Vega$ Online
222-0409
Voice of America
324-5528

703

End of the Line BBS
720-1624
The Enlightened Board
370-9528
The Info Exchange
354-1104
Missing Link
527-3175
The Potato Patch BBS
791-6411

FidoNet BBSs

704

The Big Byte
279-2295
The Exchange BBS
339-0333
Imminent Front
554-1041
The Matrix
535-7361
The Rabbit Hole
563-8474

706

The Far Side BBS
868-9726
The Last Cafe
793-1472
The Public's Domain BBS
860-5070
The Realm BBS
769-4461
The Terminal Edge BBS
571-0669

707

Darkside of the Moon
451-3321
Napa Valley Fido
257-6502
The Power Surge BBS
277-9656
Rapture BBS
573-0927
Satellite_Connection_BBS
426-4883

708

Alpha Complex
418-5805
Elysium
251-4158
Fly-by-Wire
584-5948
Precision
391-8773
Zen Arcade
934-6224

712

KYFR Radio
246-2115

713

Artichoke
978-3573
The Atomic Cafe
530-0558
Magic Window
351-9186
Satellite of Love
469-4580
The Swap Shop
777-2527

714

The Boundary BBS
963-5821
The Insanity Exchange
952-3180
The Lair
991-7928
Spider Island BBS
730-0276
Time Warp
828-1565

715

OutLand!
539-2950
Phoenix
732-7026
The Promised Land
387-0500
Super Board
845-9277
Toys in the Attic
362-8506

716

Another BBS
872-4415
Frog Pond
461-1924
Midnight Caller BBS
297-0291

The Moose BBS
646-5438
Rapid Transit
889-3261

717

Cyberia
840-1444
Cybernetics BBS
738-1976
The Money Bin
540-1418
Prometheus Unbound
626-7616
Terminal Paradise
292-5871

718

All New York City Net
726-7747
Brooklyn After Dark
782-1586
New York City Skyline BBS
597-9083
The Next Generation BBS
236-8105
The Pier
531-1657

719

Access BBS
528-1363
Global BBS
548-8483
Pikes Peak Net
599-4568
Red Sector A
547-0482
Wild Side BBS
390-6771

801

Hot Bauds
944-8055
The Iron Grid
486-0929
The Night Hawk
865-1429

Thunder Hold
756-2901
Your Roots BBS
359-0925

802

Bennington County
362-2435
Black Creek BBS
933-2417
Online World
873-9443
Socialism OnLine!
626-4103
Wintermute
656-1182

803

The Electric City BBS
226-5287
Late Night Adventure Land
750-1212
The Necropolis
762-7576
Periscope
650-9022
Zoo TV
272-2856

804

The Back Door
264-2107
The Black Planet
496-9268
Late Night BBS
685-1602
Nite Moves BBS
428-8764
The Wastelands
229-8812

805

The Bored
237-1512
Galaxy One BBS
493-0229
Lighthouse BBS
272-1812

Minnie's Basement
686-3049
Practical BBS
496-4445

806

The Barnyard BBS
353-7000
Fatevea BBS
655-5686
Lubbock Net
745-0114
The Preferred BBS
359-0876
User Friendly! BBS
381-0633

808

Coconut Telegraph
956-2626
The Daily Planet
572-4857
Enchanted Garden
423-9852
Jon's LateNite
834-1261
This Old PC BBS
239-8824

809

Caribbean Breeze
773-0195
The Island Windows
793-6121
Opus Amicus
724-0621
The Spot
793-3662
Virtual Realities I
720-8669

812

CrossRoads BBS
342-7078
Hotseat
279-2143
Party Palace
299-2983

Primetime
235-6487
Tradin' Place
334-0442

813

The Beach Board
337-5480
Hacker's Haven
442-1441
Imagine
936-4405
Reef
854-1149
Towne Cryier BBS
764-1062

814

Digital Matrix
825-3783
The Groundhog's Den
938-5218
Laser Line BBS
237-1678
The Rhythm & Blues BBS
266-9234
Sci-Link
432-8397

815

The Black Star BBS
233-5574
The Boomtown BBS
868-2422
Digital Civilization
633-2227
The Looney Bin
942-5015
Parallel Dimension
229-7069

816

Boardrooms to Bedrooms
483-7018
Micron Firefly
324-3148
The Nervous System BBS
665-4545

FidoNet BBSs

Powertrain BBS
228-1719
The Sounding Board BBS
361-9294

817

Acme BBS
383-1903
Century Alpha
772-8799
The Computer Playroom
539-5339
Maximum Overdrive
855-5420
Wonderland BBS
836-9524

818

The Bad Dog BBS
332-0100
House Atreides
965-7220
The Monolith BBS
718-0522
Open Squelch
907-7906
The Parthenon BBS
727-7070

903

Alternate Escape
883-4441
Lightning Strike BBS
894-7133
Terra-X
757-3697
Texarkana Net
838-6713
World Link
643-7607

904

Electrik Avenue
873-6360
Florida Gator Net
377-2082
The Mess
243-8376

Miami Links
651-0204
Sherwood Forest
245-3670

906

Bytes-R-Us
486-6836
Ice Castle Adult BBS
346-5848
* ! Lighthouse ! *
428-3425
Vanishing Point
475-9835
Windowed Reality
482-0724

907

Alaska Midnight Sun Net
452-1460
Alaska Mineshaft
276-2416
The Exchange
373-7520
The Pipeline
345-0147
Wilde Side
333-4039

908

The Arena BBS
272-6890
The Intelligentsian
774-3953
Pandemonium Free Port
668-7377
Shockwave Rider
294-0659
The Underground
262-9659

912

Future World
876-2453
Gate
923-2065
Green Lantern
245-0644

PowerPlex
249-9584
Way Station
387-7674

913

Beyond Recognition BBS
888-6680
Electric Dreams
832-2246
Foundation BBS
648-1412
The Manhattan Project
827-3733
The Place to Be BBS
441-3885

914

The Brewster BBS
279-2514
Delusions of Grandeur
381-2390
The Gateway BBS
934-8125
Luv at First BYTE
342-4941
People Power BBS
878-3112

915

Digital Disturbance
833-6211
The Eclipse
821-5667
Hyper Access BBS
651-5487
The Lighthouse BBS
670-0736
Swap Shop BBS
698-6242

916

Antimatter BBS
489-6421
Digital Paradise
721-1620
The Kitchen Table
684-6179

Prospector BBS
921-9949
Vortex
332-7141

918
Etcetera Etcetera
369-1053
The Glass House
749-5711
The Neutral Zone BBS
252-2236
The Wayfarer's Inn
250-3012
Wayne's World BBS
665-0885

919
Alien BBS
229-4334
The End of the Line
756-6487
InFiNiTe rEaLiTy BBS
924-2373
Private Idaho BBS
489-9446
Pure Energy
786-5549

Canada

204
The Clubhouse
489-9081
Crosstime Saloon
663-9484
Futura
255-5993
RoadHouse
774-0247
The Underground
275-0609

306
Beach House
729-4185

Dirk Gently's Holistic BBS
789-9909
Extreme Outerlimits
545-0417
Impossible Missions Force
569-9705
Technology Transfer
372-4903

403
Back to the Basics
460-1609
Brainstormer's Idea Exchange
276-2454
Power Station
963-1859
Rascal BBS
686-2550
The Ultimate BBS
249-7916

416
Alternative
662-6424
Circuit Board
579-3702
CRS Online
213-6002
Durham Net North
579-6302
Outland BBS
383-3566

418
Bab-O-Manie/Node 1
648-9590
GridPoint
695-6409
Multi-Media Lab Node 1
626-0775
PCBabillard
651-2043
Welcome Home BBS
681-1997

506
Atlantic Access
672-8543

Headhunter's BBS
642-2787
Pegasus BBS
696-3183
Supernal BBS
849-9046
The Vortex
432-6610

514
Juxtaposition BBS
364-2937
La Source BBS
378-3502
Le Chateau
691-6240
Le Courrier
336-4343
Ozzie's Fido
684-4922

519
The Digital Spectrum
570-4718
FidoNews
570-4176
Kid's Room
623-7390
Starship Enterprise
358-1561
The Village
692-5831

604
Agape
882-9107
Beyond the Bounds of Reason
985-4605
Cows BBS
820-0784
tHe eXpErImEnTaL PrOjEcT!
525-2898
The Eye of the Needle
796-9477

613
Electronic Encounters
820-0324

FidoNet BBSs

Inof Alternative
230-9519
NorthStar
739-8634
Smokey's Playground
736-7056
Ugly Twisted Nastiness
567-9633

705

Blue Orb 2
759-4831
Charlie's Place
335-6953
DogStar
942-8370
Fisherman's Scroll
253-5366
Maximus Help
494-9329

709

The Ivory Coast BBS
368-4698

NewfOnline
895-3942
Sonic Boom BBS
579-2510
Speed Pro+ BBS
634-6761
Visionz BBS
726-1752

807

CatsEye
623-5048
The Northern Connection
582-3880
OnLine Now
345-7248
Synergist
329-5210

819

Babillard Le Cafe
825-6851
Brian&Wendys BBS
827-8945

A Farewell to Kings
669-6206
The Furthest North BBS
436-7476
Le Village Normandie
776-3903

902

BoneHead's Paridise BBS
883-9438
Compu Link 2000
564-5197
Grey MaDDeR
463-6275
Nova Scotia Net
463-6275
Teds Rbbs PC
679-2258

Internet Providers

A selection of Internet providers

a2i Communications There are no startup or hourly charges. Access costs $15/month, $45/ three months, or $72/six months. For more information, send email or log in with "guest." 408-293-9020/408-293-9010 ✓**INTERNET** ...→ *email* INFO@RAHUL.NET ...→*telnet* A2I.RAHUL.NET→ GUEST/<NONE>

Anomaly (BBS) Also includes its own file archives and the Anomaly Arcade of games. There are no startup fees. For those using the system for educational purposes, costs are $75/six months or $120/ year with unlimited time. For commercial or individual users, costs are $125/six months or $200/year, which covers one hour per day. If more time is desired, additional 30-minute blocks per day may be purchased for $10/ year each. For more information, voice call 401-273-4669 or log in with "newuser." ▆▆ 401-455-0347/ 401-331-3706 ✓**INTERNET** ...→*email* INFO@ANOMALY.SBS.RISC.NET ...→*tel-net* ANOMALY. SBS.RISC.NET→NEWUSER/ <NONE>

APK (BBS) Features its own files, games, and chat features. There is a one-time $20 startup fee. Plans include $35/month for unlimited Internet access or $15/month for 20 hours. For those who use the BBS as well as the Internet features, a $50–$100/year donation is suggested. For more information, log in to the BBS with "bbs," send email to the "info" address, or send a real email question to the human at "apk." Voice calling is available at 216-481-9428 from 5 p.m. to midnight. ▆▆ ◎✿ 216-481-9436/216-481-1960 ✓**INTERNET** ...→*email* INFO@WARIAT.ORG ...→ *email* APK@WARIAT.ORG ...→*telnet* WARIAT.ORG→ BBS/<NONE>

The Black Box (BBS) This BBS with games and its own conferences provides full dial-up Internet access for $21.65/month. There is no startup fee. For more information, voice call 713-480-2684 from 6 to 10 p.m. Central, or log in as "guest." 713-480-2686

CAPCON Library Network (BBS) Costs are $150/year plus $30/month (or $24/month if a year is paid in full). There is no startup fee. Monthly fees include 20 hours of access time. An additional $2/hour is charged for every hour over 20. There is a 2-megabyte storage limit. Group rates are also available. For more information, voice call 202-331-5771 or send email. ✓**INTERNET**→ *email* CAPCON@CAPCON.NET

Colorado SuperNet (BBS) There is a $20 startup fee and a minimum monthly charge based on hourly costs of $15/month: $3/hour for Monday–Friday 8 a.m.–8 p.m.; $2/hour every day 8 p.m.–12 a.m. and Saturday and Sunday 8 a.m.–8 p.m.; $1/hour every day midnight–8 a.m. There is an added surcharge of $8/hour for use of the 800 number and $0.50/month for every megabyte of storage used over the allotted 1 megabyte. For information, voice call 303-273-3471 or send email. ✓**INTERNET**→*email* INFO@CSN.ORG

Communications Accessibles Montreal Free 15-day trial accounts available. Full Internet access costs $25/month for 10 hours a week and 4 megabytes of storage with no startup fee. For more information, voice call 514-931-0749 or send email. ✓**INTER-NET**→ *email* INFO@CAM.ORG

Community News Service There is a one-time $35 startup fee in addition to the $2.75/hour usage charges with a $10/month minimum. For those outside of the Denver region, there is also an 800-number plan with usage charges of $8/hour. For more information, send an email request or log in with "new/newuser." 719-520-1700 ✓**INTERNET** ...→*email* INFO @CSCNS.COM ...→*telnet* CSCNS.COM →NEW/NEWUSER

CRL There is a one-time startup fee of $19.50. Costs are $19.50/ month ($17.50 with a credit card) for unlimited time. For more information, send email or voice call 415-381-2800, or subscribe by logging in with "newuser." 415-705-6060/602-277-8045/404-577-3250 ✓**INTERNET**→ *email* INFO@CRL.COM

CTS Network Services There is a one-time startup fee of $15 and charges of $18/month for an average of 1 hour per day (30 hours per month) access or $25/month for an average of 2 hours per day (60 hours per month). For more information, voice call 619-637-3640, send email, or log in with "help." 619-637-3640/619-637-3660 ✓**INTERNET** ...→*email* INFO@CTSNET. CTS.COM ✍ *Type in message body:* SEND CTSNET-PERSONAL ...→*telnet* CTSNET.CTS.COM→HELP/<NONE>

The Cyberspace Station One hour a day limit. Costs include a one-time startup fee of $10 and additional fees of $20/month or $15/month for 6 months or more. Log in with "guest" and sign up online, or for more information, voice call 619-944-9498, ext. 626, or send email. 619-634-1376 ✓**INTERNET** ...→*email* ROBB@CYBER.NET ...→*telnet* CYBER.NET→GUEST/<NONE>

Delphi Besides its forums, games, chat, and news services, Delphi also provides full Internet access. There is a $19 startup fee for the 20/20 Plan. Costs for access to both the Internet and Delphi services are $13/month for 4 hours and $4/hour for additional time, or $23/month for 20 hours and $1.80/hour for additional time. Delphi offers a trial membership of 5 free hours. For more information, log in with "info" or "join delphi," voice call 800-695-4005, or send email. 🖳 📠 📼 📺 800-365-4636 ✓**INTERNET** ...→*email* INFO @DELPHI.COM ...→*telnet* DELPHI.COM →NETG1/<NONE>

Dial n' Cerf (BBS) Offers three different plans for dial up Internet access, all of which require a one-time startup fee of $50: the hourly plan costs $20/month and $5/hour on weekdays or $3/hour on weekends; the 800-number plan offers toll-free calling for $10/hour on weekdays or $8/hour on week-

ends; the flat rate—no hourly charges—is $250/month. For more information, voice call 800-876-2373 or send email. ✓**INTERNET**→*email* HELP@CERF.NET

DSC BBS (BBS) DSC carries more than 5,000 conferences from Usenet, Clarinet, FidoNet, ILink, RelayNet, Smartnet, and KinkNet and offers 10 gigabytes of files. Use of the 800 number carries an $8/hour prime-time (M–F 7 a.m. –8 p.m.) charge and a $4/hour charge at other times and includes full access to all the board's features; for non–800 usage, DSC offers a variety of plans (e.g., $15/three months for email and Usenet, $45/three months for full Internet access, $65/three months for full Internet and board access). Voice call 215-674-9290 for more information.

Eskimo North (BBS) Eskimo North also carries its own multi-user games, applications, and file archives. Offers the first two weeks free, then charges $13/month or $30/three months or $96/year with no hourly charges. There is no startup fee. Log in as "new." 📼 206-367-3837/206-838-9513 ✓**INTERNET** ...→*email* NANOOK@ESKIMO. COM ...→*telnet* ESKIMO.COM→NEW/<NONE>

Express Access There is a one-time startup fee of $20. For email and Usenet access only, charges are $15/month; for full Internet access, charges are $25/month. For those who already have *telnet* privileges, costs are $8.95/month. For more information, voice call 800-969-9090, send email, or log in as "new." 301-220-0258/908-937-9481 ✓**INTERNET** ...→*email* INFO@ACCESS. DIGEX.NET ...→*telnet* UNIVERSE.DIGEX. NET→NEW/<NONE>

HoloNet (BBS) A full-access Internet provider with its own forums, games, and services. There is no startup fee (unless you pay by check). Hourly rates are $4/hour peak-time (M–F 8 a.m. – 5 p.m. except holidays) and $2/hour off-peak-time. There are also charges for data transfer above the allotted 256K/month—this excludes email, finger, chat, and ping—$2/MB peak-time and $1/MB off-peak-time. The membership costs of $6/month or $60/year are applied toward your total monthly costs. For more information, voice call 510-704-0160, send email, or log in as "guest." 📼 📺 510-704-1058 ✓**INTERNET** ...→*email* INFO@HOLO NET.NET ...→*telnet* HOLONET.NET →GUEST/<NONE>

The IDS World Network (BBS) Besides having its own forums and chat areas, IDS is a full-access Internet provider with a menu-driven interface. There is a $15/month charge with unlimited file transfer (although there is a 24-hour time limit for a file remaining in the user's workspace). There's no startup fee. For information voice call 401-884-7856, send email, or log in as "guest." 📼 📺 401-884-9002/401-751-1067 ✓**INTERNET** ...→ *email* INFO@IDS.NET ...→*telnet* IDS. NET→GUEST/<NONE>

Maestro (BBS) Provides software, games, and full access to the Internet for $15/month, $150/year, or $400/three years based on 60 hours/month. $1/hour is charged when the 60 hours have been exceeded. There is no startup fee. For more information send email, voice call 212-240-9600, or log in as "newuser." Two hours of free online time to try out the service. 📼 📺 212-240-9700 ✓**INTER-NET** ...→*email* INFO@MAESTRO.COM

...→*telnet* MAESTRO.MAESTRO.COM→NEWUSER/<NONE>

MCSNet (BBS) Offers several different rate structures for Internet access, including $20/three months for email and Usenet access, $25/month for full Internet access without time limits, and $10/month for 15 hours of full Internet access. For those with *telnet* capabilities already, MCS charges $20/three months for full Internet access. There are no startup fees. For more information, voice call 312-248-8649, send email, or log in as "mcs." 312-248-0970 ✓**INTERNET** ...→*email* INFO@GENESIS.MCS. COM ...→*telnet* GATEWAY.MCS.COM→ MCS/<NONE>

The Meta Network (BBS) Provides full Internet access (albeit with a limited Usenet feed) for $20/month. There is a one-time $15 startup fee, with the first month free. Also includes access to its own conferences and software. For more information, voice call 703-243-6622 or send email. ✓**INTERNET**→*email* INFO@TMN.COM

MindVox (BBS) There is no startup fee. Charges are $17.50/month which includes access to the bulletin board and two hours of online time per day. Provides, besides full Internet access, more than 10 MUDs, dozens of online games, its own forums for *Wired, Mondo,* Cyberspace, Women Online, and more. For more information, voice call 212-989-2418, send email, or log in with "guest." 🖼️ 📞 212-989-1550/212-989-4141 ✓**INTERNET**→*telnet* MINDVOX.PHANTOM.COM→GUEST/<NONE> ...→ *email* INFO@PHANTOM.COM

MsenLink Offers full Internet access, including Usenet and Clarinet feeds, and access to

Msen's conferences. A startup fee of $20 and $160/month get you unlimited connect time or you can pay $20/month and $2/hour. For more information, voice call 313-998-4562 or send email. ✓**INTERNET**→*email* INFO@MAIL.MSEN.COM

NeoSoft (BBS) Provides full Internet access and unlimited connect time for $29.95/month with no startup fee. Send email, voice call 713-684-5969, or log in with "new" for more information. 713-684-5909/713-684-5900 ✓**INTERNET** ...→*email* INFO @SUGAR.NEOSOFT. COM ...→*telnet* SUGAR.NEOSOFT. COM→NEW/<NONE>

Netcom On-line Communications (BBS) Provides full Internet access for $19.50/month. There is a one-time startup fee of $20. For a list of local access numbers, voice call 800-488-2558. For more information, voice call 800-501-8649, send email, or log in as "guest." ✓**INTERNET** ...→*email* INFO@NETCOM.COM ...→*telnet* NET COM.COM→GUEST/<NONE>

Net Guide Online Net Guide Online inaugurates its national Internet service by offering 15 hours of free connect time to anyone who wants to explore the Internet. Take advantage of Net Guide's national system of local access numbers, and real-friendly-no-question-too-dumb support (Net Guide's authors are here around the clock anyway). Along with full Internet service, and its own unique forums and "electronic magazines," Net Guide Online offers the most comprehensive and easy-to-use directory of Cyberspace—all the listings in this book plus 3,000 new entries and daily updates—in an electronic format that allows for flash searches by subject, network, address,

cost, and activity. What's more, Net Guide is developing an easy Net interface: just click on an entry in any one of Net Guide's graphical menus and you'll be transported to where you want to go in Cyberspace. Join us. Charter offer: no startup fee, first month free, then $15/month with 15 free hours; $1/hour. Voice call 1-800-NET-1133 or email us for more info and local access numbers. ✓**INTERNET**→*email* INFO@GO-NET-GUIDE.COM

North Shore Access (BBS) Full Internet access for $9/month with 10 hours of connect time. Each hour over 10 hours or each megabyte over 3 megabytes costs an additional $1. There is no startup fee. Voice call 617-593-3110 or send email for more information. 617-593-4557 ✓**INTERNET**→*email* INFO@NORTHSHORE.ECOSOFT.COM

Northwest Nexus/Halcyon There is a one-time startup fee of $20; charges are $20/month or $200/year for unlimited connect time. For more information, voice call 800-539-3505, send email, or log in as "new." 206-382-6245/206-627-4554 ✓**INTERNET** ...→*email* INFO @NWNEXUS.WA.COM ...→*telnet* HALCYON.COM→NEW/<NONE>

NovaLink (BBS) Provides full Internet access. There is a one-time startup fee of $12.95, which is refundable if service is discontinued after the first month; and a monthly fee of $9.95, which includes five free daytime hours and is exempted the first month. There are also charges of $1.80/hour for local dialing or *telnet*ting into the BBS, $3.60/hour for toll-free calling from anywhere in the continental U.S., and other rates for those calling from outside the contintenal U.S. For additional

Internet providers

info, send email, voice call 800-274-2814, or log in with "info." Log in with "new" to subscribe online. 800-937-7644/508-754-4009 ✓**INTERNET** ...→*email* INFO@ NOVALINK.COM ...→*telnet* NOVALINK. COM→INFO/<NONE>

Old Colorado City Communications Service There is a one-time startup fee of $30 and $25/month charge for full Internet access; a $25 startup fee and $20/month charge for email, Usenet, and FidoNet; and a $20 startup fee and $10/month charge for email only. For more information, voice call 719-632-4848, send email, or log in with "newuser." 719-632-4111 ✓**INTERNET** ...→*email* DAVE@OLDCOLO.COM ...→*telnet* OLDCOLO.COM→NEWUSER/<NONE>

Panix There is a $40 startup fee and a charge of $57/three months for full Internet access. For email and Usenet without the interactive *telnet* services such as *telnet* and *FTP*, the charge is $10/month or $100/year with a $1/hour charge for every hour over the 60 hours/month allotted time. For more information, voice call 212-787-6160, send email, or log in with "help." 212-787-3100 ✓**INTERNET** ...→*email* INFO@PANIX.COM ...→*telnet* PANIX.COM→HELP/<NONE>

The Portal System Costs $19.95/month for unlimited connect time in addition to a one-time startup fee of $19.95. For more information, voice call 408-973-9111, send email, or log in with "info." 408-973-8091 ✓**INTERNET** ...→*email* INFO@PORTAL.COM ...→*telnet* PORTAL.COM→INFO/<NONE>

PUCnet Offers three different plans: (a) $6.25/hour; (b) $1.25/hour for 0-20 hours and $6.25/hour for time over 20 hours, with a 20-hour minimum charge; (c) $2.50/hour with a 25-hour minimum charge. In addition, interactive Internet features such as *telnet* or *FTP* incur a surcharge of $6.25/hour. For more information, voice call 403-448-1901, send email, or log in with "guest." 403-484-5640 ✓**INTERNET**→*email* INFO@PUCNET. COM

Telerama Offers a menu interface, multi-user games, and classes on how to use the Internet in addition to full Internet access for $20/month with unlimited connect time and 1 megabyte of disk space. There is no startup fee. For more information, voice call 412-481-3505, send email, or log in with "new." 412-481-4644/412-481-5302 ✓**INTERNET**→*email* SYSOP@TELERAMA. PGH.PA.US

Texas Metronet Offers three plans with no hourly charges: $10/month and a one-time $10 startup fee for email, IRC, local games and MUDs, and 1 megabyte of storage; $19/month and a one-time $20 startup fee for all previously listed features as well as *FTP*, Usenet, *telnet*, and C development tools and 2 megabytes of storage; $45/month and a one-time $35 startup fee for all previously mentioned features and 3 mailboxes. For more information, voice call 214-401-2800, send email, or log in with "info/ info." 214-705-2902 ✓**INTERNET**→ *email* SRL@ METRONET.COM

Vnet Internet Access, Inc. There is no startup fee. Rates are $25/month or $259/year for unlimited off-peak time (midnight–1 p.m.) and 2 hours/day peak time. For those who *telnet* into the system, there is a $12.50/month plan available. For more information, voice call 704-347-0779, send email, or log in with "new." 704-347-8839/919-851-1526 ✓**INTERNET** ...→*email* INFO@CHAR. VNET.NET ...→*telnet* CHAR.VNET.NET→NEW/<NONE>

The WELL (BBS) Offers its own conferences as well as full Internet access and Usenet feeds. There is a $15/month fee as well as a $2/hour charge, but no startup fee. For more information, voice call 415-332-4335, log in with "guest," or send email. ▦ ▦ ◉🐍 415-332-6106 ✓**INTERNET**→*email* INFO@WELL.SF.CA.US→WELL.SF.CA.US →GUEST/<NONE>

The World (BBS) Includes its own forums, games, and shopping. The basic plan costs $5/month and $2/hour for 1 megabyte of disk space. The 20/20 plan costs $20 for 20 hours of online time and 5 megabytes of disk space—additional time costs $1/hour. There are no startup fees. For more information, voice call 617-739-0202, send email, or log in with "new." ▦ ⬢ ▦ ◉🐍 617-739-9753 ✓**INTERNET** ...→*email* INFO@WORLD.STD.COM ...→*telnet* WORLD.STD.COM→NEW/<NONE>

Wyvern Technologies, Inc. Provides a menu featuring all of its Internet services. New users are charged a one-time startup fee of $20. For $20/month, the user gets 30 hours of connect time—any use after the 30 hours is billed at $2/hour. For $10/month, the user gets 10 hours of connect time—any use after the 10 hours is billed at $2/hour. For more information, voice call 804-622-4289, send email, or log in with "guest." 804-627-1828 ✓**INTERNET** ...→*email* INFO@WYVERN.WYVERN.COM ...→*telnet* WYVERN.WYVERN.COM→GUEST/<NONE>

Glossary

Archie   A program that lets you search Internet FTP archives worldwide by file name.

ASCII   A basic text format readable by most computers. The acronym stands for American Standard Code for Information Interchange.

backbones   The high-speed networks at the core of the Internet. The most prominent is the NSFNet, funded by the National Science Foundation.

baud   The speed at which signals are sent by a modem, measured by the number of changes per second in the signals during transmission. A *baud* rate of 1,200, for example, would indicate 1,200 signal changes in one second. Baud rate is often confused with *bits per second* (bps). See below.

binary   A file format in which data is represented by binary numbers (based on 1's and 0's); generally used to store software and pictures. One *binary* integer is called a bit (see *bits per second*).

binary transfer   A file transfer between two computers that preserves binary data.

bits per second (bps)   A measurement of the data-transfer rate between two modems. The higher the bps, the higher the speed of the transfer.

bounced message   An email message "returned to sender," usually because of an address error.

Glossary

bye A log-off command, such as "quit" or "exit."

Campus-Wide Information System (CWIS) A menu-based system on university computers that may include news, library catalogs, course listings, and email addresses of students and faculty.

cd *Change directory*, a command used at an FTP site to move from a directory to a subdirectory.

cdup *Change directory up*, the command used at an FTP site to move from a subdirectory to its parent directory. Also *chdirup*.

client A computer that connects to a more powerful computer (see *server*) for complex tasks.

compression Shrinkage of computer files to conserve storage space and reduce transfer times. Special utility programs available for all computers (including DOS, Mac, and Amiga) perform the *compression* and decompression.

cracker A person who maliciously breaks into a computer system in order to steal files or disrupt system activities.

dir *Directory*, a command used at an FTP site to display the contents of the current directory.

email The abbreviation for *electronic mail.*

FAQ *Frequently Asked Questions*, a file compiled for many Usenet newsgroups and other Internet services to reduce repeated posts about commonplace subjects in a newsgroup.

file transfer Transfer of a file from one computer to another over a network.

finger   A program that provides information about other users, either those logged in to your local system or those at a remote computer on the Internet. Generally started by typing "*finger*" and the person's user name.

flame   A violent and usually ad hominem attack against another person posting in a newsgroup or message area.

flame war   Back and forth *flames* that continue indefinitely.

Free-Net   A community-based net that provides free access to the Internet, usually to local residents, and often includes its own forums and news.

FTP   *File transfer protocol*, the standard used to transfer files between computers. On the Internet, most file transfers are performed using anonymous *FTP*.

Gopher   A menu-based guide to directories on the Internet, usually organized by subject.

hacker   A computer enthusiast who enjoys exploring computer systems and programs, sometimes to the point of obsession. Not to be confused with *cracker*.

knowbot   An experimental computer program designed to retrieve information anywhere on the Net in response to a user's request.

ls   *List*, a command that provides simplified directory information at *FTP* sites. It lists only file names for the directory, not file size or date.

lurkers   Regular readers of messages online who never post.

Glossary

matrix The worldwide combination of computer networks and their connections; sometimes used as a synonym for *the Net*.

mget An FTP command that transfers multiple files from the FTP site to your local directory. It works with a list of file names separated by spaces or an asterisk used as a wildcard. Typing "mget b*" would transfer all files in the directory with the letter *b* in their names.

Net guru A person with unimpeachable Net expertise who can answer any question.

newsgroups The Usenet message areas, organized by subject.

port number An addition to a *telnet* address that connects you to a particular application. The major-league-baseball schedule, for example, is at port 862 of culine.colorado.edu (culine.colorado.edu 862).

posting The sending of a message to a newsgroup, bulletin board, or other public message area. The message itself is called a *post*.

pwd A command used at an FTP site that prints the name of the current directory on your screen.

real-time The Net term for *live*, as in "Live from New York!" Generally applied to chat, where two or more people have a live or *real-time* conversation online.

remote machine Any computer on the Internet you reach from your original Internet location using programs such as *FTP* or *telnet*. The machine you start from is often called the *home*, or *local*, *machine*.

server A software program, or the computer running the

	program, that allows other computers, called *clients*, to share its resources.
signature	A file added to the end of email messages or Usenet posts that contains personal information—usually your name, email address, postal address, and telephone number. Net etiquette dictates that *signatures*, or *sigs* for short, should be no longer than four or five lines.
smiley	Text used to indicate emotion, humor, or irony in electronic messages—best understood if viewed sideways. Also called *emoticons*. The most common smileys are :-) and :-(
snail mail	What the U.S. Postal Service delivers.
sysop	A *system operator*—the person who owns and/or manages a BBS or other Net site.
telnet	An Internet program which allows you to log in to Internet-connected computers other than your own.
Usenet	A collection of networks and computer systems that exchange messages. It organizes these messages by subject in newsgroups.
Wide Area Information Servers (WAIS)	A system that searches by keyword through database indexes around the Internet.
World-Wide Web (WWW)	A hypertext system for searching the Internet, currently under development, that allows you to browse through a variety of Net resources, including Usenet newsgroups as well as *FTP*, *telnet*, and *Gopher* sites. You can access any of these resources directly from *WWW*.

Michael Wolff & Company, Inc.

Michael Wolff & Company, Inc., digital publishers and packagers, specializes in information presentation and graphic design, and multimedia and online publishing. The company's recent projects have included *Where We Stand—Can America Make It in the Global Race for Wealth, Health, and Happiness?* (Bantam Books), one of the most graphically complex information books ever to be wholly created and produced by means of desktop-publishing technology, and *Made in America?*, a four-part PBS series on global competitiveness, hosted by Labor Secretary Robert B. Reich. With the publication of *Net Guide*, Michael Wolff & Company, Inc., launches a national Internet and online service, Net Guide Online (info@go-netguide.com).

Michael Wolff, company president, is the author of the book *White Kids*. Peter Rutten, executive editor, is a cofounder of the magazine *Electric Word*. Albert Bayers III, senior editor, has an extensive background in online research. Kelly Maloni, senior editor, is a graduate of Mount Holyoke College and, quite possibly, the most ubiquitous woman in Cyberspace.

John Perry Barlow

John Perry Barlow, former cowboy and lyricist for the Grateful Dead, is the founder with, Mitch Kapor, of the Electronic Frontier Foundation.

Index

Index

Index

Index

Index

Index

Index

Index

Index

Index

Index

America Online's Top Ten List
What can <u>YOU</u> do with America Online?

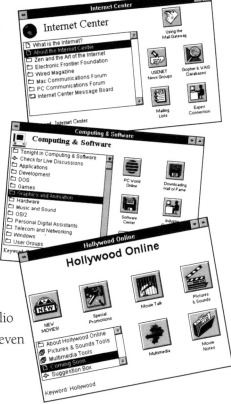

1. Access the resources of the "information superhighway" through America Online's INTERNET CENTER!

2. Send electronic mail to thousands of other subscribers on many different networks

3. Read the latest issue of TIME *before* it hits the newstand

4. Easily download files from a library of thousands

5. Tap into computing support from industry experts at online conferences and easy-to-use message boards

6. Have "real-time" conversations with other members, join clubs, and read your favorite specialty magazines

7. Monitor your stock and mutual fund investments in your own personal portfolio

8. Make airline and hotel reservations, and even do some shopping

9. Search the encyclopedia or get help with homework

10. Find out the latest information about the world of entertainment through Hollywood Online and Rocklink.

AND BEST OF ALL, YOU CAN TRY AMERICA ONLINE FREE!

If you've never experienced America Online — now is the time. There's a world of services available for you to discover and they're all at your fingertips! We'll send you free software, a free trial membership, and 10 FREE hours to explore. And all you have to do... is CALL!

A M E R I C A
Online

1-800-827-6364 ext. 8562

America Online is a registered service mark of America Online, Inc. Other names are trademarks or service marks of their respective owners. Use of America Online requires a major credit card or checking account. Limit one free trial per household.

BIX and the Internet: the ultimate power tool.

Programmers • Developers • Computer Hobbyists

Are computers how you make a living? Maybe just a serious hobby? If so, then BIX is the place for you. As the exclusive online club for development professionals, programmers, and computer enthusiasts, BIX has always been the place to go for help when you're the expert. With BIX's **full Internet access**, you can **telnet** to thousands of other sites, **FTP** files from all over the world, perform **Archie** searches, read **Usenet news**, access **Gopher** menus, access utilities like **whois** and **finger**, communicate with millions of people via **Internet mail**, and much more! **Sign up today, and you can get 5 hours of access for free through our special offer.**

New Member
5 hours for Free
Introductory Offer

And there's more to BIX than just access to the Internet - BIX is home to some of the best and brightest minds in computing and other fields. Chat with BYTE columnist Jerry Pournelle on space, computers, and current events; talk to the editors or get code from industry magazines like OS/2 Professional, Windows/DOS Developers Journal, and the C Users' Journal; get access to vendors like Commodore, Borland, and Windows developers; join the largest concentration of Amiga programmers on any online service - enter the elite of the development world! Thousands of members call BIX home, to interact with other professionals to share advice, swap code, and get help from other experts. If you're in the business, you need to be on BIX!

BIX also offers InterNav, our graphical user interface for Windows that lets you point and click your way around BIX and the Internet! Details and the option to order InterNav are available during the online registration.

Try Our Free 5 Hour Trial!

- Dial 800-695-4882
- At the login prompt type bix
- At the Name? prompt, type bix.netg1
- Full details and rates provided during toll-free registration
- Questions? Call 800-695-4775, or send Internet mail to info@bix.com

BIX

If you can hack it.

CompuServe.

The difference between your PC collecting dust and burning rubber.

No matter what kind of PC you have, CompuServe will help you get the most out of it. As the world's most comprehensive network of people with personal computers, we're the place experts and novices alike go to find what's hot in hardware, discuss upcoming advances with other members, and download the latest software. Plus, for a low flat-rate, you'll have access to our basic services as often as you like: news, sports, weather, shopping, a complete encyclopedia, and up to 60 e-mail messages a month. And it's easy to begin. All you need is your home computer, your regular phone line, a modem, and a CompuServe membership.

To get your free introductory membership, just complete and mail the form on the back of this page. Or call 1-800-524-3388 and ask for Representative 449. Plus, if you act now, you'll receive one month free unlimited access to basic services and a $15 usage credit for our extended and premium services.

So put the power of CompuServe in your PC — and leave everyone else in the dust.

CompuServe®

The information service you won't outgrow.™

Put the power
of CompuServe
at your fingertips.

Join the world's largest international network of people
with personal computers. Whether it's computer support,
communication, entertainment, or continually updated
information, you'll find services that meet your every need.

Your introductory membership will include one free month
of our basic services, plus a $15 usage credit for extended and
premium CompuServe services.

To get connected, complete and mail the card below. Or call
1-800-524-3388 and ask for Representative 449.

Yes! I want to get the most out of my PC. Send me my FREE
CompuServe Introductory Membership, including a $15 usage credit and
one free month of CompuServe basic services.

Name: _____

Address: _____

City: _____ State: _____ Zip: _____

Phone: _____

Clip and mail this form to: CompuServe
                                   P.O. Box 20212
                                   Dept. 449
                                   Columbus, OH 43220

Explore the Internet–FREE!

DELPHI is the only major online service to offer you full access to the Internet. And now you can explore this incredible resource with no risk. Join DELPHI today and get 5 hours of evening or weekend access to try it out for free!

Use DELPHI's Internet mail gateway to exchange messages with over 10 million people at universities, companies, and other online services such as CompuServe and MCI Mail.

Download programs and files using **FTP** or connect in real-time to other networks using **Telnet**. You can also meet people on the Internet. **Internet Relay Chat** lets you "talk" with people all over the world and **Usenet News** is the world's largest bulletin board with over 5000 topics!

To help you find the information you want, you'll have direct access to powerful search utilities such as "Gopher," "Hytelnet," "WAIS," and "the World-Wide Web." If you aren't familiar with these terms, don't worry; DELPHI has expert online assistants and a large collection of help files, books, programs, and other resources to help get you started.

Over 600 local access numbers are available across the country. Explore DELPHI and the Internet today. You'll be amazed by what you discover.

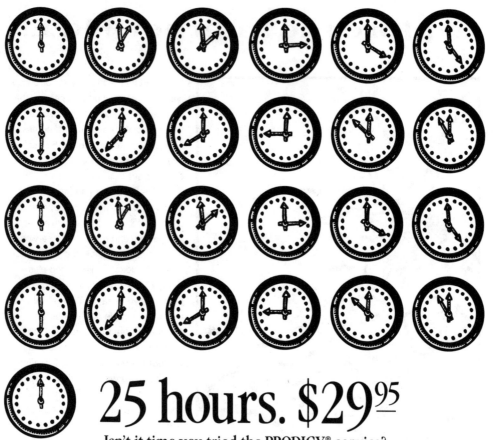

25 hours. $29⁹⁵

Isn't it time you tried the PRODIGY® service?
It's the lowest priced major online service in America.

No major service lets you spend more time online for less than the PRODIGY service. No one gives you more to *do* with your time either. More people to communicate with, the most active bulletin boards with more postings each day than the others combined, and the easiest e-mail connection to the Internet. Plus, the PRODIGY service lets you compose mail offline, send faxes, even first class letters to anyone in the U.S. And that's just the beginning.

No matter what you're interested in, you'll find something happening "Live on PRODIGY" right this second. So if the way other online services charge for their features is starting to tick (tock) you off, take a minute and call 1-800-PRODIGY x625 for your free software today. And discover the best value on the Electronic Highway.

The PRODIGY service.
For those with
unlimited imaginations.
Not unlimited budgets.

Get Wired!

"Wired looks like Vanity Fair should, reads like Esquire
used to and talks as if it's on intimate terms with the
power behind the greatest technological advance since the
Industrial Revolution."

David Morgan, Reuters

WIRED
Subscribe!

1 Year subscription (12 issues): $39.95
That's 33% off the newsstand price.
Call: 1-800-SO WIRED
Email: subscriptions@wired.com

NEIL SELKIRK